Ettie

By the same author

Dudley Docker
Sex, Death and Punishment
The Macmillans
Glaxo
Vice
Auden
Gothic
The Pursuit of Oblivion
A Night at the Majestic
(ed.) Hugh Trevor-Roper's Letters from Oxford

Ettie

The Intimate Life and
Dauntless Spirit of
Lady Desborough

RICHARD DAVENPORT-HINES

Weidenfeld & Nicolson
LONDON

First published in Great Britain in 2008
by Weidenfeld & Nicolson

3 5 7 9 10 8 6 4 2

A CIP catalogue record for this book
is available from the British Library.

ISBN-13 978 0 297 85174 5

Typeset at The Spartan Press Ltd,
Lymington, Hants

Printed and bound in the UK by CPI Mackays, Chatham ME5 8TD

Weidenfeld & Nicolson

The Orion Publishing Group Ltd
Orion House
5 Upper Saint Martin's Lane
London WC2H 9EA

An Hachette Livre UK Company

The Orion Publishing Group's policy is to use papers that
are natural, renewable and recyclable products and made
from wood grown in sustainable forests. The logging and
manufacturing processes are expected to conform to the
environmental regulations of the country of origin.

www.orionbooks.co.uk

Women's lives are *sensational.*

Elizabeth Bowen

Life is a pure flame and we live by an invisible sun within us. *

Sir Thomas Browne

We cannot choose if we will suffer or no, we can only choose whether we will suffer nobly or ignobly. *

George Eliot

* Favourite maxims of Ettie Desborough.

Contents

🙌

List of illustrations		ix
Genealogical tables		xi
Prologue		1
Chapter 1	The Orphan	9
Chapter 2	The Soul	38
Chapter 3	The Flirt	61
Chapter 4	The Mother	87
Chapter 5	The Edwardian	130
Chapter 6	The Mourner	182
Chapter 7	The Grande Dame	230
Chapter 8	The Mother-in-Law	279
Chapter 9	The Courtier	302
Chapter 10	The Dowager	327
A Poetic Appendix		370
Acknowledgements		374
Sources		377
Index		422

Illustrations

r

Section One
The Cowper family at Panshanger in 1874 (Getty Images)
The south front at Wrest (*Country Life*)
The Long Water at Wrest (*Country Life*)
The Duke of Kent's orangery at Wrest (*Country Life*)
Ettie Grenfell in her twenties (Lord Gage)
The Grenfells entertaining the Souls at Taplow (Lord Gage)
Ettie Grenfell as a young woman (Grenfell family papers)
Ettie Grenfell in the 1890s (National Portrait Gallery)
Ettie Grenfell with her sons Julian and Billy (Grenfell family papers)
Taplow in the 1890s (Lord Gage)
Julian Grenfell at Summer Fields (Lord Gage)
Billy Grenfell at Summer Fields (Lord Gage)
Willie Grenfell at Taplow with Ivo and Monica (Lord Gage)
Winston Churchill (Lord Gage)
Archie Gordon (Lord Gage)

Section Two
Nancy Astor, Pamela Lytton and Eddie Winterton (Getty Images)
Billy Grenfell at the Taplow fancy-dress ball of 1911 (Lord Gage)
Ettie and Willie Desborough with Imogen in 1908 (Getty Images)
Imogen Grenfell with Lord Desmond FitzGerald (Lord Gage)
Ivo and Imogen Grenfell at the Taplow ball of 1911 (Lord Gage)
Patrick Shaw-Stewart with Lady Massereene and Ferrard (Lord Gage)
Sargent's sketch of Adèle, Countess of Essex (Lord Gage)
Consuelo, Duchess of Marlborough (Getty Images)
Gustav Hamel standing by his Blériot monoplane (Getty Images)

Charley Castlereagh, later 7th Marquess of Londonderry (Lord Gage)
Arthur Balfour and Nellie Londonderry at Panshanger (Getty Images)
Lady Desborough photographed by Alexander Bassano in 1912
    (National Portrait Gallery)

Section Three
Panshanger in its Edwardian heyday (*Country Life*)
The Panshanger picture gallery in Lord Cowper's day (*Country Life*)
Ivo Grenfell in military uniform in 1919 (Lord Gage)
Sir Philip Sassoon around 1920 (Getty Images)
Ettie Desborough at a point-to-point in 1922 (Getty Images)
Brocket Hall in Hertfordshire in 1923 (*Country Life*)
The saloon at Brocket (*Country Life*)
Ettie Desborough and Arthur Balfour in 1924 (Getty Images)
Alice, Marchioness of Salisbury (London Library)
Mary Wemyss, Arthur Balfour and a chow in 1925 (National Portrait
    Gallery)
Winnie, Duchess of Portland in 1925 (Lord Gage)
Edward Marjoribanks with Willie Desborough in 1926 (Lord Gage)
Stanley Baldwin with Willie Desborough in 1931 (Lord Gage)
The Panshanger drawing-room in 1935 (*Country Life*)
The Desboroughs' Norfolk house, Whiteslea, in 1936 (Lord Gage)
A Desborough family portrait in 1937 (Lord Gage)
London evacuees with their babies at Panshanger in 1941 (Getty
    Images)

The Westmorlands

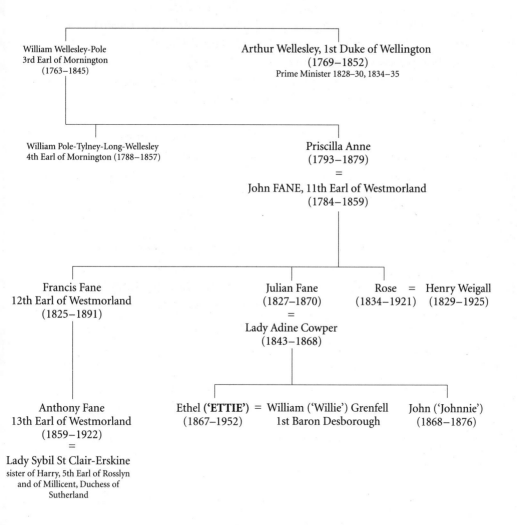

William Wellesley-Pole
3rd Earl of Mornington
(1763–1845)

Arthur Wellesley, 1st Duke of Wellington
(1769–1852)
Prime Minister 1828–30, 1834–35

William Pole-Tylney-Long-Wellesley
4th Earl of Mornington (1788–1857)

Priscilla Anne
(1793–1879)
=
John FANE, 11th Earl of Westmorland
(1784–1859)

Francis Fane
12th Earl of Westmorland
(1825–1891)

Julian Fane
(1827–1870)
=
Lady Adine Cowper
(1843–1868)

Rose = Henry Weigall
(1834–1921)   (1829–1925)

Anthony Fane
13th Earl of Westmorland
(1859–1922)
=
Lady Sybil St Clair-Erskine
sister of Harry, 5th Earl of Rosslyn
and of Millicent, Duchess of
Sutherland

Ethel ('**ETTIE**') = William ('Willie') Grenfell
(1867–1952)   1st Baron Desborough

John ('Johnnie')
(1868–1876)

The Cowpers

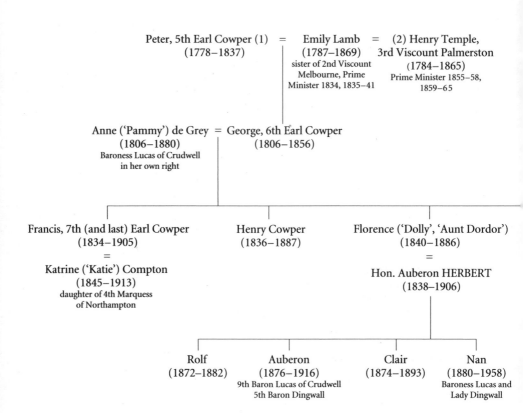

Peter, 5th Earl Cowper (1) = Emily Lamb = (2) Henry Temple,
(1778–1837)   (1787–1869)   3rd Viscount Palmerston
                               sister of 2nd Viscount   (1784–1865)
                                Melbourne, Prime   Prime Minister 1855–58,
                               Minister 1834, 1835–41   1859–65

Anne ('Pammy') de Grey = George, 6th Earl Cowper
(1806–1880)   (1806–1856)
Baroness Lucas of Crudwell
in her own right

Francis, 7th (and last) Earl Cowper   Henry Cowper   Florence ('Dolly', 'Aunt Dordor')
(1834–1905)   (1836–1887)   (1840–1886)
=   =
Katrine ('Katie') Compton   Hon. Auberon HERBERT
(1845–1913)   (1838–1906)
daughter of 4th Marquess
of Northampton

Rolf   Auberon   Clair   Nan
(1872–1882)   (1876–1916)   (1874–1893)   (1880–1958)
                  9th Baron Lucas of Crudwell   Baroness Lucas and
                  5th Baron Dingwall   Lady Dingwall

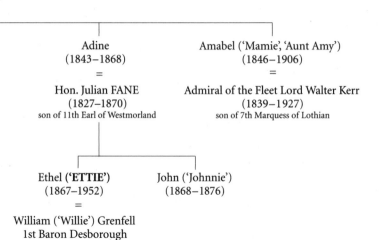

Adine
(1843–1868)
=
Hon. Julian FANE
(1827–1870)
son of 11th Earl of Westmorland

Amabel ('Mamie', 'Aunt Amy')
(1846–1906)
=
Admiral of the Fleet Lord Walter Kerr
(1839–1927)
son of 7th Marquess of Lothian

Ethel (**'ETTIE'**)
(1867–1952)
=
William ('Willie') Grenfell
1st Baron Desborough

John ('Johnnie')
(1868–1876)

The Desboroughs

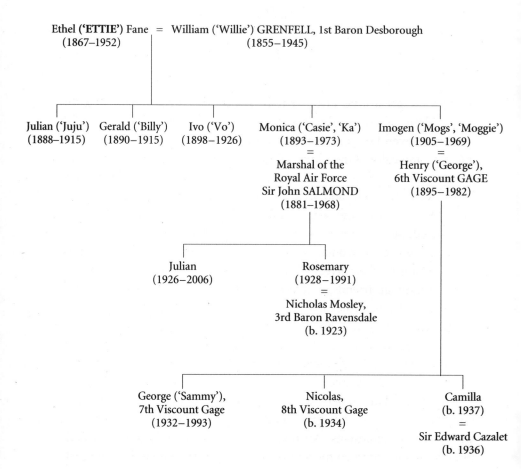

Ethel (**'ETTIE'**) Fane = William ('Willie') GRENFELL, 1st Baron Desborough
(1867–1952)   (1855–1945)

Julian ('Juju')   Gerald ('Billy')   Ivo ('Vo')   Monica ('Casie', 'Ka')   Imogen ('Mogs', 'Moggie')
(1888–1915)   (1890–1915)   (1898–1926)   (1893–1973)   (1905–1969)
                                                =   =
                                      Marshal of the   Henry ('George'),
                                      Royal Air Force   6th Viscount GAGE
                                      Sir John SALMOND   (1895–1982)
                                      (1881–1968)

Julian   Rosemary
(1926–2006)   (1928–1991)
                              =
                       Nicholas Mosley,
                    3rd Baron Ravensdale
                         (b. 1923)

George ('Sammy'),   Nicolas,   Camilla
7th Viscount Gage   8th Viscount Gage   (b. 1937)
(1932–1993)   (b. 1934)   =
                                           Sir Edward Cazalet
                                           (b. 1936)

Prologue

THIS IS A great love story. It tells of a mother's passionate love for her children, of her own burning love of life, of the privileged, grateful men who loved her, and of the women who loved her for her loyalty, intuition and calm. 'Great love', Edith Wharton once wrote, 'was wise, strong, powerful, like genius, like any other dominant form of human power. It knew itself, and what it wanted, and how to attain its ends.' Ettie Desborough's life was a story of love that was dominant, and knew itself, and what it wanted, and how to attain its ends. This is the story of a powerful woman who excited men, enthralled them, turned the direction of their lives; of a woman who amazed her elders, and inspired intimate friends, casual acquaintances and her children's contemporaries by her rules of life, her zest and her exemplary power of acceptance. It is also a story of piercing pain, shocking bereavements and utter desolation; but supremely a celebration of a woman who never yielded to self-pity, who vanquished despair and never exhausted her deep reserves of love.

An orphan shunted between the vast beautiful houses of the dowager countesses who were her grandmothers and the clever childless uncles who were her guardians. An observant, knowing child who watched, listened to and charmed the adults of the 1870s. An intensely vivid girl, who captivated London Society in the 1880s, and remained one of its most distinctive figures for sixty years. A young wife, who obtained a peerage for her husband Willie Grenfell, and in the 1890s made his house on the Thames at Taplow a favourite gathering point for the politicians, writers and wits comprising the social set known as the Souls. The heiress to great estates, the inheritor of long aristocratic traditions, the last of the Whig hostesses, concerned with the important events of her day, and the intimate friend of six prime ministers – Rosebery, Balfour, Asquith, Baldwin, Chamberlain and Churchill – and countless statesmen. The holder of an unrivalled position in the Edwardian worlds of wit and fashion, caparisoned with the glittering treasures of grace, charm and intelligence, a great lady who never lost her eminence. Wilde, Chesterton, Wells, Kipling, Yeats, Barrie and Sassoon are a few of the writers who came to play in her houses. Renowned in her own generation as a mother, and famous as a symbol of grieving maternity; the archetypal mother of the Lost Generation of brilliant young men killed in the First World War, a myth which her own writings created as much as anyone's. A woman whose whole existence seemed a cry for life, yet was dogged by death, and whose private mottoes, encapsulating her credo and experience, were '*Vivre, c'est survivre*' and 'life is a series of farewells'.

Ettie Desborough was born at the apogee of Victorian confidence in the 1860s and survived into the age of the new Elizabethans – a dilapidated but magnificently resilient remnant from an epoch that seemed irretrievably lost. Her last years were comforted by members of the house of Cecil, the great political dynasty who were the leading family of Hertfordshire, where she lived for her last thirteen years. The Cecils, at the last, knew her best.

As there are no longer any places like Taplow [Violet Cecil wrote in 1951] or people like the Grenfells, I should like to draw a picture of Mrs Grenfell (afterwards Lady Desborough) for those who did not know her in the glory of her youth or in her golden prime. In my experience she was unique . . . Mrs Grenfell had great good looks, a tall elegant figure and she dressed with taste. She had fine dark blue eyes, heavily lidded, a lovely skin and beautiful dark hair; she had a way of lowering her eyelids, when she was really attending to what was said, that was entirely seductive. She was a woman with whom men fell and stayed in love, and she was a woman who had many intimate men friends, and into the last, often close intimacies, sex never intruded . . . What distinguished her above her contemporaries, what was rare in the degree to which she possessed it, was her lovely urbanity. In looks, in voice, in speech, in approach she expressed all that can be imagined of exquisite manners and courtesy. Without being openly flattering, she said the most charming things to and about her friends, she had few equals in the conduct of easy, pleasant talk, and however witty, however spirited she was – and she could be both – she never passed the bounds of perfect manners . . . To watch Mrs Grenfell presiding over a tea-table, to see her introducing her guests to each other and leading the talk, was a lesson in the art of behaviour.

Violet Cecil was Ettie's contemporary. Her nephew David Cecil was thirty-five years younger, but knew Ettie all his life.

It is easy [he wrote] to name Lady Desborough's titles to fame in English social history: the most brilliant hostess in an age of brilliant hostesses, the intimate confidential friend to successive generations of distinguished men and women over a period of 60 years. It is harder to analyse the complex and compelling nature of her personality. Perhaps it lay in the unusual blend of the natural and civilized. The Gainsborough-like distinction of her appearance and her exquisite, elaborate grace of manner were intensely civilized. So also was the subtle art of her talk: so unegotistically concerned to bring out the best in her interlocutor that it showed as much in her listening as in her speaking; yet enchanting him, when she did speak, by its mingling of zest and *finesse*, imaginative sensibility and delicious sharp-edged humour. Civilized in another sense was her extraordinary self-discipline, most impressively apparent in the heroic courage with which she met the tragedy of her later years, but showing itself also in small things. She never broke an engagement, till late in life she was always downstairs to early breakfast even though she had been up till 4 o'clock in the morning . . . her self-control was the mode through which she expressed a robust, ardent nature, aglow with normal affections, normal ambitions, spontaneous enjoyment of normal pleasures – all energized by an astonishing vitality. Her appetite for life was insatiable. The only things she found it hard to tolerate were sourness and defeatism . . . Her rarest, most precious quality was her power of sympathy. Her friends turned first to her if they were in trouble. For they knew she would understand best. The radiant leader of fashion, the magnetic woman of the world was also the tenderest of all companions to a broken heart.

Ettie Desborough was the most patrician woman of her age. Though there were other women who preserved the traditions of sumptuous aristocratic hospitality until the 1940s – the Duchess of Portland and the Marchioness of Londonderry, for example – she was the last coroneted hostess to keep a salon at which politicians, writers and *les gens du monde* met to discuss ideas, play with words, flirt with clever women and meet the young. It was crucial to her parties that there was a mix of ages, and that all ages felt wanted. David Cecil's lifelong devotion began at the age of fifteen, when she broke off from a conversation with a great statesman, and gave him all her attention and blandishments for a full twenty minutes. There were other famed hostesses with salons in the first half of the twentieth century, but Ettie was the only English aristocrat among them. None of the others could trace their antecedents to the Holland House set, or perpetuated *ancien régime* manners, assumptions and pronunciation. Many of the other prominent London hostesses of Ettie's time had crossed the Atlantic: Adèle Essex was a New Yorker, Emerald Cunard was brought up in San Francisco by Chinese servants, Nancy Astor was a Virginian and Laura Corrigan hailed from the Midwest. Though Lady Ottoline Morrell was a Tory duke's sister, she rejected all aristocratic precedents for her salon at Garsington. As to the others, super-snobbish Maggie Greville (whom Ettie avoided) was the illegitimate daughter of a Scottish brewer, and pretentious Sibyl Colefax (whose parties Ettie thought unstylish) was a barrister's wife with her own interior decorating business.

For John Buchan, another Taplow regular, Ettie was the inspiration for Lady Flambard in his novel *The Gap in the Curtain*. 'Her interests', Buchan wrote, 'are multitudinous, and all are reflected in her hospitality, so that a procession goes through her house which looks like a rehearsal for the Judgment Day. Politics, religion, philanthropy, letters, science, art and the most brainless of fashion – she takes them all to her capacious heart.' Buchan's Lady Flambard never lets her guests slacken. 'All are put through their paces,' he said: the talk was fast and demanding; and 'good fun, if you are feeling up to it, but not quite the thing for a rest-cure'.

There was nothing impromptu about Ettie or her parties. There was no place in her scheme for unpremeditated impulses or chance events. She was expressive but not theatrical: every look, gesture, inflexion and every syllable told with her. She was a tremendous flirt, but erected impassable defences to her virtue. She wanted men to pine for her, but did not want to make her position precarious by open intrigues: she liked emotional *sensation* but shrank from scandal or even bothersome talk. When young she thought it amusing to turn herself into a masterpiece of temperament and caprice. She liked brittle pretexts for taking offence. She craved attention, admiration and even adulation, enjoyed controlling people and requisitioning their emotions. Her caprices could be unintentionally cruel until the grief of 1915 altered her for ever. Some of the men in her train were rich, others were powerful, most were wits, and a few were gloriously young and handsome; but none of them was stupid. The four who meant most to her must be named at once: her husband Willie, and her sons Julian, Billy and Ivo.

Willie Desborough, it was often said, embodied the ideal of an English gentleman, and his sons were leaders in that ill-starred generation of men for whom Wilfred Owen wrote his sonnet 'Anthem for Doomed Youth' and Sassoon wrote 'Counter-Attack'. The two eldest died heroes' deaths, within weeks of one another, in the trench warfare of 1915, and the youngest was accidentally killed eleven years later. 'They do indeed have tragedy piled upon tragedy in that family,' Lord Winterton said. Julian and Billy were undergraduates at Oxford before the war. 'These two brothers were among the most brilliant men of their generation, and both had exceptional gifts of body and mind,' the *Balliol College War Memorial Book* averred. 'Both were intensely alive: each was the joy of his friends.' Julian came up to Oxford at the age of eighteen in 1906, 'a splendid figure of a man, over six feet high, with two greyhounds, a famous Australian stock-whip, and an immense enjoyment of life'. He plunged into academic study with pugnacious zest, discovered a strong bent for philosophy, dug down to the root of things, and suffered mental agonies with his neck-or-nothing attitudes. 'There were no plains in Julian's world – it was all mountain-ranges and valleys, and anything which he could not do with his whole heart he would not do at all.' This was the first son whom Ettie made and dominated.

She commemorated Billy and him in a book, *Pages from a Family Journal*, which was never commercially published. Instead, she sent it to a few hundred of her friends; and it is proof of her influence in her times, of the emotional power that she exercised over her contemporaries, that it was formative in the literary depiction of the First World War. The dead boys were, Ottoline Morrell noted after reading her copy in 1916, 'Olympians, and their lives seem to have been one long joy-ride, for they ride over any obstacle. Death seemed to them the last joy-ride to still more glorious Elysian Fields.' The book presented the Desborough children, and the life that their mother had made for them, as an idyll – and the finest incarnation of Edwardian ideals – but Ottoline Morrell felt estranged as she read Ettie's family story. 'They had perfect health, beauty, riches and good intellects. Everything that a mortal could desire and not deserve . . . Everything was called "glorious"; nothing had a thorn in it. There were no "furies grinning through the arras". What a difference there is between their way of life and thought and that of all our friends. We seem to see the imperfections of life and to want them made better; they find it as good as it can be . . . They are never haunted by the inequalities of life, for they feel that by right they are above them all. They live in the sunshine, and when the sun doesn't shine they pretend it does. They have money, good health and every door immediately flies open to them. They never see *underneath*; their religion is never to criticize; always to see good in everything.'

There were heart-rending and even frightening reasons for the stubborn gospel of joy that Ettie had devised for herself and her children. It felt indispensable for her survival. Her mother's family were vulnerable to hereditary melancholy, which shadowed and cut short their lives. She recognised this trait in herself and fought it hard; two or perhaps three of her five children inherited it. As a young woman she determined that a veil of high spirits must be drawn across her face, but menacing depression was never entirely beaten. 'I've been so low somehow, the way life sometimes sweeps one up in its dust-pan, for no reason, & hangs firm between one's soul & all the beauty & ecstasy,' she told a friend in 1921. 'Life needs a lot of courage I think, & its prices are cruelly high.'

Several forces kept her going. One was her iron resolve. There was valiant self-discipline in everything she did. Inseparable from this was her religious faith: she prayed every day, she was convinced of the efficacy of prayer, and her Christianity was crucial to every choice and decision she made. She quoted Nietzsche's exclamation after marshalling his whole case against the existence of God: ' "O Thou, my necessity".' God was Ettie's necessity. Her sensibility, too, sustained her. She disliked music, and was a conventional philistine about the visual arts (Julian's friends thought Taplow was furnished like a hotel), but literature was indispensable to her gladness with life, and she was deeply susceptible to natural beauty. Trees, bright sunlight, strong winds, canopies of foliage or wide open skies above her head, the fast-moving shadows of scudding clouds crossing empty hillsides, swimming in the bracing sea, the colours of spring and autumn, bright flowers and exotic shrubs – these all gave her sublime joy and transcendent perceptions.

There is a letter of 1917, written on the second anniversary of Julian's death to her friend Lord Londonderry, which reaches to the heart of her. She was mourning her sons, but had felt this deathliness at her core long before they died. 'I feel often like a dead woman, still able to move & speak & eat & laugh, but the real person gone far away. It is *all wrong* – I am always fighting, & shall prevail at last. How fine Montaigne's saying is, "We must live among the living" . . . It is such a strange sensation, like being bled to death inwardly, & all the fighting-power being drained away – but after all the only real battles worth winning are against the long odds. The wonderful beauty of Spring helps, as one looks out into the light of gold, & understanding comes why men thought of the Rainbow as the *promise* of God – one feels that in a way about all beauty.'

Ettie revealed herself only to intimate friends. To those who did not know her well, she could seem, like other *femmes du monde*, hard, affected, self-satisfied, insincere. Not so to those who knew her well. 'Lady Desborough was the cleverest of us all,' wrote Margot Asquith after nearly forty years of friendship. 'Her flavours were more delicate, her social sensibility finer; and she added to chronic presence of mind, undisguised effrontery . . . She was a woman of genius . . . who created more joy for other people than anybody.' The happiness that Ettie Desborough created for others was a work of art – a precisely

7

planned, deliberately contrived appeal to other people's hearts and senses. The happiness that she made for herself was an act of will. Her gladness with life was an act of faith.

CHAPTER I

The Orphan

✍

ETTIE'S FIRST DISTINCT memory was of the sound of weeping and the taste of sweetness. It was in April 1870 and her father, Julian Fane, had just died at the age of forty-two. She was sitting on the floor with her younger brother Johnnie in a darkened room at the Portman Square home of her grandmother Lady Westmorland. 'I was not quite three years old,' she recalled over seventy years later. 'Our mother had died eighteen months before. We were both dressed entirely in black, and all the people round us were crying, but the fact that remains vivid in memory is that we were tasting chocolate for the first time.'*

The man they were mourning had been a brilliant figure. He belonged to a dynasty that had risen to power in Stuart England: the richer branch became Earls of Darlington and Dukes of Cleveland, and spelt their surname Vane; their kinsmen called themselves Fane and were made Earls of Westmorland by King James I. Altogether the Vanes and Fanes – puritans and cavaliers, soldiers and sailors, magnates and conspirators, diplomats and bishops – achieved a splendid lustre. Julian Fane's father, the eleventh Earl of Westmorland, fought against Napoleon in Egypt and the Peninsular Wars; and after the capture of Paris in 1814 was sent to Florence as Envoy Extraordinary to the Grand Duke of Tuscany. In addition to his professional distinctions – a general in the army as well as a diplomatist – Westmorland was accomplished in his avocations. He composed Italianate operas, anthems, hymns and

---

* It seems to imply a non-existent intimacy to use the nickname Ettie throughout this book, and feels presumptuous to bandy about the Christian names and diminutives of her husband, children and friends. However, the extensive use of full names and correct titles looked clumsy and mannered.

madrigals, played the violin, befriended Meyerbeer and Mendelssohn, and was founding President of the Royal Academy of Music. In 1811 he married Priscilla Wellesley-Pole, the Earl of Mornington's clever and stalwart daughter and the Duke of Wellington's niece. The Westmorlands were intimate members of the Duke's domestic circle: 'Know him?' replied Julian as a small boy, when asked if he knew Wellington, 'why I'm his near relation and very particular friend.'

Julian Fane was the youngest of five sons. He was born in Florence in 1827, spent his early childhood in Tuscany and his adolescence not at an English public school, but with his parents in Berlin, where his father was appointed Minister Plenipotentiary in 1841. The Westmorlands turned the British Legation there, said the young diplomat Robert Lytton, into a 'Continental Holland House, where Genius and Beauty, Science and Fashion, Literature and Politics, could meet each other with a hearty reciprocal welcome'. Eventually Fane left Prussia for Cambridge, where he was an undergraduate at Trinity College and one of the dozen members of the select intellectual society known as the Apostles. In appearance he was striking: he stood six feet three inches tall, and his height was accentuated by his thinness and pallor. He had a buoyant temperament, poetic sensibility and playful intellect. Everyone hailed him as a brilliant mimic, subtle tease and prodigious raconteur. He was, said Robert Lytton, 'the most graceful and accomplished gentleman of the generation he adorned': musical, with a beautiful tenor voice, and a poet, whose work was admired as vivid and supple by his friends, although nowadays it seems contrived. Julian followed his father into the diplomatic service, and was appointed Secretary of the British Embassy at St. Petersburg in 1856, at Vienna in 1858 and at Paris in 1865. He was tactful and efficient, but the very antithesis of a drudge: indeed, rather a roué, who later felt swamped by remorse that he had ruined his health by late nights.

There is a stereotype of upper-class English families as loveless, undemonstrative, emotionally inept, and unfeeling about everything except money and status. This hackneyed idea is untrue of Ettie Desborough's parents and grandparents, of her uncles and aunts, indeed of most of the individuals who mattered in her life. Julian Fane loved, respected and emulated his father; and his mother (said his best friend William Harcourt) was 'the central idol of his heart'. Mother and son adored one another's company, they were candid and trusting with each other, they depended on one another for both amusement and support; and in the terrible crises of Julian Fane's last years, Priscilla Westmorland was as magnificently unbreakable as her uncle the Iron Duke.

In 1864, while Julian was *en poste* in Vienna, his mother met a gentle, quiet, shy half-child of twenty called Lady Adine Cowper. 'There was a girl after Julian's idea of what a woman should be,' Lady Westmorland decided: 'her beauty, too, with fine dark eyes and hair was of the kind he most admired.' She wrote to him at the time that Adine Cowper was meant for him. Two years later, in August 1866, he contrived to visit Wrest Park, where Adine lived with her widowed mother Countess Cowper. After two or three days, during which Julian and Adine strolled together, chaperoned by her sisters at a tactful distance, he proposed and was eagerly accepted. He coined a new pet name for his bride: 'Deeny'.

Short engagements were the custom then. The young pair married less than two months later, on 29 September 1866, and spent their honeymoon at Panshanger, the Cowpers' neo-gothic seat in Hertfordshire. A mile from the house they were met by a mounted escort of the Cowper tenantry, who brought them to the lodge gates where a force of the local military volunteers was respectfully mustered. A lady then presented 'Deeny' with a bouquet, a local dignitary read a resounding address of welcome, and after enthusiastic cheers, Julian had to reply to the address, make a separate speech to the Volunteers, thank the ladies who had brought the bouquet and finally harangue the escort of tenants on horseback. It was from Panshanger that Julian wrote to his mother next day: 'You will be glad to hear that she calls herself "perfectly happy" and that her smiling face bears out that assertion to the full. She says that I am gentle and good with her, & I tell her that she is as tender and gracious as it is possible to be with me – so you will guess that we are getting on as well as possible together.' Deeny conceived a child in the first fortnight of the marriage.

In October the Fanes moved to Paris, where Julian resumed work at the Embassy. No marriage could have begun more auspiciously, Lady Westmorland judged, for Deeny 'delighted in literary pursuits – & (except that she had no taste for music) entered warmly into all his thoughts and occupations – indeed it may be said *she merged herself completely* in him, & had no thought or feeling but what emanated from him'.

In May 1867 the Fanes returned to London, for it was thought preferable that Adine should await her confinement near her family. As a result, Ethel Anne Priscilla Fane was born on 27 June 1867 at Lady Westmorland's town house, 29 Portman Square. Breastfeeding proved a joyous experience for Adine, and was no doubt satisfying for her daughter too. When the Fanes returned to Paris in July, the baby and her two nurses – one of them the redoubtable Mrs Matilda Wake – travelled with them. Julian's letters from Paris to his mother tell the story of Ettie's infancy with doting joy. On 23 August, for example, he wrote, 'The baby really is the most charming little thing imaginable & I adore her as does the whole household. It is charming to me to see Deeny's maternal tenderness.' And on 1 October: 'Ethel was vaccinated yesterday from a beautiful big baby who was brought here by the Doctor – just as Asses are brought to the door so that there may be no deception about the milk. She behaved riotously & put herself into a towering passion as she often does; but has seemed comfortable ever since.'

Early in 1868 Julian resigned from the diplomatic service: partly because country air was recommended for his persistently sore throat (he was a heavy smoker), but mainly because Adine's shyness made the social duties of a diplomat's wife too irksome. His brother, Lord Westmorland, lent him the family home, Apethorpe, standing in 200 acres of parkland amid the wooded plantations of Northamptonshire. Apethorpe was a large grey-stoned house built by an Elizabethan Chancellor of the Exchequer, Sir Walter Mildmay, the founder of Emmanuel College, Cambridge. The cloistered calm of Emmanuel's quadrangles resembled Mildmay's house at Apethorpe, where a great central hall separated two inner courtyards: through its deep-latticed and mullioned windows one could hear the cooing of innumerable doves. Recently the Westmorlands had built a village school, a lending library and a night school for the older boys and men – amenities that began the long, slow death of deference. 'The old feudal feeling is disappearing,' Julian Fane's sister Lady Rose Weigall wrote in 1869. 'The younger men are ceasing to touch their hats indiscriminately to

THE ORPHAN

every gentleman who passes; mere *doles* evoke no gratitude at all, but
the peasant's greeting is as respectful as ever. To half-educate the
peasant, and then expect him to remain unenvious, contented and
apathetic as before, is a great mistake.'

The timeless seclusion of Apethorpe was idyllic: Julian and Deeny
led peaceful, bookish lives, and his mind brimmed with literary
schemes. His daughter gave him daily pleasure, and he monitored her
development, teething and baby talk with close and loving pride. At
Apethorpe, on 18 July 1868, Adine gave premature birth to her second
child, Johnnie: during the flurry and anxiety of these hours Ettie was
deposited with various unsuitable manservants. 'Ethel', Julian reported
to his mother, 'was dreadfully unhappy while Mrs Wake and all of us
were engaged in bringing the brother into the world. She was left part
of the time with Duncan, and at one moment with James! The result
is that she positively refuses now to leave Mrs Wake's arms.' She
remained 'loath to let Mrs Wake out of her sight' – an early sign of her
lifelong possessiveness – and became very demanding of attention –
another lifelong trait. To ensure her parents' unwavering devotion, the
little girl embarked on the earliest of a lifetime of charm offensives.
'Altho' Ethel's adoration of Nanny is paramount, she is very dear and
cabotin [theatrical] with both of us,' Julian told his mother. 'If I pretend
to be asleep she comes & strokes my face & if I don't answer she lays
her cheek against mine till I notice her – or else she inserts her finger
(very gently) into my eye! She is very coquettish.'

Adine could not rally from her confinement. On 24 August, Julian
took her to Wrest; but there, within a few days, her condition became
so alarming that he brought her to London for medical advice. Sea air
was recommended and the Fanes went with their children to Brighton
on 21 September. 'Ettie is washed in sea-water & delights in it, & she is
enchanted with all the sights and sounds of Brighton,' Julian reported;
but Adine reacted against the town. She felt feverish, tremulous and
confused, and insisted on coming away to Canizaro, Lady Westmorland's summer villa at Wimbledon. The two little children returned
with Nannie Wake to Wrest. Adine lived a fortnight longer, 'days of
anguish unspeakable', said Lady Westmorland. As she lay dying, so
her old governess told Ettie years later, she murmured repeatedly,
'Only two years and a bit, only two years and a bit' – for that was the

13

tiny span of her happy marriage. Adine Fane died on 20 October 1868, when Ettie was sixteen months old.

Lady Westmorland brought her heartbroken son from Wimbledon to the Portman Square house, where his children were waiting for him. 'The girl, it seems, is devoted to him & her pleasure in seeing him again told upon him,' wrote Princess Mary, Duchess of Teck on 5 November after visiting Lady Westmorland. In the ensuing months Julian's sole consolation was his little daughter, who was 'joyous and amiable', he wrote on 10 November, 'pretty and attractive in all her ways'. The little child sensed her father's depression. 'Ettie sometimes startles me by her intelligence,' he wrote in January. 'She was with me just now and after pulling a lot of books off a shelf she took a photograph-book, and I said "No, Ettie, not that book. It was Mama's." She immediately let it go, and came slowly up to me, and said in a very solemn voice, "Mama's book", as if that explained perfectly to her that she was to respect it.'

Julian Fane suffered a slow physical collapse after his wife's death. He spent the summer and autumn of 1869 shifting between Wimbledon, Wrest and Panshanger before settling for the winter with his mother in Portman Square. Each month he coughed more and grew hoarser until in January 1870 his throat seized up. He lost his voice, was unable to swallow, and kept alive by sucking small pieces of fruit. Only his mother and sister Rose Weigall could interpret the low sounds that were all that were left to him of human speech. 'I used', Lady Westmorland told Robert Lytton, 'to put my ear close to his face with his dear arm round my neck & so he could talk without fatigue. Rose understood him still better by watching his lips.' For months he kept his children at Wrest, for he dreaded seeing them frightened by his wretched appearance, but six weeks before his death they were brought to London and he saw them most days for a few minutes. The anguish of the adult world, at this time, must have been palpable to Ettie. Julian Fane died on 19 April 1870.

Under Fane's will, Rose Weigall and Adine's bachelor brother Henry were appointed as guardians to his children. In accordance with his wishes, the lives of the two orphans were divided between their grandmothers. For six months of each year they were to be settled with their grandmother Lady Westmorland in Portman Square and at Wimbledon, and each July they would go to their grandmother Cowper at Wrest. Ettie and Johnnie became the objects of the Fanes' and the Cowpers' grieving devotion. 'Our parents had been the worship of their two families, and we were all that was left of them, and never can babies have been more loved and cherished,' Ettie recalled in old age. For years she was dressed in mourning black: when she was five years old, her aunt Adza Westmorland gave her a pink Paris frock, which made her grandmother Westmorland burst into sobs. The orphans came to feel that it was natural that grown-up people should often be in tears.

The Westmorland half of her childhood – spent in Portman Square and rural Wimbledon – was always remembered by Ettie with gratitude and pleasure; but Ettie felt much closer to her mother's family, the Cowpers, than to the Fanes. Temperamentally she had many Cowper traits, and liked her Cowper uncles and aunts more than their Fane equivalents: the decisive turns in her life were towards the Cowpers, and in early middle age she inherited Cowper possessions that materially meant a great deal to her. She was devoted to her Cowper cousins, but with the Westmorlands, Fanes and Weigalls she was increasingly distant. While the Fanes were staunch Tories, the Cowpers were the quintessence of Whiggery in their exclusivity, their acquisitiveness, their indifference to popular opinions, their complicated intermarriages, and their amassing of rent rolls and political sway by the honest old method of prudent marital alliances.

Whigs like the Cowpers spoke in their own dialect – Devonshire House or Holland House pronunciation as it was known – in which golden was pronounced 'goulden', yellow as 'yaller', cucumber as 'cowcumber', officer as 'orficer', apron as 'napern', bracelet as 'brasslet', chariot as 'charrt'. It was forbidden for good little Whig children to talk of coffee or of a mantelpiece: these were Tory mannerisms, and Ettie learnt to say 'cawfee' and chimneypiece. Her cousin Mabell Airlie said that Ettie's enunciation resembled their great-grandmother Lady Palmerston's. Indeed, Ettie was said, at her death, to be the last surviving speaker of the authentic Whig drawl, with its deep, slow, emphatic pronunciation of certain words; and yet her speech was clipped too, so that Panshanger was both lingered over and abbreviated – 'Pppannns' – and her husband's house Taplow was 'Tttappp'. Ettie had a more distinctive inflexion still, for she slurred the letter l so that it resembled n.

The strength of the Cowper influence partly arose from the fact that Lady Westmorland was already aged seventy-seven when the Fane orphans went to live with her. 'We loved Grandmama very, very dearly,' wrote Ettie. 'She was an angel of kindness to us, but she was then very old; still very tall, but hardly moving from her chair, surrounded by relics of the past. I think that she never got over the sorrow of our father's death, the most adored of all her children.' In the past she had entertained many eminent men, but by 1870 her only constant visitor was a dapper, elderly beau, Lord Melville, who had admired her all his life and eventually settled in her house. The little orphans called him Nana and liked him (he took snuff and rinsed his mouth publicly after meals), although in retrospect Ettie suspected he must have been dull, for Lady Westmorland rather ignored him.

The redemptive figure of Ettie's childhood was Nannie Wake. Matilda Wake (1821–1906) was a resolute little woman, with a pink face, silver hair and a great love of truth, who gave unstinting attention to Johnnie and Ettie – indeed, lavished intense protective love on them – and ensured that their existence, which might have been lonely, disrupted and uncertain, was stable, happy and thumping good fun. 'Nannie was the *clou* of all those days, our stronghold and hope; never can there have been greater devotion than she poured out on us,' Ettie recalled in old age. She thought Mrs Wake loved Johnnie most, 'partly because he was very delicate . . . and partly because he was a much nicer child than me'.

Ettie became a Londoner. Baker Street abutted Portman Square, and all the teeming street life familiar from Sherlock Holmes stories – the rattling four-wheelers and hansom cabs, the cries of street urchins, the tunes of barrel-organs, the calls of street hawkers, the bell of the white-coated muffin man, the crossing sweepers and lamplighters and marching bandsmen – made up the sights and sounds of Ettie's London childhood. Portman Square was then an elegant locality containing two important town houses built for eighteenth-century noblemen, Montagu House, designed by Athenian Stuart and destroyed by bombs in

World War Two, and Home House, which had been designed and furnished by Robert Adam. The great London landlord, Lord Portman, also had an imposing mansion on the square. Lady Westmorland's house, lying between Upper Berkeley Street and Seymour Street (now the site of an over-marbled and chandeliered American hotel), was less magnificent than Montagu, Home or Portman House; but the spacious fenced square, with its thick shrubbery, was a special pleasure for the Fane orphans. 'Best of all London fun of those days', Ettie recalled, 'were the games in Portman Square, with a screaming rout of children.'

In June of each year Grandmama Westmorland used to move to Canizaro, her large villa at Wimbledon, bringing Ettie, Johnnie, Nana Melville and the Weigalls in her train. Ettie particularly enjoyed the summer of 1871 when her little second cousins surnamed Gore – Mabell (born 1866), Alice (her exact contemporary born in 1867), Artie (1868) and Esther (1870) – were installed in a nearby house. Their mother, Edith Sudley, died of tuberculosis that autumn, and the quartet was brought up by their grandmother, Ettie's great-aunt Fanny Jocelyn (born a Cowper) and their nanny. A succession of family bereavements kept the Gore sisters, like Ettie, resentfully in perpetual mourning clothes – ugly black tarlatan dresses and pudding-basin hats. They felt secret stirrings of rebellion against Lady Jocelyn's grim relentless harping that the world was a vale of tears, most pleasures were sinful and humankind was rotten with original sin. In self-defence against this morbid, life-denying regime, the sisters fastened on to Ettie as someone vividly and intensely alive. She and Ally Gore remained the closest of friends for eighty years: the tiny girls playing under the great beech trees at Canizaro in 1871 became two superb old women, Lady Desborough and the Marchioness of Salisbury, living in large houses a few miles apart in wartime Hertfordshire, visiting and supporting one another, loving one another, enduring bombardment and rationing, bereavement and disability, a levelling social temper and slipshod new manners, with magnificent resilience and dignity.

At the end of each July the Fane orphans always returned with Mrs Wake to Wrest and their Cowper grandmother for six months or more. These visits were crucial in forming Ettie's outlook, her loyalties and her destiny. Lady Cowper proved a more decisive influence than old Lady Westmorland; and Wrest itself mattered more to Ettie than Canizaro. Indeed (to use Henry James's phrase) it was the Great Good Place of her long life.

Wrest came to the Cowpers by a complicated trail of inheritance in which heiresses unusually dominated. Henry Grey, 12th Earl of Kent – the earldom had been bestowed by Edward IV in 1465 – was a great territorial magnate who was raised to a dukedom by Queen Anne in 1710. Most of his titles became extinct on his death in 1740; but his estates passed through the female line, and were eventually inherited by the second Earl de Grey. On de Grey's death in 1859 his elder daughter, Anne, the widowed Countess Cowper, inherited the barony of Lucas (bestowed on a Countess of Kent by Charles II and transmissible through the female line) together with his great town house, 4 St James's Square (built by the Duke of Kent in the 1720s), his seat at Wrest, and other land, including Sawley on the Yorkshire–Lancashire border.

Countess Cowper was thus a great heiress. She lived, recalled Ettie, with 'the great *train-de-vie* of those days; powdered footmen and be-wigged coachmen when she was in London, and thirty gardeners at Wrest, and an immense number of indoor servants, and she spent great sums on charity. But she was very frugal about all personal indulgence (except that she always washed in elder-flower water, which smelt delicious), and I do not suppose that she spent £100 a year on herself; her clothes were all made by her maid; and her children and grand-children were all brought up on that scale of ideas.' Lady Cowper – a first-rate manager with an alert and decisive mind – disliked politically meddling women, including her mother-in-law Lady Palmerston, but was deeply inquisitive about current events. 'A very good talker, and *loved* talking, and thrashing out every detail of a subject; and liked being disagreed with, and really enjoyed a good argument,' her daughter-in-law Katie Cowper learnt. 'Honesty, straightness, intelli-gence, worth, she recognised and appreciated. And she did *not* like bores.'

Old Lady Cowper was an extreme Evangelical who reared her descendants by strict Christian precepts. 'Goodness, right-mindedness, reverence, honour, and *the Bible*, were their spiritual food,' wrote Katie Cowper, who felt her mother-in-law's religious outlook was too narrow. Lady Cowper read the Bible aloud to Ettie and Johnnie every day, and had daily prayers with them too, as did Nannie Wake. 'Looking back,' said Ettie in 1943, 'I seem to have believed at five years old exactly the same, and with the same intensity, as I believe today.' There is an elaborate chimney-piece in the Orangery at Wrest, carved with the Duke of Kent's coat of arms surmounting the Greys' motto *Foy Est Tout* – Faith is everything – and for Ettie this expressed a potent and enduring truth.

The religious ingredient in Ettie's upbringing cannot be stressed enough if her life is to be understood. She was steeped in the Christian creed: she believed that God had been incarnate in the person of Jesus Christ, that Jesus had died and risen again, that Jesus was her Saviour – that He would save her soul and bring eternal life. She kept her faith in miraculous events, in resurrection and the providence of God. Prayer and praise were not merely Christian duties, but the source for her of everyday strength. As a young woman she was confronted by and resisted 'all the inherent scepticism & doubts of the *Fin-de-Siècle*', she said; but she held to a saying of Frederic Myers that religious faith was 'the resolution to stand or fall by the nobler hypothesis'. She seldom wavered in her Christian faith (her worst crisis was in 1927, after the death of her youngest son), and always trusted Anglican doctrines, although she never made any show of religiosity. Ettie Desborough's was a Christian life: she prayed, it seems, daily; and through periods of anguish the Christian creed sustained her. One can no more understand her experiences, reactions and conduct if they are shorn of their Christian basis than one can read a novel of George Eliot's or look at a Renaissance picture without knowing their Christian context and underpinning.

As an adult Ettie was the trusted friend to whom men and women confided their loves, grief, hopes, joys and injured feelings: she was an experienced, attentive listener whose sympathy was invariably heartening. Her skills as a confidante were learnt early, for old Lady Cowper used her as a safe repository of old family episodes, Society intrigues and secrets of the heart. 'As the years went on, and her children married and scattered, I was often alone with her, and she talked to me a great deal – perhaps sometimes forgetting how young I was (just thirteen, when she died); and, looking back, some of the things she told me seem strange.' There was real devotion between the old dowager and the young orphan: 'I loved Pammy more than anyone in the world except Nannie.'

Ettie's maternal family, the Cowpers, were intelligent, charming, fatalistic and ineffective. '*Push*, in any shape, was an unknown quantity in the Cowper character,' said Katie Cowper, who was born a Compton. 'They were all undoubtedly exceptionally quick to see and quick to judge. They set the standard of worth very high; so high, indeed, that to their idea very few, if any, ever attained.' Ettie's great-aunt Minnie, who had married the philanthropic Earl of Shaftesbury, carried the Cowper melancholia into the Ashley-Cooper family: her son shot himself in a cab in Regent Street in 1886, having become depressed after succeeding to his illustrious father's titles a few months earlier.

The other great-aunt, Lady Jocelyn, a despondent creature with a puritanical religious bent, died in numb despair two months after the death of the last surviving of her four tubercular children in 1880. Fanny Jocelyn was the cheerless grandmother of Ettie's favourite cousins, Mabell, Alice and Esther Gore. 'The great beanos of our childhood were when she brought them all to stay at Wrest; Alice was exactly my age, and Mabell one year older, and they have remained the most beloved friends all my life,' Ettie recalled in old age. 'Alice was the peacemaker, and, when we were all three put to rest together on the big bed at Wrest, she was always placed in the middle, and Mabell and I fought across her body.'

Ettie was devoted to her two Cowper uncles and two Cowper aunts. The first in rank and power was Uncle Francis, the seventh and last Earl Cowper. 'When I was a very little girl', Ettie wrote after his death, 'he seemed as tall as a giant, and used to carry me about in the wastepaper-basket, up and down the long library at Wrest. One of the memories of him that comes back most of all is on the terrace at Panshanger in the sunset; he was so fond of the view of the woods and the river in that light.' There was gaiety and wit in his make-up, but he was disappointed with himself, and wrote delicate, rueful letters to *The Times* and articles in monthly magazines about the death of the Old Order, sometimes anonymously under the signature 'An Old Whig, Brooks's', and under such titles as 'The "Tap-Root" of Revolution'. He impressed his set of friends with his stately kindliness, though he did not impress his times. '*Such* a gentleman!' exclaimed Earl Grey, 'and he was so beautiful!' When he rose to address the House of Lords, 'he seemed to fill the whole House with an atmosphere of distinction'.

In 1870 Cowper had married a member of the Whig cousinhood, Katrine Compton, daughter of Admiral Lord William Compton, afterwards 4th Marquess of Northampton. It proved to be a devoted but childless marriage; and as Lord Cowper's brother and heir, Henry Cowper, showed no inclination to marry and the only other male Cowper, Lord Mount Temple, was childless, it became clear during Ettie's childhood that the family must die out, and that the Cowper estates in Hertfordshire and Kent, the de Grey estates in Bedfordshire and Yorkshire, the Melbourne lands in Derbyshire and at Brocket, would be divided and bequeathed among the children of the last Lord Cowper's three sisters: Florence, known as 'Dolly' or (by Ettie) as 'Aunt Dordor', who had married an eccentric son of the Earl of Carnarvon called Auberon Herbert; Amabel, known as 'Mamie' or Aunt Amy, the wife of Lord Walter Kerr, a veteran of the Crimean War and the Indian Mutiny, who was appointed First Sea Lord in 1899 and Admiral of the Fleet in 1904; and Ettie's mother Adine.

꒰꒱

Of all the Cowper possessions – five major houses and 38,000 acres dispersed over eleven counties – Ettie preferred Wrest. 'I was completely devoted', she said, 'to every corner of Wrest – and could never love any other place in quite exactly the same way, knowing the inside of every bush.' It was a spectacular stimulus for a child with such vivid visual receptivity and pictorial memory as Ettie. Bedfordshire is the most featureless of English counties, but the de Greys had made something rare of their possessions. In the adjacent countryside there were few buildings more substantial than farmhouses, and little in the way of woods, streams or pretty cottages; but on reaching Silsoe, the village outside Wrest's gates, the scenery changed: travellers knew at once that they were in a landscape remade by unassailable hereditary wealth. The flat, low-lying land was covered by radiating avenues of trees, and by groves with huge ash trees, massive beeches and high elms. Ettie's ancestor the Duke of Kent had employed André Le Nôtre, Louis XIV's *paysagiste* at Versailles, to lay out great gardens for him.

For the Sun King's palace Le Nôtre built a mile-long Grand Canal, which formed the axis for a system of fountains, terraces, and yew alleys ornamented with statues and vases. For the Duke of Kent Le Nôtre devised a canal called the Long Water, from which hedge-lined alleys led to enclosures containing statues, monuments or sundials. At the end of the Long Water stood a domed Baroque pavilion, and elsewhere a Palladian Bowling Green House, an amphitheatre of yew, a maze, an orangery and other follies were positioned in the grounds.

'Wrest was a Paradise for children,' Ettie averred; 'you never came to an end of the lovely surprises in those huge pleasure-grounds.' She rejoiced in and was transfigured by the beauty, romance and clandestine air of 'the little hidden pavilions, secret Lovers' Walks, Chinese temples, obelisks, sudden great still pools of water walled in by tall yew hedges, the long canal encircling all, where we fed the ducks, and fished, and – best of all in our eyes – a dogs' burial ground, with little monuments'. The miniature gravestones, with such inscriptions as 'Little Dick, Favourite Dog of Lady Amabel Cowper', still stand. The gardens contained a hundred secluded corners that were perfect for trysts; and it was at Wrest that Ettie learnt the rules that made her such an adroit and exciting flirt. Her great-grandfather Lord de Grey had shown ingenious sympathy with children's imaginations by building a pavilion, which he named Le Petit Trianon, for his grandchildren's play. It contained a drawing room, dining room and kitchen, each furnished with minuscule furniture; bygone children had painted watercolours, which hung on the walls; and frigates they had carved stood on a shelf.

As an adult Ettie owned two famous houses, Taplow and Panshanger, and often stayed in such architectural masterpieces as Houghton, Wilton, Stanway and Chatsworth. She enjoyed ducal palaces like Blenheim, Eaton, Dunrobin and Welbeck, political powerhouses such as Whittinghame and Hackwood, and the sumptuous exoticism of Rothschild and Sassoon showplaces. But Wrest remained always for her 'the ideally lovely house – of warm cream-coloured stone, the great windows set in gold like Versailles, and all the beautiful chain of downstairs rooms opening into each other, and looking south, to the big pavilion and lake, and, beyond them, the low line of the Barton Hills, seeming to us like an Alpine range as they rose out of that flat country. Every family and guest-bedroom had double-doors with octagonal ivory handles, that shut like jewel-cases, and the carpets defied the sound of any footsteps.' Lord de Grey, the first President of the Institute of British Architects, was responsible for this masterpiece. In the 1830s he had pulled down the Kents' old house and erected a building of his own design on a new site.

'Looking back to our life at Wrest, it seems like centuries ago,' Ettie noted in 1943. 'There was only one bathroom in that lovely house, and I never knew it used. Our nurseries were at the top of the house, and our nursery-maids staggered up the vast stone stairs four times a day, carrying heavy trays of meals; once a knife dropped down from the tray, and half cut off the odd-man's nose far below. The downstairs rooms were lit by lamps, wheeled round the house on trolleys, but in the upstairs rooms there were only candles – few and far between, and I well remember groping through the darkness of Pammy's sitting-room towards the two little twinkling stars by which she read.' Ettie and Johnnie were often sent to the village at Wrest's gates, Silsoe, with messages and gifts from Pammy, and knew every inhabitant. She never forgot her pleasure in the village shop, kept by the Miss Flints, whose chocolate-toffee she found delectable. She would return from Silsoe laden with gossip: 'I was a sharp little child, and knew the small secrets of the village and the household all too well, and Pammy used to laugh so.' Lady Cowper maintained all the old traditions. The Silsoe village girls wore a livery of scarlet cloaks and white hats, handed out by her in person once a year, and curtsied when they passed Ettie or her grandmother. Ettie always curtsied back to them.

Ettie learnt to read at three. 'I was an awful little bookworm as a child, and had read *Jane Eyre* by stealth, in Jane the nursery-maid's rather dark little bedroom, when I was six; and also *Oliver Twist*, when Pammy thought I was only contentedly looking at the pictures – and I woke in the night, screaming "Fagin".' Years later she loved reading aloud to her children the early Victorian tales that she had so relished: 'what a thrill & reverence the very outside bindings keep for one!' After she turned seven, in 1874, her education was taken in hand by a governess. 'Bessie Eales was only eighteen, a pretty, rather wishy-washy girl, fresh from a large family of brothers and sisters in a Devonshire rectory. It must have been very dull for her at Wrest, and rather alarming; we didn't like each other much, and I was naughty with her, and, of course, Nannie hated her. The schoolroom was at the opposite end of the big house to our nurseries, down the long long passage that we called the Red Lane, where Johnnie and I galloped, thundering along like a charge of cavalry, many times a day, over poor Pammy's unresisting head.' Little Ettie watched with wry shrewdness when her lonely governess found solace with the agent's rabbit-faced son, Henry Trethewy. 'But there was rather a to-do one day when Uncle Henry found me tied up in the ferry-boat, fishing, while Miss Eales had gone off into the woods with Henry.' The fuss seemed unnecessary to Ettie, who adored solitude and liked nothing better than to be left alone.

After a year Miss Eales was replaced by Miss Barnett, 'good, upright, plain and dull, the typical governess of story-books'. Her tenure was marred by the third overwhelming catastrophe in Ettie's childhood. In the winter of 1875 she and Johnnie went with the Weigalls to Bournemouth, where they both got whooping cough. She recovered briskly, but Johnnie never did: bronchitis came on, then inflammation of the lungs, and his health became hopeless. In December Ettie was moved with Miss Barnett to dismal lodgings elsewhere in Bournemouth. This made her 'desperately forlorn', for she had never before been separated from Nannie Wake or Johnnie, and hated being bathed by Miss Barnett.

The ailing seven-year-old boy was nursed by Nannie Wake, who seldom left his side and slept on a mattress by his bed, by Rose Weigall and Ettie's beloved 'Aunt Dordor', Dolly Herbert. 'He seems to me sinking very rapidly,' Dolly warned her brother Henry on 31 December, 'I took poor little Ettie to kiss him as he lay asleep.' But Johnnie lingered on: he wanted, he murmured pathetically, to pick primroses at Wrest at Easter. For three months Ettie's life was sad, frightening, lonely and monotonous. At last Johnnie died, gently, on 9 March 1876, and Ettie was put into black mourning clothes again and brought up to St James's Square. 'Dordor', she recalled years later, 'was my anchor and refuge, understanding so well the inarticulate wretchedness of a child in sorrow, and humouring every one of my whims.'

Ettie was helped at this time by a cousin called Hat. Adhering to the Whig tradition of intermarriage, her cousin Lord Ripon had married yet another cousin, Henrietta Anne Theodosia – 'Hat' – Vyner, granddaughter of his uncle Earl de Grey and thus one of the little children for whom Le Petit Trianon had been built at Wrest. She was lovingly supportive to the little Fane orphans, and after Johnnie's death welcomed Ettie more than ever to her London house and at Studley Royal, the Ripons' ill-furnished house in Yorkshire. In the 1880s there was far less of an exodus to the country on Saturdays and Sundays than at later dates, and the late-Victorian upper-class London Sunday was less dreary than might be expected. Once the Sunday service was over, friends walked in the smarter streets greeting one another, strolled in the royal parks or went to informal gatherings at private houses; and little Ettie, who lived so much among adults and was eager for adult pleasures, loved to visit Lady Ripon in Carlton Gardens on Sunday afternoons in London.

She would play with Hat's little dog on the balconies there, and rush downstairs with the guests to see them off. Her most exciting discovery – in 1874 when she was seven – was a handsome nobleman of twenty-seven, Lord Rosebery, who was (she said) 'very kind to me then, and ever afterwards', and whose chaffing entranced her. Her favourite visitors, after Rosebery, were her godfather Sir William Harcourt, soon to become Home Secretary; Gladstone's confidential secretary Algy West, and Reggie Brett, afterwards Lord Esher. 'Her heart went out to lame dogs and winged birds,' Brett wrote of Hat Ripon, 'she was deeply interested in [a] near relative, a small orphan girl of singular mental poise and abnormal powers of enchantment' – Ettie Fane. Brett sometimes took Ettie to London Zoo and relished his glimpses of the girl in Yorkshire. 'Ettie Fane was under the guardianship of Henry Cowper,' Brett recalled, 'and the days at Studley were red-letter ones when, with his little ward's hand resting on his knee, his delightful restrained wit flashed across the company.'

A 'strange apparition', which Ettie occasionally glimpsed at Hat Ripon's, was Benjamin Disraeli, Earl of Beaconsfield. She remembered 'Dizzy' always with distaste. 'He used to think it necessary to kiss me goodbye, and I can still remember the horror of his clammy face and greasy black ringlets; well-primed by the Liberal Cowpers, I looked upon him as the devil.' Disraeli was abominated by Pammy: 'with such a slippery Jewish pedlar one can't be too careful,' she warned.

In the spring of 1877, when Ettie was nearly ten, Miss Barnett was replaced by Fräulein Heuser, 'the very nicest kind of South-German, kind and sentimental and clever' who, as Ettie recalled, 'spoilt me dreadfully, but taught me a lot of German'. After Fräulein Heuser was crippled by a skating accident, she was replaced in May 1880 by Miss Garnett, daughter of a famous philologist and sister-in-law of Constance Garnett, the translator into English of the novels of Tolstoy and Dostoevsky. Miss Garnett was 'the most true and unselfish character', Ettie recalled, 'steeped in learning and the love of books. We were devoted to each other from almost the very first – although, quite at the beginning, I was snob enough to be a little ashamed of her, for she was very tall and very plain, and wore her hair in long ringlets (a quite outmoded fashion), and dressed in the most brilliant colours, and some of the cousins laughed about her.'

Miss Garnett, who stayed until Ettie came out in 1884, read the whole of Herodotus aloud to her, encouraged the child's love of solitude and taught her to paint on china: 'my poor family were bespattered with appalling gifts, and faithfully used them all – briar-roses and well-worn French mottoes being the favourite decoration.' She was responsible for Ettie being better educated than her friends. Mabell Gore, who longed to study masculine subjects and started teaching herself ancient Greek in secret, had her textbook confiscated and was ordered to do needlework instead.

During 1880, living in St James's Square, Ettie attended classes: Monsieur Roche's French lessons, a literature class, the fashionable Curzon riding school, and classes given by a famous dancing master called James Hervé D'Egville. She wasted many hours in joyless piano lessons, for she had not inherited the Fanes' love of music, and indeed disliked attending concerts. She spent every Saturday afternoon together with her Gore and Vyner girl cousins: they laughed so much together that (as Ettie recalled) 'we even cheered up the rather gloomy shrubberies of St James's Square, mainly tenanted by cats'. An unmitigated pleasure for Ettie and her cousins was driving out to Hyde Park with old Lady Cowper in the latter's enormous four-horse barouche with postillions. If it began to rain, a great leather apron was drawn up over the waists of the passengers, the hood was drawn down and the children at the back were huddled in with the old lady for shelter. Ettie never forgot going out in her grandmother's huge carriage, with her cousins, and the excitement of glimpsing Queen Victoria with her cross little red face being driven in Hyde Park.

In mid-July 1880, just before the annual return to Wrest, Pammy had a stroke in the depths of the night and died after a few days. Ettie was hurried out of St James's Square to stay with Hat Ripon in Carlton Gardens, and the lack of leave-taking hurt her: 'Pammy never recovered consciousness, and I never saw her again.' It was another bad time for the thirteen-year-old: 'added to the sorrow, there was all the wretched embarrassment of a child in grief; the shame of tears, the utter impossibility of expression.' She was inconsolable at the Panshanger funeral, and still numb with misery as she and her Uncle Henry (who worshipped his mother) trudged silently on their walks along the banks of the River Mimram, which winds through the grounds at Panshanger on its way to Hertford.

There was one positive aspect to this grim period. 'It was at Panshanger then that I first saw Evelyn de Vesci; she was the greatest friend of Dordor and my uncles, and came to them at once. I remember so well the first vision of her; she was twenty-eight, and most beautiful – 6 ft in height, with red-gold hair . . . She was standing, dressed in black, at the top of the little staircase leading to the west passage, and held out her compassionate hands, and opened her treasures of love to me and mine from that moment until her death, nearly sixty years afterwards.' Evelyn de Vesci created an ineffaceable impression of glamour and vitality around her. She had dauntless integrity, delicious humour and dedicated herself to enriching and exalting life. She loathed talk that belittled people and was roused to anger by any form of cruelty. In all this she was to prove a wonderful model for Ettie.

❧

After Pammy's death, Ettie did not see Wrest again until she was nearly seventeen. 'It was wound round my heart, and parting from it and from Pammy was one of the great griefs of my whole life,' she wrote many years later. Wrest (together with the Lucas barony and the house in St James's Square) passed to Pammy's elder son Francis. Ettie's guardians Rose Weigall and Henry Cowper settled that the girl's year would be divided between them as previously it had been divided between Lady Westmorland and Lady Cowper. First she went to Henry Cowper at Brocket Hall, a massive square red-brick Hertfordshire house built in the 1760s for the Lamb family, Viscounts Melbourne. After the death of the second Lord Melbourne, Queen Victoria's beloved first Prime Minister, it had passed to his sister Lady Palmerston, wife of Victoria's far-from-favourite sixth Prime Minister and Ettie's great-grandmother.

Lady Palmerston, whom Ettie dimly recalled as a decrepit old lady wearing a white fur tippet, in turn bequeathed Brocket to her grandson Francis Cowper. He had no need of it – it was only a few miles west of Panshanger in the direction of Wrest – and gave it for the use of his bachelor brother Henry. The exterior of the house looked as elegant, calm and confident as a Whig powerhouse should, and the interior had many pleasing features, including a large saloon with a magnificently decorated ceiling. Uncle Henry installed Ettie in a fine bedroom with five windows looking south over the river Lea, and gave her an adjacent sitting room. They arranged its decorations together: a white watered wallpaper with a blue border, gay chintzes, blue carpets and curtains, and Ettie's own choice of pictures.

Henry Cowper was not an obviously suitable person to bring up Ettie – although their devotion to one another was bottomless. He was tall, largely made and lame. As his sister-in-law Katie described him: 'he was not what would be called good-looking; his chief characteristic was a very large forehead, overshadowing a small nose, moustache, whiskers and rather pointed beard. His eyes were blue and quiet and kind, and he had an *immense* charm of manner.' Cowper was MP for Hertfordshire for twenty years until 1885, but no one in the family knew of him speaking in the House of Commons, except once when he seconded the Address to the Throne. Everyone said he was very able and could have done anything he liked; but (in Katie's account) 'he partook of the family dislike of publicity and advertisement, and had moreover a want of energy and a strange love of inaction. He was brilliant in conversation; quick, observant and critical. His fondness for reading was great, and his interest in people and their doings very strong. In this he resembled his mother.'

After two months at Brocket, in September 1880, Ettie was sent to stay at Southwood, the Weigalls' eighteenth-century house near

Ramsgate. There was, however, a reciprocated dislike between Ettie and her aunt Rose – an odious woman whom Sir George Sitwell likened to the death mask of Napoleon. 'It was probably a great deal my fault,' Ettie reflected in later life. 'I think that, after dear Grandmama died, she was hurt by my avowed preference for my mother's family, expressed without much reticence or tact.' After various clashes, Aunt Rose permitted a homesick Ettie to return to Brocket in January 1881; and henceforth Ettie was an out-and-out Cowper. Henry, Francis and to some extent Katie Cowper gave their orphan niece an unusual upbringing. 'Ettie had a very free undisciplined childhood, with wide open doors for sympathy to expand,' according to her friend Constance Wenlock, who was fifteen years her senior. Lady Wenlock thought the Cowpers' methods preferable to 'the freezing shrivelling puritanic discipline that I and so many others were brought up by', and had made Ettie 'almost safe from every form of unhappiness; she makes herself and everyone with her happy at the same time'.

Ettie became devoted to the four children of her beloved Aunt Dordor during a long visit to Wrest in 1879. Henry Cowper leant heavily on his favourite sister Dolly Herbert for advice about his young charge, and she effectively replaced Rose Weigall as Ettie's guardian. It was therefore yet another hard blow to Ettie when the elder Herbert son, Rolf, aged nine, fell fatally ill in 1882. ' "*Dear* Mum, *dear* Mum, I love you *so* much, better than my life," ' he murmured shortly before he died. Dolly never recovered from this tragedy.

When Ettie was fifteen, the Cowpers became disquieted by her bad posture and had her examined by Sir James Paget, a specialist in bone disease. Paget was impressed by Ettie's growth and development, defended her against suggestions that she should wear tighter stays and prescribed 'nothing but usual healthy living, nourishing food, outdoor air'. Ettie, as an adult, was admired, so Harold Nicolson recalled, for the 'dignity of her stance, the formidable carriage of her head and shoulders'. The famously ramrod-straight posture must date from nagging and training about her slouching in 1882. On one occasion in 1882 Uncle Henry took her to a house party at Panshanger, where she alarmed him by her social precocity. Once again he appealed to his sister for advice. 'Tell Ettie that you think her too young to carry on these grown-up friendships and that she is bound to let you pick & choose her friends for her at her age,' Dolly responded. 'Say that you think at 15 a girl is much better leading a child's life in the schoolroom & not making older friends & fancying herself grown up . . . you & Ettie will be happier the more you are plain & simple & tell her to do this & not do that.' Ettie had reached the 'anxious age', said Dolly.

Ettie was delighted when she was allowed to participate in the social amusements of Panshanger, Wrest and Brocket. She never forgot the Brocket party, in June 1884, held on the Saturday to Monday before her seventeenth birthday. The guests included the Liberal frontbencher John Morley, a young Tory MP called St John Brodrick and his wife Hilda, and two other rising politicians, Arthur Balfour and Alfred Lyttelton. 'The long afternoon under the trees and the charm and brilliance of their lazy talk, the excitement of rowing Arthur Balfour and John Morley on the river in my boat after tea, watching them all go down to dinner from the arch near the schoolroom, the breakfast next morning (already my favourite meal of the day), the despair of seeing them go, and – almost best of all – talking over and over every iota with Uncle Henry afterwards.' Arthur Balfour, Alfred Lyttelton and both Brodricks became lifelong friends. Ettie loved to be included in the social pleasures of her childless uncle and aunt. 'I always loved the parties at Wrest and Panshanger best of any – they had a quite unique charm and individuality – especially the long August parties at Wrest, when people came and went and stayed as they liked, for ten days or more, and life was centred in those lovely gardens and woods; and "Time seemed like a great silver bowl, from which you could ladle up the melted hours".'

At seventeen Ettie and her girlfriends, like many over-protected people with too much time on their hands, were prone to self-absorbed dramatisation of their feelings. They prided themselves on having no secrets from one another. Their upbringing had above all imbued them with consciences. 'My dear, it came on me with a rush,' Alice Gore wrote one November evening, '*how* much we have and have had, and how terribly little we do. We have money, pleasure, opportunities and what is our one thought? – ourselves; I'm not writing at you, my child, but at myself; and God help me, I'm going to try to be better.' Ettie, too, was full of resolves to be *good*. From childhood to old age she lived by ideals – though many people would have laughed at this claim. She seemed to her critics to be a hard and superficial Society hostess who lived by upper-class Edwardian conventions, and was honeyed, insincere and snobbish. Her enemies had only stumbled on half-truths about her, though. Ettie was an idealist, who fastened on to a code of behaviour when young and never relaxed her grip on it. Her code was based on ideals – admittedly rather worldly ideals – as later chapters will show.

Katie Cowper said that her generation – those of the uncles and aunts who reared Ettie – had been instilled with the rule that their feelings should never be mentioned to others, and indeed that intro-spection was impermissible. This was a healthy reaction, she thought, to the Byronic craze for 'morbid self-abandonment to public gaze'; but pushed too far, Katie conceded, 'this hard principle of smothering one's sentiments and one's aspirations in the depths of one's own breast chilled all the latent warmth of a young and ardent spirit, and dwarfed the natural growth of an upward striving mind.' The Cowpers did not try to inculcate Ettie with the old notion that emotions must be suppressed with everyone and at all costs. Although reticence and self-discipline before strangers were central to her rules of life, she was uninhibited about her thoughts and emphatic about her feelings with the people whom she loved and trusted. She believed that domestic emotions were sacred, and must be swathed in discretion; but in other respects she liked to talk and write exuberantly about her inmost susceptibilities.

Ettie, said Alice Gore, never used a comparative where a superlative would do: moreover she encouraged her friends to be similarly open, colourful and intense. They communicated, therefore, in a specialised slang that was enthusiastic, strenuous, overstated and can now seem absurdly gushing: it was their rebellion against the ice-blocked rivers of feeling, pent-up impulses, and hedged-in conversation of detestable Rose Weigall, joyless Lady Jocelyn and the Gores' anxious, staid father Lord Arran. Katie Cowper loved Ettie dearly, but had her niece in mind when she complained how seldom the younger generation 'rest content with . . . one single selected friendship! In fact, to understand a subject at all, it is considered essential to thrash it out with everyone one meets, pouring out in so doing all the inner passion of one's being, and soliciting and expecting the pouring out of everyone else's in return.'

It was Katie Cowper who chaperoned Ettie through her early London Seasons. These began in February of each year and continued until the last day of July. Three or four balls were given every weekday evening, and on Saturday nights there were often large parties – known as 'drums' – at one or other of the great families' homes in London: Devonshire House, Grosvenor House, Stafford House, Montagu House and the like. There were also two Court balls at Buckingham Palace every Season. It was fundamental that all young women, especially inexperienced unmarried girls, had to be protected from both male aggression and the temptations of feminine weakness. A girl like Ettie could not walk alone in the street, or travel unaccompanied in a cab or railway carriage, and could seldom take luncheon or tea anywhere but home: always there had to be a lady's maid or a married woman with her. Similarly, at all forms of entertainment the girl was chaperoned by her mother, father or a married woman. At balls, the chaperones would sit, with bored, weary faces, in rows along the wall, and girls were supposed to return like a homing bird to them after every dance. The duty to return to Mamma – or in Ettie's case, Katie Cowper – was invaluable in eluding unwelcome attention.

Ettie was launched on her first London Season in February 1885, when she was not yet eighteen. Helped by a generous dress allowance of £300 (the equivalent of about £22,000 in 2008), her success was swift, assured and striking. 'You did have such a roaring success my duck and all the papers talk about you: Aunt Sophy says that everyone asks her if she has seen "the beautiful Miss Fane",' Mabell Gore wrote after a ball was held for Ettie in April. 'Ducky you have been the Biggest Success (with a big S) that any girl has had for years.' In the swirl of events during her two Seasons of 1885–6 Ettie made friendships that lasted a lifetime. Alice and Mabell Gore were paramount in her life, as everyone could see. 'Oh! my darling *how* I do love you, words cannot describe it, and you have been such an angel to me all this year,' Alice gushed. 'I feel as if we had got to know each other quite differently and as if I *couldn't* live without seeing you.' And Mabell was scarcely more restrained: 'My darling I love you so and I admire you so, for although you have had such a tearing success this year, you have never been the least uppish or hoity-toity.' Many other young women doing the Season wanted to be known as Ettie's friends and became possessive of her. 'It has been a great joy & interest to me this year to have you for my *greatest* friend,' Betty Ponsonby, a courtier's daughter, wrote from Windsor Castle. 'May I come after Mabell & Alice with you? How nice it was when we were standing on that dark moonlight balcony at St James's Sq with the trees outside, my arm round your waist in your white muslin gown!'

Ettie was 'not like an everyday girl', declared a courtly old beau called Sir Arthur Ellis, but 'like the heroine of a three volume novel'. It helped that she had a habit, which delighted many men, of lowering her eyes during conversation. This gave her an air of graceful modesty, and then made her seem all the more responsive when she swept her eyes sideways. In a further tantalising contradiction, she combined a natural, eager manner with an air of contrivance, leaving men to puzzle whether there were far-reaching intentions behind quite simple remarks.

Girls of Ettie's background were brought up to matrimony: they were aimed and timed to hit their marks – rich, handsome and well-connected young men – as debutantes during their first London Seasons. Marriage was both their destiny and their vindication – although the Whig adherence to strategic and almost incestuous marital alliances was beginning to slacken. Each Season, with its dinners, dances and young ladies' balls, was a spectacle in which the fresh interest lay in the unmarried young women sampling their first Season. 'A woman's only hope of self-expression in those days was through marriage,' Mabell later wrote. 'Whether we would, or would not, succeed in getting husbands was our main preoccupation.' A girl who failed to secure a proposal within six months of coming out faced her second Season with reduced hope; and 'after the third', Mabell recalled with a shudder, 'there remained nothing but India as a last resort before the spectre of the Old Maid became a reality.' Gloriously, in her first Season, Ettie attracted three titled suitors: Lord Skelmersdale, son and heir of the Earl of Lathom; Lord Wiltshire, son and heir of the Marquess of Winchester; and Charles Harbord, son and heir of Lord Suffield.

Two of the trio were tested at a house party at Panshanger in the autumn of that year. 'A lot of people came – Lyttons, de Greys, de Vescis, Willy Comptons, Lord Skelmersdale, Lord Wiltshire,' Ettie noted. On the first night 'Wilty' bored her by talking after dinner about politics, and the next evening 'Skel' made a worse blunder. The Cowpers had hired a fashionable singer named Isidore De Lara to give an after-dinner recital. Skelmersdale (who was wearing cotton wool in his ears) sat Ettie on a sofa near the piano and harped on politics to her through the music. Nevertheless, she was exhilarated by the men's attention: 'one feels so flat after a party is over, and this one was so awfully amusing,' she told Ally Gore. The few traces of Skelmersdale in Ettie's voluminous papers are prosaic; and Wiltshire's only surviving letter is a painfully dull missive about grouse. Even his male friends found Wiltshire dull: 'more stolid than ever & sleeps peacefully immediately after dinner,' Alan Charteris told Ettie a few years later. 'He really ought to marry but I don't think he ever will: if he does his wife will only take the place of housekeeper.'

There was a fourth persistent admirer: a commoner, and the early outsider in the marriage stakes, called Willie Grenfell, a tall, handsome, muscular man who was Ettie's senior by twelve years. She had first noticed him when she was staying at Henry Cowper's house in Stratton Street, Mayfair, being prepared for confirmation. She would gaze out of its upper windows into the gardens of Devonshire House in Piccadilly. A lawn-tennis court had recently been laid out there, and in the afternoons she watched Arthur Balfour, Alfred Lyttelton, Willie Grenfell and others amusing themselves in the new fashion. Willie Grenfell was indeed a superb all-round athlete: the only man to be President of both the Oxford University Athletic Club and the University Boat Club (he was in the crew which in 1878 beat Cambridge by ten lengths), he was master of the university drag-hounds, stroked an eight across the English Channel, climbed the Matterhorn by three different routes, was punting champion on the River Thames and swam across Niagara twice – through the pool between the thundering falls and the undertow. He was also a crack fencer and cricketer.

Willie Grenfell was 'the absolutely finest man he knew', the Duke of Sutherland told Ettie, 'so clever and strong and brave, and had done every sort of thing in the world & yet never seemed to think twice about [him]self'. This intrepid sporting prodigy had been elected as Liberal MP for Salisbury in 1880. His appointment by Gladstone as a parliamentary groom-in-waiting to the Queen in 1882 had obliged him to stand for re-election, at which he was narrowly defeated. He was again returned by the Salisbury electors in the general election of December 1885: although not involved in the family business, he had a special interest in monetary policy and became private secretary to Ettie's godfather Sir William Harcourt, by then Chancellor of the Exchequer. He resigned the secretaryship in May 1886 so that it should not be thought that his vote for the Irish Home Rule Bill was that of a placeman: 'there have been four generations of (more or less silent) Grenfells in the House who have voted independently,' he told Harcourt, 'and I think I had better follow their example on an occasion of so much importance.' In the event, the Home Rule Bill was defeated in Parliament, and Willie lost Salisbury in the general election of July 1886 necessitated by that defeat.

Late in 1885 Mabell Gore accepted a proposal – her fourth that year – from the Earl of Airlie, and Ettie – as one of her bridesmaids – received her thrilling confidences about married life. 'One's honeymoon is chiefly passed in . . . feeling dreadfully ill,' Mabell reported from her new home, Cortachy Castle. 'I who never feel ill as a rule have done nothing but faint; but don't tell the others as I have concealed it from them. It is only the result of circumstances. I was nearly frightened to death & suffered *tortures*!! I am a blaze of domestic virtue; I have just come from looking over the linen, and ordering dinner. After luncheon we shall probably pursue the bucolic pastimes of the county and in the evening he in a correct evening tie reads the Leading Articles in the "Times" to me in my "best dress". And there is certainly a great repose in being married! you feel so settled & able to turn your hand to so many things. My only trouble at present is I cannot go anywhere; for some extraordinary reason, my young bowels refuse to act.'

✍

The start of Ettie's 1886 Season was marred by sadness caused by the death on 26 April of her beloved Aunt Dordor. Dolly Herbert had inherited the Cowper temperament, and since the late 1870s her letters had mentioned 'blackness & gloom', 'personal fogs and mists', 'fits of depression'. After the death of her son Rolf, her physical health began to fail, and by 1886 she was mortally ill, though Ettie strove to raise her spirits with newsy correspondence. 'It does one's heart good to read your happy beaming letter, & think that anyone so enjoys life,' Dordor told her. 'It is so much better than our grumbling way of taking it, *provided* you don't stop where you are, but go on climbing, & getting higher & higher.' Ettie's resilient joy, like her determination to achieve brilliant prominence, was inspiring for the dying woman. Yet it was part of Ettie's complexity that she never lost touch with human confusion or anguish. When, in the last weeks of her life, Dordor returned to ancestral Hertfordshire, eighteen-year-old Ettie consoled and played with the Herbert children, and received the dying woman's confidences. Her aunt's life, so Ettie told Alice Gore, was 'nothing but pain and grief to her; she said to me today that she felt so wicked to be longing so for death'.

After Dordor died, her daughter Clair – then aged eleven – sent Ettie a heartbreaking letter: 'we had been waiting & waiting for this terrible thing, & now it has come, & I can hardly realize it, everything calls up new recollections which are very beautiful & yet very painful . . . Mum may be watching over all we do, and say whether it is good or bad, but we do not know, for, all is wrapt in mystery, but even if she is not, I will try to do just what she would like, as much as if she was still here with us on this earth, she may be watching me write this letter, & she may not.' Ettie was deeply touched and never able, or willing, to evade other people's grief.

During the 1886 Season the marriage talk became more serious. By March Willie Grenfell had become a serious 'spangle', that is suitor. 'First and foremost about W.G.,' advised Mabell Airlie with the wise air of a newly married woman fully schooled in the world's ways. 'If you do not absolutely hate him I should marry him I think; first everyone says he is an absolute angel, and he may be a little dull, but after all, what a comfort it is to be cleverer than one's husband. Then he has got such awfully nice relations, and he is altogether so smart, & if you cared for that sort of thing, you could get him made a peer any time. My goodness me, you could do anything you liked.' Another spangle, Lord Greenock, began courting Ettie, but she decided he was 'rather mad and odd'. All the girls used to play together with a Planchette – resting their hands on a wooden board which purportedly provided them with predictions and advice from the spirit world – in the hope of learning their marital prospects. The Planchette had told Elizabeth Baring, 'C in August, at Cowes', and when she became engaged to Lord Castlerosse during Cowes week of August 1886 Ettie and Ally were thrilled.

At the end of July, shortly after his rejection by the electors of Salisbury, Willie gave Ettie a crystal and diamond watch. When she thanked him for his present, he asked, touchingly, 'Must I go on waiting? I *have* waited a year.' But nothing was settled. In November Ettie and Willie were both invited to stay in Hertfordshire with the Cowpers' friends Lord and Lady Brownlow. 'I am so *awfully* glad about Ashridge; I expect you will come back an engaged young person,' wrote Alice. But at Ashridge, and again during a visit to the Duke of Westminster's house, Cliveden, Willie failed to declare himself. 'I meant to try to find out on Sunday whether you cared for me at all but somehow I couldn't as I felt like an owl,' he confessed later. In December she paid a duty visit to her aunt Rose Weigall on the Isle of Thanet. 'I do like him very much,' she wrote from there of Willie to Ally Gore, '& should certainly marry him, I think, if he ever asked me – but he very likely *never* will.' But Willie inveigled an invitation to the Weigalls' house and proposed: she accepted with delight that the tense uncertainty had been dispelled.

'I cannot tell you how happy I am, and what *peace* it is,' Ettie wrote to Ally after she had returned to London with the news. 'Oh my darling little Puppy,' Alice Gore responded in their specialised private argot, 'I feel as if it was losing you, and yet I know that for you it is the very bestest thing and I feel in my inside that you will be as happy as happy can be.' Society chatterers were intrigued by the future Mrs Grenfell and began clamouring for invitations to the wedding. Ettie's launch in the world could not have been more auspicious – yet she was utterly naïve and unformed. 'I think so of the old childish days,' Mabell Airlie wrote sixty years later to Ettie: 'when we married what *children* we were; and how we leaped into our happiness with such trusting faith.'

CHAPTER 2

The Soul

ɜ~

ETTIE MARRIED ON Thursday, 17 February 1887 – two months after her engagement was announced – at St George's, Hanover Square, in the presence of one of the largest congregations ever assembled in that church. Willie's uncle Frederick Temple, Bishop of London (afterwards Archbishop of Canterbury) officiated, Ettie's former 'spangle' Lord Wiltshire was best man and Prince Albert Victor ('Eddy') of Wales signed the register. The bride entered the church at one o'clock escorted by Henry Cowper; and for all the surviving Cowpers, Ettie's marriage was a great event and a great happiness in their lives.

The newly married Grenfells stopped in Paris on their way to a happy fortnight in Cannes, where the Prince of Wales had recently arrived for the consecration of a church erected in memory of his brother Prince Leopold, Duke of Albany. Cannes was teeming with royalties, including the Grand Duke of Baden and the Duchesse de Chartres, together with their entourages. The Grenfells made a short trip along the Mediterranean coast to visit the casino at Monte Carlo, where Ettie 'won a lot at first, but lost it again'. Then, less conventionally, on leaving Cannes, they sent their servants and most of their luggage back to England, while they travelled à deux to Rome, Brindisi and Cairo. 'It is quite *delightful* you two being quite alone without any servants, & Etsie with only one gown & no maid,' Betty Ponsonby wrote. 'It just shows how well an attic person like you *can* rough it if she chooses, & you must be so independent & happy.' The Grenfells coined pet names for one another, Gent and Catts, at this time. On their return from Egypt, they were met at Taplow station by a group of tenants and employees who hauled their carriage from the station up Berry Hill to their house as a gesture of fealty. In June she was pregnant and began suffering from morning sickness.

The jubilation of early summer was soon muted, for it became evident that something was amiss with Henry Cowper. He attributed his decline to depression after the death of Dolly Herbert, and his family tended to agree. According to Katie Cowper, 'the light of his life went out when she died, and he gradually sank into apathy and ill-health, from which he made no efforts to recover.' However, his despondency became marked in 1887, following Ettie's marriage, rather than after Dolly Herbert's death a year earlier. It is hard to believe that he would have fallen so low if she had been living with him at Brocket rather than with Willie at Taplow.

Henry's family rallied at his side, but their efforts to rouse him were unavailing, and he died on 10 November. 'Poor fellow,' said Katie, 'he only died because he did not care to live.' It was harrowing for Ettie to watch him slip away and afterwards she sought consolation from Evelyn de Vesci, who had so helped her when Pammy Cowper died. It was 'too terribly sad', she wrote, '& as if the last bit of all one had loved & clung to all one's life were swept away, in him and Dolly. The only thing that comforts one is the real *belief* that for him it is the happiest: his life was so sad & lonely after darling Dolly was gone out of it, and I think that Brocket was so haunted with her that he could hardly bear it.' She felt cheated out of some precious moments of leave-taking: 'the only thing I blame my poor coming baby for is that they would not let me stay all through his illness.' She cherished, though, the memory of 'some things he said in the intervals (half in prayer and half to me) full of the most strong beautiful Faith – *most* beautiful things'.

Her guardian's death raised an inward anxiety in Ettie. For many years she worried that she might yield as he had done to a death wish: 'with Cowper lassitude in one's blood I expect one will sooner or later end by chucking *everything*,' she wrote apprehensively in 1893. The Cowper lassitude, as she called the familial depression, was a supreme failure of self-command, she decided. To fend it off, she must subject herself to iron self-rule. Her determination to think away sorrow, suffering and death, and to banish sadness or ugliness as failures of nerve, dated from 1886–7 when she watched Aunt Dordor and Uncle

Henry in turn let grief kill them. Perhaps, too, she felt that her father had lethally failed to rouse himself to survive her mother's death. Ingratitude for what life threw at you – even bereavement – was just a form of shirking, Ettie decided.

For her, Henry Cowper's death created a vacancy which was never filled. She cultivated the affection of some of his intimate friends, despite their greater age, as a way of preserving her memories of him. Her meeting, in 1888, with the American jurist Oliver Wendell Holmes, a favourite guest at Brocket of Henry Cowper's, recalled, she told him, 'so strongly old happy days with one who we both loved so deeply: I can hardly ever bear to speak of him, but to you who loved & sympathized with him so well, it was no pain (after the first) to talk of what we remembered: how one misses him at every turn of life – sometimes I think most keenly of all in one's *laughter*'. Ettie and Holmes began a correspondence that endured for forty-five years.

After Henry's death, Brocket was given on a long lease to a Canadian millionaire, Lord Mount Stephen, and Ettie revisited the house only twice in the next thirty-five years. She became even closer to her uncle and aunt at Panshanger: Francis Cowper 'adored' Ettie, according to Katie; 'she was always like a daughter to him; and he had an immense trust in and affection for Willie, and he looked upon their boys as grandsons.' The Cowpers begged the young couple to make their London home in 4 St James's Square, the imposing Georgian house they had inherited after Pammy Cowper's death. It had been built by their ancestor the Duke of Kent with high, spacious state rooms overlooking the square and a warren of gloomy back quarters. Francis Cowper felt it would be 'intolerably dreary with only two middle-aged people in it', and assured Ettie that rather than be 'condemned' to that, he would sell it to become a club premises.

From 1889 until his death in 1905 the Grenfells spent much of each Season at 4 St James's Square. Ettie was thus the only great hostess of her era who never had a permanent London home. After 1905 the Grenfells rented houses for successive Seasons: 51 Grosvenor Square in 1906, 46 Upper Grosvenor Street in 1907, 16 Queen Street in 1908, 16 South Street in 1909; and moving north of Mayfair, 19 Manchester Square in 1910 and Mansfield House in New Cavendish Street in 1911. Ettie also cultivated two rich bachelors who were happy for her to stay in their spacious London houses: Lord Revelstoke in Carlton House Terrace and later Sir Philip Sassoon in Park Lane.

༄

During June and July 1887, in the months after Ettie's marriage, the Cowpers lived chiefly in St. James's Square, going down to Panshanger and hosting parties there from Saturday to Monday. It was at this time that a clique whose members called themselves the Gang, but which became known to outsiders as 'the Souls', coalesced. They were a set of men and women who had a strong impact on London Society for five or six years, and who had enduring influence in relaxing some of its entrenched habits, in broadening its outlook and in reforming its rules. Arthur Balfour, long after his retirement as Prime Minister, said that no history of his time would be complete unless the social influence of the Souls was dispassionately recorded. This is not a history of Balfour's time, still less of the Souls, but Ettie's central role – during the formative phase when she was a newly married beauty – makes it important to describe and explain the set.

The Souls were a by-product of a critical phase in British political history. Traditionally Whigs had scorned Tories, and Tories railed against Whigs. Partisan animosity bisected London Society: Disraeli and Gladstone would have been stupefied at the idea of visiting one another's houses, and the Cowpers would never have entertained Disraeli. Adine Cowper had been unusual in marrying out of the Whig oligarchy into the Tory Fanes. Cuts and snubs were ferociously administered; but the differences between the two hostile political tribes had been as much of personnel as of policy. All this was transformed by the secession of the Whigs from the Liberal Party after Gladstone's declaration for Irish Home Rule in 1886. Francis Cowper took the chair at the decisive meeting at the Opera House on 14 April 1886 when almost 5,000 Unionists, both Conservatives and Liberals, crowded into the theatre to hear speeches and pass resolutions against Gladstone's Home Rule Bill. Politics suddenly tangled, biased and alienated people who ought to have been good friends and neighbours: Willie Grenfell, for example, was ostentatiously dropped by the Duke of Westminster for supporting Gladstone's Irish policy.

This frowning, snarling atmosphere was what the Souls opposed.

They were determined that acrimony about Ireland would not spoil their round of pleasures, and they numbered Tories, Whigs, Liberal Unionists and Gladstonians in their company. The results were emollient and informative. When the Liberal imperialist Alfred Milner, by then Governor of the Cape of Good Hope, returned to England in 1898 to stiffen political resolve to risk war against the Boers, he was invited to Panshanger and seized the opportunity to brief the Souls on his African strategy. Travelling there by train from King's Cross with a fellow Soul, the Tory imperialist Curzon, he 'talked the whole way down' about his plans. Included in the Cowpers' 'large and cheerful party', he found other political Souls, Balfour and the Brodricks for the Tories, and the Asquiths and Ribblesdales for the Liberals, as well as Ettie, Willie and some blue-blooded non-Souls, 'Wilty' Winchester and the Duke and Duchess of Portland. The men were all receptive to Milner's strategic confidences. This habit of high-level, informal amity helped to contain the verbal violence when a quarter of a century later the Liberals and Tories clashed over House of Lords reform and the two main political parties were each led by old Souls, Asquith and Balfour. It was only after Balfour's supercession as Tory leader that Britain began blundering towards civil war over Ireland.

The Souls were an urbane influence as well as a politically moderating one. They made it fashionable for Society people to be readers, and clever, amusing talkers about books. The earnestness and excruciatingly petty scruples of the mid-Victorians seemed absurd to them: they preferred the play of literary intellect to be light and sparkling. They scrutinised their world with the quizzical irony that thirty years later Lytton Strachey's *Eminent Victorians* deployed on the entire age – it was a book that Ettie devoured with relish. St John Brodrick depicted his fellow Souls as rebels against stuffy and somnolent mid-Victorianism: they were resistance workers who insisted upon even the gravest subjects being rinsed in the colouring of wit and for whom the one unforgivable sin was to be morose. 'Between us all, under AJB [Balfour], we had some share of governing the pre-war world,' Brodrick (by then Earl of Midleton) told Ettie in 1929. 'Contrast the old slumber after dinner at shooting parties of the 1870s on one side, & the rude rollicks of the 1920s on the other, & the Souls win at every point!'

By nineteenth-century standards, the women of the set were as emancipated as respectable women could be. The Souls took it as a matter of course that men and women should compete on equal terms in conversation – and indeed treated talking as the greatest sport of all. They were resolutely anti-philistine: the creed of art-for-art's-sake would have seemed to them too frivolous and selfish, but it was unique for English Society to have a materialistic, pleasure-loving clique, which found the world of ideas so exciting. Moral courage and emotional fortitude were paramount virtues in the opinion of the Souls: though they were a rich and privileged set, who were never tested by privation and whose valour was hothoused, when the war came in 1914 they vindicated themselves impressively.

In addition to the Cowpers at Panshanger and Wrest, there were two other childless middle-aged couples, Earl and Countess Brownlow at Ashridge, and the Earl and Countess of Pembroke at Wilton, who provided the gentle ambience that characterised all the favourite meeting places of the Souls. Lord Brownlow was a first cousin of Katie Cowper's, and Lady Brownlow and Lady Pembroke were sisters. 'Lady Pembroke is the rough sketch of a clever woman, but Lady Brownlow is the finished picture of an idiot,' quipped Lord Lytton. Aside from the Cowpers, Pembrokes and Brownlows, the core of the Gang comprised Arthur Balfour, George Curzon, Margot Tennant, Margot's sister Charty and her husband Lord Ribblesdale, Tommy Ribblesdale's diplomat brother Reginald Lister, Mary and Hugo Elcho, Lord Elcho's brother Evan Charteris, Willie and Ettie Grenfell, St John and Hilda Brodrick, George Wyndham and his wife Sibell Grosvenor, Frances Horner, Alfred Lyttelton, and an American diplomat called Harry White whose wife Daisy increasingly grated on Ettie. There were more occasional Gang members, among whom Ettie listed Willie's cousins Adolphus ('Doll') Liddell and Constance Wenlock, and Hat Ripon's daughter-in-law Gladys de Grey (she was George Pembroke's sister). Latecomer Souls included Alfred Milner, Lord and Lady Windsor (afterwards Plymouth) and Sir Edgar and Lady Helen Vincent (afterwards Lord and Lady D'Abernon).

The collective temper of the set is evoked by Maurice Baring's pen portrait of one of its lesser-known members. 'Reggie Lister was an artist in life and the organisation of life,' Baring wrote. 'He was radiantly sensible. He had a horror of the trashy and the affected, and his gaiety was buoyant, boyish and infectious . . . His intuition was like second-sight and his tact always at work but never obtrusive, like the works of a delicate watch.' Lister had, too, 'the gift of making the witty wittier, the singer, the talker, the musician, the reciter, do better than his best, of drawing out the best of other people by his instantly responsive appreciation'. Reggie Lister's social graces were those that the Souls – not least Ettie Grenfell – most intensely cherished.

'They shot, and ate, and drank, and flirted, and talked,' Katie Cowper said of the Gang who came to Panshanger and Wrest. 'The only unforgivable sin, it appeared to me, was to be dull or stupid. That would exclude anyone; but nothing else did.' (She was forgetting that finished picture of an idiot, Lady Brownlow, or perhaps remembering that part of the self-imposed task of the Gang was to encourage stupid people to make intelligent choices.) At the end of July, after the close of the London Season, the Cowpers would shift to Wrest, where for a month or six weeks they held summer parties. The Gang talked and played in the beautiful house, and strolled in its idyllic grounds, which seemed to reflect the elegant discipline and contrivance of their conversation. 'You were much missed at Wrest on Sunday,' Balfour wrote to Mary Elcho in August 1891. 'Shady alleys, delicious yew thickets, ponds, summer houses, and gardens make it perfect for all conversational purposes. Every taste, and every "système" is suited.' Ettie was at Wrest on this occasion, and so were the Oscar Wildes.

Most Souls (Curzon was an exception) welcomed recruits like Wilde and Asquith from outside the landowning class; but though they overlooked middle-class ancestry, they winced at middle-class furnishings. How queasy one felt, said George Wyndham, when obliged by a public-speaking engagement to stay with 'political bosses of the Midlands' in their up-to-date villas 'with their bath-rooms on every floor and no servants; vintage wines and worsted lamp-mats; early Millais and Biblical prints; Venetian blinds and smoke-smeared grass; the monkey-puzzle tree solitary in the lawn where no bird sings, and inside the brand new clock that must be interred in a drawer if you are to sleep'.

The Souls preferred venerable architectural masterpieces like Wilton as the background for their gambolling. Wilton's six magnificent gold and white Inigo Jones state rooms, with their Van Dyck portraits and intricately painted ceilings, looked out towards a Palladian bridge traversing a clear chalk river. Between the bridge and the house lay a lawn shaded by cedars, and everywhere there were murmuring waters, rustling trees, verdant walks and trim prospects. Wilton's owner, George Pembroke was, in Doll Liddell's description, 'a big, rather unwieldy man, with a richly-coloured picturesque head, a philosopher as well as a *grand seigneur*, and had a mind deeply interested in all the problems of the time, as well as keen appreciation of all that was best in literature'. He had explored the South Seas as a young man, and still loved yachting on his schooner *Black Pearl*: memorably, after several Souls on board had been discussing abstract questions, a seaman asked what they had been saying and the steward replied: 'Oh, blooming rot, *as* usual.'

Pembroke, who wrote charming letters, suffered from tuberculosis, which killed him at the age of forty-four in 1895. 'He was very attractive and clever, but just missed being a man of power,' the Society poet and *coureur des femmes* Wilfrid Scawen Blunt noted. 'There was always something incomplete, some want in him, in spite of much manly beauty, of full virility. Women were aware of this defect and, though he had many friends among them, they were friends only.' Pembroke had a *tendresse* for Charty Ribblesdale, and called Ettie 'my prop & stay in a weary & cold world'. Ettie's thinking and literary tastes matured under his influence, although she sometimes found him '*really gossipy* & tiresome'. His wife – known as Gety and ten years his senior – was 'the strangest woman', Ettie felt, 'with a wealth of heart & a good deal of shrewdness – all crossed & marred by her caprice'.

Ashridge was a flamboyant neo-gothic house built on a high ridge in Hertfordshire, with a superb interior, including a vast drawing room with marble chimneypieces and gold and marble pillars to scale, a majestic ballroom and an imposing staircase. The gardens were a blaze of gold and red in summer, with a broad blue and violet border near the house, and lay in glorious parkland, with hundreds of roaming deer and the venerable timber of a former royal forest. 'The host & hostess have special attraction,' an inveterate diner-out named Eddy Hamilton noted on a visit: 'she with all her beauty & simplicity: he with all his charm and ingenuity.' Adelbert ('Addy') Brownlow adored his wife, who was described by Scawen Blunt in 1889 as having 'lost her wonderful beauty, and now a pleasant-looking distinguished middle-aged woman with much pleasant bonhomie in her face and kindness in her character'. She was over-susceptible to other people's feelings – 'Are you a happy little couple, or not?' was one of her stock questions – and too vulnerable to their distress. 'Poor little Adelaide', said Lord Pembroke, 'has got such a terribly loving heart that life must always be more pain than joy to her.'

Mary Elcho presented the Souls as a 'protest against the Prince of Wales's set and the racing set of the Duchess of Manchester'. They were also a protest against the philistine, conglomerate house parties held by wire-pulling political hostesses like Lady Londonderry: 'vulgar to the core, & has no selection of people, books or ideas, but has energy & a good memory for pedigrees', as Margot Tennant said of her. The clever men and women of the Souls considered themselves superior in wit, originality and charm to any other social set. Quips, repartee, quotations, allusions, epigrams and flirtatious sallies were the common currency for all their dealings. To ensure the continuity of amusement, Mary Elcho and other Souls hostesses preferred that at a table with eight or fewer people, there should be general conversation rather than a division into tête-à-tête duos. Nothing, they knew, was more distracting when listening to one's immediate neighbour than to hear snatches of more brilliant, indiscreet or provocative talk further along the table.

Conversation at Panshanger, Wrest, Ashridge and Wilton was effervescent compared with the staid torpor of most Victorian country house parties. Betty Ponsonby described a visit in 1887 to Lochinch Castle in Wigtownshire as the guest of the Earl of Stair, Lord High Commissioner to the General Assembly of the Church of Scotland. She pictured to Ettie 'the stiff drawing room with a round table in the middle with the [Burke's] Peerage & *Glasgow Herald* on it, & women sitting round with pieces of fancy work or knitting, gossiping cease-lessly about the servants or, at best, their children'. Lady Stair re-sembled 'an old housekeeper', the other guests were uniformly dull, and with the men out shooting all day, she had to sit through 'silent, solemn meals'. Willie fared no better when in December that year he joined Lord Leicester's shoot at Holkham. 'This is not a comfortable house,' he wrote to his heavily pregnant wife. 'Leicester is a fearful martinet, and everything is done punctually here' (all the clocks at Holkham were set thirty minutes ahead of the correct time). The other guests 'think & dream of shooting and nothing else'; and the accommodation given to single men resembled the amenities in old-fashioned country inns: his bed was 'very narrow & . . . would not do for Gent and Catts'.

Edgar Vincent – a dashing young international financier based in Constantinople – had ample opportunity to appreciate the Souls when he was in England. 'A circle of exceptionally open-minded people effectively engaged in bursting the bonds of irksome social tradition, and in opening the way to a more rational and agreeable way of life,' he called them. 'The old society world, which they startled, was in the main territorial, traditional, and prejudiced. Its standards precluded innovation, and served to entrench dullness under the cloak of rank and station.' The Souls, however, affirmed the art and wisdom of the good life. Their 'peculiar charm', he added, thinking of Ettie, 'proceeded from the inheritors of the Melbourne tradition. The blood of the Lambs . . . remained lively enough to influence the whole group with its enjoyment of life [and] frank zest for amusement.'

According to Ettie, the epithet 'Souls' was coined in 1888 by a jaunty naval officer, Lord Charles Beresford, at a dinner party held in Lord Brownlow's London house. 'You all sit and talk about each other's souls,' Beresford declared, 'I shall call you the "Souls".' This nickname resulted, Ettie felt, in outsiders regarding the set as pretentious and even effete. Thus Lord Suffield, the sporting father of her former suitor Charlie Harbord, snorted: 'some very funny things happened when the hard-headed, practical, bluff John Bulls of either sex encountered the lackadaisical set who called themselves "Souls" and who looked upon everything that was normal and sane as vulgar and indecent.'

It was objected that the Souls were too searching and indulgent in their conversations about feelings, motives and conduct. 'Analysis of character is the favourite passion of the age,' Katie Cowper wrote in 1890 in a muted protest against her guests. 'We are overwhelmed with an avalanche of the scraps and shreds into which have been torn the feelings and desires, the speculations and calculations, the beliefs and doubts, the hopes and fears, the contemplations and realisations of each and every one in turn. No one is spared; and soul-searching and soul-pulling form the chief subject of conversation among even the comparative strangers who meet across a dinner-table or in a country-house.' Hugo Elcho, for one, turned against 'the Gossiping Souls', and during his passionate affair with the Duchess of Leinster in 1894 resented the Pembrokes and Margot Tennant gloating over his misdeeds. On some occasions, at Stanway, when bored beyond endurance by the chatter, Elcho would counterfeit an attack of hiccoughs and stride from the room with a handkerchief crammed to his mouth.

In 1893, as will be described later, the Souls were shaken by a contretemps involving Balfour and a fornicating MP called Harry Cust, and never wholly recovered their cohesion. Already by then, according to Frances Horner, 'the Souls were no longer such a phalanx.' She felt this was because middle-class politicians such as Henry Asquith and Richard Haldane were infiltrating the set, and diluting its essence. Haldane lacked the *esprit* of an authentic Soul, for he preferred keen, doctrinaire women like Beatrice Webb to laughing, playful types – he had dismissed Frances Horner herself as merely 'a woman of pleasure'. (It was Mrs Webb who disgusted a gathering at Stanway by demanding, 'Don't you agree with me, Mr Balfour, that the only excuse for a dinner-party is that it should end in a committee?')

The Souls, supremely, were *playful*. 'Games are good things, but Play is better – and quite different,' Ettie believed. 'The instinct for Play pure and simple . . . does not mingle with struggle and competition, and needs a holiday spirit of detachment and defiant idleness before it will even peep out.' Some of the Souls' play was innocuous: Styles, in which the players were given thirty minutes to write poetry or prose in the manner of, say, Blake, Browning, Carlyle or Meredith, or the guessing game Clumps, in which the answers were not solid objects like 'The Roast Beef of Old England' or 'Noah's Ark' but abstractions such as 'A Lost Cause' or 'Interval'. Other forms of play required invidious choices. There was a game in which one player was given the names of three people whom he liked equally, who were said to be trapped at the top of a tower. The player had to justify his choice as to which friend was to be led gently down by hand, which to hurl over the edge, and which to abandon to be picked by crows.

In another game one player picked the name of someone present, and the other guests had to discover the mystery individual's identity by keen, gleeful questioning about which animal, food, building or colour he or she most resembled. For the selected victims, it was not always comfortable to hear that he or she resembled a cauliflower, a toad or macaroni; but it was a game of acquired skill. 'What vegetable does this person remind you of?' tyros would demand, and be told a turnip; but expert players would produce such artfully precise questions that the player would exclaim: 'A peach melba with a little sprig of mistletoe – oh, that's *giving* it away! You *must* see who it is now!' There was also a game called Breaking the News in which one player announced in laboriously sorrowful (or perhaps cruelly tactless) language someone's death to their spouse or close friend while the other players tried to guess the identity of the defunct Soul.

The civil servant and man about town 'Doll' Liddell described the games at Panshanger in 1888. 'I liked my evening immensely gazing at such a circle of striking females' – Ettie, Mary Elcho and Frances Horner among others. They committed 'all sorts of follies', and Mrs Horner, playing Dumb Crambo, 'clothed herself in breeches & boots & appeared as Napoleon crossing the Alps, the horse being Etty Grenfell, & the Alps chairs covered with table cloths'. Ettie, however, was too modern for Liddell's taste. At a Panshanger party in 1892 he found her 'very charming and specious as usual. But, alas, she has taken to rouge . . . how sad it is to find youth & bloom flying, and to fancy that you attract less, and will attract more if you daub yourself with coloured powder.'

Wilfrid Scawen Blunt, who preferred his women to be confused and compliant, similarly found Ettie 'too noisy and painted'. Given the prevalence of acting games at Souls gatherings, it is not surprising that Ettie put on a strenuous act in her social life: in the early 1890s she was developing and perfecting the pose that people found enthralling. Liddell felt that the Souls were overly prone to slyly destructive emotional games. 'This is a regular Sunday Panshanger party,' he reported in 1893, 'Etty, Brodricks, Margot, Lady A. Portal, Harry Whites, Evan, Lord and Lady Roberts, Milner etc. There were quite the elements for a drawing room drama – Margot would play off Milner against Evan – Evan would play off Etty against Margot, and Etty would play off any man she pleased against Evan.'

Eddy Hamilton said of the Souls in 1889 that their 'primary article of creed is worship of Arthur Balfour'; and Wilfrid Scawen Blunt agreed that 'Arthur Balfour was their High Priest, Mary Elcho their High Priestess'. Balfour was the self-effacing impresario who made the Souls' conversation so brilliant. 'He allowed the talk to flow as his companion wished,' said Winston Churchill, 'appreciating in the most complimentary manner anything that was said in good will, taking up every point, and lifting the discussion step by step – yet often himself speaking very little.' He had the Souls' art – so conspicuous in Ettie too – of making his conversational partners feel that they had surpassed themselves. 'Very often they remembered the things they had said to him, which he had welcomed or seemed to agree with, better than what he had said to them,' Churchill continued. 'He loved general conversation, and knew exactly how to rule it, so that no one was left out . . . Politics, philosophy, science in all its branches, art, history, were themes upon which he embarked as readily as small-talk. He seemed to draw out all that was best in his companion.'

Ettie first met Balfour when she was aged fifteen and he was MP for Hertford, the nearest town to Panshanger. He was nineteen years her senior, and amused, charmed, impelled and guided her for the next forty-seven years. Her children, too, she was to insist, were influenced by him; and it is true that he moved with the times, liked the company of the young, listened to them and never seemed stranded by change. In all this – as in his patient, graceful manners, in his conversational art and his joyous tranquillity – Balfour set Ettie a lifelong standard, which she always sought to emulate. He was a nephew of the Cowpers' most powerful Tory neighbour in Hertfordshire, Lord Salisbury, who became Prime Minister for the second time in 1886. The following year Salisbury appointed his nephew as Chief Secretary for Ireland, with a seat in the Cabinet, and in 1891 promoted him to be Leader of the House of Commons. For the next twenty years he led either the government or the opposition in the Commons. Balfour's languid charm belied the ruthlessness with which he achieved his political ends. He deployed inexorable logic in debate, was always even-tempered and self-controlled, but capable of mordant sarcasm.

In 1902 he succeeded his uncle as Prime Minister, and among his final acts in that office was his recommendation of Willie Grenfell for a peerage – Desborough was the title that Ettie made famous. There was an Olympian nonchalance about him: he never read the political sections of newspapers, and once said that he would no more take the advice of a Conservative Party conference on policy matters than he would that of his valet, which may explain his failure as a party leader. Balfour's colossal charm and intellectual elegance made him *primus inter pares* among the Souls, although his membership of the set alienated some of his party followers: Tory MPs remembered that Gladstone and Disraeli never met socially, and mistrusted Balfour's pleasure in a milieu that included prominent and cerebral Liberals. 'The trouble with A.J.B.', they complained, 'is that he is too clever; far above the head of the man in the street.' Lloyd George's jibe that Balfour's influence on history would be no more than the whiff of scent on a lady's handkerchief has proved wrong: as Foreign Secretary, in 1917, without consulting the indigenous population or neighbouring Arab potentates, he committed the British government to the establishment of a Jewish homeland in Palestine, where 90 per cent of the population was Arab. This folly has produced conflict and misery ever since.

Balfour wrote two treatises, *A Defence of Philosophical Doubt* (1879) and *Foundations of Belief* (1895), arguing that a belief in God was sustainable in the face of evolution theory. Many Tory MPs who had not read *A Defence of Philosophical Doubt,* and those electors who had heard of it, indignantly assumed from its title that Balfour had no fixed beliefs or principles about this world or the next. When *Foundations of Belief* was published in 1895, Ettie read it 'with *intense* admiration' three times: 'it seems to me a revelation of earnestness & imagination such as no book I can remember has ever given me,' though she detected 'a faint ridge of insincerity, the twisting & forcing of metaphysical argument to ends which it somehow *doesn't* seem to support'.

Balfour's tone with Ettie was teasing, affectionate but elusive. Her admiration for him was deep and unfeigned, and she felt a strong need for the admiration to be reciprocated. It was inherent in their characters that her feelings were more intense than his, but he never disappointed her, and never felt bored by her. This was due, no doubt, to her subtle, playful handling of him. He would, at times of political stress, retreat to Taplow for a few days' respite, travelling up to London for Cabinet meetings or lying in bed till noon drafting controversial legislation. Privately, Balfour laughed at Ettie's relish at being seen and admired. Living so perpetually in the limelight of the Souls, she always needed an audience – preferably of her own kind. But her vitality seemed exceptional to him. 'Ettie's energy', he exclaimed to Mary Elcho in 1893, 'is indeed prodigious and amazing! She is never ill, never tired, never bored, always apparently with time on her hands to write to the favoured.' He thought her 'the most amusing letter writer in the world'.

Ettie's letters to Balfour were always warm, candid and relaxed but never possessive, flirtatious or intense. She sent him the best kind of letters between friends, those that are about nothing very much, with joyous descriptions of holidays in Scotland, and chirruping about her children, but flavoured with literary musings. Thus, after reading William Mallock's novel, *A Human Document* (1892), she professed 'a horror of that little brute Mallock which poisons every word he writes. He seems to me to have the instinct of a blue-bottle for the raw places of the human soul, & never to attempt one word of serious contribution towards answering the ugly questions he suggests.' She quizzed Balfour about the scientific accuracy of the theologian Henry Drummond's lectures *The Ascent of Man* (1894), an attempt to reconcile evolution theory with Christianity, which she found more attractive in its approach than Benjamin Kidd's *Social Evolution* (1894), which she had also recently read. From India, in 1892, she described travelling from Bombay to Madras: '*Oh*, such a poisonous railway-journey across, exactly like being put in a baking oven & tied behind a London dust-cart for 2 days in a strong wind!' A ball at Madras Government House was also recounted to Balfour: 'It was a very curious sight, the extraordinary English crowd, & the grave Rajahs in the background with such sad patient faces. I think R. Kipling is horribly misleading about Indian Society – the women seem so washed out, flabby, & dowdy – the men a little better, especially Generals over 82, who are quite spirited!'

All cliques are mixes of individual temperaments and inclinations;

but the Souls were made distinctive by the pervasive influence of their women. Apart from Katie Cowper, Gety Pembroke and Adelaide Brownlow, four other women shaped the Souls – united by their preference for charming informality over ceremonious dullness. These were Margot Tennant; Violet Granby; Mary Elcho; and Ettie herself. Margot once challenged Balfour with being heartless and so self-sufficient that he would not mind if she and Ettie, Violet and Mary were all to die. He paused, and replied reflectively, 'I *think* I should mind if you *all* died on the same day.'

Margot Tennant provoked many memorable moments. The sixth of ten daughters of a Glasgow industrialist, she 'came out' three years before Ettie and made an instantaneous impression. She was not a beauty – she had crinkly hair, fierce eyes, a sharp nose and an aggressive jaw – but her redoubtable character made her, in the late 1880s, the dominant woman among the Souls. It was her effrontery that seemed unique. Energetic and fearless in the hunting field, she was indefatigable and undaunted in Society. This incalculable, disconcerting, unabashed young woman's sharp, insistent veracity was stamped like a hallmark on the Souls' conversation; but after she had turned thirty, her truth-telling turned into an increasingly tedious and discordant mannerism. Margot and Ettie recognised one another's rare mettle as soon as they had been introduced by Betty Ponsonby. 'I have so little self-control & *so* much passion,' Margot wrote to her new ally. 'I'm skinned alive I think – too keen, too happy, too *miserable*.' She was clamorous for Ettie's attention: 'yr love & opinion wd turn me into an angel' and gushing with compliments: 'you are so young, so charmed with Life, you have so *much* to give.'

Violet Lindsay had in 1882 married Henry Manners, who became (by courtesy) Marquess of Granby in 1888, and succeeded as 8th Duke of Rutland in 1906. Most of the Souls women were discriminating, well-read and cultivated; but Violet Granby was exceptional in having a trained and disciplined gift. She was a portrait artist, specialising in drawing and sculpture, with abilities that surpassed those of any dilettante. Her expressive and poetic drawings, with their delicate delineation of features and subtle evocation of moods, were reminiscent of the Pre-Raphaelites, and indeed Margot Tennant likened her to a Burne-Jones Medusa. She was strikingly beautiful, with auburn hair, a delicate complexion, and dark, hollow, exaggerated eyes, and bedecked herself in a cascade of ribbons, scarves, lace and veils.

In contrast to Ettie, who liked Caribbean colour schemes of bright red, orange and yellow, Violet Granby chose bleached colours for her clothes and surroundings – cream, fawn, blue-grey or soft green – and would subdue the colour of curtains by having them laid out in the summer sunshine on her lawns. This restrained taste was the antithesis of her private life. After dutifully perpetuating the male Rutland line with two sons, Robert and John, born in 1885–6, she began to take lovers. Her daughter Letty, born in 1888, is thought to have been fathered by a boring middle-aged sentimentalist called Lord Rowton – 'rather a remnant of a man,' thought Ettie, who hoped that at Rowton's age her 'sole subject of conversation won't be the Kiss-er & the Kiss-ee!' As an adulteress, Lady Granby was indiscreet, self-pitying, histrionic and credulous.

The third leader of the Souls women was Mary Elcho. At the age of seventeen she met Balfour, whom she never ceased to love; and though he reciprocated her devotion, he never brought himself to propose. No doubt he was too self-sufficient and fastidious to enjoy the emotional intimacy and physical repletion of marriage: Clemenceau later referred to him as *cette vieille fille*, and Lord Beaverbrook mocked that he was a hermaphrodite whom no one had ever been allowed to see naked. Balfour's Scottish home, Whittinghame, was some ten miles from Gosford, the Earl of Wemyss's dramatic Robert Adam house on the Firth of Forth; and it was the Earl's eldest surviving son and heir, Hugo Elcho, whom Mary married (by her mother's instigation) at the age of twenty-one. The marriage rested on deep affection and respect; but Hugo Elcho had a sequence of affairs while Balfour remained her high-minded, unselfish cavalier. 'Mary E is too wonderful about Arthur,' Ettie felt. 'I *cannot* make it out – she never seems to see him for a moment alone, positively to avoid it . . . If it is all from the "prudence" point of view, I do admire her courage intensely, for life seems so short, opportunities so infrequent, that I think most people feel forced & driven into recklessness.' Later Mary Elcho confided her feelings for Balfour to Scawen Blunt, who was pursuing a determined and ultimately successful campaign to seduce her. 'She loves and honours and respects him, and he is constant to her, and she has always been constant to him,' Blunt recorded. 'On this understanding he has been content that their love should be within certain limits – a little more than friendship, a little less than love.'

Lord Wemyss gave his Gloucestershire house, Stanway, to the Elchos on their marriage, and Mary Elcho's spell transformed it into a magical paradise. Her own physical beauty was of the unselfconscious kind. 'Mary is very beautiful, pale, dark eyed, raven-haired, with a slight girlish figure, talking well but always with unfathomable reserve about herself, a mystery not one of her women friends pretends to have solved: her secrets are close shut, impenetrably guarded with a little laugh of unconcern,' Scawen Blunt noted in 1895. She could be as frank as Margot Tennant – she told her friends frankly when she was forced by a heavy bout of 'Eve's curse' to defer her engagements – but unlike Margot (and indeed Ettie) she seemed oblivious of her effect on others. She was innocent of any desires to defy, startle or intimidate – although she loved to be laughed at. Because of their early rivalry for Balfour's affections, Mary Elcho bestowed the nickname 'Delilah' on Ettie in her letters to AJB; but she and Ettie were devoted friends for most of their long lives. They developed a beautiful example of those intimate, loving, trusting, sincere friendships that women can attain. 'You have the wonderful gift of saying such delicious things,' Mary Elcho was to tell Ettie in 1910. 'Your friendship is such a joy and comfort to me although I never seem to do anything in return.'

People were always being effusive about Mrs Grenfell: her own intensity almost demanded it. 'Ettie seems too wonderful and delicious, with her marvellous power of diffusing mirth and making everybody happy,' Willie's cousin Lady Wenlock wrote in 1892 after the young paragon had spent several weeks staying with her. 'She has such spirits and such prodigious intention of pleasing, and all the time she is exquisitely "grande dame".' Ettie was not yet twenty-four when Constance Wenlock delivered this judgement and yet she already seemed to be an archetype. 'She really is the most perfect type of womanhood that has been evolved out of modern times,' Lady Wenlock declared. 'She combines all charms, ancient & modern. I doubt if she could have existed precisely as she is 30 years ago, when it was distinctly not allowed as the *métier* of a woman to be charming after marriage. Still, she owes very little of her perfection to modern emancipation –

freedom from restraint in intercourse with men – and nearly all of it to merits that have always been . . . appreciated in all ages. Now that she is gone, everybody in the house feels as if the sun has gone out.'

Altogether, Ettie was a striking woman – intense, intelligent and sympathetic – who watched people with more than a surface observation: whoever she was talking to felt he or she was the only person who mattered to her in the room. No guest who stayed at Taplow or Panshanger, Sir Osbert Sitwell recalled, 'did not believe when he left that he was the only person she wished to talk to'. It was not only in her own houses that she exerted this magnetism. 'Everyone is so devoted to you & you take such trouble to be nice & good,' wrote Gladys de Grey after they had both stayed with Constance Wenlock. 'It is delightful to be in the same house with you, as you have such a "rayonnement" [radiance] & such tact & such kindness, & none of the nasty small jealousies of other women, & you never never make mischief, & all this is so rare & so pleasant to live with.'

When her women friends died, Ettie lauded them with phrases that were what she hoped might be said of herself. Hilda Brodrick was 'so vivid, so vital, so needed & adored', she said – and vivid, vital, needed and adored was what Ettie, in the Souls and out, most craved to be. Her giddying efforts to live each hour to the full, like her wish to leave everyone feeling better and happier, were her devices to fend off depression. Parties were the buoys that kept her afloat. 'You know the terrible indolence and inertia that everyone with "Cowper" blood is born with,' she once wrote from Taplow to Oliver Wendell Holmes, '& here in home-life one's whole energy seems occupied in subduing it.' Yet the crowded, hurried superficiality of her life as a Society woman wearied her at times: 'I have been playing very very hard for the last year or two,' she confessed in 1892, but 'at least it is something to feel one has *lived* every minute of the time with a conscious vivid enjoyment. I am getting old now & must stop – my birthday today, a quarter of a century old!' She teased herself that she was growing 'too ugly to look at and too old to play with!'

✌

Actually, said John Baring in 1892, Ettie was 'living surrounded by clever people all of whom are very much at your feet'. George Curzon,

Oscar Wilde and Henry Asquith were foremost of these. Curzon, the personification of a 'swell' and future Viceroy of India, was a paradoxical creature: ferociously ambitious for political power, but disdainful of the House of Commons; intensely acquisitive, but contemptuous of businessmen; the audacious explorer of Asia and Persia who (because of incurable spinal curvature) writhed in agony for days if he rode a horse too long; ornate in his conversation, yet as boisterous as a puppy; absurdly touchy about his dignity, yet ruthlessly self-mocking – so high-spirited in some moods as to play the part of the Souls' buffoon. He had a 'majestic virility', said Edgar Vincent. Like Ettie, he hungered for attention, and needed a retinue of admirers. Women were a solace to him: he expected them to be yielding, to cosset him and to adulate him.

With Ettie, Curzon was bantering, exuberant and languishing by turns, which suited her perfectly. The two of them shared some moments of intimacy when young: on his last night before leaving on a world tour in 1892, he held her hand under the dinner table, and months later, from a tent in Afghanistan, recalled another moment: 'I remember kissing you in the library on a blood-red sofa in front of the fire; oh would god there were a fire now and a sofa for you and me!' On the last weekend of May 1901, when Curzon had returned to England for some months, the Grenfells entertained him at Taplow: Balfour, Milner, George Wyndham, young Winston Churchill, the Elchos, Asquiths, Vincents and Alice and Jim Cranborne made up the rest of the party. This weekend rekindled Curzon's erotic interest in Ettie, which continued smouldering after his return to India. 'For a whole night I have dreamed of you – no hope of reciprocity,' he wrote from Simla in September. 'They were wonderful dreams, lovers' dreams, in which things uncontemplated in life were realized in that glowing fancy haze. Now I am awake again and am respectable, it is a heavy shock to find there is no love, no triumph, no embrace.'

Curzon liked to keep a tight clamp on the lower orders, resented interlopers in the Souls and blamed Ettie for them. In May 1891 Harry White regaled his wife with Curzon's denunciation of 'the decadence of our circle by the introduction of the "Cosquiths", a name he has coined out of Oscar Wilde and Asquith'. Ettie led in the lionising of this pair, and had startled Balfour as well as Curzon by inviting them with their wives to Taplow. Curzon urged White to capsize them while punting in the hope of drowning them. 'I must say I am disposed to draw the line at Oscar Wilde, about whom everyone has known for years,' the American commented. Curzon was pained by Ettie's 'pursuit of notoriety in any shape (if associated with cleverness)', as he complained to White. 'The latest is giving a great Taplow party on Sunday to these new guns, including Mr and Mrs Oscar Wilde, Mr and Mrs Asquith and Mr and Mrs Beerbohm Tree . . . It means the dissolution of the fairest and strongest band of friends ever yet allied by ties of affection. Gone forever is the old Gang, and a few magnificent souls like you and Harry, Liddell, Mary Elcho and myself remain. The rest are whirling after new Gods and baring their heads in the temple of twopenny Rimmons.'

Ettie charmed Wilde, and admired his gift for taking the most unexceptional people in a room and turning them into wits. After he visited Taplow in 1891, she asked him for his photograph, which he sent together with a copy of *Lord Arthur Savile's Crime*. 'Why not a little dinner?' he asked her. 'You, Lady Elcho, Arthur Balfour and myself. It wd be entrancing.' In November that year he found the news of her departure for India 'dreadful', as depriving him of the chance of seeing her, and sent her his new volume of fairy stories, *A House of Pomegranates*. One of its stories, 'The Birthday of the Infanta', about a pampered little Spanish princess whom Velázquez painted, he dedicated to Ettie – 'as a slight return', he told her, 'for that entrancing day at Taplow'. Entrancement was a word that he often used to her. She replied from the Red Sea, and on her return, he suggested tea parties or visits to the theatre together. Wilde's wit delighted her, but the writings of this 'queer kind of literary acrobat', as she called him in 1893, left her ambivalent. She enjoyed many of his stories, but found his play *Salomé* 'repulsive' and 'hated' his novel, 'horrible *Dorian Gray*'.

Asquith was one of the six Prime Ministers – the others were Rosebery, Balfour, Baldwin, Chamberlain and Churchill – with whom Ettie enjoyed a friendship. She met him at Balliol in the spring of 1891, when they took a Sunday afternoon walk together. 'I love his steadfast undubious massive intellect, his independence and scorn, his devotion to high things, his humour – above all his heart,' Asquith's political opponent Alfred Lyttelton wrote of him to Ettie at this time. Asquith was indeed, as Churchill later said, simultaneously adamant and jocular in a crisis – a combination that was appealing to Ettie. She invited him with his wife to Taplow one Sunday with the Wildes, and a pleasant family friendship was maturing when Helen Asquith died of typhoid in September. Shortly afterwards, when the lonely widower mentioned that he was seeking solace by reading the novels of Balzac, she sent him books by Oliver Wendell Holmes; and she grew to admire his inscrutability. He would move, she thought, from acquaintance to friendship, from friendship to affection, from affection to tenderness with no outward change of expression.

In October 1892 Ettie sent him a luxuriously long letter from Schloss Eichhorn in Moravia, 'the most beautiful place I have ever seen in Europe', to which she and Willie had gone a fortnight earlier. They were staying in an ancient stone castle of the Knights Templar, perched on a rock pinnacle. 'There is a sort of flying buttress outside my window over-hanging the sheer precipice & looking down – down – on the tops of the pine trees & the river far below, & away to scarlet & gold woods on the other side of the valley. We are out the whole day long – *such* pine-woods. I love them most of all, the heavenly scent & soft carpet underfoot & the blue sky gleaming overhead.' This letter enchanted Asquith, who asked to be sent her photograph to decorate his room. 'There are only half a dozen people whose interest & approval I am really keen to have, and you know very well that you are one of them,' he assured her some months later.

Inevitably their contacts changed when, in 1894, he married Margot Tennant. 'The *great* event of course has been Margot's marriage,' Ettie reported to a friend overseas:

Poor darling little Margot I think felt very sad & strained . . . she is *not* the very least in love with him & faces it, but I do thoroughly believe it will all go well. He is *so* devoted, & has such wonderful delicacy & judgment about her . . . & she deeply likes & believes in him, & *means* to make it a success. Only just the last days were very trying, I saw a great deal of her & she was in a very overwrought state of physical strain, poor little sweet . . . I never shall forget her in the Church, she has never looked so beautiful, her little face quite white & set, as if she saw nothing, but her voice quite strong & clear: she has extraordinary self-control & kept it up to the very last. Poor Asquith as white as a *sheet* too, he has grown quite thin with emotions! It was such a lovely wedding [with] grim old St George's quite transformed – great tall white flowers & palms everywhere, & . . . all her friends crowded round her.

The Asquiths set up in Cavendish Square, and there, in July, Margot gave a luncheon to which she invited Ettie, Oscar Wilde, Wilfrid Scawen Blunt, Lord Ribblesdale and Reggie Lister. Ettie and Wilde vied for admiration and made a charming duo. 'Oscar and Mrs Grenfell were very brilliant, and all the party immensely talkative,' Blunt noted. 'Asquith was afraid to talk much, lest he should say the wrong thing.' Asquith loathed verbiage, claptrap and vehemence, and never found Ettie excessively prone to these, though Margot famously said that she told enough white lies to ice a wedding cake. He regretted that his contacts with Ettie became subdued after his marriage. 'Our talk on Sunday morning revived what I had begun to fear was past & over,' he wrote to her in 1898. 'Somehow or other you & I seem to have let slip what we once held surely & tightly.' He could never abandon his past feelings for her, but had 'felt for the last two years that a kind of veil has interposed itself'. He was delighted 'that the veil has fallen – for I count on your friendship – in its true & genuine sense, as among the best & richest things that have come into my life'. He was not exaggerating, he protested: 'over & over again I have longed to be able to say to you: "I know what you feel. I understand your encompassments (because I know my own): & if there is anything in the world that I can give or contribute, take it – it is all yours."' But by then Ettie was jaded by the sound of men offering the world.

CHAPTER 3

The Flirt

As a little child Ettie had lost her mother, her father and finally her brother. She was brought up by beloved grandmothers, who were both dead by the time she was thirteen. Before she had closed her twentieth year the aunt who had cared best for her, and the uncle who was her substitute father, had both died. Willie, too, had almost been lost to her. It was one of the stock stories of his strenuous life that he had nearly perished in 1884 during a hunting trip to the Bighorn Mountains in Wyoming. He survived three days' walking lost in the wilds, and two freezing nights without sleep, and was starving when rescued. A year after his marriage, his life was hazarded again, when he went as the *Daily Telegraph*'s special correspondent to Sudan and his camp suffered a surprise attack by dervishes. He fled a fusillade of bullets, running one of the hardest races of his life, in tennis shoes. Five years later he was gravely ill with typhoid. Thoughts of these near-escapes intensified Ettie's realisation of her deep need of Willie. Her lively imagination and high-strung responses felt steadied and levelled by marriage to this unimaginative man. His steady imperturbable view of life made her feel safe; she depended on him to chase away her phantoms and talk comforting sense to her.

Ettie knew what it meant to depend on someone, and for them to disappear. It left her afraid. When Frances Horner lost her younger son in 1908, Ettie gave such effective consolation that the grieving mother marvelled that anyone could be so tender without having known that particular sorrow. Ettie replied, 'It is fear, I think, makes me understand.' Her manner was always confiding and intimate because she feared to be abandoned or ignored. After marrying Willie, still afraid that those she loved might neglect her, or worse still die, she collected an auxiliary brigade of attendants and admirers of all ages and both sexes. It was almost as if the precocious, observant child brought up among the yew alleys, romantic groves and sequestered pavilions at Wrest had acquired there a lifelong thrill at reading hidden motives and detecting secret signals.

Intimate undertones, private allegiances, ardent confidences and delicate stratagems for discreet meetings – they all made her feel more intensely alive. Scared – particularly in the 1890s – of the depressive Cowper strain, she fought it by keeping herself always at a high emotional pitch. Willie was at first understandably unsettled by her supernumerary *tendresses*, but although she was a flirt, who craved attention and emotional intensity from men and women, she was not a practised adulteress. She might hold Curzon's hand, or kiss him on a blood-red sofa, but there was never any serious doubt about the paternity of her children, as there was with Violet Granby and Mary Elcho.

The Souls, of course, were inveterate flirts: in 1890 the Countess of Carlisle, who had a straying husband (Willie's cousin), could be heard inveighing against the 'wickedness of married flirtations and the society of Souls'; and that habitual seducer, Wilfrid Scawen Blunt, staying with George Wyndham in 1891, decided that 'the doctrine of the "Souls" is unlimited licence in love, save only the one connubial act'. Similarly, Mary Elcho averred that 'nearly all the group were married women with husbands whom they loved, and by whom they had children, but each had her "friend", who was a friend only'. The set's creed, she thought, had been well encapsulated by the Tory politician Harry Chaplin: 'Every woman shall have her man; but no man shall have his woman.'

What was the moral context of the Souls? How did Ettie react to their amatory pirouettes and ritualised ardour? She recognised her beauty as a gift to be used, enjoyed and targeted, but how did she exercise her powers to attract and command? How far did she push her love of sensation?

To answer these questions we must turn to Constance Wenlock, who provided a decisive influence on Ettie's rules of private morality. She was the daughter of the great Yorkshire magnate Lord Harewood, and in 1872, at the age of twenty, had married Beilby ('Bingy') Lawley, a rich, popular and benevolent-minded Liberal, who subsequently inherited his father's peerage and a large, cold and architecturally undistinguished house at Escrick in the East Riding. She was 'an original and pretty little woman', Scawen Blunt noted in 1890: 'a type of our modern age, a highly cultured flower of feeling, in love with beauty and virtue, but curious about love and frightened with the thought of growing old'. In 1887, after fifteen years of marriage, Constance Wenlock had become infatuated with another man. The affair left her 'miserable', and seemed at one time likely to 'destroy' her life and reputation. After its emotional storms had subsided, she had her first successful pregnancy – evidently by her husband – after seventeen years of marriage, and in 1891, on his appointment as Governor of Madras, she accompanied him to India. She was a demi-Soul, a confidential friend of Margot Tennant, George Pembroke and Violet Granby; and a woman of independent opinions, ineffaceable kindness and discriminating culture.

Lady Wenlock's crisis of 1887 made her think deeply about the romantic ideals and sexual realities of late-Victorian England. It was a favourite theme in her talk and voluminous correspondence. 'There is', she felt, 'more resemblance between our society and that of Charles II's time than between us and the generation just before us.' Modern women were divided between three categories, she said, *femmes de ménage*, *femmes de société* and *femmes de l'idéal*: 'the first is dull and virtuous, the second clever and gay, of lax morality, the third romantic with a single passion, always unhappy.' She considered herself *une femme de l'idéal*, and during 1892, when she and Ettie spent several weeks together, they talked about the snares that could trap or scar a *femme de société* and agreed on the higher calling of the Ideal in love.

Constance Wenlock found it 'strange, and cruel, in the scheme of the Universe', that so many human beings were born with 'such intense capacity for loving and belief in the right to be happy in it' because 'for an enormous number of women, and probably also of men, there is no possibility of making their life's happiness out of the feeling of being supremely in love'. Instead it was their fate that 'they *had to* give up that feeling, and build their lives without it, and even to learn to be thankful and contented for second-best'. People born with the capacity to love and 'strong instinctive expectation of its being satisfied, have to have it hammered out of them — and all the best years of life are spent in struggling, until at last they realise they *can't have* what they want — and must make the best of what they can get'.

Earlier, advising Constance Wenlock during her 1887 *crise de coeur*, her cousin 'Doll' Liddell had identified several sub-species of Society lover: Lotharios, Philanderers, *Amis caressants* and Platonics. Lotharios feigned love to achieve their driving aim of sexual pleasure, and were mostly men, he said, while philanderers feigned intellectual interests to achieve their aim of emotional excitement, and were often women. *Amis caressants* were 'common in modern life, being somewhat unnatural and the product of a refined Society'. They often attained real and durable affection, for the 'pinch of Passion in the compound gives it a strong fizz which is wanting in the Platonic, while the presence of a modified restraint prevents satiety. The weak point is a certain effeminacy, which makes it more suitable to females than to men, and more successful when the "Ami" partakes somewhat of the female disposition.' The Platonic was the most rare and artificial of all the states, but Liddell knew a few instances of 'the man of strong and passionate nature, who controls himself, for the sake of the beloved; and the man of cold and refined temperament, who prefers the more delicate conditions of the Platonic'.

Ettie, in Constance Wenlock's categories, was *une femme de l'idéal*, searching for a romantic passion and, if not supremely in love with her husband, contented and grateful for his calm, admiring companionship, even if intellectually he seemed unexciting. She was romantic in aspirations, a seeker of the Ideal, who shrank from anything mean. In Doll Liddell's categories, Ettie was a philanderer, playing up her cultural interests and seeking emotional intensity rather than physical excitement, or an *amie caressante*, somewhat too self-conscious in her affections, wanting a strong fizz in her emotions but insisting on physical restraint. As a woman in her twenties Ettie was proud and exhilarated by the power her charm and youth gave her — but also at times alarmed. She enjoyed making men the sport of her whims; she wanted to be needed and admired; but she had her grandmothers' scruples, and Nannie Wake's old-fashioned standard of good faith. She relished flirtation and excitement, but did not want the brightness of her fun to be tarnished by the need of fibbing, plotting and dodging. There would be nothing ideal about that.

The title of Balfour's book, *A Defence of Philosophical Doubt*, encouraged the misconception that the Christianity of the Souls was polite and superficial, that prayer meant little to them, that they were indifferent as to creeds and churches. This was the antithesis of Ettie's position. She never lost the simple, unquestioning faith that she imbibed in childhood from Pammy Cowper and Nanny Wake. Christianity was unique in her life: it was the one powerful influence that she did not exaggerate, dramatise or parade. She was reticent, never publicly enthusiastic, about her religion; yet it permeated all her thought and conduct, dominated her quest for ideal love, inspired her belief in her duty to be grateful for all life's experiences, sustained her unwavering trust in the afterlife. The Bible contained the eternal truths that guided her through eighty years. And so, though she thrived on emotional vibrancy in the atmosphere around her, she was an ascetic, not an adventuress, and — against superficial appearances — a faithful, unerring wife. 'I miss my darling Gent *dreadfully*,' she wrote when Willie had left on a hunting expedition in 1892. 'Nothing is nice when you are away . . . what would be the fun of a "spangle" without Gent to talk it over with?'

Ettie was impressed by reading Thomas Green's *Witness of God and Faith — Two Lay Sermons* after their publication in 1889: 'they deal with the great questions in a very noble way,' she told Oliver Wendell Holmes. The judge far away in Boston remained an important father-figure to her during the 1890s. 'It is not insincere or affected or "modern" but the very true truth when I say that I owe to you much happiness, much illumination, much encouragement, of the sort that comes from an assurance of the existence of what is true and strong.' She was particularly swayed by the speech that this thrice wounded survivor of the American Civil War had delivered to fellow veterans on the twentieth anniversary of its close. It included this resounding exordium:

Through our great good fortune, in our youth our hearts were touched with fire. It was given to us to learn at the outset that life is a profound and passionate thing . . . we have seen with our own eyes, beyond and above the golden fields, the snowy heights of honor . . . above all we have learned that whether a man accepts from Fortune her spade, and will look downward and dig, or from Aspiration her axe and cord, and will scale the ice, the one and only success which it is his to command is to bring to his work a mighty heart.

Ettie kept this Memorial Day address on her table, for it reminded her of Henry Cowper's precepts, which had guided her life. 'One's belief in a meaning to it all – somehow – somewhere – can never quite die, the hope that "Beyond the mist and the cloud-rack lies the imperishable Blue",' she told Holmes, '& it gives me a rush of happiness to recognise . . . in your writings the ring of passion & Romance & awe with which he looked out on the world.' A heart touched by fire, and stimulated by passion and romance, would, she thought, defeat the lethal Cowper indifference.

The earliest, apparently, of Ettie's attachments, during her career as *une femme de l'idéal*, was a man fifteen years her senior, Albert Grey. He and Willie, together with Lord Wenlock and Sir Francis Fletcher Vane (the founder of the Italian Boy Scouts), had formed the Anglo-Siberian Trading Syndicate, which carried on an import-export trade with Siberia in 1889–90. Like her, he was a member of the great Whig cousinhood: the grandson of the Lord Grey who had been Prime Minister at the time of the Reform Act of 1832, and heir to the earldom (to which he succeeded in 1894). A Christian missionary in politics rather than a party politician, Grey idolised the patriots of the Italian Risorgimento, especially Mazzini, and was inspired by them to a burning sense of duty and a hot patriotism. 'One of the most attractive of men,' according to Lady Battersea, Albert Grey was 'an idealist whose heart and soul were bent on social reform and the betterment of the people', and so eager that he 'caught others up in the wave of his enthusiasm and carried them with him'. Grey could easily have been a priggish and exhausting zealot, but he had a 'vivid sense of fun, [was] sparkling, gay and fervent' and, said Reggie Brett, 'lit many fires in cold rooms'.

Ettie's friendship with Grey was the prototype of her involvement with other men. By July 1888 he was holding luncheons for young Mrs Grenfell in the Grosvenor Gallery Restaurant and arranging rendez-vous at the Queen's lawn-tennis club. He beseeched and received her photograph – 'at present shedding a halo of charm all over my writing table,' he told her – and corresponded with her about books: memoirs of the revolutionary Italian patriots whom he venerated, Carlyle's *Sartor Resartus*, Green's *Witness of God and Faith* and Marie Bashkirt-seff's *Journals*. Many of these books were stiffish going, but Ettie was as earnest about self-improvement as any mid-Victorian. 'I am *absorbed* in Schopenhauer,' she told Asquith in 1892. 'I wake very early here & wrestle with his meanings on my terrace until breakfast time. It is very difficult I think & very often I cannot understand at all & when I can all my instincts are exactly the opposite to what he lays down, & yet I think he is full of a strange charm.'

'I take so deep an interest in you, & have formed so high an ideal for you,' Grey told Ettie in July 1889; and two years later he attested, 'there is *no-one* whose friendship & sympathy & help are so important as yours are to me.' In September 1892 he was greatly upset to learn that 'hateful and lying insinuations' were circulating in Society about them. From Howick, his uncle's seat in Northumberland, he sent a long, emotional explanation. 'I am very, *very* fond of you,' he averred, but 'I love my wife first & you second, both far too much to make serious love to you . . . Few people know, no one knows, I sometimes think that I don't know myself, half of all my dear wife is to me, & I shd be really miserable if it were ever thought by anyone for whose opinion either she or I care, that because of my frequent absences, or because of the pleasure I show in other People's Society (& you tell me I have a habit of getting most offensively *en evidence*) she was not loved cherished & honoured by me beyond everything else on earth.' Ettie, though, held a unique role in his life. 'I feel so happy & contented when I am with you,' he declared, 'even though the conditions . . . usually are absolutely fatal to any exchange of confidence or serious talk. You don't know, & I can't explain why in a letter, but you have been a great help to me.'

Ettie saw less of Grey after 1894, when Cecil Rhodes appointed him Administrator of Rhodesia, but in 1899 she asked him for insider's tips on promising South African mining shares – 'have just been paying all my Christmas bills, & am in the depths of blue!' He guided her to some lucrative investments, and even after 1904, when he went out to Canada as Governor-General (an appointment for which Willie had hoped), was still arranging juicy investments to satisfy what she self-mockingly called her 'greedy and impecunious soul'. They remained devoted to one another and, when he was dying of liver cancer in 1917, she cajoled old friends like Arthur Balfour into visiting him, and by her own delicate attention endeared herself to him for a final time. She found comfort in contemplating the serene Christian acceptance of Grey's last weeks: 'in complete consciousness & happiness, knowing all – & longing at the end to go – he wrote to me that it was all so *unlike* what one expected – "a gradual luring away by unseen influences to new places of beauty: one lies in a halo of the most exquisite peace & rejoicing".' This was perhaps the morphine working.

For Willie's sake, and her own, Ettie abhorred being compromised. She froze with displeasure when Margot Asquith once joked that she had the power of a royal mistress to allure and entrap. Though friends of both sexes confided their affairs to her, she recoiled from any squalid, incriminating involvement in their adultery. This is evident from her reaction when, in 1890, while travelling on the Continent, she became ensnared in the machinations surrounding Violet Granby's affair with a notorious lothario, Harry Cust. Cust – the cousin of Lord Brownlow, Ettie's host at Ashridge – and Violet arranged a clandestine Continental journey together and, on returning to England, became alarmed that their arrangements were going to be discovered. They wanted Ettie, whom they had met on their travels, to provide them with false alibis. Violet wrote beseeching Ettie '*not to mention* that you met him *travelling* but only that you met him in Venice. But you might say that you met *me* on yr way to Venice, at *a junction*, me coming from Switzerland on our way to Venice, & that we travelled together. Don't you think? And that you & I used to dine & lunch & gondola together – and that *he* was passing through Venice on his way to shoot somewhere – and was just leaving.' She had already lied to two mutual friends, Betty Montgomery and Nina Welby, about her meeting with Cust, and expected Ettie to corroborate her lies. 'Please remember,' she insisted. '*Don't* ever let Betty know more than *Venice*.'

Margot Asquith once said of Ettie, 'I would have gone to her if I was sad, but never if I was guilty': Ettie's immediate response to this incriminating plea is unknown, but it ensured the entire collapse for her of any charm that Violet Granby and Cust ever had, and she never forgave the stealthy lovers for soliciting her collusion. Her dislike of them was evident to many of their mutual friends. She strenuously supported a penurious young diplomat, Duff Cooper, when at the end of the First World War he wanted to marry Diana Manners, the love child of Cust and Violet (by then Duchess of Rutland), against her mother's wishes, and tried to get him a lucrative City berth with the Rothschilds. 'Her Grace seems to be kicking up Hades,' Ettie wrote in 1918. 'I had a letter from V.R. on Saturday that really would have melted one, if one were not so convinced of her evil character and falseness.'

George Pembroke told Ettie that their world was characterised by 'a sort of sexual warfare, a sort of hardness that often astonishes in kind natures, a sort of acknowledgment that we are in the region of natural war where the strongest must win & the weakest go under & the luckiest escape & the unluckiest perish'. At times she found the erotic crossfire uncomfortable. She relished the attention, felt stirred by the excitement and no doubt her unexplained resistances and scruples added to her attractions; but she had no wish to plumb the depths of mute instincts and unmarked desires. Indeed, as she was a woman of only twenty-three when men started targeting her in that hardened sexual warfare described by George Pembroke, the lotharios may have become oppressive.

The wolfish attentions to Ettie multiplied after the Grenfells drifted into a faster set in 1890–91. In the autumn of 1890, for example, they went to stay in Austria with Baron Hirsch. The Baron was a financial adventurer who had been sponsored in London Society by the debt-ridden young Earl of Rosslyn and consolidated his position in the Marlborough House set by clearing some of the Prince of Wales's debts. 'I grudge you to that crowd – you are much too good for them,' Albert Grey complained. These were the people for whom the phrase *cinq à sept* had a distinct meaning: the hours of the late afternoon and early evening when husbands were expected to stay safely in their clubs while their wives entertained admirers, or a special lover, in their London home.

For Ettie, the 1891 Season proved hectic and arduous. 'The fight is about to begin again,' Evan Charteris wrote in April, '& in the air is the sound of buckling armour; children are being sent out of the way into the country, stationers are scurrying with cards, houses are painted, women are painting, & men are selecting their quarry – is society much more, after all, than hostilities conducted under the disguise of friendship? – the amenities are very like those shown out hunting, where people avoid having to pick each other up, unless there's a broken limb actually in their path.' He pictured Violet Granby 'luxuriating at the rural home of Cust', Evelyn de Vesci secluded at Abbey Leix, 'Lady Pembroke piloting her yacht through the waves of Biscay', 'Lady Brownlow showing the austere refinement of her hospitality in Carlton Terrace', and 'Mrs White bumping across Europe in the Orient Express'. Ettie, shortly afterwards glimpsed by Asquith at the Marlborough House ball surrounded by a dense and imposing escort of male admirers, mixed with the racing set during the 1891 Season, fell in with bold bad baronets like Sir Charles Cradock-Hartopp and Sir John Lister-Kaye, and received gallantries from Lord Dunraven, the racing yachtsman. 'Mrs Grenfell you are a very clever woman,' Dunraven told her, 'you are the sweetest of women too.' He valued her as a privileged source of *fin-de-siècle* Society news: 'do tell me of the world, the very rotten but most amusing fag end of a materialist century.'

Ettie was attracted to other people's large, vivid, talented families – perhaps as a result of having lost all her closest relations when she was small. Two particularly, the Charteris and Baring families, she half adopted as her own. In both cases her initial intimacy was with a daughter: Evelyn de Vesci had been born a Charteris and Elizabeth Castlerosse had been born a Baring. The latter had come out with Ettie in the Season of 1885, and (as predicted by a Planchette board) had become engaged during Cowes week of 1886 to an Irish nobleman, Valentine Castlerosse, who succeeded to the earldom of Kenmare in 1905. The Castlerosses went to live in south-west Ireland, but the devotion between the two women never palled.

Elizabeth had five Baring brothers, of whom John and Maurice became crucial figures in Ettie's life, and Everard and Hugo were her friends. 'I do love them all so dearly,' Ettie said of the Barings in 1892, 'I have *never* seen a family so happy together & in each other.' To have a family that rejoiced together, and exulted in one another's company, met a deep craving in the orphan who had lost her only brother. Similarly Evelyn de Vesci, and her Charteris affiliations, assuaged Ettie's craving for continuity. 'I want to thank you Evelyn for being one of the *unchanging* ideals of this knock-about earth, & for your faithful tenderness to me,' Ettie wrote in 1912. She cherished Evelyn de Vesci as one of the last links with her grandmother Cowper, uncle Henry and aunt Dolly; and solicited the passionate admiration of Lady de Vesci's two surviving brothers, Lord Elcho and Evan Charteris.

Hugo Elcho had no compunction: he disappointed his parents, and exasperated his siblings, by fits of destructive self-indulgence. He was wayward, indecisive, petulant; but sometimes irresistibly charming. Alternating day by day between gaiety and gloom, he tried to enliven his darker moods by gambling, at which he lost large sums on the Stock Exchange, and by a hard, fast pursuit of women. Both the gambling and adultery were expressions of his compelling need to win: he advised one of his granddaughters to treat the world as a huge roulette table, and was so unscrupulous that he would even cheat when playing L'Attaque with his small grandchildren. For ten years he was MP for Ipswich, but his parliamentary successes were uniformly frivolous: an ironic disquisition on the subject of the payment of MPs and some whimsical speeches moving the Adjournment of the House on Derby Day.

During the 1889 Season Hugo's pursuit of Ettie was blatant: 'I get quite low at my repeatedly unsuccessful endeavours to accomplish the object of my desire,' he told her. Her parrying of his overtures was no deterrent: 'it only makes me moralise on my perversity in preferring being trampled by you to being caressed by anyone else.' Elcho relented in his pursuit during Ettie's second pregnancy, which began in June 1889, but soon renewed his emotional siege. 'Why do I not like you a little less or why do you not like me a little more?' he asked Ettie in December 1890. When he had realised that she was unattainable, he had resolved never to see her again. And yet: 'one makes these resolutions, & one breaks them. One sees what is best for one, & one does what is worst, & probably if temptation came in my way again I should rush to meet it. You were kind to me at Panshanger. I ought I know to estimate such kindness at its proper value, & found no false hopes on it, to be prepared when meeting you in the presence of others to be kicked in the old careless manner.' Ettie savoured her power during Elcho's temporary enslavement, but had no wish to plunge into the confused and turbid swirl of an affair with him. She answered his messages patiently and left him to make himself ridiculous with other women. She preferred instead an intimate friendship with Hugo's wise and patient wife Mary – among the deepest and most enduring friendships of her life.

There was a crisis in Ettie's life at the close of the 1891 Season when she was aged twenty-four. She admitted to being exhausted by relentless social striving – 'dismal & stale after three months hard in London,' as she wrote in July. 'I don't think the knocks one takes & gives at that game count or signify much, but I suppose it is likely to do one some harm . . . & I feel as if I had played a little too much this year, & have got a very empty head.' One day at the height of the Season, she fled London and went down on an early train full of 'haymaker trippers' to Brocket. It was 'a lovely golden June day, & the peace & fragrance of the dear place swept over me like a great tide'. She secluded herself in the walled orchard, sat amid the long grass and old, gnarled trees, and lost herself gazing at the azure sky.

Her weariness and highly wrought impressionability were evident to her friends. 'Were you tired at the end of the Season?' Alfred Lyttelton asked solicitously in September. 'Your success has been so brilliant that all nice ambitious women who are young look to your career and imitate it': she provided a 'delicious example which defeats all rules & reverses all judgements & turns round all heads', but he recognised that her 'amazing success' must have been achieved at a cost. An undated letter from Betty Ponsonby may date from this autumn. 'It did indeed tug at my heart-strings to see you cry, & I longed to hug you & take care of you as if you were a little girl.' As she feared Ettie's troubles were not yet over, she reiterated what 'hope and courage about life' all their friends derived from her example. 'You don't know how much you teach one indirectly, so that when the lowest, slackest, most reckless mood comes on, it feels utterly rebuked by the thought & remembrance of you.'

Ettie was still feeling encompassed by 'ice-bound apathy and lethargy' in November. 'Sometimes it seems as if all the joys were snatched so furtively from the very shadow of calamity, as though the only thing possible to cling to with strong faith is "Lovely & soothing Death".' She had been coarsened by constant, fashionable socialising, she confessed to her American puritan mentor Wendell Holmes. By yielding to social pressure, 'there comes day by day more amusement & "low success" into one's life, less spirit, ideal, intellect, power of self-discipline & endeavour.' She had sunk, she admitted, into 'a Valley of Desolation lately, as regards inward things'. This awkward period – about which nothing clear can be traced – closed when Willie took Ettie away to India in late November 1891. 'It was all so wretched (one's own little private thread of life) & I longed only to escape from it all,' she recalled a year later. (Willie's reactions to Ettie's 'spangles' remain inscrutable: doubtless he was unsettled by her moods at this time; but the hunting trips in Africa, north America and elsewhere that he took with other sportsmen, suggest that he was confident and trusting in his marriage, and proud rather than hurt by his wife's power over other men.)

The Grenfells landed at Bombay, where they stayed with the Governor, a famous cricketer called Lord Harris. 'The first few days of it all in Bombay were almost intoxicating, the *marvellous* colour & beauty all around one such a shock of surprise,' she reported to Alfred Lyttelton in London. 'I longed to sit all day by the dusty road & just watch.' Next the Grenfells entrained for Madras, where for six weeks in January and February of 1892 she stayed with Willie's cousins Constance and Bingy Wenlock at Guindy, where the Governor had a country house. It proved a crucial phase of Ettie's life. She fell into raptures at the sensual beauty of Madras. 'This glowing rich-coloured life seems to pour fresh vitality into one & *so* to renew one's "exhausted atmosphere",' she wrote to Judge Holmes in the depths of a Boston winter. 'I feel to have always been colour-blind before, & suddenly to have had my eyes opened to see what orange & blue &

scarlet really mean, & what colour the Sunset is.' She gloried in the shimmering noon heat, the light at dusk transfiguring the native pink houses into scarlet wonders, and the wonderful moonlight. Madras brought a permanent visual awakening: ever afterwards she had a taste for bright oranges, yellows and scarlet in her own rooms at Taplow, which some of her family found too garish. After passing so much of her childhood dressed in mourning black, the adult Ettie always felt liberated by rich, vibrant colours.

Madras also proved to be a place of emotional revitalisation. 'No words in any language will ever be found to thank you one hundredth part or even to give you any *idea* how happy I was & what a golden halo will always remain round my weeks with you!' she wrote afterwards to Lady Wenlock. 'I can never, never tell you the state of utter gloom & dejection & flatness that I have been in ever since our horrible ship steamed out of Madras.' She told Alfred Lyttelton, too, that she could never be so happy again as she had been at Guindy. Although Calcutta was less agreeable – the Grenfells stayed with the Viceroy, Lord Lansdowne, and she found Government House 'stiff, dull & solemn' – she adored the Viceroy's Camp at Darjeeling, her visits to Cooch Behar, Benares and Agra, and all the hot sensuality of the bazaars and the countryside.

It was her hostess in Madras who had put her in a mood for happiness: their talks, she told Constance Wenlock, brought 'a lasting glow for ever to the backward horizon of my life. I feel that the peace & the joy of the months here no man can take from me.' They talked often of love affairs and men. We can surmise Lady Wenlock's advice at Guindy from another fragment in Ettie's letters to her. 'I have got such a dull British nature in these ways,' Ettie wrote, 'it takes so long to care, so dreadfully long to stop caring. One ought to be wiser & take "second best" humbly & gladly – but I have never wanted wrong things, or anything underhand, only the happy friendship . . . that St Paul himself could not have condemned.'

Ettie reached England in time for the London Season of 1892 and, as Evan Charteris recounted, began 'her summer reign, with perhaps a little less zest than last year, but still with keenness enough to fill her place of supremacy'. In affirming to Constance Wenlock on 6 April that she was resolved on a new start, Ettie used phrases that suggest that her departure for India may have been triggered by unhappiness over a man. 'I saw S twice, in the street, looking *so* ill,' she reported. 'A great deal of sadness seems inevitable in pursuing a course even when the wrench of starting it is long over – but . . . this one must be preserved for the sake of all concerned. And I am a very fortunate woman & *will not regret* & repine.' She expressed similar resignation to Judge Holmes. London life seemed 'so pinched & restricted', she told him in May. 'It takes a little time to get re-reconciled to the meridian of Mayfair, & I have felt restive – perhaps the greatest waste of time of all when you know that going back into tractable Hyde Park harness is only a question of time & has *got* to be!'

Evan Charteris was the youngest and most susceptible of the Souls. As a youth, he had nursed a crush for Constance Wenlock, later he had hoped to marry Margot Tennant and he was a long-standing admirer of Lady Helen Vincent. With her 'great grace, beauty and gentleness', Helen Vincent was nearly perfect, he thought, though he cavilled at 'her painful love of smartness' and sensed that 'the diamond and plush side of life has more attractions for her than the human and sentimental'. At the start of the 1892 Season he ranked Ettie among the few women who could vie with Helen Vincent, but by the summer he was convinced that she exceeded even Helen Vincent's level of perfection. With Evan Charteris, unlike his brother Hugo, Ettie's relationship was intense, authentic, volatile and enduring.

After leaving the Coldstream Guards, Charteris had become a barrister in 1891 and was eventually to be a leader of the parliamentary bar. A man of easy grace, with a fragile appearance, he had a steely perseverance – not least in ensuring his personal comforts and convenience. He collected eighteenth-century English paintings and furniture for his rooms in Mount Street, and gained such a reputation in the art world that he was selected as Chairman of the Trustees of the National Portrait Gallery and of the Tate Gallery. Charteris had a tart sense of humour, a deep, infectious laugh and a taste for paradox, which sometimes lured him into exasperating contrariness. He was prone to melodramatic bouts of hypochondria, which Ettie cured with hoots of healthy derision, and spent hours on patient, amusing visits to invalid friends. His kindliness was coupled with an indignant temper and querulous dissatisfaction. He was a man of acute sensibility whose life was disrupted by high dudgeons. 'There, you felt, as you saw him enter a room, comes someone who will assess every shade of feeling, every nuance in this gathering, and yet will contribute more to it than he takes out,' Osbert Sitwell wrote of him. 'Injustice, oppression, vulgar thoughtlessness, the enemies of beauty, made him as angry at 70 as they might a boy of 20. Never was there a kinder or more comprehending friend, or one more willing to laugh tolerantly at the intolerance of others, but at sight of these he would charge with all the flags flying. The fires remained in him to the end imparting an enormous vitality to his conversation.'

Charteris fell deeply in love with Ettie in the summer of 1892. He deluged her with letters that were carefully written in case they were seen by other eyes, in which he expressed his feelings for her as if he were confiding his infatuation with another woman to her: 'as I know you will see her before I shall, I want you to tell her how I love her now more than I ever have in my life – she is all life to me.' He felt anguished if he did not see her constantly. 'My meetings with her are like shooting stars – I look up & she is gone – before even I have time to tell her that with my whole soul I love her. Ah, she does not know the love I have for her, the pride I take in her, the care I would watch her with.' Ettie soon settled safe terms for their love. 'My relations with her are of a nature that forbid real darkness,' he wrote in 1894. 'Our love has such native grace . . . & carries with it so much hope of an ideal, that . . . it is powerless except for good.' Charteris was the adorer, and therefore vulnerable to the caprices and absences of his adored. He felt bottomless 'despair' when Ettie went away to America in 1899: 'You do not know what a source of all things coloured & happy you are to me at every hour that we live,' he protested – lapsing in his distress from the third person. Over the years they burnished their own brand of lover's talk, hallmarked with their temperament and endeared by long use.

Ettie's contacts with Charteris were punctuated by quarrels, started by him, and eventually pardoned by her. 'I *implore* you to ask her to forgive me – tell her I was wrong & know it – & that to have hurt her & brought misery on both of us, above all through failure in our perfect truth, makes me utterly miserable,' he wrote after one such upset. On another occasion, when probably he had been too much of an *ami caressant* and too little of a platonic: 'The love you wish for is disciplined & resigned, & how little of this you have found in me I know as well as you – but still my love for you is deeper & stronger than ever before. I hunger for you. I hunger to see you there, to share the same sunshine, the same stars . . . & then it comes upon me that this hunger just interferes with your life, that its very compulsion is what has tired you so . . . I have been weak & unwise, & alienating. Will you forgive me?'

It was part of the pleasing drama for Charteris to discuss his infatuation with his confidantes. 'There's but the one view for me to take of it,' he told Constance Wenlock, 'that of gratitude for the unequalled wealth of gifts she bestows, & the feeling that monopoly is not to be – but it's not in nature to arrive at this without suffering.' His entanglement with Ettie, he added, exemplified the maxim that 'the desire of man is for a woman, the desire of the woman is for the desire of the man'. There was a pragmatic side to Evan's pursuit of Ettie. It suited him to be ostentatiously devoted to a woman who was already committed, for it seemed fearful to him as a young man without fortune to tie himself to a wife who after seven years might seem trivial, insipid and irritating. Over the years he found other married women to pine for: Lady Essex and Lady Edward Grosvenor – both friends of Ettie – later fixated, jibbed and flattered him. Ettie in turn told Lady Wenlock that she found Evan 'perfect' when he kept 'his dear best self, & love of beautiful & refined things, wonderfully unsmirched in the contact with un-ideal people'.

In 1895 Ettie went to Gosford to meet his mother Lady Wemyss, a stately old lady, always dressed in black, with a strict interdictory code of Thou Shalt Nots. They had a searching talk, which reconciled the old lady to her son's irregular affections. Afterwards she wrote a letter which 'deeply touched' Lady Wemyss. 'All you said of him sent a thrill of joy through me,' the old lady replied. 'You know that I do trust you & believe in you – therefore when you say that you "have longed & striven to keep this friendship near the high places" & with the spirit that "alone prevaileth" about it, I believe you absolutely & yet – in all this – you have not quite succeeded. There has been & is that about it which *does* cast a shadow of darkness over your own life in most sacred relations & *must* create difficulties in many ways in his – and it might have been otherwise. Why should it not have been a perfect & open friendship – that needed no concealment – a helpful influence to you both – & to use once more your own dear words an "encouragement towards all that one longs to uphold as good & ideal".'

Just as there were two Charteris brothers in Ettie's life, so there were two Baring brothers, John and Maurice. The Barings were a numerous and versatile family, cousins of Albert Grey, and their banker father had recently been ennobled as Lord Revelstoke. 'Nothing is more like itself, nothing less like anything else, than a Baring,' Edgar Vincent wrote. 'The family is one of the few that produce a similar type with regularity – a regularity only accentuated by the rare occurrence of a freak. Strong, sensible, self-reliant men, with a profound belief in themselves, in their family, and in their country . . . As long as there are Barings, England will know where to turn in an emergency.'

The eldest son, John Baring, was immaculately dressed, musical and enigmatic. Ettie met him in the late 1880s, when he had little opportunity to give her attention, for he paid a long visit in 1889 to Argentina (where he acquired a lifelong susceptibility to the Latin temperament); and shortly after becoming a partner in the family bank, Baring Brothers, in 1890, it was pitched by his father's reckless ambition into a financial crisis that almost caused a European banking collapse. The subsequent complexities meant that it was not until the summer of 1891 that John Baring had the leisure to begin sending cautious, bloodless and orotund love letters to Ettie. Like Evan Charteris, he pretended in his correspondence that Ettie was a sympathetic intermediary in his love affair with another woman, denoted by the initial C. 'I had such a heavenly blessed let: from *my* C. yesterday,' he wrote on one occasion. 'By far the most precious & prized letter that has ever been written by a woman to a man, by such a darling worshipped woman to such a humble worshipping man. I have read it through again & again & again, and it has brought such intense joy to me that I thanked God that I am alive, to have known what divine comfort & peace an absolute love for & faith in a woman can bring. Would you tell her this, if you are writing to her on Tuesday?' There are many such love letters surviving in Ettie's papers: dull and mechanical, they seem, in comparison with Charteris's, for Baring was a discreet man, without much wit or vivacity, and never indulged in colourful asides about his contemporaries. They contain, though, an emotionally servile streak: his responses to their misunderstandings and disappointments can seem abject, and probably gratified Ettie who had (said Cynthia Asquith) an 'enthralled interest in human beings combined with both the power and the desire to dominate them'.

It was, at first, confusing for Ettie to run Evan Charteris and John Baring in tandem. 'Lately I have been in the mood which hangs a query over everything one says, does or sees, and then follows mad confusion,' she explained to Constance Wenlock in the autumn of 1892. There were an 'astonishing number of alternatives': she did 'not see why one should not try each to its logical conclusion separately & then as the sum of one's experience settle down to the most successful – but what would determine the most successful?' She likened herself to 'a novice in a signal-box, surrounded by handles, with no time to learn their significance yet compelled to seize one – knowing that 9 out of 10 of them at that particular moment mean disaster. If it wasn't so exciting it would be intolerable.'

On succeeding to his father's title in 1897, John Revelstoke strove to restore Baring Brothers' unassailable standing and to affirm his own unimpeachable reputation. His father had been brusque, headstrong, overconfident and ultimately careless: the new Revelstoke cultivated, most deliberately, the reverse of all these traits. All imprudence was repugnant to him after the public humiliation of 1890–1: he was left extra-susceptible to nuances of reputation and keenly anxious about outward appearances. He leased a huge house in Carlton House Terrace and was driven every day in his chocolate-brown electric brougham to his office in Bishopsgate. He would lunch there in his room, off a chop and a glass of water, but elsewhere his tastes were sybaritic: his cigarette case was made by Fabergé, his piano by Bechstein, his jade bibelots came from Cartier, and his stable of motor cars were as expensive as the hunters he kept in the Pytchley country.

He understood that character should count for more than brains in most careers; and no one could doubt the inviolability of his character or the security of his credit after he joined the Court of the Bank of

England in 1898. He became the trusted financial adviser of King George V who regarded 'dear John' as an intimate friend. At Carlton House Terrace he gave succulent banquets cooked by the famous Rosa Lewis; but his fastidious misogyny meant that he so disliked seeing women with flushed faces that he only permitted them to be served one glass of wine at his table. This prohibition never incommoded Ettie, who drank alcohol only a few times in her life. She was more strained by the after-dinner concerts held in the drawing room. World-famous artists came over from the Continent for fabulous fees; and Ettie inwardly writhed with boredom.

Every inch of Revelstoke was suave, cosmopolitan and yet timid. He kept a beautiful apartment in Paris, at 27 rue du Faubourg Saint-Honoré, where Ettie sometimes stayed, and spoke excellent French and German, and passable Spanish and Italian. 'Lord Revelstoke is in Paris at the moment,' his rival Lord Rothschild wrote in 1906, 'enjoying the Champs Elysées and the boulevards in the company of Mr Arthur Balfour and a large number of beautiful ladies.' He loved the company of women without desiring them; he liked to be seen with them, but not to commit to them. Nicholas Mosley, who married Ettie's granddaughter, felt that her involvement with Revelstoke was 'almost certainly sexual', but the historian of Barings, Philip Ziegler, doubted if there was 'much more than parade and mutual convenience in his relationship with Ettie Desborough'. Revelstoke put Ettie and a few other favourites on a 'red list' at Baring Brothers. The red-listers were always given an allocation in any truly promising issue handled by Barings, such as the first mortgage stock of the New York Telephone Company issued in 1909 or the London Underground Electric Railway's issue of 1926.

After a 'nice & peaceable' dinner with Ettie and Revelstoke at Carlton House Terrace in 1915, Asquith (then Prime Minister) noted: 'He has been now, to my knowledge, for over 20 years more or less in love with Ettie.' Yet nothing in John Revelstoke's letters suggests that he was her lover. He felt gratitude, devotion and a somewhat habituated idolatry; yet he was not a lothario or philanderer, to use Doll Liddell's classifications, but a platonic lover who used their well-known attachment as a 'blind' to protect his reputation. After his death of a heart attack in 1929, while leading the British delegation in fraught negotiations to achieve a settlement of the issue of German war reparation payments to France, his secret was quietly betrayed. He had been shuttling between Berlin and Paris, and the young poet W.H. Auden noted in his Berlin journal that his 'sex snobbery' had been gratified to discover that a previous client of his rent boy 'Pieps' had been 'Lord Revelstoke, the banker who died in Paris, a friend of the King'. Ettie was distraught after Revelstoke's death, for his passionless adoration was what pleased her most, and she was treated as the chief mourner at his funeral.

Revelstoke's brother Maurice Baring was another of Ettie's cavaliers. He succumbed to her during the summer of 1896, when she was twenty-nine and he was twenty-two. A quarter-century later he still recalled that summer with rapture. 'I went to Ascot; I went to balls; I stayed at Panshanger; and at Wrest, at the end of summer, where a constellation of beauty moved in muslin and straw hats and yellow roses on the lawns of gardens designed by Le Nôtre, delicious with ripe peaches on old brick walls, with the smell of verbena, and sweet geranium; and stately with large avenues, artificial lakes and white temples; and we bicycled in the warm night past ghostly cornfields by the light of a large full moon.' Ettie began sending him those cool, beguiling messages to which men succumbed: 'you write *far* the best letters of anyone I know,' he told her in September 1896; and later he reproached her for neglecting her literary powers.

Maurice Baring's devotion seems more imaginative and flexible than his brother John's: 'I have been writing letters to you in my head ever since I left Taplow,' he wrote after a visit in 1901: 'your wonderfulness has haunted me like a vision.' At least once Baring angered Ettie, who cut him dead for several months: 'I am utterly miserable about it & when I was in London it really made me ill,' he wrote to her from St Petersburg in 1911, 'without yr friendship life is miserable.' Her displeasure may have been provoked by his play *Ariadne in Naxos*, published in *Diminutive Dramas* (1910). Its title character Ariadne is a gushing, capricious siren who plays off Theseus and Dionysus against each other; and Ettie-ish, in frantic form, she seems. But this 'ridge' between them, to use Ettie's epithet for ill feeling, was soon overcome.

When she was young, Ettie thought, as she later told her elder daughter, that quarrels between men and women were inevitable –

even rewarding, for so often the sudden outbreak of a hot recriminatory dispute was followed by sweet soft reconciliation. But when, thirty years later, in 1927, talking to Revelstoke, she laughingly said that she missed their rows and the accompanying vehemence, the old banker shot her back an anguished look. It made her realise – belatedly – that men hate quarrels and ultimately are estranged by them. Anger, she recognised at the age of sixty, was an impure, selfish fire that desolated rather than agreeably warmed people.

It is undeniable that Ettie enjoyed playing with younger men's emotions. During the Season of 1897, for example, she tantalised a rich 24-year-old womaniser, Ivor Guest, the future Lord Wimborne. After Guest had left on a tour of the United States and Japan, he pelted her with letters trying to escalate the flirtation. In New York he still felt 'strangely impelled to recall and interpret what you said, or to wonder what meaning lay veiled behind those looks which . . . hide the gleam of your eyes'. He was a cocksure young man, and yet she had raised a flurry of doubts in him: 'you are a very attractive woman and I think you well measure your power, but I wonder why you troubled to pour into my ears and eyes the double-distilled honey of your flattery? Why you made my last week in London a pleasure and my departure a regret?' He had enough experience to recognise her as a woman whose 'charm is not sensuous or sensual but intellectual', who was 'fooling' with him and whose only 'delight' was in giving 'innocent pleasure', yet he did not relent after returning from Japan. 'You escape me like one of your own graceful smiles,' he declared in December. 'I know you're a pious fraud but I can't believe it.'

A pious fraud? George Wyndham would not have agreed. Only four years older than Ettie, he looked lethally handsome, with romantic, smouldering eyes; spoke in booming, expressive cadences; wore his clothes well; and looked superb in spurs. He was vehement, mercurial and spoilt, a sensation seeker who lived exuberantly in every hour, a dramatiser who fancied himself as the reincarnation of a Provençal troubadour. His literary sensibility was undeniable: visiting Africa, he waded across the Limpopo with a copy of Virgil in his haversack. In 1887 he was appointed by Balfour as his private secretary, and married

an older woman, Sibell Grosvenor, the widow of the Duke of Westminster's eldest son and the mother of the Duke's heir, Lord Belgrave.
Two years later, at the age of twenty-five, Wyndham was elected MP
for Dover.

Balfour's personality drew him into politics, but he lacked the iron
will of his mentor. Wyndham was a convinced believer in custom, but
not in conscious effort. He combined ambition with negligence: at
board meetings of the London, Chatham & Dover railway company,
he whiled away his time translating into English the fifteenth-century
triolets of Charles d'Orléans. Arduous horsemanship – polo, steeple-
chasing, hunting and manoeuvres with the Cheshire yeomanry –
thrilled him, and within a few years of marriage he had become a
strenuous sexual cuirassier laying siege to various Society women.
Wyndham's admirers thought him the personification of Panache;
but Evan Charteris and Constance Wenlock agreed on his dire resem-
blances to Harry Cust. 'He has many of the component elements of a
bore,' Charteris decided, because he could be so conceited, smug and
overbearing. Ettie was devoted to the Wyndham family, but said in old
age that they were bred up with the arrogance of Plantagenets.

'He hankers for a *grande passion*,' Wyndham's cousin and confidant
Scawen Blunt noted after a frank talk in 1892. 'He is out of office and
misses the constant excitement of great affairs.' Wyndham decided that
Ettie might provide the zest that was missing from his life and
intensified his attentions to her. They exchanged photographs, and he
began sending her sonnets of his own composition, poetry by Gautier
and extracts from Malory's *Morte d'Arthur*. His letters were frothy,
overblown affairs teeming with references to chivalry, sorrows and
ladies with fair faces and sweet voices. She enjoyed the attention, but
discouraged him from taking the flirtation seriously. 'I shan't forget
a single word you have ever said,' he insisted, 'the ones you tell me
I may bury are precisely the very ones gifted with the power of
resurrection, in the night hours or during lonely walks. In my life,
since I knew you, you have always appeared upon the scene & said
something memorable at every important emotional crisis.'

By April 1893 he was smitten. 'Lying awake last night I could think
of nothing but the ghastly waste of life,' he wrote from the House of
Commons. 'I have tried to see you every day. I am telegraphing a

humble request that you will write to me.' Scawen Blunt noted on 9 May, 'George tells me that he takes a smiling view once more of life . . . by which he doubtless means that he is in love and that his love is returned.' Wyndham, though, was misreading Ettie's intentions and his buoyancy was luring him to indiscretion. On 10 May his impulses took him to Taplow to stalk her. From the back of the church he listened to her singing 'Holy, Holy, Holy'. Then he loitered outside the church in the hope of glimpsing her, and capered round to lurk near the gates to Taplow Court. In the afternoon he rowed up and down the Thames past the Grenfells' jetty, alternating between canoes and a skiff, hoping that the change of craft would make his behaviour inconspicuous. 'But the waterman, I fear, has no illusions & quite understands my fervour for aquatics. He even buoyed up my courage by telling me at about 5 that Mr Grenfell was coming directly. At 6.30 I had the hardihood to land & walk up to your tennis-courts, of course to see the tennis. But they were quite deserted & I realized that my day was done.' Ettie was horrified at the waterman's observations and dismayed by the indignity of Wyndham's conduct. He winced at her reproaches, and then compounded his indiscretions by recounting Lady Randolph Churchill's bold allusions at a dinner of Margot Tennant's to their involvement. Ettie must have been infuriated, and destroyed his next letters.

In September 1893 Wyndham exploded back into her life with a series of overheated screeds on the subject of her bugbear, Harry Cust. Violet Granby was Cust's recognised mistress, but he had also seduced his quiet, dark-eyed cousin Nina Welby and after a cousin's death made him, to his joy, heir presumptive to the Brownlow peerage and property, he reached a private understanding to marry Wyndham's sister Pamela, known as 'the Babe'. Ettie thought her a 'delicious' girl, and hoped that 'wicked Harry . . . won't break her heart'. Then the Brownlows invited both Nina Welby and Cust to stay at Ashridge, the couple spent some nights together and she, who adulated him, became convinced that she was pregnant. When she told her story in September 1893, uproar erupted among the Souls.

It was acceptable for Cust to sleep with married women of his own class or unmarried girls of a lower class; but the seduction of a baronet's unmarried daughter was intolerable to the morality of the times. Wyndham and George Curzon both deserted Lord and Lady Edmund Talbot's house party in Yorkshire after receiving urgent telegrams – leaving Loulou Harcourt and the remaining guests to attribute their disappearance to a row between the Granbys involving Cust. Wyndham convulsed Society. 'I am fighting', he proclaimed to Ettie, 'against sheer & mere worldliness so mired and corrupted by intrigue & lying that for its very rottenness it gives no purchase to an honest hand.' He could continue breathing in this 'choking miasma of lies and impurity only by the memory of your purity and truth'. Under threat of total ostracism, Cust submitted to marrying his cousin and lived discontentedly with her thereafter; and he was also obliged to relinquish his parliamentary seat at the next election.

Wyndham insisted that Ettie's example sustained him through these histrionics. 'How constantly in my trouble my heart turned to your sweet and noble friendship; how I hungered and thirsted for some short respite from pain in your dear companionship.' When it proved impossible for them to meet, he sat down and reread all Ettie's letters to him (these were later destroyed by his widow). 'This rested me & made me feel strong,' he told Ettie: 'the thought of you, & my love for all that is so lovable in you, and my respect for all that is so *good* in you, has been the well of my desert. I thank you for all your gentleness; I thank you . . . for your goodness & purity; and for your friendship to me I cannot thank you since no words can tell the ecstasy of my gratitude.' After 1893, Ettie's contacts with Wyndham settled into calm, enduring affection. Four years later he began a lifelong love affair with Gay Windsor, whose husband the future Earl of Plymouth was Commissioner of Works in the Balfour administration in which Wyndham was Chief Secretary for Ireland. Wyndham took to drink and died of a heart attack at the age of fifty.

The conventional belief is that the apogee of the Souls came in the autumn of 1898 with George Curzon's appointment as Viceroy of India. The Cowpers held a farewell Saturday-to-Monday for him at Panshanger – Curzon repaid them later with a sonorous tribute to Francis Cowper published in the *Dictionary of National Biography* – with Ettie and Willie, the Ribblesdales, Asquiths, Brodricks and Balfour among the guests. Curzon's departure for India was a significant event for the Souls; but the set had never fully recovered its playful gaiety and cohesive trust after the rage and recrimination aroused by Harry Cust five years earlier. The Souls' unifying theory of innocuous flirtation was wrecked in this storm; and indeed, the repercussions were felt outside their circle. 'The hideous scandals connected with Harry Cust', Scawen Blunt wrote in 1894 after his lover Margaret Talbot had begun repulsing his advances, 'have frightened her, as they have how many others, so that Harry, if not virtuous himself, has been the cause of virtue in others.'

Constance Wenlock likened the morals of High Society in the 1880s and 1890s to those of the English Court after the Restoration. But Ettie, far from resembling Charles II's mistresses, conjured images of purer beauty. 'Whenever one looks at her,' Edmund Gosse told Maurice Baring in 1898, 'whatever time of day, at whatever angle, she is a picture of the most finished beauty, with the most vivid and magnetic charm, like the waves on a beach dancing in and out.' She seemed to Margot Asquith 'a kind of triumphant sun-ray passing & blessing & smiling through the world'. By the last years of the Victorian age Ettie had achieved a unique position: 'socially there is nothing like you,' Ivor Guest told her in 1897, 'it's your quick and convincing optimism which throws such a spell' and had brought her, he said, 'a thousand admirers'.

CHAPTER 4

The Mother

𝒦

IN 1887, AT the age of nineteen, Ettie became chatelaine of Taplow Court in Buckinghamshire: she had married a house as well as a husband. Taplow Court – 'one of the finest residences on the River Thames' – had been built on the southernmost spur of the Chilterns by the Earl of Orkney, a military commander with Marlborough's armies who was the senior officer to be appointed as a field marshal when that rank was introduced in 1735. Willie's great-grandfather Pascoe Grenfell, who had made a fortune from the mining and smelting of copper, bought property at Taplow in 1794. A few years later he was elected as Whig member for the nearby pocket borough of Great Marlow. His son Charles, who inherited the family's copper interests and also sat in the Commons, bought Taplow Court from the fifth Earl of Orkney in 1852, and had the red-brick house heightened to four storeys and remodelled in a lively mélange of architectural styles. Its entrance front – approached by an avenue of cedars of Lebanon – was given a neo-Tudor look with a stone porch, surmounted by a heraldic carving in which the organ-rests of the Grenfell coat of arms resembled weirdly shaped seashells, and tall moulded chimneys soaring above. The garden front, though, was Frenchified with the flamboyant window tracery and corner turret of a Loire chateau.

The house's most striking feature pre-dated the Grenfells: the fifth Lord Orkney had its original central courtyard covered with a glazed roof supported by neo-medieval trusses, and turned into an imitation Norman baronial hall, which was said to be modelled on the cathedral at Kirkwall in the Orkneys. The effect was seductive and enhanced the sense that Taplow Court was a house full of light. The house was ringed by spreading cedars and there was a dark, mysterious cedar walk perched on the cliffs overhanging the Thames. With these 'sumptuous surroundings', commanding long views over Maidenhead, Taplow Court's 200 acres were 'too magnificent for words', declared Valentine Castlerosse, the heir to 118,000 acres surrounding the lakes of Killarney and therefore an expert on the picturesque.

Willie was born in 1855, lost his father, who had sat as Liberal MP for nearby Windsor, in 1861, and inherited Taplow from his grand-father when he was eleven. The house came with 3,000 acres in Berkshire and Buckinghamshire yielding annual rents in the 1880s of over £7,000. Other branches of the Grenfell family owned houses in the vicinity. Willie's uncle Henry, who served as a Liberal MP and Governor of the Bank of England, lived at Henley: his estate, Bacres, was inherited by his son Edward, a director of the Bank of England, senior London partner of the merchant bank Morgan Grenfell after its formation in 1910, and Conservative MP for the City of London until he was created Lord St Just. Other Grenfells lived a minute's walk from Taplow Court in a house called Elibank, and Willie's cousin Francis, a career soldier who was successively Governor of Malta and Commander-in-Chief in Ireland, inherited Butler's Court on the out-skirts of Beaconsfield in 1895.

In 1889–90 Willie served his year as High Sheriff of Buckingham-shire, then still a rural county with little suburban encroachment. There were market towns and railway junctions, but no conurbations with smoking chimney stacks or industrial slums. The county's proximity to London was an attraction for rich magnates who desired country house pleasures without rural isolation. After 1850 several members of the Rothschild family bought tracts of Buckinghamshire on which they erected opulent palaces – Aston Clinton, Mentmore, Ascott and Waddesdon – precisely because journeying to the City of London was so easy. The mainline of the Great Western Railway passed through Taplow, which was under an hour's train journey from London; but it owed its special character to its position above the banks of the Thames. A short distance upriver stood Cliveden, an Italianate pleasure palace built in 1849 for the Duke of Sutherland, whose other seats were too far from the centres of power in London. In 1869 it had been bought by the Duke of Westminster, who equally needed a home more accessible to Mayfair than his seat in Cheshire, and in 1893 Cliveden was sold to William Waldorf Astor, the New York Croesus. Willie was a favourite guest of the Westminsters until 1888, when he was banned from the Duke's table after fêting Charles Stewart Parnell, the Irish Home Ruler, at the Eighty Club.

✐

The first great event of Ettie's time at Taplow was a crime. At ten on the evening of Friday, 13 January 1888 a housemaid taking hot water to Ettie's bedroom found that its door, and that of her dressing room, had been shut by wedges of wood which had been shoved under the door and nailed down. The maid raised the alarm and a few moments later Willie (who had been relaxing in the smoking room with Ettie) and a footman broke down the door. Crashing into the room they found that every drawer, cupboard, dressing case, despatch box and handbag had been ransacked. Her jewel cases had been wrenched open and even the buckles cut from her waistbands and shoes. The floor was strewn with discarded clothes and letters. Willie then discovered that the main doors on the east and west fronts of the house had been wired shut, so that if the burglars had been interrupted, their pursuers would have been badly delayed, for the servants' doors at the back were the only working exits. Tripwires had also been laid across the lawns. The criminals must have been watching the routines of the house for weeks, or else possessed inside knowledge, and had known to carry out their raid during the twenty minutes after the sounding of the dinner bell. Their patient planning and ruthless execution were rewarded with a haul worth about £4,000. A pearl necklace valued at about £1,500 had been a wedding present from Willie's mother, and three other necklaces, ten bracelets, eighteen brooches, six rings and three pins – most of them wedding presents – made up the rest of the booty.

'The brutes, it makes one *cry* to think of all my poor things in their hands,' Ettie told Ally Gore next day. 'I can't help being rather thankful they had got away before W and the servants got in – a hand to hand fight would have been so awful.' The robbery caused a national hue and cry, but despite Willie's offer of a reward of £500 and the involvement of Scotland Yard, the miscreants were never caught. 'The burglary at Taplow Court is likely to remain the event of the season in the annals of criminal daring,' declared the *Daily Telegraph*. Its reporter pictured 'the audacious scoundrels . . . gloating in secret over a pile of jewels large enough to start a shop', and the villainous 'fence' wrenching the stones from their setting and melting the gold in a kitchen pot. 'Sympathy for the lady thus woefully despoiled of nearly all her cherished trinkets at one fell swoop will animate the hearts of all the feminine public,' the *Telegraph* averred. Ettie sent an account of the burglary to Betty Ponsonby, whose father Sir Henry Ponsonby, Private Secretary to Queen Victoria, read it aloud to his royal mistress, who was avid for details of the crime. 'How sad', Betty commiserated, 'for you to lose everything you have ever had great & small – all your rings, everything. But, my darling, I *am* glad that you weren't there in bed that night. It would have been awful.'

✌

Life at Taplow Court fed the local imagination with glamour and awe. The first two rows of pews in Taplow church were reserved for the Grenfells and their household, and on Sundays in summer the villagers would watch with a mixture of avidity and respect as the Saturday-to-Monday guests from Taplow Court filed into church. Willie had been appointed High Steward of Maidenhead in 1884, and for over fifty years – until 1939 – Ettie organised an annual High Steward's Banquet at Taplow Court. The menu in 1911 gives a measure of the event:

Tortue Claire
Truite au naturel
Turbot sauce cardinale
Bombes de Volaille à la voisine
Selles d'agneau
Légumes
Poulets au cresson
Pois à la Française
Soufflés à la Princesse
Tartelettes aux crevettes

'At the head of the table', declared the *Maidenhead Advertiser*, 'sat Lord Desborough, one of England's great men, who does not spare himself or his money in furthering the welfare of mankind. In Maidenhead and district Lord Desborough is highly respected and greatly loved, for he never tires of well-doing in the neighbourhood.'

Willie was elected Mayor of Maidenhead in 1895 (the first mayor there who was not a member of the town council), then re-elected for a second term so the Grenfells could superintend the Jubilee celebrations of 1897. His installation as Mayor in November 1895 was the occasion for a mammoth procession through the streets. The shops closed early, and (watched by Ettie and her two eager, bright-eyed little boys) some 4,000 people gathered to admire the trolleys, wagons, fire engines, brewery drays, bakers' carts, the butcher's fly, an old Stanhope phaeton, the trap from the Saracen's Head and a range of other vehicles process through the town exhibiting tableaux with townsmen wearing allegorical, comic or grotesque costumes. There were piercing arc-lights, fireworks, rockets, Roman candles, Japanese lanterns and braziers emitting plumes of brightly coloured smoke. Willie's initials blazed in fire from turrets above the ironmonger's shop; and there were flags, bunting and marching bands galore. His mayoral installation combined all the exuberance of an eighteenth-century carnival with the disciplined organisation and technology of the Victorians: it was a long-remembered event in what was still a country town.

As the Mayor's wife, in 1895, Ettie addressed a club for local shop girls on 'The Value of Happiness'. Like her grandmother Cowper she mistrusted political women – indeed, her dislike of public speaking rivalled her abhorrence of being photographed. 'I don't belong to the shrieking sisterhood, & delivering it really terrified me almost to death. *Never* again.' (Public speaking was unavoidable, but her speeches opening charity events were self-deprecatory, amusing and above all brief.) During 1896 she organised an August garden party for local dignitaries in the grounds at Taplow Court, held a mayoral banquet there in November, opened the newly built Maidenhead technical school with a silver key and distributed its prizes. Later she became President of a Maidenhead club for Young Women in the Professions and Business, inaugurated the Diamond Jubilee clock tower in 1900, threw the switch in 1902 that lit up the town hall from electric generators, and watched Willie open the new Public Library in 1904. She undertook district visiting, and supported clubs for local boys and girls.

There were garden parties for good causes, charity bazaars and every year the Grenfells put their grounds at the disposal of some twenty day or Sunday schools for children's outings. Ettie was indeed the Lady Bountiful of her district. 'No appeal, whether ecclesiastical, educational, municipal, social, philanthropic or athletic, is ever turned down at Taplow Court,' declared the *Maidenhead Advertiser* after she had lived there for nearly forty years. 'The records of our Hospital, the Nursing Home, the Public Library, the Technical Institute, the County Boys' School Playing Field, Grenfell Park, the Football Field, the Rifle Brigade and our beautiful Thames in many and various aspects bear evidence to the beneficent activities of the distinguished residents of Taplow Court.' Ettie took pains to imbue her children with a sense of local responsibility. At Easter of 1903 her ten-year-old daughter Monica took daffodils to the workhouse inmates while her five-year-old son Ivo brought bloaters. On a Christmas visit to the workhouse in 1907 her youngest daughter, Imogen, at the age of two, shook hands with 210 people.

Ettie was a conscientious employer, though we have no records of her interviewing scullery maids, planning menus with the cook, mollifying the said cook, instructing the butler and footmen, scolding a housemaid (for she hated books lying untidily about the house), comforting a sniffling, fidgety skivvy, despatching an undergardener to pick up tourists' litter from the woods (for she detested seeing rubbish discarded in the countryside), or arranging all the contrivances necessary for a smoothly run household. Nevertheless, her papers contain numerous letters, written in ill-educated script, with erratic spelling, from grateful ex-servants or the deserving poor whom she had helped. 'I am more than thankfull and gratefull to you for all the kindness received from you for I can assure you my dear Lady Desborough what I should have done had it not been for you I don't know,' Mary Ann Collins wrote from Maidenhead in 1911. 'You have been my *dearest friend* on earth and I can assure you I have always felt that there was no one I could trust like you . . . I often feel very lonely and I know what a high position you hold and what a lot you have got to see to but if only I could feel at any time I was at liberty to write to you it would mean so much to me.'

In Winston Churchill's papers there is a letter from Ettie, sent in

1908 when he was President of the Board of Trade and had just announced his engagement to Clementine Hozier. She realised that they would be starting a new establishment, and recommended a married couple whom she was trying to place as cook and butler. Mrs Barlow was, said Ettie, '*excellent*, & (strange to say!) economical'. Economical servants were a necessity for her: she disliked ostentation or waste in her household, and noted in her commonplace book a remark of Gladstone's that he loved splendour but hated luxury. Ettie's social successes were not boosted by lavish expenditure: she kept painstaking accounts which show, for example, that she spent a total of £2,119 on Taplow housekeeping in 1899. This is the equivalent of £160,000 in 2008 values: a considerable sum, but not inordinate given the size of the household and the extent of her entertaining.

Taplow Court was a serenely managed house, with no frets or sudden alarms. Ettie's guests were softly cushioned by her well-drilled staff: Lady Essex, staying at Taplow in 1912, was impressed at finding housemaids stoking up fires at 1.30 a.m. She liked to think of the house as her escape hatch from the 'steam-pressure of . . . seething whirling London life', as she told Wendell Holmes in 1893: 'we are here now in the blessed peaceful spring green country for 10 days holiday quite alone . . . [enjoying] the deep *intense* peace & relief of returning to a fairly natural life after that nightmare rush of London.' Atop the corner turret there was a tiny octagonal room, which Ettie converted into her private retreat: 'with a view that stretches the soul', and simply furnished, she thought, with 'a sofa, a chair, a writing-table, a bookshelf, & a Botticelli'.

Of course, Taplow Court was famed for its hospitality rather than its spiritual seclusion. Ettie held three Sunday parties in June, and kept a full house during Ascot week: her invitations were much prized. 'It was rather a nice Ascot,' George Pembroke noted in 1889, though he regretted staying with Ferdinand Rothschild rather than the Grenfells. 'They had splendid times at Taplow, bathing, boating, and wild fun of all sorts. We had engaged ourselves to Waddesdon & couldn't get off. I was so cross: those sorts of times are too rare to be missed.' It was a 'wild racket' at Taplow during Ascot week of 1894: 'we are 24 in the house,' Ettie wrote, 'most of them more or less insane – we went on the River last night till 2 this morning, such a great wonderful heavenly

June night.' Ettie illumined and irradiated every Taplow party she gave. 'You have never been more brilliant,' Sir Edgar Vincent wrote after one Ascot week, 'and I have never . . . been more completely under your wand. It really is a privilege to have lived in the same century with you.'

≈

Yet the attention she received in Society brought her no more felicity than the attention she enjoyed from her children. Posterity remembers her as a great hostess and (in the historian G.M. Trevelyan's phrase) 'the Roman Matron' of the First World War; but motherhood defined her sense of her self and gave meaning to her life. As she told Willie in 1892, 'I am such a bereaved Catts without either you or the babies or any of the things that make up the beautiful happy background of one's life.' She rejoiced in her children, and they satisfied her strong need to be adored, admired and dominant. Without her boys and girls, her existence would have seemed irredeemably frivolous and futile. Margaret Talbot – childless like her sisters-in-law Gety Pembroke and Adelaide Brownlow – was once scolded for the vanity of her days. 'It is all', she replied, 'because I have no children. I see other women of my age . . . with children growing up and happy through them. But what have I got in my future? They tell me I have everything I want in life, and it is true, all but this one thing. How gladly would I give up beauty and pleasure and social success, all for one squalling baby to keep me awake at night.'

Ettie became pregnant after four months of marriage, and gave birth to her first boy, after six hours of labour, at the Cowpers' house in St James's Square on 30 March 1888. He was baptised Julian Henry Francis, at St Paul's, Knightsbridge, his forenames commemorating Ettie's father and two Cowper uncles; but his pre-natal nickname of Max survived for many years. She was always delighted by her babies, delighted to recover in body and mind after their birth, and delighted to resume her normal life with renewed zest. The Grenfells' second son was born on 29 March 1890 – two years younger than Julian bar one day – at 4 St James's Square. 'I am very well & very pleased with the tiny new bundle that pretends it is going to be a man before it is done,' she pencilled from her bed to Judge Holmes.

Julian was already talking when his brother arrived, and seemed pleased to see him: 'What a keer little thing, a little live thing; call him Billy,' he said. It was in vain that the boy was baptised Gerald William at St Paul's, Knightsbridge, for Julian's nickname always prevailed. Once Billy had emerged from babyhood, the brothers were as close as twins, Ettie felt, and the two years' difference in age scarcely mattered. They had passionate, combative natures, and were born fighters: once, when they went to tea with an old lady, they rolled down her entire staircase, grappling together in a clinch; and once, at Stanway, Ettie found them throttling each other and both black in the face.

The secrets of family life were considered sacrosanct among Ettie's friends. Only in extreme circumstances would they consent, in Albert Grey's phrase, 'to hold up a corner of the curtain which shd conceal things too sacred to be seen'. It was not that they were frightened of expressing their feelings, repressed or inarticulate in their emotions, or stunted and deprived in their sensibility. But they understood that public figures need a private world for their ease, and therefore all shared an entrenched belief in privacy. If anything they spent too much of their abundant leisure in cultivating and analysing their own feelings, but they recoiled, as from anything filthy and contaminated, from public advertisement of them. The thought of making a spectacle of one's innermost emotions or of discussing intimate matters before strangers seemed to them feeble, ill-mannered and selfish; and they never debased cherished personal truths by public avowals.

Ettie was supportive of her pregnant friends and a safe recipient of their confidences. When Elizabeth Castlerosse was nervously awaiting the birth of her first child, Ettie paid her comforting visits: 'seeing you quite banished the deep depression one gets sitting alone thinking only of the pains of having the enfant; thank you, Ettie dearest, I shall never forget your goodness to me.' Ettie had been a bridesmaid when her skittish cousin Mollie Vyner married Katie Cowper's brother Lord Alwyne Compton in 1886, and was the later recipient of Mollie's childbearing insecurities: was it laughable that she was pregnant, were her enemies saying 'awful things', wasn't it essential to forsake Society during the last five months? 'I *certainly don't* mean to see any friends when looking awful as *I know* that means quite *losing* them. Don't you agree?' Ettie commiserated with Charty Ribblesdale's despair at becoming pregnant for the fifth time, and with friends whose pregnancies ended sadly. 'My *poor* darling,' she wrote after Margot Asquith lost a baby in 1900, 'I can guess so what the awful sterile pain must be, to have suffered it all in vain – the anguish, fear, discomfort, deprivation, sacrifice of vanity, all that one gives *so* joyfully & hopefully, with both hands, for the bliss of a child.'

Ettie's commitment to mothering was so conspicuous that her friends looked to her as a possible guardian for their own children. Margot Asquith, for example, asked Ettie to look after her daughter Elizabeth if she died. 'Margot my very darling,' Ettie responded, 'I cannot ever tell you *how* your letter has touched me. I shall keep it & love it all my life. I *know* so well how one's heart breaks at the thought of any possibility that [one] might leave one's children alone, it is the one thing that makes one unalterably & beyond all question want to live, because no one, even if far wiser, greater, nobler, cd give them the *same* we do – the love that passes understanding.' She often agonised at the thought of dying, as her mother had done, when her children still needed her. 'I pray every day to live as long as he wants me,' she wrote of Julian, '*no one* else could shield & save & cherish & encourage & adore them as we can.' She hoped her children might share the ideals and consolations of a Christian life: 'one prays so that they may keep their sunny *straight* outlook on life, & be "eager to labour & eager to be happy" – & strong & brave & merciful & joyous & kind, & have abundant life, & that they may be saved from fear & complacence & torpor – & above all learn *Resignation* – "not as I will but as Thou wilt" – & the beauty & blessedness of Death as well as the beauty & the joy of living. How one prays for them! It is like a revelation of what prayer means I think when the children come.'

As a young mother, Ettie was thoughtful, conscientious and sincere: 'I have been so very full lately of the thoughts of how to bring in to one's Children's lives the things that one longs for most for them,' she wrote to Evelyn de Vesci after Billy's birth. Happiness – or its reverse, Cowper depression – depended upon luck and temperament, but zest, pleasure and gratitude could be inculcated; and this was Ettie's intention as a mother. How much nicer children are, she knew, when they are enjoying themselves. Her children should not grow up without rapture, mystery, grace or courage. She instilled piety in her children:

from the age of thirteen Julian regularly read *The Imitation of Christ*; and his faith was never a desultory or conventional affair, but a living force, though one which he would have hated to discuss.

The trait that made Ettie special in her time was her pronounced desire to be admired as a mother. She wanted to be conspicuous in Society, of course, but she also wanted to be distinctive in her relations with her children – more intimate, attentive and exciting than most mothers of the epoch. Among her circle of friends Ettie's commitment to her children was well known. 'I do love to think of you', Alfred Lyttelton told her, 'rearing those incomparable boys so worthy of their beautiful & gracious mother.'

Julian was handed into the charge of Ettie's cherished old nanny, Mrs Wake, who was sixty-six years old when he was born. She remained defiantly active, racing about the Taplow gardens with him and later Billy, and had a gift for amusing small children. Julian and Billy were old Mrs Wake's great pride, and their homecomings from boarding school were the red-letter days in her calendar. She had her own room at the end of the nursery passage at Taplow, and when the boys returned at the end of each term, and she was too old and tremulous to go downstairs to greet them, they always rushed up to her room for a noisy, loving reunion. Julian and Billy were the antithesis of sedentary children, but they loved to sit with Nanny Wake in her old age: Billy indeed said she was the best talker in the world.

It caused tremendous sorrow to Ettie and her sons when the old lady died in her sleep in 1906, after falling ill with bronchitis while visiting her niece. Ettie was at the niece's house, in the dispiriting London suburb of Neasden, until eleven o'clock of the night that Nannie died. Mrs Wake's last words were about Julian and Billy: Ettie had mentioned them, and she murmured 'Dear boys', very tenderly, with a smile, and never spoke again. The Grenfell children, who had arranged to see her next day, were much grieved. 'I was very, very fond of her, fonder than of almost anyone,' Billy wrote from Eton after her death, 'though I fear I was sometimes impatient to her, and not grateful enough for her untiring goodness and devotion. She had a wonderful trust in God, and I am sure no one can ever have been more ready than she was.' In photographs with the children Nanny Wake always wears a warm smile.

The Grenfells wanted their sons to develop the finest of aristocratic virtues, fortitude. They wanted boys who would withstand tests of physical endurance and nerve, and gain in self-respect as they proved themselves resourceful, energetic and venturesome. From the earliest years, they set their children a regime that would encourage initiative and cheerful self-sufficiency. In the autumn of 1891, for example, they rented a forest in Sutherland – Gobernuisgach, which meant the Meeting of the Waters – for the shooting, and took Julian and Billy (then aged three and a half and one and a half) with them in Nannie Wake's charge. 'In those days, long before motor-cars and telephones,' Ettie recalled, 'it was thought rather rash to take such little children to a place 32 miles from Station or Doctor, but they loved it, and were as well as possible. Julian used to be tied to a gatepost, on a long rope, where he could not fall into the burns. Poor Billy, rather unsteady and heavy, could seldom stand on the moor without falling on his head.'

Ettie's love for her children was boundless, and her need for their reciprocation was insatiable. 'My eldest son was five years old yesterday – one fills his horizon at present & he is a very chivalrous if exacting lover, but I suppose the "Berserker" mood will descend ere long,' she wrote to Judge Holmes in 1893. 'I rejoice in his dear wholehearted devotion while it lasts, & cling to keeping *some* of it always.' He and Billy, she avowed, were 'a wonderful interest & delight.' The phrase 'pride and joy' is a cliché, and yet that is exactly what Julian and Billy were to Ettie in the 1890s: the sincerity shines out from her references to 'my dear boys, with their straight sunny eyes, who walk so happily & healthily in their bright lives'.

Ettie also loved her Herbert cousins, Aunt Dordor's children. Their father Auberon Herbert was an opinionated republican crank who disdained convention or authority. 'Not quite sane', Ettie thought him, but a man of 'chivalrous & delicate' impulses. Notoriously, in family matters, he was a wilful despot. He divided his year between a remote house in the New Forest and a villa at Portofino, and distanced his children from their Cowper relations, although Ettie once broke through his social cordon. In 1891 she managed to visit his daughters, Clair and Nan, aged sixteen and ten, when they were entirely alone in the Hampshire house, with only an old cow-man in a nearby cottage. 'You know all about the funny rough place & house, with only a track up to it,' she reported to Evelyn de Vesci, 'but I had never seen it before, & was very much struck at such a curious out-of-the-way life being still possible only three hours from London.' She was met at the station by Clair: 'I had not seen her for two years & could barely believe that the tall large young woman, with long petticoats & done-up hair, was her!' Outside the station there stood 'a little rough pony with harness tied up with string, & extraordinary trap filled as I thought with *rags*, but Clair explained these by saying "I have brought all our wraps in case you might be cold," & in we got, & drove though the Forest.' Reaching Auberon Herbert's forest refuge, a strange agglomeration of low buildings, Ettie

had an odd meal of their own cooking, poor darlings, & then a long walk in the lovely Forest, & came in to have a talk by the big wood fire before they went to bed. ('Dad has just been reading up *fresh air* again,' said Nan, so we always had to sit with the windows open, & they appeared to live chronically in many shawls & odd outer garments!). I cannot tell you *how* dear they both were, so faithful & loving & tender, remembering everything & everybody: little Nan seems perfectly happy, Clair I think is a *tiny* bit melancholy & lonely at heart, though with great spirits outwardly: a little weighed on by the cares & responsibilities of Life. She seems to lead a very solitary life, as only Nan does lessons with the governess now, & their Father is always so busy with his own things – she rides every day alone, & works away at Herbert Spencer, & draws from casts, & practices her violin; but it must be rather uphill work *quite* alone.

Eighteen months later, at Portofino, in January 1893, Clair Herbert put a desperate suicide note in her pocket and shot herself at the age of eighteen. She adored, and was frantically protective of, her surviving brother 'Bron', and had that day rowed with their father at his treatment of the boy. Her suicide was an act of 'love, self-sacrifice and unhappiness', according to her father, and an act of 'temper & cold rage', according to her aunt Amabel Kerr. Once again, in her extreme of misery, Ettie turned to Lady de Vesci. 'It breaks one's very heart to think of her gone away in all her fullness of youth – that this should be the end of the dear life which began so encompassed by love & tenderness & bright hopes: at night the horror of it all seems to suffocate one, but I try to put away the piteous human side & to remember as Dolly would have done only the great love which sanctified all her life & for which she gave it up.'

Clair Herbert's suicide, like Henry Cowper's self-willed death, and the other submissive depressions of her mother's family, more than ever convinced Ettie that she must resolve to be happy and *never* indulge in unhappiness, as some Cowpers were wont to do. The American Declaration of Independence held that the Creator had endowed humankind with a right to the pursuit of happiness, but for Ettie there was a duty to the Creator to be happy. In the words of psalm 118, 'This is the day which the Lord hath made: we will rejoice and be glad in it.' Clair's suicide strengthened Ettie's determination always to have the moral courage to be grateful. Years later she told her daughters that when young she had suffered recurrent bouts of depression, which she had determined to master by an act of will. Submitting to depression had, as she knew, proved fatal to her Aunt Dolly, to Uncle Henry, to Great-Aunt Fanny Jocelyn and to her cousins Lord Shaftesbury and Clair Herbert. Ettie *made* herself resilient. 'Her courage', said Evan Charteris (who knew about her depressions) in 1894, 'is a career in itself & . . . never due to ignorance or blind denial of the things that are.' And to friends who were prostrate with discouragement, such as Mary Curzon, Ettie would always recommend a 'joy cure'.

This tragedy tied Ettie with hoops of steel to the love of the surviving Herbert son, Bron. When his father opposed him joining the army on the outbreak of the Boer War, he went out to South Africa as a war correspondent for *The Times*. During the fighting at the relief of Ladysmith he was shot through the thigh and, after a prolonged fight against gangrene, his leg was amputated below the knee in March 1901. Bron's aunt, Eveline Portsmouth, attested that Ettie's 'tact and sweetness' during this unhappy time had been a great consolation to the family: 'how wisely & gently' Ettie had handled not only Bron but his troublesome father. The maimed youth's invincible fortitude in this period set a standard for Julian and Billy, who came to love him as if an elder brother. Bron brimmed with 'the joy-of-life', said Raymond

Asquith some years later, and conquered his disability by 'sheer vital force'. He was a misogynist: Ettie and his surviving sister Nan (who became a theosophist and moved to Cuba) were the only women he could bear. 'You have filled a place that has been vacant ever since Clair's death,' he later told Ettie, '& if you knew what that meant to me you would know what a sheet-anchor it is . . . you & she are the only two women I have ever looked *up* to for the sympathy & help & encouragement & the great gifts that a woman can give a man.'

Ettie had begun her third pregnancy around the time of Clair Herbert's suicide, and although her correspondence is peppered with other people's regrets about the birth of daughters, she craved a girl: 'I don't believe', she yearned in November 1892, 'I am *ever* going to have a baby again, which does so sadden me – I have such castles-in-the air for a daughter!' She was therefore delighted when her third pregnancy produced a tiny girl, weighing under four pounds and born at Taplow on 4 August 1893. She was enraptured to have 'a girl-baby', and one who seemed so 'pretty & pleased with life . . . though they tell me that no human being was ever quite so tiny before!' Baptised as Monica Margaret Grenfell, she soon acquired the nickname of Casie and was still known by that name by her surviving intimates when she was an old woman. For twenty years the date of 4 August resonated with joy for the Grenfells; and it was by the cruellest chance, which shadowed the rest of Monica's life, that her long-anticipated twenty-first birthday fell on 4 August 1914. Balfour was her godfather.

After Monica's birth, Harriet Plummer, the daughter of an old Taplow gamekeeper, took charge of Julian and Billy. Nicknamed 'Hawa', she was later nurse to Ettie's two youngest children, Ivo and Imogen. The devotion of Ettie and her children to Hawa was immense: they were with her when she died in 1926 and very saddened by her loss. The love between the nanny and her charges was deep and authentic at Taplow. 'I doubt', Ettie wrote, 'if the children will ever have such love given them again.'

❧

Ettie was both a young mother and a politician's wife. The Cowpers were Whigs: progressive men whose opinions were derived from their forefathers, whose political tenets were fashioned by historic sympathies, and whose tastes and associations were aristocratic. In old age she was reckoned by her protégé Lord David Cecil, the biographer of Lord Melbourne, to be the last of the Whig hostesses. In fact, as a young woman, she had such dash and originality as to seem more maverick than a Whig. 'You are by nature & temperament a good old fashioned Radical,' Albert Grey told her in 1889: 'not one of the modern humbugs & mob sycophants whose greatest ambition is to cheer with the biggest crowd, but one of the older sort who . . . vindicate for themselves & for all the world, the sacred Right of each individual to fashion his own soul.'

Having been defeated at Salisbury in 1886, in the general election necessitated by the rejection of Gladstone's first Home Rule Bill, Willie was out of the Commons for several years. In March 1890 the sitting member for Windsor, Robert Richardson-Gardner, resigned his seat in 'a huff' after being disappointed in his hopes of a baronetcy. Windsor was such a 'Royal stronghold of Toryism' that Gladstone's Liberals had not bothered to field a candidate at the previous general election, but the party managers convinced Willie that he was duty bound to contest the seat. As Eddy Hamilton noted, 'if any one can make a good fight of it, he is the man − personally popular and locally influential.' The by-election was ill-timed for Ettie, as the campaign coincided with the final stages of her second pregnancy: Billy was born on 29 March. The next day Willie wrote to her in St James's Square from the Windsor Parliamentary Election Committee Rooms: 'It was very clever of you to have another boy. I wish I could have been quietly with you instead of going through this misery.' On 2 April, polling day, Willie was defeated by 550 votes. 'Windsor certainly was a great nuisance, but it's all over now, & we must abandon it to its horrid old Tory principles,' Ettie reported to Loulou Harcourt. 'I am getting on capitally & so is Home Rule junior − he has got huge hands & prehensile feet, but is otherwise satisfactory.'

At the general election of June 1892 Willie stood as the Gladstonian Liberal candidate for the city of Hereford. He brought his wife and sons (together with the imposing family coach) to stay with him in a Hereford inn, the Green Dragon; but Ettie chafed against her constituency duties. 'Darling, I cannot possibly tell you what I am going through here,' she wrote to Constance Wenlock from the Green

Dragon. 'It does seem rather hard to spend the *only* nice English month in a horrible pot-house of an abominable country-town . . . The actual discomfort & toil are unspeakable, but the knowledge of what one would otherwise be doing – either in green peaceful country or in the "mental mill-race" of London is *worse*.' She was amused, though, by one of her admirers, Lord Cairns, who drew a sketch of Julian and Billy as sandwich men, carrying placards proclaiming, 'Vote for Grenfell and a Free Breakfast.' The allusion to free breakfasts for voters was all too apt. 'This is a very corrupt place,' Willie wrote after winning Hereford by 127 votes, 'but we congratulate ourselves on having won the first pure election.'

Willie had great sincerity and a simple, tenacious belief in doing good: he revered Great Britain and its empire, and desired to advance good causes, but not himself. In Parliament he was identified with Ettie's burly and truculent godfather, Sir William Harcourt, who returned to his old post as Chancellor of the Exchequer in August 1892. But Willie soon became disquieted by his mentor's policies. In the Regency period Pascoe Grenfell, the founder of the family fortunes, had urged that the copper and silver currency should be strengthened, and decried the Bank of England's policies for impoverishing the country. Willie, too, was a bimetallist: someone who believed that sterling should not be a monometallic currency, based on the gold standard, but bimetallic (that is, based on gold and silver). He was distressed when, in the autumn of 1892, 'two Gold Bugs' were added to the British delegation to the international monetary conference that had been convened in Brussels and warned Loulou Harcourt (who was confidential secretary to his father, the Chancellor) of the 'great indignation' of Liberal bimetallists.

In June 1893 the Cabinet allowed the Indian government to close their mints to the coinage of silver and to establish a gold standard; and in July Willie resigned his Hereford seat in protest. He denounced the government's resistance to international monetary reform as ruinous to British prosperity, and deplored the injustice perpetrated in India by suddenly closing the mints to the coinage of silver. Although, unlike most Whigs (including Francis Cowper), Willie had stomached Gladstone's Irish Home Rule policy, he also decided that he could not support the proposal to retain the full number of Irish MPs in the

House of Commons, and to allow them to vote on purely English, Scottish and Welsh matters, while giving the Irish exclusive control over their own affairs in a devolved parliament. Willie's protest was thought quixotic. 'He would not consent to take counsel with Mr G or Harcourt, perhaps for fear of being talked over,' Eddy Hamilton, who was a Treasury official, noted. 'The secession is not serious in itself, especially when the principal reason is founded on a currency quack. But what is disagreeable is that the Liberal-Radical party lose . . . a good fellow & a thorough gentleman. It is this loss of class which constitutes one of the worst outlooks for the party.' The result of the by-election necessitated by Willie's resignation, whereby the Liberals lost Hereford by forty-four votes, left Sir William Harcourt 'very much in the dumps', and decrying Gladstone's management of the Home Rule Bill: 'It had all gone pop!'

The day after Willie's resignation Balfour spoke at the Mansion House in favour of bimetallism, prompting Gladstone to pronounce that a man holding such monstrous views ought to be confined in Bedlam. Nonetheless, Balfour's influence had converted the political allegiance of one of Gladstone's favourite nephews, Alfred Lyttelton, and Willie Grenfell quietly followed. Lyttelton was a Soul, as Willie was by marriage, and their transferred loyalties exemplified the gregarious, bipartisan traditions of the Souls. A few years after Willie's 1893 resignation he was adopted as the Tory candidate for South Buckinghamshire, also known as the Wycombe division, and was elected in the Tory landslide victory of 1900. He did not much enjoy the Commons. With his conciliatory and impartial temper, he liked to facilitate constructive change, and was a temperate, steady committee-man – at one time he was serving on 115 separate committees – rather than a furious partisan.

Similarly, though Ettie had the stylish grace of a Whig hostess, she was never a political hostess with ambitions to pull strings and manipulate Cabinets. Bimetallists, she thought, were all bores; and political talk was disheartening. Lord Wiltshire and Lord Skelmersdale, her suitors in the 1880s, had both lost favour by talking politics at her; and she found dinner conversations about the Irish question as tedious as discussions of the weather. But she liked to receive confidential and privileged news in advance of the general public: Balfour's decision to resign the party leadership in 1911, strategic war plans from Kitchener, Milner and Churchill, or confidential Cabinet assessments of industrial unrest from Herbert Fisher. Her political support, as befitted an old Soul, went to her friends in the first instance and only secondarily according to party loyalties. For her, Balfour was the pre-eminent politician of her times, not because he led the Conservative Party in the House of Commons for twenty years, but because he was the lodestar of her social life. If, after 1922, all her frontbench political friends were Conservative, it was chiefly because membership of the Liberal Party so shrivelled, and subordinately because Willie in old age became explosively grumpy in the company of radicals.

ॐ

Ettie adored holidays – and supremely adored holidays with her children. In the autumn of 1894 the Grenfells with their three children went to stay at Stack, a little grey stalking lodge in Reay Forest near the west coast of Sutherland. The two boys were old enough to be perched together on an old pony, and taken with their mother for whole days by the river or at the sea. They delighted to catch river mussels and make Ettie grope in the bodies for pearls. Lord Cairns, a young man with a gentle crush on Ettie, arrived at Stack with a mountain of luggage, a crate of liqueurs, some bagpipes and a large yellow retriever called Crocus. The dog spent whole days in the sport of knocking the little boys down, and finally Julian and Billy, whenever they saw Crocus coming, used to throw themselves flat on the ground.

Ettie liked to share the joys of her holidays with her friends. 'We are having such a *very* happy time,' she reported to Balfour from Stack. 'My huge family wild with delight at anything & everything – it's a great thing to be at the stage when getting worms for the bait is quite an equal excitement to catching the fish!' She was equally enthusiastic to Oliver Wendell Holmes: 'There is the peace that passeth understanding about it all – in this wonderful *elemental* atmosphere of the beautiful, austere & utterly lonely hills, with the shrill sea-winds always about one, and the clouds quite near and friendly, not far away things as in England. I have been *so happy.*'

Ettie used these holidays to saturate herself in literature. She did not waste her time with penny romances, but like a good Soul, plunged into the world of ideas, and liked to discuss her summer reading with such intellectuals as Balfour and Holmes. At Stack in 1894 she read Samuel Butcher and Andrew Lang's translation of *The Odyssey*, Samuel Laing's *Human Origins*, Thomas Huxley's *Evolution of Ethics*, Ernest Renan's *Vie de Jésus* 'over again with renewed love', Henry Drummond's *Ascent of Man* ('well-written, but fanciful & fantastic'), George Curzon's *Problems of the Far East*, that 'marvellous & thrilling book *Wuthering Heights*', 'as always Keats, Browning & Carlyle', and the latest Stevenson novel, *Ebb Tide*. She was spellbound by Stevenson's eloquence, 'but oh what *ignominious* characters – . . . it is wretched to think of Stevenson who of all men has some hope & courage for life left, prostituting his wonderful writing to the obloquy of describing these men.' All her life she felt disappointed by novels with characters of low motivation: she wanted books to have ideals. She also preferred the classics to fashionable modern novels. 'I hate the craze for *new* books,' she exclaimed in 1892, at a time when she was rereading the *Meditations* of Marcus Aurelius, the Roman emperor and stoic philosopher. Modern French novels seemed to her 'villainously wicked & despairing . . . I can't help it, clever as they are, these *fin-de-siècle* Dead-Sea apples do leave me with a withered soul.'

Reading aloud played a large part in the Grenfells' family life. From the time that they were babies, Ettie's children loved being read to. It felt wonderful for her to command their intense, undivided attention; books brought emotional continuity as well as zest and intimacy to her life. 'I can't tell you the joy', she wrote to Judge Holmes at Christmas 1895, 'it is to read what one has loved to the next generation, in the shape of my boys – they are 7 & 5 now, & "*bouche béante*" [open-mouthed] as regards printed matter, & it's such fun watching them under Stevenson, Kipling, etc. . . . They are a wonderful joy, these absurd creatures, with their gold heads, & did truly come "trailing clouds of glory" into life.' Ettie's choice of books was imaginative and stimulating. When the boys were small, she read them Charles Kingsley's children's book on Greek mythology, *The Heroes*, as well as *Gulliver's Travels*, while Willie read them Charlotte Yonge's historical novel *The Little Duke* and Harriet Martineau's *The Crofton Boys*. A few years later, during 1897, she read R.D. Blackmore and Dickens to the boys, in the form of *Lorna Doone* and *Oliver Twist*, as well as stirring tales from Robert Louis Stevenson, Rider Haggard, Kipling and Anthony Hope: Willie that summer read extracts from *Don Quixote*. Ettie made a point of reading aloud from rousing history books: Froude's *English Seamen*, Younghusband's *Chitral*, Winston Churchill's *River War*, and H.A.L. Fisher's short biography of Napoleon. These family sessions made the Grenfell children articulate, communicative and curious. All of them associated literature with intimacy and satisfaction.

Ettie wanted her sons to be hardy, not coddled. Their upbringing taught them to test their powers of endurance. In the autumn of 1896, when the Grenfells rented a lodge in Assynt Forest in Sutherland for two months, Julian and Billy – by then aged eight and six – spent long days sea fishing with their mother. They went out all day in the little sailing boat of a tall old man called Murdoch Keir, reputedly unbalanced, but (said Ettie) 'an ideal play-fellow to the boys'. He told them Gaelic legends and stories, sang to them, played his little fiddle, and taught them to catch sea urchins, bait lobster pots and steer a sailing boat. 'When becalmed, on hot afternoons, he used to stick his knife in the mast "to bring the wind", whistle a little, and then settle down to his stories; Julian and Billy, in their little blue jerseys (as like his as possible), sitting as close to him as they could, spell-bound in hero-worship.'

As always, she wanted Balfour to share the joys of her summers. 'It is the most beautiful wild country I have ever seen,' she wrote to him from Assynt Lodge. 'A tiny grey house nestling into the big Cuniach hill . . . 43 miles from station or post-office, with Loch Assynt a stone's throw below the windows & the lovely Inver river, & the Sea only 6 miles away, *such* a beautiful bit of coast, with woods of silver birch & firs growing quite to the water's edge – then from the braes above them one sees out to the whole great sweep of the Atlantic, & coast & islands.' The colours gave her deep satisfaction: 'the sea & sky quite burning blue, & the seaweed light golden . . . & the hills every kind of orange & brown.'

The Grenfells leased Taplow Court to King Chulalongkorn of Siam for July and August of Jubilee year (1897), and embarked on their first foreign holiday together: two months at Châlet des Muguets, a small house in the Normandy fishing village of St Pierre-en-Port, near

Fécamp. The little house stood in a cornfield, with orchards and woods at the back. Ettie read essays by Jules Lemaître, Anatole France and Renan as well as old French novels, a biography of Abraham Lincoln and William James's *Will to Believe*, doubtless chosen to discuss with Arthur Balfour who visited Châlet des Muguets for a few days. This was the first of a series of seaside holidays on the west coast of France.

Perhaps the most successful of all was in 1911 when Ettie took Monica, Ivo and Imogen to Brittany. She rented Le Fort, a newly built house on a spit of land at the edge of the village of Paramé. It had a big stone terrace, with steps down on each side to the bay, so that they could bathe straight from the house, and its wide windows and balconies looked on to panoramic views of the sea, islets and distant headlands. At high tide the sea came up on both sides of the house. There was intense heat that August and September, but during the hot middle hours of the day Ettie and her children went in their little carriage, laden with books and a picnic, into the inland woods and orchards. 'How *can* people ever go to the dreary dingy English sea-side, when *this* is within a night's reach, & one can live here in luxury on about a franc a day!' she wrote from Paramé to Willie, who was touring Canada with the Duke of Sutherland.

On 3 May 1898 the first parting in the family came, when Julian, who was ten years old, went away to school at Summer Fields, a spacious, airy school of about 125 boarders with meadows leading down to the River Cherwell at Oxford. Summer Fields was pleasant enough, although the school matron made a daily distribution of just three sheets of lavatory paper to each boy, which Julian's new friend Ronald Knox found niggardly and indelicate. Nearly forty years later, when her eldest grandson Julian Salmond was going away for the first time to board, Ettie wrote in consolation to his mother about his imminent separation: 'it seems to pull at the very centre of one's being, *nothing* in life afterwards is so hard, because they are older & can face things better.' She recalled the unhappiness of taking Julian in 1898 to have his hair shorn, and of his repeated vomiting on the journey from Taplow to Summer Fields – 'but not a tear'.

Julian, as the oldest of the family, had looked large at Taplow, but at the moment of parting at Summer Fields he seemed suddenly small, and his face white and forlorn. When Willie and Ettie returned to the school a week later, they barely recognised him, playing with a host of other uniformed boys, with a filthy school cap jammed on his head. Julian seemed doubtful that he should notice his parents at school and they gazed at each other from afar for a long time. Eighteen months later, Billy joined Julian at Summer Fields, but with less composure at leaving the Taplow schoolroom. 'Leaving home was always a very great trouble to him; Julian never cried, but poor little Billy always did, every single term until he went to Eton – and the family had to show great ingenuity in never finding it out,' Ettie said.

In September 1898 the Grenfells rented a small house, Cluny, at Swanage, then a pretty resort on the Dorset coast, built in the local grey stone, standing on a fine bay with white chalk cliffs and sweeping green downs behind. There, unexpectedly, on 5 September, Ettie's third son was born. 'It was an *awful* time, but we are both doing beautifully now,' she wrote to Balfour. Ettie's admirers were distressed by her ordeal. 'Nobody who wasn't so brave & wonderful as you could have borne it,' Maurice Baring assured her. It had been like a 'sharp stab to . . . think of you suffering such horrible anguish . . . It gave me such a lump in my throat to think of your dear tired eyes, the darling Fargueil golden eyes.' The boy was hurriedly baptised at Swanage: of his forenames Ivo George Winfred, Ivo was for Evelyn de Vesci's husband, George after his godfather George Curzon (Ettie had been godmother to the Curzons' daughter Cynthia) and Winfred was the masculinised version of Winifred, the forename of his god-mother, the Duchess of Portland. Ivo was a gentle, happy, pretty baby, with a wide smile and ringing laugh. His elder brothers enjoyed playing with him and Billy was especially affectionate.

Ivo's premature birth, however, aroused the distant rustle of scandalmongers. They wondered if he had not been born early at all, and if Ettie had reasons for misleading people about dates. Though she was admired by Willie's male cousins and brothers-in-law, some of the Grenfell and Aylmer women found her patronising, competitive and over-inclined to tart remarks that put them down. She had, they complained, a 'snobbish element without the excuse of being *nouveau*'. They also mistrusted her bevy of male idolaters and scrutinised each new baby for signs that it was not Willie's. Ivo as boy and man had such a pronounced resemblance to his brothers as to belie ill-natured talk. He was also especially adored by Willie. Still, his premature arrival startled Ettie's friends. 'What an *inexplicable* thing,' Alice Cranborne wrote to her. 'Doesn't it seem strange to think that you must have begun before you came to Hatfield that time!' Like Maurice Baring, she was aghast at the peril that Ettie had endured. 'You are so much the embodiment of life and vitality to me, that danger in connection with you seems impossible,' Alice wrote.

Ettie was not physically demonstrative with her children and all the Grenfells were restrained in their touching. Monica remembered feeling pleasantly startled when she saw other families embracing. Instead, Ettie expressed her love for her children, as for her friends, in emphatic verbal endearments, intense attentive sympathy and effervescent activity: Julian once told his mother that compared to her, everyone else was like flat soda-water. Her concentration on her children impressed friends and even strangers. When, in September 1899, the family returned to Swanage for a less disrupted visit, another holidaymaker recorded her glimpses of the family at play. 'Mrs Grenfell had evidently thought it would be good to give her children a very simple seaside holiday, and to give up the whole of her time to them . . . walking, butterfly-catching, yachting, always with those boys – the two eldest – and they were such tremendous friends, all radiantly happy to be together.' One image always stayed with this summer neighbour. 'I was coming in one evening when it was dusk, and I could see through the wide open window Mrs Grenfell having a "meat-tea" with her children. They were all round her, and the light from the lamp shone on her and made her look very young. The baby was on her knee, Monica standing near her, and the two boys having their tea on either side of her. No one waiting on them – just she and the children, all supremely happy.'

In October 1899 war – engineered by Ettie's friend Alfred Milner – broke out in South Africa. 'What a grim game it is,' she wrote on 17 November to Judge Holmes, whom she always identified with warfare. 'Life & Death glare at one in letters almost too big to read.' Willie's best man at his wedding, 'Wilty' Winchester, was killed at Magersfontein on 11 December, his brother Claude Grenfell died at Spion Kop in January and later Mabell Airlie's husband was shot down while leading a charge at Diamond Hill. 'Everyone seems to be ill or dying,' Ettie wrote to Holmes again on 17 December. 'All life resolves itself into rushing between stricken houses in freezing railway-carriages, reading of fresh disaster in South Africa in each newspaper.' The jingo press horrified her. 'Willie is wild to go to the War, & I feel it will end now in *all* our men going.'

Lord Kitchener, initially the British Chief of Staff in South Africa and promoted Commander-in-Chief in 1900, had been Willie's friend since 1885. The conqueror of Sudan and victor of Omdurman always came to Taplow for his first Sunday back in England after his various undertakings in Egypt, the Sudan and India – a tall, spare figure with piercing blue eyes set far apart. For his return to Taplow in 1898, after the capture of Khartoum, the Grenfells had erected an arch with the inscription 'Welcome', and he told them, 'When I come here I feel like coming home: I have no home.' Ettie was almost the only woman with whom Kitchener felt at ease, and her sons were a joy to him. During the First World War a silver-framed photograph of Julian was the only picture displayed in his room at the War Office, and when given confirmation of Billy's death, Kitchener betrayed distress for the only time during the war.

This mutual devotion began at Taplow, one morning during the summer holiday of 1899, when Julian found an unknown man at breakfast, who took him out for an hour's walk. 'It was easy to see that he was no civilian,' Julian wrote in 1902, when he was only fourteen. 'He looked a soldier from head to foot, and there was something about his manner that showed me that he was no ordinary man, and yet he said nothing about himself or his own doings. He spoke in a way that showed me he meant what he said, and it was easy to see that he was used to being obeyed.' He personified 'self-restraint and tremendous will' for the boy, who had already resolved that he wished to be a soldier and idealised these characteristics as the supreme martial virtues. Julian studied Kitchener's idiosyncrasies – his detestation of public dinners and of being photographed – and kept a loving admiration for the great soldier all his life.

The Grenfell children were never strangers to, or shy of, the great men of the day. Their first experiences of motoring were in Balfour's car on trips to Hatfield and Wrest. During the summer of 1902 they not only saw him at Taplow, immediately after he had kissed hands as

Prime Minister, but also enjoyed Kitchener's visits to Taplow and Wrest. It was at Wrest that summer that Ivo (aged four) befriended Austen Chamberlain, who took him for a walk, fed him hothouse grapes and let him puff at his pipe. There were many other occasions when the Grenfell children mixed with the Great and the Good. At Whitsun of 1904, for example, the Grenfells took Monica and Ivo with them for a golfing holiday at Le Touquet with Balfour, Edgar Vincent, Evan Charteris and the Elchos. At a ball which Ettie gave in Mayfair in 1907, Ivo danced the Lancers as Balfour's partner.

In September 1901 Julian and Billy were again separated, when the elder boy started his Eton career. They missed each other acutely, and Julian was unhappy during his first Half, but was soon reconciled to his new surroundings and ultimately revelled in his years there. Two years later Billy came second out of seventeen Eton scholarships, though he did not take the money of his scholarship and went as an Oppidan to Arthur Benson's boarding house. Ettie's social routine was altered by being the mother of Eton sons. Taplow Court is only a few miles upstream from the school and was therefore a convenient gathering point for Julian's friends. In November 1902, during Long-Leave (half-term), Ettie held the first of many Eton parties at Taplow; and thereafter ambitious winter entertainments supplemented her annual Ascot week house party and the regular Sunday parties in summer. The guests at this inaugural Eton party comprised at least a dozen Eton pupils with their parents plus some distinguished bachelors, notably Balfour and Haldane.

This party was the birth of a new social set, with the children of the Souls at its core, which was later nicknamed the Coterie. Ettie's first big Eton Saturday-to-Monday party at Taplow took place in April 1904. Millie Sutherland came with her boys Geordie Stafford and Willie's godson Alastair Leveson-Gower, Willie Northampton with all his children, the whole Horner family, the American novelist Pearl Craigie with her son John, Norah Lindsay with her son Harry, Betty Montgomery, Bron Herbert, Winston Churchill, Raymond Asquith, Archie Gordon, Maurice Baring and others. They had a water fight on the river, in which Norah Lindsay (dressed in flimsy chiffon) was drenched.

The year 1905 was eventful in Ettie's family history. Her second daughter was born on 11 February at 4 St James's Square. Julian and Billy each came over from Eton to see the baby at Taplow: Julian cradled her like a football in the hollow of his hands, which she seemed to find comforting; and Billy celebrated his first sight of her by eating an entire chocolate cake for tea. Monica and Ivo washed the baby's face, combed her hair and wanted to brush her teeth: 'I'm not the youngest now,' Ivo said with delight, but then added anxiously, 'You won't forsake me for the new baby?' A friend joked that all Balfour's Cabinet Ministers visited Imogen's cradle and gave her rattles with Protectionist mottoes inscribed on them. Queen Alexandra, Alice Salisbury, Lord Kitchener, Bron Lucas and Julian were her godparents: she was baptised Alexandra Imogen Clair – the last forename in memory of Clair Herbert – but known as Imogen or (more often) by the nicknames of Mogs or Moggie. Imogen had a tiny face, thick golden curls, pink cheeks and blue eyes, could bray like a donkey, and was a high-speed crawler. At the Taplow Christmas of 1905, aged eleven months, she made her first appearance in the family's amateur theatricals as 'Snowball' in a white sledge. She played her part with gusto, and equally enjoyed her soft and squeaking Christmas presents. This proved to be Nanny Wake's last Christmas: she was eighty-four, happy and well, and laughed endlessly at the children's acting.

Life at Panshanger had long been dominated by Francis Cowper's crippling gout. Katie tried constant entertaining, which amused him, and change of doctors and remedies; but nothing helped, and the nights were often long and painful. He loved the quiet rooms of his house with their display of the slowly distilled accumulation of his ancestors' fastidious taste: the western sun shining on the works by Fra Bartolommeo, Rembrandt, Titian and Poussin in the gallery, the Van Dycks, Knellers and Lelys in the library, the Tintoretto on the staircase and the Reynolds portraits hanging in the dining room on the walnut panelling. He often went to gaze at them alone, and in his last years used to trundle round in his bath chair, halting before each picture in the dining room or gallery, murmuring sadly, 'I wonder which one will go first.' Cowper was devoted to his Grenfell great-nephews and liked to think that Julian would some day own Panshanger. He rejoiced, too, in their devotion to Katie, who had a particular rapport with Julian.

In July 1905 Cowper underwent an operation on an abscess and began an irreversible decline. 'It is beyond words to watch helplessly his wretchedness & discomfort,' Ettie wrote to Balfour a few hours before the end. 'He only longs to go. Katie is quite wonderful, perfectly strong & calm – she hardly ever leaves him or sleeps, but is somehow made able to go on.' Cowper was calm and dignified *in extremis*. 'Am I dying?' he asked, almost if not quite his last words; and when Katie did not reply, he added in a clear, contented voice as if to reassure her, 'I am not afraid.' He died on 19 July. 'He lay as if asleep & just breathed his life gently away – we hardly knew that it was over,' Ettie told Monica, '& just after he died there came the most wonderful look of happiness & calm.' She needed those she loved to look untroubled in death, because it helped her to feel thankful that they had gone to a better existence. She took 'Auntie Ka' as a model for her grieving – 'so strong & brave & calm,' as she told Monica.

The Earl's death broke up the Cowper estates and brought great changes to his nephews and nieces. His estate was valued at £1,179,914 gross, or £358,958 net (about £84,425,000 and £25,760,000 respectively in 2008 prices). To his widow he bequeathed £20,000 (£1,430,000 in 2008), his plate, linen, jewels, horses, carriages and his pictures in St James's Square absolutely, and the use for her lifetime of Panshanger, together with its picture collection and surroundings estates, all with remainder to Ettie. Ettie was left outright Ratling Court, a medieval house with a large thatched barn and some 2,000 acres at Adisham in Kent, and certain other properties. To his surviving sister Lady Amabel Kerr he left the estates that he had inherited from their grandmother Lady Palmerston, Brocket Hall and Melbourne Hall in Derbyshire.

Most of Lord Cowper's peerages became extinct, but the barony of Butler of Moore Park became abeyant, with Ettie as a co-heiress. Bron Herbert inherited the Lucas and Dingwall baronies, together with Wrest, 4 St James's Square and some Yorkshire estates, which derived from his de Grey ancestors; but was appalled to have this greatness thrust upon him. The unwanted magnificence of Wrest he dealt with by sending the pick of its art treasures to the National Gallery and by leasing the house to Whitelaw Reid, the US Ambassador to Britain. It had a brief but sumptuous renewal as the Americans' country embassy.

The surviving Cowper family assembled in the library at Panshanger in 1874.
Ettie (presumably upstairs in the nursery) was aged seven.

The south front at Wrest, the de Grey house where Ettie lived with her
grandmother until 1880.

The Long Water at Wrest designed by Le Nôtre, the Sun King's *paysagiste* at the palace of Versailles, and the baroque pavilion.

The Duke of Kent's orangery at Wrest was carved with the family motto, 'Faith is Everything', which remained an eternal truth for Ettie.

Ettie in her twenties – 'the most perfect type of womanhood of modern times.'

A gathering of the Souls at Taplow. Standing (l to r): Harry Cust, Ettie, Hugo Elcho, George Curzon, Henry White. Seated: (l to r): Mary Elcho, Willie, Margot Tennant.

Ettie in a diadem. She loathed looking directly at a camera.

(*Opposite*) Ettie amidst the splendour and frippery of a Rothschild house.
Lord Battersea, the photographer, forced her to look directly at him.

Taplow in the 1890s. Ettie's sanctuary 'with a view that stretches the soul' was at the summit of the tower.

Julian when a pupil at Summer Fields.

Billy as a Summer Fields boy.

(Opposite) The ideal mother with her golden boys.

Willie outside the front entrance at Taplow with Ivo and Monica.

Winston Churchill, one of the Taplow
faithful and Ettie's lifelong friend, was twice
hurled into the Thames by his fellow guests.

Archie Gordon, with his passionate joy-of-
life, was the first and most intense of
Ettie's young loves.

Lord Cowper had felt the most affectionate respect for Balfour since the 1870s, when AJB had sat as MP for Hertford, and had been pleased when, in July 1902, Balfour replaced his uncle Lord Salisbury as Prime Minister. It was expected that after leaving King Edward at Windsor Castle, Balfour would go to Hatfield to confer with his uncle. Instead, he motored over to Taplow, where there was a Saturday house party including the Devonshires, Gosfords, Tweedmouths and John Revelstoke. There he entrenched his reputation for nonchalance by discussing the Eton-and-Harrow cricket match, playing a game of croquet, and sitting under the cedars, after dinner, discussing Percy White's book *The New Christians*. He remained late at the Grenfells', and did not reach Downing Street until one in the morning: the importance to him of Ettie's company could not have been more distinctly signalled.

Willie had returned to the House of Commons as a Tory MP two years earlier and she was soon gently reminding the new Prime Minister of her husband's availability for office: 'If you thought he could be of any use in any way I know he would be only too glad to undertake anything for which you thought he was fitted,' she assured him in 1903. Yet Ettie felt *'wretched'* during the summer of 1904, when Willie was almost nominated as Lord Minto's successor as Governor-General of Canada. The Grenfells had visited the Mintos in Canada in May 1899, when Ettie had been direly bored by the official routine, and wearied by the humdrum visitors at Government House. Willie, though, desired Minto's job, which was instead entrusted to Albert Grey: perhaps it was decided that Canada needed a peer as the King's representative; or perhaps Ettie's reluctance was too manifest. It was always incomprehensible to her that people like the Mintos or Greys could leave their homes without a pang.

A significant glimpse of Ettie and Balfour at this time is provided by Beatrice Webb. On 22 November she and her husband Sidney Webb dined with Bron Lucas at his newly inherited mansion in St James's Square. This was during the death throes of the Balfour administration and there was a general expectation of a Liberal government backed by a large majority. Progressives like Mrs Webb were eagerly awaiting a period of increased influence and appraising the incoming personnel: Bron Lucas was one of the diminishing band of Liberal supporters in the House of Lords. 'Mrs Willie Grenfell and Mrs Lindsay, flippant but clever little lady, and a pleasant young Tory lawyer made up the party,' Beatrice Webb noted in her diary. The new baron seemed 'an attractive creature, dreamy and vague, with a charming veracity and gentleness of nature, with (for a *grand seigneur*) simple tastes and ways, and public-spirited and philanthropic impulses'. She found him 'a mere child in knowledge and thought on social and economic questions', with 'no notion of work', and therefore 'useless but not dangerous' to the cause of reform.

Ettie struck Mrs Webb 'as something more than the fashionable and pretty woman I took her to be. But when I sat with her and the other smart little woman in that palatial room I felt a wee bit ashamed of myself. Why was I dissipating my energy in this smart but futile world in late hours and small talk?' At the height of Mrs Webb's self-reproach, the door opened and Balfour was announced. 'The appearance of the Prime Minister dissipated my regrets,' Mrs Webb conceded. 'It is always worthwhile, I thought, to meet those who really have power to alter things . . . He was looking excited and fagged, on the eve of resignation. We chatted over the fire – Mrs Grenfell, he and I – in a disjointed fashion until twelve o'clock, when Sidney and I left the tiny party to talk, perhaps more intimately.'

It is possible that Ettie's intimate talk with the Prime Minister, once the Webbs had gone, was about the dynastic opportunities for the Grenfells created by Francis Cowper's death. Cowper's will was published around the time of Balfour's resignation. Its confirmation that the Grenfells were to receive the noble estate at Panshanger assured them of the prosperity that the King required of new peers and Balfour included Willie's name in his last honours list. 'You can imagine how thrilled I was by what Willie told me last night – it never seemed possible before to believe that it really could happen, partly because one wished it for him so very much,' Ettie thanked AJB: 'no words will at all express the gratitude that I do feel for all your goodness about it.' Once the news was announced in early December, Ettie had 'a bewildering 30 hours of opening & answering telegrams & letters. I am delighted that Willie is released from the H of C – it was so deeply uncongenial to him, & he is walking on air.'

Willie's cousin Francis, a field marshal, had taken the title of

Grenfell when he received a peerage three years earlier, and it was not sensible to court confusion by a replication of the name. After considering the titles of Marlow or St Just (the Cornish village from which the Grenfells originated), Willie plumped for Desborough – the name of one of the Chiltern hundreds in Buckinghamshire. (He could not take the title of Burnham, the hundred in which Taplow Court stood, because it had been bagged as a title two years earlier by the owner of the *Daily Telegraph*.) 'I rather hate leaving the happy shelter of the old name, & feel *deeply* "This is none of I",' Ettie wrote deprecatingly. The name Desborough, she laughed, evoked the villain of a melodrama, but she was delighted.

‮ ‬

The Cowper inheritance enabled the Desboroughs, together with Bron Lucas, who had let 4 St James's Square shortly after entertaining the Webbs, to rent a house at 51 Grosvenor Square for the 1906 Season. There, on 24 February 1906, Ettie held the first London dinner party that was all her own. Do come, she begged Max Beerbohm, to meet 'the de Greys, Soveral, Mr Balfour, Lord Rosebery, the Edgar Vincents, Evan, and a few others'. The Marquess de Soveral was the long-serving Portuguese envoy in London, and a great favourite of Ettie's. He supposedly said that no other woman could contrive, like her, to look stately and voluptuous at the same time; and she thought him 'marvellously cute & adroit & ugly'. For another London dinner party on 14 March Ettie invited Balfour, George Wyndham with Sibell Grosvenor, Alice Salisbury, the Elchos, Lyttons, Ian Hamiltons and others. Jean Hamilton enjoyed her *placement* between Hugo Elcho and Bron Lucas. 'Arthur Balfour sat opposite and talked of Mr F.E. Smith, who has made a brilliant speech in the House – his social fortune was made, for Lady Desborough was very interested – she *is* charming, really full of fascination.'

Ettie's invigorated entertaining of the smart set in London was paralleled by her heightened attention to her children and their friends. Monica and Ivo, who had never lived in London before, enjoyed driving with their mother in the victoria and stopping at a fishmonger's in Bond Street to buy shrimps for their tea. Monica had daily French lessons, German lessons three times a week with her best friend

Rosemary Leveson-Gower (Millie Sutherland's daughter), dancing classes, skating lessons and swam at the Bath Club. Ettie arranged a course of twelve lectures on English literature at Grosvenor Square for Monica, Ivo and thirteen young ladies including Rosemary Leveson-Gower, some Lister and Tennant sisters, and the exotic heiress Sybil Sassoon. Two years earlier Ettie had helped the essayist Edmund Gosse to a sinecure as Librarian of the House of Lords: 'Dear, generous & powerful Friend,' he had written, 'my real gratitude is to you who thought of it first'; and now she recruited him to make an inaugural speech to the children. Only influenza prevented Balfour from giving the prizes at the end. During March Ettie organised an outing of the Desborough, Manners, Charteris, Sassoon, Horner and Lister young to a performance of *She Stoops to Conquer*, and took an Eton party of forty to the zoo.

She also held a fancy dress party for a hundred children in the Grosvenor Square house (attended by Lord Haldane, who proved a connoisseur of babies), and a ball for some thirty teenage boys and girls, which was graced by Balfour. 'I should die rather than entertain a huge party of half-strange boys,' wrote one of her guests, Lord Aberdeen's twenty-one-year-old son Archie Gordon, 'or at any rate I shouldn't try to admix newly hatched and diffident demoiselles. The *instant* Ettie's galvanising presence was removed the thing fell into disorganisation and floaters.' Her vivacity was overdone: she had too intense an expectation that her children must enjoy themselves to the utmost; and though the Eton parties were fun, she was intruding too much into her children's friendships and forcing herself to the centre of their lives.

During this summer of 1906 a painful new phase opened in Ettie's experiences of motherhood. For years Julian's behaviour had been perfect for her. Lady Lyttelton (one of whose daughters married Willie's cousin Arthur Grenfell) recalled a beautiful summer night at Wrest in 1904, when Julian – aged sixteen – stayed out in the moonlight woods and did not appear for dinner. 'He came in suddenly through the window after dinner, among us all in our stupid evening gowns, and, looking round at us like a man in a dream, only said, "Where's Mother?" He passed through, and found you, and came back with his arm round you, telling you how wonderful it was outside in the woods, and how you must come out and feel it and see it. You went out with him, and I remember a pang of envy of you for having such a son.'

These gorgeous moments ceased shortly after Julian left Eton at the age of eighteen in July 1906. He was probably discomfited by the realisation of the intensity of his mother's emotional involvement with Archie Gordon, who was only three years older than him – an affair which, as described in the next chapter, caused a Society storm in August 1906. Certainly it was at the time of the Archie Gordon furore that he and Ettie began to have 'vehement discussions', as she wrote ten years later, 'generally on quite impersonal subjects, but not infrequently ending with both disputants in tears!' They each held strong opinions, which they could not bear the other to contradict: Ettie indeed was jealous of signs of independence in her children. She confessed to being 'mildly depressed' by the sequence of tempers, tears and truces. In fact, these blazing rows deeply distressed her and she shuddered to think how dreadful they would seem if anyone overheard them. Julian used to call them his 'fight for life', and claimed that they had been emotionally cleansing.

Ettie tried every way to cope with Julian's mutinous moods: raillery, cool explanatory reasoning, testing silence, sharp reproaches and stifling sulks – everything except hard indifference. Their clashes were not bursts of anger that produced, with frightening clarity, sudden mutual comprehension, but an incessant crossness that tired, confused and blinded them both. In late-night confidences, once he was at Oxford, Julian would deplore all the battle debris that could not be brushed away. 'There was something simple and primitive in him that was outraged by the perfection of well-bred luxury at Taplow,' concluded Lawrence ('Jonah') Jones, who had rooms under Julian's at Balliol, 'something artificial and unreal in her deft manipulation of a procession of week-end parties, lightly skimming the cream from the surface of life.'

At the end of the summer of 1906, Julian went up to his father's old Oxford college, Balliol, and Billy, returning to Eton without him, felt as if he had been widowed. Many of Julian's Eton friends went to Oxford around the same time as him: Charles Lister, Patrick Shaw-Stewart, Edward Horner, George Brodrick, Guy Benson, Ronald

Knox; and they remained a cohort throughout their undergraduate years. They were known as 'the Eton "push"' at Oxford and widely disliked. The 12th Duke of Bedford (then Lord Tavistock) was Julian's exact contemporary at Eton and Balliol. At school 'ragging and bullying' had made him miserable, and the Eton push still discomfited him at Oxford. Bedford thought Julian's set were 'not so much the flower of England's manhood, as good material, and spoiled by Eton'. He recalled one occasion when the Balliol authorities confined their undergraduates to college so as to prevent a threatened shindy with rough elements from the town. Bedford was in the same room as Julian, who was chafing at the restriction, when loud, discordant voices broke out in the street below. Julian's head shot up like a terrier's when it hears the sound of a dogfight, he retrieved a sturdy rope from some hiding place, fixed it securely and vanished out of the window to the dark street below.

Julian loved a fight, and took it as a compliment that his Balliol nickname was 'Roughers', or 'the Rough Man'. He described to his mother, in 1908, a row with an Oxford cabman who had demanded an exorbitant fare: 'I suddenly lost all control, tore him down from his seat, and shook him till bits began to drop off him. I never remember being so passionately angry in my life before, and why I can't imagine. It would be awful if murder always entered one's heart on being overcharged a shilling. Luckily I only shook him, and left him alive, gasping out wild threats of the police-court.'

The Eton push took control of the Annandale Society, a dining club, which became notorious in the college for its insolent exclusivity and intimidating rowdiness. Julian led the members of the 'Anna' in suppressing the 'plebs' at Balliol and in cowing the effete: he would drive the exquisite young Philip Sassoon out of the college by cracking a prodigious Australian stock whip within inches of his head. The Anna rowdies had their own rules: they drank deep at their dinners, but were never sottish during the day, and when they smashed up a man's rooms, they paid for the damage afterwards. George Brodrick had, perhaps, the least trained intellect of the Eton push, but all of them were articulate, well-read and stylish. They read poetry – several of them wrote it – and abominated decadents like Philip Sassoon. Billy used to tease Julian that he mixed his Christianity with everything, even racing his greyhounds; and many of the Eton push shared Julian's deep faith.

'Julian was easily the most fearless and the most direct man I ever knew,' 'Jonah' Jones later told Willie. 'He just took the whole of life in both hands, enjoyed everything in it good and enjoyable, pursued fiercely all that was false or hollow or humbugging.' At Oxford, it seemed to Jones, Julian 'did everything, and shone in them all. He rowed, and he hunted, and he read, and roared with laughter, and cracked his whip in the quad all night; bought greyhounds from the miller of Hambledon, boxed all the local champions, capped poetry with the most precious of the dons, and charmed everybody from the Master of Balliol to the ostlers at the Randolph.'

Girls were one cause of skirmishing between Julian and his mother. She would not have Violet Rutland's three daughters Marjorie, Letty and Diana Manners to stay at Taplow, and these were the three young women, Marjorie especially, whom he liked best. Her reasons for the ban are not incomprehensible. Ettie and Violet Rutland had loathed one another since their Venice visit together in 1890, Marjorie was four years older than Julian, but above all Ettie repulsed Marjorie from Taplow because the young woman was a rival. She wanted Julian's prime attention: she did not want him distracted or diverted from his devotion to her by the Manners girl, and could not yet face being a subordinate interest in his life. Ettie's determination to keep her eldest son in thraldom left him frustrated, angered and depressed: her possessiveness in 1908–10 is a dark blot, which sullies her self-image as a perfect mother.

In March 1909, a few weeks before his coming of age, Julian broke down physically and emotionally. He had been trying to improve his handicap in steeplechases by excessive dieting, Ettie explained, and had further depleted his strength by over-training. But it is not fanciful to suspect that he broke down as he faced the test of his twenty-first birthday: could he really be a self-reliant adult or would he always be harnessed to Taplow? It was to Panshanger, not Taplow, that he went to recuperate, and it was there, with Katie Cowper, that Ettie spent his birthday on 30 March 1909. It alarmed her to see him so apathetic, especially given her ancestral history of depression. She took him back to Taplow for a long-arranged coming-of-age dinner for the tenants at

Taplow, but he soon returned to Panshanger and there he began to rally.

That summer, as his strength returned, Julian sat up at night writing essays, which he hoped later to publish. They constitute the protest cries of an Eton-and-Balliol Edwardian precursor of the Angry Young Men. His chapters, with such titles as 'On Conventionalism' and 'On Calling Names by their Right Things', belittle and disintegrate much that his mother valued at a high price. He implied that she sought to buy off fate with optimistic evasions; indeed, that she had created a false narrative of her life, and by force of will was trying to make the sham of her existence seem extra real. He even attacked the sincerity of her faith. 'When Christ condemned worldliness, he condemned the conventional view that money, power, position are the important things,' Julian declared. 'He condemned the view that life consists in competition about trivialities, and he damned those who try to force this view on other people. He condemned the "worldly" man and the "man of the world"; but not the man who is in the world and who tries to make the best of it.' Ettie was hurt by what she read of these essays, and her friends were affronted.

Julian (unlike Billy) resented his mother's male admirers – John Revelstoke he compared to an obsequious draper – and was specially upset by those who were his own age. 'I hated him in the mornings,' he once wrote to Ettie of her young swain Patrick Shaw-Stewart. 'I didn't like the way he walked, even when he was walking away. I didn't like his hands or his feet or his streaky hair, or his love of money, or his dislike of dogs. Animals always edged away from him, and the more intelligent they were, the further they edged. I think there is something rather obscene about him, like the electric eel at the Zoo.' In November 1909 another of Ettie's electric eels, Archie Gordon, died with Ettie at his bedside. Her grief was deep – so strong, perhaps, as to arouse Julian's hurt rage for he relapsed into depression again.

His lethargic despair was worse than the episode at his coming of age. He lay for hours each day on the sofa in his mother's Taplow sitting room fingering the trigger of the loaded Atkins gun that his parents had given him as a twenty-first birthday present. 'Juju isn't a bit better but we won't go into that – and all the dark dispirited words that are a crime of *lèse-humanité*,' Ettie wrote. In February 1910 Julian went to Katie Cowper's rented villa at Bordighera on the Italian Riviera. His aunt never fussed him or tried to rouse him, and he enjoyed the novelty of Mediterranean life. 'The people are enchanting, they are so poor and dirty and cheerful, and the hill-villages simply wonderful,' he reported. 'Auntie Ka is too golden, and better than I have ever seen her. We generally motor in the afternoons, and get out and lie in the sun in the hills, and they sketch, and I sleep.'

Katie Cowper, and picturesque poverty rather than the red carpets and coronets of his mother's world, cured him. There was no one there whom he need be on his guard against or at his best before. His life there was not rubbed and frayed by useless contention with his mother. 'Tommy dear,' he wrote to his friend Alan Lascelles in April 1910, 'I'm at the end of the most ghastly four months of my life; I don't think I shall ever have another go – at least, it will kill me if I do. I lost my head, and rather flung myself at people's feet for sympathy. I got none, and it made it much worse; I should have done far better if I had kept it to myself and just slogged through with it.' Lascelles had been almost 'the only person who understood in the least, or who gave me any sympathy . . . an old aunt of mine was the only other person who helped me – 2 out of a million.'

The ultimate cure was to break away from Mother and become his own man. After returning from Italy, Julian fell in love with an older married woman, Pamela Lytton. Ettie had thought her lovely in the mid-1890s when she was still Pamela Plowden and Winston Churchill wanted to marry her; but had come to mistrust her as a protégé of Violet Rutland's, and because John Revelstoke held that her heartless coquetry nearly broke his brother Everard. In 1902 Miss Plowden had married the Earl of Lytton: 'she is very sweet and delicious, but so very busy getting on,' Jean Hamilton wrote two years into the Lytton marriage, that she 'would not genuinely like anyone till she was sure if they were hallmarked'. Pamela Lytton had the reputation of a vamp who made men unhappy: Billy only half-jokingly referred to her as the 'wicked Countess' and 'spider' who had entangled his brother. Julian spent several weeks of the summer of 1910 with her at Knebworth, Lord Lytton's neo-Gothic house near Panshanger, and returned there for weeks of the autumn – ostensibly to help her through an illness. This affair was more fulfilling than his flirtation with Marjorie Manners and involving, as it did, an experienced married woman, was altogether beyond Ettie's control. Julian escaped at last from maternal domination.

He had been gazetted as a second lieutenant in the Royal Dragoons, a cavalry regiment chosen because he would have long overseas postings, and he spent more of his last weeks in England at Knebworth with his lover Lady Lytton rather than at Taplow with his mother Lady Desborough. Though this affair was crucial in Julian's maturation, it was only an amusement for Pamela Lytton, who soon began an affair with Bendor Westminster and bore his son. On 4 November Julian sailed from Southampton for India and was not seen again in the family for two years. His departure was painful for Ettie, though she maintained a brave front. 'I *never* saw you', Mary Elcho declared on 27 October, 'in such *priceless* form, amusing us *all* & keeping us *all* alive, & to think all the time you have the dull pain of Julian's departure nagging at your heart.' Once Julian had sailed away, Ettie's intransigence to the Manners sisters was abandoned and they were accepted as frequent Taplow guests. Marjorie became a pleasant reminder of Julian rather than a threat to Ettie's power; and thirty years later Ettie wrote a tender, grateful obituary of her for *The Times*.

Julian's depression had forced him to renounce sitting for an honours degree, but Billy was an academic triumph. At Eton Billy proved an outstanding classicist, winning the Newcastle prize in 1909, and Ettie strained to enter into his enthusiasm, and nurture his critical intelligence. 'I am plunged in the Euripides plays – having just found them out, like discovering Hamlet at 90!' she enthused to Violet Asquith. Billy sent her Gilbert Murray's newly-published *Rise of the Greek Epic*, they discussed Walter Pater's interpretation of the Bacchae, exchanged views on Agave's punishment by Zeus and the birth of Dionysus, and together went to a memorable performance of *The Bacchae* at the Court Theatre. Ettie gloried when Billy won the top classical scholarship at Balliol. Once at Oxford he got a first in Mods and was awarded the Craven scholarship in 1911.

But Billy, too, was a bully. In his first year at Oxford he boasted to Monica of a jape in which fifty rabbits were lowered out of a college window in wicker baskets, and a bulldog set on them: 'the Dons ran after us, and afterwards collected the defunct rabbits into large piles, and buried them.' In June 1912 Billy was sent down for three terms after an Annandale Society riot in the college. The Anna had a dinner, where they dressed as prehistoric men, then half a dozen of them, led by Billy, rampaged in the college, breaking window panes, hurling beds out of windows into the quadrangle and wrecking the rooms of undergraduates against whom they thought they had a grievance.

'Of course we *did* want a scrap,' said Billy; and when the chaplain, Neville Talbot, appeared, Billy told him roundly, 'There *must* be a fight, and you may as well leave it alone.' This was not high-spirited fun, said Billy's tutor, but 'bullying' – a deliberate 'demonstration meant to annoy and insult those who had incurred their displeasure'. The Balliol dons could not tolerate civil warfare in the college and the old maids among them were aghast at a previous incident that day: 'certain women, brought over in motor-cars by men who had left the University, called at his lodgings in Beaumont Street' and Billy in his *dressing gown* escorted the visitors into the college, where (said his horrified tutor) 'these women behaved most discreditably'. To Ettie's mortification, Billy was sent down for three terms and only returned to Balliol in the summer of 1913. Shortly afterwards she had her first bout of eye strain and eye infections: physical complaints that recurred at moments of acute emotional stress for the rest of her life.

Billy resolved to put his nights of dissolute brutality behind him after dining one July evening in 1912 with another college chaplain, Henry Gibbon, once a stock-rider and steeplechase jockey in Australia, then an officer in a Sikh cavalry regiment, until 'he got a call, became a parson and settled down here in a semi-detached villa, to teach the way of God to all the little knock-kneed clever atheists up here', as Billy described. 'He is a MAN, and has risked his life a hundred times in three continents. He is so simple and brave and true, I have always loved him, and besides he has a real worship for Julian, and so I have loved him the more for that.' Gibbon 'gave it me pretty straight from the shoulder, but said at the end, "You have brains and pluck, and if you have God's help He will pull you through. And the only way to find God is to pray to Him in wide lonely places."' Gibbon had been padre to the Oxford University volunteers during the Boer War before beginning evangelical work among the undergraduates: a man of sincere piety, incapable of dreary platitudes, he was devoted to the

Grenfell brothers. 'I loved them, and I know that they loved me,' he wrote to Willie after they both had been killed. 'I taught them the Bible, and I prayed with them and for them. Heart, mind and body, they were magnificent specimens of our race.'

Billy crammed hard for 'Greats' at Oxford, and was devastated in June 1913 at achieving second-class honours after a long *viva voce* in which his chances of a first hung in the balance. Despite this blow, he set to work to compete for a Fellowship of All Souls in 1914 – though first he had to persuade his father to settle debts of £300. 'Now that Greats are over, I can think of nothing else, & I feel I shall go mad unless I get some help,' Billy pleaded. 'I can't tell you what a mean skunk I feel, having to write a begging letter to you; but I have had so many knocks and disappointments this year, I simply cannot face this alone. I know that I have always been a ghastly ass about money, & everyone has taken advantage of it. These debts have been rolling up for the last 4 years, & include everything, Battells, dinners, tennis, an enormous bill from Atkin for cartridges, spectacles, & all tradesmen. Do see me through this, if you think it right to do so.'

Ettie had a natural interest in her children's potential spouses, and indeed was bold in her interference. Though she had brought up her children to be intense, passionate creatures, she did not like it when they had quickened heartbeats for others: she wanted to remain the centre of attention in their lives and was not ready yet for outsiders to slacken her control of them. Despite talking a great deal about Love with her friends, she thought of it as an Ideal, and maintained the old Whig view of marriage in their circle as a prudential affair, in which at best the husband and wife settled after seven years into an affectionate and accommodating compromise. When Alice Salisbury's son Bobbety Cranborne married Betty Cavendish, one of the guests said, 'this is not a romantic marriage, both families want it.' Ettie did not want romantic marriages for her children when they were young: she wanted advantageous alliances, which she had enjoyed a part in achieving.

Young men who might make good husbands for Monica were added to Ettie's guest lists. The Duke of Leinster – a year older than Julian and with him at Eton – looked a promising early prospect. He had lost

his father at the age of five and his adored mother – the love of Hugo
Elcho's life – a few days after his eighth birthday. There followed
a sad, neglected childhood during which he grew obsessed by his
mother's memory. When Ettie took him up in 1906 he was already
having trouble with his 'nerves'. A few years later he was diagnosed
with epilepsy, and his obsession with the few pathetic keepsakes of his
mother's that he owned became such a monomania that in 1909 he was
confined in a bungalow at Edinburgh, with a medical attendant. From
the bungalow he sent letters of childish affection and aching loneliness
to Evelyn de Vesci, who had been his mother's dearest friend. By then
his brother and heir Desmond looked more satisfactory to Ettie. From
the age of twenty, Dessy FitzGerald was among the most faithful of
Taplow regulars and probably Ettie's first preference as a son-in-law:
she was devoted to him, and it seemed probable that he would be the
next Duke of Leinster – a very convincing duke he would have made.
But though Monica loved Dessy, too, it was only as a brother.

Ettie was no readier for her daughter to become an independent
married woman outside her control than she had been for Julian to
consort with Marjorie Manners. After Monica's début in the Season of
1911, she was courted by George Monckton, the future Lord Galway.
Ettie was friendly with him for thirty years, but rebuffed him as a son-in-
law by saying firmly that she did not think girls should marry until they
were aged at least twenty-two. Two of Julian's Eton contemporaries,
John Bigge and Montie Bertie, were also attracted by Monica during
1911. Julian wanted her to marry Bigge, and as he lay dying in 1915
asked Ettie if she thought the marriage would ever come to be. She
could not bring herself to reply that Bigge had been killed in action two
days earlier. Montie Bertie and Monica were struck by one another at the
Chesterfield House ball of 1911, and began a romance which Ettie
stopped. It is impossible to divine her objection to Bertie, who was to
inherit two separate earldoms – Abingdon and later Lindsey – and was
shrewd, humorous and personable. 'That rare creature, a man-of-the-
world who had formed his own opinions on most matters and could
express them simply,' Osbert Sitwell judged him. In old age Abingdon
said he had never been happier in his life than staying at Taplow.

Many Edwardians mistrusted brilliance, and were glad if they did
not have any; they mistrusted anything likely to derange their habits or

impede their comfort. But Ettie was dedicated to brilliance. She created a brilliant ambience by inviting expansive minds and scintillating social figures to her house, and she had ambitious but not unreasonable expectations of her children: a lustrous name for Julian, an All Souls fellowship for Billy, a splendid marriage for Monica, and shining futures for young Ivo and little Mogs.

Ettie's most cherished memories of motherhood were when her children were small, gentle, malleable and joyous. While she was having nightmarish passages with Julian and thwarting Monica's suitors, she was still able to preserve the dream of perfection with her two younger children. Ivo, as Ettie's Benjamin, had a special place in her heart, and Willie adored his youngest boy too. He was less of a scholar than his brothers, and passed his days in dreamy abstraction, but everyone found him graceful, charming and sweet-natured. Once, when Ettie asked tiny Imogen, 'You are my daughter, and what is Ivo, my — ?' she replied, 'Sweetheart.'

Ettie loved best the holidays, amateur theatricals and games with her children. She never forgot the Pied Piper tableau which starred Imogen, aged two, as Cupid, dressed in silver wings and pink roses, in a little chariot drawn by two white doves; or the tableau with Julian as a nursery-maid and Billy (by then six feet two inches tall) as a baby in white frock with blue sash and coral necklace. Ettie relished the absurd quirkiness of little children. When the Desboroughs took Vo and Mogs to the Buckingham Palace children's party of 1907, the high point for the two-year-old girl was finding a putrid dead sparrow lying in a flowerbed, and the low point when she was forbidden to kiss it. Mogs proved a nervously imaginative child: at Christmas of 1907 Bron Lucas sent her a lifelike toy tiger which, as she unwrapped it, fell on to the floor, and she screamed for hours. When, some weeks later, she had got used to it, she unluckily tugged a little ring, the tiger emitted a convincing roar and the screaming resumed, though she loved the toy eventually and used to try to milk it.

'Imogen is more fascinating than ever,' wrote a Taplow visitor when she was six, 'and took me to her nursery, and danced with grave earnestness all the delicious dances she knows.' Perhaps such scenes inspired Henry Newbolt's poem, 'Imogen (A Lady of Tender Age)', which Ettie loved:

Saw ye Imogen dancing, dancing,
Imogen dancing all in white?
Laughed she not with a pure delight,
Laughed she not with a joy serene,
Stepped she not with a grace entrancing,
Slenderly girt in silken sheen?

When Ettie took Ivo and Imogen back to Swanage in 1908, Imogen became scared of the sea, and said that the waves were whispering fearful curses at her. She said, 'You will take care of me? cos I'm only about three.' Ettie *so wanted* to take care of them. Nothing felt as elemental or pleasurable to her as the care of a little child. In other ways such a complicated woman, there was a fierce simplicity about her maternal feelings. She felt special joy over the earliest years of her youngest child. For Ettie there was abiding delight in memories of little Mogs in bed with Gollywog, Prayer the monkey, Mrs Tiggywinkle, Mutter and Jutter her two big dolls, Water and Mortar the teddy-bears, or Mogs a few years later saying, 'I do like reading the Bible, there are *such* very naughty people in it.' These were the memories that mattered to Ettie as much as her flirtations, Cabinet ministers and duchesses.

CHAPTER 5

The Edwardian

𝓚

E TTIE WAS A model of Edwardian manners, a quintessential Edwardian, even, perhaps, a great Edwardian. Her Taplow house parties seem a metaphor for the age: glorious gatherings, in gorgeous weather, at which no one was hurried or constrained, but always with the apprehension of the telegraph boy bicycling up with an ominous message in its orange envelope and the expectancy of a black thunderstorm in the evening.

Ettie was the link between many chains of relationships in that *belle époque* between the death of Queen Victoria and the outbreak of world war. She spent countless hours every year on trains travelling – third-class, with her maid Gaston, unless she was accompanying first-class friends – between the country houses whose owners clamoured for her company. She was a requisite presence at the house parties of the great political aristocrats of the age, the Salisburys at Hatfield, the Londonderrys at Wynyard, the Devonshires at Chatsworth, the Derbys at Knowsley, George Curzon at Hackwood. She was beloved by less political magnificos, such as the Portlands and Sutherlands and Westminsters – making a circuit every year 'from Duke to Duke', as a friend said. She was cherished by those stylish American heiresses who had married into great English families, Consuelo Marlborough, Adèle Essex and Eloïse Ancaster, who besought her at Blenheim, Cassiobury and Grimsthorpe.

She was an intimate friend of the leaders of both political parties, Balfour and Asquith, and of their families, and knew too many Cabinet ministers to list: her favourite cousin Bron Lucas was indeed promoted to Asquith's Cabinet. She was the woman closest to England's greatest soldier and to the Bank of England's most suave director. When she journeyed to European capitals, she stayed with the British ambassador; and at home she became a Lady of the Bedchamber to Queen Mary, and watched all the inner workings of the Court. The royal family trusted her, and her fellow courtiers relied on her humorous good sense: Lord Esher said her presence was 'a godsend' at Windsor Castle. Ettie Desborough knew few lawyers and avoided musicians, but she lionised the great authors of the era – Wells, Yeats and Kipling among them – and its actor-managers too. Her eagerness to receive emotional confidences was matched by her reputation for being safe with secrets. Political intrigues, love affairs, inner hopes and private grief – no one knew more of them in Edwardian England than Ettie Desborough, except spies in the German Embassy and blackmailers in the gutter press. Her discretion was inviolate: 'padlock' was one of her favourite words. Lady Desborough knew little of the industrial and commercial classes, and less of the labouring poor; but of the rest, she knew almost everything. The beliefs and plans of the Sovereign, of parliamentarians, high officials, noblemen, authors and idealists – they were all under Ettie's padlock.

Nonchalance was not to Ettie's taste. The stock character of the drawling, blasé man about town, pursuing an unruffled course between his tailor and his clubs, seemed pathetic to her, for she despised passivity and adored intensity. Her mettle was recognised even by that drab doctrinaire Beatrice Webb. 'Great organizing capacity; ought to be the head of a great institution,' Mrs Webb judged Ettie in 1907. 'To outward appearance she is a smart, handsome, cleverish woman. Beneath it she has an iron will, excellent temper and methodical mind, but with neither wit nor reasoning power.' Only one of Ettie's friends, Asquith, felt that she had already forfeited her best hopes. 'She might have been one of the most considerable women of her time, but she made rather a stupid marriage,' he confided to Venetia Stanley. 'Though she loves to please people, she is rather lacking in the best kinds of ambition. Still she is a remarkable person, and has made a great deal of her life.'

For the Edwardian *haute monde* Ettie was indispensable. 'No dinner was complete without her,' said Consuelo Marlborough, 'no one had a choicer circle of friends and admirers . . . and no one entertained more delightfully.' The duchess was notoriously lonely in her life at

Blenheim, and unloved in her marriage: her few satisfied memories of Edwardian England included the ease, amenity and comfort of Taplow in summer, with Willie Desborough punting on the Thames, walks in the woods with an agreeable cavalier, and diverting conversation as Ettie presided over the tea table laid out under the cedars. Tea at Taplow was justly celebrated. Max Beerbohm had an abiding image of Ettie's animated figure deftly pouring tea to brilliant guests arrayed on her lawn. Every summer afternoon, from 5.30 till 7, fresh tea and glass jugs of iced coffee were brought out on huge butler's trays as each batch of friends arrived from the station. There was a walled fruit garden at Taplow, and masses of fruit were served with tea: strawberries or raspberries and cream in the early summer, and later peaches, nectarines, apricots, gooseberries and greengages.

Breakfast was Ettie's favourite meal: it was when she was brightest; and the breakfasts at Taplow were as effervescent as champagne parties elsewhere. She and Evan Charteris were a lively combination, and the quiet of the breakfast room was broken by his barks of laughter. Harold Nicolson's description of the breakfast room in an Edwardian country house conveys the rich variety of the fare. Little spirit lamps warmed rows of large silver dishes with devilled kidneys, whiting and omelette. Hams, tongues, galantines, pressed beef, grouse, pheasant, partridge and ptarmigan would be arranged on a long table. On sideboards lay fruits, jugs of lemonade, porridge, pots of coffee, and of Indian and China tea – the China tea distinguishable by yellow and the Indian by red ribbons. The centre table, with its toast racks, would be bright with Malmaisons. Newspapers were impermissible, for Edwardian breakfasts were leisurely events from which all business duties were excluded. After the hot food, people would sample the cold meats and perhaps allow themselves a slice of melon or a nectarine. Despite these scenes of abundance, many fashionable Edwardian women kept to abstemious regimes. Some men loathed elaborate sauces as much as they would an effeminate footman – Curzon, for example, inveighed against 'costly slushes with incomprehensible names'. The favourite dinner menu of Sir Ian Hamilton, one of Ettie's soldierly retinue, was oysters, clear soup and mince.

Margot Asquith said in 1906 that Ettie was an ox who would be made into Bovril when she died – so formidable was her friend's stamina. Seizing on the metaphor, Julian quipped that his mother must have the constitution of a cartload of oxen to withstand the burden of the London Season. Edith Wharton, whose chief women friends in Edwardian England were Gladys Ripon and Adèle Essex, complained that the great London hostesses regarded the act of fighting one's way through a large and ever-varying throng of guests as the acme of social intercourse. 'Perpetual novelty was sought for, [and] the stream of new faces rushing past me often made me feel as if I were in a railway station rather than a drawing-room.' The rush and confusion made even old hands flag. Mrs Wharton once went for Sunday luncheon at Cassiobury, Lord Essex's place in Hertfordshire, at the close of a Season. There she found, 'scattered on the lawn under the great cedars, the very flower and pinnacle of the London world: Mr Balfour, Lady Desborough, Lady Poynder (now Lady Islington), Lady Wemyss (then Lady Elcho), and John Sargent, Henry James, and many others of that shining galaxy – but one and all so exhausted by the social labours of the last weeks, so talked out with each other and all the world, that beyond benevolent smiles they had little to give.' Meeting them in this depleted mood was, she commented, 'like seeing their garments hung in a row, with nobody inside'.

Ettie remained, as she had been since her first Season in 1885, one of the most brilliantly conspicuous women in Society. Forty years later Mary Elcho's eldest daughter Cynthia wrote her memoirs of the Edwardian swansong, which she sent Ettie for comments before they were published. 'I see', Cynthia Asquith wrote, 'striped awnings, linkmen with flaring torches; powdered, liveried footmen; soaring marble staircases; tiaras, smiling hostesses; azaleas in gilt baskets; white waistcoats, violins, elbows sawing the air, names on pasteboard cards, quails in aspic, *macedoine*, strawberries and cream, tired faces of cloakroom attendants, washed streets in blue dawns, sparrows pecking the empty pavements, my bedroom curtains being drawn apart to let in the late morning light; a breakfast tray approaching my bedside; bandboxes, tissue paper.'

This was Ettie's London. In the 1890s this busy, vertiginous world had sometimes exhausted or disorientated her, but by 1900 she was sufficiently hardened and habituated that it seemed central to her happiness. She thrived, like Lady Roehampton (the character based on her in Vita Sackville-West's novel *The Edwardians*), on 'the pageant of the Season, the full exciting existence in London, the crowds, the colour, the hot streets by day, the cool balconies at night, the flowers filling the rooms and the flower-girls with baskets at the street corners, the endless parties with people streaming in and out of doors and up and down stairs, the display, the luxury, the wealth, the elegance that flattered and satisfied her'.

Margot Asquith, for example, gave a dinner at her Cavendish Square house in 1906. The guests included Count Benckendorff, the Russian Ambassador in London; the Desboroughs; Lord Goschen, a former Chancellor of the Exchequer; Sir John and Lady Dickson-Poynder (later Lord and Lady Islington); the Speaker's wife, Mary Lowther; Linky Cecil; a Mrs Lester; Beatrice Webb; Raymond Asquith; and several smart young men. As Mrs Webb noted, 'The large garish rooms, the flunkeys and superlatively good dinner gave a sort of "Second Empire" setting to the entertainment. Lady Desborough, Margot, Mrs Lester and Lady Dickson-Poynder were all very *décolletée* and highly adorned with jewels. The conversation aimed at brilliancy – Margot sparkling her little disjointed sayings, kindly and indiscreet, Lady Desborough's somewhat artificial grace, Lady Dickson-Poynder's pretty folly, Mrs Lester's *outré* frankness, lending a sort of "staginess" to the talk.' As the women enthused about Shaw's plays, Mrs Webb reflected that they belonged in a comedy of manners *à la* Sheridan.

Ettie seemed factitious to Beatrice Webb, and certainly her agile graces were deliberate and self-aware, but there was nothing spurious about her poise. 'She moved always harmoniously, with the carriage of a woman who has been accustomed to feel all eyes upon her,' in Vita Sackville-West's depiction, 'as upright as an Egyptian who has borne burdens on her head, yet with the stateliness of a woman whose only burden has been a crown . . . Whatever she did, she made her circumstances appear singularly apposite and becoming.'

Under the intensity, theatricality and sensual thrill of Ettie's Edwardian London, there was always a morbid apprehension – even, at times, the semblance of a death wish. 'Wasn't it beautiful,' she asked after watching Queen Victoria's funeral in 1901, 'that triumphal procession and that note of Victory, and the blaze and colour as she passed;

and the quite *silent* crowds, more thrilling than any storm of Jubilee
cheers; wasn't it exactly "the beauty and the joy of living, the beauty
and blessedness of death"?' Ettie was quoting from the preface to
Lyra Heroica, a book of verse for boys (1891) in which the compiler,
W.E. Henley, declared that his selection of poetry about heroism would
'set forth, as only art can, the beauty of the joy of living, the beauty
and blessedness of death, the glory of battle and adventure, the nobility
of devotion – to a cause, an ideal, a passion even – the dignity of
resistance, the sacred quality of patriotism'. These were stirring sentiments, not empty sonorous rhetoric, by which Ettie and her family
lived. Always she fastened on thoughts of Death and of the void. Two
years later she was terribly struck by lines in Yeats's new play, *Where
There is Nothing*: 'Death is the last adventure, the first perfect joy, for at
death the soul comes into possession of itself, & returns to the joy that
made it'; and, 'Remember always, where there is nothing, there is
God.'

Despite her idealisation of death, Ettie reckoned herself as a woman
of beatitudes – a woman possessing supreme blessedness. She wished
her friends 'all sorts of joy & special surprise happiness . . . because it
is the people who really do adore joy who ought to get it'; and it was
this that made her such a captivating hostess, so elated, charming, and
competent, as she diffused joy among her friends. Ettie was *such* a very
good friend, according to the people whose testimony should count for
most. 'I do love you so truly,' Alice Salisbury wrote after a visit to
Panshanger. 'When I came away I nearly *cried* in the train, but I feel
better now when I think what ripping fun those last two days were . . .
It is so nice to have you to write to; it is such a comfort to feel one has
got *one* person whom one can talk to without being afraid of things
repeated.' Her influence and intuitions were pervasive with new friends
too: 'she is *so* magnetic,' Lady Hamilton wrote after a luncheon in 1904.
'She quite fascinated me, and I felt enormously stimulated and cheered
up – she is a woman one must either *love* or hate.' And remeeting her
two years later at the Leo Rothschilds' house, Ascott, Jean Hamilton
was no less enamoured. 'Even across the table her charm penetrated,
and made me happy. I wonder how she does it – she has the power of
changing one's mood and making one at one's best.'

The guests at Taplow seemed to Monica, as a young girl, uniformly brilliant: clever, elegant, unselfconscious, amusing and responsive. There was no place at Taplow for the dour, ill-disposed or pugnacious: when two young men, Alastair Leveson-Gower and Lord Castlerosse, came to blows after a Taplow weekend, it was thought extraordinary. Laughter seemed to ring through all Monica's memories of those Saturday-to-Monday parties, which were emphatically not 'weekend parties' for until the Great War, Saturday morning was part of the working week for ministers, officials, bankers and other men with offices. Monica always pictured her mother playing the Letter Game after dinner, in evening gown and evening gloves, sitting upright, scrutinising the letters through her long-handled tortoiseshell and diamond lorgnette. The hall at Taplow was a central covered courtyard with arched and colonnaded galleries up to the second storey. From their high vantage point Monica, Ivo and Mogs would spy on their parents' guests going arm-in-arm across the hall from the library in to dinner.

Ettie was Grand Panjandrum, caterer-in-chief and confidante of the brilliant children of the Souls who were known as the Coterie. Like their parents, they met at dinners and dances in London, and at Saturday-to-Mondays in select country houses – Taplow, Stanway, Avon Tyrrell above all others. Like their parents, they were playful, teasing, outspoken, flirtatious, and for the most part superbly well-read and discriminating. At their weekends they would read aloud, and have treasure hunts, amateur theatricals, mock debates, poker sessions. They secreted their ideals under a debonair cloak of cynicism, and belonged to a ruling class that seldom doubted its destiny.

'The names of nearly all of them may be forgotten now, though they were so well known then,' Violet Parsons wrote of the Coterie in 1937. 'They had something of the versatility and vigour, and also the fate, of the young Elizabethans, or King Charles's cavaliers. They were the most dazzling of the lost generation who would now, had they lived, be at the head of the country.' A few of the Coterie, such as Duff Cooper, survived the war, but most (Raymond Asquith was the oldest) did not. 'Julian and Billy,' recalled Violet Parsons (whose actor-manager father Herbert Beerbohm Tree was one of Ettie's cult), 'so beautiful each in his way, Julian more aggressive with his face like a glorified prize-fighter and the terrific charm that "got you in a moment", Billy's softer, with a more golden calm. Then Patrick Shaw-Stewart and Charles Lister, Patrick brilliant, white-faced and sharp-tongued, and Edward Horner, the real glory of the lot.'

✍

It was not mere attitudinising when Ettie insisted how much she appreciated the beauty of old trees, and walking in woods. She specially cherished her visits to Avon Tyrrell in the New Forest. Avon Tyrrell had been built in 1891 for Lord Manners on the south-westerly edge of the forest. 'Hoppy' Manners had married Ettie's cousin, Connie Fane, and had two sons, John and Francis, and twin daughters, Betty and Angie. Lord Manners was 'one of the typical figures of English social life before the war', a friend wrote of him in 1927.

> He was pre-eminently sportsman, Churchman, and country gentle-man . . . In private life he was singularly modest and unassuming, so that few people realized how original and unconventional his mind was, nor how sensitive his nature to the appeal of beauty, or to the imaginative side of life. Anything squalid or mean, or what is commonly called 'powerful' in literature, repelled him, and he would quietly ignore it when it was obtruded on the company in which he found himself. He was a most steadfast friend, and invariably loyal to the few whom he admitted to intimacy. His lovely New Forest home, Avon Tyrrell, was indeed Holiday House to many a school-boy and undergraduate, and always seemed full of the golden lads and girls he entertained so generously.

Avon Tyrrell was a fine brick house on a commanding site, from which the ground (as at Panshanger) sloped steeply southwards. It was surrounded by a wild park, with a large enclosed common covered in heather, while inside the wood panelling and marble fireplaces rep-resented the best of the contemporary crafts movement. The Desbor-oughs first visited Avon Tyrrell as a family in April 1906. They were met at Basingstoke station by Bron Lucas who took them, driving himself in a fast open car, on a windswept dash through the forest, and as they came up the steep southern slope at Avon Tyrrell, the white

137

gables of the house seemed to cut the sky like the teeth of a saw. Ettie and her children became devotees of the entire Manners family, and for Monica and Ettie, particularly, Avon Tyrrell was Arcadian. The Manners had one open motor car (the Desboroughs bought their first motor car in 1910), but preferred to go out in a carriage drawn by a superb pair of Lipizzaner horses, with two plum-pudding dogs which ran by the wheels.

The Desboroughs were regular guests of the Londonderrys at Wynyard in County Durham – a palatial house built in the 1820s with the family's colliery revenues. It had a majestic portico on the entrance front, vast reception rooms and opulent decorations: if some visitors savoured its sumptuous amenities, others felt restless under its lifeless ostentation. Charles, 6th Marquess of Londonderry, successively Postmaster General and Lord President of the Council in Balfour's government, hastened his death by drink and did not impress his civil servants. 'The woolly ineptitude that pass for *dicta* in Londonderry's official vocabulary would disgrace a schoolboy,' complained the Clerk of the Privy Council, Sir Almeric FitzRoy. 'In character & capacity Londonderry never reached mediocrity, and his popularity was due to the facile geniality that comes so readily to a man of great portion & large possessions, but is unconnected with any real qualities of heart.'

One of Ettie's fellow guests at Wynyard, the Countess of Fingall, has left a good pen portrait of her host and hostess. 'Lord Londonderry was a great gentleman,' she declared. 'He was not very clever, but did the right thing by instinct, and after all, that is the best way to do it. Lady Londonderry was a wonderful woman, with her masculine brain and warm feminine temperament. The best and staunchest friend in the world, she would back you through thick and thin. In love with Love, she was deeply interested in the love affairs of her friends, and very disappointed if they did not take advantage of the opportunities she put in their way. She used to say of herself: "I am a Pirate. All is fair in Love and War," and woe betide anyone who crossed her in either of these! Like a Queen of France, she had a private understanding with the Almighty as to what people in her position could or could not do!'

In private Lord Londonderry had rebuffed his wife (the niece of Gety Pembroke and Adelaide Brownlow) since she had become pregnant by her brother-in-law Lord Helmsley in 1879, but they were united by strong political ambitions, and in public maintained a façade that must originally have required formidable self-restraint, although in time it became a natural habit. When in London, the Londonderrys provided lavish hospitality: their luncheon table at Londonderry House was 'spread free to all comers – how often & often & how joyously we all profited', as Ettie recalled in 1946. Ettie had a weakness – gently mocked by Arthur Balfour – for being driven about Hyde Park or St James's conspicuously perched, and copiously admired, in other people's smart carriages. It was a special joy to accompany Nellie Londonderry in her smart barouche along Rotten Row and the other carriageways of the park. 'We have had such happy times & talks, & how nice it is to feel a friendship that has lasted many years is still *growing*,' Ettie wrote to the older woman in 1909. 'You know, I think, how intensely I admire you & all your splendid dealing with life. It is so utterly true what I said to you at Wynyard about the *help* you are.'

Ettie's deepest friendship among the Vane-Tempest-Stewarts was with Nellie Londonderry's son, Charley Castlereagh, who succeeded to his father's marquessate in 1915. One summer day around 1904 she sat with him in Millie Sutherland's gardens at Stafford House, and had one of those searching, intense talks that made her feel so alive. He advised her 'never, never to "hark backwards" ' – this proved, she told him over forty years later, 'one of the wisest precepts of my whole life'. They talked of other intimate matters; and Ettie was infuriated when Lady Constance Mackenzie, one of the Sutherland cousins, interrupted their tête-à-tête to show off a snake which she had coiled round her neck. Ettie believed that she and Charley enjoyed an intuitive under-standing: he was the younger by eleven years, and used her as a confidante about his political ambitions and love affairs (he eloped to Paris with Consuelo Marlborough in 1906, and had a lengthy involve-ment with another American heiress, Eloïse, the dark-eyed, determined Countess of Ancaster). In turn, he hastened to her in France, im-mediately after Julian's death in 1915, and was supportive during those anguished days, for he was a sensitive man, who liked and understood women. He had a similar effect on Ettie's life as her children had done when they were small: he made her feel admired, wanted and half-revered.

There was one place where Ettie felt shunned, Cliveden, a few miles upstream from Taplow. In 1906 young Waldorf Astor was given the estate by his father as a present on his marriage to an American divorcée, Nancy Shaw. The young Astors bought the Cowpers' old house, 4 St James's Square, from Bron Lucas two years later. Notoriously, there were – at best – chill contacts between the two chatelaines on the Thames. Their mutual mistrust dated from the period in 1904–5 when John Revelstoke had seemed to chase after Nancy Shaw and even to hint that they might marry. Mrs Astor subsequently convinced herself that Ettie had jealously sabotaged the Revelstoke flirtation, and her sharp tongue antagonised Ettie, who always disliked American brashness and huckstering sanctimony – Adèle Essex and Consuelo Marlborough were fastidious exceptions, though she found the latter's proselytising for birth control and slum clearance rather a joke. Moreover, 4 St James's Square held cherished memories for her, and she may have blanched at the tone that the American woman brought to the old Cowper town house.

The competition between the two hostesses had quickened by 1909. Balfour, Curzon, Milner, Maurice Baring, Hugh Cecil, Evan Charteris, Charley Castlereagh, Albert Grey, Kitchener and other of Ettie's best men became favoured visitors at Cliveden; and such adored women friends as Alice Salisbury, Mabell Airlie, Mary Elcho and Rachel Dudley succumbed to young Nancy Astor's blandishments and became her devotees. The overlap became so pronounced that one wonders if Nancy Astor mischievously set out to net Ettie's dearest friends. For several years the two households boycotted one another. Astor guests at Cliveden were expected to avoid Taplow during the course of their stay, and Desborough guests were likewise expected not to call at Cliveden from Taplow. It was as if, said Billy, there was a 'frontier' between the two houses. The border controls were only raised on command from high officials: on the Sunday after the Coronation in 1911, Nancy Astor was asked to entertain the prime ministers of the Dominions, and other distinguished visitors, together with their families, for luncheon at Cliveden, and the 150 colonialists were then taken by motor car and river launch, in driving rain, for tea with Ettie at Taplow. The order of the Sunday outings was a reminder that while the Desboroughs were well off and Taplow was pretty, the Astors were super-rich and Cliveden was palatial.

Bobbie Shaw, Nancy Astor's son by her first marriage, became the best of friends at Summer Fields of Ivo Grenfell. In the holidays the two boys often visited one another. Nancy Astor was a clever, determined rival, who saw an opportunity to incite disloyalty among Ettie's children as well as among the Taplow faithful. During the summer of 1910, she drew both Julian and Billy into becoming satellites in her orbit. Billy, indeed, during the course of that year, professed to fall 'madly in love' with her — she was eleven years his senior — and sent her scores of bantering, doting letters, which she preserved. The tie between them was so well-acknowledged that when Billy was killed, Alice Salisbury sent condolences to Cliveden as well as to Taplow.

In November 1911 Ettie made the experiment of inviting the Astors for luncheon on a Sunday when she was entertaining Balfour, Tommy Ribblesdale, Edmund Gosse, Adèle Essex, Betty Montgomery, the Elchos and Ian Hamiltons. After luncheon a 'shrieking' Nancy Astor seized Balfour's hand, and demanded if he knew the song 'May I hold this darling little hand?'. As Jean Hamilton noted, 'Mr Balfour laughing looked rather embarrassed. She has a rough harsh voice, and looks like a costermonger's girl. I looked at Ettie, a gracious Princess in her tight velvet gown, and wondered. Nancy Astor has said such vile things of her, saying one would get painter's colic from sitting near her, and that she was angry because she had taken a bald-headed coon [John Revelstoke] away from her, etc., but her high confident spirits are infectious.' It is not surprising that Ettie told Billy that she judged Nancy 'an excellent friend for her children', but avoided her as best she could.

The contest between the Englishwoman of 1867 vintage and the Virginian of 1879 showed the less agreeable possibilities confronting Ettie as she entered middle age. She faced the same dilemma as Vita Sackville-West's Lady Roehampton, who was mobbed in Rotten Row from the age of eighteen and grew languid under the compliments that drenched her for so long. But reaching middle age, with creases replacing the girlish smoothness, the compliments to Sylvia Roehampton, though still profuse, changed their note: 'women said — ingenious women — "No one would believe that your Margaret was eighteen";

and men said – ingenuous men – "None of your young beauties can hold a candle to you"; and even as she absent-mindedly smiled, she winced.'

It was easier to be admired as a beauty than to be congratulated because one was still so beautiful; and Ettie's friends did make invidious comparisons. 'I have been thinking of Ettie Desborough – lovely alluring Ettie,' Jean Hamilton wrote in 1907. 'Two pictures rise before me, the day about eight years ago when she was Queen of Beauty and of the Maypole, all in floating clouds of lavender, at Rose Bingham's Children's Dance at the Botanical Gardens. I can see her now in her shady hat, and the long maypole with mauve ribbons, moving towards me; and I worshipped her beauty; drank it as in a picture for ever to remain, and then last year at Ascot, the softness rather gone, a certain hardness and thickening of the lovely lines of her face – ah me! . . . and she feels it, the iron is in her soul too, her empire is slipping away through her lovely long nervous fingers – she cannot hold it much longer, she can only pretend she does not care.'

There had been phases in the 1890s when Ettie felt almost engulfed by the unstable, piteous and tragic elements of life. By 1907 she had acquired a sense of proportion, some unshakeable, comforting certainties and above all 'the courage not to be discouraged – *ever* – in self or others'. Yet she was afraid of lowering her standards and of losing her impress. The fear of weariness – 'one gets timid in middle-life about the awful pull & stress of the mill-race of living,' she told Mary Elcho in 1907 – was nearly as disagreeable as the horror of ageing: 'I mind spending so many hours with my middle-aged face in front of the looking-glass.' She fought 'the besetting tendencies of middle-life to fix & set & crystallize – in other words to cease to live.' To preserve the intensity and originality of her youth, and to ward off fixed habits and the inertia of routine, Ettie fastened on to 'the mounting joy & hope of the young generation'. She cultivated 'vital friendships' with people of her children's age. Their eagerness invigorated her, and helped preserve her supple reflexes and quick sympathy for other people's feelings and initiatives.

'Getting old is a horrid business, but tempered by the niceness of the hungry generation which so gently treads us down,' she told Balfour in 1913. As Asquith wrote when she was forty-seven, 'her vitality and

vividness of interest both in person & things are in refreshing contrast
to that of many younger people.' And so, she collected boyfriends
like Archie Gordon and Patrick Shaw-Stewart – keen and responsive
youngsters stored with strength and energy. There was nothing desultory or apathetic about them: they never stranded the talk in the
dry wastes of the commonplace. She liked taking them for walks in the
Taplow woods, and uncorking their feelings. She exchanged warming
confidences, and discouraged any simmering down of feelings: she felt
alive with young people precisely because their emotions often seethed.

'I did love my Sunday with you, & our walk together,' Horace
Nevill wrote in 1909. 'You have a key to every padlock, & it is so nice
to feel . . . that I can talk to you freely & confidently on any subject.'
Padlock was her word for a secret confidence, and 'dentist' was her
word for a searching, intimate tête-à-tête. 'It was a wonderful weekend
at Taplow,' 23-year-old Duff Cooper wrote after a dentist with Ettie in
1913. 'What I enjoyed, honestly, more than anything . . . was the too
short conversation I was allowed with you at the end of dinner on
Sunday evening. I hope we may continue it some day.' After a railway
journey with eighteen-year-old Yvo Charteris, Ettie pronounced him
'one of the most delicious talkers . . . I have ever come across, and you
know *how* grateful and delighted one is when it is possible to meet the
beloved young over the gulf of years'.

In Edwardian England it was acceptable for an upper-class young
man to start his career with an attachment to an older married woman.
If the affair was well-managed it was thought beneficial for the boy to
be trained by an older woman who kept him clear from more costly or
degrading entanglements. In 1905, a few months after coming of age,
Algy Malden, Adèle Essex's stepson, eloped with and married the
daughter of a man who kept a horse repository off Fleet Street. Just
after St John Brodrick had succeeded to his father's Midleton title in
1907, and was paying off death duties, his eldest son George – Julian's
contemporary in the Eton push – had to be extricated at some expense
from a comparable mess. 'Of course I was a fool to ever get introduced
to Miss Gates, & it came as an awful shock to Father,' George Brodrick
told Ettie. 'I'm going to pull up now I've got a fresh start, but these last
three weeks . . . things kept slipping out which made me feel an utter
cad.' (He soon relapsed, and later made a disastrous proposal to the

actress Peggy Rush – 'Poor darling, it must be about his fifteenth!' said Ettie.) In 1913, Katie Cowper's nephew Bim Compton had to pay the colossal sum of £50,000 to settle a breach-of-promise action brought by the actress Daisy Markham, star of *Glad Eye*. Bim Compton had succeeded his father as sixth Marquess of Northampton weeks before the settlement, and irritation about the case probably hastened his father's collapse.

Affinities between married women and younger men were open: there could be nothing secret, for that would have suggested contacts that were scandalous or shameful. So everyone knew that a promising young politician, Lord Percy, was in love with Ettie's friend Millie Sutherland, that the young Taplow regular Lord Vernon was the *cavaliere servente* of Norah Lindsay, that Julian was smitten by Pamela Lytton, and Billy by Nancy Astor – already jealously cherished by young Lord Winterton. (Years later Ettie gushed about the eldest Astor son to Nancy, 'I am more in love with Bill than with any man in England, he is exactly the fashionable age for me!')

Archie Gordon became Ettie's beloved friend in 1904. He was then aged twenty, the third son of Lord Aberdeen, a former Viceroy of Ireland and Governor-General of Canada, and great-grandson of the Aberdeen who had been Prime Minister during the Crimean War. There was some eccentricity among the Gordons, but Archie was a clear-headed Scot set on material success. After Oxford, he went to Berlin to work for the Dresdner Bank, and in 1908 he joined the London office of the Canadian financier Jimmy Dunn. By then, Archie and Ettie were stars in each other's firmament. 'The truth of my love & trust for you is the truest thing that I have known,' he declared; and on another occasion: 'My beloved E., I can't begin to speak of all the joy of seeing you, & seeing you *often* & *much* . . . I have the whole universe waiting to be talked about, & all my life to be submitted to you.'

For her part Ettie found their friendship so ideal because Archie was – in soul, heart, mind and body – so brimful of life. Her older friends liked him, and both Billy and Monica were devoted to him, though Julian, one senses, was upset by his mother's involvement with a boy who was only four years his senior. 'He always held the deep conviction that all that happened was for the best,' Billy said of Archie. 'Even the commonest facts of life had an enduring glamour for him, so intense was his joy of living.' Archie's conversation was everything that Taplow expected: 'full of a dancing kind of humour and quaint little jets and spurts of laughter, charming rather by its felicity than its fluency, since he would often hang becalmed, as it were, in mid-sentence.'

In August 1906 Archie's eldest brother, Lord Haddo, at the age of twenty-seven, horrified his family by marrying a Sheffield draper's widow who was old enough to be his mother. A week later Archie's devotion to Ettie suddenly became controversial. Violet Asquith, the Chancellor of the Exchequer's nineteen-year-old daughter, had a reciprocated *tendresse* for Archie. They had agreed to go together to a party given by Frances Horner, but Ettie persuaded Archie to take her to a play instead, and to chuck the party. Normally she upheld Balfour's rule never to break an engagement for something more tempting, and this proved a fatal deviation from her practice. Archie shirked explaining his arrangement with Ettie to Violet; and next morning, when Mrs Horner telephoned her in a rage, the young girl discovered the truth and felt lacerated at having been lied to. Her reproaches drove Archie into a paroxysm of anguished remorse: his letters to Violet suggest someone on the verge of a breakdown. Her stepmother Margot, her brother Raymond, Adèle Essex, Louise Sassoon all made mischievous, hurtful remarks about Ettie and Archie, and the young girl felt shocked, betrayed and humiliated. 'I am being made perfectly miserable by things those who love me think it right to tell me,' she told Archie on 19 August. 'The whole world seems to have taken this opportunity to strip me of every shred of illusion I ever had about anybody. Hoodwinking is *kindness* if this is the truth.'

Ettie meanwhile had attempted her own explanations. 'My very dear Violet,' she wrote on 17 August, 'I want to write to you really from my heart, & I can only do it knowing that you will do as I ask & not tell Margot, Raymond, Archie or anyone.' She protested that she '*always* meant *you* to know the real truth . . . because to me too it is the greatest thing in the world, & under all tiny white lies & little things that don't matter . . . it is just the one rock that stands & that all living worth the counting is lived by'. Ettie felt anguished that Violet 'had heard a story that seemed full of little mean lies & petty treachery . . . but it gave me worse pain to think of the mischief that had been made about Archie, & to see his despair – when one knew . . . his utter, utter trueness & loyalty to his friendship with you'. It was intolerable to realise that she had made such mischief in a 'precious friendship' which she had 'watched from afar with such happiness & reverence. The mischief with Frances, about which I have been utterly sick, is *nothing* near all that – & you don't know how sad I've been. But you will know now, & believe that there never was one fact or aspect of fact concerning me I could have minded you knowing – & we may hurry the imbroglio deep away.'

After reading this letter, Violet dreaded meeting Ettie, though her confidence in Archie was restored. 'Why should I be thrust into situations whose complexity bewilders me, & out of which there seems no way which doesn't involve disloyalty to & disbelief & suspicion & *méfiance* of somebody? This incident has been for me a flash of the most squalid enlightenment.' The situation was exacerbated by her rash, disruptive stepmother. 'There has been any amount of fuss between Ettie and Margot over Archie Gordon,' Mary Elcho reported to Balfour on 12 September. Margot had 'worked herself into insanity' at the thought of Ettie teaching Archie to tell lies, and seemed set on a quarrel with her old friend. 'Ettie instead of, as usual, being plausible, without joint in her harness, is humble, frightened and apologetic and has on more than one occasion been reduced to tears! She and Violet have had scenes. It's very interesting and Ettie must care a good deal surely?'

Ettie was appalled by this flare-up of passion rather than elated, as she might have been fifteen years earlier. When she had been younger, the admirers whom she collected and toyed with – Evan Charteris, John Revelstoke, Ivor Wimborne – had been treated as the vassals of an exciting but volatile feudal power. She had been able to control them because they thought they needed her. But by 1906 the power was more equally apportioned. Ettie (verging on forty) needed her Archie Gordons too much: she recruited and rewarded them as a corps of faithful young squires, and did not want sudden crises disturbing the stability of her influence.

Violet and Ettie were reconciled by their shared distress when Archie went as an ADC to Dublin Castle, the headquarters of his father Lord Aberdeen, who had been reappointed as Viceroy of Ireland. As Ettie wrote to her 'darlingest Vivi' in May 1907, 'I am thinking so much of Archie, & his going, & of you, & of all that you & I share, & of all that you possess.' By summer the two women's friendship was intense. 'You don't know the joy it is', Ettie wrote in August, 'to find a new perfect friend. *Bless you* my very dear, first of all for just being yourself, then for your perfectness to me, then for all the flood of interest you and yours have poured into my life.'

ʕ

Willie had attended the inaugural Olympic Games at Athens in 1896 as one of the British referees. The Olympic ideals chimed perfectly with his incorruptible passion for good faith and fairness. He subsequently became a member of the International Olympic Committee (by virtue of his presidency of the Epée Club and of the Royal Life Saving Society), and chairman of the British Olympic Council. He cut a splendid figure in the movement: Arthur Conan Doyle, who was active in the Olympic organisation, said that his character Lord John Roxton in *The Lost World* was 'a composite photograph' of Willie and Sir George Taubman Goldie, the buccaneering founder of Nigeria. Further Olympic Games were held at Paris in 1900, and at St Louis in 1904, but after the withdrawal of Rome as host of the projected 1908 Olympics, Willie in November 1906 announced the decision to hold them in London. An Olympic stadium costing almost £70,000 (nearly £5 million in 2008 values) was erected in the grounds of the Franco-British Exhibition at Shepherd's Bush, and Willie made a public appeal, which raised £10,000 (over £700,000 in 2008), to enable the British Olympic Committee to provide gold, silver and bronze medals, and hospitality for the entrants. Willie presided over a series of banquets at the Holborn Restaurant welcoming foreign contestants, and with Ettie held a reception on 11 July 1908 at the Grafton Galleries in Bond Street for officials and athletes.

The stadium was formally opened by Edward VII on 13 July. 'There is no one living more fitting to open . . . the fourth Olympiad than King Edward the Peacemaker,' declared *The Times*. It was a powerful impetus to 'the world's peace that 19 of the world's most civilized states should meet in the friendly rivalry of the simplest and cleanest form of sport'. Despite rain turning the route to the stadium into a sea of liquid mud, the opening ceremony was a dramatic spectacle. The King and

Queen were welcomed by Willie Desborough and Baron Pierre de Coubertin, and Ettie helped to entertain the Crown Princes and Crown Princesses of both Greece and Sweden, while over 2,000 male and female contestants paraded before the royal box in bright costumes and bearing national flags.

The stadium competitions had been preceded, since April, by racquets, tennis, polo and shooting tournaments held in Kensington, Hurlingham, Wimbledon and Bisley. Ticket sales for the stadium events disappointed Desborough and his English committee, but during a fortnight's competition there the Olympic ideal was largely upheld: the French, for example, who won only a few medals, were graceful in their unexpected defeats. A ridge of acrimony was, however, injected by the US team. They began with an unsuccessful challenge to the eligibility of Thomas Longboat, a Canadian Indian, to run in the Games, but the umpires accepted Longboat's amateur status. Then, in the 400 metres, the American J.C. Carpenter was disqualified for jostling his English rival, Halswell. The other American runners refused to participate in a rerun of the race and Halswell won by default. He was hailed for exemplifying, in contrast to the Americans, 'the real public school spirit', which meant trying one's utmost without excessive pride or egotistical gratification. Character-building was indeed at the forefront of this first English Olympiad. 'Many excellent people', reported *The Times*, 'look down upon athletic sports, on the ground that they are too individualistic and apt to breed selfishness and to encourage a taste for merely ostentatious display of physical prowess.' Desborough expected the Games to prove otherwise.

The climax of the Shepherd's Bush phase of the Olympiad was the Marathon run on Friday, 24 July – over a distance of nearly twenty-seven miles (forty-two kilometres) – on a route from Windsor Castle via Eton, Slough, Uxbridge, Pinner, Willesden and Wormwood Scrubs to the stadium at Shepherd's Bush. The start was preceded by a luncheon given by the Mayor of Windsor at Layton's Restaurant in the town for Olympic dignitaries including Willie Desborough, who had been selected as the Marathon's referee. Despite the amateur nature of the Games, there was visible sponsorship. The Oxo Company had been appointed as official caterers to the Marathon, and supplied their product gratis to competitors: flasks containing hot or cold Oxo, together with Oxo and soda, rice puddings, raisins and bananas – with stimulants available in cases of collapse. Collapses there certainly were: most famously of Pietri Dorando, a dapper, moustachioed little Italian confectioner who was front runner at the close of the Marathon. As he neared the finishing-line, he started tottering with exhaustion and all but collapsed. His distress was so pitiable that a well-meaning steward came to his rescue and guiding him by the arm, helped him to stumble through the finishing tape. Because of this intervention, Desborough was obliged to disqualify Dorando and awarded first prize to an American called J.J. Hayes. But that evening, as the Olympic Council gave a ball for 700 competitors in the Holborn Restaurant, pressure was building to give Dorando a consolation prize. He had lost the race, but won the sympathies of the English crowd.

On 26 July there was a long ceremony in which a trio of great ladies, Katherine, Duchess of Westminster, Ettie's bugbear Violet Rutland and (which must have made a frostily polite atmosphere) Ettie distributed respectively the bronze, silver and commemorative medals in each sporting category. Afterwards Queen Alexandra began her presentations to the outright winners. Suddenly, as Willie Desborough was handing the medals and cups to her, there was an outcry of 'Dorando' from the spectators and the Italian emerged – no longer broken and disorientated, but gloriously reinvigorated – from the competitors' stand. In the royal box Willie gave the Queen, and the Queen bestowed on Pietri Dorando, a valuable cup.

At the close of July there was an Olympic rowing regatta at Henley. The Desboroughs, with Ivo, Monica and Bron Lucas, watched at Henley on 31 July as the Leander Club beat the Belgians in the final, and attended a dinner given that night by Arthur Balfour at White City, where they did every 'stunt' until 11 p.m. Next day they returned to the Thames for a banquet, with illuminations, which was held at Bourne End to honour Willie and the regatta contestants. Afterwards hundreds of lit-up craft glided to and fro on the river.

✻

In November 1909 came catastrophe. On the last Sunday of the month Archie Gordon set forth in his new Daimler Silver Knight motor car to visit the Dickson-Poynders in Wiltshire. At an awkward crossroads he swerved to avoid a collision with a Renault landaulette, his car over-turned and he was trapped underneath. Rescuers took him, in agony from abdominal injuries, by horse-drawn carriage to hospital in Winchester. 'He longs all day to see Violet & me,' Ettie reported a few days later to Monica, who was in Berlin, 'but the doctors (so wisely & rightly) forbid his seeing *anyone* but his mother, & she only very, very little, as the danger of fever is so fearful.'

She felt sufficiently optimistic to go north to Chatsworth for the annual pre-Christmas house party given by the Devonshires. Her next letter, on 15 December, was scrawled in pencil on a train speeding south. 'The news of Archie was very good up to last evening, but in the night sudden symptoms of heart-failure alarmed them very much,' she warned Monica. 'Lady Aberdeen wired to me to come instantly, I *just* caught the first train, & am now on the long journey to him, but I do not think he will be alive.' She continued with the Christian resignation and insistent gratitude that she always produced in times of grief. 'We must not hold too clamorously to keeping Archie here, or feel with too much anguish that his bright spirit should leave us for a little while. His radiance is *ours*, & all his goodness & happiness & love cannot die to us. I do not want any of us who he loved ever to have a dark thought of sadness about him, it seems as if it might almost hurt & confuse *him*, in whatever land he may be.' She had no doubt of an afterlife and felt certain that the dead watched over the living. These were the thoughts that Ettie reiterated to herself as her train whistled through the wintry Midlands.

Ettie reached Winchester in mid-evening. On this last night, as Archie lay dying, some of the nursing staff assembled in the corridor outside his open door and sang 'Abide with me' – he understood the soothing message. Later, when Lady Aberdeen whispered to him, 'My Benjamin, who never brought anything but joy to his mother', his face lit up with a brilliant smile; but he was slipping towards death. Ettie stayed by his side with the Aberdeens and Violet, who had just agreed to marry him. 'We had a long talk, his voice was weak, but quite clear,' she told Balfour. 'I never saw him so happy. We all stayed with him all through the night. He wandered a little after 12, & became unconscious at 3, & the end was very quiet. It is difficult to describe the beauty of his face after then – he had grown very, very thin, so that all the lines were quite fine & clear, & the beauty of the brow & eyes seemed instinct with happiness.' She longed, she insisted to Balfour, 'that those who loved him should only think of it with thankfulness & joy, it would have hurt him so to bring *sadness* to life – he who always brought laughter & love.'

The coffin – covered with a pall of rich cream Irish poplin with a woven cross of gold – was taken from Winchester to London on a special train. Ettie went to Haddo, with the Aberdeens, for the funeral: the coffin was carried through the snow on a fine clear day to its grave. 'I know how wonderful your love for him was,' Billy told his mother, '& God knows he loved you more than anything in life or beyond. It must be happy for you to think that you never failed or disappointed him once.'

✒

Edwardian England was a royal time for Ettie. As a young woman she had known the Ponsonbys, the most influential Court family under Queen Victoria – its children resented the amount of their father's attention that was engrossed by the old monarch. But the bright young hostess at Taplow had little in common with the old Widow of Windsor, and it was not until the new reign that she was melded into the background of the Sovereign's pleasures. All the Grenfells, except Ivo, went to London for Edward VII's Coronation on 9 August 1902. They stayed in St James's Square and set forth at six in the morning for Westminster Abbey. Julian was Kitchener's page, and wore a steel-blue velvet coat with scarlet collar-band, white satin waistcoat and breeches, a sword, shoes with scarlet heels and gold buckles, and ruffles made of his great-grandmother's lace. Lord Cowper looked 'ineffably distinguished' during the Coronation, thought Violet Cecil, 'the only peer . . . able to carry off a coronet'.

Ettie told George V's biographer that she never liked Edward VII and had bored him beyond belief. She was, no doubt, too intense, too literary and too chaste for his earthy Hanoverian appetites. She enjoyed watching him, though, with his mistress Alice Keppel. Like others who were *au courant*, she used the nickname 'La Favorita' for Mrs Keppel, and devised her own soubriquet, 'Kinkie', for King Edward. In 1904 she went to Sunderland House – Consuelo Marlborough's newly built house, with marble reception rooms and thirty-six bedrooms, which brought the aesthetics of Newport, Rhode Island, to Curzon Street – for a dinner given by the Vanderbilt duchess for the King and attended by the Keppels. 'As usual,' Ettie told Balfour, 'the most fearful gaffes & "insinuendoes" were made in front of the miserable George Keppel!'

The situation was not easy for either of the Keppels. ' "La Favorita" behaved with great indiscretion, for there is a self-consciousness about her which emphasises the *equivoque* of the situation,' Sir Almeric FitzRoy observed during a visit by the King and the Keppels to Wynyard. 'She retains great beauty, but her carriage suggests an uneven blend of pride and humiliation.' Alice Keppel esteemed Ettie's brains and influence. 'Lady Desborough', she declared, 'is the cleverest woman in London.' On one occasion she scribbled an absurd letter to Ettie asking her to promote her ideas for fiscal reform with Balfour. She wanted him to target the luxuries of the rich by placing a levy of £1 per ton on pleasure yachts, £25 a year on each racehorse, and commensurate taxes on champagne, golfballs and cartridges. 'A three shilling (or more) tax per hundred cartridges would bring in a lot', or so she had been assured 'by a clever man, who is also a great shot!!'

After King Edward died in 1910, Alice Keppel begged Ettie to visit her. '*Do* come, & soon, I feel as if my life has come to a full stop . . . You are so clever, I should like to talk to you.' In time, the Keppels moved to Bellosguardo, near Florence, and there Ettie visited them during her occasional Italian holidays. When, nearly forty years after Edward VII's demise, Mrs Keppel died, her family asked Ettie to write an obituary for *The Times*. Like Ettie's other tributes to dead women friends, it says what she would have most liked said of herself: 'Alice Keppel was one of the most vivid of beings, no one can ever have enjoyed life more, or provided greater enjoyment for those who surrounded her . . . I never heard her say an unkind word, and yet how amusing she was; a living example of wit without spite, and of taking the world as it came.'

Back in the 1870s Princess Mary Adelaide of Teck, moved by the plight of motherless children, invited Ettie and Johnnie Fane, with their Gore cousins, to White Lodge in Richmond Park, where she welcomed them with a big dish of sugar plums. At White Lodge Ettie used to play with the duchess's daughter May, who was a month her senior and sometimes came to Portman Square for a children's tea party. Twenty years later May married Prince George, Duke of York who became Prince of Wales in 1901 and King George V in 1910. She recruited the eldest of the Gore sisters, Mabell Airlie, as a Lady of the Bedchamber on becoming Princess of Wales; and after her husband's accession to the throne, determined to increase her retinue again. Ettie liked to idealise situations, she enjoyed ceremony and spectacle, and her upbringing had instilled her with a deep sense of duty. This made a good recipe for a faithful courtier, and on 2 January 1911 her old childhood playfellow, Queen Mary, appointed her, Lady Minto and Lady Ampthill as three Extra Ladies of the Bedchamber.

Mary Minto had returned to England only a few months earlier, after her husband's retirement as Viceroy of India. She was the sister of Ettie's early beau Albert Grey, and had known her for a quarter of a century – indeed, had been her hostess during Ettie's boring visit to Canada in 1899. Mary Minto, as Ettie described in an unsigned tribute in *The Times* after her death, shared her brother's enthusiasm, simplicity and openness, although her marriage made her a grand Borders lady and as Vicereine she had been consummately regal. Lady Ampthill's husband had been interim Viceroy of India before Minto's appointment. The two Ampthills were conscientious servants of Empire, but unbending, conventional and monotonous in spirit.

John Revelstoke, who was the new King's most trusted friend outside the Royal Household, may have played a part in Ettie's appointment. Julian thought it absurd of his mother to become a Lady of the Bedchamber. 'It really is too disgusting for words,' he teased her from his military barracks in India; 'one looks upon all those sort of things as dead and gone, like "Chop off her head", or as only belonging to pantomime.'

Ettie's knack for amusing King George had been noticeable when he was Prince of Wales. In 1904, for example, she had been bidden to a dinner given by Consuelo Marlborough for the Waleses. One of the other guests was Gladys Deacon, the Duke's half-mad American girlfriend and future wife, who had been a Paris beauty until a gruesomely unsuccessful effort at cosmetic surgery. The Prince, Ettie told Balfour, 'looked nearly as bored as I felt at a horrible & hideous American girl who called herself by a French name & shrieked French songs at us after dinner, with a twang like a banjo. After enduring this for long, he said helplessly, "Can't she sing a coon-song?" ' Ettie with her shining undertone of happiness helped the new King to relax: he made quips to her which he would never have tried with Lady Ampthill. A few months after her Court appointment, in April 1911, the King and Queen visited Taplow with their sons. In a memorable moment of *lèse-majesté*, the young Princes climbed to the gallery of the covered real tennis court, armed with tennis balls, which they pounded down on their father as hard as they could. The Taplow experience was very different from the stock impression given by Max Beerbohm's 'Ballade Tragique' in which two courtiers disputed about the ennui of their duties:

> SHE: The Queen is duller than the King.
> HE: O no, the King is duller than the Queen.

Ettie received a salary as lady-in-waiting, which scarcely covered her expenses, and enjoyed the privilege of being taken to and from Buckingham Palace, during her waiting periods there, in a two-horse brougham: mere Women of the Bedchamber had to travel in one-horse broughams. Queen Mary's Ladies of the Bedchamber were apportioned pleasant rooms in the palace – in contrast to Queen Victoria's, who had been expected to sleep in rooms the size of cupboards. Ettie came to know the palace as an insider rather than as a guest. It is an odd building, noted Queen Mary's biographer, with its vast throne room, its ballroom, red-carpeted stairways, numerous dining rooms, long galleries displaying the royal art collection – these public rooms hugger-mugger with narrow passageways, nests of small sitting rooms and bedrooms, and cramped landings.

Ettie had hesitated at becoming a Lady of the Bedchamber, for she anticipated that calls might be made on her time that would disrupt her all-important roles as mother and hostess. The periods of waiting were divided into fortnights and apportioned by the Mistress of the Robes – traditionally a duchess and, in Ettie's time, the Duchess of Devonshire ('Evie'), a chill woman with an excessively commanding manner. Her fears were realised when – following a withdrawal by Lady Ampthill – Ettie was asked to accompany the Queen to the Coronation Durbar to be held in Delhi in December 1911. This promised to be a momentous occasion – George V was the first English monarch to visit the East since Richard the Lionheart – but although Ettie had adored her visit to India twenty years earlier, when Constance Wenlock had saved her from deadly restless despair, she declined and offered her resignation from Court. 'The Queen', replied her longest-serving lady-in-waiting, a tiny, plain-looking but vivacious woman called Lady Eva Dugdale, 'would be very sorry to lose you, & as this is rather an exceptional case, Lady Ampthill having to give up so unexpectedly at the last moment, Her Majesty *hopes* that you will try it for a little longer.'

It was settled that when Queen Mary returned to England in February 1912, Ettie would go straight into Waiting. This she did, although the royal return was marred by the death of King George's brother-in-law, the Duke of Fife. Ettie, Margaret Ampthill and Mary Minto were in attendance for the Queen's arrival at Buckingham Palace, wearing a sombre expression and Court mourning. Next day the great Thanksgiving Service for the King's return held in St Paul's Cathedral looked more like a state funeral than a public rejoicing, for everyone was swathed in black. Ettie's childhood misfortunes, when her grandmothers had dressed her in mourning clothes for years, gave her a lifelong distaste for black: yet the Court was often in mourning. In 1911, just before the Coronation, the Court went into mourning for the King's uncle, Prince Johann of Denmark, and in 1912 for a second uncle, King Frederick VII of Denmark, and in 1913 for a third uncle, King George I of Greece, who was murdered while walking in the streets of Salonica. It was the most uncongenial aspect of Court life for Ettie, though she tried to be sympathetic each time the Court was plunged into a funereal mood. 'We are very quiet & peaceful in these Royal Circles,' she wrote to Balfour from Windsor Castle after the King of Greece's assassination, '& of course sunk in crape as usual (I've never yet been in Waiting out of black clothes!). I think they've both been very sad over this last catastrophe.'

With the exception of the Indian durbar, it was impossible for Ettie to evade the royal command. 'Isn't it *Hades* about staying on here,' she wrote from Windsor Castle to Willie on one occasion, 'but there was simply nothing to be done – the K. & Q. both begged me to.' She was pleased, though, to accompany Queen Mary to Paris as her lady-in-waiting during the state visit to France in April 1914. As the *Alexandra* (flying the royal standard) followed its escort of warships out of harbour, a roll of guns sounded from Dover Castle and the King saluted from an upper deck. Overhead, with stirring notes of modernity, a seaplane, two aircraft and an airship circled in a clear sky. The royal yacht was met in mid-Channel by two French cruisers, six destroyers and – again an incongruous modern note – submarine and torpedo-boat flotillas. For the first time on such an occasion an aeroplane swooped and turned above the *Alexandra* so that a photographer could take films for cinema newsreels.

In Paris, escorted by a guard of magnificent cuirassiers, the royal party, which included Ettie's cousin Lord Shaftesbury (who was Queen Mary's Lord Chamberlain), drove in open carriages through the sunlit boulevards, with their flowering horse-chestnut and lilac trees. The King and President Poincaré went first in the *calèche présidentielle*, drawn by four black horses, followed by the Queen and Madame Poincaré in a state carriage, which had once been Empress Eugénie's. In the first of seven carriages, drawn by high-stepping and highly groomed horses, Ettie sat with Evie Devonshire and a spruce French general. If she loved being admired in Nellie Londonderry's spanking equipage in Rotten Row, how much more so in the triumphal cavalcade of the King-Emperor as it passed the whooping and cheering crowds in the Champs-Elysées.

The state visit was a triumph for the Entente Cordiale. Even King George, who loathed foreign travel and claimed to be baffled by foreigners (he could speak neither French nor German), enjoyed himself. Ettie was enraptured by the brilliant spectacle and enthusiastic crowds.

Ettie Desborough, reluctantly covered in black crape, and keeping the King amused, provides one standard image. But she was also glimpsed, dressed in apple green (a favourite shade), at a dinner of Margot Asquith's in 1905, 'beguiling fat Chesterton for all she was worth' and telling Mary Elcho afterwards that his exuberance was irresistibly appealing. G.K. Chesterton had published his acclaimed first novel, *The Napoleon of Notting Hill*, a year earlier, at the age of thirty, and

Ettie was quick to take him up. She invited him to her Taplow party after the Eton-and-Harrow cricket match of June 1905. He made one fast friendship there, with George Wyndham, who like him idealised a golden chivalric past and preferred troubadours and crusaders to manufacturers and economists.

Ettie initiated Chesterton into English high life, for George Wyndham's wife Sibell Grosvenor (the mother of Bendor Westminster) was at Taplow too, and the Portlands, the Duke of Sutherland, the Edgar Vincents, Mary Elcho with Arthur Balfour, Nellie Londonderry and Austen Chamberlain – a heady mix for a clumsy and unkempt penny-a-liner who was the son of a West Kensington auctioneer. Chesterton liked Taplow, and the Taplow faithful liked him: he joined with gusto in charades and party games. He remained a grateful occasional visitor, although deadlines and other commitments sometimes obliged him to decline her invitations. She attended his funeral in 1936.

Chesterton's politics were a rollicking brand of Catholic reaction, but on other occasions Ettie fell among progressive intellectuals. Beatrice Webb lured Ettie to a luncheon in 1907. She once proudly said that all the good in the world had been achieved by either priests or prigs, and that her husband Sidney was the champion prig of all. Her decision to pair him with Ettie for the meal was not a success. As she recalled, 'when I placed the handsome but metallic Lady Desborough beside him at a luncheon at our house, he remarked afterwards that he thought her "unpleasing with her artificial and insincere talk and silly trick of shutting her eyes at you".' The other guests included Arthur Balfour's plodding but well-intentioned brother Gerald, and his livelier wife Betty, who had been Ettie's bridesmaid, together with a young Liberal MP, Charles Masterman, later appointed to Asquith's Cabinet. George Bernard Shaw, whose plays Ettie much enjoyed, and Bertrand Russell were there with their wives; but Mrs Webb's great catch was Fridtjof Nansen, the Norwegian athlete, Arctic explorer and oceanographer. When Norway achieved political independence from Sweden in 1906, Nansen had been selected as its first diplomatic envoy in London, and he was moving towards his great humanitarian work for famine relief and refugees, which was ultimately recognised by the award of the Nobel Peace Prize. Mrs Webb was delighted by her party's successful 'mixture of opinions, classes, interests – all as jolly as jolly could be, a rapid rush of talk'.

Beatrice Webb was less gratified by the result of her other intro-duction, in 1907, of H.G. Wells to the country house set as represented by the Elchos at Stanway and the Desboroughs at Taplow: 'the British aristocracy at its best', she called them. Two years later, offended by Wells's energetic new career as an adulterer, she blamed his lapses from lower-middle-class virtue on the smart ladies before whom she had paraded him as an oracle. 'Exactly when the tide turned towards evil I do not know,' she wrote in 1909. 'Unwittingly I did H.G. a bad turn when I introduced him to the Elcho–Balfour–Desborough set. That whetted his social ambition and upset his growing bourgeois morality.' Wells began to fancy himself as a latter-day Goethe ex-perimenting with a life of sensations, she thought, 'revolted against the puritanism of the leading Fabians and was more and more attracted by the charm and glamour of smart society. We heard of him at the Sassoons, and at Taplow Court, dining with duchesses and lunching with countesses. I imagine he let himself go, pretty considerably, with women.'

When young, Wells had lived in a great house where his mother was a lady's maid, and the Desboroughs' initial welcome intoxicated him – Oliver Wendell Holmes called him 'a pet with the ladies who frequent Taplow'. But 1909 marked the apogee of his Desborough susceptibility. Perhaps Wells detected Ettie's changing view of his work. She had enthused at his novels *Love and Mr Lewisham* and *Tono-Bungay* – 'arrow-true' she thought them – but recoiled from the 'nauseous' explicitness in *Ann Veronica* (1909). 'The love-making of Ann Veronica & Capes is outside the framework of civilized literature,' she told Edward Horner. 'The utter lack of the sense of what can be written down & what can't – of what is too ugly.' Julian agreed with her that Wells's *New Machiavelli* (1911) pandered to the lower passions, and thought *The Passionate Friends* (1913), though subtle and clever, was laughable in its descriptions of country house parties à la Taplow. Certainly it was hostile to Ettie's notions of the ideal in love: 'people of our race and quality', says the upper-class narrator, 'are a little ashamed of mere gratification in love. Always we seem in my memory to have been with flushed cheeks, and discussing interminably – *situation.*' In

1922, writing *The Secret Places of the Heart*, Wells made Taplow the scene for a breakdown of manners and ideals. An urbane and disciplined man of power, Sir Richmond Hardy, loses his immaculately veneered self-control when his sports car breaks down on a road near Taplow Court. Hardy smashes up his vehicle in a rage of pent-up frustration. The pie crust of civilisation, Wells seems to say, was especially thin over the seething lava of repressed feeling at Taplow.

Since 1891 Ettie had lionised that most punctilious of Edwardian actor-managers, Sir Herbert Beerbohm Tree. Tree was a domineering talker who frowned at interruptions and bristled if he was teased. He had a high sense of his own importance and considered himself 'a baronet in the sight of God', said his spry, mischievous half-brother Max Beerbohm, who was a later and more docile Taplow recruit. The Incomparable Max rewarded Ettie by writing a story, 'Hilary Maltby and Stephen Braxton', in which she figures as the Duchess of Hertfordshire and Taplow as Keeb Hall. Beerbohm had appreciated his inclusion in the lists of Ettie's guests published in newspapers, and the Keeb guest lists were equally 'august and inspiring' in his tale of comical hallucinations. 'Statecraft and Diplomacy were well threaded there with mere Lineage and mere Beauty, with Royalty sometimes, with mere Wealth never, with privileged Genius now and then.' Beerbohm's character Maltby, a fashionable novelist, describes his first meeting with the Duchess: 'She seemed very intelligent. We got on very well. Presently she asked whether I should think her *very* bold if she said how *perfectly* divine she thought my book. I said something about doing my best, and asked with animation if she had read "A Faun on the Cotswolds". She had. She said it was *too* wonderful, she said it was *too* great. If she hadn't been a Duchess, I might have thought her slightly hysterical.' Maltby's subsequent journey to Keeb is a good description of Ettie's faithful collecting at Paddington Station, in the Desboroughs' reserved carriage on the 5.05 train, for their short journey to Taplow: the tall, the ornate, the glossy, the intimately acquainted with one another, filling the compartment; and when they alight at the little railway station, with two broughams waiting aside, and a landau and a phaeton, and dog carts and a luggage wagon.

The poetry of W.B. Yeats had been delighting Ettie for twenty years. His depiction of death as a joyous adventure went to the heart of her feelings; and around 1910–11 she was able to enlist him, for a time, as one of her guests. Billy, calling at the London house rented by the Desboroughs for the 1911 Season, was gladdened by the sight of Yeats's cloak and sombrero hanging in the outer hall. Alfred Lyttelton's widow Didi remembered him at Taplow as well. 'His hair was rather long and it seemed very grand and black, and to have a life of its own,' she recalled. 'It swayed when he spoke but often in a different rhythm from his speech, as if it were impatient of its owner's words. Then there were his eyes, burning with vehemence, smouldering with a deeper emotion than he was expressing, and finally a general sense that he did not belong to the life of London, or of England, or indeed perhaps to the life of the Earth itself.' There was a singular intensity, in both Yeats and Ettie, for delving into human souls, but Yeats liked his social context to be other-worldly, ethereal, even mystical. The Taplow regulars must have seemed too materialistic, too organised, with too many collective rites and too much private slang. Ettie tried to bewitch Yeats, but could not hold him.

Another poet gave longer-term satisfaction. 'Monica and I had a most delightful three days last week with Violet Cecil in Sussex,' she reported in August 1913 to Balfour, '& saw a great deal of Rudyard Kipling, and went to a ball at his house, an unexpected experience. How very ugly and black and hairy he is! But I minded his voice most, though now & then one did get slight verification of all that one knew must lie behind.' Having met Britain's first Nobel Prize winner for literature, she lured him and his wife to a Taplow house party in November 1913. 'Mr Kipling won everybody's heart, and *acted* most wonderfully,' Ettie said (there were charades). The comforts of Taplow seemed somehow different to him from the political effeteness and moral softness – the 'playgrounds of pleasure and leisure' – against which he had lately railed in his poem 'City of Brass', and in after years Kipling was to be a recurrent guest of Ettie's.

Ettie's love of poetry was not limited to the great lions. She used to go, incognito, 'to hear poets read aloud in the squalid loft over the Poetry Bookshop'. This bookshop opened in Bloomsbury in 1913 and was famed for its hand-coloured rhyme sheets for children. Robert Frost stayed there on a visit to London, and its private press published Richard Aldington's early poems and Ezra Pound's path-breaking anthology *Des Imagistes*. It says much for the range of Ettie's literary interests that she sneaked into the avant-garde Poetry Bookshop and knew five Nobel literary laureates: Shaw and Russell slightly; and three others rather better, Yeats, Kipling and, supremely, Churchill.

⋉

Winston Churchill became a Taplow habitué after returning from the Boer War. For a Sunday party there in June 1901 Ettie collected the Asquiths, Cranbornes, Vincents, Elchos, Balfour, Violet Cecil and her crush Alfred Milner, George Wyndham, and Churchill. Thereafter he became one of the steadiest of her irregulars, if not quite one of the faithful. He arrived late for Ettie's first big Friday-to-Monday party for Eton boys at Taplow in April 1904, while the other guests were out on the river, and having strolled through the woods to join them, he was flung into the Thames, where he swam composedly in his greatcoat, spats and top hat. Churchill shared in other high-spirited Desborough entertainments: after lunching with them in March 1907, he joined their outing to the Regent's Park Zoo, where Imogen was bitten by an antelope.

He and Ettie often met in the houses of mutual friends. Staying with the Leo Rothschilds at Ascott in 1906, Jean Hamilton watched Ettie work her spell on Winston. 'Ettie Desborough is an interesting study, she went for her long walk with Winston Churchill today. She probably has added him to her list now – what a menagerie she has. She is fascinating, and weird . . . After dinner she was talking of Maeterlinck's "La Princesse" and her wonderful power over men. I feel sure her power was that of Ettie Desborough (perhaps the magnetic charm of fearless flattery?) . . . Sidonie the sorceress she is, the charming of Winston is a large sprig of laurel for her wreath.'

After losing his Manchester constituency in a by-election in 1908, Churchill felt depressed, but revived after reaching Taplow two days later. 'This morning', he wrote after a night with the Desboroughs, 'I am again buoyant, and refreshed by a . . . cheery Sunday here.' Ettie had organised a house party for the Guards' races at Hawthorn Hill, and there was another boisterous water fight on the river, when Winston again fell in. In the evening Ettie organised charades, and won universal plaudits for writhing and twisting across a parquet floor, dressed in red velvet, as she simulated being a dragon's tail. 'Being with you *always* means happiness for me – with or without water-fights, hockey, friends, bumble puppy, charades,' wrote Violet Asquith. 'I'm afraid it must have been an exhausting party for you, but you were gloriously undefeated to the end, & never for one instant allowed *desoeuvres* [do-nothings] or stragglers.'

Ettie always relished Churchill's joy of life, shameless egotism and lovable self-mockery. As she described to Balfour on another occasion, 'Winston leads general conversation on the hearth-rug, solely addressing himself in the looking-glass – a sympathetic & enthusiastic audience. He has been *quite* splendid. They were talking last night of nicknames. Someone asked Winston if he'd ever had one: "No, except 'that young beast Churchill'."' In August 1908 Churchill announced his engagement to the Taplow household. 'Dearest Winston, we were all thrilled with excitement & delight over your telegram (so dear of you to send it),' Ettie responded. 'None can be more delighted than your many devotees in this family!' She sent him – 'with realms of hope, faith, love & blessings' – a copy of Boigne's memoirs, first recommended to her by Lord Rosebery. Clementine Hozier, Churchill's fiancée, she liked from the outset.

Ettie was an alert spectator at the wedding at St Margaret's, Westminster in September 1908. 'Winston was *so* pleased at your giving him a present,' Ettie told Balfour.

The Church was so full that Bron & I could hear nothing & only see . . . Pamela Lytton, who looked very nasty, & damnably pretty! Winston was radiantly happy, but his feet quite firm on the ground, I thought. She looked rather illuminated, & *very* beautiful. He was delighted with everything, counted every head in the crowd, & showed me all his presents one by one, & opened all the books to show the pictures. George West [Churchill's stepfather] cried in Church. All the Dundee belles [Churchill's women constituents] would stand on the seats & were pulled down by the skirts by the verger whenever the prayers began. There were two photographers, with large cameras, in Church! The Cabinet didn't bulk very well in attendance, but Lloyd George was marched round & round, like the army in the Pantomime. Altogether it was a huge success, & Linky

[Cecil] as best man, in a waistcoat of duck's egg green, was the beauty of the day.

To the groom she wrote, 'It was a delight to me to be with you yesterday, & to have anything so happy to remember and anyone so beautiful as your wife looked! I longed to tell her how we, all your "Old Guard" of friends, rejoice in your good fortune and happiness, but didn't quite like to.' As a married man Churchill had less of the Taplow high jinks: there were no more water fights.

*

Churchill had crossed the floor from the Unionists to the Liberals and sat in Asquith's Cabinet, whereas Willie had left the Liberals for the Unionists and supported Balfour loyally. In 1904 he was converted to Protectionism, became a zealous supporter of Joseph Chamberlain's campaign for tariff reform and joined the Tariff Commission. In August that year the Desboroughs were among the Portlands' guests when Chamberlain addressed a meeting of 10,000 agriculturalists on the subject of tariff reform in the great riding school at Welbeck. Ettie was on the platform, and impressed that despite a violent storm, Chamberlain's voice could be heard ringing out over the thunder across the expanse of the riding school. Also on the platform was the bombastic Earl of Lonsdale, who had a streak of the fantasist about him and a desperate need to impress. He arranged that during the speech-making he was handed a series of telegrams purporting to come from the Emperor of Germany, the Emperor of Japan and other crowned heads. These grandiloquent impostures were duly read out by Lons-dale, and excited the 10,000 agriculturalists though not, probably, the platform speakers who knew him too well. Fiscal policy meant little to Ettie, although in 1908 she was inveigled into accepting the presidency of the South Buckinghamshire branch of the Women's Tariff Reform Association.

The horseplay of English politics degenerated into a street-corner brawl after Lloyd George's budget of 1909 provoked a constitutional crisis between the Liberal-dominated House of Commons, which voted it through, and the Unionist-dominated House of Lords, which voted it out. The Souls' belief that political grudges should not contaminate social life became a persecuted creed. To Ettie's dismay, there were flurries and boycotts even among the Taplow faithful. After Prince Arthur, Duke of Connaught, resigned as High Commissioner at Malta and Commander-in-Chief in the Mediterranean, Asquith's government offered the post to Kitchener, who refused because he wanted the Indian viceroyalty. When, in June 1910, the viceroyalty was given instead to a Taplow irregular, Sir Charles Hardinge, Kitchener became incensed with Sir Ian Hamilton for having undermined his reputation for indispensability by accepting the Malta posting. Conservatives like Nellie Londonderry, who had wanted Connaught's resignation to create problems for Asquith, were equally angry with Hamilton for rescuing the Liberal government from its predicament. Hamilton and his highly strung wife Jean were put under a social ban.

Ettie was incapable of, and perhaps initially oblivious to, this vindictive ill temper spurting into social life, and invited the Hamiltons to a Saturday-to-Monday at Taplow in July 1910. As Jean Hamilton described, 'Ettie, just as she left my party the other night, said the Duchess of Sutherland had thrown her over, and she wanted a perfectly delicious woman to come, take her place and amuse her senators – wouldn't I come? I said I'd love to.' The senators proved to be Balfour, Curzon, Milner and John Revelstoke; and the other guests to include Nellie Londonderry, the Edgar Vincents, Lord Basil Blackwood, Reggie Lister, Winston Churchill's mother Jennie Cornwallis-West, Evan Charteris and Patrick Shaw-Stewart. As a group they ostracised the newly appointed High Commissioner and his wife. 'I would not have believed it possible, with so many intimate friends here, one could feel so out of it,' Jean Hamilton wrote. 'I feel as if I had the plague – everyone flies at my approach and all conversation immediately stops . . . All those people are so political and are furious with Ian . . . It has been terribly depressing, and very depressing to Ian too – there is no doubt we have been utter failures. We are both in disgrace because of Malta. I wonder very much that Ettie wanted to have us – she can't have realised how strongly the Conservatives feel about this.' Mrs Cornwallis-West also felt shunned and said bitterly to General Hamilton, 'You have to be damned nippy in this party not to be left out.'

The constitutional crisis over the House of Lords veto aroused tremendous bitterness. Ettie favoured Balfour, not Asquith, whom she began to nickname 'Old Licky', because of what he did to his lips; and at dinner with the Asquiths in November 1910, shortly before the second general election of that year, she was pleased to find him 'agitated and nervous'. She was again staying with the Portlands at Welbeck when the election results came in: they proved enough of a vindication for Old Licky to disappoint her. Balfour was 'marvellously calm' in the House of Commons in July 1911, when Asquith's announcement that he would ask the King to create sufficient new Liberal peers to pass the Budget provoked a bullying Conservative pandemonium, which Ettie watched from the peers' gallery. 'It was very horrid,' she reported to Mary Elcho, '& made me wretched to see our people give the "beau role" to the Liberals. Elizabeth Asquith's horrid hot arms were round my neck most of the time, & Margot hissing in my ear, "How I *pity* Arthur, having to lead a party made up of eunuchs like Linky & cads like F.E. Smith." '

Balfour, usually the most equable of politicians, was incensed by the perfidy, as he saw it, of the King's (Liberal) Private Secretary, Lord Knollys. 'My dear Ettie,' he replied when she asked whom he would like to meet at the next Taplow Saturday-to-Monday, 'I should enjoy meeting any man in England, except Lord Knollys: him I will not meet.' The political equanimity of the old Souls was juddered almost to pieces at this time. 'Of course we can never meet George Curzon or St John Brodrick again,' George Wyndham wrote to his wife Sibell Grosvenor after the passing of the Parliament Act in August. 'We are finished with the cosmopolitan press – and the American duchesses and the Saturday to Mondays at Taplow – and all the degrading shams. When the King wants loyal men, he will find us ready to die for him.'

Balfour's position as party leader was sapped by this prolonged crisis. 'I don't want you to learn from any lips – or pens – but mine that I intend to resign the leadership within a few days,' he wrote to Ettie on 3 November. 'Only a few people know: and I am most anxious that the matter shall not be talked about . . . please therefore keep a distant silence.' She replied next day: 'how touched I am at your finding time and thought to tell me this – in the midst of the extra burdens of life it must entail . . . I have had a sinking presentiment ever since we last met that you meant to do something of the kind! & of course you *must* be right . . . but I do feel very miserable.'

✍

In November 1910 Ettie took Monica to Paris to buy her coming-out clothes, though her daughter was a large girl who may have felt discouraged that she could never look as good in Paris frocks or long gowns as her mother. On 14 January 1911 Ettie held a ball for about 250 people at Taplow to mark Monica's début. Monica wore a silver-and-white Paris frock, with a green wreath in her hair, and a long Renaissance necklace of pearls and emeralds given to her by Katie Cowper. The county families of Buckinghamshire – the Lincolnshires from Daws Hill, the Bostons from Hedsor, the Grenfells from Butler's Court and Astors from Cliveden – all brought over parties of guests. For the Season of 1911 the Desboroughs rented Mansfield House, the Manners' spacious and imposing house in New Cavendish Street, where Ettie planned to hold Monica's coming-out ball. This had to be cancelled, however, after the invitations had been posted, because Willie's mother died on 2 February aged eighty-four, and the family went into mourning. Monica's launch suffered from this ill-timed death.

Girls of her generation could play golf, ride, or go on the river with their brothers' friends, if they were in the country, but had to submit to strict chaperonage in London. They could not cross the street alone, go shopping, travel in a taxi or take a journey without an accompanying maid. Even two or three girls could not go about together or travel without a maid or married friend. Indeed, when Monica was a nurse in France in 1914–16, seeing terrible sights and tending men's wounded bodies, Ettie still insisted that she did not travel alone and ensured that men like John Revelstoke were available to chaperone her on her cross-Channel journeys. There were other strict customs and inter-dictions. If a young man proposed and was refused by a girl, the couple were not meant to meet again. Mothers vetoed their daughters' dancing partners, and forbade dancing too often with same partner. Young people waltzed and waltzed, but only in one direction if royalty were present: reversing direction during a waltz was considered 'fast'.

For many years the Desboroughs spent each Whitsun at Hackwood with George Curzon. Ettie won the tennis tournament there in 1911 – the year in which Curzon determined to mark the Desboroughs' forthcoming silver wedding anniversary by organising a subscription to buy a present and fund a banquet for the seventy subscribers. His helpmate in this was Adèle Essex; but Ettie was aghast at the idea of the pair 'touting' for donations, and worried that the Taplow servants and tenants would feel impelled to copy their example. Moreover, Curzon's guest lists sometimes gave offence by their omissions, and Ettie felt his subscription dinner scheme smacked of eightieth birthday celebrations for a provincial alderman or a testimonial dinner for a retiring jockey. It seemed invidious to be singled out when so many other friends had married in or around 1887: Con Manners, Alice Salisbury, Elizabeth Kenmare, Betty Balfour, Winnie Portland and Alice Derby. Ettie appealed to both Balfour and Adèle Essex to stop Curzon. 'I wish I could make you realize how *eagerly* and *delightedly* . . . we all feel about Taplow & you & Willie,' Adèle Essex replied. 'The word went round to a little circle of friends who were longing to do something . . . do try & see only our great wish to offer you a small tribute to yr delicious hospitality and the many happy days you have given us.' Curzon's subscription dinner was abandoned and the Desboroughs celebrated their silver wedding on 17 February 1912 as they wished. They were photographed for *Tatler*; Sargent drew a sketch each of Willie and Ettie; and the ninety subscribers mustered by Curzon and Lady Essex paid for wrought-iron garden gates at Taplow, a fountain and a sundial.

Kitchener, who had been appointed British Agent and Consul General in Egypt following his failure to obtain the Indian viceroyalty, invited the Desboroughs to visit him there. They left England on 5 February 1913, with Monica, travelling by train to Italy and by steamer from Brindisi to Alexandria. In Cairo they found Alice Salisbury, and her daughters Mima and Moucher Cecil, already staying with Kitchener. 'I can't say *how* kind K. is, or how boundlessly funny & amusing,' Ettie said. The pro-consul gave a ball for Monica and Moucher which was 'the success of the century' – his expression was a 'mingling of ferocity, despair, triumph & infantile delight' – and a week later held a garden party for 2,000 guests. 'We have now seen nearly all the native Ministers, Princes, Grand Viziers etc., & one begins gradually to get a glimmering *guess* at the strange intricacy & complexity of the inner workings of affairs here, all the wells of intrigue by which K. is surrounded,' Ettie reported to Katie Cowper, who was wintering with her brother Willie Northampton and nephew Bim Compton at their Villa Graziella on Cap Ferrat.

Willie Desborough departed for the West Nile to hunt hippopotami and giraffes, while Ettie returned with Monica to England, which they reached on 18 March 1913. She went straight into Waiting at Windsor Castle, where a series of telegrams from Willie Northampton arrived to warn her that Katie Cowper was ill with bronchitis and that her heart was failing. Ettie decided to rush to Cap Ferrat and, with the help of her maid Rose Gaston, was throwing clothes into a travelling bag when another telegram brought the news that Katie had died. 'Too many thoughts crowd into one's heart, the stabbing one that we shall never see her again, her beautiful sad face, & that the last link with one's childhood & all the love & interest she poured out on us all is gone for ever,' she wrote to Willie away on the White Nile. 'I feel utterly forlorn & *lost* without you, & so utterly incapable of coping with all the arrangements alone, & missing you so at every turn of the way. How you lift all the weight of life off me!'

Lady Cowper's body was returned from Cap Ferrat to Panshanger, where it lay until her burial on 3 April. It was a bright spring day, and the woods between Panshanger and Hertingfordbury church were full of wild flowers as the coffin and mourners – fashionable friends and Hertfordshire tenants – passed through them. The funeral was 'unbearably sad', as Billy described. The mourners 'looked like malevolent birds of prey in our black habits', but the dark formality was alleviated by lighter touches, 'the simplicity of the white pall, and the farm wagon and horses, and all the evanescent loveliness of the sunshine and shadow over the park, and the wild flowers in the wood, and the wreathed flowers on her coffin'. The mourning seemed to Billy simple and sincere, barely post-feudal in its loyalties and sense of place, and hardly belonging in the modern world of airships, the Poetry Bookshop and the Post-Impressionists whom Julian had eagerly discussed with Ettie. 'Funerals are generally such hollow mockeries, but in her case there was no one in all that great crowd who had not really loved her, and whose heart was not filled with loss. The real grief of the village people was infinitely touching, one felt how much they had belonged to her.' Billy, like Julian and his mother, was a devout believer. 'The prayers in the Burial Service, expressing nothing but joy at the deliverance, which sometimes sound so false over the young and eager, had, one felt, a real meaning then, and expressed her own strong faith. What a glorious statement of Immortality in the Chapter of the Epistle. Her death has strengthened one's belief in it more than anything. She seemed too great and noble and vital to be put out like a candle.'

The strain on Ettie, and her bearing at the funeral, brought many commiserations. 'I must write to ease my heart, which is haunted by your little sad swollen face,' insisted Norah Lindsay, 'it makes us all so unhappy to see your radiance overshadowed, and so many of us yesterday felt a pang of wretchedness at your ill, white and tragic face.' She would always prize the memory of this trip 'to say goodbye to Katie in her wonderful home . . . the last earthly walk thro' the park, and bright spring sunshine'. From Buckingham Palace came the admiring thanks of a fellow courtier. 'You certainly gave us all a fine example this last week when, in spite of all you have been going through (& well we all knew it), you put your own feelings aside and made everything go so smoothly & happily at Windsor. I shall not forget that in a hurry, for it made a great impression on me.'

Under Francis Cowper's will, Ettie inherited Panshanger (which she abbreviated and pronounced Pppnnns), with its surrounding land stretching from Hertingfordbury in the east to Welwyn in the west and to the north Tewin Water (which he leased and then sold to the South African millionaire, Sir Otto Beit). The house's contents came to her, too, including the paintings amassed in the eighteenth century by the third earl, a virtuoso who had spent much of his life in Italy.

Panshanger had been rebuilt around 1806 in a pleasant but undistinguished neo-Gothic style. It was a low house of grey-rendered brick, 350 feet long, with battlements, turrets and bay windows. The interior had been remodelled in the 1850s in an Italianate style with a profusion of columns, a fine staircase and spacious rooms with somewhat heavy wood carvings. Its future concerned both the elder Desborough sons. Julian asked from South Africa how she was going to divide her time between Pans and Tap. 'Are you going to cleave to the one, and leave the other? I can so understand all the ghosts that Panshanger must hold for you.' He suspected it would be hard to maintain two large houses: indeed (given Lloyd George's taxes) that big houses were a thing of the past. 'I do hope', Billy urged, 'that you will give your *marvellous* vitality and joy of life a real chance after this stress.' He suggested selling a dozen Italian paintings so as to reinvigorate the family fortunes. 'Now that we have a chance, do let us put our domestic economy on an easier footing. I don't mind which it is, but I feel it would be a bad compromise, even for the Duke of Westminster, to live both at Taplow and Panshanger; for it would be a constant adverse struggle, and a fatal addition to all you already have to do.'

The Desboroughs and their younger children spent August and September 1913 at Pans. They had a succession of visitors: great men like Balfour and Milner; financiers like Leo Rothschild and John Revelstoke; middle-aged admirers like Evan Charteris; army officers like Oswald FitzGerald and Ronald Storrs; and young blades like Patrick Shaw-Stewart, Desmond FitzGerald, George Monckton, Jack Althorp and Ivan Hay. 'We are settled here,' she wrote to Balfour, 'just picnicking for a few weeks.' The house had been in suspended animation since Francis Cowper's death eight years earlier, and Ettie resolved to set up a 'Panshanger Fund' to safeguard its future. She promised George Curzon to give the National Gallery first refusal of any picture that she sold, although the nine full-length portraits known as the Panshanger Van Dycks, which Bron Lucas had inherited, had been loaned by him to the National Gallery.

There were two Raphaels of the Madonna and Child hanging in the picture gallery at Pans, and Uncle Francis's solicitor had in 1900 told Bernard Berenson, who was scouting to buy them on behalf of an American collector, that they were entailed and could not be sold unless the family could prove 'crying distress'. Ettie decided to endow the Panshanger Fund by selling the small Cowper Madonna through Duveen Brothers, the corsairs of the international art world who at this time were acquiring the art booty of Europe to sell to American millionaires, but she declined their offer for the larger picture. 'You have given me such valuable help & sympathy about all our problems here,' she forewarned Balfour on 10 September, 'that I want to tell you at once that we have today received a definite offer for the *small* Raphael

"Madonna & Child" at £70,000' (the equivalent of £4,600,000 in 2008). She was reluctant to begin the Desborough era at Pans 'by selling a picture, but I hope it will be our first & last Sale, & that the income of this sum will just make the difference to us of being able gradually to get this place into good order, & to live here part of each year, which we undoubtedly *could not* otherwise have done'. The smaller Cowper Raphael was soon hanging in the Philadelphia mansion of Paul Widener, who had made his fortune building trolley-car systems.

That autumn Ettie set in train a programme of works at Panshanger. She had long shivered in the Labradorean cold of the house so a central-heating system was installed throughout. New bathrooms were made, the drains and roof redone, electric bells wired, and five lawn tennis courts and one hard court laid out. The new bathrooms were not the spacious, sybaritic affairs, with walls and floors of imported marble, labyrinthine tubes and taps and uncosted abundance of oils and soaps, such as Consuelo Marlborough had required in Sunderland House. They were expedient insertions into the fabric of the old house, and Ettie never in her life did anything regardless of expense. 'In places like Hatfield and Belvoir and Panshanger,' wrote Helen D'Abernon, 'all the bath-rooms are after-thoughts and only by sacrificing dressing rooms and exercising ingenuity has it been possible to introduce them at all.'

These costly improvements impressed the county, and were seen as a declaration of the Desboroughs' commitment to Hertfordshire. Accordingly, when Hildred Carlile, the MP for St Albans, announced that he would not stand at the next election, the Conservatives in the constituency asked Julian to succeed him as their candidate. To Ettie's chagrin, for she longed to have Julian out of the army and back in her orbit in England, Julian replied that he was too absorbed in his soldiering to take up politics. The works at Panshanger were completed in 1914, and the house was let for the summer to Almeric Paget who, having made a fortune in the USA as a real estate developer of St Paul and railway director, had returned to England seeking a political career and a peerage. The Desboroughs intended to return to Pans in October for six months, and had invited King George and Queen Mary for pheasant shooting in December.

171

While Ettie worked hard to preserve Panshanger, Willie was striving to save the Empire. In 1913 he became President of the newly formed Imperial Air Fleet Committee, a body set on publicising the need for the aerial defence of Britain and on providing aircraft to protect its imperial territories. Willie wanted to ensure the absolute superiority of the British Empire in the skies as well as on the seas. In this work he was inspired by the achievements of one of Ettie's younger Taplow faithful, Gustav Hamel. Hamel was between Julian and Billy in age, and the son of one of Edward VII's physicians. At the age of twenty-one, in 1910, he learnt flying at Blériot's air school, and in May 1911 he flew from his friend Claude Grahame-White's aerodrome at Hendon to Farnborough, and back, at a height of 4,000 feet, carrying military despatches, to demonstrate the utility of aviation to War Office observers. He reached further fame in September 1911 when he flew the twenty-one miles between Hendon and Windsor in ten minutes to deliver the first sack of airmail letters to the Postmaster General. Hamel was a handsome, golden-haired daredevil who dashed in his racing car through the night when he was not performing heroic daytime aerial deeds. He charmed women and enjoyed their company. Ettie's friend the Countess of Dudley looped the loop with him, and Duff Cooper's sister took two piglets aloft to prove that pigs could fly. Ettie and Monica were enchanted by him, and made him a favoured Taplow guest.

Willie Desborough appreciated Hamel all the more when the youngster took him up in a monoplane and, when its engine failed, piloted to safety with consummate skill. Willie shared in the general fear of Hohenzollern Germany as the most efficient power in the world, the nation best equipped by modern science, best served by ruthless business methods, and best organised for swift action. In 1911 he was at the forefront of opposition to the Declaration of London whereby Asquith's government, hoping to salvage some ideals from the débâcle of the Hague Peace Conference, renounced the seizure in wartime of enemy goods carried on neutral ships. Willie was convinced, as were many others, that the Naval Prize Bill would hobble close blockade of Germany, and his campaigning contributed to the bill's rejection by the House of Lords. He was equally alert to the need for what he called an aerial navy. It was to publicise the strategic importance of aviation that his Imperial Air Fleet Committee sponsored Hamel in his most striking achievement: in April 1913, in the monoplane *Britannia*, he flew from Dover to Cologne in four and a quarter hours.

Everyone at Taplow was bitten by the flying bug. Monica was taken up for her first flight, with Claude Grahame-White, who had been a junior boy with Bron Lucas at Bedford Grammar School; and Ettie with difficulty kept her resolve not to go aloft. During the summer of 1913 the Desborough family attended the Hendon Aerial Derby in which aviators raced around the outskirts of London, and of which Hamel was the victor. Hamel was taken for lunch at Windsor Castle, looped the loop fourteen times, and took Winston Churchill aloft in a machine: afterwards the First Lord of the Admiralty enrolled for lessons at the Central Flying School.

Hamel was among the guests at Ettie's Taplow party – with fancy dress, cotillion and charades – on 2 January 1914. 'I don't remember a finer Taplow,' Patrick Shaw-Stewart wrote afterwards. Duff Cooper, too, 'enjoyed this Taplow more than any other Taplow,' he said. 'Everyone seemed at their best and highest.' On 19 January came what proved to be the final Taplow ball. An allure of marriageable girls were staying in the house: the Duchess of Leeds's daughter Moira Osborne, Elizabeth Kenmare's daughter Dorothy Browne, Adèle Essex's daughter Iris Capell, Winnie Portland's Vera Bentinck, Alice Derby's Victoria Stanley. Ettie also collected a promise of heirs: the heirs to three dukedoms, the Portlands' son Sonnie Titchfield, Leinster's brother Desmond FitzGerald, and Argyll's nephew, Niall Campbell; heirs to three earldoms, Harry Lascelles, Jack Althorp and Eric Ednam; heirs to lesser peerages, and presentable younger sons. 'Isn't it nice', asked the Leeds' twelve-year-old son Jack Carmarthen, 'to think of our Moira mingling with the flower of England's nobility?' Yet the ball was not unparalleled joy for uninitiated guests. George Curzon brought his eldest daughter, Irene, for her first ever ball, and forty years later she still remembered the chill loneliness of her relegation that night: 'I knew no-one, and was indescribably miserable.'

۶

Ettie went to Constantinople for a fortnight in March 1914 to stay with the British Ambassador, Sir Louis Mallet, a slightly built, distinguished-looking, fidgety gourmet and amateur of the arts, a bachelor with many close women friends, a weakness for Pekinese dogs and rare bindings, and a faithful manservant Leonard Carter who looked after him and his guests with unobtrusive devotion. Ettie travelled to Turkey with one of her favourite of the Coterie, Charles Lister, Tommy Ribblesdale's surviving son, an Oxford boon companion of Julian's and now a diplomat *en poste* in Constantinople. He was a young man after Ettie's heart, as she wrote: 'great draughts of laughter and sunshine, generous love taken and given, fine scholarship, a devotion to sport both passionate and inherited, and ecstatic delight in reading the books he cared for. But, like many an unwearied lover of life on earth, he set little apparent store by its long continuance; he was a traveller by his deepest instincts.'

She and Lister stopped in Vienna, and were joined there by Helen Vincent. In the 1890s Helen Vincent had lived in Constantinople, where her husband had been a wily Governor of the Imperial Ottoman Bank. When its headquarters was seized by Armenians in 1896 in the world's first act of modern international terrorism, he escaped over the Constantinople roofs supposedly with documents worth half a million pounds secreted in his pocket; and he certainly amassed such a fortune that on returning to England in 1897 he had bought Foley House in Portland Place (later the site of the BBC's headquarters) and employed the architects of the Ritz Hotel to build him a sumptuous house at Esher. 'Balzac', he once told Ettie, 'knew nothing of life – mere caricature.' Jean Hamilton regarded him as 'a sort of Olympian God who thinks himself entitled to have his fun where he likes'.

Ettie and Helen Vincent were met at Constantinople station by Mallet and Maurice Baring, who had been a war correspondent in the recent Balkans war and was staying in expectation of more trouble. An affable unmarried cousin of Archie Gordon's called Lord Stanmore was also staying at the Embassy, and proved so companionable that he was a regular ingredient in Ettie's later travel plans to France, Italy and Spain. 'You *would* so adore it all – the fairy beauty, & the sun, & the fun!' she wrote to Monica after settling into the Embassy. 'My head spins with all we've seen & done.' The Embassy was perched at the top of a high hill, and Ettie's windows looked down towards the Golden Horn with the St Sofia mosque in the middle distance beyond. 'Louis Mallet has been a perfect angel, & our comfort & luxury & spoiltness are beyond telling – certainly MEN are the people to stay with,' she assured Monica. 'Tonight he has a Ball for the Grand Vizier & all the most exciting of the Young Turk party – Talaat Bey (called "The Tiger"), Jemal Pasha, & Enver – the young very good-looking soldier who is now War Minister.' That afternoon she and Helen Vincent went to a seraglio party at the palace ('our clothes are *quite* all right I think'), and Mallet had arranged an expedition into Asia on the following day.

Ettie remet the Taplow irregular who later fictionalised her as 'Sylvia Roehampton', Vita Sackville-West, newly married to a young attaché at the Embassy, Harold Nicolson. Two years earlier Vita had attended one of Ettie's fancy dress balls: Julian had danced lots with her, had taken her in to supper, and helped her enjoy herself. Ettie had felt qualms about this odd-looking girl, but now, she told Monica, 'Vita is *charming*, so *pretty* & so clean! & quite tidy, & not a bit a prig or a bore, & married to a *very* nice man!'

Constantinople, in early 1914, was a cockpit of international intrigue. Turkey had been trounced by the Balkan League in the war of 1912, the Young Turk revolution had ousted the old regime, and following the second Balkan war of 1913, Turkey had ceded nearly all its European territory. Armaments dealers, concession hunters and financial adventurers were clustering in the capital. British munitions companies contracted to build a naval arsenal at the Golden Horn just as a German general with a corps of sixty officers arrived in Constantinople to re-equip the army. The plots, corruption and brutality were, however, imperceptible to Ettie. For her Constantinople was 'such fun, & every hour so crowded that I feel we've been here years instead of days. You cannot imagine the beauty of the blossom, the whole town full of it, & the fairy cupolas & minarets rising out of it like out of a mist – pink peach-blossom & white plum-blossom – so lovely when you get it against the blue sea.'

On 23 May, Hamel's monoplane fell into the English Channel as he was flying from France. He vanished, and evidently drowned, but for several days his fate caused feverish speculation. Londoners crowded around newspaper boys selling special editions put out to feed the excitement, while Duff Cooper wrote an elegy which was published in *The Times*. It is not great poetry, but its verses capture the Taplow faithful's mood after his death:

The winds of heaven were his charioteers,
He led the cohort of the sky, and dared
The elements, and the rebellious air
Knew him for long her master, and his ears
Heard thunderous melodies, and gladly heard.
He knew the roads of heaven like a bird,
And like a bird he fell, and no one knew where.

Hamel's death was to seem a prefigurative pledge of a million other deaths to come.

The English summer of 1914 was a joy for a sun-worshipper like Ettie. She and Willie went to stay near Canterbury with Milner in early June, held water parties on the Thames at Taplow later that month, and a garden party for delegates to the Imperial Chambers of Commerce's conference. After the Eton-and-Harrow match there was a big Sunday party at Taplow on 21 June attended by Balfour, Kitchener, Revelstoke, the Portlands, Sutherlands, Salisburys and others. As the political situation in his kingdom seemed so unsettled, King George had resolved to make a series of provincial tours of industrial and mining districts. In June 1914 he and Queen Mary descended on the Portlands at Welbeck Abbey from where they inspected the factories of Nottingham and coal mines of Derbyshire. Ettie and Willie were included among the Welbeck guests on 24–26 June. Only very rich men like the Duke of Portland could accommodate the royal suite on such visits, for the King and Queen were accompanied by one lord-in-waiting, one lady-in-waiting, one private secretary, two equerries, two dressers, five valets, two footmen, one lady-in-waiting's maid, two chauffeurs, two cleaners, one motor groom, one hired man from the Daimler Company, a police superintendent, the Court Postmaster and two clerks. These three days at Welbeck proved to be Ettie's last experience of the Old Order in all its magnificently armoured confidence.

The Desboroughs returned to Taplow, where on 27 June Kitchener arrived for a Saturday-to-Monday. Monday's newspapers brought the news that Archduke Franz Ferdinand, heir to the Austro-Hungarian imperial crown, together with his morganatic wife the Duchess of

Hohenberg, had been murdered in Sarajevo by a member of a Serb-trained irredentist faction called the Black Hand. In the next weeks the Austrians prepared their retaliation, for they determined to use the assassination as the pretext for a declaration of war on Serbia. On 23 July Vienna's forty-eight-hour ultimatum was presented at Belgrade. Ettie had arranged for her last Saturday-to-Monday party of the summer to begin two days later. Irish recalcitrance was the absorbing topic among her guests, for Sunday, 26 July brought news of a riot in Dublin, in which soldiers opened fire and killed three of their assailants. Murmurs about the European crisis had however already reached the Eton boys, for on Monday, when Ettie took Imogen to see Ivo at school, he questioned his mother eagerly about Serbia's refusal to submit to Austrian demands and the mobilisation of Germany and Russia. It was a sweltering hot day, and they all felt oppressed until Ettie bought ices at Layton's restaurant.

Austria declared war on Serbia next day (28 July) and bombarded Belgrade. 'God grant that we may not have a European War thrust upon us,' exclaimed Queen Mary, 'to have to go to war on account of tiresome Servia beggars belief!' There was a similar mood of exasperated denial that evening when the Desboroughs dined at Revelstoke's, with Lansdowne and Balfour as guests, and they all sat at dinner till past midnight discussing the Austrian bellicosity that was imperilling European peace. Russia, and hence France, were bound by treaty to support Serbia, but there was stout opposition in the government to British involvement.

Charles Masterman, Asquith's Chancellor of the Duchy of Lancaster, whom Ettie had first met at luncheon with Bertrand Russell, and who had since become a Grenfell connection by marriage, struggled to find the right simile to describe these last days of peace. 'It was like a company of observers watching a little cloud in the east, appearing out of a blue sky, seeing it grow, day by day, until all the brightness had vanished, and the sun itself had become obscured,' Masterman recalled. 'It was most like perhaps those persons who have walked on the solid ground, and seen slight cracks and fissures appear, and these enlarge and run together and swell in size hour by hour until yawning apertures revealed the boiling up beneath them of the earth's central fires, destined to sweep away the forests and vineyards of its surface and all the kindly habitations of man.' On 29 July, as Ettie and Monica motored back after midnight from dinner with the Salisburys at Hatfield, they felt the same disorientation as Masterman: 'a situation heading straight to misery and ruin . . . was continuing in the midst of a world where the happy, abundant life of the people flowed on unconcerned, and all thoughts were turned towards the approaching holidays and the glories of triumphant summer days.'

Throughout the escalating crisis Ettie was privileged to hear the most authoritative assessments from the principal actors. As communiqués reached London from the European chancelleries, and telegraphic alarums arrived from the ambassadors in Vienna, Berlin and St Petersburg, Ettie may have been the best-informed non-political woman in England. It was fit for this quintessential Edwardian to share in the death throes of the Edwardian epoch. Every day, it seemed, she had new glimpses into the penetralia of the trans-Continental crisis. On 30 July the Desboroughs lunched at 10 Downing Street with the Asquiths, the Foreign Secretary Sir Edward Grey, Lord Knollys and Waldorf Astor. 'The prospect is very black today,' Asquith felt. 'There is something very crude & almost childlike about German diplomacy.' Afterwards the Desboroughs went to the Commons gallery to hear Asquith postpone the Irish Home Rule Bill, and that night Willie dined alone with Kitchener.

On 31 July Kitchener, his military adviser and intimate friend Major Oswald FitzGerald, Balfour, Alice Salisbury and others dined with the Desboroughs at 9 Chesterfield Street, the Mayfair house they had taken for the Season. The gravity of the crisis weighed heavily on their mood. The next day (Saturday, 1 August) the Desboroughs vacated the house and went to stay with John Revelstoke in Carlton House Terrace. Ettie and Willie visited Balfour that morning, then she lunched at Downing Street with the Asquiths. Kitchener, Oswald FitzGerald, Hugh Cecil and Maurice Baring all called at John Revelstoke's during the day and spoke to Ettie. In the evening Balfour dined there, and the news arrived that Germany had declared war on Russia. The Royal Navy was mobilised.

This was the turning point in Monica's life. She had been to forty balls that summer. 'The last days of a very brilliant London Season were already under a shadow — a shadow in which it was difficult really to believe. Everyone behaved as usual; one could not go to meet disaster even in the realms of thought: so people behaved as usual, only with different faces.' Earlier it had been settled for her to stay with the Duke and Duchess of Beaufort at Badminton for the August Bank Holiday horse show. 'The massive beauty of the house, the serenity of the huge park, the fern, the deer, the whole picture of steadfast England gave out a feeling of security. The stables full of wonderful hunters were a real delight; we went out riding in large cavalcades, and might have been riding into the heart of an early tapestry.'

Ettie meanwhile was visiting Eloïse Ancaster at Grimsthorpe Castle in Lincolnshire. She had been met at Bytham station and in glorious weather was driven through Grimsthorpe's spacious rolling park (sixteen miles round), studded with oak woods, down the longest chestnut avenue in England, sweeping past a picturesque hundred-acre artificial lake called the Great Water, with a romantic view of the castle atop its hill. The oldest part of the castle was King John's Tower dating from the thirteenth century, the south front had been built for a visit of Henry VIII, the superb Baroque south front was Vanbrugh's last work (completed by Hawksmoor), and Lady Ancaster had just finished a modernisation programme overseen by Bendor Westminster's pet architect, Detmar Blow. Vanbrugh's Great Hall, used by Eloïse Ancaster as her main reception room, the house's other state rooms and the surrounding parterres and formal canals reified the serenity, intelligence and poise of the Age of Reason. It must have been uncanny to stay in such an immemorially reposeful house on the weekend that Europe was set ablaze.

'Darlingest,' Ettie wrote to Monica from Grimsthorpe on Sunday, 2 August, 'the news looks very bad, we have no papers today but lots of telegrams – how it twists at one's heart.' And on Monday: 'Nothing cold looks worse than the news. I am staying here quietly with Eloïse till tomorrow, then going to London to John R's . . . One can only try to keep quiet & calm, I suppose there will be a great deal of work to be done by everybody almost at once, which will be a comfort. One longs to do something instead of thinking & thinking.' On Tuesday, 4 August, when the news reached Badminton that German armies had invaded Belgium, Monica and other members of the house party watched the Duchess turn to the wall the picture of Kaiser Wilhelm, who had once stayed there with the Beauforts. It was Monica's twenty-first birthday. The following morning she travelled back to Taplow on trains packed with soldiers rejoining their units in the general mobilisation.

Ettie had already returned to John Revelstoke's. In her own words, 'the ultimatum to Germany expired at 11 p.m. and the state of War began. There was a curious sound of the tramping of crowds of people through London all that night – and very early in the morning the heavy Army wagons began to go past.' Hosts of people came to Carlton House Terrace that morning including both Mary Wemyss and Alice Salisbury: the three lifelong friends, each with sons of military age, had a long, sombre talk, with Ettie looking 'deeply moved and pale'. Kitchener joined them for lunch at Alice Salisbury's: he had been on board a steamer at Dover, on the first leg of his journey to Egypt, when a message from Asquith summoned him back to London, and he suspected that he was to be asked to take office as Secretary of State for War.

In the afternoon Ettie went to say goodbye to John Manners, whom she never saw again – he was killed a month later. Then she went to the House of Commons to hear Asquith's formal statement on the declaration of war. At 6.30 p.m. Margot telephoned Carlton House Terrace with confirmation of Kitchener's appointment to the War Office: she thought him 'a natural cad'. One of Ettie's long-term admirers, General Pulteney, who commanded the 3rd Army, came to say goodbye, as did one of the youngest of the Taplow faithful, Ivan Hay, who was destined to have his life ruined in a prisoner-of-war camp. The Desboroughs, the Russian Ambassador Count Benckendorff and Louis Mallet, who had hurried back from Constantinople, then motored down to Esher for dinner with Edgar and Helen D'Abernon – their new title, which had replaced the indistinctive surname of Vincent a month earlier.

To Monica, in retrospect, it seemed as if the next few weeks at Taplow were lived in a trance. Rosemary Leveson-Gower was there often, with Vera Bentinck and Iris Capell. Nancy Astor's son Bobbie Shaw, who was Ivo's age, would appear unheralded from Cliveden, sometimes driving over with a mule and cart, accompanied by a pack of spaniels with a chow as their ringleader. They slipped into the accustomed summer pleasures, tennis and bathing, reading aloud and enjoying delicious, confidential talks under the cedars. Bobbie Shaw was uproariously funny and would leave them choking with laughter.

Julian, of course, was already an army officer and Ettie was apprehensive for him. Billy had only recently returned from Paris, where he had been cramming for the All Souls examination in the autumn; but jettisoning his academic ambitions, he applied at the War Office for an army commission on 7 August. 'It was thought', said Ettie, 'that the whole War might be a matter of months, or even weeks.'

CHAPTER 6

The Mourner

༄

ON MEMORIAL DAY of 1895 Oliver Wendell Holmes gave an address – he entitled it 'The Soldier's Faith' – to the graduating class at Harvard University. It must have been rousing to hear, and remains stunning to read, this attestation of the beliefs that provided the crucial underpinning of Ettie's middle life. 'War,' said Holmes,

when you are at it, is horrible and dull. It is only when time has passed that you see that its message was divine. I hope it may be long before we are called again to sit at that master's feet. But some teacher of the kind we all need. In this snug, over-safe corner of the world we need it, that we may realize that our comfortable routine is no eternal necessity of things, but merely a little space of calm in the midst of the tempestuous untamed streaming of the world, and in order that we may be ready for danger. We need it in this time of individualist negations, with its literature of French and American humor, revolting at discipline, loving flesh-pots, and denying that anything is worthy of reverence – in order that we may remember all that buffoons forget. We need it everywhere and at all times. For high and dangerous action teaches us to believe as right beyond dispute things for which our doubting minds are slow to find words of proof. Out of heroism grows faith in the worth of heroism. The proof comes later, and even may never come. Therefore I rejoice at every dangerous sport which I see pursued. The students at Heidelberg, with their sword-slashed faces, inspire me with sincere respect. I gaze with delight upon our polo-players. If once in a while in our rough riding a neck is broken, I regard it, not as a waste, but as a price well paid for the breeding of a race fit for headship and command. [He did not know, Holmes continued, the meaning of the universe.] But in the midst of doubt, in the collapse of creeds, there is one thing I do not doubt . . . and that is that the faith is true and adorable which leads a soldier to throw away his life in obedience to a blindly accepted duty, in a cause which he little understands, in a plan of campaign of which he has no notion, under tactics of which he does not see the use.

Ettie was never duped by the crude war cries of August 1914 and knew from the outset how cruel the fighting would be. But she thought that there were greater challenges in life – nobler ideals, if one liked – than the safety of one's family. 'The Soldier's Faith' was an exultant credo for her, she told Holmes. She began the war in 1914 convinced of its truth. Did she end the war with the same certainty? In the intervening four and a half years she faced momentous tests of her valour. Two dead sons, amid three-quarters of a million British war dead, would challenge anyone's enthusiasm for broken necks and lives thrown away in an incomprehensible military campaign with useless tactics. What should a mother do to make sense of such loss?

On the outbreak of war Willie and Lord Lovat formed the London Volunteer Defence Force, a sort of National Guard or Home Guard comprising volunteers who relieved regular soldiers of certain duties and who were trained for mobilisation in the event of invasion. Within two years it had 10,000 members. During the early weeks of hostilities, however, the other Desboroughs were more concerned with nursing than soldiering.

On 19 August Ettie took Monica to the London Hospital in White-chapel, where their friend Angie Manners had trained as a nurse. The girls, said Clemmie Churchill, were renouncing all gaieties and ease, discarding their Paris dresses for a nurse's puff-sleeved, long-skirted, mauve-checked uniform, getting up at five in the morning, scrubbing floors and obeying orders. At first Monica's brothers were disposed to treat her initiative as a lark. 'Casie is in the London Hospital, poor lamb, washing old Yiddish women seven times a day,' Billy told Nancy Astor. 'One of them said to her, "You seem quite a superior sort of gal. I expect you walks out with a Policeman."' For Monica it was a release to escape from the overpowering perfection of Taplow into the grubbiness of the East End, just as Julian had exhaled his vast relief in the squalid dirt of South African military camps.

The late summer brought an outrush of sorrow, anxiety and solicitude. Casualties were repatriated and friends ravished of their sons. Gay Plymouth's twenty-three-year-old son Archer Clive was killed in the last week of August. On 1 September Con Manners's son John and Violet Cecil's son George (aged twenty-two and eighteen respectively) were both killed, and a few days later Voltelin Heath, one of the Taplow faithful, died of his wounds at the age of twenty-five. In this same week Ettie received the news that Desmond FitzGerald, Valentine Castlerosse and Aubrey Herbert had all been wounded. Elizabeth Kenmare believed at first that her son Castlerosse had been killed, then feared that his arm must be amputated. Some days later George Wyndham's only child Percy, lately married to Tommy Ribblesdale's daughter Diana Lister and a lieutenant in the Coldstream Guards, was killed at the age of twenty-six. A pattern had already been set: casualties throughout the war were three times heavier among junior officers than among common soldiers.

Ettie went to console Violet Cecil, who was overwhelmed by misery and loneliness. George had loved his pre-war visits to Taplow, she told Ettie. 'You gave him many delicious hours during his short life & I shall always bless you for this & for your wonderful power of loving your friends. My darling, my eyes are blinded as I write – he had so short a time for service to the country he adored with religious ardour.' Henceforth Violet Cecil felt a piercing intimacy with Ettie, which intensified after the deaths of Julian and Billy. She and Alfred Milner had long loved one another and were eventually to marry, and this coldest of men thanked Ettie warmly for her attentions to Violet. 'She is devoted to you & has few people – very very few in these days – to whom she can turn . . . That she will ever quite recover, I don't believe. But will the world ever be the same for any of us?'

Billy was commissioned on 14 September as a second lieutenant in the 8th Battalion of the Rifle Brigade; and Kitchener confided that Julian's cavalry regiment (the Royal Dragoons) would arrive on the *Dunluce Castle* on 20 September. Julian's recent letters to his mother had been jaunty. 'It must be wonderful in England now,' he wrote two days after the expiry of the British ultimatum to Germany. 'Don't you think it has been a wonderful, and almost incredible, rally to the Empire; with Redmond and the Hindus and Will Crooks and the Boers and the South Fiji Islanders all aching to come and throw stones at the Germans. It reinforces one's failing belief in the Old Flag and the Mother Country and the Heavy Brigade and the Thin Red Line, and the Imperial Idea.'

The day after the *Dunluce Castle* docked, Ettie visited Julian at Windmill Hill camp, in the middle of the British Army on Salisbury plain, and stayed with the Ian Hamiltons – '*such* fun,' she told Violet Asquith, 'I now want you to marry a General.' It was a hot, sunny Sunday, and Ettie spent the afternoon with Julian on top of the downs, in the shade of a wood, watching a sham fight on the plain below. He had never looked so happy or healthy, she felt. They were joined for a time by Charlie Nairne, her companion on the state visit to Paris a few months earlier: he was killed in October, shortly after reaching Flanders. Wartime travel was difficult, trains were always late and crammed with soldiers, and Ettie returned from Salisbury plain in the luggage van. 'Did you love our day on the hill-tops?' Julian asked next day. 'You looked so exactly the same as when I was a likka boy. I shall never be so much in love with any woman as I have always been and shall always be with you. I am hungering to see Dad and the others.' He arrived at Taplow on Friday, 25 September with two days' leave. Desmond FitzGerald was already there, lame from his wounds. Billy, Monica and Ivo all got Sunday leave, and the entire family were united in a perfect day. The following Sunday, 4 October, the Desboroughs motored to Windmill Hill to help Julian pack. He left that night.

Ettie was agonised by the parting, and by her realisation of the danger, but determined that she must be resilient rather than self-indulgent. 'We went yesterday to say Goodbye to Julian,' she told Monica in Whitechapel. 'I know how you understand & share all, my own Casie – there are things that seem beforehand quite impossible to bear. And yet we do bear them. And I feel so strongly that courage is his due, one could not be anything but brave for him. God bless you darling, & for all you are, & the comfort of thinking of you & knowing that we are at one – in the anguish of this, & yet the *uplift*.'

It was impossible to feel easy reading Julian's exhilarated but alarming letters from Flanders. 'We've got within 15 miles of them Germans now, and hope to be at them tomorrow,' he wrote to his mother on 11 October. 'It's all the best fun one ever dreamed of . . . They have got some of the London Motor-buses out here, carting about supplies and wounded: a great fat red London driver passed us the other day, and shouted at us, "Oxford Street, Bank." The buses have still got all the London playbills and advertisements on them. The roads are chock-a-block with troops and guns and supplies and transport and wounded; and aeroplanes always in the air.' A week later his martial enthusiasm was akin to his mother's exultant joy at a brilliant Saturday-to-Monday. 'It's a great war whatever. Isn't it luck for me to have been born so as to be just the right age and just in the right place – not too high up to be worried – to enjoy it the most?'

He was hyper-alert, self-masterful, understood the danger of his situation, and trying to instil self-respect in his men by imaginative leadership. 'I *was* pleased with my troop, under bad fire,' he reported in October. 'They used the most filthy language, talking quite quietly, and laughing, all the time; even after men were knocked over within a yard of them. I longed to be able to say that I liked it, after all one has heard of being under fire for the first time. But it's bloody. I pretended to myself for a bit that I liked it; but it was no good; it only made one careless and unwatchful and self-absorbed. But when one acknowledged to oneself that it *was* bloody one became alright again, and cool.'

Bombardment brought intensity of reactions and such constant challenges to purposive action as to obliterate the Cowpers' constitutional depressive apathy once and for all. 'I *adore* War,' Julian declared. 'It is like a big picnic without the objectlessness of a picnic. I've never been so well or so happy.' He encouraged Ettie in her role as a national figurehead of stoicism on the Home Front: 'you are really a great War Mother. All emotion is fatal now.' War, for Julian, was '*the* best fun; I've never felt so well, or so happy, or enjoyed anything so much. It just suits my stolid health, and stolid nerves, and barbaric disposition. The fighting-excitement vitalizes everything – every sight and word and action. One loves one's fellow man so much more when one is bent on killing him.'

Ettie circulated edited versions of these letters – 'bloody', for example, muted to 'beastly' – to friends, including Oliver Wendell

Holmes in Washington DC. The old judge 'didn't know which to admire most, the young man who wrote with such almost impersonal *bonhomie* and *sang froid*, or the mother to whom a son could write in that way of getting leave to hang his life on a hair. I take off my hat and shut up.' Ettie also sent her transcripts to Geoffrey Dawson of *The Times*, who published them anonymously in the newspaper.

After finishing three months of training at the London Hospital, Monica was sent as a probationer nurse to the British Hospital at Wimereux near Boulogne. Ettie thought it insupportable for an un-married girl to travel unchaperoned and took her to France on 12 December. This hospital had been set up by Lady Norman, the wife of an MP, in the semi-squalid Hôtel Bellevue, on a street facing on to a small river with a view of the sea 300 yards away. A vital strategic railway passed within twenty yards of the hospital so the din, day and night, was immense. Asquith sneered at Wimereux and Boulogne hospitals as 'overstaffed annexes of London Society', but that was because Venetia Stanley, with whom he was infatuated, was deserting him to nurse at Wimereux. Her account of the hospital's routine does not sound like a Park Lane ball:

All yesterday was swelteringly hot, sun streaming in on all sides, tiny wards crammed with beds, and sterilizers and kettles bubbling and steaming away. This is practically a clearing hospital, very few cases unless they are dying stay very long and through shortage of nurses and appliances one is able to do very little for them. Opera-tions go on all day long, when we went to bed last night there were 16 men waiting to be done, they pour in at all moments, are operated, dressed and as soon as possible passed on to make room for fresh ones. It's really rather ghastly . . . In the afternoon even my love of blood was satisfied as I watch[ed] for almost one hour a man have 4 different deep holes cut in him, till I turned green . . . Tonight 60 new cases have come in, one or two gas ones. They are the most harrowing to watch as they daily get worse, turn purple and blue and I suppose die quite soon. It's all very horrible.

Ettie's description of Wimereux brims with her characteristic vivid intensity:

There are eight hospitals in and about this small village. The ambulances go off at break-neck speed to the Railway Station, three miles away, and come back very, very slowly. No mud ever encountered before seems real: here it permeates all life, with a cold, clinging persistence, and penetrates into the houses and up the creaky wooden stairs. The trenches, every one says and thinks all day long. Surely no country can attain to such pewter-greyness of land, sea and sky as France when she is so inclined? The rain pours down all and every day, and the wind never seems to drop or vary . . . The hospitals are all in summer hotels or villas, queer, frail, ramshackle places, with pathetic reminiscences of gaiety, and windows that have a tendency to blow in completely if the shutters are unfastened . . . The French people are very sad, sadder than almost any in England. Nearly all the women here are in mourning . . . Every evening at 5 o'clock there are war prayers in the little church by the river. It is crowded to the doors every night, and a sprinkling of khaki-clad soldiers and orderlies. They have beautiful prayers, in French, and a sort of short litany, and sometimes a very short sermon of about five minutes. The Priest has a fine voice and preaches very well – more warlike I think than anything that would be heard in church in England.

She was staying in frowzy lodgings in the village with seven Belgian paying guests. 'The house is quite indescribably cold, smelly and stuffy; one of the most revolting features is a very dirty tame white rabbit which lopes about the rooms and up and down the stairs.' The nurses from Lady Norman's hospital who took their meals at the pension were forever bickering, or spreading tales of petty snubs, snappish retorts and festering resentment – an off-duty outlet for the gruelling strain of their work. In the hospitals, though, the 'courage and cheerfulness' was 'amazing', Ettie continued, 'never does the dark side of life even obtain a hearing. The same ubiquitous spirit possesses the patients. "I feel a treat today," a boy said who had just had his leg off yesterday. Another, very ill, said, "I am just like a king in here, my wife would jump right up in the air to see me." One man was too ill to speak, but held out a picture portrait of his wife and baby, with indescribable happiness, and patted a high pile of letters by his side.'

There was no escape from the daily reminders of death. 'The soldiers' funerals go down the village street, the Union Jack covering the coffin, and a very small party following behind. The country is as ugly as anything can be that includes cliffs and sea; the poor old village could hardly be more squalid and tawdry – it looks so singularly unfitted for this weight that it is suddenly called upon to bear.'

There was strict censorship between the Western Front and Britain, which Ettie and her friends evaded when they could. Returning from Wimereux, Ettie was aghast when eight people in front of her at Folkestone Customs House were each asked if they were carrying letters. 'I was simply trembling, with sixty-four tied round my waist, but was not asked, and I posted them all safely in London.' Monica's Christmas Eve letter to Taplow was 'much scratched out (by the Censor) and of course, just the things we were pining to read; but alas he is very efficient'. Ettie sent her uncensored replies by Evan Charteris or other friends going out to France. Her Christmas presents to Monica that year – a mackintosh apron, rubber gloves, Red Cross caps, and cocoa – were all that was desired. Her Panshanger tenants collected money to provide comforts for Julian's men.

The Desboroughs were justifiably proud when Julian's DSO was gazetted on 1 January 1915. The medal honoured Julian's courage in November when he had twice crawled out to the German lines, killing three Pomeranian soldiers by his sniping, and spying on the pre-parations for an attack: his intelligence enabled the British to decimate the Germans when the onslaught came. At the end of January Julian returned briefly to Taplow on leave. Then his unsparing letters from the Front resumed. 'The drawback to our trenches was that, in odd places in the parapet, there were buried, very very shallow, poor dead Huns, and French, and English, whose bodies were periodically resurrected by the rain, and bombs, and bullets,' he wrote on 15 February. Nights near the German lines he enjoyed best. 'Flares going up from each side all the time, and lighting up the pines like a wood in a pantomime, and intermittent rifle-firing the whole time, right along the line.'

'England is very grey in tone, but absolutely resolute,' Ettie told Judge Holmes in February; and next month she wrote to Violet Asquith of 'the dreary iron cage of anxious feeling which sometimes seems to press every bone into one's soul'. Informative letters from the theatres of war were a heartening distraction, and in London she was trusted with confidential war intelligence by Asquith, Kitchener, and later Balfour, Curzon and Milner. In mid-February, when she had tea with Kitchener, he was gratifyingly indiscreet, and she eagerly summarised his news to Evelyn de Vesci's son-in-law Aubrey Herbert, who had been posted to Cairo. '(1) That the recruiting is magnificent, a steady 35,000 a week, *more* than they can deal with; (2) That Sir J. French has now got 400,000 men in France, *ready*; (3) Thrilling possibilities of destinations of New Armies – I don't write them – but somewhere where *you gave me a letter of introduction*! Or slightly more West, as alternative . . . of course padlock all this.' Anyone intercepting this letter could have divined the armies' destination from her hint.

On the eve of the military embarkation, Ettie attended a pre-Dardanelles dinner in Downing Street. 'We dined with the Prime Minister tonight – wonderful party – all the loveliest women and nicest men London can, at present, produce,' Jean Hamilton noted on 11 March. These included Ettie, Winston and Clemmie Churchill, Gladys Ripon, Nellie Londonderry, Edgar D'Abernon, Loulou Harcourt and Kitchener. At 10.30 Churchill took Ian Hamilton – the newly appointed Commander-in-Chief of the Mediterranean Expeditionary Force – away to confer at the Admiralty about the expedition, and thirty-six hours later Hamilton embarked for the Middle East.

Ettie planned to revisit Monica before spending Whitsun of 1915 at Hunstanton with Balfour and Mary Wemyss. 'After unspeakable difficulties, which at one time seemed final, that angel Lord K. has got us permission to go to Boulogne,' she told Monica. 'I would much rather stay at Wimereux if there are any nice unsmelly rooms. I don't mind the food a bit, but think that last house was rather dangerous in the way of drains.' On 11 May Willie saw Kitchener, who was 'cheerful' about the impending landing at the Dardanelles, and Ettie dined with Asquith and Sir Edward Grey, who were 'intensely anxious'.

✌

Ettie went to Aldershot on Saturday, 15 May, just before Billy's battalion left for France. She watched them drilling and spent a happy afternoon with him in the pine woods near Grayshott. He was pleased to be going at last. Willie motored to Aldershot that evening to see Billy, and took Ettie back to Taplow. Later that Saturday evening, at eleven o'clock, the Desboroughs received a telegram from Monica stating that Julian had been slightly wounded in the head, near Ypres, on Thursday, 13 May, and was in No. 7 General Hospital at Boulogne. She was with him, the telegram explained, and he was progressing well, and would probably be moved to England on a hospital ship. As Ettie wrote a year later, 'the strain of the previous fortnight, when they had known that Julian's regiment was in the centre of the terrible fighting, had been so great that they almost felt relief at the telegram, and to hear that he was slightly wounded, and would be in safety and with them in a short time.'

Billy joined his family next day, a Sunday, as planned, for his last visit to Taplow, and Ivo was allowed back from Eton too. At 4 p.m. the Desboroughs received a telegram from Boulogne: 'Your son here wounded in head. Better come. Use this as permit.' They telephoned the Admiralty at once, obtained permission to travel that night, left Taplow by car at seven, and (accompanied by Ettie's maid Rose Gaston) barely caught the only train from Victoria to Newhaven. At 11 p.m. they were steaming out of Newhaven on a ship carrying high-explosive ammunition under escort by destroyers. It reached Boulogne at 5 a.m. on Monday, 17 May, and the Desboroughs hastened to the hospital, where Monica had never left Julian since Saturday.

At the hospital they learnt that a splinter had penetrated one and a half inches into Julian's brain. When he had reached hospital, his good spirits had deceived everyone and it was not realised how grievously he had been injured. Now he lay in a tiny room with two other desperately wounded officers. The Desboroughs visited him twice daily, but were not allowed to stay long. From various sources they heard about his last day in action. Julian had volunteered to take a message to the Somerset Yeomanry and to carry back the reply. Wilfrid Ricardo, an officer in the Royal Horse Guards, saw a figure coming coolly across under heavy fire to the Somerset Yeomanry's trenches. 'You once gave me a very good mount with the Belvoir Hounds,' the officer said in greeting, and Ricardo realised it was Julian Grenfell, whom he barely knew. Julian took back a message, which helped to turn the situation, but was hit by a splinter shell at 12.30 just after delivering it to

Brigadier-General David Campbell. To Campbell he said, 'Go down, Sir, don't bother about me, I'm done'; and to a brother officer, cheerfully, 'Do you know, I think I shall die.'

The physicians forbade Julian from wearying himself by talking. This frustrated him, for he longed to tell of his experiences, and to ask for news of his friends. Edward Horner and Bobbety Cranborne lay desperately wounded in the same hospital with Rex Benson, who had been gassed. Charlie and Lily Lincolnshire's adored son Bob Wendover (their only boy born after five daughters) was brought in with a smashed hip and arm. None of this was Julian told. Once the Lincolnshires arrived at the hospital, the Desboroughs – despite their own anxious sorrow – comforted and cared for them. The maimed viscount died on 19 May aged twenty. 'We have you & Willy in our thoughts day & night,' Lily Lincolnshire wrote from Daws Hill on 21 May. 'You are both so brave & so unselfish always thinking of others & never of yrselves, and yr trouble was the hardest to bear. I cdn't say what you and Willy were to us.' As to her Bob, it was 'a joy to think that he had such a grand and blameless life . . . It was a lovely morning and a smooth sea when we brought him home. He lies facing the rising sun in the drawing room upstairs – the greenness in front of him – and tomorrow we lay him to rest in Moulsoe Church Yard.'

On Thursday, 20 May, Billy's rifle battalion reached Boulogne, and he spent the day with his parents and Monica. He visited Julian, whom he thought very ill, and was terribly overcome after seeing him. Ettie, Billy said afterwards, was brave and calm and inspiring. Ivo had stayed at Taplow with Mogs, after his parents hurried to France, and together they waited for decisive news. He insisted on returning to Eton every evening to row for his house, sometimes shaking from head to foot, and looked utterly unfit, but his boat made a bump each of the four nights. Ivo's misery, and Mogs's, was alleviated by Nancy Astor, who treated the children with the tenderness and tact of which she was sometimes capable. 'You *have* been kind to the children, & could not do a kinder thing by me than that,' Ettie scribbled from Boulogne to Cliveden on 22 May. 'I am haunted thinking of little Ivo fretting. Julian is just the same, the doctors say, but I cannot help thinking him a *shade* less weak.'

Alas, on Whit Sunday, 23 May, Julian was found to have inflammation of the brain. The deadly septic poison seeping from his wound was slowly conquering (in Ettie's words) 'his marvellous constitution and health and strength and youth'. There was thought to be a small chance of recovery if he underwent a second operation, which was performed at eleven that morning. Afterwards, in excruciating pain, Julian was moved to a room by himself: the physicians said that a shred of hope remained.

Just before the second operation, Julian talked of the Mimram, just below the waterfall, where he had often fished, and how it rippled round the tree trunks. He recalled their holiday at Assynt in 1896, and the old fisherman, Murdoch Keir, from whose little boat they had landed such big skate. 'He prayed a great deal all those days, probably not knowing that he was speaking aloud,' Ettie described. 'He prayed sometimes to be able to bear the pain. He liked the psalms and hymns of his childhood to be said to him, and some of the George Herbert poems. The thought that he was dying seemed to go and come, but he always seemed radiantly happy, and he never saw any of the people he loved look sad. Never once through all those days did he say one word of complaint.' Towards the end, when he was lying in his hospital room, suffering in the great heat, Julian recited aloud Gilbert Murray's translation of Phaedra's song in Euripides's tragedy, *Hippolytus*. His voice was feeble, but he spoke with overpowering longing:

> O for a deep and dewy spring,
> With runlets cold to draw and drink,
> And a great meadow blossoming,
> Long-grassed, and poplars in a ring,
>   To rest me by the brink!
>
> O, take me to the Mountain; O,
> Past the great pines and through the wood,
> Up where the lean hounds softly go,
> A-whine for wild things' blood,
> And madly flies the dappled roe.
> O God, to shout and speed them there,
> An arrow by my chestnut hair
> Drawn tight, and one keen glimmering spear —
>   Ah, if I could!

Julian's condition deteriorated on Tuesday, 25 May. His Colonel, George Steele, whom he admired, had died of wounds the day before, and John Bigge (Lord Stamfordham's son who Julian hoped might marry Monica) had recently been killed. When Julian knew that he was dying, they told him about Steele, Bigge, Lord Redesdale's son Clem Mitford, and others who had died since his wounding. Ettie felt 'he looked pleased, as if they had been starting on a journey together'. To his sister he said, 'Goodbye Casie' and to his mother, 'Hold my hand till I go.' A shaft of sunlight broke through the shaded window and made a streak across his feet. He smiled at Ettie, and said 'Phoebus Apollo', and only spoke once again, his father's name. Julian died at 3.40 on Wednesday afternoon, 26 May. He knew his parents till the end and, shortly before he died, moved his mother's hands to his lips.

To Judge Holmes, Ettie wrote a fortnight later, 'We were with him the last 9 days. He died radiantly, as he lived. He seems very near to us.'

Julian was buried on a windy Friday, 28 May, in the military cemetery on the hill above Boulogne. A few friends, including Venetia Stanley, joined the Desboroughs for the funeral. His grave was lined with wild flowers: oak leaves and flowers from the Taplow gardens, which Mogs had enclosed in her last letter to him, were buried with him. No one wore mourning.

The Desboroughs and Monica went for two days' recovery in the peace of Hardelot forest. On Saturday Ettie was sitting haggard and stricken among the trees, trying to write to Billy, when suddenly she looked up and saw him in front of her like a vision. Until that morning he had been in the trenches, but Charley Londonderry had brought him over in a motor car after receiving their telegrams. Ettie wrote afterwards: 'Julian and he had been like one person, but he did not seem to have a thought that was not of faith and triumph.' He stayed for three hours, and then had to return. The Desboroughs found it almost impossible to let him go, and never saw him again.

*

Monica, Ettie and Willie were met at Victoria Station by a desolated Ivo on Monday, 31 May. 'Juju would not wish us to grieve, but only to think of him in his peace and great glory,' Ivo had written three days earlier. 'If we could only live and die like him, how beautiful a place the world would be.' Billy was equally insistent on the nothingness of death. 'How could a man end this life better than in the full tide of strength & glory,' he replied to Nancy Astor's commiserations. 'Julian has outsoared the darkness of our night, & passed on to a wider life. I feel no shadow of grief for him, only thankfulness for his bright & brave example.' Billy, though, was frustrated by the direction of the war – it was deplorable that 'the Army should be run by the stupidest of the stupid', he told his Darling Nance a fortnight later. 'Such a Chamber of Horrors we have past through, shells thicker than flies, & flies thicker than air, & our nearest & dearest neighbours 37 English & 22 German corpses of varying age & savour. However that sad strain of Negro-hunnism in my character made me really enjoy it. There is such Boche stalking & shooting for them as likes it.'

In England, on the day after Julian's death, Asquith had been forced into a coalition government with Conservative leaders. Balfour replaced Churchill at the Admiralty, Loulou Harcourt was demoted, Curzon became Lord Privy Seal and Bron Lucas left the Cabinet. That same morning *The Times* published Julian's poem 'Into Battle', which he had written in April. The carnage in Flanders had already made the unreflective, jingo rallying cries of 1914 objectionable as war poetry, although public taste during the war years regarded the bleak realism and satirical dirges of poets like Siegfried Sassoon as defeatist or seditious. The emotional self-control, technical adeptness, imagination and animal vitality of 'Into Battle' met people's needs, and the poem had an immediate national impact. 'Those extraordinarily living and breathing, ringing and stinging, verses', so Henry James told Ettie, made him feel 'almost to have known your splendid son even though that ravaged felicity hasn't come my way . . . What great and terrible and unspeakable things! but out of which, round his sublime young image, a noble and exquisite legend will flower.' Ettie and Bron Lucas had been sceptical about 'Maur' Baring's value to the war effort. There was no scoffing at Baring when on 5 June his sonnet 'Julian Grenfell' was published in *The Times*. (It is reprinted with 'Into Battle' in the appendix on pages 370–73.)

It was other parents, especially the mothers, who best understood. 'My heart stood still when Charlie came down from London & said that your beautiful beloved Julian was gone,' wrote Lily Lincolnshire. She longed to visit Ettie, but was not yet strong enough for the short journey, explained a numb Charlie Lincolnshire. 'It is curious how things go on just as usual, & yet there is an indescribable sort of aching void all the time, & now that the great shock is over one seems to realize it more & more. But yr & Lily's bravery set such a glorious example.'

Gay Plymouth, who had now lost two sons, sent a letter that was perfectly attuned to Ettie's needs: 'With such as he was, one feels there can be no real parting. He will always be there on the horizon, visible to all who knew him or heard of him, giving courage or inspiration.' So, too, did Cynthia Asquith. 'Nothing human could possibly have been more wonderful than just to have been his mother and to have given and had such a perfect love,' she assured Ettie. 'You were able to ensure him a supremely happy childhood and youth and – in spite of the aching loneliness – it must be wonderful to think of him and all his glamour as so utterly *unassailable* – to know that he "carries back bright to the Coiner the mintage of man" and yet to feel that he had already found time to fulfil himself as the perfect Happy Warrior. He was one of the rare precious interpreters who help to make the War bearable to the spectators. How *lovely* his poem is, and how happy! I think his is one of the deaths that *must* confirm one's belief in immortality. He is so obviously inextinguishable.'

Life was changed for all the Taplow faithful, Evan Charteris said, and they all had to find fresh energies to avoid being crushed. He and the pretty American-born Countess of Essex were by this time a devoted couple, and Adèle Essex, visiting Ettie on 11 June, found her in 'a most remarkable state – not even hysterical exaltedness, but of real immunity to grief of the ordinary sort. She says she feels no sense of separation, but just consciousness of his radiance and a quite un-impaired zest for life. She will not break down, wears colours, and scarcely admits she is to be pitied at all.' Ettie's reaction was not a denial of the reality of Julian's death, but an acceptant serenity based on her Christian faith, and underlain by her determination that she would not succumb to grief as previous generations of Cowpers had done.

Other commiserating visitors included Alice Salisbury, Mary

Wemyss, Norah Lindsay and Margot Asquith – the latter providing inadvertent amusement. Ettie asked, 'I have never been very frightened about my own death, have you?' and Margot replied doubtfully, 'No', but then passionately burst out, 'but it *would* be a very great *disappointment* to me if I died.' Mary Wemyss – at Taplow on 12 June – found Ettie 'wonderfully calm, and upheld by a sense of Julian's continued presence and love. She deserves the reward of her courage and faith and . . . even if the uplifting or sustaining power seems to wane as the slow days go by it is never quite forgotten.' Mary took tea with Willie too: 'my heart aches for him, he looked so crushed, so seared, so patient and so brave.' Nothing was much good (certainly not doctors), Ettie told Mary, in wrestling with jangling nerves except 'self-help'.

Ettie slept badly and was uneasy about her calm resignation. 'One feels almost a cheat not to suffer more,' she told Nancy Astor. Monica was indispensable to her that month. 'I could not have lived through these weeks without you,' she wrote on 28 June after her daughter's return to Wimereux, 'all your lovely help to him; and the revelation of strength and tenderness that you poured out.' Their bedside vigil together was unforgettable. 'My own little Casie, there are no words to say but the old words I love you. *Never* have I known all you are to me as now, the only woman I really, *really* need.'

Ettie's keen interest in the ever-revolving social merry-go-round helped a little. A month after Julian's death she amused herself at Venetia Stanley's startling engagement to Edwin Montagu. Montagu's banker father Lord Swaythling, with a moneyed man's obnoxious compulsion to control his family even beyond the grave, had stipulated in his will that his descendants would forfeit their share of the family financial settlement if they abandoned Judaism or married out of the faith. Venetia renounced Christianity, underwent a perfunctory conversion and married according to Jewish rites. 'Venetia, who has fairly joined Israel, is coming here tomorrow, an interview I look forward to with some dread, as I am so very fond of her, but feel almost beyond expression about this exploit,' Ettie gossiped in July. 'What amused me considerably was Philip Sassoon's fury on the subject, which outdid any of our Christian indignation.'

Despite her quips, Ettie was wretched from an infected eye. Her illness was especially frustrating because she was busy converting

Taplow Court into a convalescent home for exhausted nurses and as a resting place for nurses who could not return to distant homes during a short leave. She was saddened at opening spare rooms which had not been used since the last party of July 1914; but the first nurses were 'kind, simple and friendly', she told Monica. 'I am sure we shall all shake down quite alright in a day or two. Only I feel I was unimaginative not to realise more fully the sacrifice of the *privacy* of this house and garden; but it is a sacrifice so well worth making.' Between July 1915 and December 1918 just over a thousand nurses stayed at Taplow Court.

Alice Salisbury, with her invariable kindness, sent a letter to Billy in France reporting on her Taplow visit. It gladdened him to hear that his mother seemed 'lifted above sorrow', he explained in his pencilled reply from the trenches. 'Out here where the borderland is crossed so gallantly and light-heartedly by hundreds every day one can but realise that death is not a barrier but a gateway to greater joy & freedom. Julian seems even closer & more vivid & radiant than before. How fortunate to die in the full tide of youth & glory rather than old & gouty-toed & well respected & loathed by a numerous progeny.' He did not expect to survive, for he had been ten days in the salient, and as he told Alice Salisbury, was getting 'pretty well used to every form of frightfulness'.

On the morning of 2 August Ettie wrote apprehensively to Billy about the Battle of Hooge: 'it does sound the most terrible and horrible kind of fighting. I shall simply *long* to hear from you again.' Curzon was expected later that day, and was 'sure to have plenty of flesh-creeping news,' she added. This letter was promptly posted, and later returned unopened with its envelope endorsed 'Killed In Action 30/7/15'. Curzon was not Taplow's most important visitor that Monday. 'Rained all day, detestable,' Queen Mary noted in her diary. 'After luncheon drove to Taplow to see poor Etty Desborough, I had not seen her since her son was killed. I stayed with her an hour, she was wonderful . . . Half an hour after I had left they received the news of the death of their second son "Billy". It is too sad.' Billy had been killed leading his platoon in a charge, over open ground, uphill, in the face of tremendous machine-gun fire, near Hooge, on Friday afternoon. Because of terrific machine-gun fire, his body was left where it fell and never recovered. 'He is lying there now, in front of all,' said Willie in proud anguish on 6 August.

News of this second catastrophe burst like a thunderclap over London Society and its echoes resonated for days. 'Almost the only time when Lord Kitchener was ever known to break down in office', recorded his private secretary Sir George Arthur, 'was when the news of Billy's death at Hooge came through; he had to leave off work for an hour to recover himself.' Jean Hamilton was giving a luncheon that wet Tuesday for Norah Lindsay, Lord Plymouth, Arthur Stanley and Louis Mallet. 'Evan Charteris rang Norah up on the telephone as we were standing in the hall looking at the portable bed the Duchess of Somerset gave me to send to Ian at Gallipoli. I said: "Ask him to come to lunch now", but she came staggering back looking ghastly, crying out: "Billy Grenfell has just been killed", and flung herself weeping on the couch . . . we had a terribly sad lunch, Norah flying off in my motor to see Evan Charteris, when we were half way through. Poor, poor Ettie, and that darling young Billy – I liked him so much – one of the younger generation I was always happy with. Not long have they been parted, Ettie's two delicious boys.'

Charteris was one of Ettie's early visitors. 'Just as her earlier courage was sublime, so it is now, but when a wound is mortal, courage is no protection, but only inspiring to others,' he informed a desperately concerned Alice Salisbury. 'The day after she got the news (Tuesday) I had a feeling she wld not live – her life seemed to be ebbing from her in a rain of gentle uncomplaining tears – only a small flame of life seemed to be burning within. Then I think she made a supreme effort for the children, & on Thursday was up & busying herself over the nurses & doing what she could to shelter what is left of her family – & so she has remained ever since. One feels that had it not been for the children she wld neither have been able nor wld she have wished to live. There is no numbness or illusion – she realises it to the full – her faith is stedfast – her marvellous courage unshaken – her gentleness as moving & lovely as ever – but one can see that the spring of life is broken.'

It was tragic for Ettie to realise that the attack in which Billy died was a mistake, 'one of the worst of the many blunders of the war – an order given to carry out a movement which ought never to have been attempted, & which ended as it was bound to end in the loss of very nearly the whole of a battalion'. Charteris, too, gave a glimpse of the devastating effect of her brothers' deaths on little Moggie. In bed, early on the Tuesday morning, she said to her nurse Harriet Plummer, 'Hawa, you must *never never* speak of . . .' – she was going to say Julian and Billy but could not bear to name them and after a pause continued – '. . . the *war* because if you do I shall lose my mind.' That, said Charteris, was 'the measure of the tragedy coming from a child of 10'.

Alice Salisbury felt 'overwhelmed at this great sorrow,' as she wrote on 5 August to Nancy Astor, who had basked in Billy's love. 'Ever since the day they were born, underneath and nearest to her, were these two boys; her love for them, her pride in them and her hopes & thoughts for the future . . . the one thing one can do is to Pray God that she may have courage and strength to go on for the sake of Willy & those other 3.' Alice Salisbury sent, also, a touching letter of sympathy to Hawa, the Taplow nurse, and visited Ettie at Taplow. 'It is untellable how your love & strength have held me up,' Ettie told her afterwards. Her life felt perched on the edge of a precipitous mountain path 'with destruction on every side – where eyes must be fixed on the next hair-breadth turn of the way, & faith on the things that are very far off. The numbing pain & sense of dislocation seem to sink sometimes into a horrible stupor of unreality – you know how the poor people almost always say at first "I can't realize it" – & that describes a horrible form of suffering, but one must keep off the monster despair, which sometimes comes so terribly near – & know that the destruction of the living principle in this world is not the end of love but the beginning.'

It comforted Ettie when four of the nurses staying at Taplow assured her that they had never known any patient die with *dismay*. 'In the brave moments – which are the true moments – I feel happy now that Billa is gone too, even more than when it was only Julian,' she told Evelyn de Vesci, 'knowing that neither of them can ever be sad or lonely now. Monica said, "Of course they are laughing", & of course they are, as always when together.' And to Lord Kitchener, on 9 August, she wrote: 'you were always so good to Julian & Billy, I seem often to see them walking with you at Wrest, when they were very young. You used to think their home happy, and I want you to know it is happy now, and proud. They envisaged death very clearly, and went gaily to meet it, and how could we wish it otherwise, or wish to bring them back from joy and freedom. They always thought of death as a gateway, not a barrier, and the path to new life and work.' Despite these avowals she sometimes felt 'cowardly', she told Patsy Shaw-Stewart, 'but no one belonging to them could ever permanently surrender'. The Christian belief in Resurrection sustained her, she added. 'Through all the breaking anguish, one's body being torn to bits, there has never been an instant of doubt or of misgiving about them . . . I have believed all my life, but now I know.'

On 29 August Ettie went to stay at one of Bron Lucas's northern properties, Sawley Lodge, on the borders of north Lancashire and west Yorkshire. Her uncle Henry Cowper had built the house (after inheriting the estate from his mother) when Ettie was thirteen, and they had together enjoyed autumn visits there. The grey-stoned house, with its airy windows, broad gables and high chimneys, stood sheltered from the winds at the foot of a thickly wooded hill encircled by cedars and other sturdy trees. It overlooked the banks of the river Ripple, shallow, beautifully dappled and almost amber-coloured in summer, and across to luscious water-meadows traversed by glittering rivulets. A ruined Cistercian abbey rose dominant along the lane from the Lodge, and in the middle distance there were high purple moors and the Forest of Bowland.

'I am sure it will do everyone good,' Ettie wrote from Sawley to Balfour, whom she had so often sent happy accounts of earlier family holidays. 'The children are a help beyond telling, their clear faith & confidence, & the *instinct* for happiness, which I always feel to be another word for truth. There seems a strange new world before one to disentangle, & such maimed faculties to deal with it.' She had been half-stunned but at Sawley faced her pain and Willie's: 'he looks so sadly ill & thin, but is braver than can be told, & always exerting himself for the children.' To Judge Holmes she wrote a similar refrain: 'I have not been here for 32 years. Strange to look back on the dream of life since – but Hope not killed, only gone overhead.'

Everything about Sawley promised neat soothing seclusion, and the gentle setting indeed proved healing; but her month there was anything but easy. The first news that reached Sawley was that Charlie Lister, with whom she had travelled to Constantinople so happily in 1914, had died, aged twenty-seven, on 28 August of wounds received at Gallipoli. The Listers had held land in the vicinity of Sawley since 1312 and bought the nearby Gisburne estate in 1697. Several times Ettie went through the wooded hills to Gisburne to comfort Charlie Lister's father. 'I didn't think any fresh pain could hurt so much, he was worshipped by us all,' she wrote to Violet Asquith. 'I think of Julian & Billy laughing now with Charles – & Archie – & little Tommy – & John Manners – cheering us all on even more vividly than in life.' Lord Ribblesdale's other son had been killed in action in Somaliland ten years earlier; his two brothers had died unmarried, in the service of the Empire, Martin in the Straits Settlements and Reggie in Tangiers; and added to the grief for his dashing son, he knew that he was fated to be the last of his ancient family.

'I am oh so glad you are with Ld Ribblesdale, if any friend could comfort him you would,' Ettie's old bridesmaid Betty Balfour wrote to her. 'I used to think Charles Lister was one of the personalities who was going to make the new England – perhaps he will still – he & Julian together – but we shan't know it.' On a sunny September day the Desborough party all went to a service for Charlie Lister in the small church at Gisburne. Tommy Ribblesdale and his three daughters maintained brave faces, but were heartbroken. 'The children, his & ours, do so gallantly try to carry on, & not let life be shattered – but it sometimes overwhelms one to look at their faces, too young to be so stricken,' Ettie told Alice Salisbury. When Ivo left Sawley to start a new term at Eton, she missed 'his wonderfully tender & brave eyes'.

Elizabeth Kenmare's second son Dermot Browne, a Taplow familiar, was killed on 29 September at the age of twenty-one. 'My darling, we have died with them, but we must not grudge them their glory,' she wrote in anguish. 'I think of his short life full of blessings, full of love & of joy, & that was all God wanted him to know. But oh! Ettie what terrible pain – the crushing and breaking of our human hearts, and when I think of your *two*, it seems too much to bear.' Ettie went to her side as she had gone to Tommy Ribblesdale. 'Elizabeth', she told

Monica, 'helped me so, & *talking* of the pain, as she & I could, seemed to put it back into its true & secondary place, as only a faint part of the whole.'

On 17 October, during the Battle of Loos, a few days after his nineteenth birthday and after only three weeks in France, Yvo Charteris was shot down under enfilade fire, while leading his platoon over the top in an attack on the German trenches. 'How you & I have prayed that this might not be,' Ettie wrote to Balfour. 'Not little Yvo. And yet now the single glory of his life & death will hold all up, it seems to already. Mary has a lion-heart, it will make her able to triumph even over this, & prove herself indestructible.' Mary Elcho sent for Ettie on 20 October and they had a piteous talk. Later Ettie wrote her memories of Yvo: 'a most sunny and lovable little boy', and later an intellectually exciting, intuitive Etonian who understood people and ideas 'by a kind of lightning thought-reading'. She fell for him when, during a long railway journey, 'he produced several books, like a conjurer – as he had no bag with him or visible hiding-place for them – and read aloud most delightfully, both prose and poetry, with shining eyes and flushing cheeks; he looked so very young, it was startling to realise how much he knew, and how passionately he cared.'

Another of the young pre-war Taplow faithful, Charlie Mills, was killed by a shell – the sixth MP to die fighting in the war. His mother Alice Hillingdon was Lily Lincolnshire's sister and his father was Willie's cousin. Sidney Peel wrote a grave, stately memorial in *The Times*, eloquent of both the sense of near intolerable waste and of obstinate hope that made the spirit of this desolate month. Finally the news reached Sawley that George Vernon – a plump, cheerful baron popular with all his fellow Taplow regulars – had died at Malta of dysentery contracted in the Gallipoli campaign. In his final minutes he had dictated a farewell message to Diana Manners, whom he loved. With a supreme effort, said his doctor, he had feebly signed it with a capital G, and then wanting to say something more meaningful in his last moment of life, he wrote – strongly and distinctly – the single word 'love'. Everyone who knew him, and heard of the letter, wept.

Ettie was moved to write a tribute to George Vernon for the *Westminster Review*. 'He was very rich, and very delicate, and unspoilt by either accident. For money he had no care; all he possessed was at the disposal of chance or of anyone who wanted it . . . He was rather changeable and capricious in tastes, but quite unchanging to his friends. Fastidious and impulsive, his most hasty and witty criticisms were annulled by his unforgettable laugh, kind and gay . . . He was just twenty-seven when he died. But no thought of waste can enter in with regard to a life that was devoted so gaily for an overmastering cause.'

Ettie's visits to Tommy Ribblesdale, Elizabeth Kenmare and other mourners demanded tremendous courage. 'I have always looked upon you as a particularly *Gallant* person,' Betty Balfour wrote that autumn, 'you have a V.C. spirit about you.' Cynthia Asquith described a 'most touching' talk in Ettie's bedroom after George Vernon's death. 'It is so amazing the way in which she, externally, is absolutely normal in company. The same old extraordinary zest unimpaired, and the exaggerated interest in everyone and everything. One almost begins to wonder and think it inhuman, but directly she is alone with one she is just a simple, effortless woman with a bleeding heart. Tears pour down her cheeks, and she talks on and on about the boys, and yet preserving such wonderful sympathy for others . . . She seems to have no qualms about immortality, and cannot account for the fearful pain of their loss. She told me she found the complete, sudden disappearance of Billy harder to bear than the long, loving farewell of Julian.'

Ever since Archie Gordon's death, there had been a special sympathy between Ettie and Violet Asquith, who married 'Bongie' Bonham Carter in 1915. 'In all the tangled undergrowth of sorrow,' Ettie wrote to her after the crushing casualties of that autumn, 'the stupefaction & paralysis & uselessness & helplessness that is almost more bewildering than the blinding pain – you have helped me, & bound me to the knowledge that to let one element of life that they loved be spoilt for their sake & because they lived, would be the cruellest wrong by which one could betray them.' Violet replied that Ettie's valour in recent months had 'established a new standard of heroism'.

The telegrams announcing this succession of tragedies to Ettie at Sawley left her pierced and racked by loss. It was there that her thoughts turned towards a memorial to her dead sons, and by extension to other young men who, as Betty Balfour said, had been going to make a new England. She was propelled in this direction by Lord Rosebery. 'The name of Grenfell will glow', he had written on

5 August, 'in the annals of this terrible War.' Rosebery reckoned 'Into Battle' as the finest poem of the war, and wept on reading Julian's elegy to John Manners. She responded by sending him a copy of *Earl Cowper K.G., a memoir by his wife*, a sumptuously produced memorial of 731 pages of letters with interlinking passages, which Katie Cowper had compiled and privately circulated just before her death. He read it, and on 13 November suggested (as no doubt she hoped) that she should make a similar memorial to her dead sons. 'Such lives & such gifts should not die,' Rosebery urged. 'This must have occurred to yourself, but it comes more strongly from a stranger.'

A similar hint had been made in June by one of the Taplow faithful, Walter Raleigh, the Oxford literary scholar; but Rosebery's suggestion decided Ettie. 'I want to do a small book of the kind you mention,' she replied, '& have been just at the moment of intense realization of the difficulties – and your impetus *helps me on*.' She asked if she might seek his counsel while compiling the book. 'I would rather rely on your taste in literature than on any I know. And in this especial matter I know you will feel with me that no question of taste can be decided too austerely – impersonally. I want to make their own writings & sayings tell the short story, with a very sifted few of the letters about them, & hardly a word besides. It will of course be only a little private record, for closest friends.'

Rosebery issued Ettie with her instructions. 'You cannot go wrong with regard to this little memoir,' he told her. 'A mother's tender instinct is better than any other person's advice. You see at once how it is to be done. As many of the boys' letters as you select, with some connecting words from you. Let them tell their own story as far as possible . . . In this way you will produce a sacred intimate memorial for their family & friends, so intimate as to forbid the idea of publication. But it will remain an heirloom, and some day long hence when the soreness of this moment has passed and many of us with it, it may be possible for the public to be admitted to this monument of beautiful lives.' She started work on Rosebery's plan, and soon felt uplifted by the thousands of family letters evoking imperishably happy days. 'I dreaded beginning, but it is a great happiness, almost like living those years again,' she informed Rosebery on 31 March.

Ettie further consulted Walter Raleigh, who had first suggested a commemorative volume. 'Private letters, like these, are often too much edited,' he replied, 'and I hope you will keep in everything, except when it hurts you too much. Who was it said the price of a good book is to flay yourself, and sell the skin?' Raleigh gave other shrewd advice. 'What one misses in most memoirs – even good ones – is laughter. All the dearest of our dead were delightful to laugh with, and would have laughed a good deal about their own memorials. They would have been breezy . . . about it all. With us, left behind, the air is so deadeningly still.' Raleigh's emphasis on laughter heartened Ettie. 'I sometimes hope', she told Lord Kilbracken after the book's publication, 'that it contains a faint echo of their laughter. The world after seems rather silent now.'

While she was assembling her literary materials, Desmond Fitz-Gerald was killed in a grenade accident on 3 March 1916. He was attending a bomb practice on Calais beach when a military chaplain, Richard Lane Fox, asked for a chance to throw a Mills bomb. It exploded prematurely, Lane Fox lost his right eye and several fingers, and Dessy died of head injuries within an hour. 'You have always been so kind to me & we have had so many happy days together in the past,' he had written to Ettie from a train taking him back to the war after his last leave. 'I cannot express how much I admire your pluck & faith in looking on the brighter side of things for I know how terrible your loss has been. But our religion & very existence are worth nothing unless death means passing into happiness & life is given us to use for the helping of others to that happiness.'

Dessy's death was a fell blow to Ettie. 'Hardly any of the young left now could have made such a gap to us,' she wrote to Evelyn de Vesci who had been almost a foster-mother to the orphaned Leinster boys. 'But for him there can be no grief, surely no one can ever have been so ready to go into the presence of God, that wonderful natural goodness & innocence, & he had envisaged this from the very first so quietly & calmly. He was here only three weeks ago, & I had a special pang at that goodbye, because of the terrible Ypres Salient, where he was going – and told him so, we were walking in the winter woods, & he said so gently, "If it is me you must never mind." ' And a few months earlier, in November, he had told Ettie with a bright smile, 'If I see Julian and Billy before you do, I shall take them your love.' These memories were a salve. 'Darling,' she told Lady de Vesci, 'we can't wish them back in our poor world – sometimes my heart feels almost bled to death about Julian & Billy, but the thought of *them*, & of all that shining company, is always joy – and sometimes their love seems so near.'

The shining company – a phrase taken from the Communion Service – came nearer still as she collected memories of her sons from their friends. 'I seem never to have said what glorious beings they were,' Patrick Shaw-Stewart wrote from Army HQ at Salonica on 4 April, 'how curly and how big and strong and shining, and how shaded between the Greek demi-god and the young Roman emperor – Julian cracking his stock-whip in the quad, or punching a ball, or rowing; Billy running (like a great steam-engine), or lying on the grass, or volleying at tennis, or reading very far back in an armchair: these are really the things I want to remember. Oh, and Julian at Sutton, in his green silk bathing-drawers, that is almost the best.'

Raymond Asquith wrote from France that Julian was easily idealised as a 'symbolical figure of Youth and Force' who 'flung himself upon life in a surge of restless and unconquerable energy. Riding, or rowing, or boxing, or running with his greyhounds, or hunting the Boches in Flanders.' Raymond had known Billy far better: 'in every context of life a perpetual joy – I can see him now in a dozen characteristic attitudes, with a racquet or a rod, or riding off in his brown jersey on a pony-hunt, or striding from the Lido into the Adriatic, which never seemed deep enough to cover him, or shouldering lazily through a mob of Lilliputian Dagos towards his evening cocktail at Florian's.' Because of his exceptional upbringing, 'he had mixed more freely (one would say) with brilliant and exceptional people than almost any boy of his years; most certainly he had no use for fools or bores'. This made him 'intolerant of the common herd, and he moved among strangers with a kind of drowsy arrogance, which pointed delightfully the slow and simple sweetness of his way with friends. When I read what I have written here about Billy and Julian, I am shocked by the flimsiness of it. Such golden boys as these are not to be remade out of the tinsel of a few pale adjectives.'

On 6 June Raymond Asquith's newborn son – named Julian in honour of Juju – was being baptised in St Paul's Cathedral when the news reached London that Kitchener (together with his devoted

Military Secretary, Oswald FitzGerald) had been drowned when his ship struck a mine off the Orkneys. As the surviving Taplow faithful teemed down the cathedral steps, the flags across London were being lowered to half-mast, and buses were halting so that drivers and passengers could crowd round news-vendors.

'The tragedy of last Monday seems to grow worse every hour,' Ettie wrote to Monica three days later. 'It was a very wonderful death for K, coming as it did at that moment, starting eagerly and full of hope on his journey to Russia, and one really cannot wish that Fitz survived him. His life would have been so terribly empty.' Mogs – aged eleven – had known Kitchener too. 'Little Baba did not speak of it at all until last night at tea, when she began to talk to me, with her strange insight and wisdom. She said, "It was a great shock to me"; so terrible to hear those words in her little voice – then she said "K. was so much the biggest thing we have known in our lives", and then about Fitz, that she was almost glad; that he had given all his life to Lord K. and that it seemed right he should be with him at the end.' FitzGerald had written to Ettie on his last night from a train hastening to his embarkation at Scapa Flow. It felt to Willie as if a national symbol, like Nelson's Column, had collapsed, and he thought it right that Kitchener should lie with a British warship for his coffin. 'Daddy has been terribly sad, but so brave and *real* about it as he always is.'

Ettie sent off the manuscript of her book on 16 June. By then, she and her friends were in agonies of anxiety about Ego Elcho: he had been killed outright by an exploding shell on Easter Sunday, 23 April, but there was cruelly prolonged uncertainty about his fate, and the death was not confirmed until 1 July. He was the second Wemyss son to die in action. 'The thought of Mary is like a sword, I would have given the soul out of my body to save her this – one knows it too well, the long long pain, the *crushing* of the second blow,' Ettie wrote. 'I did love little Ego so all my life, & he loved me. He wrote to me about ours, "If anything ever comes my way the thought of Julian and Billy will inspire me" – and now they are together, in the shining company – but it is just the thought of *Mary* that cannot be endured.' Her last memory of him was a happy father teaching his baby son to say 'Seneca' before a portentous bust at Gosford. 'No one was ever such fun to talk to as Ego,' she said, 'his humour lit up every word that he said and every word that was said to him.' She attended his memorial service at Stanway. 'Dearest brave Ettie with the two *swords* in her heart,' Mary Wemyss exclaimed afterwards, 'who *knew* & *cared* & *understood*.'

ξ~

Originally, under Rosebery's influence, Ettie planned to print fifty copies of *Pages from a Family Journal 1888–1915*. Spottiswoode of Eton High Street eventually printed 250 copies at a cost of £375 (about £17,000 in 2008 values). At proof stage, just before the printing, Ettie became worried by 'the *chance* of the book falling here & there into stranger hands; & went through it again very carefully', she told Lord Kilbracken. 'All the more piercing intimacy of their relationship to us, the expression of it, had been left out from the very first: it *could* not go into cold print. Also all references to our private affairs, & their own private affairs (they wrote with such amazing frankness). But on going through it again I cut out every single criticism, even the mildest, of people, & discussion of people, except words of light passing praise, & hoped so to defend the book a little from within, if it ever *did* slip into non-intimate hands.'

During August 1916 she sent letters about the book to the friends, relations and neighbours who she had decided should receive it. 'Julian & Billy's book will reach you I hope this week,' she wrote to Balfour on 21 August. 'Above all people on earth I wanted you to have it.' He was at this time First Lord of the Admiralty and a member of the War Cabinet, and too busy to give it immediate attention; but Mary Wemyss urged him to set aside some time. 'Ettie's book', she explained, 'tells of all our children's (the children of the Souls!) Golden Age.' It gladdened her that 'this generation *had* a happy time, they had so short a time and it was not wasted – they were "heroes" and they had a glorious youth and their lives were lovely many-coloured skeins of vivid interests and vivid joys'. When in October Balfour spoke kindly of the book, Ettie assured him, 'You do not know what a great Idea you were in the boys' lives, as well as a most beloved presence. They most truly adored you, & in the strangest way you guided them – all unknown to yourself – as you do all of us who love you.'

Pages from a Family Journal had a potent and emotive impact on its first readers. At midnight on 25 August Diana Manners telephoned Duff Cooper in wretched misery. Reading the book had left her 'sobbing as though her heart would break'. Three days later Margot Asquith was in a similar state. 'I have been crying so much that I have come to my bedroom,' she wrote to Ettie after finishing the book. Ettie's account of Julian's death was '*perfect*, full of passionate self-restraint my darling – terribly terribly moving', and the whole book 'full of . . . vast sketches of love'. Men wept too. 'It is a most wonderful volume quite apart from its record of those two splendid boys and the home life that gave them their strength,' Rudyard Kipling wrote in September. 'We have read it ourselves and, almost every page of it, aloud and have laughed and cried together. The pure fun of it in some places, the sweetness and the character of the children throughout and the little revelations of utter family confidence . . . come very near to one's heart.' He predicted that the book would 'last for a very long time as the history and record of a whole world that the war has wiped out. Now those of us who list [*sic*] must see to it that our children shall not be made to suffer through their children as we have suffered through ours. They and we have paid for a good peace through the next three generations: my fear is that the politician, the international financier and the untouched "scum" may betray us once again.'

John Buchan found it 'such an extraordinarily *rich* book, rich in humour and feeling and thought, & it gives a living & permanent picture of two of the most wonderful of God's creatures. There is such a strong surge of happiness through it all that the tragedy is transmuted almost into something lovely and desirable.' For Maurice Baring it was 'much more than a record of Billy & Julian. It is like an emblem, a banner and microcosm . . . of all we are fighting for. It is the reflection of the soul & spirit & the *core* of the heart of England. It sums all that is best of England, & English things like a Constable landscape or a speech in Shakespeare. It is a wonderful *pageant* too of youth, courage & gaiety . . . I can't read any of it without crying . . . I shall read it again & again. It is *the* Testament of the War & for the War.' Ettie's *Family Journal* had instantly become the foundation text for that legendary cohort of heroes, the Lost Generation.

The enthusiasm of her women friends delighted Ettie. 'Ever since it came I have absolutely *lived* in it,' wrote Alice Salisbury. 'Ettie dearest

Nancy Astor (on the left), with whom Billy was smitten, and Pamela Lytton, with whom Julian had an affair, flank their host Lord Winterton at a Claridge's fancy dress ball of 1910. Ettie disliked both women, but was eventually reconciled to them.

Ettie, Willie and Moggie during the summer of the London Olympics.

Moggie adored Desmond FitzGerald, here dressed as a cowboy at the same ball.

Ivo and Mogs at the Taplow ball.

(Opposite) Billy at the Taplow fancy-dress ball of 1911.

Adèle Essex was chief of Ettie's American friends, and the most
elegant woman in her set. 'How *eagerly* and *delightedly* we all feel
about Taplow & you & Willie,' Adèle wrote.

(Opposite) Patrick Shaw-Stewart dressed as Robin Hood with
Lady Massereene and Ferrard.

Consuelo Marlborough was another amusing American friend. For her, a visit to Taplow in summer was the quintessence of Edwardian ease, grace and gaiety.

The aviator Gustav Hamel, one of the Taplow faithful, standing by his Blériot monoplane.

Charley Castlereagh – later Lord Londonderry – was
one of Ettie's most cherished men friends.

Arthur Balfour and Nellie Londonderry, Charley's mother,
at Panshanger a fortnight before the outbreak of the world war.

Ettie sat for the Society photographer Bassano around the time of her silver wedding anniversary in 1912.

what treasures you have unfolded to us!' exclaimed Adèle Essex: 'one is swept along by their joyous laughter & only when one closes the book do the tears overflow.' Elizabeth Kenmare received her copy of *Family Journal* at the first anniversary of the death of her son Dermot. Reading and rereading the book she 'seemed to have lived your life over again with you', she told Ettie. One afternoon she had come in and found her husband Val Kenmare with the book on his knees. ' "It has made me cry," he said, "they were both very splendid." There is such a note of joy & glorious life through all & darling it is a great help to us who are left.' The first anniversary of their son's death (29 September) 'was a very lovely still September morning, all the churches, right away to the hills, rang their bells for little Der. We had a mass for him & all his dear friends came, the old gamekeeper, carpenter, etc, etc for many miles round. I spent the rest of the days in the hills by the sea & looking back felt so sure all was well with him & felt comforted.'

Reacting against the enveloping grief and incomprehensible adult depressions that had darkened her upbringing, Ettie had striven to give her children an idyllic childhood and, more than ever after her sons' deaths, craved reassurance that her efforts had been a perfect success. She always needed admirers in her lifetime, and wanted future generations to extol her as a mother. Her friends realised that there was a vein of self-deception running through the book, especially as regards Julian, and that she was insistently idealising her past, but they generously affirmed her life-enhancing testament.

'You can't think how I have loved reading it – how much I have cried and how much I have laughed,' wrote Cynthia Asquith. 'You have an alchemy which transfigures sorrow for us all. What a divine goldenly happy childhood and youth you gave them – one feels that not one day was wasted or under-lived – and now you have crowned your wonderful motherhood by making them immortal.' Cynthia's sister-in-law Violet Bonham Carter 'had hardly the courage to go on – yet I could not & cannot put it down, & go on reading it over & over again', she told Ettie. 'Somehow it leaves you with much less of a sense of what you have *lost* than with an overwhelming wonder at what you have possessed – & still hold. That any woman should have *made* such beings as Billy & Julian, & held their love in the measure in which you held it! I never read such letters as theirs to you.'

Billy's Eton housemaster A.C. Benson was less enraptured by reading the *Family Journal*: 'Julian had a touch of morbidity, piety, want of balance,' he noted in his diary. 'Billy was very clever, but idle and dissolute. The book with all its talk of "golden boys" didn't wholly please me.' Lytton Strachey was lent a copy of the book by Lady Ottoline Morrell, whose brother had married a favourite cousin of Willie's. 'I felt when I'd got to the end as if I'd lived for years in that set,' he wrote, 'but oh dearie me I *am* glad that I'm *not* in it! I think it's their facility that degrades them, facility of expression, facility of sentiment, facility of thought, it's really fatal to be made like that.' Julian, he conceded, had the attractiveness of a savage. 'He seems to have done nothing all his life but kill animals (those extraordinary triumphant lists of Lady D! – "this week Julian killed 237 rabbits, 38 stags, 406 weasels" etc really *impayable*) – until he began to kill human beings which, of course, he found even more enjoyable.'

Raymond Asquith privately complained that Ettie had 'doctored' his account of the brothers: she had deleted a passage in which he spoke of Billy's insolence, and added references to Dunrobin and Wrest as places where they had fun together. 'Ettie is a snob in the same harmless sense as Patrick [Shaw-Stewart]. She meant to give her sons the best *mise-en-scène* from a worldly point of view which could be had and I suppose that she wants people to know that she succeeded.' Ten days after sending this letter, on 15 September 1916, Raymond was killed at the Somme.

Ettie felt 're-broken' by his death, 'shrivelled by the knowledge of Katharine's anguish – another home in ashes – his little boy called after Julian – what a father Raymond would have been'. She sent condolences to several Asquiths, including the Prime Minister. 'What a glorious company they are by now,' Henry Asquith replied, 'recruited every week from our best and most radiant and most loved ones: those who, we fondly imagined, were going to make & guide the future here.' He recalled visiting Taplow in the early 1890s, and playing with 'those 2 darling little boys – bright & radiant & (as one thought) destined not only for great things but for a full measure of the richest and fullest & completest life'. But like Archie Gordon, they were 'all gone – & we remain'. He felt 'a broken man – but I try to go on day by day (as you do): for the sake of what we have given'.

Wrest, Bron Lucas's house in Bedfordshire, was the paradise of Ettie's childhood. Under the protection of her Cowper grandmother, it had been the birthplace of her faith, fidelity and enduring rules of life. In April 1916 Bron Lucas turned the house, which had been vacant since the death of the American Ambassador, Whitelaw Reid, into a hospital for wounded (especially limbless) sailors and soldiers. He also offered to provide land to be worked by disabled servicemen. On the night of 14 September a serious fire broke out: 200 patients and valuable contents were evacuated; and the east wing and main roof were destroyed. The house, in its damaged state, is described in the chapter 'Luton' in one of Ettie's favourite wartime books, Logan Pearsall Smith's *Trivia*.

The destruction at Wrest hit Ettie in the same week as Raymond Asquith's death, and six weeks later the war struck again at Ettie's heart. Bron Lucas had renounced all political work after leaving the Cabinet in May 1915, and joined the Royal Flying Corps, although he was over the standard age of thirty and had an amputated leg. He trained first as an observer and then as an aviator, survived a bad crash in Egypt and finally made the authorities let him go to the Western Front. On 3 November, Bron and his machine disappeared while on a reconnoitring raid over German lines. His beloved surviving sister hastened to the side of his beloved cousin. 'Nan is here,' Ettie wrote from Taplow, 'so beyond telling good & brave', but anguished 'every time a telegram comes or the telephone-bell rings'. It was not until early in December that they received official intimation of Bron's death: he had been shot through the neck, but managed to land his machine safely before dying. The Germans had buried him near Bapaume.

Asquith made Bron Lucas the subject of the last of his famous House of Commons obsequies just before Christmas: he had been driven from office as Prime Minister a few days earlier. It was James Barrie who wrote the great public tribute – headlined ' "Bron" the Gallant' – which *The Times* published:

Everyone who knew him will be happy that if he had to die he died in the air. It is an assurance to them that he was happy to the last, pursuing and pursued up there, exulting in it all, even in the last moment when he had the supreme experience. No ill-will, I am sure, to whoever brought him down, but rather a wave of the hand from one airman to another. There is still that sort of chivalry on both sides in the sky. Having had a very good life in the years that he spent on the ground, they nevertheless seemed strange and stupid to him after his first flight. He came down a different man from the one who went up, and was different ever afterwards, as if he had made a journey into the springtime of the world and brought back a breath of it. This is what it is to be a true airman; you may see the same look in all their faces. It is not to be wondered that so many of them fly away and never come back.

He lost a leg in the Boer War, and no doubt other people had headaches that day, and the permanent effect on them and him was about the same. It is worth dwelling on for a moment for the comfort of those in similar case today and their relatives. I had known him intimately for months, seen him racing the wind on horseback, riding in races, walked with him a dozen miles a day, before I had any idea that he was even lame. Since then I have known him walk 20 miles of the stiffest country in the Hebrides, and return to play cricket or lawn tennis. It was all done by the power of his will. No one need doubt that a grim duel went on for months between him and what he had to fight, no witnesses save him and it, but it was a great victory . . . Rather a sad face at times, as if he thought the world was not so fine a place as he wished it was. The kindest of friends, he was still an elusive man whom you often thought you knew well but could never quite touch, like a character in a book. Up to the end an untamed thing that no one had ever flung a net over. Boys adored him – for his gallantry I suppose, gallant being the first and last adjective for him.

After the death in 1895 of Ettie's early mentor Lord Pembroke, the physicist Sir Oliver Lodge had received pressing invitations from Lady Brownlow to visit Ashridge, where her widowed sister Gety Pembroke yearned to consult him about psychic matters. Lodge's expertise in electromagnetic radiation had drawn him to an interest in telepathy and psychic mediums. He submitted to several talks with the widowed Countess who was, he decided, bemoaning her loss excessively; but he

never regretted his Ashridge visits, for they introduced him to Balfour
– 'the most brilliant and broadly educated man' he had ever met – and
to 'the best of the English aristocracy', as he called the Wyndham,
Charteris and Tennant complex. Intermittently before the war the
Desboroughs joined an annual Easter party at Clouds in Wiltshire
given by the parents of Mary Wemyss and George Wyndham. Lodge
was often there with Balfour. After his youngest son was killed in 1915,
he organised seances at which his boy seemed to have intimate
communication with those whom he had loved during his terrestrial
life. These psychic experiences led Sir Oliver to publish *Raymond, or
Life after Death* (1916), which claimed to demonstrate the survival of
memory and affection – that is, of human personality – after physical
death.

His views were not outlandish. Sir John French was the most
conventional of men; and in December 1915, on his final day at the
front, after he had been induced to resign as Commander-in-Chief of
the British Expeditionary Force in France, he and Winston Churchill
lunched together out of a hamper in the ruins of a cottage. They seem
to have talked of spiritual matters, and afterwards Churchill summarised what the old soldier thought. It was a stolid English version of
Wendell Holmes's 'Soldier's Faith'. French had, wrote Churchill,
'a firm belief in the immortality of the soul: if you looked over
the parapet, he thought, and got a bullet through your head, all that
happened was that you could no longer communicate with your fellows
and comrades. There you would be; knowing (or perhaps it was only
seeing) all that went on; forming your ideas and wishes but totally
unable to communicate. This would be a worry to you, so long as you
were interested in earthly affairs. After a while your centre of interest
would shift. He was sure new light would dawn; better and brighter at
last, far off, for all.'

Ettie's beliefs, like those of millions of other Christians, were
identical to those of Field Marshal French – one of the men, incident-
ally, to whom she sent a copy of her *Family Journal*. She read *Raymond*
at about the time that Bron Lucas crashed from the skies, and was
moved by the conclusion to this delicate but ambitious book. 'The
planet is surely not going to fail,' Lodge concluded on a note of
high confidence. 'Already it has produced Plato and Newton and

Shakespeare; yes, and it has been the dwelling-place of Christ. Surely it is going to succeed, and in good time to be the theatre of such a magnificent development of human energy and power and joy to compensate, and more than compensate, for all the pain and suffering, all the blood and tears, which have gone to prepare the way.' Under Lodge's influence, bereaved members of Ettie's set started to consult mediums; and probably she was among them.

Thirty years earlier she and her friends had quizzed a Planchette board about their suitors and marriage prospects, and she always liked to recruit a fortune teller to amuse the milling crowds when the Taplow grounds were opened to the public. She and Lord Ampthill – the husband of her fellow lady-in-waiting – once attended a party at which some effort had been made to reach the dead, and a message had come, which upset and shocked them both. 'That those whom we love & who have departed can hold secret spiritual communion with us, I firmly believe,' Ampthill told Ettie, 'but that it can be so in any but our most serious hours whether of joy or sorrow, is unnatural & impossible.' She had played with spiritualism, and rejected it as a profanation; but after reading *Raymond* she and Willie were tempted to return – in more reverential mood – to further seances. Rosamond Lehmann, whose family lived near Taplow, recalled Willie Desborough proselytising to her father on the subject of psychic communications with the dead. This may be the explanation of the phrases that recur in Ettie's letters after 1916: she felt her dead boys watching her, she reiterated, or near to her. She and Willie, in their aching grief, felt sure they had contacted Julian and Billy as Oliver Lodge had contacted Raymond.

Ettie reacted to Bron Lucas's death with what was intended as life-affirming defiance: she arranged a sequence of house parties at Panshanger, which she had agreed to let for two years to Almeric Paget, who had previously leased it in the summer of 1914 and was a few months away from being created Lord Queenborough. 'A few of our very special friends were home at this time,' Monica recalled, 'and we snatched the chance of seeing them . . . it was our first attempt for a long time at collecting together a few of the people we loved very dearly.' Osbert Sitwell, Duff Cooper, Millie Sutherland's daughter Rosemary Leveson-Gower and several other young women, and four eighteen-year-old Eton friends of Ivo's made up the first party.

'Lady Desborough', Duff Cooper noted in his diary for 27 December, 'is still a miracle though I seem to feel sometimes the heroic effort she makes to be the same as she was, to bear up the weight of her sorrow and the weight of her party and to make everything a success. I thought particularly after dinner when we played the old little games and nobody was really any good at them except myself. Lady Rosemary however helped a lot. I thought, perhaps wrongly, that Lady Desborough must be comparing Ivo's nice, quiet, gentlemanly almost speechless friends with the noisy, drunken, ill-mannered, audacious crew that Billy and Julian collected.' Cooper was smitten by Rosemary Leveson-Gower during this visit, and felt miserable at leaving on New Year's Day of 1917.

Panshanger was deep in snow when a few days later Ettie had a second house party. This, too, was full of the young – Curzon's three daughters Irene, Cimmie and Alexandra, Alice Salisbury's son David Cecil, St John Midleton's daughter Moyra Brodrick, Angie Manners and Moira Godolphin Osborne – as well as Evan Charteris, his sister-in-law Mary Wemyss, and her daughter Bibs (Lady Irene Charteris – soon to marry Gay Plymouth's sole surviving son). Then Violet Cecil with her teenage daughter Helen came for the night, followed by the dowdy animation of entertaining a succession of Grenfell cousins for lunch or tea, and finally a tea party for old ladies from a local rest home. It was all too much. 'I have never felt quite so anti-people,' Ettie told Monica. It had seemed best to persist with the settled arrangements, for 'in a certain stage of nerve-stupidity one really is just as harried & jangled when utterly alone so it doesn't really make any difference', but she 'felt a very useless piece of furniture on the surface of the earth'.

She consulted a London physician, Sir Sydney Beauchamp, afterwards resident medical officer to the British delegation during the Paris peace conference of 1919. 'Beauchamp was very nice & careful & kind – he examined all sorts of things, & said it was nervous exhaustion of a "severe" kind, & wondered one had got along with it so far – which was satisfactory in a way, as one always feels so "malade imaginaire" – he is *certain* of it all getting right, but really begs me to go entirely to bed for at least a fortnight, with diet & massage, & I believe it is the only thing to do. He wants me to go to *Brighton*, & live with windows open to sea.'

There was a third Saturday-to-Monday party on 20–22 January to be got through: Arthur Balfour, Consuelo Marlborough and her son Ivor, Helen and Edgar D'Abernon, Walter Raleigh, Louis Mallet, Norah Lindsay, Eddie Marsh, Evan Charteris, his niece Cynthia Asquith, Eloïse Ancaster with her husband Bertie and – 'such an unexpected joy' – Patrick Shaw-Stewart, who arrived from Salonica for a fortnight's leave in high spirits and without the strained, prematurely aged look of the young officers on furlough from the Western Front. Moggie (aged eleven) was the utmost help to her mother, and took charge of dull Lord Ancaster, saying that it was sad that nobody ever laughed at his jokes. Ettie kept hoping that she would revive, she told Monica. 'The quickest chance is to be quite alone for a tiny bit without even uttering. It is just a queer sort of silly feeling . . . a sort of nerve-fever about nothing, quite different from being unhappy.'

On the Saturday evening Cynthia Asquith sat between Willie Desborough and Raleigh at dinner. 'Poor Lord Desborough is most piteous,' she noted. 'He looks like some great animal who has been struck on the brow, neither wanting nor expecting conversation. He said naïvely to the Professor and me, "You know, Billy was a very intelligent child. He used to ask such funny questions. One night I went to see him in bed and he asked several questions quickly: 'Do rhinoceroses make a gruff noise?' 'Do fishes laugh?'."' That Sunday was bitterly cold, but the central heating (paid for by the sale of the Raphael Madonna) ensured that the house was fiercely hot: 'ox-roasting fires and hot pipes'. Cynthia Asquith felt 'queer being at a real Saturday to Monday party again . . . very much like a pre-war one', but enjoyed 'an old-time Ettie-ish vivacious breakfast' during which she, Professor Raleigh and their hostess debated about good looks and coiffures: 'always comic with a man and Ettie, in these matters, is little more knowledgeable than a man'. It proved a strain sitting between the dull, prosy Lords Ancaster and Desborough at luncheon when she longed to dive into the general conversation about Keats, Sophocles and Milton. Whenever the table talk was particularly interesting, Ancaster would dilate on his skating experiences at St Moritz, or Desborough would give point to the mention of Milton by announcing that the poet's mother had been buried at Taplow. In the afternoon Cynthia played galloping-old-maid with Moggie – 'she has grown very pretty – has extraordinary technique and charm and is very much dressed' – and she ended the night sitting up, in her dressing gown with her hair down, with Shaw-Stewart and Norah Lindsay. 'Rather an abandoned scene: Patrick toying with my tangles and rapturously exclaiming, and Norah – full of gay wit and charm such a wonderful verbal bacchante. We laughed a lot and I went to bed shortly before two, much too wound up to go to sleep.'

There is no hint in Cynthia's record that Ettie loathed this Sunday, and felt that her guests were like devils from hell. Perhaps her mood was worsened because the usual sequestered tranquillity of Panshanger was being ruined by busy noise. A gale had blown down many Hertfordshire trees, and a camp of German prisoners, all skilled woodmen, was installed in the park. They wore ignominious blue identification marks patched on their backs like bull's eyes for a marksman if they tried to escape. The usual stillness at Panshanger was broken by the ring of the German woodcutters' axes, and by the hacking and whacking of smaller branches. Thin curls of smoke wound up from fires which they had kindled. When Alice and Jim Salisbury, with their son David Cecil, came over from Hatfield for luncheon on 26 January, Ettie had a long, comforting colloquy with the marquess, who suffered bouts of religious melancholia and anxiety attacks, which he discussed helpfully with her. *Jmmm*, she always pronounced his name with lingering relish. Years later, when she wrote to Lady Salisbury – 'Ally, I really believe there were moments when I should have perished of pain and tiredness if it hadn't been for you – one or two Panshanger moments, & one at Hatfield station' – she was thinking of this time.

On 27 January the last of this bout of Panshanger parties arrived. It included Henry and Margot Asquith with their two children Elizabeth and Anthony, Ian and Jean Hamilton, Edith Wolverton, Kitty Drummond, Field Marshal French, Arthur Balfour, John Revelstoke, Linky Cecil and again Patrick Shaw-Stewart. 'Having a delicious visit,' Jean Hamilton jotted in her diary. 'It's such a small comfy party and Ettie as fascinating as ever, but one feels great sadness here, in spite of the courage and determined brightness of Willie and Ettie, both their lovely boys gone, and now Lord Lucas too . . . Imogen is a darling, growing up such sweetness and charm. Lord Hugh Cecil is always an enthralling man to talk to . . . Edith Wolverton has been the blot on the party – she represents a full stop always to me, and everything would have been much gayer without her. She has aged terribly, and has a . . . weak mumbling look about her mouth and chin, and her dowdy conventional clothes are depressing – I wonder if Lord Derby still adores her.'

Once this house party had dispersed, Ettie went, as Dr Beauchamp had instructed, to the King's Hotel, Brighton, and took enormous walks on the sunny, snowy Downs, avoiding the seafront where wounded soldiers pelted passers-by with snowballs. She resisted all visitors except Consuelo Marlborough, who had a house nearby. 'I simply can't tell you how well I feel after one week,' she reassured Balfour. 'I've literally *slept* 15 hours out of every 24, which one didn't know was possible to anyone with less intellect than you!! I *adore* the massage, eat like Hercules, have neither read, written or thought . . . I am out of bed from 12 till 5 every day, & flee straight to the Downs, & walk for miles, & have luncheon at tiny inns – far from this vile & obscure town, where rich old Jews in fur-coats *still* have very bored-looking beanos with middle-aged Poplollies.'

Soon after leaving Brighton she faced the second anniversary of Julian's death. 'Two years after is rather a bad time,' she told Evelyn de Vesci, 'one ought to have found out the new roads, & new ways of treading them, & yet reconstruction is such slow & difficult work.' If she was not to become a numb, unresponsive automaton, she must brace herself. She quoted at herself two lines from an old Scottish ballad that she had read to Julian and Billy when they were small:

> I'll lay me down and bleed awhile,
> And then I'll rise and fight again.

Again she took refuge in a hotel: the Beacon Hotel at Hindhead, close to Grayshott, where she had visited Billy on the day that the first telegram about Julian's wound had been sent from France. 'This is the day (of the week) that our darling Julian left this world, with that strange smile of rapture in his eyes,' she wrote to Monica. 'How those days will always stay, exactly the same, in our hearts. *Billa's days* too, for our farewell to him was that same week, at Hardelôt.' Her quiet retreat to Hindhead brought 'such peace' to her, especially an early morning service at a tiny church with the sun – Julian's Phoebus Apollo – pouring through the stained-glass windows.

Ettie's friendship with Lord Londonderry had intensified since the day he drove Billy over to Hardelot to see the Desboroughs after Julian's funeral. She never forgot 'all that you were to me & did for me, dearest Charley, during my worst times of anguish, your untiring pity & help . . . Every year that one lives one cares more I think about friendship – it has such secure glories, all its own, quite *different* from the other sort of thing.' She became his confidante and the booster of his surprisingly precarious morale – the only one of his women friends with whom there were no amorous undercurrents. She felt for him enduring love, gratitude and admiration; and during her depression in 1917 she sought his comfort. 'It always seems to me so wonderful that you can be so dear & patient in friendship with someone who is really only half-alive now, so strangely frozen & paralysed. I feel often like a dead woman, still able to move & speak & eat & laugh, but the real person gone far away. It is *all wrong* – I am always fighting, & shall prevail at last. How fine Montaigne's saying is, "We must live among the living." Only you don't know Charlie how touched one is by those who understand & are patient, & *trust* one to fight it out in the end.'

Ettie worried that her daughter might be caught during one of the air raids on London. Southwood, the house at Ramsgate where Ettie as a girl had paid tense visits to her aunt Rose Weigall, was wrecked in 1917 by a torpedo fired from a Zeppelin. A German aeroplane flying over Hertfordshire towards the munitions factories at Luton dropped a bomb on the lawn at Brocket, breaking all the windows on its south front. Old Lord and Lady Mount Stephen, who were sitting in the drawing room, were later asked what they had done in this crisis. 'Why, rang the bell, of course,' replied Lady Mount Stephen, 'and much to our annoyance *no one* came.'

Balfour was dining with John Revelstoke in Carlton House Terrace when three bombs fell close by. All the Salisburys' windows were broken in Arlington Street and Devonshire House was damaged. 'These raids were very noisy,' Monica recalled. 'There was a regular barrage of fire all round London, and many guns were in London itself. The searchlights were vivid, raking the sky, their beams crossing like swords; they were very beautiful.' She remembered walking once along Kingsway. 'The searchlights were dazzling across the sky, and it was a glorious, still evening. It gave me a jump of fear when I realized that the moonlight was strong enough to throw my shadow in front of me, between the very dim street lamps. The weather seemed to be inviting a raid.'

In February 1918 an air raid interrupted a dinner given in Arlington Street by Ivor Wimborne, who years before had threatened to shoot himself for love of Ettie. The guests – including Edgar D'Abernon, Venetia Montagu and Diana Manners – trooped down to a vaulted basement until the danger had passed, and amused themselves by devising a women's Cabinet, as all the political males appeared to them exhausted. The military correspondent Colonel Charles Repington, who was present, noted down their selection. Lady Desborough was to be Prime Minister and Diana Manners Vicereine of India. Ettie's Cabinet would comprise, they agreed, Adèle Essex as Foreign Secretary, Alice Keppel as Chancellor of the Exchequer, Clemmie Churchill as Home Secretary, Helen D'Abernon as Minister of Health, Pamela Lytton as Postmistress General, Consuelo Marlborough in charge of the Local Government Board and Edie Londonderry at the Board of Agriculture – with Margot Asquith Leader of the Opposition.

When Neil Primrose, Rosebery's favourite son, was killed in November 1917 in a cavalry charge against the Turks near Gaza, Ettie wrote to her old friend: 'No-one knows what the anguish is till it comes – our children, whose very existence is a part of our own.' She promised Rosebery that in time, 'there come moments when it seems only a small part of the whole that our hearts are broken to pieces'. But might not her heart be broken into pieces a third time by Ivo's death in action? Willie's cousin Arthur Grenfell had urged him after Billy's death to forbid Ivo to enlist. 'Our family has done its share,' he said. 'I don't think we should run the risk of getting wiped out as a clan, and I do hope . . . you will manage to keep him at home.'

Arthur Grenfell himself was to win the DSO at the Battle of the

Somme, and came from a heroic fraternity: his eldest brother Pascoe had been murdered in the Matabele rebellion of 1896, his brother Robert had fallen in the charge of the 21st Lancers at the battle of Omdurman in 1898, and his twin brothers Francis and Riversdale had been killed on the Western Front – Francis, who had been awarded the VC, died two days before Julian. The family became synonymous, in their class, with selfless, patriotic courage. 'The Grenfells', declared the Marquess of Winchester, 'were a symbol of that landed gentry who made England a nation of sportsmen, pioneers and warriors. When that type fails to be bred, but not till then, will England begin to sink downhill.'

Kitchener had decreed that so long as he was Secretary of State for War, Ivo would be kept back from the trenches; after he drowned, his decision was supported by his successor at the War Office, the Desboroughs' friend Lord Derby, then by their even closer friend Lord Milner, who succeeded Derby in April 1918. There was nothing irregular in this: it was the usual policy of the Adjutant-General that if two sons of a family had been killed, the third should if possible be kept back. Ivo left Eton in 1916, having turned eighteen, entered Sandhurst at the earliest possible moment and began training in the Grenadier Guards. He was desperate to prove himself equal to his brothers in front-line service. During the summer of 1917 Alice Salisbury went to see Sir Henry Streatfield, the colonel commanding the Grenadiers, to emphasise that Ivo was far too young, in every way, for the strain of action at the Front. Streatfield assured her that the War Office did not intend to send him out for some time.

Milner – a member of the War Cabinet – then asked to see Ettie, and confirmed his 'great desire to prevent Ivo going into the Trenches! He said he really considered it wd be *wrong* & he wd do anything in the world to stop it. I cannot tell you how *dear* he was.' (Ettie indeed had a special relationship with Milner: 'you were the only one who made him really human,' St John Midleton told her when Milner died.) Nevertheless, in November 1917, after dining with Ivo – 'a vision and very sweet, though not clever to talk to' – Cynthia Asquith noted that the boy felt humiliated at being kept back from the fighting and was clamouring to go out soon: 'how unthinkable for poor Ettie.' The Desboroughs were helped by the fact that Ivo's health seemed frailer than Billy's. It is impossible now to assess the diagnoses of digestive and heart weaknesses or the extent to which specialists were giving the opinions that the Desboroughs wanted; but Ettie's anguish was palpable. 'Over the possibility of Ivo going,' she told Mary Wemyss in March 1918, 'I do feel a kind of bankruptcy of courage.'

In May 1918 she took Ivo for treatment at Harrogate by a retired army surgeon, Dr Richard Morris, who pronounced that the boy would not be fit for active service for some time. In June (and again in September) Ivo was sent to the royal physician Sir Bertrand Dawson, who did not prohibit light military duties, but insisted that the boy's health must be monitored. To Ivo's chagrin he was offered work at Pirbright as a military instructor, or an appointment as ADC to the newly appointed Governor of Bombay, George Lloyd, who had married one of Willie's Lascelles cousins.

It was the same for all the mothers who had lost sons and had more to send. Elizabeth Kenmare's youngest boy Gerald went out to the Western Front in 1916 aged only nineteen: her middle son Dermot had been killed a year earlier and the eldest, Valentine, had nearly died of his wounds and psychologically was much affected. 'Little Gerald went off at 6.30 a.m. yesterday,' she wrote to Ettie, 'and I feel terribly frightened, that last hour of packing and forced cheerfulness is as bad as any on the scale. He had breakfast on a tray in my room & then I saw his great tall back fade away – just in the same frame as the last picture in my mind of Der. I didn't know how to let him go, and now, I can't help it, I feel a trembling dread through every word I speak & at the back of every minute of the day. There are times when all the courage one tries so hard to store melts and one feels a *very* cowardly wretched creature, but you understand – and know that saying it helps.'

On Christmas Eve of 1917 Ettie was taken ill with blood poisoning in her cheek. She was still weak when the news arrived that Patrick Shaw-Stewart had been killed in action near Metz on 30 December. During a heavy evening barrage he was struck through the mouth by a shell splinter and died within a few minutes by the side of the road.

'I, who never have had a presentiment, had utter foreboding about him this time,' Ettie wrote on 5 January 1918 to Margot Asquith. 'I knew that we should not see him again. We said goodbye that morning, in the street . . . I said to him "Hasn't this time been somehow even happier & more than ever?" & he said, with such a dear *childish* look of trust & affection, "You see, to me it never could be more." ' She had teased him that he would buy some cheap notepaper and write to all his 'lady loves' during his journey to the coast. 'He wrote from the train, "I did buy the notepaper, but it was to write to you, & to tell you how I adore you, & that you have never been so indispensable to me." ' She had never felt possessive or threatened by his other women, she told Margot. 'Of course he had crowds of love affairs, darling boy, but our friendship was quite steady & different & outside all that. He never minded how much I scolded & governessed him. I sometimes used to wish he would mind more!' Ettie had been shocked by Margot's ebullience after her stepson Raymond's death, but still trusted her enough to show her raw grief. 'Sometimes one feels almost quite *smashed*, but that is all wrong. It was terrible having to tell little Imogen that yet another of those she knew & loved best was gone – there was such a tight bond between her & Pat (who loathed children as a rule). She came into the room & saw the telegram in my hand, & just said "Who?".'

Friends hastened to console Ettie at this first and worst body blow of 1918. 'I can think of nothing', Con Manners wrote, 'but what you have been to him in his life; he was the only one knew & understood *everything*, & what Taplow was & is, & all it has stood for to us all.' Like many others, Con Manners attested to Shaw-Stewart's rare personality: 'that genius for friendship, that consummate knowledge of what he wanted in life, that vivid & resolute energy'; but above all his commitment to Ettie. 'He *adored* you didn't he Ettie? Surely we cannot be called upon to hear & face much more?'

After hearing of Shaw-Stewart's death Duff Cooper rushed to Taplow. He found Ettie in her room, sitting by the fire, almost in the dark. 'She adored Patrick and was perhaps the chief person in his life,' he recorded. 'She kissed me and I couldn't help crying a little. We sat and talked about Patrick until dinner. She is the most wonderful woman in the world, and the bravest.' The memory of their talk stayed forcefully with him. 'Often I think of you,' he wrote afterwards, 'and try to emulate your steel courage, your unquenchable inspiration, your dauntless endeavour to build up again with broken tools and to see in what is left something that is worth keeping. But I am made of poorer stuff, and cannot do it.' Ettie's response was branded with her bracing love. ' "Be invincible" Pat used to say,' she replied from Stanway. 'Grief makes one terribly self-absorbed & self-pitying . . . I can't get away from the pain yet, the sense of life being one gigantic bruise – but one will.' Yet she, too, needed reassurance very much: 'Duffie, you will always care for me a little? You see nearly all the young are gone now who really cared for me & who I adored.' She was slow to rally from Shaw-Stewart's death, and her intensifying superlatives seemed excessive to some friends. 'Poor Ettie is very unhappy about Patrick,' Venetia Montagu wrote after visiting her in late January. 'I can't with truth come up to her standard of praise, and am always rather forcing the note. But she is very sweet and I do love being with her.'

By June Ettie was happier, gossiping to Duff Cooper about Lytton Strachey's new best-seller, *Eminent Victorians* – 'brilliant,' she told Cooper. 'I laughed a lot, but didn't really like it. To me it gives the impression of a rather small and fundamentally inhuman man dissecting with extreme skill, but with a really rather bitter bias, men very much greater than himself.' Strachey was suddenly fashionable – lionised first by Consuelo Marlborough, and later by Ettie, Margot Asquith and Nancy Astor. Ettie praised Dostoevsky to Cooper too. 'I really do like him, divesting myself so far as is humanly possible from *Snobbisme*. I read him in a sort of maze, rarely disentangling the characters & their distracting pseudonyms, but in a contented reverie, hoping he'll never stop.' Dostoevsky's gleams of madness – 'one never feels *quite* sane again after reading *Le Crime et le Châtiment*' – were more palatable to her than the plain speaking of other Russians. 'I've read a lot of Tchekov lately, but am not so very good at the disgusting in literature. That's what stumps me with modern English novelists, say James Joyce – a fatal & Victorian tendency to physical nausea.'

For years Ettie had read in the winter evenings at Taplow, made notes and memorised what she had read. Walter Raleigh, the first Professor of English Literature at Oxford University, was impressed by her literacy. 'She knew all my books quite well,' he said, 'having read them with real interest, no bunkum. Indeed if you mentioned any poem, she could quote it mostly.' He and Ettie stayed together at Stanway in January 1918, a fortnight after Shaw-Stewart's death, and following her departure, Cynthia Asquith asked if he missed her. 'I *never* miss her,' Raleigh replied. 'I'm glad to see her, but I never *miss* her – because you see she's never a rest.' He found that 'her deliberate activity made her mechanical, and prohibited any real friendship', and he was wearied by 'her constant "battling" against life'. Some of the younger Coterie mocked what they called 'Ettyism' – the implacably positive reaction to disappointment and tragedy – and Cynthia admitted that before the war, 'one might have been irritated by her stubborn gospel of joy and attributed it largely to health and personal immunity'; but felt her wartime 'determination to go on fighting with broken tools . . . was wholly admirable'.

If Raleigh underrated her aptitude for intimacy, Cynthia Asquith's father-in-law did not. Ettie consoled him when, in January 1918, his son Arthur ('Oc') had his leg amputated – after enduring prolonged agony in the hope of avoiding dismemberment: psychologically he never recovered. In his reply, Henry Asquith ranked Ettie's as 'one of the best & most helpful friendships of my life'. She was 'the *first* person to whom I looked for loving sympathy', he told her. 'All through, you have known my secret, & shared my hopes, & cheered my despondency with your unfailing faith, & been in all times of difficulty & darkness the wisest & tenderest of counsellors. I shall never forget, and there is reserved for you a place of your own in the most sacred recesses of my heart always.'

The summer of 1918 had a high point of social comedy with the ceremonial feast given by the newly remarried Curzon after he had clawed back his great house at 1 Carlton House Terrace from serving as the headquarters of the Belgian Relief Fund.

George Curzon's dinner was really too amazing – 70 people, 60 men and 10 women, seven tables in the Ballroom and the most extraordinary pre-war banquet, one felt like a person acting in a cinematograph [Ettie told Monica]. I think he must have made quite forty enemies, as he asked all the official men without their wives, including Lloyd George and the Archbishop of Canterbury, and then put in ten extra women, and all the bigwigs looked as black as thunder, and even people like Edwin Montagu said they did think it most excessively rude. I asked George why he had done it, and he said that on these occasions the only safe rule was to take no notice at all of anyone's feelings. A.J.B. said that it seemed to him strange to take the trouble to ask 70 people to dinner in order to offend them; but George was quite triumphant. I had a lucky place between dear A.J.B. and John Morley, and talked afterwards to Winston and Bob Cecil, so the outlanders might have been in their own colonies so far as I was concerned.

Ettie had another busy London day on 21 October. She lunched à *deux* with Milner and dined alone with Balfour. 'They had been sitting in the Cabinet the entire day, and poor A.J.B. looked more annihilated by dinner time than any human being I have ever seen, but he picked up a little after oysters and champagne, and was cheerful on the whole.' Both men found this period 'almost more anxious and critical than any during the War', she said. 'The great difficulty seems to be to ascertain the exact *pitch* of exhaustion of the Germans. They know it is very great, but is it complete?'

The imminent armistice made her recall 'The Soldier's Faith' and its sustaining message. 'How often my thoughts turn to you,' Ettie wrote to Justice Holmes. 'It was you who first of all revealed to me the glory of war. I drank in your words in those happy days.' The Judge was to her a symbol of self-discipline. 'So much of what *little* I know of courage & truth,' she added later, 'of proud submission, has been learnt from you.' She had been sustained by thoughts of his faith 'so often when the waters went over my head'. Her rational self still upheld the resplendent honour of the young soldiers' sacrifice, and felt uplifted by the stupendous unselfishness of the immolation; but her instinctual and less disciplined self felt desolate at the waste. She often quoted a line from Maurice Baring's elegy to Bron Lucas: 'Something is broken that will not mend.'

She spent the morning of 11 November – 'Peace Day' as she called it – at Avon Tyrrell with Monica before returning to Taplow. 'I was *so* thankful to be with you today – how proud I am of your most splendid 4 years & a quarter, never flinching or looking back,' she wrote in the evening to her daughter. 'I did think of you, on the long strange endless journey through the rain, the inarticulate thankful crowds, looking as dislocated & dazed as one felt oneself, and as conscious of the inadequacy of human hearts & bodies to contain emotions such as these.' Monica replied from Avon Tyrrell, which had been converted into a military nursing home. 'Here it was just so right, no hysteria & such depths of thankfulness and brimming hearts,' she said. The patients and staff built a huge gorse bonfire, Lord Manners made a speech, during which his eyes filled with tears for his dead son, & then we all sat round & there was wonderful deep-voiced singing by the troops – so calm & lovely – all the war-time songs. It was really very moving. At dinner they drank a thousand and one toasts "To our fallen comrades" . . . Oh Mummie there is agonising sadness in this calm after strife.'

The bereaved mothers felt for one another and exchanged messages. 'PEACE DAY: I know, darling, that your agony *was doubled*,' Elizabeth Kenmare wrote. She was thankful to be at Dermot's home in Killarney, as Ettie was in her boys' home at Taplow, 'for we couldn't join in mad rejoicings. I walk in the golden sunshine & calm peace of lovely autumn days, through his woods, his hills, and tell him he is not forgotten, that the world is rejoicing because *they won*. I know that you are doing the same, & so is Con & Mary, and whole hosts of others.' Alice Salisbury's two sons both survived the war, but feeling the need to revivify the dead, she spent a day and part of the night with the *Family Journal* – 'with you and your children,' she wrote to Ettie, 'reading again page by page.' To Mary Wemyss, on 11 November, Ettie wrote: 'All day the thought of you has burnt in my innermost heart. Victory, & you & I look in vain for our Victors.'

Ettie felt bewilderment after the cataclysm. 'These days are very strange, I wonder if everyone feels the same sense of emptiness,' she wrote to Lord Kilbracken on 18 November. A Taplow villager had said to her, 'one can't help feeling very quiet', which seemed to Ettie exactly right. She tried to feel that 'out of the shattering, the darkness, the anguish only the Triumph *remains*', but longed ineradicably for her dead sons – and for Bron Lucas, Dessy FitzGerald, Patsy Shaw-Stewart and the rest. 'And now,' she told Kilbracken, 'the last lap comes.'

CHAPTER 7

The Grande Dame

ک

IN 1919 ETTIE turned fifty-two. The grief of the previous years
had unalterably changed her: she no longer found pleasure in the
intricate, over-artful games that she had once played with the
emotions of her men admirers; her perspective was wider; her feelings
ran deeper and more true. Ever conscious of mortality and loss, her
life-enhancing powers were undimmed. As always she remained an
inspiration to her friends. Maggie Ponsonby gossiped to a friend about
the wedding in February of John Revelstoke's nephew Jack Althorp to
the Duke of Abercorn's daughter. It was so '*mondaine* I became a
Bolshevik', she said. 'I wanted to break Bridget Keppel's teeth, pull off
Lady Herbert's hat, torture the Duke of Abercorn, & then I saw one
beautiful woman, which was Ettie. She's far more beautiful than she
ever was . . . You can see in her face that she has been at grips with
terrible reality & come out of it without bitterness – and it is her belief
in Creeds [*sic*] that saved her.'

Ettie remained indispensable to her friends. 'As years fly by,' Helen
D'Abernon wrote in April, 'one learns who are the few that really
count for one – whose love one clings to, whose presence is an unfailing . . . joy. No one in my life has filled quite the place that you
have filled, darling Etty, no one . . . has won so unreservedly my
admiration.' Ettie remained, too, a most congenial guest. 'When you
come to a house,' St John Midleton wrote after the Desboroughs had
visited him at Peper Harow in 1919, you 'bewitch everyone, make
every thing go, obscure the marriage vows in the mind of a Bishop &
almost arouse them in the heart of a celibate Senator; leaving little
heaps of feathers all round, you put a host & hostess heavily in your
debt'.

Ettie in middle age was determined to remain in the vanguard without compromising her old standards. In March 1919 she gave a dance at which the guests 'danced "jazz"' – several of them for the first time – and thus aroused *ancien régime* disapproval. At a dinner given a few days later by old Lord and Lady Lansdowne, ex-Viceroy and ex-Vicereine, 'the conversation, which included an attack on "jazz" dancing, was of rather a reactionary nature', noted the Lansdownes's thirty-seven-year-old nephew Lord Winterton. Eddie Winterton so enjoyed Ettie's dance that he promptly went for 'tango' lessons with a dancing mistress: although reminders of battlefield deaths and mutilation were inescapable, he relished this first post-war Season with its opportunities to dance with 'real pretty girls in an atmosphere almost attuned to heroism by the many empty sleeves among the men'. Alarm at the prevalent industrial unrest and fear of international Communist revolutionaries provided a disquieting backdrop to London's resumed festivities. Willie, Ettie and Winterton were among the guests of Bertie and Eloïse Ancaster at Eresby House in Rutland Gate that March. The Curzons, Hugo Wemyss, St John Midleton, Con Manners, Linky Cecil, Alan and Helen Northumberland and the French Ambassador were fellow diners. Winterton felt positively apprehensive at enjoying himself: 'Very rich & luxurious, Lady Ancaster looking like I know not what in her very artificial get-up. One could not help contrasting this with the seething unrest o'er the realm & with Germany, Petrograd, Vienna & the rest. Is it our 1788?'

On 1 May Ettie took Ivo to Paris, where Monica joined them. She stayed first in John Revelstoke's apartment in rue du Faubourg Saint-Honoré and later at the British Embassy with the Derbys. 'I cannot tell you how divine it is here, or what fun & interest we are having,' she enthused to Willie after a week. Charley Londonderry was 'an angel' to her, and his reputation as a rich English milord ensured flattering treatment when he escorted her to Antoine Rumpelmayer's *salon de thé* on rue de Rivoli or to smart dressmakers. Ettie, however, was a prudent shopper, who often wore clothes cut or trimmed by her maid Gaston, and was the antithesis of a showy Parisianised peeress. She stayed up until three in the morning when Ivor Wimborne took her to a ball at the Hôtel Majestic, then the headquarters of the British delegation at the Versailles peace conference. She thrilled to hear each day's *va et vient, poste et riposte* from Arthur Balfour, the Foreign Secretary, who viewed every momentous decision at the conference 'with the detachment of a choir-boy at a funeral service', according to one of his officials, Robert Vansittart. Ivo (aged twenty) went to lunch alone with Balfour on a day when Ettie lunched in a party with Lloyd George. She was susceptible to the Prime Minister's magnetism and wished she could cultivate him for Taplow, but this was vetoed by Willie, who abominated the little Welsh attorney both as a radical and as a crook.

After this hectic round, Ettie and Monica went to recuperate in Fontainebleau forest: 'the beauty & peace here are inexpressible, & Casie & I are so happy,' she told Willie. 'I never saw *such* beauty – the very essence of May, with summer heat super-added, & the very moment of moments for the flowers & sweet smells. The whole country is like a bower. We have hired two ramshackle bicycles in the village, & get very long distances across the Forest, very leisurely! & have dolls' tea-party meals such as we love at remote little inns. The early mornings & nights (moonlight) are very cool & lovely – the midday hours *very* hot, we usually sleep soundly in the Forest, in the afternoons.'

From Fontainebleau mother and daughter went to revisit Julian's grave. 'I dreaded coming back here in a way, as well as longed to,' she told Mary Wemyss. 'His grave is bright with tulips, rose & white & mauve, a red rose-tree at the foot. On that sunny windy hill, looking away to the far country & the battlefields, all quiet now. I sat last night on the great grey ramparts of the old town, close to where he lies at rest, the "fretful ridge" of Boulogne spinning far, far below. All the five years seemed to sweep before one, all the overpowering changes within & without. I felt more than ever, though one cannot explain why or how, that one would not surrender one moment of the anguish.' All the bereaved mothers thought tenderly of one another during their pilgrimages to the war cemeteries. That same May of 1919 Elizabeth Kenmare visited her son Dermot's grave. It was, she told Ettie, 'all so beyond comprehension, the wide battlefields, so awful, so terrible; the strange hush over all that devastation, the grim ruins, the piteous little crosses standing here and there in utter loneliness; one's mind and soul seemed to break before anything so unbelievable, unable to hold anything so immense; it was almost unbearable and yet one came away with a serenity at heart, for the splendour of the sacrifice outweighed all else.'

Ettie had a new preoccupying misery during the summer of 1919. Ivo, who felt he had been cheated out of the front-line action in which his brothers had died, volunteered to fight with the Allied Forces against the Bolsheviks in north Russia, and left England on 3 July. Ettie set to work to distance him from danger and on 5 July Churchill, the new Secretary of State for War, telegraphed to General Ironside, the Commander-in-Chief in Archangel, suggesting that he put Ivo on his staff. 'How all the anxieties old as well as new combine,' she wrote on 8 July, 'but he went forth on wings of joy, & to have failed him would have been to deny every tradition that the children have laid down for us.' In addition to Churchill, Ettie approached Sir Henry Wilson, the Chief of Imperial General Staff, who sought to dispel her fears. 'Of course war is war and one never knows but I can tell you quite honestly that I have no anxiety. I have not the time to write you my reasons for feeling confident but that is very much my frame of mind.'

It was impossible for Ettie to forget the Baltic war during her Saturday-to-Monday at Taplow on 26–28 July 1919. She had invited the historian H.A.L. Fisher, whom Lloyd George had brought into the Cabinet as a reforming Minister of Education, together with Winston and Clemmie Churchill, the Duke of Argyll, Lady Kitty Somerset, Lady Moyra Cavendish, Evan Charteris and the novelist Hugh Walpole. On the Sunday morning Walpole secreted himself upstairs finishing his story 'Absalom' – 'quite decently,' he noted in his diary. 'At lunch and afterwards studied Winston and came to the conclusion that he's not to be trusted at all – conceited, overbearing, irrational, ambitious . . . a real Prussian not a democrat at all.' He found Ettie's other guests 'not very interesting', although the Duke of Argyll was 'agreeable and friendly'. After dinner on Saturday, Churchill displayed his ebullient non-Junker side by reading aloud from *The Young Visiters*, a hilarious novel about High Society written by an eight-year-old girl called Daisy Ashford, which had been published a few months earlier. But at other times, speaking as the man in control of the War Office, he promised a September offensive in the Baltic and repudiated any idea of peace talks with Bolsheviks. On the Sunday, when Fisher strolled with Ettie down the cedar walk, he found that Winston's belligerence had cruelly frightened her about Ivo.

Churchill alarmed Ettie again with bloodcurdling predictions about the Archangel evacuation in September 1919, and Fisher again reassured her: 'Winston is, always, full of great imaginings; he has the defects of his qualities but the rest of us, who are of the common clay, neither heroes nor poets, will be quite content to cut our losses and to leave the Bolsheviks to perish of their own incurable maladies.' The great hope of the Desboroughs returned safely from Russia – 'beautiful Ivo, what a splendid boy: with not one drop of carp or nastiness in him: a perfect boy,' said Lady Islington – and went up to Christ Church Oxford to study agriculture.

In January 1920 the Desboroughs returned to Panshanger, where they lived, Ettie said, like picnickers while she superintended its tidying and cleaning after the two-year let to Lord Queenborough. When the renovations were completed in March, she determined to have a sequence of parties to inaugurate a new social era in her ancestral home. 'We hope to be there all April, will you *please* come & stay with us – in a nice clean room!' she begged Charley Londonderry. 'I should love to show you all the little things we've done – & we'll play on the newly laid *En tout cas* court, & the garden golf-course, & dance in the gallery, & fish for pike . . . & sit in the sun on the terrace.' Even the game of skittles was newly laid on. Cynthia and Beb Asquith, with Violet Bonham Carter, joined Evan Charteris, Linky Cecil, and Simon and Laura Lovat for the Saturday-to-Monday of 10–12 April. The guests were lapped and folded in ease, suffused and immersed in Ettie's warmth, and brightened by the light of her gaze. Fifteen-year-old Mogs delighted everyone, said Violet. 'It is so strange to find a *baby*, whom one remembers biting people's toes under the Taplow table, grown *suddenly* into a thrilling, lovely, complicated, mysterious & *powerful* human being.' But it was love of Ettie that drew people to Panshanger: 'as always,' Violet continued, 'I leave you with a deep sense of wonder & reverence at the way your supreme courage & faith in life have kept the flame of *joy* alive all around you.'

The second Saturday-to-Monday at Panshanger on 17–19 April sported three Cabinet ministers, Winston Churchill (with Clemmie), Edwin Montagu (with Venetia), and the debonair and witty Minister of

Labour, Sir Robert Horne. The other guests included the US Ambassador, John W. Davis, with his wife Nell; Ian and Jean Hamilton; Diana and Duff Cooper; Frances Horner and John Revelstoke's soldier brother Everard Baring and his wife Ulrica – Helen D'Abernon's sister. Jean Hamilton felt the party of twenty-four guests was unmanageably large, and her 'bedroom with its black and white panelling, and all its heavy Spanish furniture very depressing'. Her hostess, though, was all brightness. 'Ettie is as adorable as ever – wherever she comes she brings sunshine, and her Ivo is like her – a most delightful and charming boy.' Churchill's thoughts were of the dead Grenfells, and looking around at Pans, he exclaimed ruefully, 'To think Julian would have had all this!' He was painting in the orangery at the time, and Jean Hamilton found he looked 'too funny' in his smock, painting 'dull bad pictures all day long', while Clemmie stayed 'bright and sparkling as usual about nothing at all'.

Ambassador Davis thought Panshanger the sort of place that made England the envy of the world – 'a treasure-house of paintings, china and books', with a tray and ewer by Cellini especially interesting. His wife, however, looked lost, and to Ettie's surprise they left early for London, after tea on the Sunday. The Ambassadress perhaps felt slighted or neglected, for Ettie was seldom at her best with Americans: she found their sententious, self-centred prolixity was ruinous to the parries and returns of quick general conversation. Meeting Sinclair Lewis at this time, Hugh Walpole commented, 'I wish Lewis would learn to talk instead of orate – but that's what no American will ever learn'; and Ettie agreed – she wanted a concert of voices, not solo performances, from her guests. 'Americans,' Evan Charteris had recently told her, 'I find them all very much of a type – hard, totally uncultured men, without any particular suppleness of mind, but intensely sincere & independent, forming their own opinions & living entirely in a world of facts & figures, horsepower & manpower – not quick at the uptake, excessively narrow in their outlook, & without any redeeming grace of any sort or kind.' However, Charteris concluded, 'we mustn't quarrel with our bread & butter for that is what they are.'

The final Panshanger Saturday-to-Monday of this inaugural season (1 to 3 May 1920) included H.A.L. Fisher, St John Midleton and Hilaire Belloc. The guests played various games, including one which required

St John Midleton to crawl across the floor on his stomach. 'I did not think it possible to enjoy a Sunday so much,' he wrote afterwards. 'You really were in such divine form & your family, surroundings & guests so adorable.' He was lit with *feu de joie* at this time, for two months earlier, his wife had given birth to his third son: he was aged sixty-three at the time and had been raised to an earldom a fortnight before. This seemed to secure the future of his family, but both younger sons were to die childless – killed together in the battle of Salerno in 1943. Fisher was equally enthusiastic about this Panshanger visit: 'Your brilliant valour puts new life and courage into us all and I came away from the enchantment of that delightful party at Panshanger, feeling more than ever how good it was to be able to count you and yours among my circle of friends.' It meant a great deal to Ettie to have reopened Pans and to have revived its traditions of hospitality.

On 19–20 June 1920 Ettie and Adèle Essex joined Philip Sassoon at Port Lympne, his house perched on a ridge above Romney Marsh: beneath it there stretched old woods and flat green meadows bisected by a gleaming canal with Pitt's Martello towers built on the sea's edge as a defence against Napoleonic invasion. Port Lympne was originally a smallish red-brick house in the Cape Dutch manner; but under Louis Mallet's influence, it had recently been transformed into 'a luxurious, semi-oriental and wholly incoherent "Petit Palais" of peace and pleasure', in Helen D'Abernon's description. A Moorish patio was created at the centre of the house, with green marble floor, white marble columns and a central fountain with a playing jet of water. There was a great drawing room with a frescoed ceiling representing a gruesome allegory of war. Its walls were slabbed with marble, which John Singer Sargent had advised should be the colour of a chow: moss-brown, streaked with gold, Sassoon decided he meant. To balance the high windows there were high mirrors of black and oyster-coloured glass with gilded frames. Helen D'Abernon objected that the house was dwarfed by the overdose of empty magnificence in its grounds. A majestic flight of white marble steps down the hill behind the house recalled, with their plinths, the splendours of imperial Rome – but led nowhere. The huge

marble swimming pool, flanked by colossal bastions, seemed to diminish the house behind it.

Philip Sassoon – perhaps encouraged by Mallet, who was a prematurely retired ambassador – decided that it was Port Lympne's destiny to act as the diplomatic halfway house between London and Paris. In June 1920 he hosted there an Anglo-French conference deliberating on the Turkish crisis. Lloyd George, the Prime Minister, attended with Austen Chamberlain (the Chancellor of the Exchequer), Arthur Balfour, Sir Henry Wilson (the Chief of the Imperial General Staff) and Sir Maurice Hankey (the Cabinet Secretary). The French delegation led by Etienne Millerand, the French President, included Marshal Ferdinand Foch and General Maxime Weygand. The Greek Prime Minister and former Cretan insurrectionist, Eleutherios Venizelos, was in attendance, hell-bent on Anatolian aggrandisement, and was given a free hand to attack the Turks. 'The Cretan was the worst influence in Lloyd George's life, and in the end its undoing,' wrote Robert Vansittart, who was present at Lympne although his chief, Curzon, the Foreign Secretary, had been excluded by Lloyd George in a deliberate snub. 'He was a courteous, an affable barmecide of reason, the best foul weather friend we ever had, benign beneath a black skullcap. Invincible eyes glinted behind his glasses. I admired and distrusted him immensely.'

Sassoon's most important guests, including Ettie, were installed in the bedrooms overlooking the interior Moorish courtyard, while others were farmed out to Bellevue, a nearby house where Louis Mallet lived when he was not in his set of rooms at Sassoon's Park Lane house, for at this time the two men did not like to be separated. The chiefs conferred in one reception room, their officials liaised in another, the joint secretariat slaved at the paperwork in a third, and hangers-on were relegated to the hallway, with its curving central staircase flanked by columns of blue and mauve marble. Sassoon's staff served a sumptuous afternoon tea followed by a dinner with every rich delicacy, and then a cinema show. Lord Riddell, a newspaper-owning crony of Lloyd George's, was one of Ettie's fellow guests. 'Everything done regardless of expense,' he recorded. 'Fish, meat and fruit – all of the best, and plenty of everything including sugar – rather to the surprise I think of some of the higher civil servants who were there, and who no doubt find it difficult to grub along under existing conditions. The Jews are a wonderful people.'

'The Conference at Lympne was intensely interesting, a dazzle of hectic impressions,' Ettie reported to Margot Asquith. She was captivated by indomitable Marshal Foch, whose vehement gesticulations would have made him seem like a pantomime Frenchman if he had not been so palpably a heroic leader of men. When Ettie invited him to join a bathing party, 'he said he didn't like bathing, or even baths much – "*Je jette parfois un peu d'eau sur les mains*" ' [I sometimes splash a little water on my hands]. She, Adèle Essex and Sybil Rocksavage were the only women among twenty-two men – 'Philip moving in the midst, such a queer little Pharoah-like figure, with a myriad slaves,' Ettie told Alice Salisbury. 'I got off with the P.M., but did no good with Millerand . . . The French of the English was inimitable, the English of the French wisely non-existent.'

In September 1920 Ettie returned to Paris, and met up with the Churchills, Evan Charteris, Consuelo Marlborough, and Edgar and Helen D'Abernon. She intended to travel in a party to Amalfi where they were to converge with Louis Mallet and Norah Lindsay. 'My darling,' Ettie addressed Willie from Avignon on 27 September, 'since I wrote to you cosmic catastrophes have been against us! Just imagine that *as* we stepped into the train for Italy – Winston, Clemmie, Evan & I – we heard of this appalling landslide & flood on the Italian railway, near Madane, *miles* of the line washed away . . . the Winstons were too splendid – never dashed even for one second – we took a Napoleonic decision – settled to *wash* Italy – telegraphed to *stop* Norah & Louis starting from Venice to join us – took the train (with our good reserved places) as far as it could go – which turned out to be Aix-les-Bains; a most lovely place.' They arrived at eight in the morning in time for 'such a pretty sight – the choosing of "The Queen of the Vines" for the year & the procession with her round the town. She was a beautiful creature, rather like Connie Balcarres when she was young & pretty, *glowing* with pleasure!' They then entrained for Lyons, travelling through 'gorgeous vine-clad mountain-country', and after sightseeing there, proceeded by rail down the magnificent Rhône valley: the track ran close to the river, and she revelled in the evening light over the Drôme and the sunset behind the mountains of Ardèche. Learning that

Maurice Donnay was in a nearby compartment, 'I made bold & wrote him a note saying how I loved & admired his plays, & he came & sat in our carriage, & was *charming*, & told us of such interesting places to go & see.'

After twelve hours' sleep in Avignon, Ettie awoke to 'a gorgeous morning & the real real *Southern* sun pouring in. The Winstons really are splendid, in spirits like children, & *so* loving their little holiday, & ready to go anywhere & do anything, & Evan is in glorious form & not *too* contrary!' It was an advantage to travel with the Secretary of State for War – 'they work miracles for him in the hotels & trains' – and gratifyingly cheap compared to England. The party went south to Cassis: 'a lovely place, a little Provençal fishing-village on the Mediterranean – boiling hot, blue sea in which we bathe all day, & *lovely* coast & country, & millions of "subjects" for Winston to paint. Very primitive little inn! but very clean.' One day they drove over the mountains to Marseilles, and lunched there on bouillabaisse, which proved a great disillusionment; but the Churchills proved the best of holiday companions. 'Clemmie is so delicious to be with, so easy & happy,' Ettie told Willie. 'Winston's spirits & *joie-de-vivre* & the fun-per-minute that he puts into life are quite indescribable – & his *absorption* in his pictures (really very good) keeps him utterly happy from 7 a.m. till bed-time.'

~

On Armistice Day of November 1920 the Cenotaph was unveiled by the King, and after the two minutes' silence the Unknown Warrior – an unidentified corpse brought from an unnamed war grave in France – was entombed in Westminster Abbey. There were more intimate occasions of remembrance, which touched Ettie. She and Willie commissioned the sculptor Sir Bertram Mackennal to create a memorial to their dead sons in their grounds at Taplow: a representation of Apollo in his sun chariot with the words of 'Into Battle' inscribed on the reverse.

Both Desboroughs attended an unforgettable ceremony in December 1920 commemorating the war dead at their boys' school. A bronze frieze running along a wall of Founder's Quad recorded the names of

1,157 Etonians who had perished in the fighting – 20 per cent of the 5,650 Etonians who served had been killed.

> We went today to the unveiling of the names at Eton [Ettie told Mary Wemyss]. No tinge of sentimentality crept in – a few most beautiful very short prayers, & the Guards Band playing, & the whole School singing – singing low but with such curious intensity – in School Yard, where we have all watched Absence so many times – the familiar clock striking, & I thought how often Billa used to call out, 'Oh no, it *can't* be as late as that', as he heard it on long summer afternoons. How tight they held every shining moment of their lives, as if they all knew it was not to be for very long. And then they heard that far clear call, & snatched their swords, & went shouting up the pathway to the sun . . . They all seemed so marvellously near today, in that familiar happy place, as the Reveille sounded from the roof of the chapel. The piercing pain seemed only a little part of the whole, though it did tear almost to pieces.

In February 1921 Churchill succeeded Milner as Colonial Secretary. Official opinion in Ottawa had plumped for Willie as the man to succeed Victor Devonshire as Governor-General of Canada – the idea had already been trailed in *The Times* of 4 February and *Sunday Times* two days later – and Churchill took up the idea with his usual gusto. Willie had greatly desired this post in 1905 and still had some hankering for it. Ettie went 'through HELL', she told Mary Wemyss. 'I should LOATHE it with every fibre of my body . . . but you know what his sense of duty is, & I think he will be persuaded to go. Of course I could stop it by moving an eyelid, but would not for the world. I *couldn't* do that, & if we go I shall go with a morning-face, & should abhor posing as victim & martyr.' She felt Willie had so much absorbing work in England – among other responsibilities he was Chairman of a Home Office inquiry into the police forces as well as of the Thames Conservancy Board – and that the governor-generalship was a job 'for someone who *hasn't* much to do . . . No real power or initiative possible – the jealous Canadian government sees to that – only tactful carrying out of orders from home, & endless functions & "entertaining" of that dreariest kind, which surely he'd hate – *never* being alone or having any home life.' Geordie and Eileen Sutherland '*long* to go to Canada, & I feel they'd be the very people – young & keen, & very rich, & tactful, & wanting to "make their way" in life'. She had disliked her visit to the Mintos in Canada in 1899: Ottawa was detestable, the Canadian countryside was soulless and 'the mere sound of a Canadian voice is to me like a slate-pencil'.

To Alice Salisbury, too, she poured out her horror of being a governor-general's wife: 'I LOATHE Canadians' with their 'crude aggressive trite cocksure suspicious natures utterly obvious & yet full of shoddy sentimentality just like the Yanks'. Shortly after Willie declined Churchill's offer, Ettie attended the Curzons' Whitsun party at Hackwood: the other guests included Adèle Essex, Peggy Crewe, Robert Vansittart of the Foreign Office and the Churchills. 'Winston', she reported to Willie, 'was most understanding & nice – he said he certainly would *not* have gone in your place, but that he felt bound to offer it to you, as he thought you far the best candidate.'

The Churchills were among the Taplow guests in June 1921. A few days later Winston's mother, Lady Randolph Churchill, whom Ettie had known for nearly forty years, died suddenly of a haemorrhage. 'Your spirit is brave & will stand fast, but I cannot bear to think of you in the dark country of grief,' she wrote to him. Two months later the Churchills' little daughter Marigold died. Ettie sent one of those letters vibrating with sympathetic comprehension that moved recipients, who could hear her distinctive voice in the written sentences. 'The news has just reached us on coming in tonight about the darling baby,' she told Winston. 'I cannot express to you what I feel about dearest Clemmie and you – there was something quite special about her of radiance & delight, & I am so miserable to think of this great sorrow falling on your happiest home-life, & on the other dear children. The baby of the family always seems in a way the focus-point, & Marigold was such a wonderful, darling & beautiful little child – everything that was bright seemed to lie open before her, the little Duckadilly . . . my deepest heart is with you – no one, no one knows what the pain of losing a darling child is but those who have borne it.' After a little time the Churchills were restored to equilibrium and visited the Desboroughs for a painting weekend: 'we had a happy & funny little picnic – Winston & Sir John Lavery – painting in the unbelievable October sunshine – house very partially open, & kitchen-maid in control – it was *great* fun.'

In October 1921 Sir Henry Newbolt published *The Book of the Grenvilles*, a weird novel reflecting the prevalent interest in spiritualism aroused by Oliver Lodge's *Raymond*, and written under the inspiration of John Buchan's *Francis and Riversdale Grenfell* (1920) and of Ettie's *Pages from a Family Journal*. Three young brothers become psychic time travellers who witness scenes of reckless courage: one brother dives into the river Cherwell and joins Sir Richard Grenville fighting sixteenth-century Spaniards on the *Revenge*, another brother unlatches a church door and becomes the Cornish royalist Sir Bevil Grenville's companion during the English Civil War, and the third brother takes flight in an aeroplane to the Western Front in 1914–15 and meets Riversdale, Julian, Francis and Billy Grenfell at their most inspiring. 'My book', Newbolt explained, when sending a copy to Ettie, 'shows the four Grenfells as four atoms flashing for an instant in the Storm of Chaos.' The last boy is traumatised by his Flanders experiences. 'There was a kind of beauty in what I saw that woke one up quite painfully – it was even more painful than the ugliness,' he concludes. 'We were always given to understand that time is a cure for anything, but there are some things that no-one could want to be cured of. When I remember the things that Francis and Billy said – and the others too – the extraordinary intensity of their love and the way everybody loved them, I feel I would much rather go after them at once than stay behind and lose the sense of it.'

The Grenfells, especially Julian, became totemic figures for Conservative England in the inter-war years. Arthur Bryant, the Tory historian, conjured two patriotic images in 1933. 'Wren, dying full of years, sitting upright in his chair, left behind him a glorious legacy of work accomplished – St Paul's dome, riverside Greenwich, Hampton Court, Chelsea and the belfries and spires of a hundred churches; Julian Grenfell falling in battle in early youth, a trumpet call in men's hearts to remind them how valiant, how beautiful, how generous man at his best could be.' And nearly a quarter of a century after Juju's death, during another war in which he held high responsibilities, Eric Ednam (by then Earl of Dudley) told Ettie: 'I always think of Julian when I'm scared – it's the only thing that stops me running away till I drop!'

The surviving Grenfell boy, Ivo, had gone up to Christ Church Oxford for a course in agriculture in 1920. He had a broad, disarming smile but a vague, forgetful manner and none of his brothers' fierce focus. People liked him immensely, but no one thought of him as a leader. Both his brothers had been ferocious boxers, and though Ivo had a gentler temperament, he was determined to honour their memory and prove his own worth in the ring. He got his boxing blue in 1921. Unfortunately when Willie visited Oxford to watch him box against Cambridge, Ivo delegated the dining arrangements to his flamboyant and sybaritic American friend, Henry Channon. 'Chips', as he was known, reserved a magnificent room for Willie at the Randolph Hotel, ordered a Rabelaisian feast, and invited some boon companions to dine. Willie was shocked by the precocious luxury and profligate tastes of the young men, and cannot have been surprised when he was shortly afterwards called upon to settle a parcel of Ivo's debts – run up, the Desboroughs realised, under Chips's influence. 'Thank you most awfully for sending me that magnificent cheque, it really has saved my life and reputation,' the boy wrote to Taplow, 'I shall never trust America again.' Perhaps in consequence of the high living, or probably because he lacked the studious temperament, Ivo left Oxford later in 1921, without taking a degree, and went first to tour Australia, then game-hunting in British East Africa.

'Business is bloody, and politics are worse,' Ivo said. He determined to become a farmer and, wanting to fit himself for his ultimate inheritance of Taplow and Panshanger, in October 1922 began a year's training at Lydney in Gloucestershire on the home farm of Lord Bledisloe, an agricultural authority who every year took a few pupils. During his year at Lydney, Ivo 'endeared himself to all, and especially the farm-workers, by his energy, his modesty, his indomitable pluck, and above all by his unvarying and infectious cheerfulness', Bledisloe averred. 'I have never known a more lovable young man, or one who, to a greater extent, radiated happiness in his environment.' Like Julian in the army or Monica in the Whitechapel hospital wards, Ivo was reacting against the de luxe sophistication of Taplow, and needed earthier companions than his mother's manicured, perfumed and pomaded guests. 'Simplicity of life seemed for him to be a condition of true happiness,' Bledisloe felt. 'He lived with his fellow pupils in a small farmhouse in the humblest style, and never asked for anything better. No farm work was too unimportant or too dirty for him.'

After training, Ivo began farming with Stanley ('Joe') Clarke – who had been a fellow pupil with him under Lord Bledisloe – at Alderden Manor, near Hawkhurst in Kent. The Desboroughs put some money into the venture, but grudgingly. Perhaps they were disappointed that Ivo's ambitions were limited to agriculture, or felt he was too vague to be a good organiser of the project. They seem to have been so stinting in their support, and the farm so starved of Ivo's portion of capital, that in July 1926 Clarke sent an appeal to Willie Desborough: 'I shall be very, very sorry to lose Ivo as a partner as we get on so well together, but I cannot see how we carry on like this.'

The seventh anniversary of Julian's death fell in May 1922. 'One's heart goes out to you just at this time, and I know it is a sacred moment,' St John Midleton wrote. On the Sunday, sitting under a chestnut tree at Taplow, with Mogs stretched on the grass beside her reading Spenser, she opened her heart to Alice Salisbury. 'One always feels glad that it was May . . . when he died, & that it is the May days that are consecrated to him, because he always had that overwhelming love of the Spring, ever since he could speak.' He and Billy still 'seemed so marvellously near, in the beauty of this month this year – seven of the years of our separation gone, & the blessed sense of their *vital* continuing & nearness so utterly the same as the very first day . . . The longing for them can never grow less, but I can think of them without that almost physical torture that always seemed so cruelly incongruous with them, with the power they had of turning every experience they met into the best. I always felt that in some mysterious sense it was through them that some sort of power to fight down the suffering came, they both had such a strong sense of duty & loyalty to *this* world, binding on all the people still in it. And Juju would have thought any renunciation of happiness what he used to call a poor affair.'

Outwardly Ettie did not retreat or repine. Instead, she organised a Taplow Saturday-to-Monday (20–22 May 1922) to celebrate a rare visit by Betty Montgomery from Ireland. She collected Balfour, Evan Charteris, Maurice Baring, Jack Stanmore, Mary Wemyss, Elizabeth Kenmare, Linky Cecil, Norah Lindsay, H.A.L. Fisher, Eddie Marsh,

Desmond MacCarthy, Ronald Storrs, Ian and Jean Hamilton and a few more. 'Everyone charming and in their best moods,' Jean Hamilton said of this glorious May party; and fellow guests like Jack Stanmore agreed. 'Everything was absolutely perfect. The people, the weather, the food, the lilac, the river, the bluebells and every moment of the time between 6 p.m. on Saturday & 9.30 on Monday morning.'

Lord Stanmore was a middle-aged bachelor, affectionate, discreet and harmonious, who had befriended Ettie while they were both Louis Mallet's guests in Constantinople in 1914. When the war broke out four months later, Asquith had appointed Stanmore as a Lord-in-Waiting to King George V, and Ettie was much with him at Court until he lost that post with the fall of Lloyd George in 1922. Thereafter he was the Liberals' Chief Whip in the House of Lords: he performed his duties conscientiously, despite year by year more peers forsaking the Liberal Party for the Conservatives. He was 'a good fitter-in', Ettie said: 'I am very fond of him, & he is easy.' Stanmore, like his friends Norah Lindsay and Louis Mallet, had sensibility, talent and vitality, but the trio cared most for the affection of their friends, and never chose to descend into the dust and strife of the public arena. Many of Ettie's younger friends, like Monica's ex-suitor Montie Bertie (Earl of Abingdon from 1928) were like cases: droll and deprecating, with a passive receptivity to the finer pleasures and whimsical fatalism about the future.

They were not time wasters who had to fill wide intervals of vacuity in their lives (Bertie was a trustee of the British Museum and Stanmore chairman of the management committee of a London hospital); but they *were* too contented with their lives to incise their mark on their times. Norah Lindsay was a vivacious letter writer whose conversation sparkled with unexpected analogies, lightning repartee and conspiratorial intimacies. More than that, she was one of the most instinctive gardeners of her generation: if she had wished, she might have been the peer of Gertrude Jekyll in gardening literature, and if her books had proved as racy as her talk, they would have become best-sellers. Instead, she dissipated her possibilities in conversation and friendship. Philip Tilden, the architect whom Mallet persuaded Philip Sassoon to employ at Port Lympne, found the waste unbearable. 'Sociability takes up too much energy; a hundred men and women of that generation and the one before it could have written, painted and created in some way, more than they ever did, a hundred times over. So much of what they thought and said, imagined, and suggested is lost, and I cannot for the life of me understand why Norah Lindsay could not have written half a dozen books, why Lord Stanmore could not have sculpted big and impulsively, why Louis himself could not have written the most intimate and Lamb-like essays.'

The deaths of Ettie's friends were not just sad incidents in the year, common to all people as they grow older, but indelible markers in her life. Ever since those terrible months of 1915, Ettie had made a conscious, daily affirmation of life against death, and of glad joy against despondent apathy. Death provided the context of living for her now. Grief accentuated her brio. Survival gave meaning to her zest. On the eve of the seventh anniversary of Billy's death, Ettie had a sharp shock. Adèle Essex, who had been born in the same year as Ettie, startled her friends by dying on 28 July 1922. After an evening of bridge she was motored home to Brook Street by Margot Asquith, and found by her maid next morning submerged in an overflowing bath. Early suspicions of suicide were squashed by the coroner's verdict that she had suffered a heart attack.

Evan Charteris, who had loved Adèle for years, flew at once for comfort to Ettie, who had accompanied them both on an Italian holiday as long ago as 1903. He resented the least crease in the smooth surface of his life and made a selfish fuss, though he was already more in love with Elizabeth Kenmare's daughter Dorothy, whom he married as soon as decently possible after the death of her husband, Lord Edward Grosvenor, in 1929. Ettie reckoned Adèle as 'top' for elegance of any woman she ever knew. The countess's fastidious, fragile beauty seemed the antithesis of her late husband George ('Sulky'), whose ribald conversation once made Balfour leave the room: Ettie coined 'Essex' as a synonym for coarseness. Though she had upset Ettie by meddling in the Society storm of 1906 over Archie Gordon's mendacity to Violet Asquith, Adèle's sympathy was so unfailing that no claims seemed too heavy and no confidences too irksome. She had Ettie's gaiety and Ettie's love of bright colours and flowers; and their friends had expected that of all those who figured in the social life of their generation, she would show them all how to age gracefully.

The Essexes had lived at Cassiobury, an Elizabethan house on the outskirts of Watford, for 300 years: it had been remodelled around the same time as Panshanger, and its grounds also landscaped by Repton. They could no longer afford to live there as the result of Sulky's bad investments, and its contents had been dispersed in a ten-day sale just a month before Adèle's death: the Grinling Gibbons carved staircase (admired by Edith Wharton on her visits) is now in the Metropolitan Museum in New York. 'London will never be the same without Adèle,' Jean Hamilton declared on the day after her death. 'One could depend on Adèle. I can't believe she can be gone, all that sweetness and beauty passed for ever – it was too cruel, too sudden a wrench.'

Lady Essex rested overnight in her coffin at St Margaret's, Westminster, before being cremated at Golders Green in the presence, by her request, of only one mourner – the family's agent at Cassiobury. Next day Charley Londonderry accompanied Ettie to the memorial service at St Margaret's. 'What a wonderful friend you are,' she wrote to him afterwards. 'I have been so tired lately, just too tired – not one damned thing after another but the whole lot together, that is what flummoxes me, & I long to lean my head against the wall and howl.' It was 'one of the curious cold crude contrasts of life' that only a month before Ettie had been in St Margaret's, all dressed up, for the wedding of Adèle's daughter; and she felt strange returning from the service to Taplow, where she faced 'three hundred clamorous happy little schoolchildren & their ecstasy over Punch & Judy'.

Three weeks after Adèle Essex's death Cassiobury with 435 acres was sold. The house was stripped of its fittings and demolished in 1927; part of the park was developed into a golf course, and the rest covered with small houses. The Cowpers' beloved Hertfordshire of thickhedged fields, leafy coppices and neat red-brick cottages was vanishing. Three years earlier, in May 1919, the Desboroughs had put up for auction some 2,817 acres of the outlying portion of the Panshanger estate at Welwyn. Altogether they raised £106,735 (the equivalent of about £3,270,000 in 2008), which enabled Ettie to continue living there until her death over thirty years later. The social reformer Ebenezer Howard, who had instigated the pre-war transformation of Letchworth into the first English 'Garden City', hastily raised enough money to cover the deposit for some 1,500 acres at Welwyn. During the 1920s, on the west of the development, Howard's company laid out pleasant, trim housing in leafy, curving lanes.

By the time that Evelyn Waugh wrote his novel *Scoop*, Welwyn Garden City was synonymous with blameless domesticity, cosy horizons and monthly pay cheques. The eastern edge of the development, closest to Panshanger, was reserved as an industrial area. Its factories never impinged on the Desboroughs' peace. Indeed, the Shredded Wheat factory, built in 1925 to the designs of the distinguished architect Louis de Soissons, was an object of beauty: white, clear-cut, confident and salubrious. More significant, as it proved, was the Garden City's decision, as early as 1919, to build 'an aeroplane station' intended to put Welwyn in effective touch with London. When war broke out twenty years later, the Panshanger Aerodrome made Ettie's days and nights all too lively.

The Desboroughs let Taplow for July and August of 1922 for a huge rent to the New York financier Otto Kahn and spent six weeks in Hertfordshire before going north to Scotland. 'I am so glad about this,' she told Alice Salisbury at Hatfield. 'We *couldn't* let Pans, people all seem to think it too big & difficult to manage, & I shall be enchanted to be there for a bit, & W & the children are resigned!' (None of the Desboroughs liked Panshanger as Ettie did: her children found it gloomy and grimy.) Hugh Walpole described a Saturday-to-Monday there that July of 1922. 'Down to Panshanger with Evan Charteris. Had not expected so huge a place, the Park miles long and it literally takes me nearly ten minutes to walk from my room to the dining-room. And what a house-party! Balfour, Robert Horne, the Portlands, the Sutherlands, the Salisburys, the John Wards, etc. Like the Portlands hugely: kindness shines from their eyes.' A day of pelting rain did not matter in a house like Pans. 'The pictures are marvellous especially two lovely Andrea Del Sartos and an equestrian Rembrandt. All fading from lack of attention.' Balfour discussed his favourite childhood books, *Robinson Crusoe*, *Pilgrim's Progress*, Captain Marryat's novels and Miss Yonge's, and Horne confided that 'he never went anywhere without expecting a romance. Not bad for the Chancellor of the Exchequer.' Walpole preferred Lady Desborough to Lady Colefax – 'Sibyl with her cliché phrases, resentments and intrigues and hard little curls' – and Ettie, too, felt an 'insurmountable instinctive shrinking' from the Coalbox and her methods.

Brocket had been leased to Lord Mount Stephen for many years, and after his death in 1922, Ettie's Kerr cousins decided to sell the estate. 'It is a bit of a wrench,' Lord Walter Kerr wrote, 'but we have fallen on evil times.' During this Panshanger summer of 1922, Ettie revisited Brocket. She entered the house for the first time since Henry Cowper's death in 1887: it seemed utterly unchanged, and evoked memories that felt more vivid and living than the life of the 1920s. Brocket was bought in 1923 by a cheerful brewer called Sir Charles Nall-Cain, who was duly created Lord Brocket in 1933. Ettie was soon on closer terms with the new family than she had ever been with the Mount Stephens.

Wrest (which had been held by Ettie's Grey ancestors since the thirteenth century) had previously been sold – in 1917 – to John Murray, the chairman of breweries and collieries in north-east England, whom Ettie regarded as a war profiteer. Murray hunted a pack of basset hounds, and was High Sheriff of Bedfordshire in 1923, but after sustaining financial reverses, he felled timber in the park, sold some of its monuments and retreated to a corner of the house, which sank into a forlorn condition.

There were convulsive political changes, too, and – what counted for most with Ettie – changes that involved the happiness of her friends. She had been swiftly reconciled to Venetia Stanley's marriage to Edwin Montagu, whom she sent long gossipy letters during his tour as Secretary of State for India in 1917–18; and Montagu valued her as a source of up-to-date news of the ins and outs of high office: 'you who have been seated these long years in the hub of the political wheel, spreading those wonderful tentacles of yours into the secret places of almost every plot and counter plot, and sapping information from the most unpromising quarters.' In March 1922 he was dismissed from the Cabinet after clashing with the Foreign Secretary, Curzon, over policy towards Turkey. When he went to Buckingham Palace to hand over his seals of office, Ettie coached the King to be agreeable to him and Montagu abased himself by bursting out crying in her room.

On 23 October 1922 Bonar Law became Prime Minister following the disintegration of the Coalition government and Lloyd George's resignation. Law had firmly disclaimed her acquaintance since succeeding Balfour as Tory leader in 1911, and she thought his Cabinet unimposing: 'what little stunted plants . . . dragged into the flashing light of high office'. Victor Devonshire replaced Churchill at the Colonial Office and Jim Salisbury succeeded Balfour as Lord President of the Council: the newly created Marquess Curzon of Kedleston remained at the Foreign Office. Ettie was exultant when Charley Londonderry was asked to join the Cabinet as Secretary for Air, and distraught after he decided that he was bound by a previous commitment to serve as Minister of Education in the Northern Ireland government. 'I do believe', she told him, 'that our country is very near the edge of doom, & that you could have given help that is real.' The old Liberal Party was fast decaying, and as to the Conservatives – 'F.E. greeted as Judas outside the Carlton Club; Austen no longer Leader; AJB rejected; & the Marquis triumphant. The Marquis triumphant! that to me is the irony of the situation. Nothing disturbs one's mind so much in this kaleidoscopic picture.'

Curzon's disproportionate reactions amused Ettie. As Foreign Secretary, at the height of the Lausanne conference in January 1922, he sent a letter marked '*Very secret*' to the woman he addressed as Dearest Ett. He had heard that 'young Westmorland' was 'running after' his youngest daughter. 'I am sure that he has not a bob in the world & his antecedents do not fill me with enthusiasm. Neither of course do I know if he is steady or wild, grave or gay, a money-hunter or a — .' Could she give a character reference for her cousin? Around this time George Gage reported Curzon addressing a thunderous remonstrance to the board of directors of a railway company complaining that their stationmaster at Rugby had met him wearing a bowler hat instead of a top hat.

Less amusingly, Curzon had previously vetoed Charley Londonderry's appointment as Under-Secretary for Air as petty revenge for Londonderry's refusal to support the early demobilisation of a favourite Curzon footman: 'George Curzon's manner', said Helen D'Abernon delicately, 'has become rather disconcertingly consequential.' Curzon did himself lasting damage by a haughty, irritable outburst in April 1923 to the ailing Prime Minister, Bonar Law, about the Marquess of

Winchester – the brother of Ettie's spangle of 1885. Winchester was fronting a financial syndicate, which was offering a large loan to Turkey, and Curzon declared that it was impossible to support the project because he had been forced to resign as Lord-Lieutenant of Hampshire after decamping from his wife. It was hard to think that this disputatious, pettifogging magnifico could manage a Cabinet without ructions.

A month later a party gathered at Sheringham for the Whitsun weekend of 19–20 May: Ettie, Balfour, Mary and Hugo Wemyss, Edgar D'Abernon, Evan Charteris, and Edwin and Venetia Montagu. Bonar Law had learnt that he was dying of throat cancer and on the Sunday the King received his resignation as Prime Minister. Lord Stamfordham immediately sought the views of Balfour, as the senior Conservative statesman, and of Jim Salisbury as hereditary keeper of Tory folk memory, on whether the King should appoint Curzon as Prime Minister, or the Chancellor of the Exchequer, Stanley Baldwin.

In the early hours of Monday morning Salisbury – clad in frock coat and top hat – travelled up from Devon on a milk train: a new exploit for him, upon which he dilated with pardonable pride. His advice inclined towards Curzon. Balfour went to London on the Monday morning by a more orthodox conveyance. His talk with Stamfordham was subtle but decisive: he said nothing of Curzon's eccentricities, but stressed that it was inexpedient to have a prime minister who sat in the House of Lords. 'And will dear George be chosen?' Ettie asked when he returned to Sheringham on the Tuesday. 'No,' he famously replied, 'dear George will not.' On the Tuesday Curzon met Stamfordham expecting to be asked to form a government, but was told instead that Baldwin was at the palace with the King. For some hours his dis-appointment was unbearable, but as Ettie reported to Charley London-derry, 'G.N.C. (after behaving incredibly) took a real pull on Wednesday afternoon, and made a speech at the informal Cabinet that brought soppy tears to his hearers' eyes, completely obliterating him-self, and *really* behaving very well.'

Ettie and her set were 'vastly amused' by the pretensions of the political pygmies who sat in Cabinets of the 1920s. They were especially disdainful of Sir Laming Worthington-Evans, who filled the shoes of Kitchener, Lloyd George, Derby, Milner and Churchill at the

War Office – '25th rate & bursting out of his skin with importance & the idea that he is a great international figure,' as Philip Sassoon laughed with Ettie. 'What a dull Cabinet – not a tingle anywhere,' she wrote of Baldwin's second administration formed in 1924. 'I wish they hadn't got cads like W. Evans though. I always remember him doing conjuring tricks to Lord Kitchener at Cairo – the sort of conjuring tricks that end in "Sucks for you".'

Ettie was famous in her lifetime as the mother of dead sons, but she was just as much the mother of daughters. Talk of the Lost Generation, reminders of Julian's and Billy's contemporaries who survived the fighting but never fully recovered, make it easy to forget the irreparable effect of the war on young women. It was declared on Monica's twenty-first birthday in 1914 and filled every crevice of her being. During four years of nursing she saw heartbreaking and gruesome scenes on a daily basis. Scores of the young men with whom she had danced and flirted at Taplow during the Edwardian swansong perished: several of them had courted her and a few were expected to propose before the war changed everything. When young, Monica combined tact with sympathy, enthusiasm and affection; during the war she proved to have her mother's courage; but after 1918 her life went slowly, almost imperceptibly, awry. She remained unmarried throughout her twenties, which disappointed her and worried her parents. From being a dangerously tiny baby, she had grown into a broadly built debutante; and as a wartime nurse she had snatched food at irregular hours, eaten for comfort at times of stress, and developed a taste for sweet or starchy ballast. No one thought of her as a depressive in the way that Julian had been; yet there was a trace of passivity, an air of smiling gracious lassitude, that was reminiscent of the nineteenth-century Cowpers.

Mogs had been only nine when war was declared, but it affected her life deeply. As the last child of a family spaced over seventeen years, she had been specially cherished by her mother, and they were deeply susceptible to one another's moods. She had an anxious, bewildering fortnight at Taplow when her parents were away at Julian's bedside; she was at Taplow during the unbearable, incomprehensible week after the telegram came about Billy; and she was with her mother at Sawley in that cruel month of September 1915 when Charles Lister and so many other of the young Taplow faithful were killed – she had much to bear at the age of ten. Many others of the war dead had been looming beautiful figures in her childhood. The fighting ended when Mogs was thirteen, but it changed her profoundly. She could never be a creature of skin-deep reactions or placid content. She inherited her father's athletic prowess – she was a dauntless tennis player, swimmer and rider to hounds – and her mother's effervescence, vitality and zest. But she was shy and lacked her mother's faith: life to her was more fragile, more mutable and she lived it with a romping gaiety that did not always ward off her unnamed scourges and unnameable apprehensions.

Was Ettie an officious mother? Was it a strain for her daughters always to stay fresh, attractive and amusing? Did she debilitate or demoralise their lives, or were they invigorated and enriched by her example? A general answer emerges from the many hundreds of surviving letters exchanged between the three women. Ettie liked to control people and her surroundings, she had deep fathoms of emotional experience and clear ideas about what other people should do next. But she had abundant emotional imagination, too much subtlety to browbeat and too much tact to meddle. She enormously wanted her daughters to be happy, and was thoughtful, firm and supportive in guiding them towards happiness. They turned to her for help at critical moments, and thought her a wonderful person, whom they remembered always with passionate gratitude. But her generation had high standards of self-discipline and high expectations of achievement; and though both Ettie's daughters were valiant and charming, with her skating quickness of intuition, they could not comfortably match her resolution.

Ettie and her contemporaries tried to adapt to the 1920s: at the Taplow Whitsun house party of 1925 John Revelstoke played ragtime music on the piano while Norah Lindsay led the dancing. That was the year of Noël Coward's *Hay Fever* and of Scott Fitzgerald's *Great Gatsby*; and though Ettie was game for change, her tightly controlled focus on her guests, her languid grace and her unquenchable thirst for intense and intimate Souls conversations had no meeting point with the random impulses and frenetic pace of the Jazz Age. Some of Ettie's guest lists – at Taplow as well as in London – suggest that her social net now had wider meshes, and that mundane guests sometimes slipped through. Post-war Seasons seemed to lack the self-possessed grandeur and grace of Edwardian London. The old reserve and discriminations were succumbing to a new spirit of concession. Monica's generation had endured the Victorian system of chaperonage in its unrelenting rigour; but all the traditional social mandates were relaxed by the war. Though girls were still chaperoned at balls, they went to parties and other entertainments without vigilant mammas or other female protectors. The new forms seemed *déclassé* to some sturdy matrons. 'They go about anywhere and everywhere with any male friend whom they choose,' noted Mary, Countess of Lovelace. 'In fact, they "walk out" and "keep company" just as our friends in the servants' hall do.'

With hindsight, one can recognise the Season of 1921 as a turning point. Its climax in July was 'metallic, glittering, flashy, noisy', Helen D'Abernon noted; and significantly this was the Season when Laura Corrigan first descended on London. Born Laura-Mae Whitrock, a lumberjack's daughter from Stevens Point, Wisconsin, she had married a steel magnate from Cleveland, Ohio and by the late 1920s commanded a tax-free annual income of $800,000. This fortune she deployed to push her way on to the London scene, which mocked but did not successfully repulse her. Genuinely kind, absurdly snobbish and horrendously blatant, her ideas of hospitality were not Ettie Desborough's. She was willing to spend £6,000 on a single party, and lured guests to her house in Grosvenor Square (rented from Alice Keppel) by holding a tombola, in which the tickets and prizes were rigged so that dukes and duchesses won presents from Cartier, while commoners got baubles from Selfridges. She employed cabaret artists rather than old-fashioned bands, and whereas Ettie's idea of play involved word games and intuitive wit, Mrs Corrigan had Lord Weymouth, Lord Brecknock and a pair of young titled ladies performing bicycle tricks while singing 'Daisy, Daisy, give me your answer do'.

Ettie was celebrated for her *mots justes*, but Mrs Corrigan was relished for her faux pas. She referred to the Duke of Westminster as Bend Up, Richard the Lionheart as Richard Gare de Lyon, and greeted the Aga Khan as the brother of Ettie's Taplow tenant, Otto Kahn. When it was suggested that a ballet troupe perform *L'après-midi d'un faune* at one of her parties, she was incredulous that anyone would wish to watch a ballet about a telephone; and asked after a Mediterranean cruise if she had seen the Dardanelles, she replied no, but she had had a letter of introduction to them.

Laura Corrigan's brash galas were very different from the small dance Ettie held at Taplow on Monday, 15 January 1923 to launch Mogs's first Season. It was a much anticipated event. Her guests – the 'young Beans', she called them using Mogs's dialect – were the *jeunesse dorée*, but emphatically not the wildly carousing Bright Young People of the period. 'For weeks the journalistic pen has been proclaiming the coming rout,' Edwin Montagu wrote next day, 'and this morning I read of the beautiful young women and the young hopes of noble houses; I read of Mr Clifford Essex's Band . . . of the early spring flowers, of the white and yellow dominating all other colours. I think of the party that was brought by Sir Maurice and Lady de Bunsen . . . I see the list of young soldiers who doubtless carry Field Marshal's batons in their knapsacks.'

The 1923 Season was hectic for Ettie. As she enthused to Mary Wemyss, 'Life has been so new and strange, with darling Moggie out, and average bedtime a quarter-to-five, and sleep a mere superstition! She is *so* happy, and her little ball here was so pretty, with masses of spring flowers.' The Desboroughs rented 8 Hill Street in Mayfair for the 1923 Season, and on 14 March Ettie gave a dance there attended by the Prince of Wales and his rakish young brother, the Duke of Kent. Ettie's friends took delighted interest in her daughter throughout the Season. 'It was a brilliant scene,' noted Jean Hamilton of a dance at Dudley House on 26 June. 'Winston Churchill *solemnly*, most solemnly and painstakingly footing a jazz, Sir Robert Horne gigotting through it like a pork butcher was quite worth going to see – I pitied their poor partners.' She felt Ettie looked 'battered by age – Imogen young and happy, but *not* as striking-looking amongst her lovely compeers as I had hoped.'

Elizabeth Kenmare, economising in Ireland (the family had been extricated from entangled debts by her brother John Revelstoke at Ettie's instigation), yearned to see Imogen in her Paris clothes: 'how I envy you having a daughter to bring out, those first years of sheer dancing enjoyment are the happiest that can be.' Ann Islington thought Moggie had 'so much charm, is so wise & poised: & sensible: & *so* very pretty [with] her lovely head & curly hair, her little straight nose & round chin'. Ettie looked back on the 1923 Season as 'a happy whirl, and the children so radiant and delicious'; but there were excitements in Monica's year even more momentous than Imogen's.

Since 1919 there had been a growing attachment between Monica and a widower twelve years her senior, Sir John Salmond. Jack Salmond had joined the Royal Flying Corps in 1912, at its inception, took out a squadron as a captain in August 1914, and at the age of thirty-six, with the rank of major-general, commanded the Royal Air Force in France during the last year of the war: this amounted to a hundred squadrons and about 200,000 men. In 1922 he reorganised the RAF in India, and was then posted to the Middle East, where he took command of the campaign in Kurdistan against the Turks, and consolidated the new kingdom of Iraq. Salmond had an only child, Joy, on whom he doted: he wanted her to have a pleasant home to grow up in, and was lured by the hope of introducing her to the elegant ambience and charming people that the Desboroughs provided at Taplow. He was, indeed, responsive to Ettie, and appreciative of her social arts, as well as attracted by her daughter.

In September 1923, while Ettie was staying with Balfour at Whittinghame, Monica became engaged to Salmond. 'I have always felt, in the most literal sense of the words, that you deserved happiness, as no one else in the world had ever done,' Ettie told her, 'but one never quite knew *what* the joy would be.' She thought of how happy the news would make Julian and Billy. 'Isn't Jack exactly the man Julian would have chosen, & would admire? Do you remember almost his last words about you – "Here is the girl with the sunlight in her hair, the sunlight lingering in her hair" – now it will always be about you, my darling. How those days we shared together come back . . . that most strange revelation both of the extreme of human anguish & what transcends it. All the real meaning of our lives seems gathered into them.'

Salmond was *en poste* in the Middle East, and the engagement was negotiated and clinched by telegrams. 'It's a tremendous day for us, & I just *must* tell you – although it is still utterly secret,' Ettie wrote to

Ottoline Morrell. 'We are all so tremendously happy, & she is dancing on stars. He is a wonderful man, as well as a wonderful hero, & he has adored her for four years – but she had been so unhappy – Julian & Billy killed – & *all* the people who loved her & who she loved – she suffered *too* much & was too young – & I used to fear that the smash was too complete – that she would never recover.'

The engagement was publicly announced in October 1923 and made such a stir among the newshounds that it was blazed in electric lights in Trafalgar Square. Congratulatory letters deluged Taplow. 'Give my best love to Monica – she is a treasure for any man to find,' wrote Churchill, who had been Minister for Air in 1919–21 and found Salmond 'charming & vy able. He will no doubt be head of the Air Force, when Trenchard retires.' Women like Ann Islington found Salmond 'so good-looking and romantic', and everyone agreed that he had a great future. Eric Ednam was 'overjoyed' at the news. 'Of course I know the fellow quite well by name & reputation, like the Prince of Wales and Mussolini; but have my *Who's Who* open before me and whew! my hat, what a swell. I have measured him with the Marquis Curzon's column and he wins easy!'

Salmond, as commander of British forces in Iraq, was based in Cairo, and in January 1924 Ettie took her daughters to Egypt – she had last been there eleven years earlier as Kitchener's guest. 'How charming Jack has been in every possible way, so gentle & considerate – & they really are so *wonderfully* happy & radiant,' she trilled to Willie. 'He is simply full of energy, & stirs Ca up like anything! . . . He is so exactly *right* with her in every way . . . He is so straight & simple & *sensible*, such a pleasure to deal with.' To Ivo, Ettie enthused about her expedition to Jericho and swimming in the Dead Sea. 'Oh! we've had such fun-fun, the most wonderful Beano there's ever been, not a second of one hour wasted . . . Mogs has drunk it to *the dregs*.'

Monica and Jack married on 2 June 1924 at St Margaret's, Westminster. Beforehand there had been presentations to the bride from the tenantry in Buckinghamshire and Hertfordshire, and on the Saturday before the wedding Ettie was At Home, and gave a Taplow garden party, for locals to view the presents. She had the chancel of the church ablaze with flame-pink gladioli and scarlet azaleas. Sitting in the front pew with Monica's godfather Balfour, she was resplendent in an amber chiffon dress veiled with cinnamon golden lace; a full-length cape of soft gold, copper and cocoa-brown taffeta brocade with a feathery neck border; and a brown hat trimmed with green, brown and russet plumage.

Ettie recuperated from the wedding by visiting Mary Wemyss and Gay Plymouth at Stanway. 'I never so deeply realized all that you stand for in all our lives,' she wrote to Mary, 'the symbol of beauty & sympathy, love & stimulus, & utter unshakeable understanding & trust – it was like a mountain dew to be with you & Gay – Gay in her exquisite beauty & dignity & gentleness, the dark waters one felt & feared very near her spirit, but nothing could *harm* her nobility.' Monica's marriage felt a terrible severance of old ties, she continued to Mary. 'I cannot speak even to you without an almost strangling physical pain that leaves one shattered. But then there is the all-compensating thought of Monica's happiness, & one can anchor in it – one's actual own life does literally get to matter very little . . . in comparison to the burning longing for the children's well-being.' It was a marvellous compensation that she still had Mogs, and still had intense feelings: 'Thank God middle-life has not *dulled* our sensitivities.'

Ettie never lost her enthusiasm for the company of high-spirited young men, although in the 1920s they probably seemed less idealistic and poetical than the Coterie. Foremost among the new generation was Ivo's Oxford contemporary Lord Gage. At the age of sixteen he had inherited Firle, a house nestling under the South Downs in Sussex, built around a central courtyard by his Tudor ancestors and beautifully refaced and extended in the eighteenth century. Wounded while serving in the Coldstream Guards, he was appointed as a Lord-in-Waiting by Baldwin in 1924 and held a position at Court until 1939. Ettie found him funny, dashing and intelligent, and eventually he married Mogs; but what did he think of his mother-in-law?

In 1979, at the age of eighty-three, George Gage recorded his estimate of Ettie – partly to contradict some impressions given in Nicholas Mosley's biography of Julian, which had been published a few years earlier. 'I only met her for the first time in 1920 when she was about fifty-six [actually fifty-two] and I was a fairly unsophisticated twenty-four,' Gage wrote. 'She may have been quite different in her youth, but I very much doubt that "*la vie amoureuse*" in its usually accepted sense was ever the main preoccupation of her life, as has been suggested.' It seemed improbable to him not least because of her looks. 'E.D. had the face of an ascetic, relieved indeed by frequent and happy laughter, but I have never seen a face so indicative of self-control. Her daughter and my wife, Imogen, told me her mother had suffered early in life from congenital melancholia – as apparently did Julian – and that she had cured it by sheer will power, and this I can believe. She did not smoke and she did not drink, except on one single unhappy occasion when she had a "White Lady" at a party and said to her friend, "Jack, I think I am drunk. Will you help me downstairs?" She liked men friends, and was somewhat possessive of them, and that in my view was all.'

Gage found Ettie alarming when he first met her. 'She obviously had a strong character and had a disconcerting habit of suddenly concentrating it all on you. But then I found that in spite of the alarm she was making me laugh. And then I found I was being very amusing myself. Later, I discovered that this was her great gift. She herself was not only brilliant in conversation, but she made everyone else feel brilliant.' Her only gifts were social, he thought. 'She knew little of the arts. She detested music. She decorated her bedrooms in a style we must now call African; vivid reds, oranges and yellows. The curtains and cushions were probably made from her old evening dresses. She might add to the embellishment with a vase of sham poinsettias.'

As a young bachelor, after Oxford, Gage shared a house near Buckingham Palace with Chips Channon and Prince Paul of Serbia. Ettie knew both young men. There was little in Channon – a social climber, an intriguer, a scrappy letter writer, an American and a bad influence on Ivo – to please her. He was not prompt in sending his thanks after visiting Taplow or Panshanger, but would wait until a subsequent weekend when he was staying at an even grander address like Arundel Castle, and could use his host's ducally coroneted notepaper. This ploy was too crude for Ettie. Channon, who realised her distaste for him, was surprised when Margot Asquith described her as one of the best women letter writers since Madame de Sévigné. Prince

Paul she found too much of a *petit maître*: 'what a very queer diseased little mental'.

Her doubts about Channon and Prince Paul were exceptional. Otherwise, in the 1920s, Ettie renewed her powers of friendship in Moggie's generation. She especially liked Antony Knebworth, although she had long mistrusted his mother Pamela Lytton for taking Julian away from her in 1910 and for her cruel vamping of Everard Baring. Knebworth was a hero from Willie's mould – a champion boxer and skier, an aviator and a MP at the age of twenty-eight – and Ettie felt nothing short of reverence for men of action. He was equally responsive to her charm. 'I have had a most amusing weekend at Taplow – A.J.B., Maurice Baring and Linky Cecil, all in killing form,' Knebworth reported to his mother in 1923. 'We played the two-people-talking-and-having-to-guess-who-they-are game, and she was quite, quite brilliant, knowing exactly who you were after two words. Linky said he was going to discuss an event with her and she was to guess who she was meant to be. He said, "I think you were so wonderful under very trying circumstances", and she answered, "Yes, I minded the smell most", and then the conversation went on for ages. She was meant to be Mrs Noah and guessed it at once.' Ettie's intuitions were always so quick and right. Spoken words, as she often told her men friends, were unnecessary.

Ettie's devotion to Antony lifted the fog of abhorrence from his mother. The Lyttons' house, Knebworth, was only a few miles from Pans, and it seemed absurd to prolong the old reserve of cool civility. Victor Lytton had been appointed Governor of Bengal in 1922, and was acting Viceroy of India during 1925 when Pamela sent a warm invitation to the Desboroughs. 'It would be a most tremendous joy to us all to go to India and see you all again,' Ettie replied; but the plan had to be shelved when Harriet Plummer, the old family nurse, suffered a series of strokes, and became distressed and confused. Ettie and Mogs were both as attentive to 'Hawa' as sisters, and with her when finally she died. (No one who reads Ettie's letters to Hawa, signed 'your affectionate friend Ethel Desborough', can doubt the deep sincerity of the feelings between the two women – Ettie inspired real devotion in Rose Gaston and Mildred Lear, her lady's maids, too.)

Antony Knebworth's accidental death, while flying with the RAF in

1933, drew heartfelt letters from Ettie to both his parents. '*He* was your son,' she wrote to Lord Lytton, 'that is your pride for evermore' – perhaps not a tactful opening, for the other Lytton boy, John, who now became heir to the earldom, had been fathered by Bendor Westminster. 'Billy said, when Julian was killed, that it made him realize the nothingness of death. That is what I feel about Antony – that he has just outsoared our shadows, beautiful and young for evermore.'

There were other new squires for Ettie: a young soldier called Gervase Blois, for example, and Helen D'Abernon's great-nephew Sim Feversham, whose hunting cry as Master of the Simmington hounds was *Gret-a Gar-bo, Gret-a Gar-bo*. She adored Osbert Sitwell's badinage, gallantry and provocative opinions, and he basked in her enthusiasm for his writings and wit. Sitwell's insolent playfulness – as when on a tour of China he called at the Anglo-American Golf Club in Peking and enquired of the club steward if it was the Refuge for Distressed Eunuchs – was indeed reminiscent of Julian and Billy. She began by disliking his touchy, antagonistic approach to life, derived, she thought, from early tribulation, but having pierced his defensive reserve, they became fast friends. She felt lifelong pride after he told someone that she was his favourite reader.

Two other younger friends must be mentioned: Archie Gordon's first cousin Edward Marjoribanks, and Alice Salisbury's younger son David Cecil.

Edward Marjoribanks had been seven months old when his father died in 1900. Archie Gordon adored his mother, and resented his stepfather, 'a small, pale & insignificant barrister' called Hogg, who eventually became Lord Chancellor Hailsham. Marjoribanks won a scholarship to Eton at the age of twelve, was captain of the school and by dint of working by candlelight until two in the morning achieved an open scholarship at Christ Church. There he overlapped with Ivo, but had a more brilliant career, including a double first and the presidency of the Oxford Union. He was tall and slender, with a fine forehead overhung by a rebellious lock of hair and something of the features of Julian and Billy – but supremely he reminded Ettie of dead Archie.

Marjoribanks turned to Ettie during his recurrent emotional crises, especially after his mother's death in 1925. Her sympathy and advice helped him to survive a love affair with an erratic brunette called

Pamela Beckett, who accepted his proposal, then refused it, accepted a second proposal and then finally repudiated him while they were cruising together in the Mediterranean in 1926. His uncle Lord Tweed-mouth (a Cabinet colleague of Asquith's) had died of brain disease, and Marjoribanks was haunted by the fear of going mad. 'I feel inexpressibly cold and weary; the only thing that could really warm and revive me would be to see you,' he told Ettie after being taunted about his ancestral history by Margot Asquith. 'Of course, if one *has* had a lunatic or a maniac in one's family, Lady Oxford is sure to . . . face one with it'; but Ettie's letter on the subject helped him to laugh away his worries for a time.

Marjoribanks aspired to be steely and accomplished, but achieved only a distraught intensity. 'I have heard two voices in myself for the last years,' he wrote to Ettie on his twenty-sixth birthday. 'The old, childish voice which made me want to be Captain of the School at Eton, President of the Union at Oxford and Prime Minister at 60, and another voice, more fastidious, more mature, much more critical . . . now I realise if I am ever going to be of material importance in this world, it is the old childish voice I must obey. I would rather die than not be a great person in the world's eye.' In 1929 he was elected to Parliament, where he identified himself with elderly blimps, and struck attitudes of Mussolini-like machismo. He yearned to enter the Cabinet, but must have known that his hopes of occupying 10 Downing Street were nil: as he was heir presumptive to his elderly cousin Lord Tweed-mouth, who was unlikely to father a son, his political future would inevitably be confined to the House of Lords. His reckless, over-excitable egotism earned him the nickname of Clarence. 'Clarence made a speech which filled me with consternation,' George Gage reported in 1930. 'He foamed at the mouth, his arms waving wildly & nearly knocking out Lord Salisbury, & all because of the Quota which nobody understands.'

When Marjoribanks's second fiancée came to feel overwhelmed by his highly charged personality and jilted him, he succumbed to insomnia, despair and self-doubt. Ettie tried to calm and console her young protégé; but in April 1932 he shot himself in the chest with a double-barrelled twenty-bore shotgun in the billiard room of his stepfather's house in Sussex. 'How very sad, sad, sad,' Mary Wemyss wrote to Ettie, who was stunned by this catastrophe. 'I'm glad you have been seeing him lately – tho' it makes the mystery more baffling – for never has anyone done for their friends *more* than you. You *did save* him *once*. Remember that! Never has there been a friend with a more *sane* & inspiring influence than you.' In retrospect the life of this gifted, rich young man seemed tragically futile.

David Cecil was another Christ Church contemporary of Ivo's. He was Alice Salisbury's youngest child – a sickly, imaginative, unstoppably talkative boy who only survived Eton by spending a day each week in bed. After his election as a Fellow of Wadham College Oxford in 1924, Ettie encouraged him to write his first book – a biography of her kinsman the poet William Cowper, entitled *The Stricken Deer*, which was awarded the Hawthornden prize. *The Stricken Deer* celebrated the gentle, jokey, cosy, cultivated world of the Cowpers, and delved into the family's black pits: the cycles of lethargy, depression and anguish that the poet suffered, which Ettie knew well, and the constitutional defeatism which she so robustly rejected after it killed her uncle. Desmond MacCarthy, one of the Taplow faithful, hailed the book as the work of a clear head and a clever heart; and was delighted when a few years later Cecil married his daughter. David Cecil was a witty conversationalist with a stuttering, enthusiastic delivery which endeared him to Ettie. He was gentle, sweet-tempered and combined an almost childish sense of wonder with an emphatic manner and resilient powers. 'Whenever I see you I feel encouraged about life,' Cecil told her. He always remembered that she got him started as an author. His next major book, *The Young Melbourne*, focused on Ettie's Lamb ancestors, whose portraits still hung at Panshanger – people commented on how closely Mogs resembled Lord Melbourne.

Already, at the time of the Salmond engagement, Ettie divined signs that her other daughter might marry George Gage. 'The Viscount & Mog have just gone to London,' she wrote to Monica in October 1923 when Imogen was eighteen. 'George was *so* delightful. I don't know if it will be staved off much longer, & don't exactly know what to wish; she does seem *too* young, doesn't she – & yet could one ever both love & like anyone more than him.' She gulped at the prospect of both daughters marrying and leaving home in the same year, but was touched by Gage's devotion to Mogs: 'I saw them come walking over the grass this morning before breakfast in the lovely early sunshine & they did look very happy hand in hand.' Ettie loved George Gage 'inexpressibly dearly' because he made her laugh – telling her, for example, of Philip Sassoon's parrot, which took a fancy to Winston Churchill, and to which he heard the Chancellor of the Exchequer declaring, 'I love you, parrot; I'll marry you, and breed the Holy Ghost.'

During the summer of 1924 Moggie had proposals from John Fremantle, Edward Rice and others: 'somehow she is so utterly true & direct to them all – & takes it all so simply & with so much sunshine,' Ettie wrote; but she worried 'whether the life is too exciting & in a sense spoiling for her. She has such worship poured at her feet by every post.' Ettie took Mogs for winter sports at St Moritz in January 1925, and enjoyed every moment – except when Mogs risked a broken neck on the Cresta Run twice. 'The little town looks magical,' she wrote in a description that was published in *The Times*, 'half Russian Ballet, half fairyland – the lights on the snow, the sleighs with their white furs and jingling bells, the coloured gaudy plumes fastened upright on the horses' collars, the children of every size on every species of toboggan, who dash with perfunctory cries of "Achtung" under the sleighs and between the legs of horses, the confectioner's shop proudly pointed out as "the most expensive tea-place in the world".' She adored the approach of dusk in the Alps. 'Down their white sides tiny streams of black ants are homing, to the houses and hotels, to eat and sleep, to laugh and make ephemeral love. Human existence seems to be put very surely in its place out here.'

Ettie and Willie remained great Thames-side figures during the 1920s. Photographs of Willie punting down to Boulter's Lock on Ascot Sunday appeared every year in the illustrated newspapers until 1929; and Ettie gave zest to the whole district. In 1922, for example, she organised a great jumble sale in her covered tennis court in aid of the National Society for the Prevention of Cruelty to Children – having first implored all her women friends to help. 'If you have any *real rubbish* that you could spare to me,' she had written to Jean Hamilton, 'I shd be *so* grateful. *Anything* – above all old clothes & boots & shoes,

& Ian's ditto! or tattered bits of chintz or carpet or old cushions or broken ornaments – it is astonishing what they buy!'

On the afternoon of the sale, all the local roads were thronged with people flocking towards the flag-tipped tower of Taplow Court. A dense crowd mustered patiently at the gates, awaiting the three strokes from the clock tower that signalled the start of the stampede for bargains. Once inside the building, 'it was not possible to turn back, and one had to undergo a very uncomfortable and suffocating ordeal, churned and charged about by the frenzied people dashing about from stall to stall,' reported a visitor. 'Women rushed and pushed, pushed and rushed, struggled and squeezed in the pell-mell scramble.' Outside the tennis court, the bargain hunters had stacked their barrows, prams and bicycles on which to carry home their cheap spoils – the hats, caps, cages, traps, mattresses, walking sticks, parlour lamps, table linen, dresses, dusters, and even a pedigree pig. Monica managed the dress department, Mogs the flower stall, and Willie sold boots, shoes and gaiters; 400 teas were served, and Ettie had devised other fund-raising ploys: 'the ever-present, ever-circulating, ever-smiling Jumble Queen was flitting round to press you to have your fortune told up in the gallery.' The event raised £175 (about £6,370 in 2008 values) and was a triumph for Ettie. ' "Wish dear Lady Desborough would have a jumble sale every Week," said a man going down the hill with a mattress, a bird-cage, two decanters and a tennis racket, "it's much more exciting than getting married." ' Ettie made herself, reported the *Maidenhead Advertiser*, 'so kind and unbending, so thoughtful, that as the woman with the carpet-roll and the Paris hat said, "You can't 'elp a-liking of 'er." '

The jumble sale had a less boisterous sequel. In May 1924 Ettie hired a famous puppeteer to stage a marionette show in Maidenhead Town Hall – again in aid of the NSPCC. She invited many distinguished friends and neighbours – Charley Londonderry and Geordie Sutherland were there, together with Lady Linlithgow, Lady Lincolnshire, Field Marshal Grenfell and Antony Knebworth – as well as towns-people, and raised the princely sum of £110 (about £4,180). On a Lilliputian stage the most authentic-looking, all-alive marionettes imaginable, Pantaloon, Harlequin, Columbine, Old Mother Slipper-slopper, Sam the samiosaurus, Mumbo Jumbo and others, strutted, danced and performed their antics. The hour's show was gentle and picturesque with a charming satirical vein. 'Learned men and ladies, high-placed and lowly people alike, and the kind who easily find boredom in ordinary entertainments stuck to the seats as though glued,' reported the *Maidenhead Advertiser*. 'Everybody present appeared to share Lady Desborough's delight with these super-marionettes.' It was important to Ettie that the preparations and execution of her events looked calm and effortless. To call oneself 'very busy', she thought, 'sounds so bourgeois & fussy'.

🙶

What impression did Ettie make on strangers and acquaintances? George Gage remembered driving with the Desboroughs when suddenly a bus swerved across Oxford Street to avoid a woman who had fallen in the road and hit their car with considerable impact. The bus driver started to make profuse apologies, but Ettie interrupted him with pleasant courtesy: 'Oh no, I saw it. You couldn't possibly have done anything.' They were, said Gage, 'simple words, but she said them in a manner that might have been reserved for her most distinguished friends'. The busman turned to Gage in amazement. 'Who was that?' he asked. 'We don't often get talked to like that these days.' Of course Ettie's conversational style, like her Holland House accent, was distinctive. Back in the 1880s she and her coevals – Alice Salisbury, Mabell Airlie, Helen D'Abernon and the rest – had acquired the habit of emphatic, extravagant ways of talking and writing as a reaction against their buttoned-up Victorian parents. The Grenfells never lost this tendency to verbal excess. George Gage remembered Barrett Good, the Taplow butler, being asked to send a telegram accepting an invitation. Knowing the family style, he did so in the words: 'Yes how perfectly wonderful love love love.' Usually this would have been appropriate, but not in this case, as the invitation came from a prosaic official of the Thames Conservancy Board.

Ettie charmed bus drivers; but writers can be harder to please. The anti-war poet Siegfried Sassoon, the jingo poet Rudyard Kipling, the camp belle-lettrist Lytton Strachey and the novelist-sensation Rosamond Lehmann can all be summoned to testify.

Ettie was introduced to Siegfried Sassoon at a lunch in Bloomsbury given by Margot Asquith in 1923: she sat opposite him, with Maynard

Keynes next to her. Nearly two years later, in May 1925, Winnie Portland's sister-in-law Lady Ottoline Morrell, the earliest and most steadfast of Sassoon's literary champions, asked him to join her for tea at Taplow, where she was weekending. Everyone was out when he arrived. Good the butler solemnly intoned, 'her ladyship is on the water', and directed Sassoon to the boathouse; but instead he strolled along the high cedar walk perched above the Thames, listening to the sound of the weir below. Ottoline Morrell greeted him on his return, and reintroduced him to Ettie, who led him into a room full of people and introduced him to his cousin Sir Philip Sassoon, whom he had never met. 'He looks a bit of a bounder, but has a remarkable face,' the poet recorded of the baronet. 'I was introduced to Lord Balfour and several titled dowagers – old Lady Wemyss, Lady Kenmare, etc. Sat down at a long table, between Ottoline and Lady Desborough, with Lord B on Lady D's left. About twenty people at the table. I felt very shy and self-conscious. Lady D made conversation hectically, asking whether I wrote at night or by day, and did I alter my poems much afterwards. I explained my methods ponderously, and Lord B joined in, very amiably. He is plump and pink-faced under his white hair, and wore white flannel trousers (had been on the river and was about to play tennis). His face looked prim, and lacks nobility.' Ettie's tea-table magic failed with Siegfried Sassoon: 'conditions were impossible for conversation, with Lady D pouring out cups of tea all the time and a terrific cackle going on all around us.' After tea he watched Eddie Marsh playing Mah Jong with Norah Lindsay and Desmond Mac-Carthy, then drifted to another room where he listened to 'a feeble conversation between P. Sassoon, Lady Londonderry and Lord Hugh Cecil (a soft-looking man)'. As soon as they could, he and Ottoline 'escaped from that too-prosperous house-party and went down to the de la Mares, which was like coming to life again'.

Ottoline Morrell claimed to have felt shy at this house party in May 1925: the other guests, not mentioned by Sassoon, were Betty Montgomery, John Revelstoke, Norah Lindsay, old Lady Minto and two young friends for Moggie, Betty Jolliffe and Edward Rice. She fled several times to call on Walter de la Mare, who lived by the main gates to Taplow Court. De la Mare occasionally accepted, but often evaded, invitations across the road, and showed his horror of Ettie's entertainments in his gothic-nightmare poem, 'The Feckless Dinner Party'. The de la Mares' simple domesticity and understated manners were for Ottoline Morrell an antidote to what she called 'the Grand Opera at the Big House'. But though she professed to avoid social drama, she enjoyed the scene when she introduced Siegfried Sassoon to his cousin Philip – 'they looked at each other as two dogs of the same breed would look' – and succumbed to her hostess's blandishing conversation: 'I am more & more impressed by her good sound knowledge of History, & Life, & Literature. She is *very* remarkable.' During this Saturday-to-Monday, so Ottoline Morrell testified, 'all the food was of the Gods', though the one dish she describes – 'salmon with green jelly trimmings & horseradish sauce' – sounds outlandish.

Ettie reciprocated Ottoline Morrell's admiration. 'What burning intellectual zeal she has,' she wrote to Betty Montgomery after this Whitsuntide visit of 1925. 'She never "passes by", always tests & samples, and always has treasures of discovery, and always gets *interest* into the most trite or ordinary topics.' She was especially drawn by her guest's account of D.H. Lawrence, one literary lion whom she could never get to Taplow. Lawrence might seem an unlikely interest for Ettie until one recalls that the central figure of one of his novels is an intelligent, idealistic woman with tremendous love and ambitions for her children. Her eldest son dies with her at his bedside, she falls into a listless despair that seems certain to kill her, and is only roused by the need to nurse her next son through pneumonia. '*Sons & Lovers* is one of my most favourite books,' she told Ottoline. There were scenes of torrid adultery, and plunges into emotional dereliction, but she thought it best 'to take no notice at all of some of the later aspects – they were utterly negligible, & all the talk just set them out of all proportion'.

After Sassoon's visit to Taplow, Ettie borrowed a copy of *Lingual Exercises*, his latest volume of poetry, from Walter de la Mare, read it conscientiously and copied passages from 'When I'm Alone' into the commonplace book she had been compiling since 1895:

> I thought of age, and loneliness, and change.
> I thought how strange we grow when we're alone,
> And how unlike the selves that meet, and talk,
> And blow the candles out, and say good-night.

Alone . . . The word is life endured and known.
It is the stillness where our spirits walk
And all but inmost faith is overthrown.

In May 1926 Ettie invited Sassoon, with Ottoline Morrell, to Panshanger. Times had changed at the house. Ten years earlier Willie had disapproved when, at a Panshanger party, Norman Douglas's teasingly risqué new novel *South Wind* had been discussed in front of the ladies, but now he cheerfully announced at dinner that one of his cows was lesbian, and there was a cross-dressing girl among the guests. Ettie took Sassoon walking in the woods, and subjected him to one of her intense tête-à-têtes. He responded by giving her a handwritten copy of a newly written poem, which was published a few years later in *The Heart's Journey*, the book that marked his apogee as a poet. She wrote to him in 1929, when she was fighting to rally from Ivo's death, about *The Heart's Journey*: 'There are words of yours that have brought strength these two years when there seemed to be no strength. Only smash.' He responded kindly, and she tried to lure him back to Taplow: 'it isn't really "a party" – only tiny – Rudyard Kipling & Violet Bonham Carter are coming.' Sassoon was contentedly reclusive and like de la Mare, he seems to have evaded some of Ettie's invitations, though he returned to Taplow in 1933 and maintained contact with her for another twenty years.

Despite Sassoon's initial doubts, he had much in common with Ettie. They were, after all, the two creators of some of the most resonant legends of the First World War, and themselves iconic figures among the war's survivors. The tall, bereft, unbendingly proud noblewoman, whose literary memorial to her dead sons and their friends created the Lost Generation, paced through the woods at Panshanger with the tall, thin officer-poet decorated with the Military Cross, the man who, by his poems, created the myth of the callous, stupid, chateau-based High Command sacrificing innocents in the carnage of trench warfare. The Roman Matron of the Great War walked side by side with its foremost protest-poet, and talked of other things – the Flower Show cricket-match scene in Sassoon's *Memoirs of a Fox-hunting Man*, for example – rather than recalling the Flanders landscape of tangled wire, muddy craters and rotting corpses.

It is regrettable that Ettie failed to bring Sassoon together with Kipling, whom she continued to see during the 1920s. After a Saturday-to-Monday at Pans in October 1925, Kipling noted her refusal to abandon summer time until November of each year. 'One gets up at ungodly hours and lives in a world of confusion and unease. She said serenely that most of Monday morn's departing guests had taken a train an hour earlier than they thought.' The house impressed him, as it had done Hugh Walpole, but not its servants:

> Panshanger is a most beautiful place, with untold pictures of all kinds – six Sir Joshuas 'skied' in one room; Titians; Lelys, Rembrandts, Vandykes and similar trifles and more priceless china and books than I've ever seen in one place outside of a museum. But they don't live there much and so it's understaffed and a bit dirty. Guests look after their own arrangements and maids aren't met at the station with any regularity. The Park on that beautiful Sunday was full of colour; but the timber has been neglected for generations and about a third of it seems to be dying. The company was young. Monica (*very* fat and *exceedingly* plain) and her Air-Marshal husband were about the oldest. Then Imogen; a black haired amazing long girl called Peggy Ward; one Charles Gough, a nice barrister man whom one had met at the Cazalets at Fairlawn; the Lady Betty Harris . . . a big-eyed infant just engaged to one Fremantle, a thin, nice boy who said his family business was carpets. Then two other children – Hopes – Lady Mary Hope, *very* silent except when she exploded into an imitation of a parson that she knew; and her brother who is brother to some earl (I *can't* write with a *Debrett* on the table) or other – he wasn't very eloquent. And there was a steady small drift of people in to tennis and tea – Oh, and Lady Algy Gordon-Lennox (Orient boat, last year, wasn't it?) looked in and I rather liked her.

One evening he strolled in the park with Ettie, who seemed 'less insincere' than usual – 'p'raps she doesn't think it worth while with me. Anyway they were all as nice as could be and we played fool paper-games after dinner and that was *that*.'

Lytton Strachey, though, was struck by the ageing of Ettie's retinue rather than by the conversational genius when he was tempted to Taplow in 1930. The other guests included 'a knot of dowagers and Barrie', he wrote. 'Also Lord D. Cecil, who struck me as being too much at home among the female antiques. Desmond was there too – a comfort; but I came away feeling pretty ashy. Lord Desborough himself was really the best of the crew – a huge old rock of an athlete – almost completely gaga – I spent the whole of Sunday afternoon with him *tête-à-tête*. He showed me his unpublished books – "The History of the Thames" – "The History of the Oar", etc. He confessed he had read the whole of Shakespeare. "And, you know, there is some pretty stiff stuff in it." ' Strachey did not note Willie's idiosyncrasy when bored by excessively brittle conversation at dinner: he used to shut off from the repartee, and practise punting strokes to himself at the end of the table.

Rosamond Lehmann had first been invited to Taplow – for a children's fancy dress ball – in 1909 at the age of eight, and had been awed by Julian (aged twenty-one) striding godlike through the room. She and the other Lehmann children accompanied the Desboroughs on wartime theatre outings, and three characters in her first novel *Dusty Answer* (1927), Roddy, Charlie and Julian, are modelled on the Grenfell brothers. *Dusty Answer* was a best-seller, on which Ettie congratulated its author while commiserating on the break-up of her marriage. Lehmann sent Ettie a copy of her next novel, *A Note in Music*, as soon as it arrived from the printers, for she never forgot Ettie's letter about *Dusty Answer*, and 'what a difference it made to me at an awful moment of my life'. She was '*terribly* anxious' for Ettie to like *A Note in Music*, which Ettie praised to other people as 'marvellously well-written and clever'.

Ettie was the model for Lady Spencer in Lehmann's third novel, *The Weather in the Streets* (1936): 'She lives by the most rigid standards herself – and has almost complete tolerance for everybody else . . . She's one of the people who've chosen a behaviour long ago and stick to it.' In addition to her stalwart husband, there is a loyal family friend – Evan Charteris mixed with John Revelstoke – whom Lehmann depicts as a lisping, snobbish, complacent old booby. The Ettie character is effusive but formidable: 'Lady Spencer was in the doorway, was bearing down, full-rigged, confined in an ample severity of black, with diamonds, with heroic shoulders bare, with white austerely sculptured cheeks and hair, with both hands outstretched. "My dear! This is delightful!"' She lives for the memory of her dead son Guy and for the future of her live son Rollo. Guy is a version of Julian, 'an Edwardian dream-child with romantic hair', who has been commemorated by a version of *Pages from a Family Journal*. 'He died for England: going over the top, at the head of his men, shot through the heart. All as it should be. And they'd done what could be done: worn white for mourning; put a memorial window in the church; collected his letters and poems and all the tributes to him, had them printed for private circulation. All bore witness – nurses, governesses, schoolmasters, broken-hearted friends – all said the same: gay, brilliant, winning, virtuous, brave Guy: pattern of the eldest son.'

Once, in 1919, Lehmann had gone for an evening at Taplow, where she had danced interminably with Ivo. She saw Ettie sitting out, scrutinising them with a basilisk's eye, and realised that Ettie would loathe Ivo falling for her, the daughter of middle-class neighbours. In the novel Lady Spencer deprecates Rollo's love affair with the novel's heroine, and breaks them up with ruthless delicacy. Her intervention is gently spoken but unanswerable.

On 6 September 1926 Ettie and Willie left for Ireland. They – together with Alice Salisbury – stayed first with Val and Elizabeth Kenmare at Killarney, then went to the Lansdownes' nearby house at Derreen. The house stood on a conical hill at the centre of a rocky peninsula stretching into the Atlantic, amid grounds that had been laid out as an evocation of a Himalayan landscape, with contiguous views of sea, mountain and woodland. 'This place is lapped & surrounded by sea & gold & orange sea-weed, & fuchsias growing like hedges, & palm-trees & bamboos – blindingly beautiful. We are quite alone with the darling Lansdownes, they are *too* wonderful – both about 80 now, & so *full* of zeal.' Maud Lansdowne's grandson Lord Waterford had recently declared himself to Mogs as George Gage's rival to marry her and the devoted old lady urged his suit; but Ettie was anxious that the girl should not be rushed. After Ireland they moved to lodgings at 1 Great

Bedford Street, Bath, so that Willie could have treatment for rheumatism.

In the early hours of 26 September Ivo was driving his little two-seater Saxon car from Wadhurst to Alderden Manor, where he lived and farmed with 'Joe' Clarke. At Flimwell School, cornering a bend, the steering wheel came sheer off its pin, the car swerved across the road and bumped along the side of a wall for some yards before stopping in a hedge. Ivo was so vague that the accident may have been caused by lack of concentration; but both his sisters felt that Ivo was driving a cheap, badly made little car, and that cut-price engineering and parental cheeseparing were contributory causes of the accident. A heavy coping stone was dislodged from a gatepost and smashed the front of his skull. He was rushed to Hawkhurst Cottage Hospital, where quick action saved his life for the moment; and before dawn Ettie was woken by the sound – never forgotten – of a policeman knocking hard on the front door of her lodgings in Bath and asking for Lord Desborough.

The Desboroughs hastened to Kent, where they spent every waking hour in a vigil at the hospital. The doctors 'cannot say *very* much yet, except that his youth & strength are greatly in his favour', Ettie reported at the end of the first day to Monica, who was seven months pregnant. 'I know how calm, brave & strong you will be, you know our Vo would want that more than anything in the world.' Two days later she allowed herself some faint optimism. 'Ivo has now lived 60 hours since the accident, & I think the doctors now begin to have a *shade* of hope. When we got the first message they said it was a matter of moments.' The bedside vigil was excruciatingly similar to Ettie's experiences with Archie Gordon and with Julian. Moggie arrived, distraught but trying to repress every trace of her anguish, and was a superb comfort to her parents. Whenever Ettie saw her bending over Ivo in his coma, she was vividly reminded of Monica at Julian's bedside in 1915. Hawkhurst felt so similar to Boulogne eleven years earlier that Ettie found herself calling Vo and Mogs by the names of Juju and Casie.

King George and Queen Mary asked Willie to send regular bulletins to them, and instructed Lord Stamfordham to send messages of agonised sympathy to the stricken parents. It is no exaggeration to say that during the days and nights that the Desboroughs spent at Hawk-hurst, the lives of their friends went into semi-paralysis: of dread, hope, horror and prayer. By 1 October Ivo's symptoms were increasingly favourable, and he seemed to be recovering consciousness; but four days later bouts of restlessness brought on a deadly exhaustion, and he died on the night of 8 October. 'Ivo never suffered & was never dismayed – he went smiling to death, his lovely look of serenity & trust undimmed,' Ettie wrote to Ottoline Morrell.

Asquith (by now Earl of Oxford and Asquith) was weeping when he brought Margot the news. The Desboroughs were overwhelmed by a cascade of commiseration. 'I know that the very foundations of your lives are shattered and that your anguish must seem past endurance,' Elizabeth Kenmare wrote from Ireland. 'Ivo has gone to join Julian and Billy, those splendid three are all together but you, my poor darling, are left with a heart broken to bits. You know, my darling, what my love is for you, so true & faithful, we have lived through so much together, & now I feel your grief is mine & I feel utterly crushed, only grieving, *grieving* for you both.'

On 12 October there was a private funeral, for immediate family, in the old closed graveyard next to the walled kitchen gardens of Taplow Court. The King and Queen sent a telegram and the Prince of Wales a wreath. On the same day there were memorial services in Maidenhead and at St Margaret's, Westminster.

The St Margaret's service was full and brought a further deluge of letters. Helen D'Abernon cherished 'golden memories' of Ivo: 'First as the loveliest curly-haired Cupid, later as one whose extraordinary personal beauty was . . . enhanced and made rarer . . . by the charm of completely unconscious, unconstrained manliness and simplicity.' She had been deeply moved by the reading from Robert Louis Steven-son, the trumpet calls, the muffled drums and the buglers of the Grenadier Guards sounding the Last Post to conclude the service. The Earl of Birkenhead – whom Ettie in 1906 had recruited to the Taplow faithful when he was the newly elected MP, F.E. Smith – was so moved that he wrote twice that day. Ivo's death was an 'unspeakably cruel thing', he declared. At 'this terrible moment in your life' he needed to tell her 'how deep & general the sympathy is with you all, even among those who do not know you'. As to the dead boy, 'I liked

Ivo far more than any young man now alive. His simplicity, gaiety, warm-heartedness & courage made an appeal to me which no other has made since the War killed all my younger friends. I am sorry now that I never let him see how much I liked him.' After returning from St Margaret's to the India Office, where he was Secretary of State, Birkenhead wrote again. He had found the service 'impressive, sweet & solemn. But I was absolutely out of sympathy for I said to myself all the time: if God is omnipotent why did he allow this malignant cruelty? and if he is not why is he God?'

These were not questions that the Desboroughs wished to ask. Their faith, and the assurances of their friends, made this period bearable for them. Sir George Arthur, the sentinel of Kitchener's reputation, felt '*sure* that in His own good time God will bring you and your splendid boys face to face again'. Willie, too, was sure. 'One thing about the three boys was their glowing and rock rooted faith which they all shared, & feared death not at all,' he told Nancy Astor. She and her husband Waldorf, together with their children, gave unremitting kindness to the Desboroughs at this time; and though Ettie had always blanched at Lady Astor's showiness, discordant voice and jarring impulses, she was determined on a final reconciliation. 'We'll never refer to "bygones",' she wrote, 'but I suppose the world has never taken so much trouble in its life to make mischief between two people as between you and me! & I do want to tell you, dear Nancy, that I am so *so* glad that we have got it all right, directly we got to know each other.'

Moggie at this time was in a tumult of misery. Ivo's last day had been devastating for her, and she felt crushing responsibility for her parents in their grief. 'I often think Imogen very reminding of Julian,' Ettie wrote to Tommy Lascelles at this time. 'She carries on their torches — all through those twelve days and nights at Hawkhurst she never let one trace of her own anguish appear, as she leant over Ivo, flushed & radiant.' Bendor Westminster, *Le Roi Soleil* as Ettie called him, realised that Taplow would be insufferable for the mourners, and put the Woolsack, his hunting-lodge at Mimizan in the Landes, at their disposal. The Desboroughs left for France with Mogs and her friend Betty Jolliffe on 18 October.

From there, on 21 October, Ettie wrote to Monica of 'the utter beauty, utter peace, beyond all imagination – just at first it seemed to make it all worse, the longing greater, but this is so ungrateful, so utterly unlike Ivo'. Moggie frightened Ettie one morning by finally breaking down in uncontrollable tears; 'but', Ettie said, 'it may have relieved the terrible tension & strain.' Betty Jolliffe was superbly tactful, and the two girls went for long rides in the pine woods, swam and fished in the lake, and played tennis. 'Bendor's kindness beyond all telling – ordering every tiniest thing himself, in his own writing – & telegraphing daily.' Ettie was immeasurably relieved at being away from Taplow; 'and things we don't generally personally care about, like being very comfortable, & lovely food, do oddly make a little difference just now'. She did not hide from Monica that the pain this time 'has been almost greatest of all', that during 'those 12 days & nights' all the old wounds were 'torn open & bleeding together . . . the cup of agony could hold no further drop'. Willie had adored Ivo: 'Only you & I & Mogsie know what this is to him – the cumulative anguish.'

Ettie took long walks through the pine woods every afternoon with Willie, and read a batch of new novels: reading, she found, was the best opium for racked nerves. From the Woolsack, she wrote to Charley Londonderry on 1 November at the end of 'a fortnight of wonderful respite, the beauty & peace & sunlight – today most lovely – I love the pinewoods, & this wild Atlantic coast'. She longed to see him. 'Our friendship is the one most wholly independent of words that I have ever known. Yet there are sometimes very simple ones that I want to say – that I love you, thank you, trust you, need you.' That same Monday she wrote to Alice Salisbury admitting her 'intensity of anxiety about Moggie'. Though 'her faith is so sure & radiant . . . you & I have the same passionate instinct to save – to shield – our children'.

Ivo's death had raised a great deal of newspaper publicity; and on returning to Taplow, Ettie found several letters from strangers transmitting spiritualistic messages supposedly from the dead boy. The experience was repugnant, as she described in a letter which was printed above the signature 'X' in *The Times*. The letter writers sincerely intended to be helpful, 'except in a few very horrible instances where the question of earning money comes in', she felt; and she therefore hoped 'they may listen to an entreaty, made by one in great sorrow', that they should elicit whether their communications would be welcome before sending them. 'The sudden opening of these so-called messages', she warned from first-hand experience, 'may cause a very terrible sense of shock and desecration to the recipients.'

While staying at the Woolsack, Ettie received long, considerate letters from both Maud Lansdowne and Evie Devonshire about 'Tyrone' Waterford's devotion to Mogs and willingness to wait until she had made up her mind about his proposal. George Gage, too, remained a patient suitor; and when Mogs, already quite battered, felt cornered (she was only twenty-two), and could not make a decision, Ettie had to act as an intermediary with both Gage and the Waterford connections. Moggie hedged and hesitated, and the strain was so bad on a Saturday-to-Monday at Taplow that Tyrone disappeared just at the moment when he was supposed to be taking her for a walk. Jack Salmond found him hidden in a lavatory weeping. There was a hereditary strain of instability in the Waterford family: Tyrone's grandfather the 5th Marquess had shot himself at Curraghmore in 1895; his father the 6th Marquess had drowned in an ornamental pond there in 1911; and other members of the family lacked equipoise.

In the spring of 1927 Tyrone, taut with uncertainty about Mogs, had a bad breakdown. This convinced her that her doubts about marrying him were justified, but filled her with miserable guilt; and it was many weeks before the doctors permitted him to be told of her decision. Ettie supported her daughter, had a series of distressing consultations with Tyrone's mother Lady Osborne Beauclerk, and made several painful visits to his nursing home at Wadhurst. Waterford begged to be allowed to see Mogs, who felt agonised by responsibility for his breakdown, but this was forbidden by the doctors. Ettie throughout showed delicacy and patience with all sides, including Waterford's physicians; but her efforts had a cost she could not meet. 'I have been sair hadden down,' she wrote to Mary Wemyss at the end of May. 'Our feeble questionings & doubts are so puny – but just lately mine have pushed up their wicked heads. One never knows beforehand what is going to be "the last straw", but to see Tyrone, so young & innocent, so beautiful & unselfish & brave, suffering like this – & Moggie, the innocent agonised cause, has been almost too much.' Like Lord Birkenhead, she questioned why an omnipotent God would allow such sadness. Her painful doubts continued through the summer of 1927.

This episode had a tragic sequel. In 1930 Waterford married, and delighted journalists by spending his honeymoon travelling with his bride through Ireland in a horse-drawn caravan – cooking for themselves, making the beds and scrubbing the floors as it was incredulously noted. He fathered two sons, but in 1934 was found dying behind the locked door of his gunroom at Curraghmore with a bullet wound in his right temple. A coroner's inquest, with six of his estate employees sitting as the jury, was held at the house, and discreetly concluded that he had gone to the gunroom at 5.45 a.m. to shoot a hare he had seen on his lawn, and accidentally discharged the rifle after slipping on the stone floor. Mogs's painful decision seemed vindicated.

As the anniversary of Ivo's death approached, Ettie went to the Norfolk Broads for her first long visit to Whiteslea Lodge, a little house built by Bron Lucas, which he had bequeathed to Ivo, and which Willie had inherited from Ivo. She went there to be alone and stare her situation in the face, and to collect herself before facing the searching looks of the outer world. It is not therefore surprising that she suffered a recurrence of eye strain and eye infections. The trouble became so acute that she consulted a Norwich oculist who said she was suffering from 'shock & strain' – 'glib, meaningless words,' she thought – and recommended her to lie for days on end in the dark. Each morning she woke at four with the memory of the police knocking on the door at Bath.

On 26 September 1927, the first anniversary of Ivo's accident, she unburdened herself to Willie. 'You know my own darling we have said to each other with truth that our spirits have never capitulated – this summer mine did. I say it to you only. The torture had seemed long in reaching one's consciousness, but this summer I went under.' But at Whiteslea she had recovered. 'In those first days here, lying ill in darkness, it had to be one way or the other, & I do believe that some help from Ivo himself came to set one's spirit free – to make the wonderful healing & peace of all this beauty avail. *Souffrir, mais souffrir debout* [Suffer, but suffer standing upright]. You *always* have, my most darling.'

CHAPTER 8

The Mother-in-Law

W

HITESLEA WAS ETTIE'S place of redemption in the autumn of 1927, and for eleven further summers it was – she said – her 'Paradise of PEACE'. The chatelaine of the great houses at Tap and Pans acquired a third house to cherish – a modest modern dwelling, which she adored both as her sequestered retreat and as a keepsake from her beloved dead.

The history of Whiteslea can be briefly told. Back in 1908 Bron Lucas, Edwin Montagu and the then Foreign Secretary, Sir Edward Grey, decided to form a bird sanctuary, bought a small section of the Norfolk Broads called Ball's Corner and appointed a redoubtable Broadsman called Jim Vincent as their keeper. In 1909 Bron additionally bought Hickling Broad, Heigham Sound and subsequently Horsey Mere. After his death in 1916 his Norfolk property, including a small house called Whiteslea on Hickling Broad, passed under his will to Ivo Grenfell; and the family soon grew to love it. 'This place really is divine, & we are so happy here,' Monica wrote in 1919 once Ivo had taken possession after his return from Archangel. 'It is on a bog, in the middle of the vastness of the broad, incredibly far from the mainland: the house is just a bungalow with a very jolly big living-room which Bron built on.' Willie inherited Ivo's estate in 1926, and thus took responsibility for some 3,000 acres of the Broads heritage.

Jim Vincent, who continued to run the sanctuary until his death in 1944, became an admired figure in the Desboroughs' lives. With his customary energy, Willie started writing about ornithology and became a vice-president of the Royal Society for the Protection of Birds. He and Ettie stopped going to Geordie Sutherland's shooting lodge at Loch Merkland in late summer, and reduced their autumn tours of friends' country houses. A routine began in 1928, and survived until the outbreak of war, whereby the Desboroughs, with available children and grandchildren, went each August and September to Whiteslea, between their summers at Taplow and their winters at Panshanger.

For eleven years the Whiteslea visit was a point in the year around which Ettie's emotional life revolved. The remote little Norfolk lodge became a precious sanctuary for her. Its importance to her well-being was clear to those who knew her well. Desmond MacCarthy, for example, wrote of 'your yearly retreat without which you could not keep your sorrows out of that part of life which cannot reflect them'. He recognised the necessity for Ettie to have 'a time when you can be alone with your thoughts & memories. I admire you very much for always having made a place for them.'

There were two Salmond grandchildren, Julian and Rosemary, born in 1926 and 1928. Ettie doted on them, both for their own sakes and as poignant reminders of the golden years of the 1890s when her dead sons were small, happy creatures with their attention fixed on her. 'I am writing in the lovely August peace of the garden,' she wrote from Taplow to Siegfried Sassoon in 1929, 'lavender & bumble-bees & white magnolias – & the two babies (Monica's children) asleep in their perambulators near by – so like very long ago days here.' But Whiteslea was the place where Ettie plunged deepest into the joys of being a grandmother. Each summer Monica's children, and later Moggie's, joined her there; and her pleasure in their play was rapturous and unaffected. The Salmond children, accompanied by their nurse, were at Whiteslea with their grandmother, for example, in September 1933 while their mother revisited Venice. 'Your sweet babies', Ettie reported, 'were *perfect* – luncheon here on fish & partridges & black-berries – a great excitement! They "rested" in the sitting-room . . . & we made lovely pot pourri bags, & they sailed, & swam in the Broad . . . & then we blackberried, & had tea in the summer-house.'

Julian, as the eldest grandchild, was her obvious favourite. She loved playing with him as a baby, giving him his bottles of orange juice and milk, even monitoring the regularity and healthiness of his daily functions. Her preference for the boy may have jarred with his sister, to whom she was the least close of her five grandchildren. Rosemary was alarmed by Ettie – by her exacting standards even more than by the incident when the old lady shut her in a cupboard for being noisy – and felt ambivalent about her. Sailing at Whiteslea changed the direction of Julian's adult life; for though, after leaving the RAF in the 1950s, he farmed in Wiltshire, his real devotion was to his yacht in the Caribbean, which he sailed for his own pleasure and skippered for fee-paying American millionaires.

Yet even the idyllic peace of Whiteslea was jeopardised. 'This secret corner of England' was being despoiled, complained a wildfowler called Wentworth Day who visited the Desboroughs in September 1930. 'Its solitudes are prostituted by gramophone and guitar, its waterways invaded by pestiferous young men in flannel trousers and stocking caps, its Broads alive with ill-sailed craft and ill-mannered hooligans. It is all no doubt done in the name of democracy and, as such, inviolable.' Fenland villages were already, Day protested, 'so ruined by trippers, so vulgarised by bungalow and petrol-pump development, that Hickling will be the last large area where the ordinary decent citizen will be able to fish, sail, and watch birds'. Day's fulminations against the summer visitors who 'wear practically no clothes, scream and shriek, play banjos and gramophones, get drunk and terrorise whole villages' were too puritanical for Ettie, though she may, like him, have deprecated launches 'full of factory youths, clerks, medical students (who ought to know better), and horrid young men of the chinless beret type tearing up the rivers at full speed, oblivious of other boats, ignorant of seamanship, and raising a wave which washes away the banks'.

Ettie and her friends had to face disfiguring changes everywhere. Electrical pylons were installed across the Sussex Downs, near George Gage's house at Firle. The Brighton Corporation proposed to build a racing-car track nearby. Gage, who served for fifty years on East Sussex County Council, became expert in the planning for what he called the 'intermediate countryside' of south-east England with its 'ribbon development, advertisement nuisances and bungalow atrocities'.

It was perhaps with Gage that Ettie went for her walk on the South Downs in March 1930. She started west of Firle, probably in Worthing. 'The mean streets of the town stretched back a long way,' she reported in an article for *The Times*, 'and gradually gave way to asphalted field-paths, and an area of surely the most atrocious bungalows in England. These horrible little mushrooms were mostly in course of construction, surrounded by the squalid flotsam and jetsam of building, but here and there window-curtains betokened occupation, and one gate had already been painted with the title "Bo-peep".' Shuddering inwardly, she took a grass track to the top of the Downs and thence walked the eight miles to Chanctonbury, an Iron Age hill fort (standing at 783 feet above sea level) with a ring of great beeches planted round it. 'Very soon all the dirt and mess and clangour were left behind, and the great distances of the Downs began to appear. It was a tremendous landscape, with snow still in the crevices, grey and icy . . . In a sudden glint of sunshine a lark began to sing, and Beachy Head and the Seven Sisters could be seen very dimly and very far away, across the flying lights and shadows on land and sea . . . It seemed so swift a transition from the poor towns below to these great spaces, wholly unaffected by man for hundreds of years.'

The democratisation of leisure that Wentworth Day railed against shook the Desboroughs' life by the Thames too. In 1922 H.G. Wells published a novel, *The Secret Places of the Heart*, containing a prudish chapter entitled 'Maidenhead'. It offended Maidonians by stressing the town's popularity as a trysting place for adulterers, and particularised Skindle's Hotel as a hot spot for illicit honeymooners. Willie owned Skindle's, which in the 1880s had been an irreproachable venue for boating parties of young people of Ettie's class. The river had been the one place where they might go in groups without chaperones and, as a result, Skindle's eventually became as popular a resort as Brighton for fornicators and adulterers. Indeed, when the hotel was inherited by Ettie's granddaughter Camilla Gage in 1952, her father insisted that it was an unsuitable property for a fifteen-year-old girl to own, and it was sold.

Wells, in his novel, made his protagonist row up-river past 'piled-up woods behind which my Lords Astor and Desborough keep their state' into a sullen hinterland of cheated hopes. Trippers, Wells wrote, imagine themselves at Taplow reach, 'rowing swiftly and gracefully, punting beautifully, brandishing boat-hooks with ease and charm. They expect romantic assignations, glowing evenings, warm moonlight, and distant voices singing.' The reality was harsh and meagre. 'Boats bump and lead to coarse ungracious quarrels; rowing can be curiously fatiguing; punting involves dreadful indignities. The romance here tarnishes very quickly. Chilly mists arise from the water and the magic of distant singing is provided, even excessively, by boatloads of cads.' The Thames near Taplow had a combative temper, he felt. 'People on the banks jeer at anyone in the boats. You hear people quarrelling in boats, in the hotels, as they walk along the towing-path. There is remarkably little happy laughter here.'

Wells, no doubt, over-egged his pudding, but as early as the 1890s the Grenfells had been annoyed in summer by trippers' steam launches, racing up the Thames from Cookham to Boulter's Lock, competing in speed and noise with one another, sounding off sirens, whistles and foghorns, which Willie complained were better suited to an Atlantic liner off the shoals of Newfoundland than a pleasure steamer on the reaches of the Thames. The crowds of day trippers at Maidenhead on Ascot Sunday grew more swollen and ugly with every year after 1919. According to a police census, 10,191 cars passed Boulter's Lock on Ascot Sunday of 1925, the pavements of the lower town were scarcely passable and Skindle's served over 1,200 meals. Desborough and his house party punted down to the lock as usual that Ascot Sunday and were photographed for the picture magazines; but the packed, gawping crowds did not edify. Mass motoring was spoiling the idyll. On any summer Sunday the newly built Great West Road coming out of London was loud with the roaring, throbbing, hooting and clattering of cars of all shapes, sizes, sounds, and colours. It all made for a mass of agglutinated humanity descending on the Thames.

It is not surprising that the Desboroughs came to prefer Whiteslea in late summer. Swaths of Buckinghamshire were being suburbanised. Everywhere, it seemed, genteel Londoners were erecting villas that aped manor houses, with pretentious belfried garages. Willie, Lord Hambleden and H.A.L. Fisher became the vice-chairmen – with Lord Astor as chairman – when the Thames Valley branch of the Council for the Preservation of Rural England was inaugurated in 1928 in response to the feeling that the beauties of the riverside were being thoughtlessly spoilt. Everyone agreed that the delicate old savour of Taplow reach had coarsened. On the festive Ascot Sundays of the palmy pre-war years thousands had flocked to the lock to gaze at the luxurious river craft and richly dressed women; but by 1930, Ascot Sunday at Boulter's Lock was a commonplace affair with undistin-guished visitors and mediocre launches. The wealthier classes recoiled from the rough, almost intimidating fairground scenes that now took place, according to the *Maidenhead Advertiser*. 'Even Lord Desborough relaxed his usual practice of punting down to the Lock.'

Taplow was Willie's personal heaven, and Ettie loved it for his sake and for the memory of the children she had reared there. But her plans for her descendants focused more than ever on Panshanger. The old Cowpers had longed for her sons to succeed them at Pans, and Ivo's death did not extinguish her hopes that it would remain a family home – to be occupied eventually by her grandson Julian Salmond. Though there is no great river running through Hertfordshire to compare with the Thames, the countryside was friendly and placid with quiet mysterious woods. There were no large towns or cities either: the county town, Hertford, a few miles east of Pans, was pretty, intimate and welcoming, and remains largely unspoilt today. Undeniably, there was a proliferation of bus routes through the country lanes, of gaudily painted petrol pumps in village streets and of crass advertising hoard-ings clamouring for attention on the high roads. Ettie's letters to visiting friends began to recommend that their drivers use the route of the Hatfield bypass. Still, though the Great North Road was busier than the Great West Road, there were no picnickers with portable gramo-phones in the woods at Pans. Hertfordshire had in one respect changed little since the Romans built Watling Street across it: it was a county that most people travelled through on their way to somewhere else.

In 1927, so as to secure the future of the Panshanger estate, which was being supported by the proceeds of the Welwyn land sales of 1919, the Desboroughs recontacted the art-dealing firm of Duveen about further sales from the Cowper art collection. Sir Joseph Duveen (a few years from becoming Lord Duveen) was interested in acquiring Raphael's *Madonna and Child* still held at Pans, and selling it to an American collector. One of his firm's experts went to Pans and scrutinised its contents. He noted the large Rembrandt portrait of Frederick Rihel on horseback, which, if cleaned, might attract a buyer; the Rembrandt portrait of a young man with a red cap; Frans Hals's

portrait of a young man with finely painted hands; an apple-green
Sèvres porcelain set; a landscape by Cuyp; and a murky, indifferent
Rembrandt of a boy's head.

Joe Duveen did not expect any bargains from Ettie and had his
sights fixed on the Raphael: the Rembrandt equestrian portrait, he
sneered, he would not have as a gift. His firm also consulted the art
appraiser Bernard Berenson, who was staying with Edith Wharton at
Hyères. Berenson had last visited Panshanger in 1909, and did not
highly value the pictures there beyond the Raphael and Fra Bartolommeo's masterpiece of the Holy Family. As Ettie was loath to sell the
Raphael, Duveen settled on a strategy of approaching her about one
picture at a time, and when appraisers from two rival firms, Knoedler
and Colnaghi, also called at Panshanger, he advised her that, as Pans
was a showplace, she should not denude the collection, but only sell
one or two pictures at a time – not over a dozen, as Knoedler was suggesting.

Eventually, in May 1928, after secret bidding by the rival dealers,
the Desboroughs sold the Raphael to Duveen for $875,000 (about $39
million in 2008 values). This was the highest figure ever paid for a
single painting – far exceeding the price Duveen had paid Bendor
Westminster for Gainsborough's *Blue Boy* in 1921. The picture passed
to the Secretary of the US Treasury, Andrew Mellon, and now hangs
in the National Gallery of Art in Washington DC. Ettie lived on the
proceeds of its sale for two decades.

❧

Ettie, who was ambitious for the Salmonds, felt that Monica exerted
herself insufficiently to advance her husband's career. Salmond's service pay as Commander-in-Chief of Air Defence was not lavish, and
in 1927 the couple determined to relinquish the Crown Estate lease
of their York Terrace house overlooking Regent's Park. They thought
of economising by taking a house at Holyport, a few miles down-
stream from Taplow: Monica felt it would be pleasant to be near her
mother, and Jack favoured his elder daughter's exposure to the agreeable manners and smart connections of the Desboroughs. But Ettie was
'aghast', she wrote, 'at the idea of you & Jack renouncing London
altogether!' She had lived since the 1880s in a sphere in which one had

at all costs to keep going, or else drop out. Opportunities only came to those who made themselves visible, she stressed. 'All the charming people (including political people & *useful* people) are open armed to you & Jack, but if you make no response, or are never there, they must inevitably forget, in the swift rush of life. It isn't just parties, but all the chances of keeping the old friends & making the new ones.' She thought, too, of her one-year-old grandson's social opportunities: surely, she asked, 'you'd love Julian to grow up with your own friends' babies, & not with horrible little Holyporters . . . I do really think that tiny children are as well & happy in London as anywhere.' It is not clear if she yet realised that the Air Marshal, when overtired, could be irritable and caustic, but she warned that the added strain of daily train commuting was another consideration. 'In the terrible rush of life,' she concluded, 'one does *so* quickly drift into the quiet peaceable back-water, & Jack *must* keep in the burning vital centre of it all.'

Monica was inclined to be dumpy even before her pregnancies, and by her mid-thirties had ballooned as the result of comfort-eating. Ettie was pained by this indiscipline about food, and from time to time incited her to diet. 'You looked *so* well, & *so* much thinner!' she urged in October 1927. 'Oh do persevere now, & remember that you can have the loveliest figure *in the world* – like in 1923 & 1924 – & what a prolonger it is of *youth*.' Walk fast for at least two hours a day, she urged. '*Eschew* all tea bread butter potatoes cream puddings cakes sweets. I believe in 3 months you'd be a wreath! & oh *remember* Daddie's mother & aunts!!! You don't know the difference thin-ness makes to *your* looks, & chic!' Monica was listless, too, and Ettie must have feared the growing manifestations of hereditary Cowper apathy.

Ettie had such clear ideas of perfection for her children, and such expectations that they would submit to her priorities, that Monica's complaisant slackness was exasperating. After Christmas of 1927 mother and daughter had an explosive row – apparently their first. 'I cannot forgive myself for being so hurt & furious on Thursday,' Ettie wrote from Pans on New Year's morning. 'What a strange thing anger is – shrivelling up in an instant (but mercifully only *for* an instant) all the deep tenderness & trust of years – so that for the moment one feels *only* hatred & malice & deep desire to wound. I was so utterly taken by surprise – but that is *no* excuse really, & I do so deeply grieve about it.'

She ended her peacemaking with a declaration of her lifelong credo: 'it *is*, one knows, the first duty to try to keep serene.'

Ettie had resumed her social round in 1927. She tried to return to what she called 'the kind of gaiety that has nothing to do with what lies beneath, but makes the actual business of living easier'. In June 1927, when she was at her lowest over the imbroglio between Mogs and Lord Waterford, she acquired an exciting new friend who was to make the business of living, and especially travelling, easier for her. Mogs made the introduction, after being returned to Taplow from a party in a resplendent Rolls-Royce, driven by a spruce chauffeur, belonging to one of the other guests. Her benefactor was Frederick Lindemann, the Professor of Experimental Philosophy – that is, physics – at Oxford University.

Lindemann, who had turned fifty-one that year, was a man of many parts. In 1916 he had learnt to fly, and as an experimental pilot had first calculated in principle, then confirmed by his own empirical tests, how aviators could get aircraft out of deadly spins. He was a rich man with too much discipline to be a dilettante of the Jack Stanmore or Norah Lindsay type: his work on low-temperature physics and astronomy resulted in his election as a Fellow of the Royal Society at the age of thirty-four. Lindemann was a teetotaller and vegetarian, an excellent pianist and a dedicated concert-goer. He was a big man, with aquiline features and a dominating presence, and a first-rate tennis player: he had the unique distinction of competing at Wimbledon when already the tenured holder of an Oxford chair. It was through tennis that he met Bendor Westminster, whose invitation to him to compete in a tennis tournament at Eaton in 1921 had momentous consequences. Clemmie Churchill was a fellow Eaton competitor, and Winston a spectator. The two men became fast friends: during the 1930s Churchill relied on Lindemann as his adviser on weaponry, and on becoming Prime Minister made him Paymaster General and obtained a barony for him.

Lord Cherwell, as Lindemann became, was a ferociously loyal friend, an implacably violent enemy and a prickly, selfish bachelor who was ruthlessly effective in protecting his comfort and convenience. For democratic forms he felt brisk contempt; and for titled ladies of all ages he had infinite patience. He charmed Bendor Westminster's flighty wives and illiterate daughters; Gladys and later Mary Marlborough welcomed him to Blenheim; the Londonderrys had him to Wynyard and Mount Stewart, the Midletons to Peper Harow, the D'Abernons to Esher and – above all of these – Winnie Portland to Welbeck. The gregarious duchess adored him, and claimed that it was she and Ettie who coined for him the nickname 'Proff'. Lindemann had been a don at Christ Church when Ivo was an undergraduate there, and had taken an avuncular interest in Edward Marjoribanks. To Ettie, Marjoribanks wrote of 'the English Einstein, one Professor Lindemann, who used to like me very much when I was here, altho' we cared and care for none of the same things . . . He is rather pathetic in character, rich, brave, learned, and, I believe, in science brilliant, & the youngest professor at Oxford, yet somehow without attraction & quite sexless.'

After being sent home in Lindemann's Rolls-Royce, Mogs – doubtless at her mother's behest – contacted him at Christ Church. Her parents, she explained, 'have heard so much about you from many mutual friends', and would be 'so delighted' if he could visit Taplow in the said Rolls-Royce. 'Wouldn't it be possible for you to come to luncheon on Sunday? If so, could you be most terribly kind & let us know, so that we may get some nuts of the Tennis world – & every other – to meet you. It would be the greatest fun.' Lindemann came to meet the tennis nuts, and to add a new *grande dame* to his visiting list. Ettie was delighted by him as a conversationalist (they talked 'all kinds of cabbages and kings') and amused by his food fads – 'a little cold potato and a haricot-bean' for luncheon; and he became a Taplow regular. In 1928 she introduced him to Panshanger with a carefully baited invitation. 'Would November 10th till Monday be possible, when A.J.B. and the Devonshires and Salisburys and a few more can come; or November 24th which would be equally delightful for us?'

In August 1929 she and Mogs joined Lindemann at the Hôtel d'Angleterre in Touraine, and accompanied him on a motoring tour of the Loire valley. He exerted himself tirelessly on their behalf, and Ettie was appreciative. She thought him 'an old Sly-Boots' but 'the best courier ever invented'. The following year he invited mother and daughter to visit Sicily with him; but Ettie's commitments prevented this. In 1931 it was her turn to moot a foreign journey. Lindemann had been thinking of visiting Palermo. 'If you do find it possible to get away, would you feel the least inclination to change your venue to *Spain*, and join Jack Stanmore and me there, somewhere about the middle of March, and go for a little tour wherever you and we liked? I think that this would be the very greatest fun if possible for you, and we might possibly persuade the Islingtons to bring their motor too, and all travel about together???' Lindemann savoured Ettie's glamour, loved to saunter down the green paths leading to the river at Taplow reach and hailed Willie as 'the Beau Ideal of English Manhood'.

In April 1928 George V announced three new Knights of the Garter to fill the vacancies created by the deaths of King Ferdinand of Romania, 'Clan' Lansdowne and Henry Oxford: the Duke of Abercorn, Queen Mary's brother the Earl of Athlone and Willie. 'After this last triplet of Garters it can never be said again that honour is dissociated from merit,' Sir George Arthur judged. Having assessed Abercorn's achievements as Governor of Northern Ireland and Athlone's as Governor-General of South Africa, he concluded, 'Desborough combines in himself every good quality an Englishman is said to possess.' In the summer of 1928, after Charlie Lincolnshire's death caused a further vacancy, Buckingham Palace and Downing Street discussed whether future Garters should be awarded on a less class-bound basis. The Prime Minister, Baldwin, consulted Lord Salisbury, who summarised the precedents: 'Broadly speaking Garters were only given to men of high rank and what is rather absurdly known as good family. All these sort of things have in the present days a rather out of date appearance,' Jim Salisbury felt. 'Men of high rank and good family nowadays are I am sorry to say in general singularly undistinguished. Nevertheless there is a certain advantage in limiting the field of those who are possibles instead of flinging it open to the scramble for honours and the inevitable gradual degeneration that the scramble ultimately may involve. And also men of the old category look the part perhaps rather better.' The next Garter nomination was of the King's suitably picturesque crony Lord Lonsdale.

On the morning of 19 April 1929 John Revelstoke was found dead in his bed in his apartment in rue du Faubourg Saint-Honoré. For two months he had been working at a high pitch on behalf of the British government to resolve the international crisis over German war reparation payments, though in Berlin he had found secret opportunities to relax with a pliable mercenary youth called Pieps. On the day before his death he had mediated in fraught negotiations between German and French representatives. The Revelstoke house in Devon, Membland, was being demolished at the time, but his body was taken for burial at the nearby church of Noss Mayo. Ettie, accompanied by Mogs, was 'more shattered than I have ever known her', Maurice Baring said, and at the funeral she was treated almost as the grieving widow. Afterwards she went into purdah at Panshanger. 'The last thing one could bear would be to "make a fuss", or to dramatise in any way – but it is such a great piece of life torn away, 37 years of the closest friendship,' she wrote to Charley Londonderry. 'I feel such poor company – just blank – but shall soon fight back to the standing-ground. You know how with each fresh pain the old griefs come rushing back, flooding & overwhelming, & John was always my rock of defence.'

Ettie mourned Revelstoke all that year; and had already had a forewarning of another great loss. On Sunday, 17 March 1928 Balfour was staying at Taplow, as Ettie later described. 'He sat out for a short time before luncheon, watching the tennis on the red court. After luncheon we sat on at "coffee" in the library, until four o'clock, and he and Winston and Mr Fisher had an enthralling conversation – starting with Napoleon. Mr Fisher has often reminded me of how brilliant Arthur was that day. Then I went out for a walk with Winston, and A.J.B. started to walk round to the tennis court with Venetia Montagu. It was then that he had the sudden difficulty in finding the right words, and used the wrong ones. He was much troubled, and went up to his room to rest. I went up there on returning, a little after five. His speech was then all right, but he was very agitated.' Four months later Balfour celebrated his eightieth birthday, and his health was sufficiently strong for him to remain in the Cabinet until the defeat of the Baldwin government in the general election of 1929. After returning the seals of his office to the King, he went to stay at his brother's house near Woking, where he was attacked by phlebitis in his leg. It became evident that circulatory disease had begun to weaken and kill him.

Ettie realised that her beloved friend was 'near to the great starting-point', and once again the omnipresence of death intensified her feelings. 'How one longs to know what lies in front of us all. I have given up guessing, but hope seems to grow even stronger.' She visited him almost to the last: he died on 19 March 1930 holding the hand of his brother. 'All the pain is for one's self, for his sake there can only be thankfulness,' she wrote from Windsor Castle to Judge Holmes in Washington. 'The last six months were perfectly serene – he was still working, still witty, though kept in bed by the doctor – still loving the society of his greatest friends (those of us who were left) & the end came very gently.' Again Ettie sought Charley Londonderry's comfort. 'I don't think', she wrote to him of Balfour, 'one single important decision was taken ever without being influenced (consciously or unconsciously) by his standard. I don't think the joy & *excitement* of being with him ever grew less.'

Churchill consulted Ettie when writing his chapter on Balfour for *Great Contemporaries*. 'I shall always think of AJB as the supremely perfect friend,' she replied, 'always nearest when need was sorest – no one who he loved could have been with him in anguish & have failed to realize that. He had treasures of devotion & tenderness, & his austerity to any nonsense-griefs made the gift even greater of his pity when it came. I adored him from the age of fifteen until his death last year – 47 years – & I don't think that the loss of anyone (except my sons) has ever or could ever have left such a sense of bereavement.' Churchill sent the draft of his Balfour chapter to her for comments, and embodied her corrections in some crucial revisions. She recalled her activity in 1903 as a 'go-between' taking messages between Balfour and Austen Chamberlain at the time of Joseph Chamberlain's resignation from the Cabinet, and corrected his account of George Wyndham's retirement in 1905: 'Arthur backed George with the whole power of his strength, & absolutely refused, time after time, to allow him to resign'; but ultimately, 'poor George's health and nerves completely broke down, & it was only at the *entreaty* of Sibell Grosvenor & all George's family, heavily backed by the doctors, that Arthur at long last, most reluctantly accepted his resignation.' Churchill rewrote this paragraph almost in Ettie's words.

She always revered Churchill's powers, exulted in his company and devoured his books. Every page of *My Early Life* was 'intoxicating', she told him when it was published in 1930. 'The "attaque" is brilliant, sweeping one instantly into delighted & intimate communion. It is marvellous in seizure – the swiftness, the life in every syllable, the outrush, the uproar . . . & humour always underlying & leaping out in such glorious flashes – there isn't one ounce of vanity . . . in the whole caboodle – that is why it's such fun.'

ↄ

In October 1930, at the age of twenty-five, Mogs finally engaged herself to George Gage. 'I do feel *so* happy about them,' Ettie enthused to Monica. 'All the slight nuances seem to have completely vanished, ever since it was settled – he has been so absolutely *charming*, & looks so happy – not a bit fussed, though he was here the worst morning of all, on Tuesday, when the telephone never stopped for one single second, & the house was surrounded by photographers!' George Gage had been 'Ivo's greatest friend', she told Judge Holmes, and had admired Mogs 'since she was a little schoolroom girl'.

They married at St Nicholas's church, Taplow on 26 February 1931 – a day that marked the apogee of the Desboroughs at Taplow. Ettie's preparations were painstaking, and created a tremendous stir in the district. As the *Maidenhead Advertiser* reported, 'Lord and Lady Desborough graciously permitted the villagers and people from Maidenhead to view the presents during the Sunday afternoon, when close on 600 availed themselves of the much-prized privilege. The groups of visitors were shepherded by Mr Barrett Good (the stalwart faithful butler to the family for nearly half a century) and Mr Kemble Cheek, a servitor at the Court for about 30 years . . . there were mountains of things to be seen, admired and envied – something like 900 presents.' (Barrett Good, who had begun to work for Willie in 1875, was still working as his butler at the age of eighty-six in 1943.) George Gage gave his bride a jewel case containing three diamond necklaces, an emerald and diamond necklace, four diamond rings, four pairs of diamond earrings, a diamond tiara, a diamond crescent brooch and a diamond brooch in the form of a butterfly set in the style of Queen Anne's reign. The Desboroughs gave two large pieces of old French tapestry to be hung in the great Stone Hall at Firle; and examples from the long list of gifts give a vivid glimpse of a Society wedding in AD 1931:

Queen Mary – motoring dress-case in green crushed morocco with
   white jade ornament
Philip Sassoon – diamond and sapphire arrow-shaped hat ornament
Sybil and Rock Cholmondeley – oval topaz brooch set with diamonds
Helen D'Abernon – emerald and diamond brooch
Alice Salisbury – a settee
Winnie Portland – a silver fox fur
Margaret Ampthill – jade green feather fan set in ivory
Stanley Baldwin – twelve brandy goblets
Maurice Baring – a set of his own works bound in red morocco
Maidenhead Fire Brigade – a silver inkstand
The chauffeurs at Taplow – a hunting crop

George Gage had chosen Chips Channon – not Ettie's favourite
American – as his best man. There were eight pages (including Julian
Salmond) who wore ivory-satin suits based on the Raeburn portrait at
Panshanger, and the four bridesmaids (including Rosemary Salmond)
were dressed in long high-waisted Raeburn frocks with bodices of
ivory satin and frilled skirts of ivory net and lace, with wreaths of
mixed flowers in their hair, and carrying long golden staves adorned by
flame-coloured and yellow azaleas and tulips tied with peach-coloured
ribbon. The church was decorated with spring flowers of orange, flame
and yellow – a colour scheme of Ettie's making. The bride wore a
long-sleeved ivory satin gown with a long ivory tulle veil held in place
by a double wreath of apple blossom finished with clusters of orange
blossom on either side; and Ettie wore a frock of pale brown georgette
shot with gold and a pale brown velvet cloak with lynx collar. This
indeed was *marriage à la mode*.

One journalist has left a vivid account of the wedding day. 'The
Desboroughs', he overheard a local woman pronounce on the Taplow
bus, 'are the finest lot of people on earth. I have often heard Lady
Desborough speaking at the Town Hall, and she is extremely nice and
a perfect human being – without any starchiness or side or pretence.
She must be loved by everybody, and her family too. Some rich people
make themselves really absurd and disliked; but the Desboroughs are
so totally different.' Even the hard-bitten reporter was impressed; and
on arriving in the village, he was charmed by the triumphal arches

erected over the narrow lane leading down from the court to the church. More buses from Maidenhead and charabancs from distant parishes unloaded burgeoning crowds. As the church clock struck two, the invited guests began to arrive, and there was soon a chain of cars curving up the hill.

By 2.15 the village green skirting the churchyard was congested with jostling bystanders – in proportion of twenty women to one man – surging forward as each car halted, craning their necks to glimpse the guests ambling through the churchyard, and shuffling their feet in the dull intervals of waiting. The guests, by contrast, not huddled together outside the railings but loitering under the yew trees in the spacious amplitude of the churchyard, smiled and nodded to their friends, complementing one another's distinction, in the moments before they filed into the church. Bishop Talbot narrowly escaped being crushed between a charabanc and a newspaper van as he lumbered towards the church.

Ettie's arrival at 2.27 was greeted by loud shouts of welcome and agitated waving of handkerchiefs. 'She oscillated and bowed with her inimitable smile to the people right and left,' reported the journalist. 'It was a happy but touching passing; the remarks I heard from the spectators as she glided past to the church were really enough to make one's heart melt.' After the bride had been escorted into the church by her father, the spectators rushed for the church gates, which were shut on them, then set siege to the railings; the police became overpowered and a young woman who fainted was carried to safety. A horde of Fleet Street photographers busied themselves erecting platforms for their cameras, scrambling up trees and walls to secure their vantage points, feverish to snap the bride. After the ceremony, Ettie left the church beaming with smiles: 'you could feel between her and the villagers and the people from the town who cheered her, the silent union of hearts, the true spirit of sisterhood which unites whether the bonds be drawn by strands of gold or the threads of poverty. It was to some sensitive natures deeply touching – remembering things past.'

The names of the wedding guests were a litany of Ettie Desborough's world. They included great territorial families, Ancasters, Brownlows, Beauforts, Cranbornes, Dalkeiths, Devonshires, Lansdownes, Linlithgows, Londonderrys, Lyttons, Northamptons, Plymouths, Portlands,

Rutlands, Westminsters, Westmorlands and many others. There were political couples like the Astors, Duff Coopers, Cunliffe-Listers and Neville Chamberlains; and literati, including the G.K. Chestertons, Walter de la Mares, Rudyard Kiplings, Professor Lindemann, Osbert and Sacheverell Sitwell, and the Maynard Keyneses, who were George Gage's tenants in Sussex. Shortly after the Gage wedding Winston Churchill inserted a few elegiac lines in *Great Contemporaries* – he was writing of an ex-Soul. 'The leadership of the privileged has passed away,' he declared, 'but it has not been succeeded by that of the eminent. We have entered the region of mass effects.' The Gage wedding guests were a fine balance of the privileged and the eminent. They made one of the high-pedestalled moments in Ettie's life.

Ettie was delighted by the marriage. '*George* – what luck it is to have one's greatest (young) friend for a son-in-law,' she said later. Immediately after the wedding, she went to the Côte d'Azur with those soothing, contented bachelors, Louis Mallet and Jack Stanmore. They stayed at Mortefontaine, Mallet's house near Grasse, a 'lovely eyrie in the hills, 12 miles from all the crowd & noise, with *divine* mountain walks & wild flowers'. They were visited there by Consuelo Marlborough and her French husband Jacques Balsan, who had been guests at the wedding, and some evenings drove the twelve miles down the mountains to Cannes ('everyone carries a loaded revolver in their car at night!'). One Saturday she sat next to Eddy Derby at a dinner given by Philip Sassoon's sister and brother-in-law the Cholmondeleys. Derby 'was charming, & very, very fat. We were dining with Sybil & Rock at the Cannes Casino – a "Gala" night & immense crowd & noise & a most startling Cabaret – the mania seems to be for the *entièrement nu*! I glanced now & then rather apprehensively at Alice Derby, but she appeared quite accustomed to it. It was great fun.'

For one weekend Ettie accompanied Mallet and Stanmore on a visit to Edith Wharton at Sainte Claire le Château, near Hyères, and had 'a HEAVENLY happy restful peaceful stimulating time' despite unremitting rain. Mrs Wharton's *The Age of Innocence* had disappointed Ettie when she read it in 1921: '*L'infiniment petit* carried to a scale that H. James alone could handle', though various Wharton novellas, 'Ethan Frome', 'The Old Maid' and 'New Year's Day', delighted her. Her earliest meeting with her hostess, as Adèle Essex's guests at Cassiobury, had been flat, but in 1931 these two intelligent women charmed one another. Edith Wharton said that she was born happy every morning, and the same was true of Ettie: for both women happiness was a matter of resolve as well as temperament. 'Will-power', Wharton had written in *The Glimpses of the Moon* (which Ettie had read in 1922), 'was not a thing one could suddenly decree oneself to possess. It must be built up imperceptibly and laboriously out of a succession of small efforts to meet definite objects, out of the facing of daily difficulties instead of cleverly eluding them, or shifting their burden on others. The making of the substance called character was a process about as slow and arduous as the building of the Pyramids; and the thing itself, like those awful edifices, was mainly useful to lodge one's descendants in.' She might have been writing of Ettie.

The marriage of their youngest child led Ettie and Willie to finalise arrangements for the succession to their estates at Pans and Tap. Ettie signed her final will in July 1931; and though its details were modified by six codicils between 1934 and 1951, the framework remained unchanged. It was Ettie's hope – indeed, her assumption – that the Panshanger estate, together with the house and its contents, would ultimately be enjoyed by Julian Salmond, and that he would be the continuer of the Desborough and Cowper lines (their wills, however, contained the option for the Hertfordshire property to be held intermediately by Monica). The Taplow estates were allotted to Mogs and the Gages. Ettie's will of 1931 also reveals who she thought her best friends were. Her bequests included:

> *To Alice Salisbury*, a pink enamel clock given to her by Edward VII.
> *To Mary Wemyss*, two silver bowls given to her by Arthur Balfour.
> *To Elizabeth Kenmare*, a small violet and green enamel clock (always kept on her writing table) given to her by John Revelstoke.
> *To Betty Montgomery*, a small gold watch given to her by Philip Sassoon.
> *To St John Midleton*, nine volumes of morocco-bound Shakespeare.
> *To Alice Hylton*, a diamond and emerald watch.
> *To Violet Leconfield*, an oval brooch of amethysts and diamonds.
> *To Violet Bonham Carter*, an emerald and diamond Cartier pendant.

She also left an unspecified book or object as a keepsake to Charley Londonderry, Hugh Cecil, Maurice Baring, the Duke of Portland, Sir Philip Sassoon, Lord Stanmore, Edgar D'Abernon, Helen D'Abernon, Winston Churchill, Cynthia Asquith, Irene Plymouth, Rose Lascelles, Marie de Rothschild and Louise Sassoon. These were people in whose hearts and memories Ettie hoped to be carried when she was dead.

Mogs's two sons, Sammy and Nicky Gage, who were born in 1932 and 1934, were a joy to Ettie, and from their first years were annual visitors to Whiteslea, where they lived in their bathing suits. 'The two tinies', Ettie enthused in 1936, 'are such divine toys. How nice it would be to bottle them at those ages.' Their sister Camilla, who was born in July 1937, became the unadulterated joy of Ettie's old age: her letters sing with pride and pleasure at the little girl's latest quip or social conquest of her elders. As she told Queen Mary, 'one never quite realized beforehand the delight that grandchildren would be.'

She began in time to welcome a small ration of distinguished visitors – Stanley Baldwin and Neville Chamberlain, for example – to Whiteslea. In 1937 she spent eight 'happy eventless weeks in this heavenly country', she told Charley Londonderry. 'I love its calm spaces & the unbroken circle of the horizon, & I've read & walked (& slept) & bathed a lot, & we've had Moggie's three delicious babies.'

This, however, is to anticipate. A few months after Sammy Gage's birth in July 1932, Ettie was confronted by a family crisis: the Salmond marriage had proven only a mirage of happiness. Jack Salmond – by now an air chief marshal – had been appointed Chief of Air Staff, the most senior post in the RAF, in January 1930. In the eighteen months that followed he had to cope with the R101 airship disaster, in which several of his friends perished, with harsh Treasury curbs on RAF expenditure, with clashes on the Committee of Imperial Defence over the fortification of Singapore, and with the World Disarmament Conference of 1932. Cumulatively this was a great strain; and Monica was unsteady and variable in her support. In the early years of the marriage she had enjoyed a good relationship with her stepdaughter; but Joy was an ill-starred adolescent, and the two women drifted on to the reefs of umbrage. Miserable quarrels began between husband and wife; and in November 1932 Ettie heard with dismay that the Salmonds had separated.

Her Salmond grandchildren came to stay at Pans – their mother went for a respite on the Riviera – and Ettie invited the Air Marshal to bring Joy and join them for Christmas. 'We will all try to make it the happiest time we have ever had together,' she told him. 'I think you must know how deep a hold you have on us, on our love & admiration & trust, & how proud we are of you.' She offered, delicately, to act as intermediary. 'If you would ever like to talk to me, you know that I am yours . . . You may think silence best, which I should utterly understand. But I can never forget what you were to me in 1926, & if I could be of one iota of help now to you & yours, it would be the truest gladness that life could hold.' Salmond visited his children at the Desboroughs' and in January the couple were reconciled. 'I feel sure it all arose from the terrific nervous strain, worry & disappointment (about the Air Force),' Ettie told Monica. 'Oh darling, I *am* so thankful, & what it must have cost him to "make the move". Do embrace & hold fast.'

There were other family vexations: the inevitable extinction of the Desborough title, and the possible perpetuation of peerages among Ettie's descendants. For a time it had seemed possible that she might become a peeress in her own right. Bron Lucas's baronies had been inherited in 1916 by his surviving sister Nan, and for three years Ettie was heiress presumptive to them – until, at the age of thirty-nine, Nan gave birth to her daughter Anne. Ettie, though, was also co-heiress to the barony of Butler of Moore Park, which had been abeyant since Lord Cowper's death in 1905. She could have petitioned for its revival in her favour: so, indeed, could Monica, or later Julian Salmond, at any date before 2005. After Ivo's death, there was a feeling among Ettie's fellow courtiers – led by Lord Stamfordham – that the patent of Willie's peerage should be adjusted so that Monica and then her son could perpetuate the Desborough name. Willie was 'a magnificent Englishman and an example to the youth of this country of what a man should be', declared Lord Wigram, Stamfordham's eventual successor as Private Secretary to the King. 'It is tragic to think that the Title will become extinct.' King George endorsed the idea, but the College of Arms evidently made objections. Sadly, Ettie was not advised of the availability of the Butler barony (heralds, as Edith Wharton once teased, sometimes do not even know their own silly business).

Jack Salmond took early retirement from the RAF in 1933, in order to ease promotion for some of the younger hopefuls crowding at his heels, and a few months later in August Ettie addressed Ramsay MacDonald, the Prime Minister, whom she often met when he came for audiences with the King while she was in Waiting to the Queen. 'I am sorry to bother you with a letter, but there is a subject about which I have greatly wished to talk to you for some time, only I could not bear to trouble you during these last weeks, when I knew how terribly busy you were.' This was a reference to the World Economic Conference, which had been convened in London in an effort to alleviate the global economic depression, but which was killed off by the Americans' refusal to stabilise the dollar. 'It is about our son-in-law, Jack Salmond. When he gave up the command of the Air Force last spring, we were told by several outside people . . . that there was a question of a peerage being bestowed upon him: then I believe that some difficulty with regard to precedent arose? but I heard a little time ago that the matter was not finally decided.'

Ettie recapitulated Salmond's service in France, Iraq, India and Whitehall. 'My husband & I are intensely anxious that all Jack has done should be recognised,' she continued. 'And there is one quite separate aspect of the case that enters strongly into my own mind, & that *you* will, I know, understand': the King's and the Court's hope that the Desborough name would be continued by 'Jack Salmond's boy'. Though the technical difficulties in a modified patent had proved insurmountable, an alternative was possible. 'If the little boy was to succeed in time to his own father's peerage, it would seem to consummate all those wishes – & it would be a great joy to us to think that this would happen.' MacDonald resisted these blandishments, and replied that a peerage for Salmond was impossible, as it would raise a train of similar claims. Was it fair of Ettie to unload so much of the past and place such expectations on a six-year-old child?

Ettie did more than tout for a peerage for Jack Salmond. He had only a directorship of Imperial Airways to keep him occupied, and she asked Lindemann to scout for additional work. The tensions between him and Monica were smothered and forgotten, she hoped. She so wanted to buttress his marriage that in 1934 she endowed a trust fund with £8,000 (the equivalent of about £378,000 in 2008 values) and nominated Joy, Monica's stepdaughter, as the primary beneficiary. For Ettie, who was usually close with her money, this was a considerable step; but it proved unavailing. The Salmond marriage soon relapsed, ostensibly because of continued rows about Joy, though there were other reasons for reproach and disappointment. In January 1935 the couple separated and henceforth, despite behaving decently together on family occasions, developed a strong inward aversion for one another. Ettie seems to have concluded that further efforts to reunite the Salmonds would be wrong. When Siegfried Sassoon told her that he had separated from his wife, she replied that she was 'unspeakably sorry, but one *must* decide these things by one's own best judgment, it would be both cowardly & fatal to decide them by any other means'.

The failure of the Salmond marriage so subdued and perhaps even abashed Ettie that she never mentioned it when writing to her friends. She was sufficiently old-guard to be relieved that the Salmonds kept out of the divorce courts, and were never sullied by the dirty fingering of a *Daily Express* reporter satisfying public prurience. Monica's position as a separated woman was more amorphous and disempowered than that of a divorcée: she entered a social limbo, in which it was impossible to be purposive; and with the passing of the years, living quietly in Sussex, acquired the air of a desert-island castaway who has given up watching for a sail. She was generous to her children and roused herself in times of crisis (notably in 1968 when Mogs was dying), but it seemed as if the great excitement of her life was provided by meringues.

Although Ettie's trust in Monica's judgement was shaken, the devotion between mother and daughter was unfading. She was gratified when Monica proposed dedicating her memoirs of wartime nursing, which Faber were publishing, to her; but she made a counter-suggestion. 'Wouldn't you like to dedicate it "To my brothers", or to your Julian,' she asked. 'All in us that is worth anything belongs to the boys . . . They set the pitch, & called the tune, for us all.' Monica's book, entitled *Bright Armour*, was nevertheless published in the autumn of 1935 bearing a plain, resolute dedication to 'My Mother'. It was her attempt to make sense of experiences that had transformed her life, and to commemorate an indispensable part of the war experience that was almost ignored – because it had been women's work. Unlike Ettie's *Family Journal*, *Bright*

Armour was void of intensity, emphasis, self-consciousness and ideals. Instead, it recounted in steady, modest terms a tale of courage and self-control: one extract, describing her bewildered 'horror' when one day she found herself crying while putting surgical dressings on a wounded soldier, is representative. 'I suddenly felt the whole sum of pity for everybody, and just at that moment it overcame me,' she recalled, but self-discipline was swiftly reasserted: 'it wasn't for *me* to cry, after all, and I was dismayed at having done anything so unhelpful.' She resolved that weeping must never recur, and only cried once more at a patient's bedside, when a fellow nurse lost consciousness.

Bright Armour's reviewers were amiable; and David Cecil's piece in the *Spectator*, though written by someone with intimate ties to the author, is fair rather than corrupt. 'A winning, a profoundly touching book,' Cecil judged. 'She tells the story of her career as a nurse in France and England as simply and colloquially and personally, with as little apparent consciousness of an audience, as if she were writing a letter to a friend.' Precision was combined with restraint. 'The petty details of life in the ward, the trouble she had sweeping it, the little jokes that relieved its strain, are all exactly recorded for us', but in describing the 'nauseating horror' of a military hospital, she was austerely factual: 'she never tries to make our flesh creep.' The novelist L.P. Hartley – not yet a family friend, but a visitor to Panshanger in the 1940s – was another reviewer. 'Lady Salmond's attitude to herself is one of the chief charms of the book. It is utterly free from affectation, from the desire to impress, from the wish to appear a heroine or a martyr – indeed, from all the irritating tricks of self-consciousness.'

In December 1935 Ettie motored over from Panshanger to open a bazaar at Silsoe, the village lying at the gates of her old home, Wrest. The recent despoiling of her childhood paradise appalled her: John Murray had sold Wrest with 2,126 acres to the Essex Timber Company in 1934, the park was ploughed up and the surrounding trees cut down. She did not enter the house, but was made wretched by what she saw. Everywhere the Old Order had been overturned; as Churchill said, 'the tidal wave of democracy and the volcanic explosion of the War have swept the shores bare.' And the future threatened worse convulsions than felled timber or chinless youths in berets tearing past Whiteslea in speedboats.

CHAPTER 9

The Courtier

🙠

T HERE WERE A few isolated redoubts where the Old Order was not overwhelmed between the wars: ducal palaces like Welbeck and Eaton, where Winnie Portland and Bendor Westminster still lived in pomp, and supremely in the Royal House-hold, of which Ettie remained a member until her death.

Even so, Court life had been transformed during the war. The King gave himself to war duties, toiling at Buckingham Palace for long hours at the contents of his red leather despatch boxes, leaving only for tours of inspection and patriotic events, permitting himself but short holidays at Windsor or Sandringham. The Queen, too, took up strenuous war work. She and her ladies, who had all led protected and rarefied lives, confronted scenes that would have been unthinkably brutal in the long years of peace.

Ettie's first exposure to the Court's harrowing new duties came on 1 May 1915 when she accompanied the King and Queen on their visit to forty-eight wounded and maimed officers in Guy's Hospital by London Bridge. Some of them were suffering from the after-effects of gassing, and their stories were so fearsome that Ettie promptly bought six respirators and sent them to Julian. Hospital visits were an ordeal for the Queen, who had always been squeamish, but she trained herself to talk calmly to mutilated or hideously disfigured servicemen. 'Some-times when we left the ward I would see tears glistening in her eyes but she never allowed them to fall,' Mabell Airlie recalled. The Queen's self-discipline was absolute. She had always been gun shy, but trained herself to endure a 101-gun royal salute with a smile. During Zeppelin raids she would join the King on the Buckingham Palace balcony despite her terror of the booming guns in Green Park and the explosion of falling bombs across the capital.

Ettie was unfailingly cheerful and tractable throughout her twenty-eight years of active courtiership, and rather than flinch at her wartime duties, made light of them. All courtiers had to rally under the flood of disheartening news and accustom themselves to unprecedented austerity. One aspect of the wartime regime at Court even amused Ettie. The King's booming voice and hearty manner sometimes misled his subjects into thinking that he was a drunkard although, in truth, he had abstemious habits. In April 1915 he was cajoled by Lloyd George, then Minister of Munitions, who believed that armaments productivity was hindered by inebriate factory workers, into setting an example for the nation by renouncing alcohol and enforcing abstention throughout his household for the duration of the war. This did not matter to Ettie, who disliked alcohol, but her graphic account to Patrick Shaw-Stewart of Windsor Castle on the 'water-wagon' shows the strain on her male colleagues. 'Tempers were but little improved by temperance, a crepe wreath was fastened to the cellar door, and Charlie Cust fainted the first night after dinner; the only cheerful person being Margot, who took copious swigs from a medicine bottle, and talked a great deal, but no one else spoke except to contradict her.' Lord Rosebery, after swallowing an unaccustomed glass of ginger beer, got such hiccoughs that he could not continue talking to the Queen. There were other light moments for Ettie, as when Prince John, the King's epileptic youngest son, declared, ' "David's gone to the Front, & Bertie's gone back to Sea, & I sit here & knit, knit, knit. I call this a *bloody* War." '

Mabell Airlie accompanied Queen Mary on a visit to France in 1917. 'We visited many hospitals – British, Australian, French, Belgian – the endless succession of beds had a terrible sameness of young faces and broken bodies. Some of them were cheerful places, clean and well organized, but others were old and grimy Hôtels Dieu with layers of dust on the floors and the indescribable stench of Death and sickness hanging in the air,' Mabell recorded. 'The most harrowing sight of our tour was the battlefield: a vast stretch of land that had once been fertile and smiling, covered with crops, but was now only a tumbled mass of blackened earth fringed by sparse and splintered trees. The ground was strewn with rocks and stones and mounds of soil flung up by the mines, and pitted with deep craters that had swallowed up farms and villages. We climbed over a mound composed of German dead . . . over this devil's charnel house Nature had thrown a merciful veil of gently creeping plants.'

Similar sights dazed Ettie, Elizabeth Kenmare and other bereaved war mothers who were able to visit their sons in the cemeteries after the Armistice; and Helen D'Abernon had worked for months as an anaesthetist in field hospitals amid comparable terrain. No previous generation of Englishwomen of their background had endured such scenes. The memories were ineffaceable. As Mabell Airlie recalled of Queen Mary's battlefront tour, 'scattered everywhere in the ineffable desolation were the pathetic reminders of human life – rifles fallen from dead hands, old water bottles, iron helmets. And in the distance the guns boomed relentlessly . . . We stood there speechless. It was impossible to find words. The Queen's face was ashen and her lips were tightly compressed. I felt that like me she was afraid of breaking down.'

From the moment of her appointment as a lady-in-waiting in 1911 Ettie proved a nimble courtier whose sincere admiration for her Sovereign and his consort was spiced with judicious flattery. Ettie did not know George V well before her appointment, but soon felt devoted to him. 'My passion for him grows to an obsession,' she told Balfour in 1913. 'It is to be hoped he reciprocates, as I've sat next him at dinner 5 nights running, poor creature, & shall in all probability do so for 9 nights more!' She was not insincere: she truly revered the King's self-discipline, sense of duty and dogged industry. His storms of temper she thought rather masculine and they did not ruffle her.

The King and Queen's wartime self-mastery moved Ettie. 'It is sad to see what a very heavy burden is carried there,' she wrote in 1917 after a spell in Waiting at Windsor. 'Very mournful impressions, & the great beauty & nobility of the surroundings add to the sense of irony. There is such an intense desire to do right – it is like the piteous spectacle of watching a very good child under an almost insurmountable handicap.'

Ettie was right to liken the King and Queen to well-behaved children. The monarch's weekly schedule, and his consort's, were as tightly planned and rigidly controlled as any boarding house pupil's. The days of the King and Queen were portioned and packed with duties. Each hour was arranged to eliminate the possibility of chance occurrences; every minute was allotted. It was no wonder that a man whose time was so regimented as the King's started a private collection of clocks, and that the undertone of their ticking could be heard through his houses. King George and Queen Mary were like the star pupils of a tense, austere, highly controlling housemaster – very good children, but labouring under the handicap of never being able to relax their guard, seldom permitted to think of their own feelings and enforcedly inarticulate under the duress of their tight routine. The great quasi-boarding houses that were the royal palaces were indeed very tightly run. Every move in the royal household was governed by a strict routine based on precedent. There was an inflexible hierarchy in each department from Lord Chamberlain to the stables.

Ettie was conspicuous among the Queen's ladies-in-waiting: more vivid and original than most of her colleagues. St John Midleton was 'delighted' that she was one of the Bedchamber ladies as he thought it important 'for H.M. to have the best brains & feelings around her'. Ettie was not advanced in her social views, but she liked the young, and Mogs's 'Beans' and 'nuts' kept her up to date. The resumption of the old pattern began for Ettie with a party at St James's Palace in February 1919 to celebrate the impending marriage of Princess Patricia of Connaught to a Scottish naval officer. The King and Queen did not attend the party in person, as they were in mourning after the death of their thirteen-year-old son Prince John, but by royal command, Court mourning was not worn. Someone asked beforehand if women were to wear tiaras and to Ettie's delight was told, 'second-best tiaras'. She quipped to Margot Asquith that Winnie Portland had to send her fourth groom-of-the-chambers to fetch her second-best tiara.

The old boundaries had been demolished during the war and hallowed certainties were scattered in the noisy, disturbing, headlong rush of change; but the Court tried to preserve some continuities from the Old Orders of the day. Queen Mary epitomised the forces of immutable stability: instinctively opposed to change, she faced it with grim forbearance. Her manner was inimitable – reserved, elegant and invincible – and reflected the calm decorum of her days. She was called at 7.15 and breakfasted with the King at nine – a meal often disturbed by his aggressive parrot, Charlotte, with whom he liked to take breakfast and luncheon. At 9.30 Queen Mary would summon by bell the lady-in-waiting currently on duty. Ettie would find the Queen sitting upright at her desk, with a pile of opened letters before her (for the Queen opened every letter addressed to her personally) and hand her further general correspondence, and help her with the replies. The Queen had a retentive memory, was tidy and businesslike, and liked to make direct interventions in the running of her household. She felt the Edwardian Court had been surfeited by gold plate and orchids: her guest lists were less promiscuous and her hospitality less meretricious. She had a more flexible mind than the King's, but never contradicted him, and submitted to his prejudices about colours and clothes, though she longed to break away from the hats, clothes and sober tones associated with her.

Queen Mary had (as Duchess of York and Princess of Wales) always been ruled by one abstract passion – for the British monarchy. After her husband's accession, she sublimated herself to the ideal of the Crown, and Ettie, who was a great proponent of sublimating oneself for ideals, admired her for this. As Queen she never relaxed. She might lie down for an hour before dinner, being read to by her lady-in-waiting, but resting to conserve one's strength was different from remittance of her duties. Like Ettie she was deeply religious, with a simple faith, and punctilious in her prayers. She held fast to the strict tenets of her upbringing: these were indistinguishable from the faith and principles that old Lady Westmorland and old Lady Cowper had instilled in Ettie in the 1870s. The Queen had unbending views of right and wrong, despised gossip and imposed a staid, impersonal taste in small talk on her Bedchamber ladies. She was acquisitive rather than introspective, and had proved a hard bargainer with Ettie's godfather Sir William Harcourt, the Chancellor of the Exchequer, in the negotiations over her marriage settlement. She never repined over the past, and thus made herself immune from the worries that dismay most other people. Her parents had enjoyed a stormy marriage in which she had often had to act as a discomfited peacemaker: in consequence she recoiled from any sort of emotional scene.

'The Queen', said Mabell Airlie, 'had an eager enjoyment of life, and a sense of fun, carefully controlled like all her emotions, but always rippling beneath the surface. I can remember her laughing over the jokes in *Punch*, and even in *La Vie Parisienne*; sending me comic postcards (in an envelope); learning the words of "Yes, we have No Bananas" . . . and singing it with me at the top of our voices for the joy of shocking a particularly staid member of the Household; hopping in a green and white brocade dress round one of the drawing-rooms at Windsor in a game of Dumb Crambo after dinner.' Queen Mary's playfulness is well caught by the doggerel verse about Prohibition which she wrote out and gave to Ettie:

> Twenty little Yankees feeling very dry
> Went off to Canada to fetch a keg of rye.
> When the keg was opened,
> The Yanks began to sing,
> Who the hell is Hoover? —
> God Save the King.

Ettie's clamp on royal gossip was tight: she was unwavering in her submission to the Court rule never to repeat any direct remarks made by the Sovereign or his consort. Her discretion was inviolate. Doubtless she spoke to Willie under the strictest confidence, but she allowed herself only the most superficial mention of royal doings in her letters. 'He continues *wonderfully* well, & in tip-top spirits – all the old fun with him! He is shooting again.' These two sentences about the King, in a letter from Sandringham to Willie, are as informative as she ever got. Or, to Herbert Fisher, after George V's grave illness in 1928–9, 'Our Sovereign is most marvellously better, & in excellent spirits.' She greatly respected Queen Mary for keeping confidences, and repressing gossip: for being, indeed, 'a "tomb" for any indiscretion'. She was alarmed when in 1941 Charley Londonderry told her that in writing his memoirs he was going to use a letter she had sent him at the time of George V's death. 'You know all the queer point of honour about being a deaf mute when in Waiting (which I was then),' she replied immediately. 'Anything I may have written to you in those last sad days at Sandringham . . . was solely & sacredly for *you*.' She was not wholly immune, however, from the temptation to raise a laugh. At a Wiltshire house party in 1936, she told 'Royal Family stories' at breakfast. The sole occasion, she said, when she saw Queen Mary 'really angry' was when Winnie Portland brought her own bed sheets on a visit to Windsor.

Ettie was astonished by the unkind indiscretions, as she saw it, about Queen Victoria that were published by Arthur Ponsonby (brother of her lifelong friend Betty Montgomery) in his biography of his courtier father Sir Henry Ponsonby. She complained about the book to Queen Mary and to others. 'It seemed to me that he lessened Q.V. – made her shrink; emphasised her foolishness, stubbornness, capriciousness, & – while giving a faint glimpse of her strange charm – obliterated her greatness.' The repetition of unguarded remarks upset her most. 'That is what I mind in A's book – a disagreeable sense of listening at the key-hole. All those foolish peevish little notes of irritation, published after all these years, written in utter confidence to her devotee & *souffre-douleur* & safety-valve, H.P. It seems to me like putting into cold-print what someone says when they bang their funny-bone.'

Her friendship with Lady Oxford had begun to deteriorate with the publication of the self-promoting, inaccurate *Autobiography of Margot Asquith* in 1922, which was unfailingly flattering to Ettie but wounded many of their mutual friends. Their affection was destroyed by the time Lady Oxford published her last indiscreet and ill-remembered memoir, *Off the Record*. ' "Off the Rocker" ', as Ettie called it, 'has profoundly shocked me . . . not to speak of its colossal sales-success. It does seem the very nadir of literature. And I *was* so fond of her – the only friendship of any kind that I have ever lost.'

On afternoons when the Royal Household was installed at Buckingham Palace and Queen Mary had no hospital-visiting or other duties to perform, she would sally forth after luncheon to visit a gallery, museum or art dealer – leaving punctually at 2.45 and returning in good time to take tea with the King. Before dinner the Queen would rest on a sofa, wrapped in a brightly coloured kimono, with embroidered cushions behind her immaculately coiffured head, working on her embroidery, while her lady-in-waiting read aloud. Ettie had begun reading aloud to her children when Julian and Billy were small, continued to read aloud on family holidays during the 1920s, and in the 1930s had the joy of her grandchildren as a new audience: it was a task for which her expressive and harmonious voice was especially suited. King George loathed to dine out in London more than four or five times a year, and did not share the Queen's love of theatre and dancing (he exploded with rage when he surprised her being taught modern dance steps by Fritz Ponsonby). A typical London day for the Queen and Ettie, which was followed by a less typical evening out, is recorded in the Queen's diary for 20 July 1925. 'Very dull day with some rain,' she wrote. 'Went with Ly Desborough to the Burlington Fine Arts Club to see a good collection of Annibale Carraccis etc – then to Goode's shop. Sat out later. Dined with the Portlands to meet Elizabeth of the Belgians. We had music afterwards. The Russian quartette sang too divinely. Mme Edwina also sang & a French lady played.'

Queen Mary travelled in a massive slow-moving Daimler with a high roof, which enabled women to alight without adjusting their tall hat or toque. It exhibited its passengers like a conservatory on wheels, and was fitted with a Silent Knight engine, which fulfilled its promise of quiet, but emitted a haze of oily exhaust smoke in the faces of onlookers as it pursued its sluggish course. One journey that Ettie took with the Queen went hilariously awry. The Daimler carrying them from Sandringham to an official engagement at Cambridge broke down. And – in a glorious moment that deserved a Max Beerbohm cartoon – Ettie and Queen Mary hitched a lift. They squeezed, Ettie described, into a 'very small car which was half full of onions, & the little owner who drove it asked me "whether Your Majesty liked going very fast indeed?".' Ettie evidently replied, no, for they reached Cambridge safely, and drove to the Queen's destination, where at first 'the little car was waved away angrily by the Police & others who were waiting to receive Your Majesty'. On the return journey, in a regulation Daimler, the Queen and Ettie laughed and laughed; and ever afterwards, 'onions' was a code word between them.

For longer journeys they travelled in the royal train, painted in a livery of carmine and cream: the head stocks behind the buffers were shaped like lion's heads and painted with gold leaf; and frosted glass engraved with the insignia of chivalric orders protected the occupants of bedroom and bathroom from vulgar gaze. There was a special compartment for the ladies-in-waiting. The true meaning of the phrase 'a royal progress' was shown by the arrangements. Travelling south from Balmoral to London, seventeen engines would wait with steam up along the route in case the royal locomotive broke down. Elaborate printed orders covered every eventuality. There was a predestined time and order for each incident of the journey: even the deceleration of the train at 6.30 so that the Queen could take her evening bath without water slopping on the floor.

Ettie saw much of King Alfonso of Spain and his Queen during their informal visits to Britain in the 1920s, but there were two foreign royalties whom she encountered regularly. Grand Duchess Xenia, sister of the last czar, had been rescued from the Crimea by a British warship sent to Yalta by her cousin King George. She lived first at Frogmore Cottage in Windsor Park and later in a grace-and-favour house near the maze at Hampton Court Palace. Of all the exiled royalty in England, she was the favourite of King George and Queen Mary: she had an air of high distinction, great simplicity and unblinking honesty; and the King nicknamed her the Owl because of her large, beautiful eyes. Another exile much received at the Court was Manoel, the deposed King of Portugal, who lived at Twickenham. He had succeeded to his throne at the age of eighteen in 1908 after his father and elder brother were gunned down before his eyes, and went into exile thirty-two months later, following riots caused by the murder of the super-intendent of Lisbon lunatic asylum by one of his patients. King George liked Manoel because he had been trained for a naval career, and evidently did not know that the Portuguese was so prone to seasickness that ships to which he was posted seldom put to sea.

Queen Alexandra, Edward VII's stone-deaf and amnesiac widow, died of a heart attack in November 1925. Impulsive and unpunctual, the old Queen had been the antithesis of her daughter-in-law, of whom at times she had shown petulant jealousy. It was a hard, cold day when her coffin was carried from the chapel at St James's Palace, ablaze with lights, flowers and gold vessels, to Westminster Abbey: snow hushed the sound of wheels, hoofs and tramping feet. 'All last week', Ettie wrote afterwards to Mary Wemyss, 'seemed taken up with the lovely Fairy Queen's funeral. How one's thoughts rushed back to the days when she was so lovely and supreme . . . I thought the Abbey service very, very wonderful, the dim winter light and obscure shadows, and the great mass of colour of the scarlet and gold uniforms everywhere.

The streets and park very striking, with the deep snow and black trees and black crowds, and the funeral dirges of the bands coming muffled through the snow.'

The old lady's death meant that Ettie now became a regular visitor to an old Cowper house. In 1862, at the age of twenty, when still Prince of Wales, Edward VII had paid £220,000 to buy the 7,000-acre Sandringham estate belonging to Ettie's great-uncle Spencer Cowper, who lived abroad because his wife's sexual reputation ensured that she was ostracised in England. The Prince hired undiscerning provincial architects to convert Spencer Cowper's elegant Georgian house into a large, exuberantly mock-Jacobean royal residence. Its surrounding acreage, which had been neglected by its absentee Cowper landlord, was lavishly improved, and became a model sporting and agricultural estate. Edward VII bequeathed Sandringham to his widow for her lifetime, but after her death, King George and Queen Mary left their commonplace villa, York Cottage, and moved into the main house in October 1926. 'You would be surprised to see how comfortable the Queen has made this beastly house,' Ettie wrote from Sandringham to Balfour, 'my great-uncle's, as you will remember, and sold at a ramp price by Lord Palmerston.' In winter the Sandringham estate was sallow, mud-stained country; and in summer, when it was bright, the Royal Household were usually at Balmoral. There were no outstanding pictures and the furniture was unremarkable, but Ettie always felt a lazy sense of well-being there: it was a well-ordered, amply servanted and properly heated establishment. Overstaffing indeed was the key to the smooth success of royal households. Employ the equivalent of a servant and a half for every job that needed doing, and the amenities would seem flawless.

Ettie's duties at Windsor and Sandringham were those of a hostess. She visited newly arrived guests in their rooms, and answered questions about form posed by those who had not stayed in a royal residence before. She had to be down early for dinner, so as to line up all the ladies in strict order of precedence so that the King and Queen might walk down the line shaking hands; then she had to pair them off with partners before they processed in to dinner. Winnie Portland insisted that she had precedence before all other duchesses because she had been Queen Alexandra's Mistress of the Robes; and although this was correct protocol, it sometimes riled duchesses of earlier creations. Ettie could not go to bed until she had seen all the other guests to their rooms.

A typical Sandringham Waiting began on 16 January 1934 when Ettie succeeded Lady Ampthill in Waiting there. The little Princesses, Elizabeth and Margaret, were staying in the house, and that evening her friends Sybil and Rock Cholmondeley, who owned the great Norfolk house of Houghton, came to dine with the King. During the next few days Stanley and Lucy Baldwin, and the King's third son the Duke of Gloucester arrived at Sandringham, and the newly appointed High Commissioner for Egypt, the Governor of the Seychelles and the envoys to China and Peru had audiences before leaving England to assume their appointments. On Saturday, 27 January, Princess Mary, her husband Lord Harewood and the Lord Chancellor, Lord Hailsham, arrived until the Monday. Ettie accompanied the Queen on various forages into the Norfolk countryside, and after concluding this period in Waiting she addressed one of her courtly letters to her royal mistress. 'Madam, May I trouble Your Majesty with just one syllable, with my humble duty, to thank Your Majesty most gratefully for all your goodness & kindness at Sandringham, & for the lovely & happy days there. I came away, as always, feeling that I had learnt so much from Your Majesty – this sounds rather like "Mrs Fairchild", but is most deeply true. One did so wish that a foreigner could have been there to see the perfect relationship between Your Majesty & those village women: their devotion & respect & admiration so plain to see, & yet they were absolutely at their ease, & *trustful* of your kindness, & interest in them.'

Women at Sandringham – in the shooting season at least – had to change four times daily: they came down to breakfast in day clothes, donned thick tweeds for luncheon with the guns, changed into smart Ascot dresses for tea and put on evening dress for dinner. Indoors, smoking cigarettes through a holder, the King would stand with his grey-pink parrot Charlotte perched on his left wrist. 'Life at Sandringham was but country-house life all over England,' averred Ettie's friend and the King's biographer, John Gore. 'Tea-time was a friendly, informal meal even for an arriving guest introduced straight from the car into the royal circle, and when to the guests, assembled in the drawing-room before dinner, the Royal Family appeared in the hall, it was a prelude to another quite informal occasion. The fare was never elaborate, and swift service shortened the meal still more. When the Queen rose and the ladies followed her out, each curtseying to the King as she retired and receiving from him a bow, he would beckon the latest guest to his side and . . . put him instantly at his ease with a suitable gambit.'

The King liked to fill his after-dinner hours at Sandringham by listening to his gramophone, which must have taxed Ettie, who disliked music, and perhaps (Gore conceded) pained his more discriminating guests: 'he had that touch of sentimentality which did not rule out popular airs, even sugary, and he would play and replay such old favourites, innocently regardless of the tastes of his audience.' There was none of the high-stake gambling that had caused such difficulties in his father's time: bridge was too difficult for the King to play, though he managed poker.

Usually there were clear demarcations between Ettie's periods of Waiting at the three chief royal residences, Buckingham Palace, Windsor Castle and Sandringham. Always there were audiences for the Prime Minister, for senior Cabinet ministers and for officials taking leave of the King before going abroad as newly appointed ambassadors or colonial governors. Buckingham Palace fortnights were full of public ceremonies, ribbon-cutting and the Queen's enthusiastic darts to art galleries and furniture dealers. At Windsor Ettie could expect visits from the extended royal family, from pillars of the Church, and commanding officers of crack regiments. Sandringham was most relaxed of all: small family parties with an admixture of sporting friends from the great families of England.

A busy Buckingham Palace Waiting was inaugurated on 1 March 1932 when Ettie succeeded Mabell Airlie in Waiting. On the first day, her cherished friend Philip Sassoon came to the palace for an audience with the King. Next day Ettie attended the Queen on a visit to the Royal Home for Officers' Widows and Daughters at Wimbledon, and another of her friends – Charley Londonderry – had an audience with the King. On 3 March the King, Queen and their courtiers were shown a film of the Mount Kemet expedition by the expedition leader; and Ettie attended a luncheon given for Sir John Anderson on his appointment as Governor of Bengal. She escorted Queen Mary on a Friday visit to the British Legion Poppy Factory at Richmond; and on 6 March the widowed Queen Augusta Victoria of Portugal came over from Twickenham for a Sunday luncheon at the palace. Afterwards Ettie accompanied the royal couple to an exhibition of antique walnut furniture held in aid of the Royal Northern Hospital by Philip Sassoon at his house at the Buckingham Palace end of Park Lane's expensive length.

The royal party were joined at Sassoon's by Marjorie Anglesey, whom Julian had courted twenty years earlier, together with her husband and the art connoisseur Lord Crawford.

We went all round the show, [Crawford reported] and as we came to a room the public were discreetly pushed to one side, and seemed to enjoy getting in advance of the Queen and being pushed on or off again. After a longish peregrination we retired to the dining room and sat down to a magnificent tea. I never remember such a tea. The King was offered an egg, a boiled egg, tactfully prepared in anticipation. He refused it and it disappeared. Then Marjorie Anglesey asked if she might have it – Sassoon called for its return – but it didn't arrive and Sassoon got more and more fussy – we all laughed. Marjorie then begged him not to bother about it, but the huge butler bestirred himself and after some minutes – presumably three – the egg or its substitute reappeared, and was put on her plate. We began to laugh again. Some wonderful grouse sandwiches arrived – the King refused them because he could not stop eating haddock sandwiches: more laughter, and then I suddenly realised I was in the noisiest party I could recall. The whole house might have shaken with the shindy which reached its height when the King denounced the new tariffs which cause him to pay an extra ten per cent on any foreign stamps he buys abroad. 'Who is responsible,' he cried out, 'the Treasury, or the B. of Trade or the three Tariff Commissioners?' He turned to me defiantly as if I was answerable, bawled his questions again right at me, and I said, 'The authority for this is in the statute Your Majesty signed a few days ago.' Whereupon the Queen said, 'You see, George, you should not sign papers without reading them', and the King ended the passage by a tremendous guffaw, and the remark, 'Oh, that silly thing.' Then we fell to again and a chocolate cake of unique and incomparable distinction was handed round in quarter pound slabs. I could not eat it having partaken so freely of the grouse: but Lady Desboro' was undaunted, and the conversation resumed its lurid tone. We must have sat at that table nearly an hour, and I confess I was immensely amused, though nothing witty was said from beginning to end. I am quite sure the King was thoroughly amused (with himself).

This period of Waiting continued on Monday, 7 March with Prince Chula Chakrabongs of Siam lunching at the palace: Ettie then attended the Queen on a visit to the Young Women's Christian Association club in Bloomsbury. On 10 March there was a huge afternoon palace party for parliamentarians, judges and other worthies with the string band of the Scots Guards playing a selection of music. On 11 March Ettie attended the Queen on a visit to the British Museum. Next day she was in attendance when the King and Queen visited India House, and on 14 March when the Queen had a private view of the Royal Amateur Art Exhibition at Chesterfield House.

Ettie wrote in 1929 of 'the strange pause & peace that prevails in Royal residences – "isled from the fretful hour" – (and from so much else!)'. She was then ensconced for a fortnight at Sandringham, which had been enlivened by a noisy Sunday visit from Winston Churchill and Lord Birkenhead. Both men had recently lost Cabinet office with the fall of the Baldwin government, and had seized the opportunity to embark on lucrative lecture tours in the USA. At Sandringham, Ettie described, 'they started on fairly even conversational terms, not having met since their separate journeys to America, & each professing a wish to hear the other's experiences. But in an incredibly short space Winston was fairly *yelling* F.E. down – shouting over his prostrate body just like the pictures in today's newspapers of the Prize Fight – F.E. lolling limply in an arm-chair, a large cigar hanging from his lips.'

Like his father, George V was prone to bronchial catarrh aggravated by his smoking. He nearly died in December 1928 of virulent septicaemia, and Sister Catherine Black was thereafter in permanent attendance on him. She became the loyal accomplice of Lord Dawson, the chief royal physician, in stratagems to trick the obstinate monarch back into health. In Dawson's opinion, boredom was as lethal as over-tiredness to the King, and he founded an Anti-Boredom League at the Court in which Ettie was one of the liveliest conscripts. Dawson instigated private cinema shows at the royal residences to keep the King amused in the evenings, and the King became a movie buff whose taste for lowbrow farces the Queen and her ladies had to feign to share.

In 1939 the Court commissioned a personal memoir of the late monarch: a book which showed him in his domestic surroundings rather than a political history. Its author John Gore – a cousin of Alice Salisbury and Mabell Airlie – had been introduced to Ettie at a shooting party of St John Midleton's at Peper Harow a few years earlier, but they barely knew one another. After his appointment to write the memoir, both King George VI and Queen Elizabeth insisted that he consult Lady Desborough at the outset, and he made an appointment to see her. 'She took me on trust almost at once,' he recorded years later. 'She was most insistent that no mention of her name must ever appear in the preface. She was a devoted and utterly loyal admirer of the late King and of Queen Mary and what she told me, point by point, at that single interview breathed life into the portrait of the man who ultimately emerged. She had the rare gift of word painting, seemed to know exactly where light was wanted, what strokes would tell and how to make them.'

Gore was the first royal biographer who truly attempted candour or achieved authenticity in his portrait. He tested the truth of various tales about the King; and despite Queen Mary and King George VI returning their copies of the proofs with comments clipped to many sections requesting reticence or revision, provided an intimate personal portrait and a study of kingship that were unrivalled for years. Gore's *George V* – published in 1941 – bears many signs of Ettie's perceptive intellect. Where other people saw the King as boorish, choleric and narrow, Ettie saw humility and a simple, all-governing dedication to his duty. And so Gore celebrated the King's 'straightness, his frankness, his simplicity, his deep loyalty to country and friends, his silent devotion to duty, his uncomplaining endurance of physical disability and pain, his constant under-emphasis of his difficulties and labours'. He pictured him as tense, touchy, a worrier; but not deep or subtle. 'He was not broadly a sentimentalist, but he was always emotional,' Gore explained. 'With none of his father's powers to divert his thoughts into easier channels, with only a little of his father's elasticity and *joie de vivre*, he found doubt and anxiety in half the decisions he was called on to make and he could not shake the anxiety off.'

King George was aware of having been astonishingly poorly educated, compared with almost all of the men with whom he had official dealings, and knew that he lacked the trained mind necessary to analyse data, assess situations and take decisions. The popular sense of the monarch as unbookish and even boorishly ill-informed is belied by Gore's evidence. He showed King George to have been a systematic, conscientious reader who, like a diligent pupil, kept careful lists of the books he had read: Gore prints extracts from the list which suggest that the King was far better read and informed than most of his subjects.

Like the overgrown schoolboy confined within bounds whom he resembled, the King enjoyed 'ragging' of an adolescent sort. 'His method of joking was that "downright to rudeness" method which tried friends appreciate,' Gore explained; the older the jokes, the better he liked them. Gore's efforts to give the rich savour of the King's repartee seem unpersuasive. 'Some of his remembered sayings possessed the point of wit, as when Mr Baldwin congratulated him on his looking fit again after his illness and he replied: "Yes, I'm pretty well again"; hastily adding, "but not well enough to walk with the Queen round the British Industries Fair." '

Gore presented the King as a demonstrative parent who ' "bathed" his babies in turn, weighed them, played with them, took them for walks, instructed them in country lore, treasured their sayings, delighted in all genuine praise of them, and felt constant pride in the success of their first flights with a gun, a rod or on horseback'. Historians have judged the King's parenting skills more harshly. In good moods he adopted a clumsy jocularity with his children that made them squirm; but the permanent effects of his riding accident in 1917 often made him irascible with his adolescent sons. 'He distrusted new or foreign fashions in music, dress and dancing,' as Gore explained. 'A cigarette lit before some ceremonial occasion, a young man coming out to ride in jodhpurs and a collared jumper, a girl riding astride, the latest methods of dancing imported from America, painted finger-nails – such innovations distressed, even shocked, him and constantly irritated him. And since he was impetuous by nature, he gave vent to his feelings instantly and without reserve. His trust in the discretion of all his Household, high and humble, moreover, was so complete that he did not stop to mince his words even in the presence of the servants, and his loud and trenchant chaff or criticism would ring out, not sparing the object of his wrath.'

Ettie thought Gore's memoir 'a very beautiful book, so vividly recalling that beloved figure & showing how he moved from strength to strength all his life, & the wonderful *goodness*', she told Queen Mary. She liked it most for emphasising King George's dedication to his royal vocation. 'I once asked The King if some (very dull) duty bored him. He said so simply, "I have never thought of it in that way." ' She felt she had learnt much from his royal exámple. There were no debauchees at Court: in 1917 Lord Winchester was required to resign as Lord-Lieutenant of Hampshire after deserting his wife for another woman, in 1920 Bendor Westminster was required to resign as Lord-Lieutenant of Cheshire after his divorce, and the King had qualms about Sunny Marlborough retaining the Oxfordshire lord-lieutenancy after he was divorced by Ettie's friend Consuelo. Lloyd George's nomination of Sir George Riddell for a peerage was at first rejected because the owner of the *News of the World* had been divorced for adultery – and it was a sign of receding standards when King George relented in 1920. 'His', declared the Master of the King's Household, 'was the straightest Court there ever was and the cleanest, and King George the straightest man I ever knew.'

The King's close friends were John Revelstoke above all men, and other magnificos whom Ettie knew well: Portland and a clutch of other dukes (Buccleuch, Devonshire and Roxburghe); some lavish-living earls – Bob Crewe (whom he made a marquess), Rosebery, Eddy Derby, Jack Durham, Osbert Sefton and that boisterous fantasist Hugh Lonsdale; and men with lesser fortunes, including Luke Annaly, Simon Lovat and Bertie Vane-Tempest (whose death in a railway accident obsessed the King for months). John Gore heard it said that the King might have 'gained much if he had possessed his father's penchant for constant conversation on every variety of topic with women of the world'; but, Gore added, thinking of Ettie, 'among the Queen's ladies were women of high ability and wide influence, who were always well informed in current thought.' George V drew them out, and sought from them what was quaintly termed 'the women's point of view'. Ettie was an antidote to a baneful feminine influence in the King's life: he spoke every day on the telephone to his spinster sister Princess Victoria, and trusted her judgement, which was inexperienced and narrow. She was an expert at insinuating criticism of Queen Mary, whose self-confidence was oddly vulnerable to her sister-in-law's pinpricks.

Ettie had many contacts with young members of the royal family. She stood in a distant familial relationship to them for the King's daughter Princess Mary married Willie's cousin Lord Lascelles in Westminster Abbey in 1922. During the 1920s Ettie felt attracted by the dashing young Prince of Wales, who attended a dance she gave in London during Mogs's first Season. Yet privately she also found him rather odd. On three occasions, separated by several years, he addressed her at dinner with the same opening remark, prepared beforehand, and intended to interest a hostess whom he knew to be a discriminating amateur of literature: 'Lady Desborough, I know you're a bookish sort of person: I'm reading *such* an interesting novel. I think it would appeal to you: it's called *Dracula*.' He did not seem to be teasing her; and it seemed a vacuous piece of prattle. Their other literary talk was equally bewildering. 'Look at this extraordinary little book which Lady Desborough says I ought to read,' the Prince of Wales once said to Alan Lascelles. 'Have you heard of it?' The extraordinary little book was *Jane Eyre*.

Ettie liked the diffident, stuttering second son, to whom she sent fulsome congratulations when he was created Duke of York in 1920. 'I do want to add my duty & most true gladness & congratulation to all the tributes that will be pouring in to you. I am so very, very glad about your honour, & that you will bear such a beautiful name – the best one of all.' She admired his bride, Lady Elizabeth Bowes-Lyon, especially after she sent a heartfelt letter about Ivo's death; and Ettie, who loved the company of little children, rejoiced when the two York girls were with their grandparents at Windsor or Sandringham.

Julian Salmond was born in the same year (1926) as Princess Eliza-beth, and Ettie adored their occasional contacts. At Windsor, in 1929, so Ettie reported, 'the tiny Princess Elizabeth' led Julian up to her grandfather the King, and 'putting her hand on his red curls said, "Isn't he nice?"' On another occasion, when Julian (aged three) was in the motor car which came over from Taplow to collect Ettie from Windsor, 'little Lillibet immediately took off her gloves "to feel his 'air" – such a good way to break the ice with a new young man.'

Before Christmas of 1931 Ettie organised a party for Monica's children and other toddlers. 'The only babies I would tentatively sug-gest,' she wrote from Pans, 'are the little Yorks (as they are so much the nicest babies in the world except ours) but perhaps you think that would turn it into rather a different kind of party, and I have *no* strong feeling on the subject *at all.*' This was not true: she held ardent views on the subject and was determined to gain her point. 'If you would like me to write to the Duchess, I joyfully will, or I expect you will write to her yourself (much better), saying that it is only a tiny homely little party of tea and games; as I know she does not much like Princess Elizabeth to go to too many "real" parties.' In the event, the Duchess of York accepted Ettie's invitation for Princess Elizabeth, but judged Princess Margaret too young.

Ettie involved her Gage grandchildren as well as the Salmonds with the royal family. 'Madam,' she wrote to Queen Mary from Taplow in 1932,

I do hope that Your Majesty, in your great kindness, will forgive me for troubling you, with my humble duty – but I promised Imogen & George Gage that I would ask Your Majesty something, very privately. They are so longing to ask His Majesty the King if he possibly could & would consent to have the little new baby as a Godson – but they are wondering if they *could* do so, without great presumption?, & I said that Your Majesty was always so kind, & that I thought I might perhaps ask your opinion in the matter? They would so absolutely understand if it were better not to trouble His Majesty with the request – but on the other hand, *if* Your Majesty thought that he would not mind, I cannot possibly say how grateful & happy they would be – if such an honour *could* be granted to their little first-born son. Queen Alexandra was so very kind in accepting Imogen as a God-daughter ('Alexandra Imogen Clair'), & it would indeed be a happiness & pride if so lovely an association might be carried on.

The Gage baby was duly baptised George John St Clere Gage, with the King as his sponsor, but was always known as Sammy.

ಜ್

The death of his favourite sister Princess Victoria on 3 December 1935 proved a fatal blow to the King's health. Her overlong funeral at Windsor was an ordeal for him; and he was short of breath and overtired when he reached Sandringham for Christmas. The icy weather kept him mainly indoors, where the household remained in mourning for Princess Victoria. A house party of old friends assembled for the shooting, but the King's heart was failing, and it was evident, when Ettie arrived at Sandringham from Panshanger on 16 January 1936, that the King had fired his last cartridge. She had enjoyed 'such a lovely happy Christmas' at Panshanger, followed by a sherry-and-sausage party for their Hertfordshire neighbours on 3 January, and a Shoot to which the Portlands came: she had been looking forward to her fortnight in Waiting at Sandringham: 'always a very nice peaceful time, nearly alone with them generally, & early hours'. Instead, she arrived to find an atmosphere of restrained but deadly apprehension. On her first evening she had to sit through the screening of a film which the King wished to see: it was a hectic farce, starring the ex-jockey-turned-comedian Tom Walls, called either *Pot Luck* or *Foreign Affaires*, and its vulgar, fast-paced nonsense chimed grotesquely with the mood of the audience.

Queen Mary realised the gravity of the King's condition, and felt *distraite*. The royal physician, Lord Dawson, and Lord Wigram, who had been the King's Private Secretary since Stamfordham's death, arrived at Sandringham to join a reduced party of the Duke of York, Ettie, Lady Elizabeth Motion, Lord Claud Hamilton, Sir Stanley Hewett (the Royal Apothecary) and two senior courtiers, Alec Hardinge and Tommy Lascelles. One of Ettie's friends dubbed the equerry Lord Claud Hamilton the 'arch-spoil-sport', whose perpetual look of cold boredom was comparable to a wet midsummer day; but for once his joylessness was justified. The King spent the next two days sitting in front of a crackling fire in his bedroom, which was furnished like the cabin of a yacht, gazing through the bay window across the leafless winter trees to the square tower of Sandringham church. The first medical bulletin was issued to the nation, the Prince of Wales arrived at Sandringham by air, and on Sunday, 19 January he and his brother the Duke of York motored to London to tell Baldwin, the Prime Minister, that their father was dying.

Queen Mary decided not to attend Sunday service at Sandringham church, for journalists and their photographers were waiting in heartless ambush. Silent crowds at Liverpool Street Station watched the arrival and departure of the trains for Sandringham – one carried the King's youngest son, the Duke of Kent, with Cosmo Lang, the Archbishop of Canterbury. On this sombre Sunday Ettie scribbled a note to the Queen reporting that Evie Devonshire, Mary Minto and Sibyl Cholmondeley had telephoned with sympathetic enquiries. She added a more personal paragraph: 'In the great desire not by one word or look to make preserving Your Majesty's miraculous fortitude even harder I think that one must appear callous & unmindful, but I know too well how one word may upset control – when all depends upon preserving calm & strength – only may I just lay my most reverent admiration & devotion at your feet, dearest dearest Madam. I would give anything in the world if there were one single thing I could do for Your Majesty. Ettie.'

On Monday morning, the Archbishop of Canterbury, Edward Marjoribanks's stepfather Lord Hailsham, Ramsay MacDonald as Lord President of the Council, Sir John Simon the Home Secretary, Lord Wigram, Sir Maurice Hankey as Clerk of the Council, and Bertrand Dawson filed past Charlotte, the King's parrot, into the King's bedroom. He was seated in a chair in a bright floral dressing gown. His right hand had become helpless, and for five minutes he struggled to sign the order-in-council establishing a Council of State to rule in his place. Finally he achieved a few indecipherable marks. He dismissed his councillors with a little nod of the head and a weak smile: when they left his room, most were in tears.

Queen Mary insisted that all the men lunched with her – Ettie in

'Panshanger last night was glorious,' Billy wrote, 'but it is peopled with ghosts.'

The Panshanger gallery. 'I'm so glad you've decided to sell the little Raphael,' Julian told Ettie.

Sir Philip Sassoon in whose pleasure-palaces Ettie loved to stay.

Ettie the country woman at a point-to-point in 1922.

Brocket Hall, where Ettie had lived as a child, just before its sale by her cousins in 1923.

(Opposite) Ivo in uniform in 1919 just before going to fight in the Baltic war.

Ettie and Balfour attend Lady Ursula Grosvenor's wedding in 1924. She described the bride: '6 ft high, lovely lithe figure & skin like apple-blossom. Very childish & simple & ... the most curious mixture of almost ultra Grosvenor refinement & then just a touch of Wild West. Beautiful hands & rather barmaid golden hair.'

Alice Salisbury was Ettie's dearest girl cousin and staunchest friend for eighty years.

Mary Wemyss snapped at Taplow with her *cavaliere servente* Arthur Balfour by Ottoline Morrell in 1925.

Winnie Portland, the most unaffectedly magnificent of duchesses, in 1925.

Edward Marjoribanks – whom Ettie could not save from suicide – on the Thames with Willie in 1926.

Stanley Baldwin with Willie at a university sports match in 1931.

The drawing-room at Panshanger in 1935.

Ettie's Norfolk refuge, Whiteslea, in September of Abdication year.

A family portrait after Camilla Gage's christening in 1937. Ettie and Willie are seated with Camilla and Nicky, whose brother Sammy is perched on the back of the bench. Julian, Jack and Monica Salmond are standing to the left; George Gage and Rosemary Salmond to the right.

London evacuees with their new-born babies at Panshanger in 1941.

attendance – and kept the conversation on neutral subjects. All of the Council of State save the Archbishop then left for London, and Dawson wrote on the back of a menu card the message for the nine o'clock BBC news bulletin which became so famous: 'The King's life is moving peacefully towards its close.' Dawson's warning, wrote John Gore, 'was heard at regular intervals during that dark and bitter night all over Britain and the Empire, solemn, inexorable, peaceful, as the tolling of a passing bell. In the King's room the Queen and his children kept vigil round his bed and, as he drew his last breaths, the Archbishop offered up the commendatory prayers.' At five minutes before midnight on Monday, 20 January 1936, George V died. His widow immediately took her eldest son's hand in her own and, stooping in obeisance, kissed it. The dead King was embalmed at dawn.

There had been other, more devastating death scenes for Ettie, but the King's passing was a profound, enduring memory. 'I can't tell you how sorrowful these days have been, but the end came very gently last night,' she wrote to Annie Chamberlain, wife of the Chancellor of the Exchequer. Next evening she followed the royal cortège to Sandringham church. 'We walked behind him,' Ettie reported to Bertrand Dawson, 'a tiny procession, to the Church – his grenadiers behind him, the pipers leading. It was pouring with rain, and very dark, a wild wind blowing.' Willie Desborough wrote an appreciation of the late King for the Primrose League incorporating Ettie's observations. It ended with her account of 'the pathetic procession from Sandringham to the Church, formed by his Family, retainers and friends, and his white pony with the empty saddle, which brought tears to many eyes, the last lament of his faithful piper, all a prelude to the wonderful manifestation of respect and affection which greeted his earthly remains when they arrived in London'.

Ettie accompanied the widowed Queen to London, was installed in Buckingham Palace and made herself indispensable. Sir Stanley Hewett, the Court Apothecary, said that he could not imagine what the Royal Household would have done without her. 'One hasn't had time to think of personal grief – yet – in absorption in the Queen's infinite desolation,' she told Mary Wemyss on 26 January. Her in Waiting fortnight expired, but the Queen asked her to remain at Buckingham Palace and she gladly assented. She replied on the Queen's behalf to the plethora of condolences sent by personal friends. 'The Queen is most deeply touched by your letter, & commands me to send you Her Majesty's true and heartfelt thanks,' she told Linky Cecil. 'She is *really* pleased.'

Behind a façade of self-control the Queen felt passionate grief and often broke down after reading letters that evoked old memories. One such – magnificent in its cadences – was from Winston Churchill: 'The nation has found the means of giving vent to its grief, and the tributes it has paid have moved the world. But for the one on whom the blow falls directly with all the human pain of any humble home, there can be no relief from the awful severance.' Ettie replied to Winston on 4 February. 'The Queen told me that she had received a most beautiful & touching letter from you . . . & commands me to send you her heartfelt gratitude. She said that it was a most lovely & perfect letter, & I know that what you have said has *really* given her consolation. You can guess what her fortitude & unselfishness have been – unconquerable in this infinite desolation.' She appended her own personal message to Churchill. 'Dearest, how I would love to see you both – I have been with her ever since the fatal illness began, on Jan 15th – it has been a momentous time, tragic & yet uplifting! I can never forget his face after death – young & calm & happy – "Now, when all safety's lost, safest of all".'

One incident during this week at the palace Ettie confided to Mary Wemyss, whose loving support meant so much to her. 'To you alone I must tell one other tiny thing: the only tangible way in which one could help the darling Queen was by answering *special* letters that she entrusted to one. There were very many, & one night my eyes went, & I thought all the old . . . trouble was beginning again. And I prayed hard, & the next morning they were all right, & stayed so.' She had no doubt of Divine support. 'This I could *only* tell to you, the children would be worried about my eyes, & others would think it just nonsense, & Groupy.' Here again is proof of the indispensable importance to her of daily prayer. Ettie's faith was intense; but she evidently found the ostentatious display of Frank Buchman's Oxford Group – a Christian revivalist movement which had ensnared Jim Salisbury and was more interested in 'moral rearmament' than divinity – distasteful. Her religion was much more attuned to Lord Salisbury's brother, Linky Cecil. 'Many people in England', Cecil chided, 'think of a Church as a kind of a spiritual chemist's shop to which one may send for a bottle of religious grace whenever one happens to want it; they have no sense of belonging to an unseen Kingdom with a loyalty to an unseen King.'

There was Court mourning (all-black) until 21 July, and half-mourning (in which black, white, grey and mauve were permitted) till 21 October, which Ettie found painfully prolonged. 'It has all been rather confused,' she explained to Annie Chamberlain in March, 'but the Queen asks me to say that Her Majesty feels that the wives of members of the Cabinet *should* wear Court mourning. This was always the Custom, I believe, at any rate before the War, & Her Majesty thinks it right and "seemly".' Before the period of half-mourning had expired, Queen Mary and her retinue left Buckingham Palace for nearby Marlborough House on 1 October. Queen Mary's household was henceforth known as the Old Court.

The first cloud puffs of surmise about Wallis Simpson had been espied by Ettie in 1935. At first her set regarded the American interloper as a rather shocking joke: her old friend Alice Keppel – an excellently behaved royal mistress – on a visit to Norah Lindsay at Sutton Courtenay, declared it was 'her want of class that mattered so much'. The situation became less amusing after the old King's death a month later, and by the summer of 1936 Ettie was worried about the appropriate response if she was asked to meet Mrs Simpson at Sibyl Colefax's salon. In May 1936 Ettie and the Churchills had been part of a Rothschild house party that went on an outing to Whipsnade Zoo – 'Winston has never been before, and behaved exactly like a child of seven'; and on 10 November she sent him rich praise of the new volume of his biography of his great ancestor the Duke of Marlborough: she was 'rolling every syllable' in her ears. This letter contains possibly the earliest mention in the vast Churchill archives of Wallis Simpson. 'Never could there be another hero like Marlborough,' Ettie added. 'Each actor in the drama is as present in one's eye as Mrs S!'

Edward VIII's abdication appalled Ettie, as it did all those attached to Queen Mary. She was shopping in Oxford Street on 10 December 1936 when news-vendors began displaying posters announcing the news. There was a rush to buy papers, and she managed to buy the last one on a vendor's stand: strangers came crowding round her to read the news. 'One mustn't write,' she wrote to Monica, ever discreet about the family she served, 'but I know how our thoughts have been together. London has been so sad & grave, rich & poor – *no* Schadenfreude.' Stanley Baldwin had been for years an established guest at Taplow, Panshanger and Whiteslea. On 4 July 1937, after his final retirement as Prime Minister, he came to Taplow, and gave Ettie a 'brilliant . . . hour by hour' account of the Abdication crisis. 'You know how good he can be when he lets go,' she told Churchill.

Revisiting Windsor Castle seven months into the reign of George VI, Ettie felt almost disorientated, so she told Linky Cecil. 'So strange being here under the new régime. They are all that is most charming, but of course memories come rushing back.'

CHAPTER 10

The Dowager

Ӄ

O N 17 FEBRUARY 1937 Ettie and Willie celebrated the fiftieth anniversary of their marriage. She was in Waiting at the time, and between attending Queen Mary on visits to the British Cotton Textile exhibition at White City and the British Industries Fair at Olympia, she attended a golden wedding party at 18 Carlton House Terrace. The Duke of Portland made an affectionate speech extolling the continuing 'vim' of the Desboroughs, and ended with a special tribute to Ettie: 'her charm is magnetic; her friendship is constant and true; her kindness is unfailing . . . no wonder that, men and women alike, all love and adore her.' She had opposed the plan of George Curzon and Adèle Essex to raise a subscription and hold a banquet to mark her silver wedding in 1912, because it seemed to snub their other friends with similar anniversaries at that time. But she welcomed the suggestion of her fellow Lady of the Bedchamber, Mary Minto, of an afternoon party to mark the golden weddings of the Desboroughs, Kenmares and Salisburys. This was held on 1 June at Winnie Portland's house in Hill Street, Mayfair. Queen Mary attended; and all three couples were presented with gold gifts subscribed by their friends.

Ettie at seventy retained her keen intelligence but had a less dominating will: barring her recurrent eye infections, she was still hardy and hale. Conrad Russell, the Somerset landowner with an aptitude for friendship, described a country ramble with her at this time: 'across hill, dale, briar, barbed wire, ankle-deep cow dung, savage bull in field, gates to climb. It was immense fun, talk and jaw.' She had also adapted herself to change. When she sent the Dowager Lady Lansdowne an invitation to a 'Sherry and sausage party – 6–8', the old lady rang for her butler, and asked him to read it, which he did several times before explaining what it meant. 'What a nice party,' she said eventually, 'I should like to go.'

There was a renewal in the 1930s of Ettie's contacts with the Chamberlain family. In July 1936, always keen to catch a rising star, she invited Neville Chamberlain, the Prime Minister-in-waiting, to a Taplow party. He was not too bruised by a dispute there with his fellow guest Churchill about the government's policy towards the European dictators. 'At least Winston showed sport,' H.A.L. Fisher commented. 'How hugely he enjoys his role of Cassandra! I wonder if the sky is nearly so black?' Long before, during the tariff reform crisis of 1903, she had acted as a confidential messenger between Balfour and Austen Chamberlain, and she always retained an affectionate respect for that most diligent, dutiful and upright of men. He was numbered among the select who received a copy of *Pages from a Family Journal* in 1916. 'We are linked by the memories of so many happy days, and you know the great love and admiration we had for your Father,' she wrote to him at that time. She grieved when he dropped dead in March 1937, and wrote a short tribute that was published in *The Times*. 'How much of one's youth goes too with the people one knew in those happy far-off days,' she told his half-brother Neville.

A month later Ettie lost one of her most cherished friends when Mary Wemyss died after a day's illness on 29 April. 'You really do *not* know what you represent in the world – the light & life,' Ettie had assured her a few years earlier. 'You are the essential help & joy of all our lives.' Although Mary Wemyss exuded calm and harmony, and had made Stanway into an oasis of peace, there had been tempestuous phases in her life. She could be fey and was intensely self-critical. 'In a sort of queer selfish way,' Ettie had told her in 1921, 'it comforts me that *you too* should have self-downs, & that *awful* sense of *fraud* – oh, how I know it – the most insidious temptation to despair that old morbid Satan has to offer. I have such *appalling* bouts of it, such attacks of nausea about myself, but I believe one must treat & ignore them just like bouts of physical sickness. Even though of course they contain *sub-strata* of truth. But they would paralyse not only effort but Faith if we let them prevail.'

Ettie was pledged to the cause of peace, and devoutly committed to

Neville Chamberlain who, after succeeding Baldwin as Prime Minister in May 1937, saw his vocation as a peacemaker. She invited him to Panshanger and Whiteslea as well as Taplow: he liked to discuss books with her, and bird-watching and sports with Willie. She was 'filled with the utmost admiration', she told him after his two days at Panshanger in January 1938, 'because I am certain that you were besieged by endless worries, and you never gave a damn. "Central peace subsisting at the heart of endless agitation", or someone's good prescription for living – "You must never be tired, & never in a hurry".' Ettie loved to marvel at her guests – she never stopped needing heroes to idolise – and ladled out her compliments to Chamberlain. 'You must possess a very strong & serene philosophy – or faith,' she told him. They had missed their usual conversation about Shakespeare, but had examined the European outlook: Mussolini was directing a drum fire of invective against Chamberlain's government; Hitler was making aggressive moves, which soon culminated in the Nazi annexation of Austria; and civil war raged in Spain. 'I like what you say about crises cancelling out,' she told Chamberlain. '*That's* the way to fight them.'

On 30 June 1937 the Desboroughs were invited to the third of Annie Chamberlain's receptions at 10 Downing Street, and on 19 July they attended a luncheon given by the Chamberlains there: the Argentine Ambassador, the Dowager Duchess of Grafton, and the newly ennobled owner of the *Sunday Times*, Lord Kemsley, were among the other guests. 'It was an immense pleasure to me to see that well-known house looking so rejuvenated and delightful under its present occupancy,' Ettie wrote. She tried to tempt the Chamberlains to Taplow during the summer, and when that proved impossible hoped for 'better luck at Panshanger in the autumn'. But by then the Prime Minister was duelling with Hitler over the fate of central Europe.

All emotion is fatal now, Julian had told Ettie after the 1914 war broke out; but she could not restrain her misery at the looming horror of a Continental war fought over the Sudeten districts on the German–Czech frontier. On 15 September Chamberlain flew to Berchtesgaden, and there began the process of capitulation to Hitler's demands for the territorial dismemberment of Czechoslovakia. Ettie was full of admiration. 'What a magnificent enterprise,' she wrote from Whiteslea to Annie Chamberlain. 'The very idea must have lifted up the hearts of all

Europe – you must feel proud.' During the next fortnight, under the hovering dread of war, she prayed daily for Chamberlain's mission, which was seldom out of her mind. He returned to Germany for further negotiations and, after their collapse, prepared a statement to give to the House of Commons on 28 September. A German invasion of Czechoslovakia, and an Anglo-French mobilisation against the Nazis, seemed certain.

In order to hear Chamberlain's statement first-hand, the Desboroughs travelled up from Panshanger. Getting off their train at Liverpool Street Station, they were told that most of the London taxis had been commandeered, and Ettie's 'heart dropped like a stone'. For a moment she feared the fighting had already begun. Listening from the peers' gallery in the Commons, the Desboroughs heard Chamberlain give a sombre recapitulation of recent negotiations: the logic of all his words meant that there was no honourable alternative but for Britain to support France in resisting a German invasion of Czechoslovakia just as they had resisted a German invasion of Belgium in 1914. As he neared the end of his speech, he was handed a typed sheet and, after reading it, announced that he and Mussolini, with the French Prime Minister, Edouard Daladier, had been invited by Hitler to a conference at Munich on the following day. 'I need not say what my answer will be,' he told the House. It was 'a breathless moment', said Ettie. 'It was curious to see all the most hardened old salts crying. One of the Labour whips said, "This means an election, & it means the end of the Labour party, but it is the greatest occasion of my life." '

Chamberlain for a third time flew to Germany – 'if at first you can't appease, fly, fly, fly again,' quipped Ettie's young friend Bob Boothby – and on 30 September an agreement was signed, which sacrificed Czechoslovakian integrity but seemed to make a future war with Germany unnecessary. Ettie was at Whiteslea when Chamberlain returned this final time from Munich with his promise of 'Peace in our Time'. From there she wrote to him 'to say how deeply & affectionately the gratitude of the whole world is echoed in our hearts – one can only gradually believe in the reprieve'. She was pleased to think what his late father 'must feel', and told how she had been in the Commons gallery when he made his historic declaration and repeated the Labour whip's remark that it was the greatest occasion of his life. 'I don't think', she continued to Chamberlain, 'there ever can have been such a universal emotion against war, throughout the whole world, every best & every worst human quality enlisted against it – but I don't believe that anyone but you could have saved Peace with Honour.' Another grateful message went to Annie Chamberlain. 'I simply cannot help telling you', Ettie wrote, 'how you have both been in our thoughts & hearts all these interminable weeks – or the true & enthusiastic admiration that we feel. I woke up feeling so happy this morning – couldn't think why – & then knew that it was because you were both safe in Scotland!'

Ettie exhaled her relief to other friends. 'How deeply I have thought of you all these days of terror,' she wrote to H.A.L. Fisher from Whiteslea on 30 September. She had a single doubt: 'will all the Winston & Co begin snarling now? Surely not . . . As Imogen said, [war] would be the absolute negation of all her generation had been taught to believe – besides their early memories.' Ettie thought the national mood was very different from last time. 'All that held us up in 1914 utterly & totally absent'; and the London parks and squares battened down in anticipation of heavy air raids. The reality of the danger hit her when she called on Alice Salisbury, whose small Arlington Street garden had been converted into a bomb-proof shelter. 'Neville had the courage & the imagination to do the simple & most direct thing,' she told Fisher. 'Willie has been so steady & calm all through: I said to him, after the gleam of hope on Wednesday, "What shall we do if it breaks down again *now*?" He said, "Go through the war as well we can." '

The leading denunciator of capitulation to the Nazis was Churchill, but Ettie always thought it absurd for political differences to jeopardise friendships. She had 'a lovely time' with Clemmie in late November, and sent a message to Winston after he had indicted the Chamberlain government as 'kindly, humane, well-meaning men' with 'the fault, very grievous in persons of high station – it is a fault which amounts to a crime – of not being able to make up their minds'. 'We think differently about things just now,' Ettie told Winston, 'but that could never make any alteration – you know how fondly I shall always regard you, bound up as you are with a world of happy days.' She vowed her 'unchanging love'. In March 1939 the German conquest of

Czechoslovakia – despite all the vainglorious guarantees of September – shattered the policy of appeasement. Next, Hitler seized territory from Lithuania, and in April Mussolini's troops invaded Albania.

In August the Desboroughs tempted fate by inviting the Prime Minister and their Norfolk neighbour Sir Samuel Hoare (formerly Foreign Secretary) for a day at Whiteslea. 'I am delighted', Willie wrote to Hoare, 'that, under Hitler, there is every chance of the P.M. (and, of course, yourself) being able to come to Whiteslea on September 22 . . . come as early as you can in the afternoon so as to have a look at the Marshes & Broads – I have a launch that can take us round. I pray that nothing may happen to prevent this visit. The P.M. is a marvel!' The last ever entries in the Taplow visitors' book, for August 1939, include the signatures of the Portlands, Charley Londonderry, Baldwin and Churchill. Ettie hurtled about on visits: she had a Sunday in Esher at the D'Abernons' with Winston and Clemmie, Herbert Fisher, Jack Stanmore, and Edgar D'Abernon's successor as British Ambassador in Berlin, Horace Rumbold; then to Arundel Castle for the wedding of the Duke of Norfolk's sister; and finally to Christabel Aberconway's place at Bodnant in Wales. 'A *heavenly* visit,' she told Monica: all the Aberconway family plus Norah Lindsay, Rex Whistler, and three artistic noblemen, Evan Tredegar (whom she thought '*quite* mad'), Lord Berners and Gerry Wellesley (the future Duke of Wellington). 'We never went indoors for *any* meal, & lived in the mountains, which were like a drop-scene to that inspired garden. Rex even more heavenly than he's ever been.'

On the day (21 August 1939) that Ettie wrote her happy description of the Bodnant party, Nazi Germany signed its non-aggression pact with Soviet Russia. War became inevitable – 'I never thought it would come, did you, two Armageddons in one generation,' she asked Pamela Lytton – and the Desboroughs fell in with prearranged war plans. They evacuated Taplow – packing up fifty-two years of life in four days. On 1 September 190 newborn London babies began arriving at the house, refugees from the anticipated saturation bombing, and the weary Desboroughs left on a sad, slow journey to Whiteslea. At Newmarket, en route, they heard that Warsaw and Cracow had been bombed by German airmen, and that Polish soldiers were fighting German invaders on the ground. There was no chance now that, 'under Hitler', the PM would be joining them on the Broads, for on Sunday, 3 September war was declared. The Desboroughs' three Gage grandchildren were already at Whiteslea. 'The babies here, so happy & unconscious, are an enormous comfort, & there is heaps to be done, the villages all swarming with evacuees,' Ettie told Monica, who had taken in eight evacuated children at her Sussex home. 'Dad is marvellous, but his face was sad as he watched his Taplow turning into workhouse wards,' she added. The calm courage of the Norfolk villagers as their young men left to join the forces impressed Ettie. Everyone's lives were being requisitioned for the war and fitted into a national destiny.

*

George Gage was called up into the Coldstream Guards, Jack Salmond returned to the Air Ministry, and the War Office indicated that it wished to take over Panshanger. 'Dad & I do so greatly hope to do *some* War work, decrepit as we are!' Ettie told Monica. 'No one could have minded seeing their homes evacuated more than Dad & George, or behaved more beautifully. I cannot tell you what the work was, or *how* marvellously all played up. All the young gardeners – of fighting age – carrying carpets & bits of china with equal care, & whistling away so cheerfully – one wondered so if one would ever see it restored again, & thought of all the happy years & all the sorrow.'

At Whiteslea, in the shimmering heat, there were three air-raid warnings, of which no one took much notice. The Desboroughs 'skewered up' their Rolls-Royce for the duration, and were using a tiny car belonging to their keeper Jim Vincent, consuming forty miles to the gallon instead of ten, 'for essential purposes, but of course as little as possible'. Time, Ettie wrote, was 'passing in a strange sort of mist, in the extraordinary beauty & peace of these surroundings in the halcyon weather & heat, & then all that underlies, the anguish in store for *all* one loves best, & for all the world. I don't think it could be borne but for the inspiration of faith & courage that is all around & they call this an irreligious age!' From Whiteslea, at the end of September, Ettie reported again to Monica: 'all the people here very steady & calm & good. We hang on the wireless like all Europe.' There were swirls of rumours, all swiftly contradicted, and the temporising disarray of the war effort exasperated her: 'How utterly bewildering & incomprehensible all the War news is, why are we doing *nothing*???'

What were the British fighting for? The Cambridge historian G.M. Trevelyan predicted to Ettie in September that this new war certainly meant 'the end of the England we have known – will Taplow and Panshanger ever be reopened? The only reason one can bear it is that, tho' old England may be ending, there must be hope of some new England that will arise in its place; the new England will not be yours or mine.'

On 1 October Churchill (by now First Lord of the Admiralty) made his first wartime radio broadcast. This was the oration in which he spoke of the Russian strategy as inscrutable – 'a riddle wrapped in a mystery inside an enigma' – and of the imponderable duration of the war, which depended upon how long Hitler 'and his group of wicked men, whose hands are stained with blood and soiled with corruption, can keep their grip upon the docile, unhappy German people'. Ettie thought his words superbly united the nation. 'Your broadcast last night was a touchstone lifting up our hearts,' she wrote from Whiteslea. 'You made me feel that all that matters most is unconquerable, serenely sheltered somewhere – to hold us all together.' It would all be unbearable 'but for the spirit everywhere, the selfless service & sacrifice – "the spirit alone availeth".' She had been rereading the Book of Isaiah: 'it might have been written for the Poles & that epic of heroism,' she told Churchill.

Ettie was still energetic, resourceful and valiant: fitted to dominate any scene or situation; and resolved never to be tired, disheartened or disgusted by remembrance, but always grateful. Nor could war abate her relentless lion hunting. In November Churchill appointed Lindemann as his personal assistant at the Admiralty. 'I have just read – delightfully – about you in the *Evening Standard*, & the memory of many happy days comes back,' she wrote instantly to the Prof. 'I know how intensely busy you are, but if you *ever* had a free day or night to run down here, what a pleasure it would be to us both. We are packed away in the West-wing, but have a nice spare room-cum-bath.'

It delighted Ettie to return to her Hertfordshire woods in October 1939. 'This country is looking so lovely in the October sunshine,' she reported. 'The west-wing here makes such a compact charming small house, using the back-door, & cutting off *everything* east of Dad's sitting room.' Although the London evacuees had been well looked-after, '*all* the mothers rushed back at once, horror-struck by the dullness of the country! It is comforting to know how in love they are with the slums, about which we pitied them so much.' The War Office decided at Christmas that the house was unsuitable for either an officers' convalescent home or the billeting of troops. For weeks of January and February 1940 the Desboroughs were snowbound at Panshanger, almost without coal or coke, and later surrounded by floods. The Gages' 'heavenly little children are our fellow-captives here', she told Charley Londonderry. 'One can only go slogging on. I have at last realized that I can't think to any purpose about this war. Life as we used to know it seems a strange battered abstraction, can it ever bloom again?'

Most of the other great houses that Ettie knew were being battened down, commandeered and damaged. Alice and Jim Salisbury were confined to a few rooms at Hatfield, which had been converted into a military hospital. 'Gosford', Evan Charteris reported in November of the Wemyss house near Edinburgh, 'is an incredible desolation – a devastated area – had the Prussians been in occupation it could not look more dismayed & broken – the basement rings with the voices of sergeants & sergeant majors – nailed boots (army pattern) plough up the floors – dart targets have taken the place of Madonnas on the walls – sofas & armchairs have all been removed – trestle beds, trestle tables, kitchen chairs have taken their place . . . I cannot think it will ever be inhabited again.' At Welbeck, Winnie Portland was 'very cosy & happy' under wartime conditions. 'We have shut up all the 5 Drawing rooms & have furnished the Smoking Room as a Drawing room, & the nice big Billiard Room next door as a Dining Room . . . George & Barbara Mercer Nairne we have "billeted" here with us, & they are so charming & gay! & all their Scottish Horse officers (here) love her!' The old duke was cheerfully taking them on shoots, 'but oh! the cold is fearful out! We have a charming Brigadier J. Scott Cockburn MC, was in 4th Hussars & the best pig sticker in India.'

The Duchess's high-handed elation was exceptional: most proprietors looked askance at the officers billeted on them. Gladys Ripon's grandson 'Mikie' Duff – known at this time as Flying Officer

Assheton-Smith — was one of the most vivid, amusing and stylish of Ettie's younger friends: on the basis of their common, but remote, de Grey ancestry, his sparkling letters were always addressed to Darling Cousin Ettie. 'Vaynol is a Military Hospital, filled with our men from Dunkirk, none of them badly wounded, thank God,' he reported to her in 1940 of the great house that ballasted his baronetcy. 'The Colonel in charge of the hospital here is *such* a bore, & no matter how I try, he always talks about bears! I have tried everything — talking of trivial things like match-sticks, heather, Scotland, the Dardanelles, Turkey, white wine, the Dorchester Hotel — but he brings it round to bears — great black, white, & Polar bears!'

Although an absentee Lady of the Bedchamber, Ettie maintained contact with the Old Court. In September 1939 a convoy of cars had carried Queen Mary, together with multitudinous servants and heaped luggage, to Badminton, the ducal palace where Monica had been staying when the 1914 war erupted. Queen Mary was a metropolitan creature, with little previous interest in country matters: on being shown a hayfield, shortly after arriving at Badminton, she scrutinised it keenly and said, 'so *that's* what hay looks like.' She was bored at first, but recovered her spirits by organising work parties to tear down the ivy enveloping trees and outhouses on the Badminton estate.

Queen Mary is most flourishing [her lady-in-waiting Lady Cynthia Colville wrote from Badminton to Ettie in 1940] and I think the amount of fresh air and exercise she takes nowadays really makes her very fit indeed. It is curious, in a way, what a kind of hold country life has taken on her so late in life, and we go out most afternoons, say from 2 p.m. till 4.30, and work in shrubberies or coverts, chopping, burning, cleaning up generally. Of course H.M. does not do hard physical work herself, but she is standing the whole time, constantly snipping ivy, dragging branches to the bonfire, etc. Many days when I feel that the weather would entitle me to take a day off, stay indoors, read a book, write letters etc., the Queen will say: 'Oh! I don't think this rain will be much, I expect we shall be able to go out. It *is* a very cold wind, but . . . we shall be fairly sheltered!' Really rather wonderful, when you think how static and indoor the Queen's London life used to be! Of course, she *does* miss

Marlborough House and all her own things round her, also here she feels terribly out of things, hears nothing, & is altogether lonely & cut off. An occasional *cri de coeur* escapes her, but for the most part she is wonderfully cheerful, plucky and serene.

The failure of the British expedition to Norway, and Hitler's armoured invasion of the Netherlands precipitated Chamberlain's resignation as Prime Minister on 10 May 1940. Churchill, walking with destiny as he said, replaced him. At the moment of this upheaval the Desboroughs were travelling for a ten-day visit to Whiteslea: it proved to be their last. 'Dearest Winston,' Ettie wrote after their arrival, 'your old, old friends must be among the very first to rejoice with you, & how truly we do – what a pinnacle it is, the summit of so many dreams, attained by how few. My whole heart goes out to wish you well in the tremendous undertaking. God bless you & darling Clemmie.'

Few of Ettie's set doubted Churchill's aptitude for such a crisis, though some of them might have baulked at him in milder times. 'His star suffers frequent and semi-total eclipse,' Helen D'Abernon had written in 1921, 'but I still think it will rise at length supreme. He is one of those rare people who seem to gather fresh strength from every reverse . . . He has amazing talent, spirit and vitality, is full of expedients for every situation, and although he has sometimes shown a lack of judgement he is endowed with rare gifts of imagination and vision. On the human side he is kindly and good-natured, so long as people do not stand directly in his path.' His sensitivity with women, she added, was 'coupled with a sense of humour that is witty and mischievous but never malignant or mean'. With all this Ettie agreed.

Neville Chamberlain was stricken with galloping cancer after leaving Downing Street, although in July he apparently motored to Panshanger for tea with the Desboroughs. Ettie sent him a last message near the end. She was 'truly grieved to hear that you may have to rest for a bit longer, how sad Winston will be, we were at Chequers last month & he spoke with such deep appreciation of all your help to him personally as well as to the country', she wrote. 'What an *incalculable debt* we all owe you for the years as Prime Minister, & all that you saved us from – but the strain must have been overwhelming, & alas those tests take their physical toll.'

During that flawless summer of 1940, when Ettie never went indoors except to sleep, the Battle of Britain raged in the skies. Ettie was delighted when Evan Charteris told her of waiting in a dark air-raid shelter when an Air Raid Precautions warden looked in. 'Are there any expectant mothers here?' the ARP man asked; and having no answer, repeated his question, at which a young cockney shouted back, 'Give us time, guv, we've only been here ten minutes.' This story Ettie gleefully repeated to Eddie Marsh, Charley Londonderry and her other burgeoning wartime correspondents.

Summer sunshine had always seemed to crown Ettie's days with meaning, and for the citizenry on the ground during an aerial war, summer and daylight were welcome friends. As Ettie and Monica had realised in 1917, it was autumn, night-time and especially moonlight that were the enemies. On Saturday afternoon and evening of 7 September, over 200 German bombers struck at London: the Blitz had begun. The Desboroughs were with the Churchills at Chequers either that weekend or the next, and found the Prime Minister absorbed by discussions about aerial defence and the practicality of evacuating essential government offices to a subterranean warren at Dollis Hill.

'Oh dear I feel so *cross* – an unfitting mood for the War, but they do pester us so all round with bombs (12 on one side of us last night & 2 the other) – all falling harmlessly, but all within 3 miles, & I do feel a little nervous about keeping the babies here,' Ettie complained on 23 September after returning to Pans. That very evening a German parachute mine was dropped on Hertford killing three people, demolishing a row of cottages and wrecking another eighty houses. Two days later the Desboroughs went into the market town. 'The heroism and cheerfulness and extraordinary good humour were beyond belief, but this is of course universal throughout England,' she wrote in a patriotic impulse to *The Times*. (Overall 30,500 incendiary bombs, 4,421 high-explosive bombs and eighty-five parachute mines fell on Hertfordshire in 1939–45; 256 people were killed.)

The telephone line to Panshanger was bombed out twice in October. In three weeks there were forty-nine bombs, plus a landmine, within half a mile of the house; windows were broken and ceilings collapsed. This aerial bombardment was especially upsetting because that winter seventy evacuee women with newborn babies were moved into the east wing. The bombers seldom targeted the mainline railway, but inundated the little branch line from Hertford to Hatfield: the station names were all erased from the platform signboards to prevent enemy parachutists from discovering where they had landed. The Salisburys, at Hatfield, were in an unenviable location near the de Havilland aircraft factory, and felt at night as if they were sleeping in the front lines. Jack Stanmore's cherished manor house, Goldings, a few miles from the Enfield munitions works, was destroyed by a landmine one night in mid-November and he was hospitalised by his injuries for weeks. Mabell Airlie was bombed out of her flat in Cumberland Mansions and once, when the air-raid sirens sounded unexpectedly, spent the night underground on a tube station platform. Sleep was impossible, so she chatted to a man who kept a stall in Berwick Street market and could explain to her why her asparagus had never been successful.

Hearing that the Desboroughs retreated with their mattresses to their cellars on bad nights, the old Dowager Duchess of Devonshire wrote to congratulate Ettie on the 'wonderful sleeping arrangements' at Pans, and report on her visit to Welbeck. 'It *was* partly shut up – for ever Portland said – but Winnie has evidently been unable to resist the craving for more entertaining, as the whole house is now open, except the drawing room and library, & she has large parties all the time. Very pleasant for all of us, but not good for the family finances.' Winnie Portland, however, bemoaned to Lord Cherwell, as Professor Lindemann now became, that the war seemed unending. 'I never see my old friends alas! Salisburys, Mabell Airlie, Desboroughs – I hear they sleep (the latter) in cellars every night!!'

Eric Dudley, the Regional Commissioner for the Midlands, whose mother had been one of Ettie's closest girlhood friends, gave a BBC broadcast about the Civil Defence organisation during the bombing raids. His talk fired Ettie's enthusiasm: she congratulated him profusely and sent copies of the text to her friends. Dudley described every phase of a raid. 'Early in the evening comes the mournful wail of the sirens, the distant drone of planes, and a few seconds later the shattering crack of the guns.' He described the falling bombs, collapsing buildings, the fires, the trapped people and the rally to their aid. 'With the rescue and first-aid parties', Dudley said, 'toil their fellow-citizens, the passers-by, the housewives, their own relatives and neighbours, and fellow-workers who are off shift. You need highly organised teamwork when the streets are cumbered with debris, blocked with bomb craters, the muck and the smoke and the smell of escaping gas, smouldering fires and shattered buildings – the only light a cold unreal beam of the moon, and the vivid glare of the fires, leaving tricky patches of darkness where you most need to see.'

Ettie was charmed by her local bomb squad, especially when they let her and Willie detonate an unexploded 500-kilo bomb that had fallen behind their red-bricked stables. 'The time-bomb behind the stables was grand, *we* exploded it by electric wire – all wrapped up in tin helmets & cotton wool, you'd have laughed,' she boasted to Evan Charteris. 'A Liverpool boy, not yet 21, is in charge of the 90 men, all about the same age . . . He came one morning – beaming – and staggering under an enormous piece of jagged iron, saying, "I got this tail for you." The sergeant told me afterwards that it was at grave personal risk, & you never saw a more detestable lurid possession . . . We have now got a land-mine in the carriage-drive, & another unexploded bomb in front of the house by the river, but have been very much quieter the last 2 or 3 nights.'

This was her last letter to Evan – it was returned after his death, on 16 November 1940, of kidney failure. 'I knew him first when he was 17, & since 1892 he has been a most precious part of my life,' she wrote to Charley Londonderry – now more than ever her standby in times of grief. 'He never lost youth, or the rebellion of youth – never grew resigned, or dimmed the edge of his eagerness.' Evan had been vain, irritable and selfish; but also compassionate, and *so* funny. She was full of grateful sad memories, and other members of her family recalled the couple's revels together: Evan's hairpiece slipping off while he was swimming in the pool at the Bath Club and Ettie calling out in her piercing Holland House accent, *Evan, your hair has come orff and is swimming behind you like a little daug.*

Ettie's grieving letter to Mount Stewart began a candid exchange with Lord Londonderry. He was bitter at his exclusion from political power (he was generally thought to have coquetted with the Nazis), and depressed at his enforced idleness. '*I* always want you to have the universe for your toyshop & the stars for your rattle – but Life, grim terrible Life, does not work in that way, & all we can strive after is to suffer nobly,' she wrote in one letter. And then, on a slow train journey to visit her Gage grandchildren in Wales, she shared her own poor guesses at the philosophy of life' with him:

To me it seems that almost everyone's life is sooner or later an unhappy thing. Even those most envied have probably had their own anguish to endure, & perhaps it could hardly be borne but for the faith that there is no enduring city, that all the suffering here is the fiery trial for some future beyond our imagination or conception – that there is a power controlling all, & that only in His will is there peace. Submission is not enough; it is enforced & does not count. It must be surrender. 'Though He slay me, yet I will trust in Him', & how beautiful the Prayer-book words are, 'we offer & present unto Thee ourselves, our souls & bodies, to be a reasonable holy & lively sacrifice.' Once the sacrifice is complete, I think that peace does dawn, & even joy, because every fragment of happiness that is granted becomes a bonus to be eagerly thankfully grasped . . . even in the darkest hours consolation comes. As I watched Julian and Ivo die – each time it was thirteen days – I used to pray to be able to hold out to the end for them. And strength & help came flooding – pouring – like a miracle – & a sense of utterly incredible tranquillity. I always believed, but then I *knew*. And that if it is just our share of the Sacrifice, it does not matter if our hearts are broken to pieces here.

On 5 February 1941 the Desboroughs went for luncheon with Winston in an underground room at Downing Street, and found him 'immensely cheered' after conferring with President Roosevelt's adviser Harry Hopkins. Around this time David Balniel, who had been recruited as a Taplow regular after his marriage to Ettie's young friend Mary Cavendish and had recently come into his inheritance as Earl of Crawford, wrote to Ettie from his house at Haigh. He asked if Winston saw much of her. 'I hope so, as I fear the flattering Ditchley set cannot be particularly good for him, & you could help him so much & he is so devoted to you. At the last Taplow weekend, he settled down with Mary to Chinese Chequers immediately after Saturday tea: again after Saturday dinner: again Sunday morning & Sunday afternoon – do you remember? Mary won every game & Winston said he would go on until he won one. I said to Mary in one of the intervals "Why don't you let him win?" "I would," she said, "if he didn't cheat, & will do so the moment he stops cheating." How like Winston – & how like Mary. Now Winston is going on till he wins every game – and if he cheats, God bless his cheating!'

The publication in March 1941 of John Gore's authorised memoir of King George V, for which Ettie had given such a crucial preliminary interview, was a great excitement for her. 'I cannot tell Your Majesty what the enjoyment has been, or how one's admiration for His Majesty grows with every word,' she told Queen Mary. 'I don't think anyone could read it without being touched to new endeavour. Your Majesty will guess how happy recollections rushed back at many points, & deep & truest gratitude for the great, great privilege of being sometimes near to Your Majesties. Every moment of those last days at Sandringham is graven on one's memory.'

Ettie also sent a laudatory letter to Gore. 'I read it very slowly and carefully – but with such intense, almost indescribable interest and enjoyment . . . you have done it quite perfectly – and with such very great courage.' She thought Gore's royal portrait was 'marvellously built up, the gradual emergence of that beautiful character traced line by line. I did not feel beforehand that my admiration of the man *could* be increased, but your book has heightened it.' It was the 'exquisite candour *and* reticence' of Gore's depiction of the philistine, anxious, duty-bound King that Ettie admired – all handled, she thought, with 'austere restraint'. Gore had received 'generous letters from strangers & friends, Statesmen, Churchmen & literary men', he replied, 'but none which gave me more pleasure & pride than yours, for none was more understanding. After all, you supplied in almost every chapter some vital aids to life & light & truth, & did more than any other to give the memoir such of those necessities as it has.'

An epistolary friendship between Gore and Ettie ripened during the war years. He wrote to her of his training of the Home Guard in Hampshire, the cases that came before him as a magistrate, his toil as a journalist, wartime privations, his despair for the future, his pride in his children and struggles to pay their school fees. She replied to him with social and Court news, anecdotes of Churchill, Rosamond Lehmann and mutual friends, book talk and doting tales of the latest witticisms and antics of her Gage grandchildren. They addressed one another as Dear Cousin Ettie and Dear Cousin John, but seldom met: he paid his first and only visit to Panshanger in July 1945. Nevertheless, the letters that came winging to him were a precious gift. 'I look back with thankfulness over seven years when I have gained from you a liberal education in the things that matter – a correspondence course beyond price,' he told her in 1947. 'How I wish this education could have started earlier; I think it might have made me better able to face the years when middle age turns to old age, & change & decay & goodbyes mark the stages of our road. To me, as to so many, you have been a light to my eyes & a lantern to my feet & yours is an undying fire.'

Ettie was a heartening wartime companion and made Pans as welcome an oasis as Taplow had been a revel. In June 1941, for example, Stanley Baldwin motored over from Hatfield. 'Your part breathed peace and the house looked just as I remembered it,' he wrote afterwards to Ettie, 'but as I drew up at the front door there was something that seemed unfamiliar and a large placard hit me in the eye bearing the legend "POST NATAL CLINIC".' (The east wing of Pans had been opened in January 1941 as a home for seventy mothers and newborn babies; many of the women were unmarried. Ettie often helped them to find work and secure their futures.) Baldwin wandered into the house 'to find His Lordship reading a book, smoking a pipe and looking aside at moments with affectionate pride on his cups and medals and other trophies of his amazing life. We had a most agreeable chat but I felt it really wasn't fair to disturb him for long and I had another engagement at half past four, so I pushed on, not without a brief sight of your Mogs who is always an enchanting vision.' A few weeks later Ettie entertained Mary Wemyss's two daughters Cynthia Asquith and Bibs Plymouth – 'such a Joy', Cynthia found it. 'Panshanger is like a blessed life-line, and you do make it such a paradise . . . I loved our undergraduates' talk under the trees Sunday night.'

Ettie gave other succour at this time. In the spring of 1941 Elizabeth and Val Kenmare came to live in a small house at Essendon a few miles south of Pans. Elizabeth had a weak heart, was frail, and Ettie often went over to help the old couple. Their daughter Dor, the widow of

Evan Charteris, felt the burden of her ailing parents would have been insupportable without Ettie. Elizabeth Kenmare was beginning to rally when in September Val Kenmare had a bad heart attack. He spent six weeks 'slowly dying – the end always expected in a few hours', as Ettie informed Queen Mary. 'It was all so piteous – Elizabeth, the nurses, the servants all became *completely* worn out. She hardly left him, & – five hours before his death came last Friday morning – she completely collapsed, & is still very ill.' The Kenmares' wastrel gossip-columnist son Valentine Castlerosse took the body to Killarney, and Ettie helped Dor Charteris to write an obituary tribute that they jointly published in *The Times*. Afterwards Dor opened her heart to Ettie. She doubted 'anyone has ever before done quite so much to rescue – to help – to heal – as you have done for me, & indeed for us all. I cd not have survived the shocks & difficulties, apart from the depths of sorrow, without your wise counsel & your unfailing steadiness & calm. How we leant on you my darling, & how instantly & with what utter selflessness you responded . . . I do pray you are not utterly exhausted, sometimes you did look so tired, & these weeks were so heart-rending for you.'

In August 1941, during a latent phase of the Kenmare crises, the Desboroughs were able to return to Taplow for a month. St Stephen's College, a girls' school run by an Anglican order of nuns, had been evacuated from a coastal area threatened by invasion and now occupied the house; but during the pupils' summer holiday it was arranged that the owners could return. Their five grandchildren joined them and it proved the last time that all the Desboroughs assembled there. George Gage was working in the Special Operations Executive and living nearby in Eton, where Mogs' 'spirit of flame, shining with wit and gaiety, charm, intelligence and courage' enlivened the depleted war-time community, according to another inhabitant. In August Churchill steamed in the newest battleship, the *Prince of Wales*, to the Newfoundland coast, where he conferred with President Roosevelt on war strategy. Ettie had other hopes for him: not Placentia Bay but Taplow. 'I suppose', she wrote in mid-August, 'you *couldn't* both come over from Chequers one day for old sake's sake? It is impossible to say what a joy it would be to us.' To Queen Mary she sent photographs of her grandchildren at Taplow. 'It was lovely to be there again, after 2 whole years, & to see all our own people . . . I think of you so very often, &

realize how the strange life of these days must seem more changed to Your Majesty than to *anyone.*'

Ettie adored reading *The Worst Journey*, Apsley Cherry-Garrard's trenchant and compelling account of the Scott expedition to Antarctica of 1911–12, and was delighted to find that he lived nearby at Wheathampstead. She invited him to Panshanger, where a German aeroplane had recently crashed in the grounds, killing the pilot, and Ettie quizzed him while Willie took his wife punting on the Mimram. Cherry-Garrard, like other visitors, was breathtaken by the Panshanger magnolias: 'the park', he told her, 'is still a bit of the real old England – like the Druid's Grove near Box Hill.' The Desboroughs and Garrards exchanged further visits until petrol rationing made journeys impossible. Thereafter Ettie sent the explorer letters in increasingly spidery handwriting, and quoted to him Tennyson's rousing injunction: 'To strive, to seek, to find, and not to yield.'

ɞ

She found other mottoes for herself at this time. Her pocket diary for 1942, which survives, is inscribed with three epigraphs drawn from her extensive reading:

> Howsoever men approach me, so do I accept them; for on all
> sides the paths they choose leads them to me. – Bhagavadgita.

> Cry courage, & away! *Henry VI*, pt 3, v/3

> Valour's Steel – *Julius Caesar*, II, 1.

These were rallying cries with which Ettie bestirred herself as she approached her seventy-fifth year. 'I am cut off from the *Etties* of life!' Winnie Portland complained in January 1942 from Welbeck, but Ettie did not yet feel isolated. That month she played croquet almost every day, even during sharp frosts, and enjoyed visits from Alice Salisbury and Helen D'Abernon. On her fifty-fifth wedding anniversary in February she wrote again to Churchill: 'I have tried for days not to write you – fearing to add one feather-weight to your burden – but it has become impossible not to send you thoughts & love & trust . . . How proud one feels of the nation, & of belonging to it.'

Ettie spent ten memorable May days at Badminton. 'Queen M is really astonishing,' she reported to Charley Londonderry, 'cut off from all the things that she likes best, but utterly uncomplaining, & without self-pity, & *so* charming.' She felt inspired by her mistress. 'The talks with Your beloved Majesty were such a help,' she wrote afterwards. 'I came back to the myriad little bothers that usually greet one's return . . . & felt quite strong to cope with them after that lovely little change, & all the realization of how Your Majesty is facing life as it is & making it strong & real & useful, & *cheerful* for all.' Humour, she thought, was 'one of the very first duties now – & oh how "a good laugh", as the maids say, does help one'. The invitation to Badminton followed a letter from the Queen commiserating on the Desboroughs being forced to sell the Cowper collection of seventeenth- and eighteenth-century silver, which was auctioned by Christie's on 18 March.

Violet Bonham Carter was a regular wartime visitor. '*Never* – in all our heavenly Sundays with you – have I loved every single hour with you quite as intensely as this time,' she wrote in May. 'I shall never forget our walk through that lovely wood where the bluebells floated like a mist under the trees & the white & purple lilac hung . . . and I did so love my walk with Willie after tea – he was so *angelic* to me – & talked of the old, dead, lovely days *so* amusingly, & without a veil or a trace of repining . . . one feels so many values are in the melting pot (some *rightly* so of course), & such confusion of mind & feeling about them.' Though Violet's walk with Willie had been a success, their conversations were sometimes fraught. Her opinions on men and events were vehement, and Ettie had to beg her not to discuss war news or post-war prospects as her combination of personal animosity and Liberal meliorism enraged Willie. Violet's handsome soldier son enchanted Ettie. 'I was so deeply struck by Mark & the intense interest of his face, & longed to have a few *days* of talk with him. What a son to possess – oh my darling, what is it that holds one up to face life?'

Until the war Alice Salisbury had never taken a meal in a London restaurant, and Ettie had usually eaten in her friends' or her own home. Now on her London day trips she became a habitué of the restaurant at the Ritz Hotel: the food was rationed, of course, but she had a favourite table in a quiet corner of that gilt and mirrored room overlooking Green Park. She invited John Gore for luncheon in November –

adding a typically eager, up-to-date question: 'have you seen some *lovely* poems by a young Frenchman called Aragon?' Tommy Lascelles had a talk with Ettie at a wedding reception in November: 'can't be far off eighty and looks little different from what she did thirty years ago,' he noted. 'She had written me that morning one of her highly confidential notes, asking me in effect if I thought Lady Leconfield (a friend of hers) was potty, or not potty.' In the next months Ettie was much involved with trying to help Violet Leconfield, whose eccentricities had become impossibly disruptive. She went to visit her in the nursing home where she was kept at Pinner, and was distressed by what she found.

The Gage children had settled at Pans for the duration of the war, and Ettie's affinity with Camilla Gage was a heart-warming version of the ties between old Lady Cowper and little Ettie Fane at Wrest three-quarters of a century earlier. There was a world of difference, though, between Wrest in the 1870s and the privations of wartime Hertfordshire: Ettie gleefully reported the response of Camilla, aged five, to her question what she had had for dinner: 'Fat, with gristle in the middle.' There was a great 'hullabaloo' for Christmas of 1942. In addition to all the Gage family, several hundred East End mothers and babies by now occupied the east wing. 'The Hospital was bursting with holly and Father Christmasses (Osbert Sitwell says that holly makes him feel as desolate as a robin), & we had the three youngest grandchildren here, & I wrote a Play for them to act – a mingling of Shakespeare & Noël Coward: Camilla Gage, aged 5, was a cross old Sea-Captain in full uniform, but making her accustomed goo-goo eyes. She is exactly like Lady Melbourne, but with a deeper sense of the Way of the World.'

This was her account to John Gore; and with a characteristic change of key, she turned from children's play-acting to her visit on 8 January to the Churchills. 'I went to luncheon alone with Winston, he was super-fine. I said, with truth, that the War had destroyed the last fragment of my brain. He said that his on the contrary had never been so good; that he made better speeches than ever before, with less preparation, & that his memory was a miracle. I asked – rather boringly – if he didn't find anxiety very tiring? He said "I am never anxious." He then began a close analysis of his own character – "I am arrogant but not conceited" etc, & was so entranced (& so was I) that he missed his indispensable afternoon snooze.'

Again Ettie's pocket diary for 1943 survives with its minuscule epigraphs neatly inscribed with a thin nib. And again they are characteristic of Ettie's gospel:

Strange power, I trust thy might,
Trust thou my constancy.
                    Emily Brontë

Le vierge, le vivace et le bel aujourd'hui [The pure, the deep-rooted and the beautiful today: the opening line of a sonnet by Stéphane Mallarmé].

Fear knocked at the door. When Faith opened the door, there was no one there.

A hammer shivers glass but forges steel – Russian proverb.

Woe unto him who has lost patience – Ecclesiastes.

Desmond MacCarthy had recommended her to read the final, lately published edition of T.S. Eliot's *Four Quartets*. She 'sweated away over "Little Gidding"', she wrote, and decided that MacCarthy's fear of seeming old-fashioned had led him to praise 'such awful rot'. She found it inexplicable that Eliot, having become a communicant of the Church of England, still wrote poetry with futility as its theme. She became a keen reader of the *Times Literary Supplement*. It led her to many ambitious books (loaned to her by the London Library), including Jacques Maritain's *Redeeming the Time*, and Rilke's *Letters*, which baffled her. 'I've been reading such highly-commended disgusting novels: I am quite robust about such things when they're necessary, but it is all the abominations that seem to be just dragged in as trimmings that revolt one.'

Ettie invited Linky Cecil to stay for 'a "week-end" (vile word)' in January 1943. 'We have still got a comfortable guest-room (& room for your servant), & the house is fairly warm, but bring warm clothes,' she urged him. Churchill had recommended him for a peerage, and he was now called Lord Quickswood, having taken his seat in the Lords with Willie as his sponsor. They were joined on the Sunday (10 January) by a young American with huge eyes and a drawling, bassoon-deep voice called Stuart Preston. He and Ettie took a long walk in the wet thaw, and he made himself agreeable to Linky in the evening. Preston had come to London in 1942 as a sergeant in the US Army, sleeping on a straw mattress in his North Audley Street billet, but often visiting Pans on Sundays or weekends. His boyhood readings of Proust had imbued him with a lifelong absorption in class distinctions and avidity for social arcana. Accordingly, in England, he had endeared himself to various elderly or eminent people. He recurs throughout James Lees-Milne's war diaries as an indefatigable party-goer called 'The Sergeant' and less flatteringly as a character called 'The Loot' in Evelyn Waugh's *Sword of Honour* trilogy.

Preston was part of 'a rather naughty crew', Logan Pearsall Smith informed Hugh Trevor-Roper in January 1943, who 'splash about [in] Mayfair gutters . . . or, it was hinted, on the darker dead-sea waters that lave the police-walls of the Cities of the Plain'. He had first been taken up by Harold Nicolson and was known as 'Harold's American', which for Smith '*ne présage rien de bon*'. Apart from Nicolson, his best friends in England were 'Lady Cunard & Lady Desborough; & Sibyl Colefax is trying wildly to hunt him down'. Despite succumbing to Preston's dashing charm and eager receptivity, Smith felt a residual caution: 'I am an old bird, & suspect that he has a low-down, shady side. He must have it, for he is much too good to be true.' A month later, after a long stay at Pans, Preston succumbed to jaundice, as Smith again reported to Trevor-Roper: 'the all-conquering American charmer is in hospital for an indigestion of lobster-salad & champagne & iced coronets. But his window opens on a prospect of ducal residences & millionaire homes.' Later Preston used his friendship with Ettie to justify arriving unheralded at the Paris home of Millie, Duchess of Sutherland, whom he beguiled; but there seems eventually to have been a cooling between Ettie and Preston. Willie perhaps grew exasperated by him, and certainly other members of the family talked of him as a bore.

The journey to London was tedious but not impossible for Ettie, and she punctuated her seclusion at Pans with busy day outings to the capital. While she was there with her lady's maid Mildred Lear on

20 January 1943, the sirens sounded as they shopped in Oxford Street, an air raid began and there were volleys of gunfire above the great department stores with their taped and shuttered windows. Nothing daunted she went to see Brydie Amery (the wife of the Colonial Secretary, Leo Amery) to discuss what they might do to help Violet Leconfield in her madness.

Ettie returned to London with Willie on Monday, 25 January. She went to the National Gallery to look at the Constables, then to the memorial service at the church of St Martin-in-the-Fields for Richard Hillary, who had recently been killed in a flying accident at the age of twenty-three. His hands and face had been badly burnt when his Spitfire was shot down over the North Sea in 1940, and his pungent memoir, *The Last Enemy*, was a minor masterpiece. His handsome daring was so reminiscent to Ettie of Gustav Hamel, his lyrical accounts of aerial dogfights were in the same chord as Julian's scarifying letters from the bedlam of the Western Front, and his long sojourn in war hospitals evoked Monica's nursing memoir *Bright Armour*. 'When something really tragic happens – the cutting-off of a man at a moment when he has most reason to live,' Hillary wrote, 'the result for those who love him isn't a whimpering pathos; it's growth, not decline. It makes you a richer person, not a poorer one; better fitted to tackle life, not less fitted.'

From Hillary's memorial service Ettie had a brisk ten minutes' walk to her table at the Ritz and luncheon with Osbert Sitwell. They were joined by Mogs Gage, Mikie Duff and David Herbert; and afterwards Ettie went shopping with her daughter. In the early evening they attended a party at the Dorchester Hotel given by Liz Kenmare and Dor Charteris for obese, grasping, dissipated Valentine Castlerosse (as everyone still thought of the new Earl of Kenmare) and a chic, vulnerable, paper-thin Australian called Lady Furness: the couple married next day. Ettie returned to Pans with Willie on a pitch-dark evening train.

At Panshanger there was always croquet, letter writing, long walks in the woods alone, afternoons of joyous laughter with Alice Salisbury, and voluminous reading. Ettie spent many hours in her tent overlooking the slope down to the gentle water-meadows of the Mimram valley with its shimmering river. There, during the summer of 1942, she had written a short memoir of her girlhood. Monica and Imogen encouraged her to have a few copies privately printed, and on May Day of 1943 she sent out copies of her *Eyes of Youth* to choice friends. It was a beautifully printed and crisply written book, which celebrated her strange orphan childhood in her grandmothers' houses with the clear immediacy of an intelligent child's vision. There was no cheapening nostalgia or complicating adult retrospection: only a gracious, contented evocation of a way of life that seemed beguiling but archaic.

Ettie received many appreciative letters in early May, of which John Gore's can stand for the rest. 'A gem,' he told her. 'It wasn't my lot to live in great houses, but I danced on the fringe of Privilege. It may be that red cloaks & soup & curtseying to the squire were "all wrong" but when I think of modern successors, the *Daily Express* & movies & tinned foods, I can't help feeling that the Age of Privilege shd have survived even longer & covered the gap between the beginnings & the *results* of public education. You have brought it all back in its essence & at its best, vivid as memories of childhood revived by the smell of damp towels drying on the nursery fireguard . . . it is a longing, lingering look you cast back, & I don't wonder. And I think only Eyes of Eternal Youth cd have written *Eyes of Youth*.'

Ettie's content was short-lived. The calamity that came upon her is best given in her own words from her pocket diary. 'Tues 11 May 1943: A very cold day but out in tent & croquet. Dropped W[illie] at Mrs Franklyn's, & on to Hertford shops. Walking slowly across a quite empty street I fell down & broke my thigh. Do not remember falling, but came to in the midst of an enthusiastic Hertford crowd who were *enchanted*! & got taxi & me into it – literally shrieking w pain. It took three hours to get up stairs. I backwards up stairs & *very painful* night. Dr Lamb came at 11 & gave me morphia & got X Ray. Had morphia again & a very good night.'

She had fractured her right femur, which never mended. Over the next few days her pain was controlled by morphine, and she was heartened by daily visits from Alice and Jim Salisbury. The weather was intolerably hot, and at night, with hundreds of aircraft droning overhead, she could not sleep without opiates. She tried to distract herself by reading Chris Massie's novel about a clothes fetishist who murders his mistress, *Corridor of Mirrors*, but decided that it was a disgusting book. After family convocations with their physician John Lamb, Ettie was taken on 19 May by motor ambulance to University College Hospital in London, where she underwent an operation the following day. She was in miserable agony; it was feared that she might die. Willie was in faithful attendance at the hospital, with a hurt, puzzled look on his face, and Ettie had a host of visitors. Jack Stanmore, Alice Salisbury, Helen D'Abernon, Violet Bonham Carter, Dorothy Charteris, Osbert Sitwell, Linky Quickswood, Winnie Portland, Charley Londonderry, John Gore, George Gage, Stuart Preston, Sybil Cholmondeley, the Princess Royal, Walter de la Mare, Christabel Aberconway, Violet Leconfield (released from confinement) and many others of the privileged and the eminent trooped to her bedside.

A high point – which aroused a thrill throughout the hospital – was a sudden amazing visit from Winston Churchill on 21 June. He was responding to a hint from Willie: 'If your pressing & glorious occupations ever permit you, she would be delighted if at any time you could manage to see her'; though Willie reminded the War Overlord that there were more formidable autocrats in London even than him: 'it is best to telephone first to the sister in charge, Private Ward, University College Hospital.' Churchill was grieved to see how ill Ettie was, and worried that his visit overexcited her, as well it may have done. She never forgot him coming to the hospital that day: it was a wonderful tribute to his love for her, and testimony to the humane, stalwart friendship of the man.

Ettie was unable to leave her bed to sit in a chair until 15 July; and not until 27 July could Willie bring her back to Pans in an ambulance. 'Lovely evening & drive, trees still pale green & untarnished. Straight to bed in White Room & W had tea with me,' she recorded with deep satisfaction. She had a cheery, unladylike nurse who called her 'ducky' and seldom left her room without the parthian injunction to be a good girl. Her return to Pans was 'better news than the fall of Mussolini', John Gore told her. 'I have hated so long to think of you in those dingy surroundings, though I knew they were the setting for the best of medical science. But it is absolute joy to think of you in yr more familiar rooms, looking out on the trees & lawns you know & love, &

taking up again yr life & interests among your own.' Ettie was not allowed to try to stand on her own feet until September ('Blow & blast!'), and even then she was limited to ten minutes a day, using crutches.

Her life henceforth was to follow the sad course of encroaching infirmity, although this was not yet certain. Almost every day she was pushed in her wheelchair to her tent on the ridge above the Mimram valley where she wrote her letters, read her books and received visitors. The Gage grandchildren cheered her, though: 'Camilla said to me this morning "You *will* have me & all my children to stay here, won't you, if you're alive?"'

Unfortunately, shortly after her return home, Willie succumbed to an attack of jaundice and was in bed for nearly four months. Throughout the autumn he was sunk in despondency. 'I've been through a bad patch,' she wrote in November 1943, 'of ignoble self-pity – that most deadly of all spiritual assaults – but somehow the terrible depression coming to Willie, and lasting so many weeks, seemed like a curtain hung between us: the only isolating factor in 56 years. And I felt so utterly emptied & depleted & *utterly* useless to him.' The depression lifted before the effects of the jaundice, as Christabel Aberconway recollected of a visit to Willie in this period. 'He was in bed, in pyjamas, which you were coaxing him to change from when he got up to exercise gently up and down the passage; and I had a long talk with him afterwards about *clothes* – men's & women's – and what classical writers had said of them, and whether Byron would have had any success in plus fours! He was so gay, acting and imitating the parts and people described, and pretending to be shocked if I quoted unseemly statements by Gibbon.'

Ettie and her cousin Alice Salisbury – still 'Ally' to her in private – had known and loved one another for over seventy years. Now that Ettie was crippled and marooned, hobbling on crutches or confined in her wheelchair, the humour and intelligence of the Marchioness became an indispensable, selfless comfort to the household at Pans. 'You know what you have meant to me all your life, a beacon of hope,' Ettie wrote in January 1944 after Alice had made one of her countless visits from Hatfield. 'It is difficult to tell you what our talk meant to me – how hard it is to put it all into words, & yet how words, or communion of spirit, help, define, strengthen that wonderful sense of certainty & peace' that she drew from the first four words of the Apostles' Creed and the four last – 'I believe in God . . . and the life eternal' – 'though epochs must be faced when clouds *veil* the light'.

'What a knock-about turn life has become, I often feel very like Aunt Sally, don't you? But hope on hope,' Ettie said to Linky Quickswood shortly before returning to University College Hospital for a further operation in February 1944. It did no good.

On a Sunday in May Elizabeth Kenmare finally died – 'so peacefully at the end, no one could have wished to hold her back,' Ettie wrote to Charley Londonderry to whom she had long resorted at times of mourning. Liz Kenmare had been 'such a dearest friend to me our whole lives long . . . We were born, "came out", married, & our eldest children were born, in identical years; & there never was one shadow between us. It is one of the sad things about being very old, that the last of the bright candles are blown out so swiftly.'

In the campaign after D-Day, to the sorrow of Ettie and especially Mogs, Rex Whistler was killed at the age of thirty-nine – his neck broken when he was hurled from the side of a tank by a mortar explosion. 'The bomb that killed Rex has shattered many houses,' Ettie told Pamela Lytton. 'I dreadfully miss him,' Mogs wrote. 'Just as happiness is composed of parts of everything one has ever loved – so is sorrow *one* wound.' All her grief for her brothers and her other precious dead revived 'each time someone adored dies'.

The obstacles to Ettie exchanging visits with her friends were becoming insurmountable. 'I have thought of you often in this long War of Separation,' she wrote to Siegfried Sassoon in June 1944, '& always with happy memories.' She lived in hope of seeing him again, 'though I am 77 this month, & a little village child asked me yesterday when I thought I should die'. Now that Ettie was confined to Pans, her letter writing became inveterate and her friends' replies were a lifeline. Younger friends like John Gore and Mikie Duff became treasured messengers from the world beyond Ettie's gates and woods. Duff was an occasional visitor to Pans – 'so peaceful, & calm, & delicious', he always found it, and from RAF headquarters of the British North African Force, wrote yearningly of 'that lovely park at Pans, filled with copper beeches and repose and that lovely drive up to the house'.

Duff loved Ettie, as his letters shiningly prove; and knowing what she craved, he enchanted her with delicious Society letters after being invalided home in 1944. In July that year, for example, he reported an evening in Buckinghamshire. The widowed Duchess of Kent came to dinner, 'bringing Prince Philip of Greece, who is CHARMING, and I consider just right to perform the role of Consort for Princess Elizabeth. He has everything in his favour, he is good looking, intelligent, a good sailor, and he speaks ONLY English.' Duff knew the Prince was often at Windsor, 'but whether he likes P.E. or she him I can't say'. He also chattered about the 'race going on between Mrs Wessel (Lady Churston of the old days) and Lady Kenmare' — Valentine Castlerosse's widow — 'to see which can catch the Duke of Leinster. It seems that Mrs Wessel has had a good year's start, and so far there are no signs of it being neck and neck, though Lady Kenmare gains ground and holds it daily like our troops in Normandy. How pleased *your* Lady Kenmare must be to be rid of all this stupidity.' Chips Channon had taken his eight-year-old son Paul, just repatriated from America, 'to make his bow before the Duchess of Kent . . . The Duchess asked him if he was pleased to be home again. Says Master Channon "I am sure I am, it's God Save the King for me, and God bless Your Royal Highness, also Their Royal Highnesses, your children".' Mikie Duff amused Ettie with tales of that clumsy American snob, Laura Corrigan. Mrs Corrigan had accosted Winnie Portland in Claridge's saying, ' "You are the Dowager Duchess of Portland aren't you? You have a great following in America, where your *Press* is good." Winnie, much overcome, murmured like Queen Victoria at her Diamond Jubilee, "How kind, how kind", & disappeared into the lift hurriedly.'

Charley Londonderry spent Saturday, 14 October 1944 at Pans to Ettie's joy: she only let him out of her sight to stroll in the woods with Willie. Willie had been frailer since his jaundice, but felt in good fettle for a man of eighty-nine after his walk with Charley. It was therefore a shocking blow when a few days later he suffered a serious heart attack. The cardiologist Sir Maurice Cassidy was called in and gave a depressing prognostication. The next weeks proved grim. 'Darling Dad', Ettie assured Monica on 7 December, 'is really & truly a *little* better, sleeping most certainly better, looking better, stronger, the weakness & great depression & distaste for "company" continues — but he did see Jack Stanmore, by own wish, on Monday . . . I feel about 90 years older in the last nearly-eight weeks, which brings my age to 167.' In the week between Christmas and New Year Willie felt wretched and constantly scratched a real or imaginary itch on his skin. He would see no one but Ettie and Mogs. 'I have been so worried about Willie, he doesn't seem to get on, & suffers so much from many ills, & one feels so utterly at a loss as to what to do – & I am such an idiotic cripple, & so *useless*,' she complained to Charley Londonderry on 3 January 1945. 'Then there's been trying (oh so inadequately) to make Christmas nice for the children & the Hospital, & to struggle against self-abhorrence (which is merely *more* tiring).'

Early in the New Year Willie's discomfort ceased. He had four peaceful days, and on 8 January was delighted to have the strength to dictate five letters and sign two cheques. He said to Ettie that evening, 'I should like to live two more years.' Instead, he died next day, peacefully at Panshanger, of myocardial degeneration, arterio-sclerosis and oedema. For Ettie this was the end of fifty-eight years of common memory – grateful and heartening memories weighed with sadness but unladen by admonitions or reprisals. Their marriage had been a confederacy with a secret history that only the two of them knew.

Willie's death was a public event. His passing at Panshanger was broadcast on the BBC news bulletin, and there was a universal sense that the English had lost 'the prototype of the Great English Gentleman of our great days'. This was the refrain of so many messages to Ettie: she found herself replying to over fifty letters of condolence a day, and did not finish her answers until 6 February. Willie, declared Lord Crawford in one of them, had ennobled everyone around him. 'His were the best manners I have ever known: but they were not artificial manners: they were the perfect and natural expression of the whole of his character . . . I think of him on a hot Sunday afternoon, in his straw hat, blazer & white trousers, striding in his strength and beauty across the lawns of Taplow, as an example and symbol of England – England of the past . . . calm, strong, good, courageous, wise, tolerant & great.'

Willie was buried in the closed graveyard at Taplow beside Ivo – where Ettie would join them seven years later. Only Monica and Jack Salmond, Imogen and George Gage, Julian Salmond in his blue battledress and Rosemary Salmond were there with her. There was a packed memorial service at St Margaret's, Westminster, as there had been for Ivo; and on the Sunday after Willie's death, at St George's Chapel at Windsor, a march was played at the end of the service, as was the immemorial custom when a Knight of the Garter had died. Sir William Harris, the organist, chose the mighty 'Nimrod' march from Elgar's *Enigma Variations* – 'a strikingly impressive tribute', Alan Lascelles told Ettie, 'in that lovely place, with the banners above to remind one that Chivalry never dies in England.'

༞

The Desboroughs had befriended a great medical man called Sir Charles Wilson, who accompanied Churchill as his personal physician on his momentous wartime overseas journeys. When Wilson was granted a barony on Churchill's recommendation in 1943, Willie and Linky Quickswood acted as the new Lord Moran's sponsors as he took his seat in the House of Lords. In February 1945 Moran's exceptional book *The Anatomy of Courage* was published. Its acknowledgements thanked 'first the Prime Minister, who has taken me where I might learn from those who are doing the fighting', then 'Group Captain Corner, who, until he was killed, acted as my pilot in more senses than one', and Lady Desborough and Desmond MacCarthy for their criticism and advice. The book is studded with extracts from Moran's diary as a medical officer of the first war: he wrote the preface in a bomber flying over the Libyan desert and finished the final chapter in a flying boat above the Atlantic. It is a study of the nature of courage, of the management of fear and the art of command – which, he convinces his readers, is the art of impressing the imagination. 'War is only tolerable when one takes part in it, when one is a bit of the target & not a pensioned spectator,' Moran wrote. 'Courage is will-power, whereof no man has an unlimited stock; and when it is used up, he is finished.' Helen D'Abernon found it a 'hair-raising book'.

The coming of spring in 1945 buoyed Ettie's spirits. 'Oh such a perfect April day, I wish I could send you all the sights & scents & sounds – cuckoos & chaffinches shouting each other down, & everything out at once,' she exclaimed. She enjoyed many visitors from London, though most of their stories were sad; and on the evening of 8

May she heard a broadcast of Churchill's impromptu oration – dressed in his siren-suit – to the crowds in Whitehall confirming the German capitulation and the end of the war in Europe. She wept when he roared the triumphant words at his audience, 'And it's your victory too!' The first days of peace were disorientating. 'So queer isn't it, like a very long illness,' she wrote on 12 May. 'Jim Salisbury has just been here, what an angel, but utterly bewildered too – & we just sat in the blinding sunshine & wondered together.'

On 22 July Queen Mary (dressed in white from head to foot) gave Ettie the joy of a visit – it was the last time that the two magnificent old women met. 'All the happy days came rushing back, & the absolute unfailing kindness of Your Majesties through dark days & bright days,' she wrote afterwards to the Queen. 'It was so delightful to talk again of the early days; so often one mentions some well known & loved name & the response (however kindly) is absolutely blank!' They were joined by Alice Salisbury – 'she has had much sorrow & anxiety in these last years, but her courage never flags – & I can never say what she & Jem have been to us all.' The reduced staff at Pans adored the royal visit – 'our old "Alfred" spoke of your kindness with literal tears in his eyes.'

'Saturday afternoon,' she wrote to Charley Londonderry on 18 August, '& my treat is going to be writing to you – dear Alice S just gone, & the sun pouring in to my tent, & the wood pigeons cooing away, & the August honeysuckle smelling heavenly. I have thought of you so much in these strange days, how numb one feels, & rather far from jubilation & coloured-paper. I suppose it's the bruising & battering of the long six years – but thankfulness *must* come, or it would be too ungrateful.' Her greatest joy that summer was long visits from 'the darling & riotous holiday grand-children . . . I cannot tell you of their sweetness to this poor old crock, or the joy & laughter they bring to life.' Her friends knew that admiring allusions to the little Gages were the best way to hearten her. 'Isn't Nicky a perfect demon-angel?' Christabel Aberconway asked with her usual tact. 'I find him bewitching, and Christopher says that he is the greatest "adventurer" in the whole school.' In mid-September she was visited by loyal Jack Stanmore, next day by Jim Salisbury, then Lucia Galway, by Stanley Baldwin, who seemed tired and sad, John Winant, the US Ambassador, and finally Osbert Sitwell, in the midst of writing his sumptuous and lordly memoirs, of which he sent the proofs of each volume to Ettie, although, alas, he barely mentioned the Desboroughs.

The autumn of 1945, however, brought anxiety and sorrow. Violet Leconfield relapsed into insanity, and Betty Montgomery, with whom Ettie had been exchanging weekly letters for fifty-nine years, was burnt after tumbling into her gas fire, and died after six terrible weeks. 'I do feel so ashamed of sometimes being depressed,' Ettie wrote in December. 'Oh isn't it annihilating to be unable to move under one's own steam?' Four years earlier she had written a tribute in *The Times* when Edgar D'Abernon died. 'Life itself was the art that he loved best, and as the terrible illness that seized upon him increased its hold the invincible sweetness and valour of his nature shone out,' she had written in 1941. 'There was never a touch of resentment, never a syllable of complaint.' Near the end he had whispered, 'I enjoy every minute of my life' and when after unpleasant treatment he was asked if he was comfortable, 'he was just able to breathe one word: "Perfect".' Edgar D'Abernon was one of her models for facing creeping decrepitude.

Her frustration with her disability, the loss of self-respect that came with her loss of self-reliance, and the precepts by which she tried to cope with her new conditions of life, are implicit in the obituary she contributed to *The Times* when Maurice Baring died that month after ten harrowing years of Parkinson's disease – latterly he was quite helpless. It was anonymous, but the opening sentence revealed its authorship to Desmond MacCarthy and others. 'To those who read his poems about "Bron" Lucas and Julian Grenfell, all the sides of his nature must be revealed,' it began. 'He believed in the best in human nature, and he succeeded in producing it in his friends. Even those who have found consolation through other gates can never fail to know what his allegiance to the Roman Catholic church meant to him, in peace and security; it was his faith which inspired the courage which withstood all the suffering and physical humiliation of his last years . . . Life never became a habit with him, it was always a miracle; the inevitable was accepted by his unfailing qualities of gentleness and strength; and "the brave battle of his laughter ended", he went back without regret to the source of his belief.' This was a very personal tribute from another noble invalid. Ettie was resolved to make what was left of her life feel miraculous, not routine, to face suffering and humiliation with fortitude, and live to the brave battle sound of laughter.

'I haven't been very grand,' Ettie wrote on New Year's Day of 1946, but '*must* try to pull together for whatever short time is left'. Now confined in stately solitude at Pans, she was still a lively hostess upholding the great Souls tradition of brilliant conversation. 'Those 3 hours flew like lightning,' Violet Bonham Carter enthused after a visit in the summer of 1946, '& I went away bursting with things I hadn't told you – & wanted to – things I longed to hear & hadn't asked. Talking to you is such unspeakable luxury & delight – my topmost treat in the world.' She sent her son Mark to enjoy the conversational luxuries at Pans: Ettie, and indeed little Camilla Gage, adored him. 'He did bring such charm & delight – & spread enjoyment all round. I *adored* talking to him, what vivid reminders of Raymond . . . I haven't had such eager (& constantly agree-ing) talk with anyone for ages & ages. His effect on Camilla was instant, she said to me "he took away my eyesight".'

The affinity between Ettie and her youngest grandchild remained especially close, and in these years the two were important figures in one another's lives. Ettie was a strong influence on anyone she truly loved, and by the 1940s her brand of love was no longer despotic. Camilla Gage, for her, was a fount of hope and laughter. 'Fun seems to have vanished from the world – for anyone older than your & my friend Camilla,' she wrote to Londonderry in August. 'Camilla, not yet very good at the letter-game, only got one word the other evening – it was pox. Very Restoration? She said it meant "a kind of fox".'

Ettie's famous tent on the ridge was replaced by a wooden hut in which she could still read, write and (at harvest time) watch the sturdy grapplers with the corn. In September intrepid Helen D'Abernon came all the way to Pans by Green Line bus – a two-and-a-quarter-hours journey each way from Stoke D'Abernon. 'I am enchanted but ter-rified, as she always falls down when she goes in a bus, & generally breaks a bone,' Ettie told Londonderry; and to Linky Quickswood: 'Helen came, most marvellously, by *bus* from Stoke D'Abernon . . . She looked quite beautiful & was in her very best mood of personal sweetness & general stiletto, quite undimmed by the years, in a little

brown hat, with one exquisite orange ostrich feather, perfectly poised.'
It was a marvel of aplomb that the ostrich feather had not suffered from
such a journey; and breathtaking for Ettie to think of Helen, whose
Foley House had been the most commanding house on Portland Place
and whose house at Esher (designed by the architects of the Ritz Hotel)
had been the acme of Edwardian opulence, being shuddered across
country on a packed Green Line bus.

Charley Londonderry paid a last visit: full of complaints, quarrelling
with his family, en route to Wynyard, which he and his wife loathed.
Other visitors included Dorothy Charteris, Violet Bonham Carter,
Ann Islington, Grace Curzon, Violet Leconfield and Katherine Drummond, aged eighty-four, who arrived in an ambulance, with two male
and two female attendants, after a seventy-seven-mile journey, over
Tilbury Ferry, from Sissinghurst. Ettie felt ill as the second anniversary
of Willie's death approached in January 1947, but by February she was
wading out to her hut on her sticks over the snow and ice 'like Captain
Scott'. Some days a few stubborn men friends braved their way to Pans
in freezing trains or over ice-bound roads.

It was a great moment when the maternity hospital left Pans on
25 March 1947. The hospital authorities had been able to obtain fuel for
the house's central-heating system, but these supplies immediately
ceased; and the house was so freezing in April that Ettie shut up almost
everything but her sitting room and bedroom. The east wing was never
reopened and, already worn by hospital use, became decayed. The west
end of the long house where Ettie lived, closest to the orangery,
became increasingly a twilight world. Knowing how she craved bustle
and laughter in her muffled rooms, her granddaughter Rosemary, who
had met George Curzon's grandson Nicholas Mosley when they were
both Oxford undergraduates, took him to meet her grandmother. He
had no idea who her grandmother was and did not dare to ask.

They motored into Hertfordshire, and eventually reached the closed
gates to a great park. They sounded their horn, an old lady came out of
the lodge, and for a moment, until she opened the gates and they swept
past up the long drive, Mosley thought she was Rosemary's grandmother. They reached a house, which looked as long as a battleship,
entered by a back door, and padded down sombre stone passages
where life seemed to have halted. He was left waiting while Rosemary

went into her grandmother's small sitting room. Then he was ushered in. An old lady in a wheelchair said, 'Ah! I was such a friend of your grandfather's.' He had no idea who she was until he glimpsed an envelope lying on a desk addressed to Lady Desborough. 'She gave Rosemary a huge old-fashioned key and we went down a central corridor of tattered grandeur and into a long high picture gallery where, when Rosemary had opened a creaking shutter, there appeared – through cobwebs – a Van Dyck? An Italian Renaissance Holy Family? A huge portrait of a soldier on a horse that could be – surely not! – a Rembrandt? (Rosemary said, "Yes, they say it is.")'

On later visits Ettie charmed Mosley with stories of long ago. When Oscar Wilde sued Lord Queensberry in 1895 for describing him as a sodomite, Willie had taken Wilde's side protesting that Queensberry's accusation was impossible – such vices could not happen. As the case progressed, and the facts became clearer, Willie's innocence was shocked. Whatever the outcome of the civil case, he said before Wilde was arrested, we can never have him to Taplow again. 'I liked Ettie Desborough because out of the world of old gods and goddesses, she seemed to be one of the best; her wit, even her gospel of joy, seemed to have some virtue in a world in which expressions of despair were commonplace,' Mosley recalled thirty years later – though when he became engaged to Rosie, his father Sir Oswald Mosley, ex-leader of the New Party and of the Blackshirts, said Ettie was worse than his sisters-in-law: 'That woman is more affected than all the Mitfords.'

Ettie turned eighty in June 1947. The inveterate diner out and house party guest was seeing, in her last years, no other house but her own. She was increasingly isolated, especially after widowed Lady Salisbury left Hatfield for a small house in a Chelsea square, though Alice bought a typewriter on which she hammered out chaotic but unquenchably warm-hearted messages to the friends she could no longer easily visit. Ettie's isolation never made her plaintive, but she became a trifle importunate in her calls for attention. 'I do long to see & talk to you, how I wish that you were here now, in this undying Summer, looking over the river,' she told Siegfried Sassoon.

'My beloved Winston,' she wrote at this time, 'I know too well how untellably busy you are, & this is only one syllable to say that if there ever ever ever appeared a niche in this Summer when you & darling

Clemmie could slip down to see me here, it would be an untellable joy to me. But you are *not* to bother about it, I think of you so often, & of all the old days, & of all you meant to me & mine.' She was writing from her hut, overlooking the Mimram valley, and promised that he would make a lovely painting of the view. Osbert Sitwell was coming tomorrow, she added, '& who do you think on Sunday, Nick Mosley (son of my dear Cynthia Curzon & the unspeakable one)'. Asquith, Balfour and even Chamberlain had relished chatty social letters from Ettie, but party leaders were no longer permitted the old relaxations, and Churchill, Leader of the Opposition, had no spare time for Ettie's way of life. He telegraphed back, 'Clemmie and I would love to come down to see you but cannot manage it just now. Much love.'

The growing remoteness of old age did not diminish Ettie's curiosity. Her life might be dwindling but her interest in other people was not. In July 1947 came the excitement of the engagement – predicted by Mikie Duff in 1944 – of Princess Elizabeth to Prince Philip of Greece. 'I spent the weekend with the Duchess of Kent, & the newly betrothed came to lunch on Sunday,' Duff reported. 'Princess E looked radiant, & he not quite so much. I have known him for years & think him charming in a rather dull way. I don't think he has very endearing qualities but they may grow, he's a bit "Naval", if you know what I mean, & has none of the gaiety of Dickie Mountbatten (or what we all thought gay) and his manners are a trifle rough . . . Philip of Greece gives me the impression of taking all the wrong & trivial things to heart, & not the things that *really* matter . . . He *scowls* a bit as though a fly were a permanent guest on his nose! I think all Royalty scowl, the male members especially. I suppose it's done in self-defence! . . . The Duke of Gloucester looked quite stuffed at the Garden Party, as though he had been bedded out for the summer to be looked at but not touched. The Queen looked *sweet*, & Margaret Rose as painted as any inmate in a chic brothel! Mabell Airlie was *enchanting* & Lady Ampthill much less so.' These were the sort of Society snapshots that sustained Ettie through the late 1940s.

She was too disabled to accept her invitation to the royal engagement party, and was touchingly animated by Rosemary Salmond's acceptance in July of Nicholas Mosley's proposal. Ettie had been godmother to his mother Cynthia Curzon, and his grandfather George

Curzon had been Ivo's godfather, so there were many pleasant links, but she and Monica were mortified by the Blackshirt associations of the Mosleys. Nicholas, after his mother's death, had been chiefly brought up by his aunt Irene Ravensdale, Curzon's eldest daughter, and Ettie was relieved that Nicholas would one day inherit her Ravensdale peerage and, she hoped, shed the Mosley name. She stressed to friends that he had been awarded the Military Cross for valour in the Italian campaign; and Monica similarly always emphatically intoned, 'Captain Nicholas Mosley *MC*', when introducing him at this time, to stress that he had fought for his country rather than been incarcerated in Brixton prison as an enemy sympathiser like his father.

The couple married in November at the historic church of St Bartholomew-the-Great, Smithfield: all around the church lay City streets razed by German bombs. They went to live in a bamboo hut, by a beach of white coral sand, on a Caribbean islet owned by a Mrs Snowball. They stayed there for months, and talked of staying for ever, to escape the nuclear war between Soviet Russia and the USA that seemed to be looming.

꜒

The shabbiness, rationing, shortages and enveloping priggishness of post-war England made Lady Desborough into a symbol of all that had been lost. Austerity conditions heightened rather than annihilated the memories of the dowagers. 'There *never* has been anyone like Ettie – and there never will be again!!' exclaimed Lady Joicey from her refuge in the Dorchester Hotel. Violet Bonham Carter broadcast a radio talk on the Souls in October 1947. 'They all indulged with passionate zest in talk on every kind of subject – politics, religion, literature, art, scholarship, human relations, last night's play or last Sunday's sermon – all was grist that came to their mill. They were intellectually ambitious, they were adventurous, unconventional, tolerant at everything except stupidity – and silence . . . They met each other constantly, not only in London at innumerable dinners, great and small, but also in the loveliest country-houses in England – Wilton – Wrest – Stanway – Panshanger (what visions those names conjure up to those who knew them, of grey and golden stone, of green lawns in the shade of great trees!).'

Violet had discussed the contents of the broadcast with Ettie, and added some dewdrops to the dear friend with whom she had shared Archie Gordon's love forty years earlier: 'Lady Desborough – a woman of genius – genius for life itself and for every relationship it holds; one whose eternal youth still flowers, rooted in joy undimmed, unconquerable courage.' Violet's talk ended with heart-churning poignancy. 'The great houses are crumbling into hydros, the long green avenues are lying low, the fountains have ceased playing, and that old, exquisite, consummate art that played with them, and flowed from them, is dying too. We are living in the twilight of an age, an age on which the darkness is fast closing in. The Souls were the last shaft of glory from its setting sun – the final flowering of a now deserted garden.' Ettie listened spellbound to every word and was enchanted: 'I thought it *so* lovely, you seemed to have caught the very essence . . . & oh how exquisite & all-undeserved the words about me.'

Ettie had an attack of shingles in January 1948 that proved hard to shake off: it took over six months for her to hobble back to her sitting room. The horror of illness, she found, was not only the boredom but the fear of burdening other people. At times she felt overmastered by physical weakness and drained by the exactions of monotony. Once again Alice Salisbury came to her aid, and warned her friends how poorly she was. 'Queen Mary', wrote Alice's sister Mabell Airlie, 'thinks of you constantly and knows how sore are your trials & how *wonderfully* you bear them. Darling you were with her in one of the darkest hours of her life, and those things are not forgotten.' The shingles left her weaker and more alone: few of her friends had the strength for the journey, or the fortitude to face her in her helpless state. As Ettie became feebler, she amused herself by rereading, sorting and sometimes deliberately mislabelling old letters. Passionate billets-doux from Evan Charteris were docketed 'Alice' and 'Letters from E to A' in the tremulous scratchy script of her extreme old age, though they had nothing to do with Lady Salisbury.

After Willie's death Ettie was beset by business decisions of which she had no experience, and felt the value of her estate shrink with every announcement from the lawyers. Under his will, signed in June 1944, she inherited the Whiteslea estate outright, and a lifetime interest in Taplow and Panshanger and their contents. The family solicitors,

Manisty Nicholl, now laid careful plans for her death. The Desborough Settlement Trust, which had been set up in 1910 following Lloyd George's egalitarian budget, bought farmland in order to minimise the liability for death duties. Properties in Derbyshire, Lancashire and Yorkshire were bought for the trust, and in 1949 the Campsea Ashe estate in Suffolk following the death of Lord Ullswater. Under Ettie's will of 1931 and a codicil of September 1944, the Panshanger estate, together with its mansion house and contents, were left to Monica if she resided in the house; or to Julian, if he instead lived in the house; or failing that arrangement, to Rosemary Mosley under like conditions. The Taplow estate was left with similar provisos to Mogs and the Gage grandchildren.

Following Ettie's death in 1952, the total value of her estate, including the settled land, was assessed at £406,685 gross, or £380,971 net – respectively £8,080,975 and £7,570,028 in 2008 values – with death duties payable of only £12,426 (£246,909). The northern estates were sold in March 1953 for about £250,000 (the equivalent of about £4,670,000 in 2008), and Campsea Ashe in September 1953. The house at Campsea Ashe was then demolished, the estate was broken up, and its famous gardens and parkland, with long formal canals and avenues of trees, were ploughed up. The Mosleys were tempted to take over Panshanger if it came to them, but Monica and her son had prior choice. Neither of them liked the house, which had rot in the roofs and was dilapidated after the war, and in July 1953 they sold the Panshanger estate for about £120,000 (£2,241,000 in 2008). The house and eighty-nine acres were bought for £17,750 (£331,500 in 2008) by a demolition contractor, who set about his devastating work in the following winter. The estate was subsequently acquired by a gravel excavation company, which has dug up much of the grounds but has treated Repton's landscaping with surprising sensitivity. Only the orangery – battered by the depredation of vandals – and the stable block still stand. In October 1953, Christie's sold 154 lots of paintings and pictures from Panshanger totalling £7,808 (£145,830). All the sales of Pans land and contents were made near the bottom of the market.

Taplow Court was sold by the Gages, who already owned their much-loved house at Firle, and became the headquarters of British Telecommunications Research, which developed civilian and military

communication systems. The pick of the Taplow contents were transferred to Firle. After the privatisation of British Telecom by the
Thatcher government, Taplow Court was bought in 1988 by a
Japanese Buddhist society, which campaigns for world peace and has
maintained the house and grounds immaculately.

Ettie was unwell in January 1949 – perhaps she had a small stroke –
and for some time all her letters were dictated to Mogs. 'I have been
incapable of either speaking or hearing for weeks, but am better now,'
she wrote on 9 February to Lord Cherwell, whom she besought for a
visit. Linky Quickswood, like her, was infirm, immobile and losing his
reading memory, but felt his failing body had nothing to do with the
survival of his personality, and was looking forward to his interesting
experiences after death, as he told Ettie. 'You write so contentedly,' she
replied through her amanuensis Mogs, 'a lesson to me for I do often
feel restive, just about the things you mention, like complete oblivion
about what one reads, however absorbed at the moment, also of what
one hears! It is disturbing, but one's great duty after 80 is acceptance –
however hard to learn . . . one can only try one's bad best: & I am
surrounded by such kind care & enchanting grandchildren.' Some of
her letters deeply moved their recipients. 'Oh! my darling how *wonderful* of you to write to me!' Mabell Airlie responded. 'The tears came to
my eyes as I read your dear letter, and thought of all the long years we
had known and loved each other. I do think of you so often, and *long*
to see you.'

The testimony of King George V's two official biographers, John
Gore and Harold Nicolson, shows that even in decrepitude Ettie was an
inspiration:

> The lesson her letters offer [wrote Gore], is the virtue of courage, of
> unquenchable zest for living & undefeated human sympathy in the
> face of constant tragedy & shattering losses . . . She lived in
> discomfort in a corner of Panshanger. But she continued to
> correspond with vivacity & enthusiasm with a score of friends, new
> & old, young & not so young, & could supply to each the comfort
> & stimulus appropriate to their condition . . . After her accident in
> 1943, she became virtually a cripple and very rarely left that corner
> of Panshanger which was reserved to her. In summer and autumn

she sat half the day in her summer house overlooking the lake and there received her friends and wrote her letters. She kept up an enormous correspondence and her letters were of a kind to be read and read again. She loved good talk and promoted but never dominating it. No trace of malice ever pointed her wit . . . The last decade of her life was one long triumph of the spirit.

Ettie helped Nicolson with his biography of the dead King, as she had Gore a decade before. 'A less vital character might have been subdued by the slow malady of her final years,' wrote Nicolson. 'She gave to illness itself a calm and lovely elegance. Even when confined to a single room at Panshanger she retained her splendid curiosity in the varied doings of the outside world; from her bed she would write pathetically illegible letters, sharing with others the treasures of her miraculous and varied past.'

About the time that Rosemary Mosley was giving birth to Ettie's first great-grandchild, Shaun Mosley, in August 1949, Ettie suffered a major stroke that left her face twisted and reduced her adeptness – though her brain was unimpaired. 'I have now got a great grandchild,' she wrote in September to Winston Churchill, 'such a beautiful little boy, lying with me here now, under the big chestnut tree, in the unending summer. *Do* come, and dearest Clemmie, to see him & me when you can. Your old old friend Ettie. How many happy days rush back.' She asked that Shaun should be christened at Panshanger, and the ceremony took place in her bedroom there. She lay in her wig raking the room with sharp looks from her bed. It was the last full-dress event of her life: thereafter, as she wrote in her final message to Queen Mary in 1950, she was 'very feeble . . . & still laid-up'.

Ettie was now a magnificent, forlorn relic proclaiming her stubborn gospel of joy. Dorothy Charteris often called at Pans in these last years, and recognised her resilient bravura as part of the glorious entirety of the Lady Desborough story. 'As a hostess she was an inspiration; as a friend she was true as steel. Some, who knew her little, may have thought her hard, but in the trials that came to her she needed the quality of proven metal, and in great suffering her high courage never failed. There are those who will remember her not only as the sparkling queen of a brilliant, vanished world, but also as a lady of great age, lying half paralysed in a huge empty house and saying with the heart-rending ghost of a gay smile: "We did have fun, didn't we?".'

George VI died in February 1952. On the day of the King's funeral, Mabell Airlie – then living in two cold and draughty rooms at Airlie Castle (the rest was shut up) and chopping her own firewood to keep warm – joined Queen Mary at Marlborough House. 'We sat alone at the window, looking out into the murk and gloom. As the cortège wound slowly along, the Queen whispered in a broken voice, "Here *he* is," and I knew that her dry eyes were seeing beyond the coffin a little boy in a sailor suit. She was past weeping, wrapped in the ineffable solitude of grief. I could not speak to comfort her. My tears choked me. The words I wanted to say would not come. We held each other's hands in silence.' One of the last letters Ettie received was from loyal John Gore marvelling that Tommy Lascelles had been twice at Sandringham for the death of a King. 'God bless you,' he ended. 'I think of you most days with affection & gratitude & admiration.'

Lord Moran had written a paragraph on death in his chilling masterpiece, *The Anatomy of Courage* – perhaps one of the passages that Ettie helped him to complete. 'Old people with slow thoughts pass beyond the doubts and fears and hesitations of their middle years into the silence of great age, and when at last death comes to them quietly they hardly know their friendly visitor. Arteries harden, blanching the seat of reason; men see life dimly as through a film, and find on the brink of dissolution the peace that passeth understanding.'

Ettie died at Panshanger on 28 May 1952, aged eighty-four, of cerebral thrombosis and cerebral arterio-sclerosis. To the end she was deliberate and eloquent. The date of her death was the thirty-seventh anniversary of the day that she had buried Julian in France. She never forgot her dead: her choices always were controlled: she did nothing by accident.

A Poetic Appendix

✍

JULIAN'S BEST-REMEMBERED poem was written in April 1915 two weeks before he was wounded and four weeks before he died. His nephew-by-marriage Nicholas Ravensdale has written wisely about it. 'It is almost unique among poems of the First World War in that it shows no outrage against war and yet its luminousness and serenity do not seem false. Because it is a poem about love of life in time of war, it was once loved much; later, when there was peace and life was again loved less, it was loved less too.'

'Into Battle'
BY JULIAN GRENFELL

The naked Earth is warm with Spring,
And with green grass and bursting trees
Leans to the Sun's gaze glorying,
And quivers in the sunny breeze;

And Life is Colour and Warmth and Light,
And striving evermore for these;
And he is dead who will not fight;
And who dies fighting has increase.

The fighting man shall from the sun
Take warmth, and life from the glowing earth;
Speed with the lightfoot winds to run,
And with the trees to newer birth;
And find when fighting shall be done,
Great rest, and fullness after dearth.

All the bright company of Heaven
Hold him in their high comradeship,
The Dog Star and the Sisters Seven,
Orion's Belt and sworded hip.

The woodland trees that stand together,
They stand to him each one a friend;
They gently speak in the windy weather;
They guide to valley and ridges' end.

The kestrel hovering by day,
And the little owls that call by night,
Bid him be swift and keen as they,
As keen of ear, as swift as sight.

The blackbird sings to him: 'Brother, brother,
If this be the last song you shall sing,
Sing well, for you may not sing another;
Brother, sing!'

In dreary, doubtful, waiting hours
Before the brazen frenzy starts,
The horses show him nobler powers;
O patient eyes, courageous hearts!

And when the burning moment breaks,
And all things else are out of mind,
And only Joy of Battle takes
Him by the throat and makes him blind,

Through joy and blindness he shall know,
Not caring much to know, that still
Nor lead nor steel shall reach him, so
That it be not the Destined Will.

The thundering line of battle stands,
And in the air Death moans and sings;
But Day shall clasp him with strong hands,
And Night shall fold him in soft wings.

Maurice Baring was primarily an elegiac poet, as he indicated by placing his proudly exultant elegy to Bron Lucas, 'In Memoriam, A.H.', on the opening pages of his *Selected Poems*. His sonnet to Julian Grenfell celebrates the adventurous courage of his dead friend, and eleven years later he commemorated Ivo with verses that rallied to Ettie's faith that her dead were gone away but not out of touch. These poems were iconic in their time.

'Julian Grenfell'
BY MAURICE BARING

Because of you we will be glad and gay,
Remembering you, we will be brave and strong;
And hail the advent of each dangerous day,
And meet the last adventure with a song.

And, as you proudly gave your jewelled gift,
We'll give our lesser offering with a smile,
Nor falter on that path where, all too swift,
You led the way and leapt the golden stile.

Whether new path, new heights to climb, you find,
Or gallop through the unfooted asphodel,
We know you know we shall not lag behind,
Nor halt to waste a moment on a fear;
And you will speed us onward with a cheer,
And wave beyond the stars that all is well.

'Ivo Grenfell'
BY MAURICE BARING

'What have they done to you, where have they taken you?
    Answer us, Ivo, my son.'
'I have sailed far away on a marvellous voyage,
    With Julian and Billy and Bron.'

'Shall there not come to us, news of you, word from you,
    Sign of you, Ivo, my son?'
'I am nearer to you than the closest of whispers,
    With Julian and Billy and Bron.'

'The autumn wind blows and the leaves are deserting us,
    Summer leaves, Ivo, my son.'
'The same wind came blowing in Springtide and Autumn,
    For Julian and Billy and Bron.'

'Breathe but a message to say all is well with you,
    Just a word, Ivo, my son.'
'Our word to you is: "Let God have His way with you":
    Ivo and Julian and Billy and Bron.'

Acknowledgements

CONVERSATIONS WITH ETTIE Desborough's two surviving grand-children, Lady Cazalet and Lord Gage, and with her former grandson-in-law Lord Ravensdale, have been the utmost pleasure. They are the chief begetters of this book, for although they bear no responsibility for its contents, their encouragement and enthusiasm have animated its research and writing. Regrettably the death of Ettie Desborough's eldest grandchild, Julian Salmond, in November 2006, during the early research of this book, prevented me from meeting him.

Among my other debts, I must first express my gratitude to Her Majesty Queen Elizabeth II for her gracious permission to quote from the diaries and correspondence of her grandmother Queen Mary and her father King George VI.

In response to my importunities, Mr Charles Gore found Ettie Desborough's letters to his father squirrelled away in his house, sent me copies and commented on those draft passages of the book that I sent him: he was unfailingly patient with the calls I made on his time, and shrewd and tactful in his advice. I am grateful to him and to his sister Elizabeth, Lady Cave for their permission to use material of which they hold the copyright.

Jenny Davenport, David Gelber, Philip Mansel and Christopher Phipps read parts of the penultimate draft of my manuscript, and made invaluable suggestions for its improvement. In Mr Gelber's case, I received ferociously attentive comments, which must have taken him many long days and ascetic nights to prepare, and which were of untellable help in honing my ideas and discarding superfluities.

For information or assistance I thank Mrs Ursula Aylmer; Patric Dickinson, Richmond Herald; Lord Egremont; Lady Selina Hastings;

Lord Monteagle; Lord Norwich; Peter Parker; Jane Ridley; the Marquess of Salisbury; Professor David Watkin, who showed me the Panshanger gates now at Peterhouse; and Professor Blair Worden, executor of the literary estate of Lord Dacre. Kristen Davis acted as my proxy researcher at the Harry Ransom Center, Peter Woolgar supplied me with illustrations from the photograph albums at Firle and Christopher Phipps has compiled a first-class index. My editor at Weidenfeld, Benjamin Buchan, and my agent at A.M. Heath, Bill Hamilton, were the most practical of helpmates and abettors.

During the summer of 2006 I often travelled to the endearing county town of Hertford, and worked on the great collection of Cowper and Desborough papers which are preserved in the Hertford Archives and Local Records Office there – partly as a result of the constructive aid of the Friends of National Libraries under their chairman Max Egremont and estimable treasurer Charles Sebag-Montefiore. The Hertford archivists were unfailingly helpful, good-humoured and painstaking: after thirty years' experience of county record offices, I cannot name a better one than that at Hertford. My productivity was doubled by their efficiency; and I marvelled at the staff's tact and versatility in dealing with other researchers in their holdings.

I am grateful to the custodians of the following repositories for access to the archives held in their care:

Birmingham University Library: papers of Sir Austen Chamberlain, and of Neville Chamberlain.

Bodleian Library, Oxford: papers of 1st Marquess of Lincolnshire, 6th Earl Winterton, 1st Earl of Oxford and Asquith, Sir William Harcourt and 1st Viscount Harcourt, 1st Viscount Milner, Baroness Asquith of Yarnbury (Lady Violet Bonham Carter) and H.A.L. Fisher.

British Library: papers of 1st Marquess of Ripon, 1st Earl of Balfour, 1st Viscount D'Abernon, 1st Baron Avebury, 1st Baron Riddell, Lady Battersea, Lady Ottoline Morrell, Sir Edward Hamilton, G.K. Chesterton and Lytton Strachey.

Cambridge University Library: papers of 1st Marquess of Crewe, 1st Earl Baldwin of Bewdley, 1st Viscount Templewood and Siegfried Sassoon.

Christ Church, Oxford: papers of Lord Dacre of Glanton.

Churchill College, Cambridge: papers of 1st Viscount Norwich, 1st

Viscount Chandos, Sir Winston Churchill, Leo Amery, Sir Alan Lascelles, Alfred Lyttelton and Reginald McKenna.

Eaton Hall, Cheshire: papers of Countess Grosvenor.

Fitzwilliam Museum, Cambridge: papers of Wilfrid Scawen Blunt.

Getty Research Institute Library, Los Angeles: Duveen papers.

Harry Ransom Center, University of Texas at Austin: papers of Lady Ottoline Morrell and diaries of Sir Hugh Walpole.

Harvard University Law Library: papers of Oliver Wendell Holmes.

Hatfield House, Hertfordshire: papers of Alice, Marchioness of Salisbury and of Lord Quickswood.

Hertford Archives and Local Records Office: papers of 7th Earl Cowper, Countess of Westmorland and of Lady Desborough.

House of Lords Record Office: papers of 5th Earl Cadogan and 18th Lord Willoughby de Broke.

Hull University Library: papers of Constance, Lady Wenlock.

India Office Library: papers of 1st Marquess Curzon of Kedleston.

Knebworth House, Hertfordshire: papers of 2nd Earl of Lytton.

Liddell Hart Centre, King's College, London: papers of Sir Ian and Lady Hamilton.

Liverpool Record Office: papers of 15th and 17th Earls of Derby.

National Archives: papers of 1st Earl Kitchener of Khartoum, 1st Earl of Midleton and of Ramsay MacDonald.

National Library of Scotland: papers of 5th Earl of Rosebery and 1st Viscount Haldane.

Nuffield College, Oxford: papers of 1st Viscount Cherwell.

Public Record Office of Northern Ireland: papers of 1st Marquess of Dufferin and Ava, of Theresa, Marchioness of Londonderry, of Edith, Marchioness of Londonderry and of 7th Marquess of Londonderry.

Reading University Library: papers of Viscountess Astor.

Royal Archives, Windsor: correspondence of King George VI, and letters and diaries of Queen Mary.

Somerset Record Office: the papers of Evelyn, Viscountess de Vesci and of Mary Herbert of Pixton.

Trinity College, Cambridge: papers of Edwin Montagu.

Sources

><

PROLOGUE

1 'Great love was wise' Edith Wharton, *Glimpses of the Moon* (1921), 340.

2 '*Vivre c'est survivre*' Brian Masters, 'Lady Desborough', *Great Hostesses* (1982), 15; Lord Egremont, 'Lady Desborough', in Peter Quennell (ed.), *Genius in the Drawing Room* (1980), 117–28.

2 'As there are no longer' Viscountess Milner, *My Picture Gallery* (1951), 218.

3 'It is easy to name' Lord David Cecil, *The Times*, 3 June 1952.

4 'Her interests are multitudinous' John Buchan, *The Gap in the Curtain* (1932), 13.

5 'They do indeed have tragedy' Diary of Lord Winterton, 9 October 1926, Bodleian, Winterton 34.

5 'These two brothers were' *Balliol College War Memorial Book 1914–1919* (1924), 197–201.

6 'Olympians and their lives' Lady Ottoline Morrell, *Ottoline at Garsington* (1974), 159.

6 'I've been so low' ED to Charley Londonderry, 12 April 1921, PRONI D3099/2/6/79.

7 ' "O Thou, my necessity" ' ED to Alice Salisbury, 25 January 1944, Salisbury papers, Hatfield.

7 'I feel often like a dead' ED to Charley Londonderry, 29 May 1917, PRONI D3099/2/6/2.

7 'Lady Desborough was the' Margot Asquith, *Autobiography*, I (1920), 188.

CHAPTER 1: *The Orphan*

9 'I was not quite three' ED, *Eyes of Youth* (1943), 7.

10 'Know him? Why I'm' Robert Lytton, *Julian Fane* (1871), 144–5.

10 'Continental Holland House' Lytton, *Fane*, 11.

10 'the most graceful accomplished gentleman' Lytton, *Fane*, 3.

10 'The central idol of his heart' Lytton, *Fane*, 271.

11 'There was a girl' notes prepared for Robert Lytton by Lady West-morland, D/EFa/F21.

11 'You will be glad' Julian Fane to Lady Westmorland, 30 September 1866, D/EFa/C54/70.

11 'delighted in literary pursuits' notes by Lady Westmorland, D/EFa/F21.

12 'The baby really is' Julian Fane to Lady Westmorland, 23 August 1867, D/EFa/C55/3.

12 'Ethel was vaccinated yesterday' Julian Fane to Lady Westmorland, 1 October 1867, D/EFa/C55/2.

12 'The old feudal feeling' Lady Rose Weigall, 'Our Friends in the Village', *Macmillan's Magazine*, XX (1869), 526.

13 'Ethel was dreadfully unhappy' Julian Fane to Lady Westmorland, 19 July 1868, D/EFa/C56/25.

13 'loath to let Mrs Wake' Julian Fane to Lady Westmorland, 25 July 1868, D/EFa/C56/14.

13 'Altho' Ethel's adoration of Nanny' Julian Fane to Lady Westmorland, nd, D/EFa/C56.

13 'Ettie is washed in sea-water' Julian Fane to Lady Westmorland, 25 September 1868, D/EFa/C56/3.

13 'days of anguish unspeakable' Lady Westmorland's notes, D/EFa/F21.

13 'Only two years and a bit' *Eyes of Youth*, 13.

14 'The girl, it seems' Princess Mary, Duchess of Teck, to Duchess of Cambridge, 5 November 1868, D/EFa/C84.

14 'joyous and amiable, pretty and attractive' Julian Fane to Lady West-morland, 10 November 1868.

14 'Ettie sometimes startles me' Julian Fane to Lady Westmorland, 9 January 1869, D/EFa/C58/16.

14 'I used to put my ear' Lady Westmorland notes, D/EFa/F21.

15 'Our parents had been' *Eyes of Youth*, 16.

16 'We loved Grandmama very, very dearly' *Eyes of Youth*, 29, 32.

16 'Nannie was the *clou*' *Eyes of Youth*, 34.

17 'Best of all London fun' *Eyes of Youth*, 33.

18 'the great *train-de-vie*' *Eyes of Youth*, 17.

18 'A very good talker' Countess Cowper, *Earl Cowper K.G.* (1913), 74–5, 386–7.

18 'Goodness, right-mindedness, reverence, honour' *Earl Cowper K.G.*, 77.

19 'Looking back, I seem' *Eyes of Youth*, 18.

19 'all the inherent scepticism' EG to Oliver Wendell Holmes, 7 November 1891.

19 'As the years went on' *Eyes of Youth*, 19.

20 '*Push* in any shape' *Earl Cowper K.G.*, 76.

20 'great beanos of our childhood' *Eyes of Youth*, 20–1.

20 'When I was a very little girl' *Earl Cowper K.G.*, 720.

20 'An Old Whig, Brooks's' 'The Position and Prosperity of the Whig Party', *The Times*, 10 May 1866; 'Desultory Reflections of Old Whig', *Nineteenth Century*, XIII (1883), 729–39.

20 'The "Tap-Root" of Revolution' *The Times*, 9 July 1895.

21 '*Such* a gentleman! . . . so beautiful!' *Earl Cowper K.G.*, 713.

21 'I was completely devoted' *Eyes of Youth*, 16–17.

22 'Wrest was a Paradise' *Eyes of Youth*, 25–6; *Country Life*, 9 July 1904, 54, 56, 63.

22 'the ideally lovely house' *Eyes of Youth*, 26–7.

23 'Looking back to our life' *Eyes of Youth*, 22–3.

23 'I was a sharp little child' *Eyes of Youth*, 35.

23 'what a thrill & reverence' EG to Oliver Wendell Holmes, Easter Sunday 1893.

23 'Bessie Eales was only eighteen' *Eyes of Youth*, 36.

24 'good, upright, plain and dull' *Eyes of Youth*, 37.

24 'desperately forlorn' *Eyes of Youth*, 38.

24 'He seems to me' Dolly Herbert to Henry Cowper, 31 December 1875, DERV 1290/3.

24 'Dordor was my anchor' *Eyes of Youth*, 39.

25 'very kind to me' *Eyes of Youth*, 40–1.

25 'Her heart went out' Lord Esher, *Cloud-Capp'd Towers* (1927), 131–2.

25 'strange apparition' *Eyes of Youth*, 41.

25 'a slippery Jewish pedlar' *Earl Cowper K.G.*, 235.

26 'the very nicest kind' *Eyes of Youth*, 42–3.

26 'the most true and unselfish character' *Eyes of Youth*, 46.

26 'we even cheered up' *Eyes of Youth*, 47.

27 'Pammy never recovered consciousness' *Eyes of Youth*, 48.

27 'It was at Panshanger' *Eyes of Youth*, 49.

27 'It was wound round my heart' *Eyes of Youth*, 50.

28 'he was not . . . good-looking' *Earl Cowper K.G.*, 650.

29 'a great deal my fault' *Eyes of Youth*, 52.

29 'very free undisciplined childhood' Constance Wenlock to Adolphus Liddell, 15 February 1892, Wenlock papers DDFA3/5/4.

29 '*Dear* Mum, *dear* Mum' Dolly Herbert to Henry Cowper, 10 April 1882, DERV C1290/17.

29 'nothing but usual healthy living' Dolly Herbert to Henry Cowper, 4 October 1882, DERV C1290/22.

29 'dignity of her stance' Sir Harold Nicolson, 'Marginal Comment', *Spectator*, 6 June 1952, 742.

29 'Tell Ettie that you think' Dolly Herbert to Henry Cowper, 2 November 1882, DERV C1290/23.

30 'The long afternoon under the trees' *Eyes of Youth*, 54–5.

30 'My dear, it came on me' Lady Alice Gore to EF, 30 November 1884, DERV C428/6.

31 'morbid self-abandonment to public gaze' Countess Cowper, 'The Decline of Reserve among Women', *Nineteenth Century*, XXVII (1890), 65–7.

32 'such a roaring success' Lady Mabell Gore to EF, 8 & 14 April 1885, DERV C1981/9 & 18.

32 'Oh! my darling *how*' Lady Alice Gore to EF, 31 July 1886, DERV C428/22.

32 'My darling I love you' Lady Mabell Gore to EF, September 1885, DERV C1981/24.

33 'a great joy & interest' Betty Ponsonby to EF, 1 August 1886, DERV C1886/15.

33 'not like an everyday girl' Lady Mabell Gore to EF, nd, DERV C1981/11.

33 'A woman's only hope' Mabell, Countess of Airlie, *Thatched with Gold* (1962), 40.

34 'A lot of people came' Diary of EF, 1 & 2 November 1885, DERV F31/1.

34 'one feels so flat' EF to Lady Alice Gore, 7 November 1885, Salisbury papers.

34 'more stolid than ever' Alan Charteris to EG, 7 February 1890, DERV C464/11.

34 'the absolutely finest man' EG to Willie Grenfell, *c.* 1887, DERV C1070/4.

35 'there have been four' Willie Grenfell to Sir William Harcourt, 27 May 1886, Harcourt ms 215/110.

35 'One's honeymoon is chiefly passed' Mabell Airlie to EF, 29 January 1886, DERV C1981/25.

36 'blackness & gloom' . . . 'personal fogs and mists' Dolly Herbert to Henry Cowper, D/EFa/C20, D/EFa/C23.

36 'It does one's heart' Dolly Herbert to EF, 7 March 1886, DERV C1291/3.

36 'nothing but pain and grief' EF to Lady Alice Gore, nd [1886], Salisbury papers.

36 'we had been waiting' Clair Herbert to EF, May 1886, DERV C1289/3.

36 'First and foremost about W.G' Mabell Airlie to EF, 6 March 1886, DERV C1981/26.

36 'rather mad and odd' EF to Lady Alice Gore, 24 August 1886, Salisbury papers.

37 'Must I go on waiting' Betty Ponsonby to EF, August 1886, DERV C1886/18.

37 'I am so *awfully* glad' Lady Alice Gore to EF, 20 November 1886, DERV C428/28.

37 'I meant to try' Willie Grenfell to EF, 7 & 9 December 1886, DERV C1159/4 & 5.

37 'I do like him' EF to Lady Alice Gore, Southwood, Sunday, Salisbury papers.

37 'I cannot tell you' EF to Lady Alice Gore, 8 December 1886, Salisbury papers.

37 'Oh! my darling little Puppy' Lady Alice Gore to EF, 9 December 1886, DERV C428/29.

37 'I think so of the old' Mabell Airlie to ED, 13 January 1945, DERV C1891/78.

CHAPTER 2: *The Soul*

38 'won a lot at first' EG to Henry Cowper, 15 March 1887, DERV C1068/1.

38 'It is quite *delightful*' Betty Ponsonby to EG, 28 March 1887, DERV C1886/1.

39 'the light of his life' *Earl Cowper K.G.*, 651.

39 'too terribly sad' EG to Evelyn de Vesci, 16 or 23 November 1887, de Vesci papers DD/DRU/103.

39 'with Cowper lassitude' EG to Oliver Wendell Holmes, Easter Sunday 1893.

40 'so strongly old happy days' EG to Oliver Wendell Holmes, 5 January 1889.

40 'adored . . . like a daughter' *Earl Cowper K.G.*, 708.

40 'intolerably dreary with only two' Lord Cowper to EG, 3 January 1890, DERV C599/3.

42 'talked the whole way' Diary of Lord Milner, 24 November 1898, Bodleian Library.

42 'Between us all, under AJB' Lord Midleton to ED, 21 January 1929, DERV C299/51; Earl of Midleton, *Records and Reactions* (1939), 50–1.

43 'Lady Pembroke is the rough sketch' EG to Oliver Wendell Holmes, 9 August 1894.

43 'Reggie Lister was an artist' Maurice Baring, *The Puppet Show of Memory* (1922), 188, 190.

44 'They shot, and ate' *Earl Cowper K.G.*, 645–6.

44 'You were much missed' Jane Ridley and Clayre Percy (eds.), *The Letters of Arthur Balfour and Lady Elcho 1885–1917* (1992), 77–8.

44 'political bosses of the Midlands' Guy Wyndham, *Letters of George Wyndham*, I (1915), 401.

45 'a big, rather unwieldy man' Adolphus Liddell, *Notes from the Life of an Ordinary Mortal* (1911), 197.

45 'Oh, blooming rot' Frances Horner, *Time Remembered* (1933), 160; Viscountess Milner, *My Picture Gallery* (1951), 42.

45 'He was very attractive' Wilfrid Scawen Blunt, Secret Memoirs XVII, 4 May 1895.

45 'my prop & stay' Lord Pembroke to Lady Wenlock, 31 May 1892, Wenlock papers DDFA3/5/6.

45 '*really gossipy* & tiresome' EG to Lady Wenlock, 9 June 1892, Wenlock papers DDFA3/5/13.

45 'the strangest woman' EG to Oliver Wendell Holmes, 9 August 1894.

45 'The host & hostess' Diary of Sir Edward Hamilton, 18 November 1888, Add ms 48649.

46 'lost her wonderful beauty' Wilfrid Scawen Blunt, Secret Memoirs XIII, 31 October 1889.

46 'Are you a happy little couple' Sarah Bailey, *The Letters of Sybil Cust* (1939), 101.

46 'Poor little Adelaide' Lord Pembroke to Lady Wenlock, 14 February 1888, Wenlock papers DDFA3/5/6.

46 'protest against the Prince' Wilfrid Scawen Blunt, Secret Memoirs XVII, 4 May 1895; cf Secret Memoirs XIV, 2 June 1891.

46 'vulgar to the core' Lady de Grey to EG, 31 December 1890, DERV C2202/2.

46 'the stiff drawing room' Betty Ponsonby to EF, 2 October 1887, DERV C1886/68.

47 'This is not a comfortable house' Willie Grenfell to EG, 13–15 December 1887, DERV C1159/26, 28 & 29.

47 'A circle of exceptionally open-minded people' Viscount D'Abernon, *Portraits and Appreciations* (1931), 40, 92–3, 94–5.

47 'You all sit and talk' ED, *Flotsam and Jetsam* (1949), 38.

47 'some very funny things' Lord Suffield, *My Memoirs 1830–1913* (1913), 322.

47 'Analysis of character' Countess Cowper, 'Decline of Reserve', 66–7.

48 'the Gossiping Souls' Hugo Elcho to Evelyn de Vesci, nd, de Vesci papers DD/DRU/90.

48 'the Souls were no longer' Frances Horner to ED, 21 January 1929, DERV C1346/17.

48 'Don't you agree with me' Lady Cynthia Charteris, *Haply I may remember* (1950), 14.

48 'Games are good things' ED, *Flotsam and Jetsam*, 23.

49 'What vegetable does this person' Angela Lambert, *Unquiet Souls* (1984), 93.

49 'I liked my evening' Doll Liddell to Lady Wenlock, 16 December 1888, DDFA3/5/3.

49 'very charming and specious' Doll Liddell to Lady Wenlock, 10 December 1892, DDFA3/5/3.

49 'too noisy and painted' Wilfrid Scawen Blunt, Secret Memoirs XVI, 29 July 1894.

49 'This is a regular Sunday' Liddell to Lady Wenlock, 2 July 1893, Wenlock papers DDFA3/5/3.

50 'primary article of creed' diary of Sir Edward Hamilton, 27 July1889, Add ms 48651.

50 'Balfour was their High Priest' Wilfrid Scawen Blunt, Secret Memoirs XIV, 2 June 1891.

50 'He allowed the talk' Winston Churchill, *Great Contemporaries* (1937), 241.

51 'The trouble with A.J.B' Earl Winterton, *Orders of the Day* (1953), 3.

51 'with *intense* admiration' EG to Oliver Wendell Holmes, 8 March 1895.

52 'Ettie's energy is indeed prodigious' Ridley and Percy, *Balfour Elcho Letters*, 92.

52 'horror of that little brute' EG to Arthur Balfour, 18 September 1892, DERV C1085/23.

52 '*Oh*, such a poisonous railway-journey' EG to Arthur Balfour, 10 January 1892, DERV C1085/20.

53 'I *think* I should mind' Countess of Oxford, *Off the Record* (1943), 52.

53 'I have so little self-control' Margot Tennant to EG, April 1890, DERV C71/7.

54 'rather a remnant of a man' EG to Arthur Balfour, 18 September 1892, DERV C1085/23.

54 'Mary E is too wonderful' EG to Lady Wenlock, 8 December 1892, Wenlock papers DDFA3/5/13.

54 'She loves and honours' Wilfrid Scawen Blunt, Secret Memoirs XVII, 24 January 1895.

55 'Mary is very beautiful' Wilfrid Scawen Blunt, Secret Memoirs XVII, 9 January 1895.

55 'Eve's curse' Mary Elcho to Evelyn de Vesci, 10 June 1901, DD/DRU/87, de Vesci papers.

55 'You have the wonderful gift' Mary Elcho to ED, 27 October 1910, DERV C477/25.

55 'Ettie seems too wonderful' Constance Wenlock to Doll Liddell, January 1892, DERV C1550/1 and 15 February 1892, DERV C1550/2.

56 'did not believe when he left' Sir Osbert Sitwell, 'Lady Desborough', *The Times*, 9 June 1952.

56 'Everyone is so devoted' Lady de Grey to EG, 19 November 1894, DERV C2202/2.

56 'so vivid, so vital' EG to Oliver Wendell Holmes, 11 August 1901.

56 'You know the terrible indolence' EG to Oliver Wendell Holmes, 7 May 1892.

56 'I have been playing very very hard' EG to Oliver Wendell Holmes, 27 June 1892.

56 'living surrounded by clever people' John Baring to EG, 1 December 1892, DERV C157/26.

57 'majestic virility' D'Abernon, *Portraits and Appreciations*, 26.

57 'I remember kissing you' Nicholas Mosley, *Julian Grenfell* (1976), 52.

57 'For a whole night' David Gilmour, *Curzon* (1994), 224.

57 'the decadence of our circle' Allan Nevins, *Harry White* (1930), 82–3.

58 'Why not a little dinner?' Merlin Holland and Sir Rupert Hart-Davis (eds.), *The Complete Letters of Oscar Wilde* (2), 477.

58 'queer kind of literary acrobat' EG to Oliver Wendell Holmes, Easter Sunday 1893.

58 'I love his steadfast' Alfred Lyttelton to EG, 23 May 1891, DERV C1661/8.

59 'the most beautiful place' EG to Henry Asquith, 2 October 1892, Bodleian ms Eng c 6715.

59 'There are only half a dozen' Henry Asquith to EG, 12 February 1893, DERV C72/17.

59 'The *great* event of course' EG to Albert Grey, May 1894, DERV C1090/1.

60 'Oscar and Mrs Grenfell' Wilfrid Scawen Blunt, Secret Memoirs XVI, 17 July 1894.

60 'Our talk on Sunday' Henry Asquith to EG, 9 August 1898, DERV C72/19.

CHAPTER 3: *The Flirt*

61 'It is fear, I think' Frances Horner, *Time Remembered*, 164.

62 'wickedness of married flirtations' Wilfrid Scawen Blunt, Secret Memoirs XIV, 18 October 1890.

62 'the doctrine of the "Souls" ' Wilfrid Scawen Blunt, Secret Memoirs XIV, 31 August 1891.

63 'an original and pretty little woman' Wilfrid Scawen Blunt, Secret Memoirs XIII, 14 September 1890, and Secret Memoirs, XIV, 6 October 1890; diary of Lady Hamilton, 18 October 1903.

63 'miserable' Doll Liddell to Lady Wenlock, 20 November 1887, Wenlock papers DDFA3/5/3.

63 'There is more resemblance' Lady Wenlock to Doll Liddell, 4 April 1892, Wenlock papers DDFA3/5/4.

64 'common in modern life' Doll Liddell to Lady Wenlock, 5 December 1887, DDFA3/5/3.

65 'I miss my darling Gent' EG to Willie Grenfell, 17 January 1892, DERV C1070/6.

65 'they deal with the great questions' EG to Oliver Wendell Holmes, 23 October 1889.

65 'Through our great good fortune' Oliver Wendell Holmes, Speeches (1891), 11.

66 'One's belief in a meaning' EG to Oliver Wendell Holmes, 21 February 1891.

66 'One of the most attractive' Lady Battersea, Reminiscences (1922), 205.

66 'vivid sense of fun' Lord Esher, Cloud-Capp'd Towers, 37, 44.

67 'at present shedding a halo' Albert Grey to EG, 6 January 1889, DERV C1175/2.

67 'I am absorbed in Schopenhauer' EG to Asquith, 2 October 1892, Bodleian ms Eng c 6715.

67 'I take so deep an interest' Albert Grey to EG, Friday 10 [Aug 1889?], DERV C1157/7.

67 'There is no-one whose friendship' Albert Grey to EG, 28 July 1891, DERV C1175/33.

67 'hateful and lying insinuations' Albert Grey to EG, 11 September 1892, DERV C1175/39.

68 'have just been paying' EG to Albert Grey, 11 February 1899, DERV C1090/3.

68 'greedy and impecunious soul' ED to Albert Grey, 14 February [1905–6?], DERV C1090/14.

68 'in complete consciousness & happiness' ED to Evelyn de Vesci, 30 August 1917, DD/DRU/103, de Vesci papers.

68 'not to mention that' Violet Granby to EG, 31 October 1890, DERV C1764/2, 31 October 1890.

69 'I would have gone to her' Margot Asquith, Autobiography, I (1920), 189.

69 'Her Grace seems to be kicking' ED to MG, 2 & 16 December 1918, DERV C1078/238 & 241.

69 'a sort of sexual warfare' Lord Pembroke to EG, 7 January 1891, DERV C1293/11.

69 'I grudge you to that crowd' Albert Grey to EG, 11 September 1890, DERV C1175/27.

70 'The fight is about to begin' Evan Charteris to Lady Wenlock, 20 April 1891, DDFA3/5/9.

70 'Mrs Grenfell you are a very clever' Lord Dunraven and Mountearl to EG, 17 February 1892, DERV C2135/26.

71 'I do love them all' EG to Lady Wenlock, 20 October 1892, Wenlock papers DDFA3/5/13.

71 'I want to thank you' ED to Lady de Vesci, 1912, Herbert papers DD/DRU/103.

71 'I get quite low' Lord Elcho to EG, 6 May 1889, DERV C474/3.

71 'Why do I not like you' Lord Elcho to EG, 7 December 1890, DERV C474/5.

72 'dismal & stale after three months' EG to Oliver Wendell Holmes, 29 July 1891.

72 'Were you tired at the end' Alfred Lyttelton to EG, 28 September 1891, DERV C1661/9.

72 'It did indeed tug' Betty Ponsonby to EG, nd, DERV C1886/147.

73 'ice-bound apathy and lethargy' EG to Oliver Wendell Holmes, 7 November 1891.

73 'It was all so wretched' EG to Lady Wenlock, 24 November 1892, Wenlock papers DDFA3/5/13.

73 'The first few days' EG to Alfred Lyttelton, 12 February 1892, CHAN 92/7.

73 'This glowing rich-coloured life' EG to Oliver Wendell Holmes, 8 January 1892.

74 'No words in any language' EG to Lady Wenlock, 12 February 1892, Wenlock papers DDFA3/5/13.

74 'stiff dull & solemn' EG to Lady Wenlock, 12 February 1892, Wenlock papers DDFA3/5/13.

74 'a lasting glow for ever' EG to Lady Wenlock, 11 March 1892, Wenlock papers DDFA3/5/13.

74 'I have got such a dull' EG to Lady Wenlock, nd, Wenlock papers DDFA3/5/13.

74 'her summer reign with less zest' Evan Charteris to Lady Wenlock, nd [spring 1892], Wenlock papers DDFA3/5/9.

75 'I saw S twice' EG to Lady Wenlock, 6 April 1892, DDFA/3/5/13.

75 'so pinched & restricted' EG to Oliver Wendell Holmes, 7 May 1892.

75 'great grace, beauty and gentleness' Evan Charteris to Lady Wenlock, nd [1892], Wenlock papers DDFA3/5/9.

76 'There, you felt, as you saw him' Osbert Sitwell, *The Times*, 27 November 1940, 7f.

76 'as I know you will see' Evan Charteris to EG, nd, DERV C467/30.

76 'My meetings with her' Evan Charteris to EG, nd, DERV C467/29.

76 'My relations with her' Evan Charteris to EG, 27 November 1894, DERV C467/90.

76 'despair' . . . 'a source of all things' Evan Charteris to EG, [March 1899], DERV C467/5.

76 'I *implore* you to ask' Evan Charteris to EG, nd, DERV C467/72.

77 'The love you wish for' Evan Charteris to EG, nd, D/ERV C467/97.

77 'There's but the one view' Evan Charteris to Lady Wenlock, nd, Wenlock papers DDFA3/5/9.

77 'perfect' . . . 'dear best self' EG to Lady Wenlock, 6 April 1892, Wenlock papers DDFA3/5/9.

77 'deeply touched' Lady Wemyss to EG, 12 December 1895, DERV C465/2.

78 'Nothing is more like itself' D'Abernon, *Portraits and Appreciations*, 14–15.

78 'I had such a heavenly blessed let:' John Baring to EG, nd [summer 1891?], DERV C157/1.

79 'enthralled interest in human beings' Lady Cynthia Asquith, *Remember and Be Glad* (1952), 51.

79 'Lately I have been' EG to Lady Wenlock, 19 November 1892, Wenlock papers DDFA/3/5/13.

80 'dear John' 'The King and the late Lord Revelstoke', *The Times*, 23 April 1929, 9c.

80 'Lord Revelstoke is in Paris' Philip Ziegler, *The Sixth Great Power* (1988), 269.

80 'almost certainly sexual' Nicholas Mosley, *Julian Grenfell* (1976), 44.

80 'much more than parade' Ziegler, *Sixth Great Power*, 270.

80 'nice & peaceable' Michael and Eleanor Brock (eds.), *H.H. Asquith: Letters to Venetia Stanley* (1982), 592.

81 'sex snobbery' Richard Davenport-Hines, *Auden* (1995), 60.

81 'I went to Ascot' Sir Maurice Baring, *The Puppet Show of Memory* (1922), 167–8.

81 'you write *far* the best letters' Maurice Baring to EG, Thursday September 1896, DERV C160/4.

81 'I have been writing letters' Maurice Baring to EG, 9 February 1901, DERV C160/16.

81 'I am utterly miserable' Maurice Baring to ED, 29 January 1912, DERV C160/31.

82 'strangely impelled to recall' Ivor Guest to EG, 12 July 1897, DERV C1196/3.

82 'You escape me like' Ivor Guest to EG, 29 December 1897, DERV C1196/8.

83 'component elements of a bore' Evan Charteris to Constance Wenlock, nd, Wenlock papers DDFA3/5/9.

83 'He hankers for a *grande passion*' Wilfrid Scawen Blunt, Secret Memoirs XV, 30 August 1892.

83 'I shan't forget a single word' George Wyndham to EG, 25 September 1892, DERV C2800/3.

83 'Lying awake last night' George Wyndham to EG, 14 April 1893, DERV C2800/27.

84 'George tells me that' Wilfrid Scawen Blunt, Secret Memoirs XV, 9 May 1893.

84 'Holy, Holy, Holy' George Wyndham to EG, 11 May 1893, DERV C2800/32.

84 'delicious' . . . 'wicked Harry' EG to Lady Wenlock, 8 December 1892, Wenlock papers, DDFA3/5/13.

85 'I am fighting . . . worldliness' George Wyndham to EG, 27 September 1893, DERV C2800/38; see also diary of Lewis Harcourt, 14, 15 & 19 September 1893, Harcourt ms 395; and Wilfrid Scawen Blunt, Secret Memoirs XVI, 16 October 1893.

85 'How constantly in my trouble' George Wyndham to EG, 19 September 1893, DERV C2800/37.

86 'The hideous scandals connected with Harry' Wilfrid Scawen Blunt, Secret Memoirs XVI, 27 June 1894.

86 'Whenever one looks at her' Maurice Baring to EG, 16 December 1898, DERV C160/15.

86 'a kind of triumphant sun-ray' Margot Tennant to EG, nd, DERV C71/11.

86 'socially there is nothing like you' Ivor Guest to EG, 29 December 1897, DERV C1196/8.

CHAPTER 4: *The Mother*

87 'one of finest residences' *Maidenhead Times*, 9 November 1895.

88 'sumptuous surroundings' . . . 'too magnificent' Valentine Castlerosse to ED, 14 January 1912, DERV C309/1.

89 'The brutes, it make one *cry*' EF to Lady Alice Gore, 14 January 1888, Salisbury papers.

89 'The burglary at Taplow' *Daily Telegraph*, 16 January 1888; *Maidenhead Advertiser*, 18 January 1888.

90 'How sad for you to lose' Betty Ponsonby to EG, [mid-January 1888], DERV C1886/127.

90 'At the head of the table' *Maidenhead Advertiser*, 9 August 1911.

91 'I don't belong to the shrieking sisterhood' EG to Oliver Wendell Holmes, 27 December 1895.

92 'No appeal . . . ever turned down' *Maidenhead Advertiser*, 13 October 1926.

92 'I am more than thankfull' Mary Ann Collins to ED, 23 May 1911, DERV C554/1.

93 '*excellent*, & (strange to say!) economical' EG to Winston Churchill, 30 August 1908, CHAR 1/74.

93 'steam-pressure of . . . seething London' EG to Oliver Wendell Holmes, Easter Sunday 1893.

93 'with a view that stretches the soul' EG to Oliver Wendell Holmes, 10 April 1904.

93 'It was rather a nice Ascot' Lord Pembroke to Edith Balfour, 26 June 1889, CHAN 5/18.

93 'wild racket' . . . '24 in the house' EG to Oliver Wendell Holmes, 24 June 1894.

94 'You have never been more brilliant' Sir Edgar Vincent to EG, nd, DERV C2630/2.

94 'the Roman Matron' George Macaulay Trevelyan to ED, 25 September 1939, DERV C2586/1.

94 'I am such a bereaved Catts' EG to Willie Grenfell, 14 January 1892, DERV C1070/9.

94 'It is all because I have no children' Wilfrid Scawen Blunt, Secret Memoirs XV, 12 October 1892.

94 'I am very well & very pleased' EG to Oliver Wendell Holmes, 14 April 1890.

95 'to hold up a corner of the curtain' Albert Grey to EG, 11 September 1892, DERV C1175/39.

95 'seeing you quite banished' Elizabeth Castlerosse to EG, 18 May 1891, DERV C307/2.

95 'awful things' Mollie Compton to EG, 5 August 1891, DERV C1877/1.

96 'My *poor* darling, I can guess' EG to Margot Asquith, 21 August 1900, Bodleian ms Eng c 6676.

96 'Margot my very darling' EG to Margot Asquith, nd [1900], Bodleian Mss Eng c 6676.

96 'I have been so very full' EG to Evelyn de Vesci, 11 December 1890, DD/DRU/103.

97 'I do love to think of you' Alfred Lyttelton to EG, 31 May 1904, DERV C1661/4.

97 'Dear boys' ED, *Pages from a Family Journal* (1916), 91.

98 'In those days long before motor-cars' *Family Journal*, 3.

98 'My eldest son was five years old' EG to Oliver Wendell Holmes, Easter Sunday 1893.

98 'my dear boys with their straight sunny eyes' EG to Oliver Wendell Holmes, 24 April 1894.

98 'Not quite sane' EG to Oliver Wendell Holmes, 4 October 1902.

99 'the funny rough place' EG to Lady de Vesci, 24 May 1891, DD/DRU/103.

99 'love, self-sacrifice and unhappiness' Lady de Vesci to EG, 10 January 1893, DERV C2623/6.

99 'temper & cold rage' Lady Amabel Kerr to EG, 14 January 1893, DERV C1475/13.

99 'It breaks one's very heart' EG to Lady de Vesci, 21 January 1893, DD/DRU/103.

100 'This is the day' King James's Bible, psalm 118, verse 24.

100 'Her courage is a career' Evan Charteris to EG, 27 November 1894, DERV C467/90.

100 'joy cure' Mary Curzon to Jennie Churchill, 18 May 1903, CHAR 28/78.

100 'tact and sweetness' Lady Portsmouth to EG, 24 March 1901, DERV C2659/1.

100 'the joy-of-life' John Jolliffe (ed.), *The Letters of Raymond Asquith* (1980), 60.

101 'You have filled a place' Lord Lucas to ED, 28 July [ny], DERV C1284/15.

101 'I don't believe I am *ever* going' EG to Lady Wenlock, 24 November 1892, Wenlock papers DDFA3/5/13.

101 'a girl-baby' EG to Oliver Wendell Holmes, 19 August 1893.

101 'I doubt if the children' ED to Lord Londonderry, 4 September 1926, Londonderry papers, PRONI D3099/2/6/18.

102 'You are by nature' Albert Grey to EG, 29 September 1889, DERV C1175/10.

102 'a huff' diary of E.W. Hamilton, 27 March 1890, Add ms 48652.

102 'Royal stronghold of Toryism' diary of E.W. Hamilton, 4 April 1890, Add ms 48652.

102 'It was very clever' Willie Grenfell to EG, 30 March 1890, DERV C1159/48.

102 'Windsor certainly was a great nuisance' EG to Lewis Harcourt, 7 April 1890, Harcourt ms 452/170.

102 'Darling, I cannot possibly tell you' EG to Lady Wenlock, 9 June 1892, DDFA/3/5/13.

103 'This is a very corrupt place' Willie Grenfell to Sir William Harcourt, 6 July 1892, Harcourt ms 220/51.

103 'two Gold Bugs' Willie Grenfell to Lewis Harcourt, 16 October 1892, Harcourt ms 166/122.

104 'He would not consent' diary of E.W. Hamilton, 3 August 1893, Add ms 48661; 'Mr W.H. Grenfell and the Government', *The Times*, 3 August 1893, 4e.

104 'very much in the dumps' Sir Algernon West, *Private Diaries* (1922), 189.

105 'We are having such a *very* happy time' EG to Arthur Balfour, 2 September 1894, DERV C1085/27.

105 'There is the peace' EG to Oliver Wendell Holmes, 28 September 1894.

106 'over again with renewed love' EG to Oliver Wendell Holmes, 11 November 1892.

106 'I can't tell you the joy' EG to Oliver Wendell Holmes, 27 December 1895.

107 'an ideal play-fellow' *Family Journal*, 33.

107 'It is the most beautiful wild country' EG to Arthur Balfour, 29 September 1896, DERV C1085/32.

108 'How *can* people ever go' ED to WD, 25 August 1911, DERV C1070/79.

108 'it seems to pull' ED to MS, 30 April 1936, DERV C1078/1099.

109 'Leaving home was always a very great trouble' *Family Journal*, 47.

109 'It was an *awful* time' EG to Balfour, 14 September 1898, DERV C1085/22.

109 'Nobody who wasn't so brave' Maurice Baring to EG, 20 September 1898, D/ERV C160/14.

109 'snobbish element without the excuse' conversation with Ursula Aylmer, 23 April 2007.

110 'What an *inexplicable* thing' Alice Cranborne to EG, 16 September 1898, DERV C428/8.

110 'Mrs Grenfell had evidently thought' Flora Howard to George Russell, 10 June 1915, DERV C1366/1.

110 'What a grim game' EG to Oliver Wendell Holmes, 17 November 1899.

110 'Everyone seems to be ill' EG to Oliver Wendell Holmes, 17 December 1899.

111 'It was easy to see' Lord Desborough, 'Lord Kitchener as I knew him', 4.

113 'I'm not the youngest' *Family Journal*, 79.

113 'I wonder which one will go' *Earl Cowper K.G.*, 712.

114 'It is beyond words' EG to Balfour, 19 July 1905, DERV C1085/56.

114 'Am I dying?' *Earl Cowper K.G.*, 717.

114 'He lay as if asleep' EG to Monica Grenfell, 20 July 1905, DERV C1078/12.

115 'If you thought he could' EG to AJB, 8 October 1903, DERV C1085/18.

115 *'wretched'* ED to Oliver Wendell Holmes, 26 January 1907.

116 'Mrs Willie Grenfell and Mrs Lindsay' Norman and Jeanne MacKenzie (eds.), *The Diary of Beatrice Webb*, III (1984), 11–12.

116 'You can imagine how thrilled' EG to Balfour, 19 November 1905, DERV C1085/53.

116 'a bewildering 30 hours' EG to Sir Arthur Godley, 10 December 1905, DERV C1085/55.

117 'I rather hate leaving' EG to Albert Grey, 28 December 1905, DERV C1090/10.

117 'the de Greys, Soveral' Max Beerbohm, *Letters to Reggie Turner* (1964), 164–5.

117 'marvellously cute & adroit' EG to Oliver Wendell Holmes, 7 June 1901.

117 'Arthur Balfour sat opposite' diary of Lady Hamilton, 14 March 1906.

118 'Dear, generous & powerful friend' Edmund Gosse to EG, 6 February 1904, DERV C1006/2.

118 'I should die rather' Archie Gordon to Violet Asquith, 30 April 1906, Bodleian, Bonham Carter, 133.

118 'He came in suddenly' *Family Journal*, 649–50.

119 'vehement discussions' . . . 'mildly depressed' *Family Journal*, 99.

119 'There was something simple' Sir Lawrence Jones, *An Edwardian Youth* (1956), 55–6.

120 'the Eton "push" ' Duke of Bedford, *The Years of Transition* (1949), 72–3.

120 'I suddenly lost all control' *Family Journal*, 138.

121 'Julian was easily the most fearless' L.E. Jones to WD, 30 May 1915, DERV C1435/1.

122 'When Christ condemned worldliness' Mosley, *Julian Grenfell*, 152.

122 'I hated him in the mornings' Kate Thompson, *Julian Grenfell, Soldier and Poet* (2007), 81–2.

122 'Juju isn't a bit better' Mosley, *Julian Grenfell*, 169.

123 'The people are enchanting' *Family Journal*, 169.

123 'Tommy dear, I'm at the end' Julian Grenfell to Alan Lascelles, 10 April 1910, LASL 5/5/1.

123 'she is very sweet' diary of Lady Hamilton, 3 December 1903.

123 'wicked Countess' Billy Grenfell to Nancy Astor, nd [1910], Astor papers 1416/1/4/42.

124 'I *never* saw you' Mary Elcho to ED, 27 October 1910, DERV C477/25.

124 'I am plunged in the Euripides' ED to Violet Asquith, 19 September 1908, Bonham Carter papers 175.

124 'the Dons ran after us' Billy Grenfell to MG, November 1909.

125 'Of course we *did* want a scrap' Billy Grenfell to Lord Desborough, [June 1912], DERV C1108/48.

125 'There *must* be a fight' J. Strachan Davidson to Lord Desborough, 23 June 1912, DERV C646/1; Strachan Davidson to Lord Desborough, 10 December 1912, DERV C646/3.

125 'he got a call' *Family Journal*, 275–6.

126 'I loved them, and I know' *Family Journal*, 626.

126 'Now that Greats are over' Billy Grenfell to Lord Desborough, [June 19], DERV C1108/52.

126 'not a romantic marriage' Viscountess Gage, quoting Nancy Astor, in Hannah Cranborne, *David Cecil* (1990), 24.

127 'nerves' Duke of Leinster to Lady de Vesci, 29 October 1905, DD/DRU/90.

127 'That rare creature' Sir Osbert Sitwell, 'Lord Abingdon and Lindsey', *The Times*, 25 September 1963, 14f.

128 'You are my daughter' *Family Journal*, 110.

128 'Imogen is more fascinating' diary of Lady Hamilton, 19 November 1911.

129 'Saw ye Imogen dancing' Sir Henry Newbolt, *Poems New & Old* (1912), 199.

129 'You will take care' *Family Journal*, 135.

129 'I do like reading' *Family Journal*, 172.

CHAPTER 5: *The Edwardian*

130 'from Duke to Duke', Hugh Godley to ED, 30 November 1910, DERV C968/1.

131 'a godsend' Lord Esher to ED, 26 April 1911, DERV C280/1.

131 'Great organizing capacity; ought' B. and J. Mackenzie (eds.), *Diary of Beatrice Webb*, III, 68.

131 'She might have been' Brock, *Asquith Letters*, 515.

131 'No dinner was complete' Consuelo Vanderbilt Balsan, *The Glitter and the Gold* (1953), 157, 161.

132 'costly slushes with incomprehensible names' Norman Rose, *Superior Person* (1969), 285–6.

133 'Perpetual novelty was sought' Edith Wharton, *A Backward Glance* (1937), 221–2, 263.

133 'I see striped awnings' Lady Cynthia Asquith, *Remember and Be Glad*, 64.

134 'the pageant of the Season' V. Sackville-West, *The Edwardians* (1930), 94–5.

134 'The large garish rooms' MacKenzie, *Webb Diary*, III, 34.

134 'She moved always harmoniously' Sackville-West, *Edwardians*, 124–5.

134 'Wasn't it beautiful, that' Mosley, *Grenfell*, 81.

135 'Death is the last adventure' Russell Alspach (ed.), *The Variorum Edition of the Plays of W.B. Yeats* (1966), 1160, 1164.

135 'all sorts of joy' ED to Marchioness of Londonderry, 3 January 1909, PRONI D2846/2/25/56.

135 'I do love you' Alice Salisbury to EG, December 1904, DERV C428/91.

135 'she is *so* magnetic' diary of Lady Hamilton, 15 February 1904.

135 'Even across the table' diary of Lady Hamilton, 8 April 1906.

136 'The names of nearly all' *Alan Parsons' Book* (1937), 50–1.

137 'one of the typical figures' 'The Late Lord Manners', *The Times*, 26 August 1927.

138 'The woolly ineptitude that pass' diary of Sir Almeric FitzRoy, 1 July 1905, Add ms 48374, and 8 February 1915, Add ms 48378.

138 'Lord Londonderry was a great gentleman' Elizabeth, Countess of Fingall, *Seventy Years Young* (1937), 208–9.

139 'spread free to all comers' ED to Charley Londonderry, 30 January 1946, PRONI D3099/2/6/64.

139 'We have had such happy times' ED to Nellie Londonderry, 18 December 1909, Londonderry papers D2846/2/25/55.

139 'never, never to "hark backwards"' ED to Charlie Londonderry, 24 September 1947, PRONI D3099/2/6/76.

140 'frontier' Billy Grenfell to Nancy Astor, nd, Astor papers 1416/1/4/42.

141 'shrieking' . . . 'May I hold' diary of Lady Hamilton, 19 November 1911.

141 'women said – ingenious women' Sackville-West, *Edwardians*, 94.

142 'I have been thinking' diary of Lady Hamilton, 15 February 1907.

142 'the courage not to be' ED to Oliver Wendell Holmes, 26 June 1907.

142 'one gets timid in middle-life' ED to Mary Elcho, [December 1907?], DERV C1100/33.

142 'Getting old is a horrid business' ED to Arthur Balfour, 21 December 1913, DERV C1085/86.

142 'her vitality and vividness' Brock, *Asquith Letters*, 514.

143 'I did love my Sunday' Horace Nevill to ED, 1907–8, DERV C1948/1.

143 'It was a wonderful weekend' Duff Cooper to ED, 15 January 1913, DERV C579/3.

143 'one of the most delicious talkers' Countess of Wemyss, *A Family Record* (1932), 259.

143 'Of course I was a fool' George Brodrick to ED, nd, DERV C292/1.

144 'Poor darling, it must' ED to MG, 9 June 1916, DERV C1078/151.

144 'I am more in love' ED to Lady Astor, nd, Astor papers 1416/1/2/17.

144 'The truth of my love' Archie Gordon to ED, 8 May 1908, DERV C982/6.

144 'My beloved E' Archie Gordon to ED, 12 August 1908, DERV C982/5.

144 'He always held the deep conviction' *Family Journal*, 162–3.

145 'I am being made perfectly miserable' Violet Asquith to Archie Gordon, 19 August 1906, Bodleian, Bonham Carter ms 147.

145 'My very dear Violet' ED to Violet Asquith, 17 August 1906, Bodleian, Bonham Carter ms 175.

146 'Why should I be thrust' Violet Asquith to Archie Gordon, 19 August 1906, Bodleian, Bonham Carter ms 147.

146 'There has been any amount of fuss' Ridley & Percy, *Balfour–Elcho Letters*, 234.

146 'darlingest Vivi . . . thinking of Archie' ED to Violet Asquith, 18 May 1907, Bodleian, Bonham Carter ms 175.

147 'You don't know the joy' ED to Violet Asquith, 1 August 1907, Bodleian, Bonham Carter ms 175.

147 'a composite photograph' Arthur Conan Doyle to Lord Desborough, 30 August 1912, DERV C702/1.

147 'There is no one living' 'The King and the Olympic Games', *The Times*, 14 July 1908.

148 'the real public school spirit' 'The Olympic Games', *The Times*, 27 July 1908.

150 'He longs all day' ED to Monica Grenfell, 3 December 1909, DERV C1078/22.

150 'The news of Archie' ED to Monica Grenfell, 15 December 1909, DERV C1078/24.

150 'My Benjamin, who never brought' Marquess and Marchioness of Aberdeen and Temair, *We Twa*, II (1925), 196–7.

150 'We had a long talk' ED to Balfour, 17 December 1909, DERV C1085/69.

151 'I know how wonderful' Billy Grenfell to ED, 17 or 18 December 1909, DERV C1110/356.

151 'ineffably distinguished . . . only peer' Milner, *Picture Gallery*, 119.

152 'As usual, the most fearful' ED to Arthur Balfour [25 February 1904], DERV C1085/10.

152 '"La Favorita" behaved with great indiscretion' diary of Sir Almeric FitzRoy, 18 October 1903, BL Add ms 48372.

152 'Lady Desborough is the cleverest woman' Lady Cynthia Asquith, *Diaries 1915–1918* (1968), 415.

152 'A three shilling (or more) tax' Alice Keppel to ED, [1905? 1909?], DERV C1468/1.

152 '*Do* come, & soon' Alice Keppel to ED, nd [1910], DERV C1468/2.

152 'Alice Keppel was one of the most vivid' ED, 'Mrs George Keppel', *The Times*, 20 September 1947, 6e.

153 'It really is too disgusting' Julian Grenfell to ED, 12 January 1911, DERV/C1135/565.

153 'looked nearly as bored' ED to Arthur Balfour, [25 February 1904], DERV C1085/10.

155 'Queen would be very sorry' Lady Eva Dugdale to ED, 18 October 1911, D/ERV C713/1.

155 'We are very quiet' ED to Arthur Balfour, Easter Sunday 1913, DERV C1085/80.

155 'Isn't it *Hades* about staying on' ED to Willie Desborough, nd, D/ERV C1070/124.

156 'beguiling fat Chesterton' Ridley & Percy, *Balfour–Elcho Letters*, 225.

157 'when I placed the handsome' Beatrice Webb, *Our Partnership* (1948), 9.

158 'mixture of opinions, classes' *Webb Diaries*, III, 69.

158 'the British aristocracy at its best' *Webb Diaries*, III, 123–4.

158 'a pet with the ladies' James Bishop Peabody, *The Holmes–Einstein Letters* (1964), 49.

158 'arrow-true' . . . 'The love-making' ED to Edward Horner, [1909], DERV C 1091/3; Kate Thompson (ed.), *Julian Grenfell, Soldier and Poet* (2007), 31–2.

158 'people of our race' H.G. Wells, *The Passionate Friends* (1913), 155; Julian Grenfell to ED, 23 October 1913, DERV C1135/634.

159 'a baronet in the sight of God' Gilbert Murray to ED, 13 July 1920, DERV C1929/3.

159 'Statecraft and Diplomacy were well threaded' Max Beerbohm, *Seven Men* (1919), 70, 74.

160 'His hair was rather long' Joseph Hone, *W.B. Yeats* (1942), 260.

160 'Monica and I had' ED to Arthur Balfour, 19 August 1913, DERV C1085/84.

160 'Mr Kipling won everybody's heart' *Family Journal*, 355.

160 'to hear poets read aloud' Wemyss, *Family Record*, 259.

161 'Ettie Desborough is an interesting study' diary of Lady Hamilton, 8 April 1906.

161 'This morning I am again buoyant' Lady Soames (ed.), *Speaking for Themselves* (1998), 9.

162 'Being with you *always* means happiness' Violet Asquith to ED, 28 April 1907, DERV C407/2.

162 'Winston leads general conversation' ED to Arthur Balfour, 27 November [1901?], DERV C1085/50.

162 'Dearest Winston, we were all thrilled' ED to Winston Churchill, 15 August 1908, CHAR 1/73.

162 'Winston was *so* pleased' ED to Arthur Balfour, 13 September 1908, DERV 1085/67.

163 'It was a delight' ED to Winston Churchill, 13 September 1908, CHAR 1/75.

164 'Ettie, just as she left' diary of Lady Hamilton, 9–11 July 1910.

165 'agitated and nervous' ED to Monica Grenfell, 10 November 1910, DERV C1078/51.

165 'marvellously calm' . . . 'very horrid' ED to Mary Elcho, 27 July 1911, DERV C1100/41.

165 'My dear Ettie . . . Lord Knollys' Randolph Churchill, *Lord Derby* (1959), 119; Kenneth Rose, *King George V* (1983), 143.

165 'Of course we can never' Max Egremont, *The Cousins* (1977), 278–9.

165 'I don't want you' Arthur Balfour to ED, 3 November 1911, DERV C32/44.

165 'how touched I am' ED to Balfour, 4 November 1911, DERV C1085/76.

167 'I wish I could make you realize' Adèle Essex to ED, nd [1911–12], DERV C390/2.

167 'I can't say *how* kind' ED to Willie Desborough, 22 February 1912, DERV C1070/127.

168 'Too many thoughts crowd' ED to Willie Desborough, 25 March 1913, D/ERV C1070/132.

168 'unbearably sad' . . . 'malevolent birds' *Family Journal*, 301.

169 'I must write to ease' Norah Lindsay to ED, 4 April 1913, DERV C1600/30.

169 'You certainly gave us' Sir Derek Palmer to ED, 2 April 1913, DERV C1469/1.

169 'Are you going to cleave' Kate Thompson (ed.), *Julian Grenfell, Soldier and Poet* (2007), 148.

170 'I do hope that you will give' *Family Journal*, 302.

170 'We are settled here' ED to Balfour, 19 August 1913, DERV C1085/84.

170 'crying distress' Rollin Hadley (ed.), *The Letters of Bernard Berenson and Isabella Stewart Gardner 1887–1924* (1987), 204.

170 'You have given me' ED to Balfour, 10 September 1913, DERV C1085/85.

171 'In places like Hatfield and Belvoir' Viscountess D'Abernon, *Red Cross and Berlin Embassy* (1946), 120.

173 'I don't remember a finer Taplow' Patrick Shaw-Stewart to ED, 12 January 1914, DERV C2491/26.

173 'enjoyed this Taplow more' Duff Cooper to ED, 8 January 1914, DERV C579/4.

173 'Isn't it nice to think' Lady Guendolen Osborne to Alan Lascelles, 13 January 1914, LASL 5/4/1.

173 'I knew no-one' Baroness Ravensdale, *In Many Rhythms* (1953), 31.

174 'great draughts of laughter' ED, 'Charles Lister', *The Times*, 29 December 1916, 9c; ED, *Flotsam and Jetsam*, 67.

174 'Balzac knew nothing of life' Edgar D'Abernon to ED, 7 or 14 November 1917, DERV C2630/9.

174 'a sort of Olympian God' diary of Lady Hamilton, 8 April 1906.

174 'You *would* so adore it' ED to MG, 19 March 1914, DERV C1078/67.

175 'such fun & every hour so crowded' ED to MG, 24 March 1914, DERV C1078/68.

177 'God grant that we may not' James Pope-Hennessy, *Queen Mary* (1959), 486.

177 'It was like a company' Lucy Masterman, *C.F.G. Masterman* (1939), 266.

178 'The prospect is very black' Brock, *Asquith Letters*, 136.

178 'The last days of a very brilliant London Season' Monica Salmond, *Bright Armour* (1935), 1, 15.

179 'Darlingest, the news looks very bad' ED to Monica Grenfell, 2 August 1914, DERV C1078/71.

179 'Nothing cold looks worse' ED to Monica Grenfell, 3 August 1914, DERV C1078/72.

180 'the ultimatum to Germany' *Family Journal*, 440.

180 'deeply moved and pale' Wemyss, *Family Record*, 240.

180 'a natural cad' Margot Asquith to Lord Crewe, [1914], CUL, Crewe papers C/40.

181 'It was thought that the whole War' *Family Journal*, 441.

CHAPTER 6: *The Mourner*

182 'War, when you are at it' Oliver Wendell Holmes, *An Address – The Soldier's Faith* (1895), 6, 11.

183 'Casie is in the London Hospital' Billy Grenfell to Nancy Astor, nd, Astor papers 1416/1/4/42.

184 'You gave him many delicious hours' Violet Cecil to ED, 27 November 1914, DERV C1866/5.

184 'She is devoted to you' Viscount Milner to ED, 27 June [?] 1915, DERV C1863/5.

184 'It must be wonderful' JG to ED, 6 August 1914, DERV C1135/676; Thompson, *Julian Grenfell*, 213.

185 '*such* fun . . . marry a General' ED to Violet Asquith, misdated 15 August [*recte* September] 1914, Bodleian, Bonham Carter papers 176.

185 'Did you love our day' *Family Journal*, 466.

185 'We went yesterday to say Goodbye' ED to Monica Grenfell, 5 October 1914, DERV C1078/73.

186 'We've got within 15 miles' Mosley, *Grenfell*, 236–7; Thompson, *Julian Grenfell*, 223–4.

186 'I *was* pleased with' Mosley, *Grenfell*, 239; Thompson, *Julian Grenfell*, 229–30.

186 'I *adore* War' Thompson, *Julian Grenfell*, 231.

186 '*the* best fun' *Family Journal*, 480; Thompson, *Julian Grenfell*, 237.

187 'didn't know which to admire' H.B. Peabody (ed.), *The Holmes–Einstein Letters* (1964), 105.

187 'overstaffed annexes of London Society' Brock, *Asquith Letters*, 427.

187 'All yesterday was swelteringly hot' Venetia Stanley to Edwin Montagu, 25 May 1915, Montagu II A1/118.

188 'There are eight hospitals' *Family Journal*, 494–6.

189 'I was simply trembling' ED to MG, 21 December 1914, DERV C1078/74.

189 'The drawback to our trenches' *Family Journal*, 515.

189 'England is very grey' ED to Oliver Wendell Holmes, 3 February 1915.

189 'the dreary iron cage' ED to Violet Asquith, 30 March 1915, Bodleian, Bonham Carter papers 175.

190 'the recruiting is magnificent' ED to Aubrey Herbert, 12 February 1915, DD/HER/62.

190 'We dined with the Prime Minister' diary of Lady Hamilton, 11 March 1915.

190 'After unspeakable difficulties' ED to MG, 7 & 12 May 1915, DERV C1078/78 and 79.

190 'cheerful' . . . 'intensely anxious' ED to MG, 12 May 1915, DERV C1078/11.

191 'strain of the previous fortnight' *Family Journal*, 546.

191 'You once gave me' *Family Journal*, 549.

192 'We have you & Willy' Marchioness of Lincolnshire to ED, 21 May 1915, DERV C399/3.

192 'You *have* been kind' ED to Nancy Astor, 22 May 1915, Astor papers 1416/1/2/17.

193 'his marvellous constitution and health' *Family Journal*, 553–4.

193 'He prayed a great deal' *Family Journal*, 555–6.

194 'We were with him' ED to Oliver Wendell Holmes, 10 June 1915.

194 'Julian and he had been' *Family Journal*, 557.

194 'Juju would not wish' Ivo Grenfell to Willie Desborough, 29 May 1915, DERV C1123/11.

195 'How could a man' Billy Grenfell to Nancy Astor, 2 July 1915, Astor mss 1416/1/4/42.

195 'the Army should be run' BG to Nancy Astor, postmarked 14 July 1915, Astor mss 1416/1/4/42.

195 'Those extraordinarily living and breathing verses' Mosley, *Grenfell*, 266.

195 'My heart stood still' Marchioness of Lincolnshire to ED, 30 May 1915, DERV C399/4.

196 'It is curious how' Marquess of Lincolnshire to ED, 4 July 1915, DERV C400/1.

196 'With such as he was' *Family Journal*, 574.

196 'Nothing human could possibly' Lady Cynthia Asquith to ED, 30 May 1915, DERV C69/7.

196 'a most remarkable state' Cynthia Asquith, *Diaries*, 41.

197 'I have never been' ED to Monica Grenfell, 30 June 1915, DERV C1078/103.

197 'wonderfully calm and upheld' Wemyss, *Family Record*, 289.

197 'self-help' ED to Mary Wemyss, nd [July 1915], DERV C1089/4.

197 'One feels almost a cheat' ED to Nancy Astor, 8 June 1915, Astor mss 1416/1/2/17.

197 'I could not have lived' ED to MG, 28 June 1915, DERV C1078/83.

197 'Venetia, who has fairly joined' EM to MG, 19 July 1915, DERV C1073/8.

198 'kind, simple and friendly' EM to MG, 27 July 1915, DERV C1078/97.

198 'lifted above sorrow' Billy Grenfell to Alice Salisbury, nd [June or July 1915], Salisbury papers.

198 'it does sound the most terrible' ED to Billy Grenfell, 2 August 1915, DERV C1073/10.

198 'Rained all day, detestable' RA QMD, 2 August 1915.

199 'He is lying there' Willie Desborough to Nancy Astor, 6 August 1915, 1416/1/2/17.

199 'Almost the only time' Sir George Arthur, *Further Letters from a Man of No Importance* (1932), 224.

199 'Evan Charteris rang Norah' diary of Lady Hamilton, 3 August 1915.

199 'Just as her earlier courage' Evan Charteris to Alice Salisbury, nd [August 1915], Salisbury papers.

200 'overwhelmed at this great sorrow' Alice Salisbury to Nancy Astor, 5 August 1915, 1416/1/4/84.

200 'It is untellable how' ED to Alice Salisbury, 8 or 15 August 1915, Salisbury papers.

200 'In the brave moments' ED to Evelyn de Vesci, 6 or 13 August 1915, DD/DRU/103.

200 'you were always so good' ED to Lord Kitchener, 9 August 1915, DERV C1094/1.

201 'cowardly . . . no one belonging to them' ED to Patrick Shaw-Stewart, 15 October 1915, DERV C1097/52.

201 'I am sure it will' ED to Balfour, 30 August 1915, DERV C1085/93.

201 'I have not been here' ED to Oliver Wendell Holmes, 20 September 1915.

202 'I didn't think any fresh pain' ED to Violet Asquith, 6 September 1915, Bodleian, Bonham Carter ms 175.

202 'I am oh so glad' Betty Balfour to ED, 24 September 1915, D/ERV C134/14.

202 'The children, his & ours' ED to Alice Salisbury, 19 September 1915, Salisbury papers.

202 'My darling, we have died' Elizabeth Kenmare to ED, [2 October 1915], DERV C307/11.

202 'Elizabeth helped me so' ED to MG, probably 6 October 1915, DERV C1078/105.

203 'How you & I have prayed' ED to Balfour, probably 18 October 1915, DERV C1085/5.

203 'a most sunny and lovable little boy' Wemyss, Family Record, 338.

203 'love' Viscount Norwich (ed.), The Duff Cooper Diaries (2005), 20–1.

203 'He was very rich' ED, 'Lord Vernon', Westminster Review (November 1915).

204 'I have always looked' Lady Betty Balfour to ED, nd, DERV C134/15.

204 'most touching' Cynthia Asquith, Diaries, 103.

204 'In all the tangled undergrowth' ED to Violet Asquith, 25 January 1916, Bonham Carter mss 175.

204 'established a new standard' Violet Bonham Carter to ED, 31 January 1916, DERV C407/27.

204 'The name of Grenfell' Family Journal, 634.

205 'Such lives & such gifts' Lord Rosebery to ED, 13 November 1915, DERV C2124/3.

205 'I want to do' ED to Lord Rosebery, 15 November 1915, Rosebery ms 10128.

205 'You cannot go wrong' Lord Rosebery to ED, 19 November 1915, DERV C2124/4.

205 'I dreaded beginning but' ED to Lord Rosebery, 31 March 1916, Rosebery ms 10125.

206 'Private letters like these' Sir Walter Raleigh to ED, 15 April 1916, DERV C2144/15.

206 'I sometimes hope that' ED to Lord Kilbracken, 21 August 1916, DERV C1092/3.

206 'You have always been' Lord Desmond FitzGerald to ED, nd, DERV C820/12.

206 'Hardly any of the young' ED to Evelyn de Vesci, 12 March 1916, DD/DRU/103.

207 'I seem never to have said' *Family Journal*, 311.

207 'symbolical figure of Youth' *Family Journal*, 357–60.

208 'The tragedy of last Monday' ED to MG, 9 June 1916, DERV C1078/151.

208 'The thought of Mary' ED to Evelyn de Vesci, 3 July 1916, DD/DRU/103.

208 'No one was ever such fun' Wemyss, *Family Record* (1932), 266–7.

209 'Dearest brave Ettie' Mary Wemyss to Evelyn de Vesci, 23 July 1916, DD/DRU/87.

209 'the *chance* of the book' ED to Lord Kilbracken, 21 November 1916, DERV C1092/9.

209 'Julian & Billy's book' ED to Balfour, 21 August 1916, DERV C1085/95.

209 'Ettie's book tells of all' Ridley and Percy, *Balfour–Elcho Letters*, 341.

209 'You do not know' ED to Balfour, 7 October 1916, DERV C1085/97.

210 'sobbing as though her heart' Norwich, *Duff Cooper Diaries*, 36.

210 'I have been crying' Margot Asquith to ED, 28 August 1916, DERV C71/43.

210 'It is a most wonderful volume' Rudyard Kipling to ED, 8 September 1916, DERV C1497/1.

210 'such an extraordinarily *rich* book' John Buchan to ED, 29 August 1916, DERV C319/1.

210 'much more than a record' Maurice Baring to ED, 5 September 1916, D/ERV C60/86; Jocelyn Hillgarth and Julian Jeffs (eds.), *Maurice Baring Letters* (2007), 115.

210 'Ever since it came' Alice Salisbury to ED, 29 August 1916, DERV C428/15.

210 'Ettie dearest what treasures' Adèle Essex to ED, nd [September 1916], DERV C309/9.

211 'seemed to have lived' Elizabeth Kenmare to ED, Killarney, 8 October [1916], DERV C307/13.

211 'You can't think how' Lady Cynthia Asquith to ED, 19 September 1916, DERV C69/9.

211 'had hardly the courage' Violet Bonham Carter to ED, 4 September 1916, DERV C407/28.

212 'Julian had a touch' David Newsome, *On the Edge of Paradise* (1980), 334.

212 'I felt when I'd got' Lady Ottoline Morrell, *Ottoline at Garsington* (1974), 160.

212 'doctored' . . . 'Ettie is a snob' Jolliffe, *Raymond Asquith*, 291.

212 're-broken . . . shrivelled by knowledge' ED to Lord Kilbracken, 26 September 1916, DERV C1092/7.

212 'What a glorious company' Henry Asquith to ED, 27 September 1916, DERV C72/22.

213 'Nan is here' ED to Evelyn de Vesci, Sunday, DD/DRU/103.

213 'Everyone who knew him' J.M. Barrie, 'Bron the Gallant', *The Times*, 4 December 1916, 11e.

215 'the most brilliant and broadly educated' Sir Oliver Lodge, *Past Years* (1931), 220–3.

215 'a firm belief in immortality' Winston Churchill, *Great Contemporaries* (1937), 68–9.

215 'The planet is surely' Sir Oliver Lodge, *Raymond* (1916), 394.

216 'That those whom we love' Lord Ampthill to ED, 20 December 1890, DERV C2266/1.

216 'A few of our very special friends' Salmond, *Bright Armour*, 184.

217 'Lady Desborough is still a miracle' *Duff Cooper Diaries*, 44.

217 'I have never felt' ED to MG, 16 January 1917, DERV C1078/171.

217 'Beauchamp was very nice' ED to MG, 19 January 1917, DERV C1078/172.

218 'such an unexpected joy' ED to MG, 23 January 1917, DERV C1078/173.

218 'Poor Lord Desborough is most piteous' Cynthia Asquith, *Diaries*, 258.

219 'Ally, I really believe' ED to Alice Salisbury, 28 May 1922, Salisbury papers.

219 'Having a delicious visit' diary of Lady Hamilton, 28 January 1917.

220 'I simply can't tell' ED to Balfour, 8 February 1917, DERV C1085/102.

220 'Two years after is' ED to Evelyn de Vesci, 22 June 1917, DD/DRU/103.

220 'This is the day' ED to MG, 23 May 1917, DERV C1078/191.

221 'all that you were' ED to Charley Londonderry, 8 August ny [?1918], PRONI D3099/2/6/80.

221 'Why, rang the bell' Lady Helena Gleichen, *Contacts and Contrasts* (1940), 36.

222 'These raids were very noisy' Salmond, *Bright Armour*, 229–31.

222 'No-one knows what' ED to Lord Rosebery, 18 November 1917, Rosebery ms 10125/320.

222 'Our family has done its share' *Family Journal*, 619.

223 'The Grenfells were a symbol' Marquess of Winchester, *Statesmen, Financiers and Felons* (1934), 167.

223 'great desire to prevent' ED to Willie, 17 October 1917, D/ERV C1070/ 158.

223 'you were the only one' Earl of Midleton to ED, 17 May 1925, DERV C299/61.

223 'a vision and very sweet' Cynthia Asquith, *Diaries*, 362, 425.

224 'Over the possibility of Ivo' ED to Lady Wemyss, 29 March 1918, DERV C1100/62.

224 'Little Gerald went off' Elizabeth Kenmare to ED, nd [1916], DERV C307/18.

224 'I, who never have' ED to Margot Asquith, 5 January 1918, Bodleian mss Eng c 6676.

225 'I can think of nothing' Lady Manners to ED, 5 January 1918, DERV C1751/29.

225 'She adored Patrick' Norwich, *Duff Cooper Diaries*, 64.

225 'Often I think of you' Duff Cooper to ED, 9 January 1918, D/ERV C579/2.

226 ' "Be invincible" Pat used to say' ED to Duff Cooper, [11 January 1918], DUFC 12/14.

226 'Poor Ettie is very unhappy' Venetia Montagu to Edwin Montagu, 27 January 1918, Montagu II A1/182.

226 'brilliant . . . I laughed a lot' ED to Duff Cooper, 20 July 1918, DUFC 12/14.

226 'She knew all my books' Nicola Beauman, *Cynthia Asquith* (1987), 40.

227 'I *never* miss her' Cynthia Asquith, *Diaries*, 396.

227 'one of the best' Asquith to ED, 23 February 1918, DERV C72/18.

227 'George Curzon's dinner' ED to MG, 28 June 1918, DERV C1078/289; Randolph Churchill, *Lord Derby* (1959), 372–3.

228 'They had been sitting' ED to MG, 22 October 1918, DERV C1078/260.

228 'The great difficulty seems' ED to MG, 29 October 1918, DERV C1078/ 252.

228 'How often my thoughts' ED to Oliver Wendell Holmes, 17 October 1918.

228 'So much of what *little*' ED to Oliver Wendell Holmes, 1 September 1922.

228 'Peace Day' . . . 'I was *so* thankful' ED to MG, 11 November 1918, DERV C1078/249.

229 'Here it was just so right' MG to ED, 13 November 1918, DERV C2305/ 555.

229 'PEACE DAY: I know' Elizabeth Kenmare to ED, 20 November 1918, DERV C307/21.

229 'with you and your children' Alice Salisbury to ED, 22 November 1918, DERV C428/127.

229 'All day the thought' ED to Mary Wemyss, 11 November 1918, DERV C1100/68.

229 'These days are very strange' ED to Lord Kilbracken, 18 November 1918, DERV C1092/15.

CHAPTER 7: *The Grande Dame*

230 '*mondaine* I became a Bolshevik' Maggie Ponsonby, fragment of a letter of February 1919, DERV C2103/1.

230 'As years fly by' Helen D'Abernon to ED, 4 April 1919, DERV C2632/14.

230 'When you come to' Lord Midleton to ED, 4 December 1919, DERV C299/25.

231 'danced "jazz"' diary of Lord Winterton, 26 March 1919, Winterton 22.

231 'the conversation, which included' diary of Lord Winterton, 1 April 1919, Winterton 22.

231 'real pretty girls' diary of Lord Winterton, 25 May 1919, Winterton 23.

231 'Very rich & luxurious' diary of Lord Winterton, 3 March 1919, Winterton 22.

231 'I cannot tell you' ED to WD, 8 May 1919, D/ERV C1070/191.

232 'with the detachment of a choir-boy' Lord Vansittart, *The Mist Procession* (1958), 218.

232 'the beauty & peace' ED to WD, 16 May 1919, D/ERV C1070/192.

232 'I dreaded coming back' ED to Mary Wemyss, 24 May 1919, DERV C1100/74.

232 'all so beyond comprehension' Elizabeth Kenmare to ED, 26 May 1919, DERV C307/23.

233 'How all the anxieties' ED to Lord Kilbracken, 8 July 1919, DERV C1093/10.

233 'Of course war is war' Sir Henry Wilson to ED, 1 August 1919, DERV C2763/1.

233 'quite decently . . . At lunch' diary of Hugh Walpole, 27 July 1919.

234 'Winston is, always, full' *Coalition Diaries of H.A.L. Fisher*, II (2006), 462–3.

234 'beautiful Ivo, what a splendid' Ann Islington to ED, 6 April 1920, DERV C21114/12.

234 'We hope to be' ED to Lord Londonderry, 6 February 1920, D3099/2/6/6.

234 'It is so strange' Violet Bonham Carter to ED, 17 April 1920, DERV C407/41.

235 'Ettie is as adorable' diary of Lady Hamilton, 18 & 20 April 1920.

235 'a treasure-house of paintings' *The Ambassadorial Diary of John W. Davis* (1993), 89–90, 267–8.

235 'I wish Lewis would' diary of Hugh Walpole, 3 February 1922.

235 'Americans . . . I find them' Evan Charteris to ED, nd, D/ERV C467/ 261.

236 'I did not think' Lord Midleton to ED, 3 May 1920, DERV C299/26.

236 'Your brilliant valour puts' H.A.L. Fisher to ED, 4 May 1920, DERV C814/6.

236 'a luxurious semi-oriental . . . "Petit Palais"' Viscountess D'Abernon, *Red Cross and Berlin Embassy*, 66–7.

237 'The Cretan was the worst' Vansittart, *Mist Procession*, 217.

237 'Everything done regardless of expense' diary of Lord Riddell, 20 June 1920, BL Add ms 62985; cf. Lord Riddell, *An Intimate Diary of the Peace Conference and After* (1933), 205.

238 'The Conference at Lympne' ED to Margot Asquith, 12 August 1920, Bodleian mss Eng c 6676.

238 'Philip moving in the midst' ED to Alice Salisbury, 12 August 1920, Salisbury papers.

238 'My darling, since I wrote' ED to WD, 27 September 1920, D/ERV C1070/211.

239 'a lovely place, a little' ED to WD, 5 October 1920, D/ERV C1070/212.

239 'Winston's spirits & *joie-de-vivre*' ED to MG, 5 October 1920, DERV C1078/364.

240 'We went today to' ED to Mary Wemyss, 6 December [1920], DERV C1100/80.

240 'through HELL . . . I should LOATHE' ED to Mary Wemyss, 12 February 1921, DERV C1100/81.

241 'I LOATHE Canadians' ED to Alice Salisbury, 10 or 17 February 1921, Salisbury papers.

241 'Winston was most understanding' ED to WD, 14 May 1921, C1070/32.

241 'Your spirit is brave' ED to Churchill, 29 June 1921, CHAR 1/141.

241 'The news has just' ED to Churchill, 24 August 1921, CHAR 1/141.

241 'we had a happy' ED to Mary Wemyss, 12 October 1921, DERV C1100/84.

242 'My book shows the four' Margaret Newbolt, *The Later Life and Letters of Sir Henry Newbolt* (1942), 409.

242 'There was a kind' Sir Henry Newbolt, *The Book of the Grenvilles* (1922), 261.

242 'Wren, dying full of years' Earl of Lytton, *Antony, Viscount Knebworth* (1935), 368.

242 'I always think of Julian' Eric Dudley to ED, 27 January 1941, DERV C2676/4.

243 'Thank you most awfully' IG to ED, nd [February–March 1921], DERV C1123/21.

243 'Business is bloody' Lord Gage to ED, 2 August 1926, DERV C892/38.

243 'endeared himself to all' *The Times*, 12 October 1926, 19d.

244 'I shall be very, very sorry' Stanley Clarke to ED, 29 July 1926, DERV C518/1.

244 'One's heart goes out' Earl of Midleton to ED, 19 May 1922, DERV C299/32.

244 'One always feels glad' ED to Alice Salisbury, 28 May 1922, Salisbury papers.

245 'Everyone charming and in their' diary of Lady Hamilton, 21 May 1922.

245 'Everything was absolutely perfect' Lord Stanmore to ED, 25 May 1922, D/ERV C985/1.

245 'a good fitter-in' ED to Mary Wemyss, 3 February 1936, DERV C1100/172.

245 'Sociability takes up too much' Philip Tilden, *True Remembrances* (1954), 34.

246 'top' ED to Lord Quickswood, 16 April 1947, Quickswood papers 58/171.

247 'London will never be' diary of Lady Hamilton, 29 July 1922; 'Adèle, Lady Essex', *The Times*, 2 August 1922, 14d; diary of Lord Winterton, 4 August 1922, Winterton 30.

247 'What a wonderful friend' ED to Charley Londonderry, 3 August 1922, PRONI D3099/2/6/8.

248 'I am so glad' ED to Alice Salisbury, 28 May 1922, Salisbury papers.

248 'Down to Panshanger with Evan' diary of Hugh Walpole, 15 July 1922.

248 'The pictures are marvellous' diary of Hugh Walpole, 16 July 1922.

248 'Sibyl with her cliché' diary of Hugh Walpole, 27 January 1922.

249 'insurmountable instinctive shrinking' ED to Mary Wemyss, 9 February 1925, DERV C1100/96.

249 'It is a bit' Lord Walter Kerr to WD, 2 March 1922, DERV C1484/1.

249 'you who have been' Edwin Montagu to ED, 24 October 1922, DERV C1882/8.

250 'I do believe that' ED to Charley Londonderry, 27 October 1922, PRONI D/3099/2/6/12.

250 '*Very secret*' . . . 'young Westmorland' Lord Curzon of Kedleston to ED, 17 January 1922, DERV C623/19.

250 'George Curzon's manner' D'Abernon, *Red Cross and Berlin Embassy*, 51.

251 'And will dear George' Churchill, *Great Contemporaries*, 287.

251 'G.N.C. (after behaving incredibly)' ED to Charley Londonderry, 25 May 1923, PRONI D/2099/2/6/13.

252 '25th rate & bursting' Sir Philip Sassoon to ED, 6 July 1920, DERV C2345/10.

252 'What a dull Cabinet' ED to Lord Kilbracken, 8 November 1924, DERV C1093/20.

254 'They go about anywhere' Mary, Countess of Lovelace, 'Fifty Years', *The Times*, 9 March 1932, 13f.

254 'metallic, glittering, flashy, noisy' D'Abernon, *Red Cross*, 91.

255 'young Beans' ED to Oliver Wendell Holmes, 29 October 1924.

255 'For weeks the journalistic' Edwin Montagu to ED, 16 January 1923, DERV C1882/9.

255 'Life has been so new' ED to Mary Wemyss, 23 January 1923, DERV C1100/88.

255 'It was a brilliant scene' diary of Lady Hamilton, 26 June 1923.

255 'how I envy you' Elizabeth Kenmare to ED, 20 June 1923, DERV C307/24.

256 'so much charm' Ann Islington to ED, 16 October 1925, DERV C2114/16.

256 'a happy whirl' ED to Lady Wemyss, 29 December 1923, DERV C1100/89.

256 'I have always felt' ED to MG, 1 October 1923, DERV C1078/449.

256 'It's a tremendous day' ED to Lady Ottoline Morrell, 18 October 1923, HRC Morrell papers.

257 'Give my best love' Winston Churchill to ED, 21 October 1923, D/ERV C508/6.

257 'so good-looking and romantic' Ann Islington to ED, 22 October 1923, DERV C2114/15.

257 'overjoyed' . . . 'Of course I know' Eric Ednam to MG, 23 October 1923, DERV C2677/1.

257 'How charming Jack has been' ED to WD, 27 January 1924, DERV C1070/270.

257 'Oh! we've had such fun' ED to IG, 12 February 1924, DERV C1074/5.

258 'I never so deeply realized' ED to Mary Wemyss, 15 June 1924, DERV C1100/91.

258 'I only met her' Viscount Gage to Mark Bonham Carter, received 22 January 1979, Bodleian, Bonham Carter ms 764.

260 'What a very queer' ED to MG, 12 September 1922, DERV C1078/410.

260 'I have had a' Earl of Lytton, *Antony*, 161–3.

260 'It would be a most' ED to Pamela Lytton, 23 September 1925, Lytton papers.

261 '*He* was your son' ED to Victor Lytton, 3 May 1933, Lytton papers.

261 'small, pale & insignificant' Archie Gordon to Violet Asquith, 17 August 1905, Bodleian, Bonham Carter papers 132.

262 'I feel inexpressibly cold' Edward Marjoribanks to ED, nd, DERV C 1774/17.

262 'I have heard two voices' Edward Marjoribanks to ED, 14 February 1926, DERV C1774/28.

262 'Clarence made a speech' Lord Gage to ED, 31 October 1930, D/ERV C892/48.

262 'How very sad, sad' Mary Wemyss to ED, 4 April 1932, DERV C447/155.

263 'Whenever I see you' Lord David Cecil to ED, nd, DERV C432/5.

263 'The Viscount & Mog' ED to MG, 31 October 1923, DERV C1078/454.

264 'inexpressibly dearly' ED to Mary Wemyss, 15 June 1924, DERV C1100/91.

264 'I love you, parrot' ED to MG, 10 April 1924, DERV C1078/459.

264 'somehow she is so utterly' ED to MS, 11 August 1924 DERV C1078/470.

264 'The little town looks magical' ED, 'The Winter Journey to Switzerland', *The Times*, 23 January 1925.

264 'If you have any' ED to Lady Hamilton, 20 April 1922, Hamilton 20/1/4.

265 'it was not possible' 'The Jumble Queen', *Maidenhead Advertiser*, 3 May 1922.

266 'Learned men and ladies' 'The Puppet Show', *Maidenhead Advertiser*, 14 May 1924.

266 'very busy sounds so bourgeois' ED to Lady Ottoline Morrell, 20 October 1933, HRC.

266 'Oh no, I saw it' Viscount Gage to Mark Bonham Carter, received 22 January 1979, Bodleian, Bonham Carter ms 764.

267 'her ladyship is on the water' Sir Rupert Hart-Davies (ed.), *Siegfried Sassoon Diaries 1923–1925* (1985), 255–6.

268 'the Grand Opera' diary of Lady Ottoline Morrell, 23 May 1925, British Library.

268 'What burning intellectual zeal' ED to Betty Montgomery, 29 May 1925, HRC Morrell papers.

268 '*Sons & Lovers* is' ED to Ottoline Morrell, 28 March 1930, HRC Morrell papers.

269 'There are words of yours' ED to Siegfried Sassoon, 9 February 1929, CUL Add 9375/211.

269 'it isn't really a "party"' ED to Siegfried Sassoon, 15 August 1929, CUL Add 9375/212.

270 'One gets up at ungodly hours' T. Pinney (ed.), *Rudyard Kipling Letters*, V (2004), 268–9.

271 'a knot of dowagers' Michael Holroyd, *Lytton Strachey*, II (1968), 653.

271 'what a difference it made' Rosamond Lehmann to ED, 4 June 1927, DERV C1571/1.

271 '*terribly* anxious' Rosamond Lehmann to ED, 21 August 1930, DERV C1571/2.

271 'marvellously well-written and clever' ED to MS, 22 August 1930, DERV C1078/770.

271 'She lives by the most rigid' Rosamond Lehmann, *The Weather in the Streets* (1936), 32, 78, 99.

272 'This place is lapped' ED to MS, 14 September 1926, DERV C1078/544.

273 'cannot say *very* much yet' ED to MS, 26 September 1926, DERV C1078/546.

273 'Ivo has now lived' ED to MS, 28 September 1926, DERV C1078/547.

274 'Ivo never suffered' ED to Ottoline Morrell, 30 November 1926, HRC.

274 'I know that the very foundations' Elizabeth Kenmare to ED, 9 October 1926, DERV C307/28.

274 'golden memories' . . . 'curly-haired Cupid' Helen D'Abernon to ED, 12 October 1926, DERV C2632/18.

274 'unspeakably cruel thing' Birkenhead to ED, 12 October 1926, DERV C2426/5.

275 'impressive, sweet and solemn' Birkenhead to ED, 12 October 1926, DERV C2426/4.

275 '*sure* that in His own' Sir George Arthur to WD, 17 December 1926, DERV C571/1.

275 'One thing about the three' Willie Desborough to Nancy Astor, 15 October 1926, Astor papers, 1416/1/2/37.

275 'We'll never refer to "bygones"' ED to Lady Astor, 19 October 1926, Astor papers, 1416/1/2/37.

275 'I often think Imogen' ED to Alan Lascelles, 4 December 1926, LASL 5/5/1.

275 'the utter beauty, utter peace.' ED to MS, 21 October 1926, DERV C1078/550.

276 'and things we don't' ED to MS, 23 October 1926, DERV C1078/551.

276 'Only you & I' ED to MS, 26 October 1926, DERV C1078/552.

276 'a fortnight of wonderful respite' ED to Lord Londonderry, 1 November 1926, PRONI D/3099/2/6/19.

276 'intensity of anxiety about Moggie.' ED to Alice Salisbury, 1 November 1926, Salisbury papers.

276 'except in a few' 'Ill-Judged Sympathy', 'X', *The Times*, 15 November 1926, 15e.

277 'I have been sair' ED to Mary Wemyss, 23 May 1927, DERV C1100/107.

278 'shock & strain' . . . 'You know my own darling' ED to WD, 27 September 1927, DERV C1070/284A.

CHAPTER 8: *The Mother-in-Law*

279 'Paradise of PEACE' ED to Mary Wemyss, 7 September 1929, DERV C1100/122.

279 'This place really is divine' MG to ED, 5 November 1919, DERV C2305/588.

280 'your yearly retreat without' Desmond MacCarthy to ED, 3 August 1935, DERV C1078/8.

280 'I am writing in' ED to Siegfried Sassoon, 15 August 1929, CUL Add 9375/212.

280 'Your sweet babies were *perfect*' ED to MS, 13 September 1933, DERV C1078/938.

281 'This secret corner of England' J. Wentworth Day, 'Whiteslea – The Enchanted Marsh', *The Field*, 29 November 1930, 777.

281 'intermediate countryside' 'Bungalows and Town Planning', *The Times*, 2 September 1936, 8c.

281 'The mean streets of the town' ED, 'On the South Downs', *The Times*, 1 April 1930, 19f.

282 'piled-up woods behind' H.G. Wells, *Secret Places (1922)*, 48–50.

284 'Even Lord Desborough relaxed' *Maidenhead Advertiser*, 25 June 1930.

285 'aghast at the idea' ED to MS, 7 August 1927, DERV C1078/596.

286 'You looked *so* well' ED to MS, 2 October 1927, DERV C1078/607.

286 'I cannot forgive myself' ED to MS, 1 January 1928, DERV C1078/616.

287 'the kind of gaiety' ED to Oliver Wendell Holmes, 13 March 1930.

288 'the English Einstein' Edward Marjoribanks to ED, nd, DERV C1774/27.

288 'have heard so much' Imogen Grenfell to Frederick Lindemann, 7 June [1927], Cherwell papers K95/29.

288 'all kinds of cabbages' ED to Frederick Lindemann, 29 June 1927, Cherwell papers K95/1.

288 'Would November 10th till Monday' ED to Frederick Lindemann, 15 October 1928, K95/2.

288 'an old Sly-Boots' ED to Lord Londonderry, 27 February 1947, D3099/2/6/75.

288 'If you do find' ED to Frederick Lindemann, 9 February 1931, K95/8.

289 'the Beau Ideal of English' Frederick Lindemann to ED, 10 January 1945, DERV C1595/1.

289 'After this last triplet' Sir George Arthur, *Further Letters from a Man of No Importance* (1932), 224.

289 'Broadly speaking Garters were' Lord Salisbury to Stanley Baldwin, 28 September 1928, Baldwin papers 163.

290 'more shattered than I' Emma Letley, *Maurice Baring* (1991), 212.

290 'The last thing one' ED to Charley Londonderry, 9 May 1929, D3099/2/6/20.

290 'He sat out for' Blanche Dugdale, *Arthur James Balfour*, II (1936), 394–5.

290 'near to the great' ED to Oliver Wendell Holmes, 13 March 1930.

291 'All the pain is' ED to Oliver Wendell Holmes, 15 April 1930.

291 'I don't think one' ED to Charley Londonderry, 22 March 1930, PRONI D3099/2/6/22.

291 'I shall always think' ED to Winston Churchill, 20 September 1930, CHAR 8/267.

291 'go-between' . . . 'Arthur backed George' ED to Winston Churchill, 27 September 1931, CHAR 8/267.

291 'intoxicating . . . "attaque" is brilliant' ED to Winston Churchill, nd [1936], CHAR 1/214.

292 'I do feel *so* happy' ED to MS, 18 December 1930, DERV C1078/789.

292 'Ivo's greatest friend' ED to Oliver Wendell Holmes, 15 December 1930.

292 'Lord and Lady Desborough graciously permitted' 'Tomorrow's Wedding', *Maidenhead Advertiser*, 25 February 1931.

293 'The Desboroughs are the finest' 'The Grand Taplow Wedding – Dense Crowds Besiege the Church', *Maidenhead Advertiser*, 4 March 1931.

295 'The leadership of the privileged' Winston Churchill, *Great Contemporaries* (1937), 77.

295 '*George* – what luck' ED to Mary Wemyss, 8 December 1933, DERV C1100/151.

295 'lovely eyrie in the hills' ED to Willie Desborough, 9 March 1931, DERV C1070/284B.

295 ('everyone carries a loaded revolver') ED to Willie Desborough, 11 March 1931, DERV C1070/285.

295 'A HEAVENLY happy restful' ED to Mary Wemyss, 15 March 1931, DERV C1100/137.

295 '*L'infiniment petit* carried' ED to Oliver Wendell Holmes, 21 February 1921.

296 'Will-power was not a thing' Edith Wharton, *The Glimpses of the Moon* (1922), chapter 20, 243.

297 'The two tinies are such divine toys' ED to Mary Wemyss, 16 September 1936, DERV C1100/175.

297 'one never quite realized' RA GV/CC 47/1950, 18 September 1941.

297 'happy eventless weeks' ED to Lord Londonderry, 1 October 1937, PRONI D3099/2/6/26.

298 'We will all try' ED to Sir John Salmond, nd, DERV C1076/2.

298 'I feel sure it' ED to MS, 18 January 1933, DERV C1078/893.

298 'a magnificent Englishman' Lord Wigram to ED, nd, DERV 2730/3.

299 'I am sorry to bother you' ED to Ramsay MacDonald, 9 August 1933, PRO 30/69/679.

300 'unspeakably sorry, but one *must* decide.' ED to Siegfried Sassoon, 14 April 1946, CUL Add 9375/216.

300 'Wouldn't you like to' ED to MS, 24 June 1935, DERV C1078/1045.

301 'I suddenly felt the' Salmond, *Bright Armour*, 120.

301 'A winning, a profoundly' Lord David Cecil, 'Undertones of War', *Spectator*, 20 September 1935, 436–7.

301 'Lady Salmond's attitude to herself' L.P. Hartley, 'The Literary Lounger', *The Sketch*, 18 September 1935.

301 'tidal wave of democracy' Churchill, *Great Contemporaries*, 77.

CHAPTER 9: *The Courtier*

302 'Sometimes when we left' Countess of Airlie, *Thatched with Gold*, 132.

303 'water-wagon' . . . 'Tempers' ED to Patrick Shaw-Stewart, 21 April 1915, DERV C1097/49.

303 ' "David's gone to the Front" ' ED to Aubrey Herbert, 12 February 1915, DD/HER/62.

303 'We visited many hospitals' Airlie, *Thatched*, 138–9.

304 'My passion for him' ED to Balfour, 23 March 1913, DERV C1085/80.

304 'It is sad to see' ED to Lord Kilbracken, 13 August 1917, DERV C1092/20.

305 'delighted . . . for H.M. to have' Earl of Midleton to ED, 30 January 1925, DERV C299/45.

305 'second-best tiaras' ED to Margot Asquith, 26 December 1919, Bodleian ms Eng c 6676.

306 'The Queen had an eager enjoyment' Airlie, *Thatched*, 146–7.

307 'Twenty little Yankees feeling' ED's commonplace book, III, April 1930, Cazalet papers.

307 'He continues *wonderfully* well' ED to Willie Desborough, 22 January 1935, DERV C1070/292.

307 'Our Sovereign is most' ED to H.A.L. Fisher, 21 November 1929, Fisher 67/73.

307 'a "tomb" for any indiscretion' ED to Queen Mary, 29 October 1942, RA GV/CC 47/2014.

307 'You know all the queer point' ED to Charley Londonderry, 16 September 1941, PRONI D3099/2/6/42.

307 'Royal Family stories' Georgiana Blakiston, *Letters of Conrad Russell* (1987), 140.

308 'It seemed to me' ED to John Gore, 3 November 1942, Gore papers.

308 'That is what I mind' ED to John Gore, 7 November 1942, Gore papers.

308 'Off the Rocker' ED to John Gore, 18 February 1944, Gore papers.

309 'Very dull day' RA QMD, 20 July 1925.

309 'very small car' ED to Queen Mary, 3 March 1950, RA GV/CC 47/2458.

310 'All last week' ED to Mary Wemyss, 1 December 1925, DERV C1100/98.

311 'You would be surprised' Kenneth Rose, *King George V* (1983), 291.

312 'Madam, May I trouble' RA GV/CC 47/1255, 3 February 1934.

312 'Life at Sandringham was' John Gore, *King George V* (1941), 378.

314 'We went all round' John Vincent (ed.), *The Crawford Papers* (1984), 544–5.

315 'the strange pause & peace' ED to H.A.L. Fisher, 21 November 1929, Fisher 67/73.

316 'She took me on trust' John Gore, typescript memoir of Lady Desborough, Gore papers.

316 'straightness, his frankness, his simplicity, his deep loyalty' Gore, *George V*, 292, 300, 359, 367–8, 371.

318 'a very beautiful book' RA GV/CC 47/1956, 16 November 1941.

318 'His was the straightest Court' Gore, *George V*, 372.

318 'gained much if he' Gore, *George V*, 364.

319 'Lady Desborough, I know' Sir Osbert Sitwell, *Rat Week* (1986), 33–34.

319 'Look at this extraordinary little book' Lascelles, *King's Counsellor*, 111.

319 'I do want to add' ED to Duke of York, 11 June 1920, RA GVI/PRIV/04/8.

320 'the tiny Princess Elizabeth' ED to Mary Wemyss, 4 June 1929, DERV C1100/118.

320 'little Lillibet immediately took' RA GV/CC 47/1950, 18 September 1941.

320 'The only babies I' ED to MS, 26 November 1931, DERV C1078/841.

320 'Madam, I do hope' ED to Queen Mary, 31 July 1932, RA GV/CC 47/1183.

321 'such a lovely happy Christmas' ED to Mary Wemyss, 3 January 1936, DERV C1100/169.

321 'arch-spoil-sport' Sir Michael Duff to ED, 23 July 1947, DERV C711/17.

322 'In the great desire' ED to Queen Mary, 19 January 1936, RA GV/CC 47/1372.

323 'The King's life is moving' Gore, *George V*, 443.

323 'I can't tell you' ED to Annie Chamberlain, 21 January 1936, NC/11/1/
252.

323 'We walked behind him' Francis Watson, *Dawson of Penn* (1950), 281.

323 'the pathetic procession from Sandringham' Desborough, 26 January
1936, DERV F132/6.

323 'One hasn't had time' ED to Mary Wemyss, 26 January 1936, DERV
C1100/197.

324 'The Queen is most deeply touched' ED to Lord Hugh Cecil, 23 January
1936, Qui 50/57.

324 'The nation has found' Winston Churchill to Queen Mary, 3 February
1936, CHAR 1/284.

324 'The Queen told me' ED to Churchill, 4 February 1936, CHAR 1/284.

324 'To you alone I must tell' ED to Mary Wemyss, 3 February 1936, DERV
C1100/172.

325 'Many people in England' Kenneth Rose, *The Later Cecils* (1975), 233.

325 'It has all been rather confused' ED to Annie Chamberlain, 30 March
1936, NC 11/1/253.

325 'her want of class' diary of Lady Hamilton, 15 December 1935.

325 'Winston has never been' ED to MS, 5 May 1936, DERV C1078/1101.

325 'rolling every syllable' ED to Churchill, 10 November 1936, CHAR 8/
531.

326 'One mustn't write' ED to MS, 5 December 1936, DERV C1078/1134.

326 'brilliant . . . hour by hour' ED to Winston Churchill, 5 July 1937,
CHAR 8/548.

326 'So strange being here' ED to Lord Hugh Cecil, 12 June 1937, Qui 53/
167.

CHAPTER 10: *The Dowager*

327 'vim' Duke of Portland, *Men, Women and Things* (1937), 77–8.

327 'across hill, dale, briar' Georgiana Blakiston, *Letters of Conrad Russell*
(1987), 140.

327 'Sherry and sausage party' Blakiston, *Conrad Russell*, 117.

328 'At least Winston showed sport' H.A.L. Fisher to ED, 21 July 1936,
DERV C814/39.

328 'We are linked by the memories' ED to Austen Chamberlain, 9 October
1916, AC 12/78.

328 'How much of one's youth' ED to Neville Chamberlain, 18 March 1937,
NC 7/1/5; *The Times*, 18 March 1937; ED, *Flotsam and Jetsam*, 76.

328 'You really do *not* know' ED to Mary Wemyss, 12 October 1921, DERV
C1100/84.

329 'filled with the utmost admiration' ED to Neville Chamberlain, 15 January 1938, NC 7/11/31/97.

329 'It was an immense pleasure' ED to Annie Chamberlain, 23 July 1938, NC 11/1/254.

329 'What a magnificent enterprise' ED to Annie Chamberlain, 16 September 1938, NC 13/12/189.

330 'heart dropped like a stone' ED to Herbert Fisher, 30 September 1938, Fisher ms 77/36.

330 'to say how deeply' ED to Neville Chamberlain, 30 September 1938, NC 13/11/645.

331 'I simply cannot help' ED to Annie Chamberlain, 7 October 1938, NC 11/1/255.

331 'How deeply I have' ED to Herbert Fisher, 30 September 1938, Fisher ms 77/36.

331 'a lovely time' ED to Churchill, 25 November 1938, CHAR 1/324.

332 'I am delighted that, under Hitler' WD to Sir Samuel Hoare, 1 August 1939, Templewood XVII/12/2.

332 'A *heavenly* visit' ED to MS, 21 August 1939, DERV C1078/1275.

332 'I never thought it' ED to Pamela Lytton, 16 September 1939, Knebworth archives.

333 'The babies here, so happy' ED to MS, 5 September 1939, DERV C1078/1279.

333 'Dad & I do' ED to MS, 9 September 1939, DERV C1078/1280.

333 'passing in a strange sort of mist' ED to Charley Londonderry, 10 September 1939, PRONI D3099/2/6/28.

333 'all the people here' ED to MS, 25 September 1939, DERV C1078/1284.

334 'How utterly bewildering' ED to MS, 25 September 1939, DERV C1078/1285.

334 'the end of the England' G.M. Trevelyan to ED, 25 September 1939, DERV C2586/1.

334 'Your broadcast last night' ED to Winston Churchill, 2 October 1939, CHAR 2/364.

334 'I have just read' ED to Lindemann, 29 November 1939, Cherwell papers K95/15.

334 'This country is looking so lovely' ED to MS, 8 October 1939, DERV C1078/1286.

335 'heavenly little children are fellow-captives' ED to Charley Londonderry, 7 February 1940, PRONI D3099/2/6/29.

335 'Gosford is an incredible desolation' Evan Charteris to ED, 22 November 1939, DERV C467/248.

335 'very cosy & happy' Duchess of Portland to ED, 21 January 1940, DERV C215/13.

336 'Vaynol is a Military Hospital' Sir Michael Duff to ED, 24 August 1940, DERV C711/1.

336 'so *that's* what hay' Pope-Hennessy, *Queen Mary*, 598.

336 'Queen Mary is most flourishing' Lady Cynthia Colville to ED, 15 December 1940, D/ERV C560/1.

337 'Dearest Winston, your old, old friends' ED to Churchill, 11 May 1940, CHAR 2/393.

337 'His star suffers frequent eclipse' D'Abernon, *Red Cross*, 88.

337 'truly grieved to hear' ED to Neville Chamberlain, 3 October 1940, NC 13/18/832.

338 'Are there any expectant mothers' Christopher Hassall, *Edward Marsh* (1959), 625.

338 'Oh dear I feel so *cross*' ED to Marquess of Londonderry, Monday, 23 September 1940, PRONI D/3099/2/6/32.

338 'The heroism and cheerfulness' Ethel Desborough, 'The People's Spirit', *The Times*, 28 September 1940, 5e; *Flotsam and Jetsam*, 51.

339 'wonderful sleeping arrangements' Evie Devonshire to ED, 13 February 1941, DERV C415/1.

339 'I never see my old friends' Duchess of Portland to Lord Cherwell, 7 January 1941, Cherwell papers K240/26.

339 'Early in the evening' Earl of Dudley, 'Civil Defence in Action', *The Listener*, 16 January 1941, 81–2.

340 'The time-bomb behind the stables' ED to Evan Charteris, 2 November 1940, DERV C1087/2.

340 'I knew him first' ED to Charley Londonderry, 19 November 1940, PRONI D3099/2/6/34.

340 '*I* always want you' ED to Charley Londonderry, 15 January 1941, PRONI D3009/2/6/38.

341 'own poor guesses at philosophy' ED to Charley Londonderry, 16 January 1941, PRONI D3099/2/6/39.

341 'immensely cheered' ED to Charley Londonderry, 6 February 1941, PRONI D3099/2/6/41.

341 'I hope so, as I fear' Earl of Crawford to ED, nd [1941?], DERV C1598/3.

342 'I cannot tell Your Majesty' RA GV/CC 47/1911, 1 April 1941.

342 'I read it very slowly' ED to John Gore, 1 May 1941.

342 'exquisite candour *and* reticence' ED to John Gore, 28 October 1942.

342 'austere restraint' ED to John Gore, 3 November 1942.

342 'generous letters from strangers' ED to John Gore, 6 May 1941, DERV C995/2.

343 'I look back with thankfulness' John Gore to ED, 22 January 1947, DERV C995/32.

343 'Your part breathed peace' Earl Baldwin of Bewdley to ED, 9 June 1941, D/ERV C128/4.

343 'such a Joy' Lady Cynthia Asquith to ED, 30 June 1941, DERV C69/21.

344 'slowly dying – the end' RA GV/CC 47/1956, 16 November 1941; see also ED's tribute to Valentine Kenmare, *The Times*, 18 November 1941.

344 'anyone has ever before' Dorothy Charteris to ED, 19 November 1941, DERV C1337/11.

344 'spirit of flame, shining' G.W.G.A., 'Viscountess Gage', *The Times*, 8 January 1969, 10f.

344 'I suppose you *couldn't*' ED to Churchill, 22 August 1941, CHAR 2/417.

344 'It was lovely to be there' RA GV/CC 47/1950, 18 September 1941.

345 'the park is still' Apsley Cherry-Garrard to ED, nd [post August 1948], DERV C914/3.

345 'To strive, to seek' Sara Wheeler, *Cherry: a life of Apsley Cherry-Garrard* (2001), 267.

345 'I am cut off' Duchess of Portland to Lord Cherwell, 6 January 1942, Cherwell papers K240/36.

345 'I have tried for days' ED to Churchill, 17 February 1942, CHAR 2/441.

346 'Queen M is really astonishing' ED to Marquess of Londonderry, 14 May 1942, PRONI D3099/2/6/43.

346 'The talks with Your beloved Majesty' RA GV/CC 47/1985, 16 May 1942.

346 '*Never* – in all our heavenly Sundays' Lady Violet Bonham Carter to ED, 27 May 1942, DERV C407/52.

346 'I was so deeply struck' ED to Lady Violet Bonham Carter, 18 November 1942, Bodleian, Bonham Carter ms 175.

347 'have you seen some *lovely* poems' ED to John Gore, 19 November 1942, Gore papers.

347 'can't be far off eighty' Duff Hart-Davis (ed.), *King's Counsellor* (2006), 78.

347 'Fat, with gristle' ED to John Gore, 13 October 1943.

347 'hullabaloo' . . . 'The hospital was bursting' ED to John Gore, 19 January 1943.

348 'sweated away over "Little Gidding"' ED to John Gore, 26 February 1943.

348 'I've been reading such' ED to John Gore, 22 January 1944.

348 'a "week-end" (vile word)' ED to Lord Quickswood, 16 December 1942, Qui 7/57.

349 'a rather naughty crew' Logan Pearsall Smith to Hugh Trevor-Roper, 21 January 1943, Dacre papers.

349 'the all-conquering American charmer' Logan Pearsall Smith to Hugh Trevor-Roper, 26 February 1943, Dacre papers.

350 'When something really tragic happens' Richard Hillary, *The Last Enemy* (1942), 185–6.

351 'A gem . . . It wasn't my lot' John Gore to ED, 7 May 1943, DERV C995/9.

352 'If your pressing & glorious occupations' WD to Winston Churchill, 15 June 1943, CHAR 2/464.

352 'better news than the fall of Mussolini' John Gore to ED, 26 July 1943, DERV C995/10.

353 '('Blow & blast!')' ED to Charley Londonderry, 8 August 1943, PRONI D3099/2/6/48.

353 'I've been through a bad patch' ED to John Gore, 12 November 1943.

353 'He was in bed' Christabel Aberconway to ED, 27 January 1945, DERV C1718/3.

353 'You know what you have meant' ED to Alice Salisbury, 25 January 1944, Salisbury papers.

354 'What a knock-about turn' ED to Lord Quickswood, 15 January 1944, Qui 58/1.

354 'so peacefully at the end' ED to Marquess of Londonderry, 24 May 1944, PRONI D3099/2/6/52.

354 'The bomb that killed Rex' ED to Pamela Lytton, 10 August 1944, Knebworth archives.

354 'I dreadfully miss him' Mogs Gage to Pamela Lytton, 23 August 1944, Knebworth archives.

354 'I have thought of you' ED to Siegfried Sassoon, 12 June 1944, CUL Add 9375/213.

354 'so peaceful, & calm' Sir Michael Duff-Assheton-Smith to ED, 7 October [1940], DERV C711/2.

354 'that lovely park at Pans' Sir Michael Duff-Assheton-Smith to ED, 28 December [1944?], DERV C711/5.

355 'bringing Prince Philip of Greece' Sir Michael Duff-Assheton-Smith to ED, 12 July 1944, DERV C711/12; ibid., 27 July 1944, D/ERV C711/13.

355 'You are the Dowager Duchess' Sir Michael Duff-Assheton-Smith to ED, nd, D/ERV C711/14.

355 'Darling Dad is really' ED to MS, 7 December 1944, DERV C1078/1344.

356 'I have been so worried' ED to Charley Londonderry, 3 January 1945, PRONI D3099/2/6/57.

356 'I should like to live' ED to Duff Cooper, 12 February 1945, DUFC 12/14.

356 'the prototype of the Great' John Gore to ED, 11 January 1945, DERV C995/23.

356 'His were the best manners' Earl of Crawford to ED, 28 January 1945, DERV/C1598/7.

357 'a strikingly impressive tribute' Sir Alan Lascelles to ED, 19 January 1945, DERV C1534/8; Hart-Davis, *King's Counsellor*, 288.

357 'War is only tolerable' Lord Moran, *The Anatomy of Courage* (1945), xiv.

357 'hair-raising book' Helen D'Abernon to ED, 25 February [1946?], DERV C2632/24.

357 'Oh such a perfect' ED to Charley Londonderry, 21 April, 1945, PRONI D3099/3/6/59.

358 'And it's your victory' ED to Churchill, 8 May 1945, CHAR 2/530.

358 'So queer isn't it' ED to John Gore, 12 May 1945.

358 'All the happy days' RA GV/CC 47/2240, 23 July 1945.

358 'Saturday afternoon & my treat' ED to Charley Londonderry, 18 August 1945, PRONI D3099/2/6/60.

358 'the darling & riotous holiday' ED to Charley Londonderry, 22 September 1945, PRONI D3099/2/6/65.

358 'Isn't Nicky a perfect demon-angel?' Christabel Aberconway to ED, 27 January 1945, DERV C1718/3.

359 'I do feel so ashamed' ED to Charley Londonderry, 11 December 1945, PRONI D3099/2/6/66.

359 'Life itself was the art' ED, 'Lord D'Abernon', *The Times*, 7 November 1941.

359 'To those who read' ED, 'Maurice Baring', *The Times*, 19 December 1945.

360 'I haven't been very grand' ED to Charley Londonderry, 1 January 1946, PRONI D3099/2/6/61.

360 'Those 3 hours flew' Violet Bonham Carter to ED, 5 July 1946, Bodleian, Bonham Carter ms 204.

360 'He did bring such charm' ED to Violet Bonham Carter, 29 July 1946, Bodleian, Bonham Carter ms 175.

360 'Fun seems to have vanished' ED to Charley Londonderry, 14 August 1946, PRONI D3099/2/6/73.

360 'I am enchanted but terrified' ED to Charley Londonderry, 2 September 1946, PRONI D3099/2/6/74.

361 'like Captain Scott' ED to Charley Londonderry, 27 February 1947, PRONI D3099/2/6/75.

362 'Ah! I was such a friend' Nicholas Mosley, *Time at War* (2006), 164–5.

362 'I liked Ettie Desborough' Mosley, *Julian Grenfell*, 182.

362 'That woman is more affected' information from Lord Ravensdale.

362 'I do long to see' ED to Siegfried Sassoon, 15 October 1947, CUL Add 9375/220.

362 'My beloved Winston' ED to Churchill, 9 May 1947, CHUR 2/148.

363 'I spent the weekend' Sir Robin Duff-Assheton-Smith to ED, 14 July 1947, D/ERV C711/19.

364 'There *never* has been' Kitty Joicey to ED, 27 April [1945?], DERV C1425/1.

364 'They all indulged with passionate zest' Lady Violet Bonham Carter, 'The Souls', *The Listener*, 30 October 1947, 769–70.

365 'I thought it *so* lovely' ED to Violet Bonham Carter, 26 October 1947, Bodleian, Bonham Carter ms 175.

365 'Queen Mary thinks of you' Mabell Airlie to ED, 18 March 1946, DERV C1891/83.

367 'I have been incapable' ED to Lord Cherwell, 9 February 1949, Cherwell papers K95/23.

367 'You write so contentedly' ED to Lord Quickswood, 26 February 1949, Qui 59/99.

367 'Oh! my darling how *wonderful*' Mabell Airlie to ED, 13 March 1949, DERV C1891/85.

367 'The lesson her letters offer' John Gore memoir.

368 'A less vital character' Harold Nicolson, 'Marginal Comment', *Spectator*, 6 June 1952, 742.

368 'I have now got' ED to Winston Churchill, 7 September 1949, CHUR 2/162.

368 'very feeble . . . & still laid-up' RA GV/CC 47/2458, 3 March 1950.

368 'As a hostess she was an inspiration' Lady Dorothy Charteris, *The Times*, 30 May 1952.

369 'We sat alone at' Airlie, *Thatched with Gold*, 236.

369 'God bless you' John Gore to ED, 9 May 1952, DERV C995/45.

369 'Old people with slow thoughts' Moran, *Anatomy of Courage*, 154.

Index

𝒦

'Lord Campbell, the Lord Chancellor of 50 years ago, used to say that anyone who published an interesting book without an index ought to be put to death.'

Lord Kilbracken to Lady Desborough, 27 August 1916

Abbey Leix, 70

Abdication crisis, 325–6

Aberconway, Christabel, Lady, 332, 352, 353, 358

Abercorn, James Hamilton, 3rd Duke of, 230, 289

Aberdeen and Temair, John Hamilton-Gordon, 1st Marquess of, 118, 144, 146, 150, 151

Aberdeen and Temair, George Gordon, 2nd Marquess of (*earlier* Lord Haddo), 145

Aberdeen and Temair, Ishbel, Marchioness of, 150, 151

Aberdeen and Temair, Mary, Marchioness of, 145

Abingdon, Montagu ('Montie') Bertie, 8th Earl of Abingdon and 13th Earl of Lindsey, 127, 245

Adam, Robert, 17, 54

Adisham, 114

Afghanistan, 57

Aga Khan, 255

Agave, 124

Age of Innocence, The (Wharton), 295

Agra, 74

air raids: First World War, 221–2, 302; Second World War, 331, 332, 333, 338–40, 350, 364

Airlie, David Ogilvy, 11th Earl of, 35, 110

Airlie, Mabell, Countess of (*née* Gore): character, 266, 363; childhood, 17, 20, 26; death of her husband, 110; debutante, 32–3; during Second World War, 339; on Ettie, 15, 302; friendship with Ettie, 367; Lady of the Bedchamber to Queen Mary, 153, 302, 303–4, 306–7, 313, 365, 369; marriage, 35, 36, 37; and Nancy Astor, 140; war work, 302, 303–4

Airlie Castle, 369

airships, 156, 168, 221, 297, 302

Aix-les-Bains, 238

Albania, 332

Albert Victor, Prince of Wales ('Eddy'), 38

Alderden Manor, 244, 273

Aldershot, 190, 191

Aldington, Richard, 160

Alexandra, Queen, 113, 148, 149, 310–311, 321

Alexandra (ship), 156

Alexandria, 167

Alfonso XIII, King of Spain, 310

All Souls College, Oxford, 126, 181

Althorp, Albert ('Jack') Spencer, Viscount (*later* 7th Earl Spencer), 170, 173, 230

Althorp, Cynthia, Viscountess (*née* Hamilton, *later* Countess Spencer), 230

American Civil War, 65

American Declaration of Independence, 100

Americans, Ettie's views on, 140, 235, 241

Amery, Brydie, 350

Amery, Leo, 350

Ampthill, Margaret, Lady, 153, 154–5, 293, 363

Ampthill, Oliver Russell, 2nd Baron, 153, 216

Anatomy of Courage, The (Moran), 357, 369

Ancaster, Eloïse, Countess of, 130, 139, 179, 218, 231, 294

Ancaster, Gilbert ('Bertie') Heathcote-Drummond-Willoughby, 2nd Earl of, 218, 231, 294

Anderson, Sir John (*later* 1st Viscount Waverley), 313–14

Anglesey, Charles Paget, 6th Marquess of, 314

Anglesey, Marjorie, Marchioness of (*née* Manners), 118, 121, 123, 124, 127, 314

Anglo-Siberian Trading Syndicate, 66

Ann Veronica (Wells), 158

Annaly, Luke White, 3rd Baron, 318
Annandale Society, 120, 125
Anne, Queen, 18
Antarctica, 345
'Anthem for Doomed Youth' (Owen), 5
Apethorpe, 12–13
Apostles, the (society), 10
appeasement, 329–32
Après-midi d'un faune, L' (ballet), 255
Aragon, Louis, 347
Archangel, 233, 234, 279
Ardèche, 238
Argyll, John Campbell, 9th Duke of, 173
Argyll, Niall Campbell, 10th Duke of, 173, 233
Ariadne in Naxos (Baring), 81
Armistice (1918), 228–9
Arran, Arthur Gore, 5th Earl of, 31
Arran, Arthur ('Artie') Gore, 6th Earl of, 17
Arthur, Prince, Duke of Connaught, 164
Arthur, Sir George, 199, 275, 289
Arundel Castle, 259, 332
Ascent of Man, The (Drummond), 52, 106
Ascot, 81, 93–4, 142, 264, 283–4
Ascott House, 88, 135, 161
Ashford, Daisy: The Young Visiters, 233
Ashridge: decoration and grounds, 45; Ettie visits, 37; Harry Cust and Nina Welby stay at, 84; Sir Oliver Lodge visits, 214–15; the Souls gather at, 43
Asquith, Anthony, 219
Asquith, Arthur ('Oc'), 227
Asquith, Lady Cynthia (née Charteris): on Edwardian Society, 133; on Ettie, 79, 204; in Ettie's will, 297; and Ivo Grenfell, 223; and Julian Grenfell's death, 196; and Pages from a Family Journal, 211; visits Panshanger, 218, 219, 234, 343; and Walter Raleigh, 227
Asquith, Elizabeth (later Princess Antoine Bibesco), 96, 219
Asquith, Helen, 57, 58, 59
Asquith, (Herbert) Henry (later 1st Earl of Oxford and Asquith): character, 58–9; death, 289; on death of Bron Lucas, 213; and death of Ivo Grenfell, 274; on death of Raymond Asquith, 212; on Ettie, 131, 142–3, 227; Ettie first meets, 58; and First World War, 178, 180, 190; as intimate friend of Ettie, 2, 58–9, 60, 130, 227; on John Revelstoke, 80; and Lord Stanmore, 245; at Marlborough House ball, 70; marriage to Margot Tennant, 59–60; political career, 42, 130, 157, 163, 164, 165, 172, 195, 213; and the Souls, 42, 43, 44, 49–50, 57–8, 85; and Venetia Stanley, 131, 187; visits Panshanger, 219; visits Taplow, 57, 58, 59, 161; wounding of his son, 227; letter to, 67
Asquith, Herbert ('Beb'), 234

Asquith, Julian (later 2nd Earl of Oxford and Asquith), 207, 212
Asquith, Katharine (née Horner), 212
Asquith, Margaret ('Margot'; née Tennant, later Countess of Oxford and Asquith): appearance and character, 53, 55; children, 96; and Constance Wenlock, 63; death of her stepson, 225; deterioration of friendship with Ettie, 308; dinner parties, 134, 156; and Edward Marjoribanks, 262; on Ettie, 7, 53, 60, 68, 69, 86, 132–3, 259; and Ettie's relationship with Archie Gordon, 145, 146; and Evan Charteris, 75; and imaginary women's Cabinet, 222; and Ivo Grenfell's death, 274; and Julian Grenfell's death, 197; and Lady Essex, 246; and Lady Randolph Churchill, 84; and Lytton Strachey, 226; marriage, 58–9; miscarriage, 96; on Nellie Londonderry, 46; and outbreak of First World War, 180; and Pages from a Family Journal, 210; and Siegfried Sassoon, 266; and the Souls, 42, 43, 48, 49, 53, 58, 85; visits Panshanger, 219; visits Taplow, 161; at Windsor Castle, 303; Autobiography of Margot Asquith, 308; Off the Record, 308; letters to, 224–5, 238, 305
Asquith, Raymond: on Bron Herbert, 100–101; death, 212, 213, 225; and Ettie's relationship with Archie Gordon, 145; at Margot Asquith's, 134; and Pages from a Family Journal, 207, 212; reminders of, 360; visits Taplow, 112
Asquith, Violet see Bonham Carter, Lady Violet
Assynt Forest, 107, 193
Aston Clinton, 88
Astor, William Waldorf, 1st Viscount, 89, 140
Astor, Waldorf, 2nd Viscount, 140, 166, 178, 275, 295
Astor, William ('Bill'; later 3rd Viscount), 144
Astor, Nancy, Viscountess (earlier Shaw): background, 4; and Billy Grenfell, 141, 144, 183, 195, 200; at Imogen Grenfell's wedding, 295; and Ivo Grenfell's death, 275; and Julian Grenfell's death, 192, 195, 197; and Lytton Strachey, 226; rivalry with Ettie, 140–41, 275; visits Taplow, 166; letter to, 197
Athens, 147
Athlone, Alexander Cambridge, 1st Earl of, 289
Auden, W. H., 81
Augusta Victoria, Queen of Portugal, 314
austerity, post-war, 364
Australia, 243
Austria, 69, 176–7
Autobiography of Margot Asquith, 308
aviation, 156, 172–3, 248, 287, 322, 350
Avignon, 238, 239
Avon Tyrrell, 136, 137–8, 228–9

Bacchae, The (Euripides), 124
Bacres, 88
Baden, Frederick I, Grand Duke of, 38
Badminton House, 179, 336, 346
Balcarres, Constance ('Connie') *see* Crawford, Constance, Countess of
Baldwin, Lucy (*later* Countess Baldwin of Bewdley), 312
Baldwin, Stanley (*later* 1st Earl Baldwin of Bewdley): and Abdication crisis, 326; appointed Prime Minister, 251; defeat in 1929 election, 290, 315; final retirement, 326; and George Gage, 258; his Cabinet, 252, 290; Imogen Grenfell's wedding gift, 293; as intimate friend of Ettie, 2, 58; and King George V, 251, 317, 322; and Knights of the Garter, 289; at Sandringham, 312; visits Panshanger, 326, 343, 358; visits Taplow, 326, 332; visits Whiteslea, 297, 326
Balfour, Arthur (*later* 1st Earl of Balfour): and Albert Grey, 68; appearance, 267; at Ashridge, 215; and Baldwin's appointment as Prime Minister, 251; at Cassiobury, 133; character, 50–51, 54, 83, 215; at Cliveden, 140; at Clouds, 215; and the Coterie, 112; at Curzon's banquet, 228; death, 290–91; Ettie first encounters, 30, 34, 50; at Ettie's children's parties, 118; at Ettie's London dinner parties, 117, 178; and Ettie's reading, 106; during First World War, 177, 178, 190, 195, 209, 221, 228; and George Wyndham, 82–3; godfather to Monica Grenfell, 101, 257; and Harry Cust, 48; as intimate friend of Ettie, 2, 50, 51–2, 58, 105, 115, 116, 130, 139, 328; and John Revelstoke, 80, 177, 221; and Mary Elcho, 54–5, 146; and Olympic Games (1908), 149; at Paris peace conference, 232; political career, 42, 50–51, 104–5, 115–16, 165–6, 195, 209, 232, 250, 290; at Port Lympne, 237; recommends Willie Grenfell for a peerage, 51, 116; at Sheringham, 251; and the Souls, 41, 42, 43, 44, 50, 51, 53, 57, 85; summer holidays with the Grenfells, 107, 108, 111–12; visits Panshanger, 170, 218, 219, 248, 288; visits Taplow, 57, 111–12, 115, 141, 157, 161, 164, 176, 244, 260, 267, 290; at Whittinghame, 54, 256; writings, 51, 65; **letters to**, 105, 109, 114, 142, 150–51, 152, 155, 160, 162, 165–6, 170–71, 201, 203, 209, 220, 304
Balfour, Lady Elizabeth ('Betty'; *later* Countess of Balfour), 157, 167, 202, 204
Balfour, Gerald (*later* 2nd Earl of Balfour), 157
Balkan League, 175
Balkans Wars (1912–13), 174, 175
Balliol College, Oxford, 5, 58, 119–20, 124–5
Balliol College War Memorial Book, 5
Ball's Corner, 279

Balmoral, 311
Balniel, David, Lord (*later* 28th Earl of Crawford), 341–2, 356
Balsan, Jacques, 295
Baltic war (1918–19), 233–4
Balzac, Honoré de, 59, 174
Bank of England, 79–80, 88, 103
Bapaume, 213
Baring family, 70–71, 78
Baring, Elizabeth *see* Kenmare, Elizabeth, Countess of
Baring, Everard, 71, 123, 235, 260
Baring, Hugo, 71
Baring, John *see* Revelstoke, John Baring, 2nd Baron
Baring, Maurice: Balkan war correspondent, 174; on birth of Ivo Grenfell, 109; at Cliveden, 140; in Constantinople, 174; death, 359; and death of John Revelstoke, 290; and Edmund Gosse, 86; elegy to Bron Lucas, 228, 372; Ettie's obituary for, 359; in Ettie's will, 297; family background, 70–71, 78; Imogen Grenfell's wedding gift, 293; and outbreak of First World War, 178; on Reggie Lister, 43–4; relationship with Ettie, 81; visits Taplow, 112, 244, 260; *Ariadne in Naxos*, 81; *Diminutive Dramas*, 81; 'Ivo Grenfell', 372–3; 'Julian Grenfell', 195, 372
Baring, Lady Ulrica, 235
Baring Brothers (bank), 78, 79, 80
Barnett, Miss (governess), 24, 26
Barrie, J. M., 2, 213–14, 271
Bartolommeo, Fra, 285
Barton Hills, 23
Bashkirtseff, Marie, 67
Basingstoke, 137
Bath, 273
Bath Club, 118, 340
Battersea, Constance, Lady, 66
Beaconsfield, 88
Beauchamp, Sir Sydney, 217–18, 220
Beauclerk, Lady Osborne (*earlier* Marchioness of Waterford), 277
Beaufort, Henry Somerset, 9th Duke of, 179
Beaufort, Henry Somerset, 10th Duke of, 294
Beaufort, Louise, Duchess of, 179–80
Beaufort, Mary, Duchess of, 294
Beaverbrook, Max Aitken, 1st Baron, 54
Beckett, Pamela, 262
Bedford, Hastings Russell, 12th Duke of, 120
Bedford Grammar School, 173
Bedfordshire, 21; *see also* Wrest Park
Beerbohm, (Sir) Max: at Ettie's parties, 117, 132, 159; on Herbert Beerbohm Tree, 159; 'Ballade Tragique', 154; 'Hilary Maltby and Stephen Braxton', 159
Beerbohm Tree, Helen, Lady, 58

Beerbohm Tree, Sir Herbert, 58, 136, 159
Beit, Sir Otto, 169
Belgian Relief Fund, 227
Belgium, 179, 330
Belgrade, 177
Belloc, Hilaire, 235
Bellosguardo, 152
Belvoir Castle, 171
Benares, 74
Benckendorff, Alexander, Count, 134, 180
Benson, A. C., 112, 212
Benson, Guy, 119
Benson, Rex, 192
Bentinck, Lady Victoria ('Vera'; later Erskine-Wemyss), 173, 180
Berchtesgaden, 329
Berenson, Bernard, 170, 285
Beresford, Lord Charles (later 1st Baron), 47
Berkshire, 88
Berlin, 10, 81, 144, 150, 289–90
Berners, Gerald Tyrwhitt-Wilson, 14th Baron, 332
Bertie, Montagu ('Montie'; later 8th Earl of Abingdon and 13th Earl of Lindsey), 127, 245
Bhagavadgita, 345
Bible, 19, 65, 125, 129, 334, 348
Bigge, John, 127, 194
bimetallism, 103, 104
Bingham, Rose, 142
bird-watching, 279, 329
Birkenhead, F. E. Smith, 1st Earl of, 117, 165, 250, 274–5, 277, 315
'Birthday of the Infanta' (Wilde), 58
Bisley, 148
Black, Catherine, 315–16
Black Hand faction, 177
Black Pearl (schooner), 45
Blackmore, R. D.: Lorna Doone, 106
Blackshirts, 362, 364
Blackwood, Lord Basil, 164
Bledisloe, Charles Bathurst, 1st Viscount, 243–4
Blenheim Palace, 22, 130, 288
Blériot, Louis, 172
Blitz, 338–40
Blois, (Sir) Gervase, 261
Blow, Detmar, 179
Blunt, Wilfrid Scawen: on Adelaide Brownlow, 46; on Asquith, 60; on Balfour and Mary Elcho, 54–5; on Constance Wenlock, 63; on George Pembroke, 45; on George Wyndham, 83, 84; on Harry Cust, 86; on Oscar Wilde, 49; on the Souls, 50, 62, 86
Bodnant, 332
Boer War, 42, 100, 110–111, 125, 161, 214
Boigne, Comtesse de, 162
Bombay, 52, 73

Bonham Carter, Mark (later Baron Bonham-Carter), 346, 360
Bonham Carter, Sir Maurice ('Bongie'), 204
Bonham Carter, Lady Violet (née Asquith): and Archie Gordon, 145–7, 150, 204; on Ettie, 162, 204; in Ettie's will, 296; friendship with Ettie, 146–7, 204; marriage, 204; and Pages from a Family Journal, 211; radio talk on the Souls, 364–5; visits Ettie in hospital, 352; visits Panshanger, 234, 346, 360, 361; visits Taplow, 269; letters to, 124, 145–6, 146–7, 185, 189–90, 202
Book of the Grenvilles, The (Newbolt), 242
Boothby, Robert ('Bob'), Baron, 330
Bordighera, 123
Boston, Cecilia, Lady, 166
Boston, George Irby, 6th Baron, 166
Botticelli, Sandro, 93
Boulogne, 187, 190, 191, 192, 194, 232
Boulter's Lock, 264, 283, 284
Bournemouth, 24
Bowes-Lyon, Lady Elizabeth see Elizabeth, Queen (consort of George VI)
Bowland, Forest of, 201
Brecknock, John Pratt, Earl of (later 5th Marquess Camden), 254
Brett, Reginald (later 2nd Viscount Esher), 25, 66, 131
Bright Armour (Monica Salmond), 300–301, 350
Brighton, 13, 220, 282
Brighton Corporation, 281
Brindisi, 38, 167
Britannia (monoplane), 173
British Cotton Textile exhibition, 327
British East Africa, 243
British Industries Fair, 317, 327
British Legion Poppy Factory, Richmond, 314
British Museum, 245, 315
British Olympic Council, 147, 148, 149
British Telecom, 367
British Telecommunications Research, 366–7
Brittany, 108
Brocket, Charles Nall-Cain, 1st Baron, 249
Brocket Hall: decoration, 28; Ettie flees to after the 1891 Season, 72; Ettie's girlhood at, 28, 29, 30; First World War bomb damage, 221; Henry Cowper at, 28, 29, 39, 40; inheritance of, 21, 28, 40, 114; let to Lord Mount Stephen, 249; orchard, 72; sold to Sir Charles Nall-Cain, 249
Brodrick, Francis, 236
Brodrick, George (later 2nd Earl of Midleton), 119, 120, 143–4
Brodrick, Lady Hilda, 30, 42, 43, 49, 56, 85
Brodrick, Michael, 236
Brodrick, Moyra, 217

Brodrick, St John *see* Midleton, St John Brodrick, 1st Earl of

Brontë, Charlotte: *Jane Eyre*, 23, 319

Brontë, Emily, 348; *Wuthering Heights*, 106

Browne, Dermot, 202, 211, 224, 232

Browne, Lady Dorothy (*later* Lady Edward Grosvenor, *then* Charteris), 77, 173, 246, 343–4, 350, 352, 361, 368–9

Browne, Gerald, 224

Browning, Robert, 106

Brownlow, Adelbert ('Addy') Cust, 3rd Earl: at Ashridge, 37, 43, 45–6, 84; Evan Charteris on, 70; and Harry Cust, 68, 84; marriage, 46; and Sir Oliver Lodge, 214; and the Souls, 43, 47

Brownlow, Adelaide, Countess: appearance and character, 43, 44, 45–6; at Ashridge, 37, 43, 45, 84; childlessness, 94; and Nellie Londonderry, 138; and the Souls, 43, 44, 53

Brownlow, Peregrine Cust, 6th Baron, 294

Brownlow, Katherine, Lady, 294

Bryant, (Sir) Arthur, 242

Buccleuch, John Montagu-Douglas-Scott, 7th Duke of, 318

Buccleuch, Walter Montagu-Douglas-Scott, 8th Duke of (*earlier* Earl of Dalkeith), 294

Buchan, John (*later* 1st Baron Tweedsmuir), 210; *Francis and Riversdale Grenfell*, 242; *The Gap in the Curtain*, 4

Buchman, Frank, 324

Buckingham Palace, 32, 128, 154, 155, 249, 302, 308, 313–15, 323–4

Buckinghamshire, 87, 88–9, 104, 117, 166, 283; *see also* Cliveden; Taplow Court

Bunyan, John: *The Pilgrim's Progress*, 248

Burlington Fine Arts Club, 309

Burnham, Edward Levy-Lawson, 1st Baron, 117

Butcher, Samuel, 106

Butler of Moore Park (barony), 114, 298–9

Butler's Court, 88, 166

Cairns, Herbert, 3rd Earl, 103, 105

Cairo, 38, 167, 190, 252, 257

Calais, 206

Calcutta, 74

Cambridge, 309

Cambridge University, 34, 243; *see also* Emmanuel College; Trinity College

Campbell, (Sir) David, 192

Campbell, Niall (*later* 10th Duke of Argyll), 173, 233

Campsea Ashe, 366

Canada, 68, 108, 115, 153, 240–41

Canizaro, 13, 17, 18

Cannes, 38, 295

Canterbury, 176

Canterbury, Randall Davidson, Archbishop of, 227

Canterbury, Cosmo Lang, Archbishop of, 322, 323

Canterbury, Frederick Temple, Archbishop of, 38

Cap Ferrat, 168

Capell, Lady Iris, 173, 180

Capell, Lady Joan (*later* Viscountess Ingleby), 247

Caribbean, 364

Carlile, Sir Hildred, 171

Carlisle, Rosalind, Countess of, 62

Carlton Club, 250

Carlyle, Thomas, 106; *Sartor Resartus*, 67

Carmarthen, John ('Jack') Osborne, Marquess of (*later* 11th Duke of Leeds), 173

Carpenter, J. C., 148

Carracci, Annibale, 309

carriage-riding, 26–7, 117, 138, 139, 154, 156

Carter, Leonard, 174

Cassidy, Sir Maurice, 355

Cassiobury House, 130, 133, 247, 295

Cassis, 239

Castlereagh, Charles ('Charley') Vane-Tempest-Stuart, Viscount *see* Londonderry, Charles Vane-Tempest-Stuart, 7th Marquess of

Castlerosse, Elizabeth, Viscountess *see* Kenmare, Elizabeth, Countess of

Castlerosse, Valentine Charles Browne, Viscount *see* Kenmare, Valentine Browne, 5th Earl of

Castlerosse, Valentine Edward Browne, Viscount (*later* 6th Earl of Kenmare), 184, 224, 344, 350, 355

Cavendish, Elizabeth ('Betty'; *later* Marchioness of Salisbury), 126, 294

Cavendish, Mary (*later* Countess of Crawford), 341–2

Cavendish, Lady Moyra, 233

Cavendish-Bentinck, Lady Victoria ('Vera'; *later* Erskine-Wemyss), 173, 180

Cecil, Lady Beatrice ('Moucher'; *later* Lady Harlech), 167

Cecil, Lord David: career, 263; character, 263; on Ettie, 3–4, 102; reviews *Bright Armour*, 301; visits Panshanger, 217, 219; visits Taplow, 271; *The Stricken Deer*, 263; *The Young Melbourne*, 263

Cecil, George, 184

Cecil, Helen, 217

Cecil, Lord Hugh ('Linky') *see* Quickswood, Hugh ('Linky') Cecil, 1st Baron

Cecil, Lady Mary ('Mima'; *later* Duchess of Devonshire), 167

Cecil, Lord Robert (*later* 1st Viscount Cecil of Chelwood), 228

Cecil, Violet (Lady Edward Cecil, *later* Viscountess Milner): death of her son, 184; on Ettie, 2–3; Ettie visits in Sussex, 160; on Francis Cowper, 151; friendship with Ettie, 184; visits Panshanger, 217; visits Taplow, 161

Cellini, Benvenuto, 235

Central Flying School, 173

Cervantes, Miguel de: *Don Quixote*, 107

Chamberlain, Anne, 295, 329; **letters to**, 323, 325, 329–30, 331

Chamberlain, (Sir) Austen, 112, 157, 237, 250, 291, 328

Chamberlain, Joseph, 163, 291

Chamberlain, Neville: appeasement policy, 329–32; at Imogen Grenfell's wedding, 295; as intimate friend of Ettie, 2, 58; Prime Minister, 329–32; resignation, 337; visits Panshanger, 329, 337; visits Taplow, 328; visits Whiteslea, 297, 329; **letter to**, 337

Chanctonbury, 282

Channon, (Sir) Henry ('Chips'), 243, 259, 293, 355

Channon, Paul (*later* Baron Kelvedon), 355

Chaplin, Henry (*later* 1st Viscount), 62

Charles, duc d'Orléans, 83

Charles II, King, 18, 86

Charlotte (the King's parrot), 305, 312, 322

Charteris family, 70, 71, 118, 215

Charteris, Alan, 34

Charteris, Lady Cynthia *see* Asquith, Lady Cynthia

Charteris, Lady Dorothy ('Dor'; *née* Browne, *then* Lady Edward Grosvenor), 77, 173, 246, 343–4, 350, 352, 361, 368–9

Charteris, (Sir) Evan: and Adèle Essex, 77, 196, 246; appearance and character, 75–6, 340; and Billy Grenfell's death, 199–200; career, 75; at Cliveden, 140; death, 340; on Ettie, 100; at Ettie's London dinner parties, 117; French holiday with Ettie (September 1920), 238, 239; on George Wyndham, 83; golfing holiday with the Grenfells (1904), 112; on the London Season, 70, 74–5; marriage, 246; relationship with Ettie, 71, 75, 76–8, 79, 146, 365; relays letters during First World War, 189; during Second World War, 335, 338; at Sheringham, 251; and the Souls, 43, 49–50, 75; views on Americans, 235; visits Panshanger, 170, 217, 218, 234, 248; visits Taplow, 132, 164, 233, 244

Charteris, Lady Irene ('Bibs'; *later* Countess of Plymouth), 217, 294, 297, 343

Charteris, Yvo, 143, 203

Chartres, Duchesse de, 38

Chatsworth, 22, 130, 150

Cheek, Kemble, 292

Chekhov, Anton, 226

Chequers, 337, 338

Cherry-Garrard, Angela, 345

Cherry-Garrard, Apsley, 345

Cherwell, Frederick Lindemann, 1st Viscount ('the Prof'), 287–9, 295, 299, 334, 339, 367

Cherwell, River, 108

Chesterton, Frances, 295

Chesterton, G. K., 2, 156–7, 295; *The Napoleon of Notting Hill*, 156

Chiltern Hills, 87

Cholmondeley, George ('Rock'), 5th Marquess of, 293, 295, 312

Cholmondeley, Sybil, Marchioness of (*née* Sassoon), 118, 293, 295, 312, 322, 352

Christ Church, Oxford, 234, 243, 261, 263, 288

Christianity, 7, 19, 52, 65, 96, 150, 196, 201, 215–16, 324–5

Chula Chakrabongs, Prince of Siam, 315

Chulalongkorn, King of Siam, 107

Churchill, Clementine (*née* Hozier, *later* Baroness Spencer-Churchill): at the D'Abernon's, 332; death of daughter, 241; French holiday with Ettie (September 1920), 238, 239; at Hackwood, 241; in imaginary women's Cabinet, 222; marriage, 93, 162–3; at pre-Dardanelles dinner in Downing Street, 190; tennis tournament at Eaton, 287; trip to Whipsnade Zoo, 325; visits Panshanger, 234, 235; visits Taplow, 233, 241, 332; on wartime nurses, 183

Churchill, Lady Randolph (*later* Mrs Cornwallis-West), 84, 164, 241

Churchill, (Sir) Winston: on Asquith, 59; and Balfour, 50, 290, 291; and Baltic war, 233–4; at Curzon's banquet, 228; at the D'Abernon's, 332; dancing, 255; death of his mother and daughter, 241; on death of King George V, 324; declines invitation to Panshanger, 363; in Ettie's will, 297; during First World War, 190, 195, 301; flying lessons, 173; and Frederick Lindemann, 287; French holiday with Ettie (September 1920), 238, 239; at Hackwood, 241; as intimate friend of Ettie, 2, 58, 105, 161–2, 291; and Ivo Grenfell, 233; Leader of the Opposition, 363; lecture tours, 315; marriage, 93, 162–3; on Monica Grenfell's marriage, 257; offers Willie Desborough governor-generalship of Canada, 240–41; as painter, 235, 239, 241–2; and Pamela Plowden, 123; parliamentary career, 161, 163, 195, 233, 240, 250, 257, 315, 334; and Philip Sassoon's parrot, 264; at Sandringham, 315; during Second World War, 334, 337, 338, 341–2, 344, 345, 347–8;

and Sir Charles Wilson, 357; on Sir John
French, 215; trip to Whipsnade Zoo, 325;
visits Ettie in hospital, 352; visits Panshanger,
234, 235; visits Taplow, 57, 112, 161–2, 233,
241–2, 290, 328, 341–2; *Great Contemporaries*,
291, 295; *My Early Life*, 291–2; *River War*,
107; letters to, 92–3, 324, 325, 326, 331, 334,
337, 344, 345, 362–3, 368
'City of Brass' (Kipling), 160
Clarke, Stanley ('Joe'), 244, 273
Clemenceau, Georges, 54
Cleveland, Ohio, 254
Clive, Archer, 184
Cliveden, 37, 88–9, 139–40, 166, 180
Clouds, Wiltshire, 215
Colefax, Sibyl, Lady, 4, 248–9, 325, 349
College of Arms, 298–9
Collins, Mary Ann, 92
Colnaghi (art dealers), 285
Cologne, 173
Colville, Lady Cynthia, 336
Committee of Imperial Defence, 297
Communism, 231
Compton, Lord Alwyne, 95
Compton, Lady Alwyne (*née* Vyner, 'Mollie'),
95
Compton, William ('Bim'), Earl *see*
Northampton, William ('Bim') Compton,
6th Marquess of
Conan Doyle, Sir Arthur: *The Lost World*, 147
Conservative Party, 104–5, 164, 165, 245, 250;
see also Tories
Constable, John, 350
Constantinople, 47, 173, 174–5, 245
Cooch Behar, 74
Cookham, 283
Cooper, Anne (*later* Palmer and 10th Baroness
Lucas of Crudwell), 298
Cooper, Lady Diana (*née* Manners, *later*
Viscountess Norwich): banned from Taplow,
121, 124; childhood, 118; and George
Vernon, 203; in imaginary women's Cabinet,
222; at Imogen Grenfell's wedding, 295;
marriage, 69; and *Pages from a Family
Journal*, 210; visits Panshanger, 235; visits
Taplow, 124
Cooper, Duff (*later* 1st Viscount Norwich):
elegy for Gustav Hamel, 175–6; Ettie
supports, 69; friendship with Ettie, 143; at
Imogen Grenfell's wedding, 295; marriage,
69; and *Pages from a Family Journal*, 210;
visits Panshanger, 216–17, 235; visits
Taplow, 173, 225–6; letter to, 226
copper smelting, 87
Cornwallis-West, George, 162
Cornwallis-West, Jennie (*earlier* Lady
Randolph Churchill), 84, 164, 241

Corridor of Mirrors (Massie), 352
Corrigan, Laura, 4, 254–5, 355
Cortachy Castle, 35
Coterie, the, 112, 136–7, 227, 258
Coubertin, Baron Pierre de, 148
Council for the Preservation of Rural England,
283
'Counter-Attack' (Sassoon), 5
Court Theatre, 124
Coward, (Sir) Noël: *Hay Fever*, 253
Cowes, 37
Cowper, George Clavering-Cowper, 3rd Earl,
169
Cowper, Francis, 7th Earl: and Balfour, 115;
character, 20–21; Curzon's tribute to, 85;
death, 113–14, 116, 249, 298; at Edward VII's
Coronation, 151; and Ettie's upbringing, 29;
his and Ettie's mutual devotion, 20, 40;
inherits Brocket, 28; inherits Wrest and 4 St
James's Square, 27, 40; marriage, 21; political
career, 21, 41, 103; his will, 116, 169; *Earl
Cowper K.G., a memoir by his wife*, 205
Cowper, Anne ('Pammy'), Countess, 11, 15,
17–20, 23, 25, 26–7, 39, 65, 71, 91, 347
Cowper, Henry: builds Sawley Lodge, 201;
death, 39–40, 100; death of his mother, 27;
and Evelyn de Vesci, 71; guardian of Ettie,
14, 24, 25, 27–8, 29–30, 34, 38; heir to
Cowper estates, 21, 201; Member of
Parliament, 28
Cowper, Katrine ('Katie'), Countess: on the
Cowpers, 18–19, 20, 28, 30, 39, 40; death,
168–9; and Ettie's upbringing, 29, 31–2; her
husband's death, 113, 114; and Julian
Grenfell, 113, 121, 123; and Lord Brownlow,
43; marriage, 21; and Monica Grenfell, 166;
and the Souls, 44, 47–8, 53; *Earl Cowper
K.G., a memoir by his wife*, 205; letter to, 168
Cowper, Spencer, 311
Cowper, William, 263
Cracow, 332
Cradock-Hartopp, Sir Charles, 70
Craigie, John, 112
Craigie, Pearl, 112
Cranborne, James Gascoyne-Cecil, Viscount
see Salisbury, James Gascoyne-Cecil, 4th
Marquess of
Cranborne, Robert ('Bobbety') Gascoyne-
Cecil, Viscount *see* Salisbury, Robert
('Bobbety') Gascoyne-Cecil, 5th Marquess of
Cranborne, Alice, Viscountess *see* Salisbury,
Alice, Marchioness of
Cranborne, Elizabeth ('Betty') , Viscountess *see*
Salisbury, Elizabeth ('Betty'), Marchioness
Crawford, David Lindsay, 27th Earl of, 314–15
Crawford, David Lindsay, 28th Earl of (*earlier*
Lord Balniel), 341–2, 356

Crawford, Constance ('Connie'), Countess of, 238

Crawford, Mary, Countess of, 341–2

Cresta Run, 264

Crewe, Margaret ('Peggy'), Marchioness of, 241

Crewe, Robert ('Bob') Crewe-Milnes, 1st Marquess of, 318

Crimea, 310

Crimean War, 21, 144

Crocus (dog), 105

Crofton Boys, The (Martineau), 106

croquet, 345, 350

Cuba, 101

Cunard, Maud ('Emerald'), Lady, 4, 349

Cunliffe-Lister, Mary (*later* Countess of Swinton), 295

Cunliffe-Lister, Philip (*later* 1st Earl of Swinton), 295

Curraghmore, 277, 278

Curzon of Kedleston, George Curzon, 1st Marquess: banquet at Carlton House Terrace (1918), 227–8; character, 57, 250, 251; at Cliveden, 140; compared with Jack Salmond, 257; and Edwin Montagu, 249; and Ettie's silver wedding anniversary, 167, 327; during First World War, 190, 195; Foreign Secretary, 237, 249, 250–51; and George Wyndham, 165, 241; godfather to Ivo Grenfell, 109, 364; at Hackwood, 167; intimacy with Ettie, 57, 62, 250; at Lord and Lady Ancaster's, 231; Lord Privy Seal, 195; and Panshanger art collection, 170; rejected for premiership, 251; snubbed by Lloyd George, 237; and the Souls, 42, 43, 44, 56–8, 85; taste in food, 132; Viceroy of India, 85; visits Taplow, 164, 198; *Problems of the Far East*, 106

Curzon of Kedleston, Grace, Marchioness, 231, 241, 361

Curzon of Kedleston, Mary, Lady, 100

Curzon, Lady Alexandra, 217, 250

Curzon, Lady Cynthia ('Cimmie') *see* Mosley, Lady Cynthia

Curzon, Lady Irene (*later* 2nd Baroness Ravensdale), 173, 217, 364

Cust, Sir Charles, 303

Cust, Henry ('Harry'), 48, 68–9, 70, 83, 84–5, 86

Cuyp, Aelbert, 285

Czechoslovakia, 329, 330

D-Day, 354

D'Abernon, Edgar Vincent, 1st Viscount: on Balzac, 174; on the Barings, 78; career, 47, 174; in Constantinople, 174; on Curzon, 57; death, 359; dines at Downing Street, 190; at Esher, 180, 332; at Ettie's dinner party in London, 117; Ettie's tribute to, 359; in Ettie's will, 297; and Frederick Lindemann, 288; French holiday with Ettie (1920), 238; golfing holiday with the Grenfells (1904), 112; at Ivor Wimborne's, 222; at Sheringham, 251; and the Souls, 43, 47; visits Panshanger, 218; visits Taplow, 57, 94, 157, 161, 164

D'Abernon, Helen, Viscountess (*earlier* Lady Helen Vincent): on *The Anatomy of Courage*, 357; appearance and character, 266, 360–61; in Constantinople, 174, 175; on Curzon, 250; and death of Ivo Grenfell, 274; at Esher, 180, 332; on Ettie's improvements at Panshanger, 171; at Ettie's parties, 117; in Ettie's will, 297; and Evan Charteris, 75; and Frederick Lindemann, 288; French holiday with Ettie (September 1920), 238; friendship with Ettie, 230; in imaginary women's Cabinet, 222; Imogen Grenfell's wedding gift, 293; on the London Season, 254; on Port Lympne, 236; and the Souls, 43; visits Ettie in hospital, 352; visits Panshanger, 218, 345, 360–61; visits Taplow, 57, 157, 161, 164; war work, 304

Daily Telegraph, 61, 89–90, 117

Daladier, Edouard, 330

Dalkeith, Molly, Countess of (*later* Duchess of Buccleuch), 294

Dalkeith, Walter Montagu-Douglas-Scott, Earl of (*later* 8th Duke of Buccleuch), 294

dancing, 26, 118, 128–9, 231, 253, 255, 309, 318

Dardanelles, 255

Dardanelles Campaign (Gallipoli), 190, 199, 202, 203

Darjeeling, 74

Davidson, Randall, Archbishop of Canterbury, 227

Davis, John W., 235

Davis, Nell, 235

Daws Hill House, 166, 192

Dawson, Sir Bertrand (*later* 1st Viscount Dawson of Penn), 224, 315–16, 321, 322, 323

Dawson, Geoffrey, 187

Day, J. Wentworth, 281, 282

de Bunsen, Berta, Lady, 255

de Bunsen, Sir Maurice, 255

de Grey, Frederick Robinson, Earl *see* Ripon, Frederick Robinson, 2nd Marquess of

de Grey, Gladys, Countess *see* Ripon, Gladys, Marchioness of

de Grey, Thomas, 2nd Earl, 18, 22, 23, 25

de Havilland factory, 339

de la Mare, Constance, 267, 268, 295

de la Mare, Walter, 267–8, 269, 295, 352; 'The Feckless Dinner Party', 268

De Lara, Isidore, 34

de Soissons, Louis, 248

de Vesci, Evelyn, Viscountess: and Duke of Leinster, 127, 206; Ettie first meets, 27; Evan Charteris on, 70; family background, 70, 71; as model for Ettie, 27, 71; **letters to**, 39, 96, 99, 200, 206–7, 220

de Vesci, Yvo Vesey, 5th Viscount, 109

Deacon, Gladys see Marlborough, Gladys, Duchess of

debutantes, 32–3, 166, 254

Declaration of London (1911), 172

Defence of Philosophical Doubt, A (Balfour), 51, 65

Defoe, Daniel: *Robinson Crusoe*, 248

D'Egville, James Hervé, 26

Del Sarto, Andrea, 248

Depression, the, 299

Derby, Alice, Countess of, 167, 231, 295

Derby, Edward Stanley, 17th Earl of, 220, 223, 231, 295, 318

Derbyshire, 21, 176, 366; *see also* Melbourne Hall

Derreen, 272

Desborough, Ettie, Lady: birth, 12; infancy, 13; death of her mother, 9, 13–14; death of her father, 9, 14; orphaned childhood, 14–15, 16–18, 20, 22, 23, 25–7, 152–3; death of her brother, 24–5; girlhood, 28–32, 351; debutante, 32–4; courted by Willie, 34, 36–7; their marriage, 38–9, 61, 64, 73, 131; chatelaine of Taplow, 38–9, 74, 87, 91–4, 284; first pregnancy, 39, 94; death of Henry Cowper, 39–40, 249; burglary at Taplow (1888), 89–90; birth of Julian, 94; second pregnancy, 71, 94, 102; birth of Billy, 94–5, 102; visits Austria (autumn 1890), 69; emotional crisis at end of 1891 Season, 72–3; visits India (1891–2), 52, 58, 73–4, 155; visits Moravia (October 1892), 59; suicide of Clair Herbert, 99–101, 113; politician's wife, 101–3, 104–5, 115; birth of Monica, 101; Mayor's wife, 90–92; holidays with her young family, 105, 107–8, 109, 110, 112, 128, 129, 193; birth of Ivo, 109–110; visits United States and Canada (1899), 76, 115, 153, 241; birth of Imogen, 113; death of Francis Cowper, 113–14, 116, 249, 298; Willie's peerage, 1, 51, 116–17, 298, 299; death of Archie Gordon, 122, 149–51; appointed Lady of the Bedchamber to Queen Mary, 131, 153–6, 168, 304; silver wedding anniversary, 167, 327; visits Kitchener in Egypt (1913), 167–8, 252, 257; death of Katie Cowper, 168–9; visits Constantinople (March 1914), 173–5, 202, 245; state visit to Paris (April 1914), 155–6, 185; war work as Lady in Waiting, 302; Julian's death, 139, 191–7, 204, 206–7, 216, 229, 341; Billy's death, 198–201, 204, 206–7,

216, 229; writes *Pages from a Family Journal*, 6, 204–6, 207, 208, 209–212, 215, 229, 242, 300–301, 328; death of Patrick Shaw-Stewart, 224–6, 229; post-War life at Court, 305–6, 307–8, 309; visits France with Ivo and Monica (May 1919), 231–3, 304; attends Port Lympne conference (June 1920), 236–8; French holiday with the Churchills (September 1920), 238–9; Monica's marriage, 256–8, 297–8, 299–300; holiday in St Moritz with Imogen (1925), 264; Ivo's death, 269, 273–7, 278, 319, 341; Royal duties after death of Queen Alexandra, 311–15, 316, 319; birth of grandchildren, 280, 297, 320–21; deaths of Revelstoke and Balfour, 289–91; Imogen's marriage, 292–5; writes her will, 296–7, 366; French holiday with Louis Mallet and Jack Stanmore (1931), 295–6; and death of King George V, 321–5; golden wedding anniversary, 327; supports Chamberlain's appeasement policy, 328–32; wartime in Hertfordshire, 334–5, 338–40, 343–4, 345, 346–7, 348–9, 350; writes memoir of her girlhood, 351; falls and fractures her femur, 351–3, 354; Willie's death, 355–7; failing health, 353, 354, 356, 359–60, 365, 367–8; death, 369; her estate, 366

Character & characteristics: abstention from alcohol, 80, 259, 303; accent, 4, 15–16, 169, 266, 340; ageing, 142–3, 230, 255, 343, 369; appearance, 2, 3, 86, 117, 142, 230, 259, 347; archetype of her age, 55–6, 130, 178, 368–9; attention-seeking, 5, 13; capriciousness, 5; charity work, 92, 264–6; close with money, 93, 299; complexity, 3, 36; confidante, 19–20, 62, 68, 131, 139, 143; conversationalist, 3, 50, 56, 60, 143, 253–4, 259, 266; courage, 100, 142, 224, 225–6, 228, 236, 334, 365, 367; as courtier, 131, 151, 153–6, 303, 304, 305, 307–8, 312, 316, 319, 322; dislike of being photographed, 91; dislike of music, 7, 26, 80, 259, 313; dislike of ostentation, 93, 324; enjoyment of young people's company, 142–3, 146, 258, 260, 305; expressiveness, 5, 31; eye complaints, 125, 197, 278, 324, 327; flirtatiousness, 5, 13, 22, 33, 62, 64; friendship, 33, 55, 62, 135, 142, 230, 367, 368; 'gospel of joy', 6, 7–8, 36, 135, 227, 246, 348, 367; as hostess, 4, 5, 40–41, 56, 90, 92–4, 112, 128, 131–2, 368; idealism, 30–31, 135; intelligence, 7, 56, 152, 327; investments, 68, 80; letter-writing, 52, 81, 259, 354, 368; love of literature, 7, 45, 58, 67, 105–7, 118, 124, 158, 159–61, 226, 268, 347, 348; love of nature, 7, 137, 357; manners, 2–3, 4, 50, 56; melancholy, 6, 39–40, 56, 62, 73, 100, 196, 259, 263, 328; morality, 62, 64–6, 183;

motherhood, 94–8, 110, 117–19, 128–9, 211, 253, 308; mottoes, 2, 287, 345; organisational capacity, 93, 131; philistine about visual arts, 7, 259; politics, 102, 104–5, 163–5; possessiveness, 13, 121, 126, 127, 259; posture, 29, 134; public speaking, 91; quarrelsomeness, 81–2, 119; religious faith, 7, 19, 65, 68, 96, 150, 196, 201, 206–7, 277–8, 324–5, 341; resolve, 6–7, 30, 39–40, 100, 196, 225–6, 253, 334; restraint, 110; self-discipline, 3, 7, 31, 39–40, 228, 259; serenity, 287; slang, 31, 37, 143, 309; snobbery, 109, 212, 226; stamina, 132–3; sympathy, 3–4, 19, 56, 61, 367; urbanity, 2, 55; views on Americans, 140, 235, 241; views on death, 135, 159–60, 196, 201, 215–16, 246; visual receptivity, 21, 54, 73–4, 259; vitality, 3, 52, 56, 142–3, 367; white lies, 60, 145; wit, 3, 368

Writings: commonplace book, 93, 268–9; contributions to *The Times*, 124, 152, 153, 264, 276, 281–2, 328, 338, 359; *Eyes of Youth*, 351; *Pages from a Family Journal*, 6, 204–6, 207, 208, 209–212, 215, 229, 242, 300–301, 328; pocket diary, 345, 348; tribute to George Vernon for *Westminster Review*, 203–4

Desborough, William ('Willie') Grenfell, 1st Baron: appreciation of King George V, 323; and Billy's death, 199, 201, 218; and Boer War, 110–111; and burglary at Taplow, 89; business career, 66; Chairman of Thames Conservancy Board, 240; character, 5, 34–5, 103, 105, 269, 271, 289, 298, 356; and children's upbringing, 106, 128; and Consuelo Marlborough, 132; and Council for the Preservation of Rural England, 283; courting of Ettie, 34, 36–7; death, 355–7; and death of Kitchener, 208; and Duke of Westminster, 41, 89; and Ettie's charity work, 265; and Ettie's fall (1943), 351, 352; family background, 87, 88; during First World War, 183; golden wedding anniversary, 327; and governor-generalship of Canada, 68, 115, 240–41; High Sheriff of Buckinghamshire, 88; High Steward and Mayor of Maidenhead, 90–91; hunting trips, 61, 65, 73, 168; inherits Taplow, 88; and Ivo's death, 275, 276, 278, 279; jaundice, 353, 355; and Julian's death, 191–4, 197, 201; Knight of the Garter, 289; and Lord Quickswood, 349; marriage, 38–9, 61, 64, 73, 131; memorial service, 357; Olympic Games (1908), 147–9; ornithology, 279, 329; and Oscar Wilde, 362; owns Skindle's Hotel, 282; at Panshanger during Second World War, 343, 345, 346; parliamentary career, 35, 37, 41, 102–4, 115, 163; peerage, 1, 51, 116–17, 298, 299; President of Imperial Air Fleet Committee,

172–3; psychic beliefs, 216; punting, 264, 271, 283, 284, 345; rheumatism, 273; and the Souls, 42; special correspondent to Sudan, 61; tours Canada with Duke of Sutherland (1911), 108; typhoid, 61; unpublished books, 271; visits Holkham (1887), 46–7; visits India (1891–2), 73–4; visits Ireland with Ettie (1926), 272; visits Ivo at Oxford, 243; visits Kitchener in Egypt (1913), 167–8; his will, 365

Desborough Settlement Trust, 366
Devon, 23, 251, 290
Devonshire, Spencer Cavendish, 8th Duke of, 115
Devonshire, Victor Cavendish, 9th Duke of, 150, 240, 288, 294, 318
Devonshire, Evelyn ('Evie'; *née* Fitzmaurice), Duchess of, 150, 154, 156, 277, 288, 294, 322, 339
Devonshire, Louise, Duchess of (*earlier* Duchess of Manchester), 46, 115
Devonshire, Mary, Duchess of (*earlier* Lady Mary ('Mima') Cecil), 167
Diamond Hill, 110
Dickens, Charles: *Oliver Twist*, 23, 106
Dickson-Poynder, Ann, Lady *see* Islington, Ann, Lady
Dickson-Poynder, Sir John *see* Islington, John Dickson-Poynder, 1st Baron
Dictionary of National Biography, 85
Diminutive Dramas (Baring), 81
Dingwall (barony), 114
Dionysus, 124
Disraeli, Benjamin, Earl of Beaconsfield, 25, 41, 51
Ditchley Park, 341
Don Quixote (Cervantes), 107
Donnay, Maurice, 239
Dorando, Pietri, 149
Dorian Gray (Wilde), 58
Dorset, 109, 110, 129
Dostoevsky, Fyodor, 226
Douglas, Norman: *South Wind*, 269
Dover, 83, 156, 173, 180
Dracula (Stoker), 319
Dresdner Bank, 144
Drôme, 238
Drummond, Henry: *The Ascent of Man*, 52, 106
Drummond, Katherine ('Kitty'), 219, 361
Dublin, 177
Dublin Castle, 146
Dudley, Rachel, Countess of, 140, 172
Dudley, Eric Ward, 3rd Earl of (*earlier* Viscount Ednam), 173, 242, 257, 339–40
Duff, Sir Michael ('Mikie'), 335–6, 350, 354–5, 363
Dugdale, Lady Eva, 155

Dunkirk, 336
Dunluce Castle (ship), 184, 185
Dunn, (Sir) James ('Jimmy'), 144
Dunraven and Mount-Earl, Windham Wyndham-Quin, 4th Earl of, 70
Dunrobin Castle, 22, 212
Durham, County, 138
Durham, John ('Jack'), 5th Earl of, 318
Dusty Answer (Lehmann), 271
Duveen, Sir Joseph (*later* 1st Baron), 284-5
Duveen Brothers (art dealers), 170, 284-5

Eales, Bessie, 23-4
East Sussex County Council, 281
Eaton Hall, 22, 287, 302
Ebb Tide (Stevenson), 106
Edinburgh, 127
Ednam, Eric, Viscount (*later* 3rd Earl of Dudley), 173, 242, 257, 339-40
Edward IV, King, 18
Edward VII, King, 115, 147-8, 151-2; buys Sandringham from the Cowpers, 311; Coronation, 151; as Prince of Wales, 46, 69, 311
Edward VIII, King: abdication, 325-6; and death of his father, 322, 323; military career, 303; as Prince of Wales, 154, 255, 274, 319, 322
Edwardians, The (Sackville-West), 134, 141-2
Egypt, 9, 38, 111, 167-8, 180, 213, 252, 257
Eighty Club, 89
Elcho, Hugo Charteris, Lord *see* Wemyss, Hugo Charteris, 11th Earl of
Elcho, Hugo ('Ego') Francis Charteris, Lord, 208-9
Elcho, Mary, Lady *see* Wemyss, Mary, Countess of
Elcho, Lady Violet ('Letty'; *née* Manners), 54, 121, 124
Elgar, Sir Edward: *Enigma Variations*, 357
Elibank, 88
Eliot, T. S.: *Four Quartets*, 348
Elizabeth, Princess (*later* Queen Elizabeth II), 312, 319-20, 355, 363
Elizabeth, Queen (consort of George VI; *earlier* Lady Elizabeth Bowes-Lyon), 316, 319, 363
Elizabeth, Queen of the Belgians, 309
Ellis, Sir Arthur, 33
Eminent Victorians (Strachey), 42, 226
Emmanuel College, Cambridge, 12
Enfield, 339
English Seamen (Froude), 107
Enver Pasha, 175
Epée Club, 147
Escrick, 63
Esher, Reginald Brett, 2nd Viscount, 25, 66, 131
Esher Place, 174, 180, 288, 332, 361

Essendon, 343
Essex, George ('Sulky') Capell, 7th Earl of, 133, 246, 247
Essex, Algernon ('Algy') Capell, 8th Earl of (*earlier* Viscount Malden), 143
Essex, Adèle, Countess of: appearance and character, 246; background, 4; death, 246, 247; and Edith Wharton, 133, 295; and Ettie's relationship with Archie Gordon, 145, 246; and Ettie's silver wedding anniversary, 167, 327; and Evan Charteris, 77, 196; friendship with Ettie, 130, 140, 246; at Hackwood, 241; in imaginary women's Cabinet, 222; and *Pages from a Family Journal*, 211; at Port Lympne, 236; visits Taplow, 93, 141
Essex, Clifford, 255
Essex Timber Company, 301
Eton, 148, 209, 344
Eton College, 261, 263; Billy Grenfell at, 97, 119, 124, 217; the Eton 'push', 120-21, 143; Ettie's Eton parties, 112, 118, 157, 161, 176; Ivo Grenfell at, 177, 192, 202, 216, 217, 223; Julian Grenfell at, 112, 119, 126, 127, 217; war memorial, 239-40
Euripides, 124; *Hippolytus*, 193
Evening Standard, 334
Evolution of Ethics (Huxley), 106
evolutionary theory, 52, 106
Eyes of Youth, 351

Fabians, 158
Fane, Lady Adine (*née* Cowper; Ettie's mother), 9, 11-14, 21, 40, 41
Fane, Constance ('Connie') *see* Manners, Constance ('Connie'), Lady
Fane, John ('Johnnie'; Ettie's brother), 9, 13, 16-17, 19, 23, 24, 152
Fane, Julian (Ettie's father), 9-14, 40
Farnborough, 172
Fécamp, 108
'Feckless Dinner Party, The' (de la Mare), 268
Ferdinand I, King of Romania, 289
Feversham, Charles ('Sim') Duncombe, 3rd Earl of, 261
Fife, Alexander Duff, 1st Duke of, 155
Fingall, Elizabeth, Countess of, 138
Firle, 258, 281, 292, 295, 366, 367
First World War: air raids, 221-2, 302; Battle of Hooge, 198-9, 199-200; Battle of Loos, 203; Battle of the Somme, 212, 222-3; Dardanelles Campaign (Gallipoli), 190, 199, 202, 203; Ettie's war work with King and Queen, 302; outbreak of, 177-8, 179-81; Ypres Salient, 191, 206; *see also* Armistice (1918); Paris peace conference (1919); reparations
Fisher, H. A. L.: on Churchill, 234, 328; and Council for the Preservation of Rural

England, 283; at the D'Abernons, 332; Ettie as confidante, 105; Minister of Education, 233; visits Panshanger, 235, 236; visits Taplow, 233, 244, 290, 328; *Napoleon*, 107; **letters to**, 307, 331

Fitzalan-Howard, Lady Rachel, 332

FitzGerald, Lord Desmond ('Dessy'), 127, 170, 173, 184, 185, 206, 229

Fitzgerald, F. Scott: *The Great Gatsby*, 253

FitzGerald, Oswald, 170, 178, 208

FitzRoy, Sir Almeric, 138, 152

Flimwell School, 273

Florence, 9, 10, 152

flying, 156, 172–3, 248, 287, 322, 350

Foch, Ferdinand, 237

Folkestone, 189

Fontainebleau forest, 232

Foundations of Belief (Balfour), 51

France, 38, 107–8, 112, 156, 168, 238–9, 275–6, 288, 295, 299; First World War, 177, 187–9, 303–4; Second World War, 330; *see also* Paris

France, Anatole, 108

Francis and Riversdale Grenfell (Buchan), 242

Franz Ferdinand, Archduke of Austria, 176–7

Frederick VII, King of Denmark, 155

Freeman-Mitford, Clement, 194

Fremantle, John (*later* 4th Baron Cottesloe), 264, 270

French, Sir John (*later* 1st Earl of Ypres), 190, 215, 219

Frogmore Cottage, 310

Frost, Robert, 160

Froude, James: *English Seamen*, 107

Furness, Enid, Viscountess (*later* Countess of Kenmare), 350, 355

Gage, Camilla (*later* Lady Cazalet), 282, 297, 333, 335, 347, 353, 358, 360

Gage, George ('Sammy'; *later* 7th Viscount), 297, 320–21, 333, 335, 347, 353, 358

Gage, Henry ('George'), 6th Viscount: county councillor, 281; on Curzon, 250; early relationship with Imogen Grenfell, 263–4, 272, 277, 292; on Edward Marjoribanks, 262; on Ettie, 258–9, 266; marriage, 292–5; military career, 258, 333, 344; planning expertise, 281; at Willie's burial, 356

Gage, Imogen, Viscountess *see* Grenfell, Imogen

Gage, Nicolas ('Nicky'; *later* 8th Viscount), 297, 333, 335, 347, 353, 358

Gainsborough, Thomas: *Blue Boy*, 285

Gallipoli, 199, 202, 203

Galway, George Monckton-Arundell, 8th Viscount, 127, 170

Galway, Lucia, Viscountess, 358

Gap in the Curtain, The (Buchan), 4

Garnett, Constance, 26

Garnett, Miss (governess), 26

Garter, Knights of the, 289

gassing, 302

Gaston, Rose, 130, 168, 191, 231, 260

Gautier, Théophile, 83

Gaza, 222

George I, King of Greece, 155

George V, King: and Bonar Law's resignation and Baldwin's appointment, 251; character and life at Court, 303, 304–5, 308–310, 313–15, 316–19, 321; Coronation, 140, 155; death, 307, 321–5; and Desborough peerage, 298, 299; and Edwin Montagu's resignation, 249; Gore's *George V*, 312–13, 316–19, 323, 342; illness (1928–29), 307, 315–16, 317; invited to Panshanger (1914), 171; and Ivo Grenfell's death, 273, 274; and John Revelstoke, 273, 318; makes Willie Desborough Knight of the Garter, 289; marriage, 153; his parrot, 305, 312, 322; as Prince of Wales, 153–4; at Sandringham, 311–13, 321–2; sponsor of 'Sammy' Gage, 320–21; state visit to Paris (April 1914), 155–6; tours Midlands (June 1914), 176; visits Welbeck (June 1914), 176; war work, 302, 303

George VI, King: accession, 326; death, 369; and death of his father, 321, 322; as Duke of York, 319, 321; and Gore's *George V*, 316; marriage, 319; military career, 303; as Prince Albert, 154, 303

George, Prince, Duke of Kent, 154, 255, 322

Germany: militarisation before First World War, 172; First World War, 178, 179, 228, 330; post-First World War unrest, 231; reparations, 81, 289–90; Nazi annexation of Austria and Czechoslovakia, 329–30, 332; non-aggression pact with Russia, 332; Second World War, 332–3, 358; *see also* Berlin

Gibbon, Henry, 125–6

Gibbons, Grinling, 247

Gisburne, 202

Gladstone, William Ewart, 25, 35, 41, 51, 93, 102, 103–4

Glimpses of the Moon, The (Wharton), 296

Gobernuisgach, 98

Godolphin Osborne, Lady Moira (*later* Viscountess Chandos), 173, 217

Goldie, Sir George Taubman, 147

golf, 112, 166, 247

Good, Barrett, 266, 292

Goode, Thomas (shop), 309

Gordon, Archibald ('Archie'): character and career, 144–5, 146; death, 122, 149–51, 202,

204, 212; and Edward Marjoribanks, 261; at
Eton parties, 112, 118; relationship with Ettie,
119, 143, 144–7, 151, 246, 365
Gordon-Lennox, Lady Algernon, 270
Gore, Lady Alice *see* Salisbury, Alice,
Marchioness of
Gore, Arthur (*later* 6th Earl of Arran), 17
Gore, Lady Esther (*later* Viscountess
Hambleden), 17, 20
Gore, John, 342–3, 346–7, 351, 352–3, 367–8,
369; *George V*, 312–13, 316–18, 323, 342;
letters to, 342, 347–8, 354
Gore, Mabell *see* Airlie, Mabell, Countess of
Goschen, George, 1st Viscount, 134
Gosford, Archibald Acheson, 4th Earl of, 115
Gosford, Louisa, Countess of, 115
Gosford House, 54, 77, 208, 335
Gosse, (Sir) Edmund, 86, 118, 141
Gough, Charles, 27
Grafton, Susanna, Duchess of, 329
Grahame-White, Claude, 172, 173
Granby, Henry Manners, Marquess of *see*
Rutland, Henry Manners, 8th Duke of
Granby, Violet, Marchioness of *see* Rutland,
Violet, Duchess of
Grasse, 295
Grayshott, 190, 220
Great Contemporaries (Churchill), 291, 295
Great Marlow, 87
Great North Road, 284
Great West Road, 283, 284
Great Western Railway, 88
Greece, 155, 237
Green Line bus, 360, 361
Green, Thomas: *Witness of God and Faith*,
65–6, 67
Greenock, Alan, Lord (*later* 4th Earl Cathcart),
36–7
Grenfell family, 87, 88, 223
Grenfell, Arthur, 118, 222–3
Grenfell, Charles ('Willie's grandfather), 87
Grenfell, Charles William ('Willie's father), 88
Grenfell, Claude, 110
Grenfell, Edward (*later* 1st Baron St Just), 88
Grenfell, Francis, 1st Baron, 88, 116–17, 166,
265
Grenfell, Francis Octavius, 223, 242
Grenfell, Georgiana ('Willie's mother), 89, 166
Grenfell, Gerald William ('Billy'): appearance,
128, 207; and Archie Gordon, 144–5, 151;
birth, 94, 96, 102; character, 5, 6, 95, 124–5,
136–7, 207, 244; childhood, 91, 95, 96, 97–8,
101, 103, 105, 106–8, 110, 111–12, 113;
commemorated in *Pages from a Family
Journal*, 6, 207, 209–212; death, 5, 141,
198–201, 204, 221, 229; and Ettie's
inheritance of Panshanger, 170; features in

The Book of the Grenvilles, 242; and Julian's
death, 192, 194, 195, 221, 261; on Katie
Cowper's funeral, 168–9; and Kitchener, 111;
military service, 181, 184, 185, 190–91, 192,
220, 221; on Monica's wartime nursing
career, 183; and Nancy Astor, 141, 144, 183,
195, 200; on Nannie Wake, 97; at Oxford, 5,
124–6, 181; on Pamela Lytton, 123; religious
faith, 169; schooldays, 97, 109, 112, 119, 124,
217; and W. B. Yeats, 160
Grenfell, Henry, 88
Grenfell, Imogen ('Mogs', 'Moggie'; *later*
Viscountess Gage): appearance, 113, 219,
256, 263, 270, 343; birth, 113; character, 128,
220, 234, 235, 253; childhood, 92, 101, 108,
128–9, 161, 177, 218, 219, 220, 252–3; her
children, 297, 320–21; death, 300; debutante,
255–6, 319; early relationship with George
Gage, 263–4, 272, 277, 292; Ettie's
amanuensis, 367; and Ettie's charity work,
265; and *Eyes of Youth*, 351; father's death,
356; and Frederick Lindemann, 287, 288;
girlhood, 234, 244; godparents, 113, 128, 321;
holiday to St Moritz with Ettie (1925), 264;
and Ivo's death, 273, 275, 276; at John
Revelstoke's funeral, 290; and Julian's and
Billy's deaths, 192, 194, 200, 252–3; and
Kitchener, 208; and Lord Waterford, 272,
277, 287; marriage, 292–5; in parents' wills,
296, 366; and Patrick Shaw-Stewart, 225; and
Rex Whistler, 354; during Second World
War, 343, 344, 350
Grenfell, Ivo: agricultural training, 243–4, 273;
appearance, 109–110; birth, 109; character,
109, 128, 234, 243, 275; childhood, 92, 101,
108, 110, 111–12, 113, 117–18, 128–9, 149;
death, 5, 269, 273–4, 319, 341, 356, 357;
game-hunting in British East Africa, 243; and
George Gage, 292; godparents, 109, 364;
health, 223–4; inherits Whitesea Lodge, 278,
279; and Julian's death, 191, 192, 194–5;
Maurice Baring's poem for, 372–3; military
service, 222, 223–4, 233, 234, 279; at Oxford,
234, 243, 288; and Rosamond Lehmann, 272;
schooldays, 141, 177, 185, 191, 192, 202, 216,
217, 223; tours Australia, 243; visits Paris
with Ettie (1919), 231–2, 232–3
Grenfell, Julian ('Max', 'Juju'): appearance,
108–9, 136, 207, 271; awarded DSO, 189;
birth, 94; character, 5, 6, 95, 119, 120, 121,
136, 207, 244; childhood, 91, 95, 97–8, 101,
103, 105, 106–8, 110, 111–12, 113, 118–19;
commemorated in *Pages from a Family
Journal*, 6, 207, 209–212; death, 5, 139, 191–5,
204, 220–21, 229, 244, 341; depressions,
121–2, 122–3, 124, 259; on Ettie, 110, 133, 153;
and Ettie's inheritance of Panshanger,

169–70; features in *The Book of Grenvilles*, 242; godfather to Imogen, 113; on H. G. Wells, 158; his grave, 194, 232; his greyhounds, 9, 121; in India, 124; and John Bigge, 127; and Katie Cowper, 113, 121, 123; and Kitchener, 111, 151; love for Pamela Lytton, 123–4, 144; and Marjorie Manners, 121, 123, 124, 127, 314; Maurice Baring's sonnet to, 195, 372; military career, 124, 169, 171, 181, 184–6, 189, 243, 302; on Monica, 256; and Nancy Astor, 141; Nicholas Mosley's biography of, 258; at Oxford, 5, 119–21, 124; religious faith, 97, 120–21, 193; resentment of Ettie's male admirers, 119, 122, 144; rows with Ettie, 119; schooldays, 108–9, 112, 217; as totemic figure, 242; twenty-first birthday, 121–2; and Vita Sackville-West, 175; wartime letters, 184–5, 186–7, 189, 350; writings, 122, 195, 205, 239, 370–71

Grenfell, Monica ('Casie'; *later* Lady Salmond): appearance, 101, 166, 252, 270, 285, 286; and Archie Gordon, 144; on Armistice day, 228–9; birth, 101; character, 252, 286; childhood, 92, 108, 110, 111–12, 113, 117–18, 135–6, 138, 149; her children, 108, 280–81, 320; daughter's marriage, 364; debutante, 127, 166, 178–9, 180–81, 252, 254; engagement, 256–7; and Ettie's charity work, 265; and *Eyes of Youth*, 351; father's death, 355, 356; first flight, 172, 173; on First World War air raids, 222; godparents, 101, 257; and husband's career, 285; and Imogen's death, 300; and Ivo's death, 273; and Julian's and Billy's deaths, 191, 192, 194, 200; marriage, 257–8, 297–8, 299–300; in parents' wills, 296, 366; prospective husbands for, 126–7, 194, 252; rows with Ettie, 286–7; schooling of her son, 108; during Second World War, 333; twenty-first birthday, 101, 180, 252; visits Berlin (1909), 150; visits Kitchener in Egypt (1913), 167–8; visits Paris and Julian's grave with Ettie (1919), 231–2; wartime nursing career, 166, 183–4, 185, 187–9, 197, 216, 229, 243, 252, 300–301; at Whiteslea Lodge, 279; *Bright Armour*, 300–301, 350; **letters to**, 114, 150, 174–5, 179, 185, 190, 197, 198, 203, 208, 217, 218, 220–21, 227–8, 228–9, 256, 263, 275–6, 292, 298, 320, 326, 332, 333, 355–6

Grenfell, Pascoe (Willie's cousin), 223
Grenfell, Pascoe (Willie's great-grandfather), 87, 103
Grenfell, Riversdale, 223, 242
Grenfell, Robert, 223
Greville, (Dame) Margaret ('Maggie'), 4
Grey, Charles, 2nd Earl, 66
Grey, Henry, 3rd Earl, 21

Grey, Albert, 4th Earl, 66–8, 69, 78, 95, 102, 115, 140, 153
Grey, Sir Edward (*later* 1st Viscount Grey of Fallodon), 178, 190, 279
Grimsthorpe Castle, 130, 179
Grosvenor, Lord Edward, 246
Grosvenor, Lady Edward (*née* Browne, *afterwards* Lady Dorothy Charteris), 77, 173, 246, 343–4, 350, 352, 361, 368–9
Grosvenor, Sibell, Countess: and Balfour, 291; at Ettie's parties, 117, 157; marriage, 83, 85, 157, 291; and the Souls, 43, 165
Grosvenor Gallery Restaurant, 67
Guest, Ivor (*later* 1st Viscount Wimborne), 82, 86, 222, 231
Guindy, 73–4
Gulliver's Travels (Swift), 106
Guy's Hospital, 302

Hackwood Park, 22, 130, 166–7, 241
Haddo, 151
Haddo, George Gordon, Lord (*later* 2nd Marquess of Aberdeen and Temair), 145
Haggard, (Sir) Henry Rider, 107
Hague Peace Conference (1907), 172
Haigh Hall, 341
Hailsham, Douglas Hogg, 1st Viscount, 261, 312, 322
Haldane, Richard, 1st Viscount, 48, 112, 118
Hals, Franz, 284–5
Halswell, Wyndham, 148
Hambleden, Esther, Viscountess (*née* Gore), 17, 20
Hambleden, Frederick Smith, 2nd Viscount, 283
Hamel, Gustav, 172–3, 175–6, 350
Hamilton, Lord Claud, 321–2
Hamilton, Lady Cynthia (*later* Viscountess Althorp, *then* Countess Spencer), 230
Hamilton, (Sir) Edward ('Eddy'), 45–6, 50, 102, 104
Hamilton, Sir Ian: Ettie visits, 185; at Ettie's parties, 117, 141, 164, 219; favourite dinner menu, 132; during First World War, 190, 199; High Commissioner at Malta, 164; social ban on, 164; visits Panshanger, 235; visits Taplow, 245
Hamilton, Jean, Lady: and Billy Grenfell's death, 199; on death of Adèle Essex, 247; dines at Downing Street, 190; at Dudley House, 255; on Edgar D'Abernon, 174; on Ettie, 117, 135, 142, 161; Ettie visits, 185; at Ettie's parties, 117, 135, 141, 164, 219–20; on Pamela Lytton, 123; social ban on, 164; visits Panshanger, 235; visits Taplow, 245; **letters to**, 264–5
Hampshire, 98–9, 137, 190

Hampton Court Palace, 310
Hankey, Sir Maurice (*later* 1st Baron), 237, 322
Harbord, Charles (*later* 6th Baron Suffield), 33
Harcourt, Lewis ('Loulou'), 1st Viscount, 85, 102, 103, 190, 195
Harcourt, Sir William, 10, 25, 35, 103, 104, 306
Hardelot forest, 194, 221
Hardinge, Alexander ('Alec'; *later* 2nd Baron Hardinge of Penshurst), 321
Hardinge, Charles, 1st Baron Hardinge of Penshurst, 164
Harewood, Henry Lascelles, 4th Earl of, 62
Harewood, Henry ('Harry') Lascelles, 6th Earl of (*earlier* Viscount Lascelles), 173, 312, 319
Harris, Lady Elizabeth ('Betty'; *later* Fremantle), 270
Harris, George, 4th Baron, 73
Harris, Sir William, 357
Harrogate, 224
Harrow School, 157, 176
Hartley, L. P., 301
Harvard University, 182
Hatfield: bypass, 284; de Havilland factory, 339; station, 219, 339
Hatfield House, 110, 111, 130, 171, 178, 335, 339
Hawkhurst, 244, 273–4
Hawksmoor, Nicholas, 179
Hawthornden prize, 263
Hay, Ivan, 170, 180
Hayes, J. J., 149
Heart's Journey, The (Sassoon), 269
Heath, Voltelin, 184
Hebrides, 214
Hedsor House, 166
Heigham Sound, 279
Helmsley, William Duncombe, Viscount, 138
Hendon, 172, 173
Henley, W. E.: *Lyra Heroica*, 135
Henley-on-Thames, 88, 149
Henry VIII, King, 179
Henry, Prince, Duke of Gloucester, 154, 312, 363
Herbert, Auberon, 21, 98, 99
Herbert, Auberon ('Bron') *see* Lucas, Auberon Herbert, 8th Baron Lucas of Crudwell
Herbert, Aubrey, 184, 190
Herbert, Clair, 36, 98–100, 101, 113
Herbert, David, 350
Herbert, Lady Florence (*née* Cowper; 'Dolly', 'Aunt Dordor'), 21, 24, 27, 29–30, 35–6, 39–40, 71, 98, 100
Herbert, George, 193
Herbert, Lelia, Lady, 230
Herbert, Nan (*later* Baroness Lucas of Crudwell), 98, 99, 101, 213, 298
Herbert, Rolf, 29, 36
Hereford, 102–3, 104

Herodotus, 26
Heroes, The (Kingsley), 106
Hertford, 50, 115, 284, 338, 339, 351
Hertfordshire, 2, 21, 171, 247–8, 284, 334, 338; *see also* Ashridge; Brocket Hall; Cassiobury House; Hatfield House; Knebworth House; Panshanger
Hertingfordbury, 168
Heuser, Fraulein (governess), 26
Hewett, Sir Stanley, 321, 323
Hickling Broad, 279, 281
'Hilary Maltby and Stephen Braxton' (Beerbohm), 159
Hillary, Richard, 350
Hillingdon, Alice, Lady, 203
Hillingdon, Charles Mills, 2nd Baron, 203
Hindhead, 220–21
Hippolytus (Euripides), 193
Hirsch, Baron Maurice de, 69
Hitler, Adolf, 329, 332
Hoare, Sir Samuel (*later* 1st Viscount Templewood), 332
Hogg, Douglas (*later* 1st Viscount Hailsham), 261, 312, 322
Hohenberg, Sophie, Duchess of, 176–7
Holkham Hall, 47
Holland House set, 4, 10, 15, 266, 340
Holmes, Oliver Wendell: begins correspondence with Ettie, 40; and Billy Grenfell, 94, 98, 106, 201; and Boer War, 110, 111; at Brocket, 40; and the 'Cowper indolence', 56; and death of Balfour, 291; and death of Henry Cowper, 40; Ettie sends his books to Asquith, 59; and Ettie's crisis in 1891, 73; and Ettie's India trip, 73, 75; and Ettie's reading, 106; and Ettie's Scottish holidays, 105; as father-figure to Ettie, 65–6; and First World War, 186–7, 189, 228; and George Gage, 292; on H. G. Wells, 158; and Julian Grenfell, 98, 106, 186–7, 194, 201; and Taplow, 93; 'The Soldier's Faith', 182–3, 215, 228
Holyport, 285, 286
Home Rule Bill (1886), 35, 41–2, 102, 103–4
Homer: *The Odyssey*, 106
Hooge, Battle of, 198–9, 199–200
Hope, Anthony, 107
Hope, Lady Mary, 270
Hopkins, Harry, 341
Horne, Sir Robert (*later* 1st Viscount Horne of Slamannan), 235, 248, 255
Horner family, 112, 118
Horner, Edward, 119, 137, 158, 192
Horner, Frances, Lady: death of her son, 61; and the Souls, 43, 48, 49; and Violet Asquith, 145, 146; visits Panshanger, 235
Horsey Mere, 279

Houghton Hall, 22, 312
House of Lords: Librarian, 118; reform of, 42, 164–5
House of Pomegranates, A (Wilde), 58
Howard, (Sir) Ebenezer, 247–8
Howick, 67
Human Document, A (Mallock), 52
Human Origins (Laing), 106
Hunstanton, 190
Huxley, Thomas: *Evolution of Ethics*, 106
Hyères, 285, 295
Hylton, Alice, Lady, 296

Imitation of Christ, The, 97
'Imogen (A Lady of Tender Age)' (Newbolt), 128–9
Imperial Air Fleet Committee, 172–3
Imperial Airways, 299
Imperial Chambers of Commerce, 176
Imperial Ottoman Bank, 174
India, 52, 57, 63, 73–4, 85, 103, 111, 124, 155, 256, 260, 299
Indian Mutiny, 21
Institute of British Architects, 23
International Olympic Committee, 147
'Into Battle' (Julian Grenfell), 195, 205, 239, 370–71
Inver River, 107
Ipswich, 71
Iraq, 256, 257, 299
Ireland, 88, 177, 229, 244, 255, 272; Home Rule, 35, 41–2, 89, 102, 103–4
Ironside, Edmund (*later* 1st Baron), 233
Islington, Ann, Lady (*earlier* Lady Dickson-Poynder), 133, 134, 149, 234, 256, 257, 289, 361
Islington, John Dickson-Poynder, 1st Baron, 134, 149, 289
Italy, 38, 66, 123, 152, 169, 238, 246
'Ivo Grenfell' (Baring), 372–3

James I, King, 9
James, Henry, 133, 195, 295
James, William: *Will to Believe*, 108
Jane Eyre (Brontë), 23, 319
Japan, 82
jazz, 231, 253, 255
Jekyll, Gertrude, 245
Jemal Pasha, 175
Jocelyn, Frances ('Fanny'), Lady, 17, 20, 31, 100
Johann, Prince of Denmark, 155
John, Prince, 303, 305
Joicey, Katherine ('Kitty'), Lady, 364
Jolliffe, Elizabeth ('Betty'), 267, 275, 276
Jones, Inigo, 45
Jones, (Sir) Lawrence ('Jonah'), 119, 121

Joyce, James, 226
Judaism, 197
'Julian Grenfell' (Baring), 195, 372

Kahn, Otto, 248, 255
Keats, John, 106
Keir, Murdoch, 107, 193
Kemsley, Gomer Berry, 1st Viscount, 329
Kenmare, Valentine Browne, 5th Earl of (*earlier* Viscount Castlerosse): death, 343–4; engagement, 37, 70; golden wedding anniversary, 327; in Ireland, 272; marriage, 70; at Taplow, 88, 136
Kenmare, Valentine Browne, 6th Earl of (*earlier* Viscount Castlerosse), 88, 184, 224, 344, 350, 355
Kenmare, Elizabeth, Countess of (*née* Baring, *then* Viscountess Castlerosse): on Armistice day, 229; birth of children, 95; death, 354, 355; death of second son, 202–3, 204, 224, 232–3; engagement, 37, 70; in Ettie's will, 296; failing health, 343–4; family background, 70–71; golden wedding anniversary, 327; in Ireland, 229, 255, 272; and Ivo Grenfell's death, 274; marriage, 70, 167; and military service of youngest son, 224; moves to Essendon during Second World War, 343–4; and *Pages from a Family Journal*, 211; son's marriage, 350; visits military cemetery after Armistice, 304; visits Taplow, 244, 267; and wounding of elder son, 184, 224
Kenmare, Enid, Countess of (*earlier* Viscountess Furness), 350, 355
Kent, 21, 29, 37, 114, 176, 236, 244, 273
Kent, Henry Grey, 1st Duke of, 18, 19, 21, 40
Kent, Princess Marina, Duchess of, 355, 363
Keppel, Alice, 151–2, 222, 254, 325
Keppel, Bridget, 230
Keppel, George, 152
Kerr, Lady Amabel (*née* Cowper; 'Mamie', 'Aunt Amy'), 21, 99, 114
Kerr, Lord Walter, 21, 249
Keynes, John Maynard (*later* 1st Baron), 266–7, 295
Keynes, Lydia, 295
Khartoum, 111
Kidd, Benjamin: *Social Evolution*, 52
Kilbracken, Arthur Godley, 1st Baron, 206, 209, 229
Killarney, 88, 229, 272
Kingsley, Charles: *The Heroes*, 106
Kipling, Carrie, 160, 295
Kipling, Rudyard: Ettie reads to children, 106, 107; Ettie's views on, 52, 131, 160; at Imogen Grenfell's wedding, 295; and *Pages from a*

Family Journal, 210; visits Ettie, 2, 160, 266, 269, 270; 'City of Brass', 160
Kirkwall, 87
Kitchener, Herbert, 1st Earl: and Billy Grenfell, 111, 199, 200–201; career, 105, 111, 164; at Cliveden, 140; death, 207–8; Desboroughs visit in Egypt (1913), 167–8, 252, 257; and First World War, 178, 180, 190, 223; friendship with Willie and Ettie, 111; godfather to Imogen Grenfell, 113; and Ivo Grenfell, 223; and Julian Grenfell, 111, 151, 184, 200–201; visits Taplow, 111, 112, 176; **letters to**, 200–201
Knebworth, Antony Bulwer-Lytton, Viscount, 260–61, 265
Knebworth, John Bulwer-Lytton, Viscount, 261
Knebworth House, 123, 260
Kneller, Sir Godfrey, 113
Knoedler & Company (art dealers), 285
Knollys, Francis, 1st Viscount, 165, 178
Knowsley Hall, 130
Knox, Ronald, 108, 119–20
Kurdistan, 256

Ladysmith, 100
Laing, Samuel: *Human Origins*, 106
Lamb, John, 351, 352
Lancashire, 366
Landes, 275
Lane Fox, Richard, 206
Lang, Andrew, 106
Lang, Cosmo, Archbishop of Canterbury, 322, 323
Lansdowne, Henry ('Clan') Petty-Fitzmaurice, 5th Marquess of, 74, 177, 231, 272, 289
Lansdowne, Henry Petty-Fitzmaurice, 6th Marquess of, 294
Lansdowne, George Petty-Fitzmaurice, 8th Marquess of (*earlier* Mercer Nairne), 335
Lansdowne, Barbara, Marchioness of (*earlier* Mercer Nairne), 335
Lansdowne, Elizabeth, Marchioness of, 294
Lansdowne, Maud, Marchioness of, 231, 272, 277, 327–8
Lascelles, (Sir) Alan ('Tommy'), 123, 275, 319, 321, 347, 357, 369
Lascelles, Henry ('Harry'), Viscount *see* Harewood, Henry ('Harry') Lascelles, 6th Earl of
Lascelles, Rose, 297
Last Enemy, The (Hillary), 350
Lausanne conference (1922), 250
Lavery, Sir John, 241–2
Law, Andrew Bonar, 249–50, 251
Lawrence, D. H., 268
Le Nôtre, André, 21–2, 81
Le Touquet, 112

Lea, River, 28
Lear, Mildred, 260, 349
Leconfield, Violet, Lady, 296, 347, 350, 352, 359, 361
Leeds, Katherine, Duchess of, 173
Lees-Milne, James, 349
Lehmann, Rosamond, 216, 266, 271–2, 342; *Dusty Answer*, 271; *The Weather in the Streets*, 271–2
Leicester, Thomas Coke, 2nd Earl of, 47
Leinster, Gerald FitzGerald, 5th Duke of, 127
Leinster, Maurice FitzGerald, 6th Duke of, 126–7, 173
Leinster, Edward FitzGerald, 7th Duke of, 355
Leinster, Hermione, Duchess of, 48, 127
Lely, Sir Peter, 113, 270
Lemaître, Jules, 108
Leopold, Prince, Duke of Albany, 38
Lester, Mrs (dinner party guest of Margot Asquith), 134
Leveson-Gower, Lord Alastair, 112, 136
Leveson-Gower, Lady Rosemary (*later* Viscountess Ednam), 118, 180, 216, 217
Lewis, Rosa, 80
Lewis, Sinclair, 235
Liberal Party, 41, 42, 102, 105, 115–16, 163, 164, 165, 245, 250
Liddell, Adolphus ('Doll'): on Ettie, 49; on George Pembroke, 45; on Society lovers, 64; and the Souls, 43, 49–50, 58
Limpopo River, 82
Lincoln, Abraham, 108
Lincolnshire, Cecilia ('Lily'), Marchioness of, 166, 192, 196, 203, 265
Lincolnshire, Charles ('Charlie') Wynn Carrington, 1st Marquess of, 166, 192, 195–6, 289
Lindemann, Frederick (*later* 1st Viscount Cherwell; 'the Prof'), 287–9, 295, 299, 334, 339, 367
Lindsay, Henry ('Harry'), 112
Lindsay, Norah: and Billy Grenfell's death, 199; at Bodnant, 332; character, 116, 245–6; gardening career, 245; and Julian Grenfell's death, 197; on Katie Cowper's death, 169; and Lord Vernon, 144; and Louis Mallet, 238; at Sutton Courtenay, 325; visits Panshanger, 218, 219; visits Taplow, 112, 244, 253, 267
Linlithgow, Doreen, Marchioness of, 265, 294
Linlithgow, Victor Hope, 2nd Marquess of, 294
Lisbon, 310
Lister family, 118, 202
Lister, Barbara, 202
Lister, Charles, 119, 137, 174, 202, 253
Lister, Diana (*later* Wyndham), 184, 202
Lister, Laura, 202

Lister, Martin, 202
Lister, (Sir) Reginald, 43–4, 60, 164, 202
Lister, Thomas, 202
Lister-Kaye, Sir John, 70
Lithuania, 332
Little Duke, The (Yonge), 106
Lloyd, Blanche (*née* Lascelles, *later* Lady Lloyd), 224
Lloyd, George (*later* 1st Baron), 224
Lloyd George, David, 1st Earl Lloyd George of Dwyfor: on Balfour, 51; budget of 1909, 163, 366; at Churchill's wedding, 162; at Curzon's banquet, 227; fall from power, 245, 250; and H. A. L. Fisher, 233; lunches in Paris with Ettie, 232; Minister of Munitions, 303; nomination of Sir George Riddell for peerage, 318; at Port Lympne, 237; tax policies, 170; Willie Desborough abominates, 232
Loch Merkland, 279
Lochinch Castle, 46
Lodge, Sir Oliver, 214–15, 216; *Raymond, or Life after Death*, 215–16, 242
Lodge, Raymond, 215
Loire valley, 288
London: air raids (First World War) 221–2, (Second World War), 331, 332, 338–40, 350, 364; Arlington Street, 222, 331; Berwick Street market, 339; Bishopsgate, 79; Bloomsbury, 160, 266, 315; Bond Street, 117, 147; Brook Street, 246; Buckingham Palace, 32, 128, 154, 155, 249, 302, 308, 313–15, 323–4; Carlton Gardens, 25, 27; Carlton House Terrace, 41, 70, 79, 80, 178, 180, 227; Cavendish Square, 60; Cenotaph, 239; Chelsea, 362; Chesterfield House, 127, 178, 315; Cumberland Mansions, 339; Curzon Street, 152; Devonshire House, 15, 32, 34, 222; Dollis Hill, 338; Dorchester Hotel, 350, 364; Dudley House, 255; Eresby House, 231; Foley House, 174, 361; Golders Green, 247; Green Park, 302, 346; Grosvenor Square, 40, 117, 118, 254; Hill Street, 255, 327; Holborn Restaurant, 147, 149; Hurlingham, 148; Hyde Park, 26–7, 139; India House, 315; Kensington, 148; Kingsway, 222; Liverpool Street Station, 322, 330; Londonderry House, 139; Manchester Square, 40; Mansfield House, 40, 166; Mansion House, 104; Marlborough House, 337, 369; Montagu House, 16–17, 32; Mount Street, 75; Neasden, 97; New Cavendish Street, 40, 166; North Audley Street, 349; Olympia, 327; Olympic Games (1908), 147–9; Oxford Street, 266, 325–6, 350; Park Lane, 41, 237, 314; Portland Place, 174, 361; Portman Square, 9, 12, 14, 15, 16–17, 153; Queen Street, 40; Regent's Park, 285; Ritz Hotel, 346, 350, 361; Rotten Row, 139, 141; Rutland Gate, 231; St Bartholomew-the-Great, Smithfield, 364; St George's, Hanover Square, 38, 60; St James's Palace, 305, 310; St James's Square 26, 33 (*see also under* St James's Square (No. 4)); St Margaret's, Westminster, 162, 247, 257, 274, 357; St Martin-in-the-Fields, 350; St Paul's Cathedral, 155, 207–8; St Paul's, Knightsbridge, 94, 95; Shepherd's Bush, 147, 148; South Street, 40; Stafford House, 32, 139; Stratton Street, 34; Sunderland House, 151–2, 171; 10 Downing Street, 178, 190, 329, 341; Trafalgar Square, 257; University College Hospital, 352, 354; Upper Grosvenor Street, 40; Westminster Abbey, 239, 310, 319; White City, 149; Whitechapel, 184–5; Willesden, 148; Wormwood Scrubs, 148; York Terrace, 285
London, Chatham & Dover railway company, 83
London Declaration (1911), 172
London Hospital, 183, 187
London Library, 348
London Underground Electric Railway, 80
London Volunteer Defence Force, 183
London (Regent's Park) Zoo, 25, 118, 161
Londonderry, Charles Vane-Tempest-Stuart, 6th Marquess of, 138–9
Londonderry, Charles ('Charley') Vane-Tempest-Stuart, 7th Marquess of (*earlier* Viscount Castlereagh): affair with Eloïse Ancaster, 139; audience with the King (1932), 313; at Cliveden, 140; elopes with Consuelo Marlborough, 139; in Ettie's will, 297; excluded from political power, 340–41; and Frederick Lindemann, 288; friendship with Ettie, 139, 221; at Imogen Grenfell's wedding, 294; and Julian Grenfell's death, 139, 194, 221; and King George V, 307; at Maidenhead puppet-show, 265; at memorial service for Adèle Essex, 247; in Paris, 231; political career, 250; visits Ettie in hospital, 352; visits Panshanger, 234, 355, 361; visits Taplow, 332; letters to, 7, 221, 247, 251, 276, 290, 291, 297, 307, 335, 338, 340–41, 346, 356, 358, 360
Londonderry, Edith ('Edie'), Marchioness of, 4, 222, 267, 288, 294, 361
Londonderry, Theresa ('Nellie'), Marchioness, 46, 138–9, 157, 164, 190
Longboat, Thomas, 148
Lonsdale, Hugh Lowther, 5th Earl of, 163, 289, 318
Loos, Battle of, 203
Lord Arthur Savile's Crime (Wilde), 58
Lorna Doone (Blackmore), 106

Lost World, The (Conan Doyle), 147
Louis XIV, King of France, 21–2
Lovat, Laura, Lady, 234
Lovat, Simon Fraser, 14th Lord, 183, 234, 318
Love and Mr Lewisham (Wells), 158
Lovelace, Mary, Countess of, 254
Lowther, Mary, 134
Lucas (barony), 114, 298
Lucas, Auberon ('Bron') Herbert, 8th Baron
    Lucas of Crudwell: and 4 St James's Square,
    115, 117, 140; at Avon Tyrrell, 137; his
    baronies, 114, 298; bird sanctuary, 279;
    career, 100, 114–15, 130, 195, 213; character,
    100–101, 116; at Churchill's wedding, 162;
    death, 213–14, 215, 220, 228; at Ettie's
    London dinner parties, 117; godfather to
    Imogen Grenfell, 113, 128; influence on
    Julian and Billy Grenfell, 100; J. M. Barrie's
    tribute to, 213–14; Maurice Baring's elegy to,
    228, 372; and Panshanger art collection, 170;
    relationship with Ettie, 100–101; rents 51
    Grosvenor Square with the Desboroughs,
    117; schooling, 173; sister's suicide, 99; visits
    Taplow, 112; watches Olympic regatta
    (1908), 149; and Whiteslea Lodge, 278, 279
Lucas, Nan Cooper, 9th Baroness Lucas of
    Crudwell (*earlier* Herbert), 98, 99, 101, 213,
    298
Luton, 213, 221
Lydney, 243
Lyons, 238
Lyra Heroica (Henley), 135
Lyttelton, Alfred: on Asquith, 59; on Ettie, 72,
    97; Ettie first encounters, 30, 34; politics, 104;
    and the Souls, 43; **letters to**, 73, 74
Lyttelton, (Dame) Edith ('Didi'), 160
Lyttelton, Katharine, Lady, 118–19
Lytton, Robert Bulwer-Lytton, 1st Earl of, 10,
    14, 43
Lytton, Victor Bulwer-Lytton, 2nd Earl of, 117,
    123, 260, 261, 294
Lytton, Pamela, Countess of (*née* Plowden),
    117, 123–4, 144, 162, 222, 260, 294, 332, 354

MacCarthy, (Sir) Desmond, 245, 263, 267, 348,
    357
MacDonald, Ramsay, 299, 322
Mackennal, Sir Bertram, 239
Mackenzie, Lady Constance, 139
Madras, 52, 63, 73, 74
Maeterlinck, Maurice, 161
Magersfontein, 110
Maidenhead, 88, 90–92, 265, 274, 283, 292, 293,
    294; Skindle's Hotel, 282, 283
Maidenhead Advertiser, 90–91, 92, 265, 266, 284,
    292
Maidenhead Fire Brigade, 293

Malden, Algernon ('Algy') Capell, Viscount
    (*later* 8th Earl of Essex), 143
Mallarmé, Stéphane, 348
Mallet, Sir Louis: appearance and character,
    173–4, 245–6; at the D'Abernons, 180; Ettie
    visits in Constantinople, 173–5, 245; French
    holiday with Ettie (1932), 295; at Jean
    Hamilton's, 199; and Norah Lindsay, 238;
    and Philip Sassoon, 236, 237, 245; at Port
    Lympne, 236, 237, 245; visits Panshanger,
    218
Mallock, William: *A Human Document*, 52
Malory, Sir Thomas: *Morte d'Arthur*, 83
Malta, 164
Manchester, Louise, Duchess of *see* Devonshire,
    Louise, Duchess of
Manisty Nicholl (solicitors), 366
Manners, Angela ('Angie'), 137, 183, 217
Manners, Betty, 137
Manners, Constance ('Connie'), Lady (*née*
    Fane), 137, 167, 184, 225, 231
Manners, Lady Diana *see* Cooper, Lady Diana
Manners, Francis (*later* 4th Baron), 137
Manners, John, 137, 180, 184, 202
Manners, John ('Hoppy'), 3rd Baron, 137, 229
Manners, Lady Marjorie (*later* Marchioness of
    Anglesey), 118, 121, 123, 124, 127, 314
Manners, Robert, Lord Manners of Haddon, 54,
    118
Manners, Lady Violet ('Letty'; *later* Lady
    Elcho), 54, 121, 124
Manoel II, King of Portugal, 310
Marcus Aurelius: *Meditations*, 106
Margaret, Princess, 312, 319, 320, 363
Marina, Princess, Duchess of Kent, 355, 363
Maritain, Jacques: *Redeeming the Time*, 348
Marjoribanks, Archibald, 261
Marjoribanks, Edward, 261–3, 288, 322
Marjoribanks, Elizabeth (*later* Hogg), 261
Markham, Daisy, 144
Marlborough, John Churchill, 1st Duke of, 87,
    325
Marlborough, Charles ('Sunny') Spencer-
    Churchill, 9th Duke of, 153, 318
Marlborough, Consuelo, Duchess of: elopes
    with Charley Castlereagh, 139; on Ettie, 131;
    French holiday with Ettie (September 1920),
    238; friendship with Ettie, 130, 140; in
    imaginary women's Cabinet, 222; at Imogen
    Grenfell's wedding, 295; and Lytton
    Strachey, 226; marriage, 131–2, 318; and the
    Prince of Wales, 153; proselytising, 140; and
    Sunderland House, 151–2, 171; meets Ettie in
    Brighton (1917), 220; visits Ettie on Côte
    d'Azur (1932), 295; visits Panshanger, 218
Marlborough, Gladys, Duchess of (*née*
    Deacon), 153–4, 288

Marlborough, Mary, Duchess of (*née* Cadogan), 288

Marlborough House set, 46, 69, 70

Marlow, 117

Marryat, Frederick, 248

Marseilles, 239

Marsh, (Sir) Edward, 218, 244, 267, 338

Martineau, Harriet: *The Crofton Boys*, 106

Mary, Queen ('May'): appoints Ettie Lady of the Bedchamber, 131, 153, 154–5, 304; at Badminton during Second World War, 336–7, 346; character and life at Court, 302, 304–5, 305–310, 313–15, 319, 325; childhood playfellow of Ettie, 152–3; on death of Billy Grenfell, 198; at Ettie's golden wedding party, 327; and Gore's *George V*, 316, 318, 342; Imogen Grenfell's wedding gift, 293; invited to Panshanger (1914), 171; and Ivo Grenfell's death, 273, 274; and the King's death, 321–5, 365; the 'Old Court', 325, 336; and outbreak of First World War, 177; at Sandringham, 311–13, 321–2; state visit to Paris (April 1914), 155–6; tours Midlands (June 1914), 176; visits Panshanger, 358; visits Taplow after Julian's death, 198; visits Welbeck (June 1914), 176; war work, 302, 303–5, 305–6; widowhood, 325, 327, 336–7, 342, 344–5, 346, 369; **letters to**, 297, 312, 320–21, 322, 342, 344–5, 346, 358, 368

Mary, Princess, Duchess of Teck, 14, 152

Mary, Princess Royal and Countess of Harewood, 312, 319, 352

Massie, Chris: *Corridor of Mirrors*, 352

Masterman, Charles, 157, 177–8

Matabele rebellion (1896), 223

Matterhorn, 34

Mazzini, Giuseppe, 66

Meditations (Marcus Aurelius), 106

Melbourne, Elizabeth, Viscountess, 347

Melbourne, William Lamb, 2nd Viscount, 28, 102, 263

Melbourne Hall, 21, 114

Mellon, Andrew, 285

Melville, Robert Dundas, 4th Viscount, 16, 17

Membland House, 290

Memoirs of a Fox-hunting Man (Sassoon), 269

Mendelssohn, Felix, 10

Mentmore, 88

Metz, 224

Meyerbeer, Giacomo, 10

middle-classes, 44, 48

Midleton, St John Brodrick, 1st Earl of: on Alfred Milner, 223; on death of Julian Grenfell, 244; on Ettie, 230, 305; Ettie first meets, 30; in Ettie's will, 296; and Frederick Lindemann, 288; and George Wyndham, 165; host at Peper Harow, 230, 288, 316; at

Lord and Lady Ancaster's, 231; and the Souls, 42, 43, 49, 85; succeeds to father's title, 143; visits Panshanger, 235–6

Midleton, George Brodrick, 2nd Earl of, 119, 120, 143–4

Midleton, Madeleine, Countess of, 288

Mildmay, Sir Walter, 12

Millerand, Etienne, 237

Milner, Alfred, 1st Viscount: and Boer War, 42, 110–111; at Cliveden, 140; and First World War, 105, 190, 223, 228; relationship with Ettie, 223; and the Souls, 42, 43, 49–50; and Violet Cecil, 184; visits Panshanger, 170; visits Taplow, 57, 161, 164

Milton, John, 218–19

Mimizan, 275

Mimram, River, 27, 193, 345, 350, 363

mining, 68, 87

Minto, Gilbert Elliot-Murray-Kynynmound, 4th Earl of, 115, 153, 241

Minto, Mary, Countess of, 115, 153, 155, 241, 267, 322, 327

Mitford, Clement, 194

Monckton, George (*later* 8th Viscount Galway), 127, 170

monetary reform, 103

Montagu, Edwin: bird sanctuary, 279; career, 249; at Curzon's banquet, 227; friendship with Ettie, 249; marriage, 197, 249; at Sheringham, 251; visits Panshanger, 234; visits Taplow, 255

Montagu, Venetia (*née* Stanley): and Asquith, 131, 187; and death of Patrick Shaw-Stewart, 226; at Ivor Wimborne's, 222; at Julian Grenfell's funeral, 194; marriage, 197, 249; at Sheringham, 251; visits Panshanger, 234; visits Taplow, 290

Montaigne, Michel de, 7, 221

Monte Carlo, 38

Montgomery, Alberta ('Betty'; *née* Ponsonby): on the burglary at Taplow, 90; death, 359; debutante, 33; on Ettie, 38, 72–3; in Ettie's will, 296; introduces Ettie to Margot Asquith, 53; and Violet Granby, 68; visits the Earl of Stair, 46; visits Taplow, 112, 141, 244, 267; **letters to**, 26, 359

Moran, Charles Wilson, 1st Baron, 357, 369

Moravia, 59

Morgan Grenfell (bank), 88

Morley, John, Viscount, 30, 228

Mornington, William Wellesley-Pole, 3rd Earl of, 10

Morrell, Lady Ottoline, 4, 6, 212, 257, 267–8; **letter to**, 274

Morris, Richard, 224

Morte d'Arthur (Malory), 83

Mortefontaine, 295

Mosley, Lady Cynthia ('Cimmie'; *née* Curzon), 109, 217, 363
Mosley, Nicholas (*later* 3rd Baron Ravensdale), 80, 361–2, 363–4, 370; *Julian Grenfell*, 258
Mosley, Sir Oswald, 362
Mosley, Rosemary *see* Salmond, Rosemary
Mosley, Shaun, 368
Motion, Lady Elizabeth, 321
Mount Stephen, George Stephen, 1st Baron, 40, 221, 249
Mount Stephen, Gian, Lady, 221
Mount Stewart, 288
Mount Temple, William Cowper-Temple, 1st Baron, 21
Mountbatten, Lord Louis (*later* 1st Earl Mountbatten of Burma), 363
Munich Agreement (1938), 330–31
Murray, Gilbert, 193; *Rise of the Greek Epic*, 124
Murray, John, 249, 301
Mussolini, Benito, 329, 330, 332, 352
My Early Life (Churchill), 291–2
Myers, Frederic, 19

Nairne, Barbara Mercer (*later* Marchioness of Lansdowne), 335
Nairne, Lord Charles, 185
Nairne, George Mercer (*later* 8th Marquess of Lansdowne), 335
Nall-Cain, Sir Charles (*later* 1st Baron Brocket), 249
Nansen, Fridtjof, 157
Napoleon I, 9, 107, 290
National Gallery (London), 114, 170, 350
National Gallery of Art (Washington, DC), 285
National Portrait Gallery (London), 75
National Society for the Prevention of Cruelty to Children (NSPCC), 264, 265
Naval Prize Bill (1911), 172
Netherlands, 337
Nevill, Horace, 143
New Christians, The (White), 115
New Forest, 98–9, 137
New Machiavelli (Wells), 158
New York, 82; Metropolitan Museum, 247
New York Telephone Company, 80
Newbolt, (Sir) Henry: *The Book of the Grenvilles*, 242; 'Imogen (A Lady of Tender Age)', 128–9
Newfoundland, 344
Newhaven, 191
Newmarket, 332
News of the World, 318
Niagara Falls, 34
Nicolson, (Sir) Harold, 29, 132, 175, 349, 368
Nietzsche, Friedrich, 7
Nigeria, 147
Nile, River, 168

Norfolk Broads, 278, 279, 281, 332
Norman, Florence, Lady, 187
Normandy, 107–8
Northampton, William Compton, 4th Marquess of, 21
Northampton, William ('Willie') Compton, 5th Marquess of, 112, 144, 168
Northampton, William ('Bim') Compton, 6th Marquess of, 144, 168, 294
Northampton, Emma, Marchioness of (*née* Thynne), 294
Northumberland, Alan Percy, 8th Duke of, 231
Northumberland, Helen, Duchess of, 231
Norway, 157, 337
Noss Mayo, 290
Nottinghamshire, 176; *see also* Welbeck Abbey
NSPCC (National Society for the Prevention of Cruelty to Children), 264, 265

obituaries: by Ettie, 124, 152, 153, 359
Odyssey, The (Homer), 106
Off the Record (Asquith), 308
Oliver Twist (Dickens), 23, 106
Olympic Games: Athens (1896), 147; Paris (1900), 147; St Louis (1904), 147; London (1908), 147–9
Omdurman, 111, 223
Orkney, George Douglas-Hamilton, 1st Earl of, 87
Orkney, Thomas FitzMaurice, 5th Earl of, 87
Orkneys, 87
Orme, Denise *see* Wessel, Denise
ornithology, 279, 329
Osborne, Lady Moira (*later* Viscountess Chandos), 173, 217
Ottawa, 241
Owen, Wilfred: 'Anthem for Doomed Youth', 5
Oxford, 121, 125; Randolph Hotel, 121, 243; Summer Fields, 108–9, 141
Oxford Group, 324
Oxford University, 34, 125, 243, 261, 287; *see also* All Souls College; Balliol College; Christ Church; Wadham College
Oxo Company, 148–9

Pages from a Family Journal, 6, 204–6, 207, 208, 209–212, 215, 229, 242, 300–301, 328
Paget, Almeric (*later* 1st Baron Queenborough), 171, 216, 234
Paget, Sir James, 29
Palermo, 288
Palestine, 51
Palmerston, Emily, Viscountess, 15, 18, 28, 114
Palmerston, Henry Temple, 3rd Viscount, 28, 311
Panshanger: architecture and decoration, 169,

235, 248, 270; art collection, 113, 114, 169, 170–71, 235, 248, 270, 284–5, 366; bomb damage, 338; Christmas and New Year at, 216–17, 321, 347; demolished, 366; Ettie's girlhood at, 27, 29–30, 33–4; Ettie's improvements and renovations, 171, 234; Ettie's parents at, 11, 14; Ettie's plans for its future, 284, 296; First World War prisoners' camp, 219; inheritance of, 114, 116, 169–70, 365, 366; let to Almeric Paget, Lord Queenborough, 171, 216, 234; park, 27, 137, 168, 169, 248, 270, 345, 346, 352, 354, 360, 363; sale of land, 247, 284; 'Saturdays-to-Mondays' at, 41–2, 85, 216–17, 218–20, 234–6, 248, 270, 348–9; Second World War home for mothers and babies, 333, 334–5, 338–9, 343, 347, 361; silver collection, 346; sold by the Salmonds, 366; the Souls gather at, 44, 49–50, 85; terrace, 20

Panshanger Aerodrome, 248

Panshanger Fund, 170–71

Paramé, 108

Paris, 9, 10, 11, 12, 38, 80, 81, 139, 166, 181, 231–2, 238, 349; Olympic Games (1900), 147; state visit (April 1914), 155–6, 185

Paris peace conference (1919), 217, 231–2

Parliament Act (1911), 165

Parnell, Charles Stewart, 89

Parsons, Violet, 136–7

parties: annual High Steward's Banquet at Taplow, 90–91; balls for Monica's and Imogen's débuts, 166, 255; Christmas and New Year parties, 113, 173, 216–17, 321, 347; Eton parties, 112, 118, 157, 161, 176; Ettie as hostess, 4, 5, 40–41, 56; Ettie's children's, 118; of Ettie's girlhood, 30, 32, 33–4, 153; Ettie's London dinner parties, 117, 178; garden party for Monica's wedding, 257; golden wedding party, 327; 'Saturdays-to-Mondays' at Panshanger, 41–2, 85, 216–17, 218–20, 234–6, 270, 348–9; 'Saturdays-to-Mondays' at Taplow, 57, 90, 112, 130, 135–6, 164, 165, 176, 177, 233–4, 244–5, 253–4, 267–8, 277, 341–2; sausage-and-sherry parties, 321, 327–8

Passionate Friends, The (Wells), 158

Pater, Walter, 124

Patricia of Connaught, Princess (later Lady Patricia Ramsay), 305

Paul, Prince of Serbia, 259–60

Peel, (Sir) Sidney, 203

Pembroke, George Herbert, 13th Earl of: on Ascot week at Taplow, 93; character, 45; and Constance Wenlock, 63; death, 45, 214; and the Souls, 43, 48, 69

Pembroke, Gertrude ('Gety'), Countess of: childlessness, 94; Ettie's view of, 45; Evan

Charteris on, 70; and Nellie Londonderry, 138; and the Souls, 43, 48, 53; and spiritualism, 214

Peninsular Wars, 9

Peper Harow House, 230, 288, 316

Percy, Henry, Earl, 144

Persia, 57

Petrograd (St Petersburg), 10, 81, 231

Philadelphia, 171

Philip, Prince of Greece (later Duke of Edinburgh), 355, 363

Picture of Dorian Gray, The (Wilde), 58

'Pieps' (rent boy), 81, 290

Pinner, 148, 347

Pirbright, 224

Pitt, William, the Younger, 236

Planchette boards, 37, 70, 216

Plowden, Pamela see Lytton, Pamela, Countess of

Plummer, Harriet ('Hawa'), 101, 200, 260

Plymouth, Robert Windsor-Clive, 1st Earl of (earlier 16th Baron Windsor), 43, 85, 199

Plymouth, Ivor Windsor-Clive, 2nd Earl of, 217, 294

Plymouth, Alberta ('Gay'), Countess of, 43, 85, 184, 196, 258

Plymouth, Irene ('Bibs'), Countess of (née Charteris), 217, 294, 297, 343

Poetry Bookshop, 160–61, 168

Poincaré, Raymond, 156

Poland, 332, 334

Ponsonby, Alberta ('Betty') see Montgomery, Alberta

Ponsonby, Arthur (later 1st Baron Ponsonby of Shulbrede), 308

Ponsonby, Sir Frederick ('Fritz'; later 1st Baron Sysonby), 309

Ponsonby, Sir Henry, 90, 151, 308

Ponsonby, Magdalen ('Maggie'), 230

Port Lympne, 236–7, 245; Anglo-French conference (1920), 237–8

Portal, Lady Alice, 49

Portland, William Cavendish-Bentinck, 6th Duke of: and Desboroughs' golden wedding party, 327; dines with Queen Mary, 309; in Ettie's will, 297; at Imogen Grenfell's wedding, 294; and King George V, 318; during Second World War, 335, 339, 345; and the Souls, 42; visits Panshanger, 248, 321; visits Taplow, 157, 176, 332; at Welbeck, 163, 165, 176, 335, 339, 345

Portland, William ('Sonnie') Cavendish-Bentinck, 7th Duke of (earlier Marquess of Titchfield), 173

Portland, Winifred ('Winnie'), Duchess of: and Desboroughs' golden wedding party, 327; dines with Queen Mary, 309; and Frederick

Lindemann, 288; godmother to Ivo Grenfell, 109; as hostess, 4; at Imogen Grenfell's wedding, 293, 294; and Laura Corrigan, 355; marriage, 167; Mistress of the Robes to Queen Alexandra, 311–12; and Ottoline Morrell, 267; at Princess Patricia of Connaught's wedding, 305; during Second World War, 335, 339; and the Souls, 42; visits Ettie in hospital, 352; visits Panshanger, 248, 321; visits Taplow, 157, 176, 332; at Welbeck, 163, 165, 176, 302, 335; at Windsor Castle, 308

Portman, Edward, 1st Viscount, 17
Portofino, 98, 99
Portsmouth, Eveline, Countess of, 100
Portugal, 310
Pound, Ezra, 160–61
Poussin, Nicolas, 113
Preston, Stuart, 349, 352
Primrose, Neil, 222
Primrose League, 323
Prince of Wales (battleship), 344
Problems of the Far East (Curzon), 106
Protectionism, 113, 163
Proust, Marcel, 349
Prussia, 10
'psalm 118', 100
psychic mediums, 214–15, 216
Pulteney, (Sir) William, 180
Punch (magazine), 306
punting, 264, 271, 282, 283, 284, 345

Queenborough, Almeric Paget, 1st Baron, 171, 216, 234
Queen's Club, 67
Queensberry, John Douglas, 9th Marquess of, 362
Quickswood, Hugh ('Linky') Cecil, 1st Baron: Churchill's best man, 162–3; at Cliveden, 140; and death of King George V, 324; in Ettie's will, 297; at Lord and Lady Ancaster's, 231; at Margot Asquith's, 134; in old age, 367; and outbreak of First World War, 178; peerage, 348–9; on religion, 325; and Sir Charles Wilson, 357; visits Ettie in hospital, 352; visits Panshanger, 219, 220, 234, 348–9; visits Taplow, 244, 260, 267; letters to, 326, 354, 360–61, 367

R101 (airship), 297
Raeburn, Sir Henry, 293
RAF (Royal Air Force), 256, 281, 297, 298, 299, 354
ragtime music, 253
railway travel, 130, 143, 150, 159, 167, 185, 251, 309–310, 350

Raleigh, Professor Sir Walter, 205–6, 218, 226–7
Ramsay, Sir Alexander, 305
Ramsgate, 29, 37, 221
Raphael, 170–71, 284, 285
Ratling Court, 114
Ravensdale, Irene, 2nd Baroness (née Curzon), 173, 217, 364
Ravensdale, Nicholas Mosley, 3rd Baron, 80, 361–2, 363–4, 370; Julian Grenfell, 258
Raymond, or Life after Death (Lodge), 215–16, 242
Reay Forest, 105
Red Sea, 58
Redeeming the Time (Maritain), 348
Redesdale, Algernon Freeman-Mitford, 1st Baron, 194
Reform Act (1832), 66
Reid, Whitelaw, 114, 213
Relief of Chitral, The (Younghusband), 107
Rembrandt, 113, 248, 270, 284, 285, 362
Renan, Ernest, 108; Vie de Jésus, 106
reparations, 81, 289–90
Repington, Charles, 222
Repton, Humphry, 247
Revelstoke, Edward Baring, 1st Baron, 78, 79
Revelstoke, John Baring, 2nd Baron: appearance and character, 78, 79–80; career, 78, 79–80; as chaperone, 166; death, 80–81, 289–90; Desboroughs dine with, 177; on Ettie's coterie, 56; family background, 70–71, 78; gift of a clock, 296; his house in Carlton House Terrace, 41, 79, 80, 178, 179, 180, 221; his Paris apartment, 231, 289; and Kenmare family debts, 255; and King George V, 80, 153, 318; and Nancy Astor, 140, 141; and outbreak of First World War, 177; relationship with Ettie, 78–9, 80, 82, 122, 146, 290; sexuality, 80, 81, 290; visits Panshanger, 170, 219; visits Taplow, 115, 164, 176, 267
Reynolds, Sir Joshua, 113, 270
Rhodes, Cecil, 67
Rhodesia, 67
Rhône valley, 238
Ribblesdale, Charlotte ('Charty'), Lady, 42, 43, 45, 85, 95–6
Ribblesdale, Thomas ('Tommy') Lister, 4th Baron, 42, 43, 60, 85, 141, 202, 204
Ricardo, Wilfrid, 191
Rice, Edward, 264, 267
Richard I, the Lionheart, King, 155, 254
Richardson-Gardner, Robert, 102
Richmond, 314
Richmond Park, 152
Riddell, George, 1st Baron, 237–8, 318
riding, 26

Rilke, Rainer Maria, 348

Ripon, George Robinson, 1st Marquess of, 24

Ripon, Frederick ('Olly') Robinson, 2nd Marquess of (earlier Earl de Grey): at Ettie's parties, 117

Ripon, Gladys, Marchioness of (earlier Countess de Grey): dines at Downing Street, 190; and Edith Wharton, 133; on Ettie, 56; at Ettie's parties, 117; and the Souls, 43

Ripon, Henrietta ('Hat'), Marchioness of, 24–5, 27, 43

Rise of the Greek Epic (Murray), 124

River War (Churchill), 107

Roberts, Frederick Roberts, 1st Earl, 49

Roberts, Nora, Countess, 49

Rome, 38, 147

Romney Marsh, 236

Roosevelt, Franklin D., 341, 344

Rosebery, Archibald Primrose, 5th Earl of: death of his favourite son, 222; Ettie first meets, 25; at Ettie's parties, 117; as intimate friend of Ettie, 2, 58, 162; and King George V, 318; recommends Ettie writes Pages from a Family Journal, 204–5, 209; at Windsor Castle, 303

Rosslyn, James St Clair-Erskine, 5th Earl of, 69

Rothschild family, 22, 69, 88, 325

Rothschild, Baron Ferdinand de, 93

Rothschild, Leopold de, 135, 161, 170

Rothschild, Marie de (née Perugia), 161, 297

Rothschild, Nathan, 1st Baron, 80

Rowton, Montagu Corry, 1st Baron, 54

Roxburghe, Henry Innes-Ker, 8th Duke of, 318

Royal Academy of Music, 10

Royal Air Force (RAF), 256, 281, 297, 298, 299, 354

Royal Amateur Art Exhibition, 315

Royal Flying Corps, 256

Royal Home for Officers' Widows and Daughters, Wimbledon, 313

Royal Life Saving Society, 147

Royal Navy, 178

Royal Northern Hospital, 314

Royal Society, 287

Royal Society for the Protection of Birds, 279

Rumbold, (Sir) Horace, 332

Rumpelmayer, Antoine, 231

Rush, Margaret ('Peggy'; later Brodrick), 144

Russell, Bertrand (later 3rd Earl Russell), 157, 161, 177

Russell, Conrad, 327

Russia, 177, 178, 310, 364; Bolsheviks, 233–4; non-aggression pact with Germany, 332

Rutland, Henry Manners, 8th Duke of, 53, 85

Rutland, John Manners, 9th Duke of, 54, 295

Rutland, Kathleen, Duchess of (née Tennant), 295

Rutland, Violet, Duchess of (née Lindsay, then Marchioness of Granby): appearance and character, 53–4; and Constance Wenlock, 63; Ettie's loathing of, 69, 121, 123, 149; and Harry Cust, 68–9, 70, 84, 85; her lovers, 54, 62, 68–9; marriage, 53, 54; at Olympic Games (1908), 149; paternity of her children, 54, 62, 69; and the Souls, 53

Sackville-West, Vita, 175; The Edwardians, 134, 141–2

St Albans, 171

St James's Square (no. 4), 18, 24, 26, 27, 33, 40, 41, 94, 113, 114, 115, 117, 140, 151

St Just, 117

St Just, Edward Grenfell, 1st Baron, 88

St Louis, Missouri, 147

St Moritz, 218, 264

St Paul, Minnesota, 171

St Paul's Cathedral, 155, 207–8

St Petersburg (Petrograd), 10, 81, 231

St Pierre-en-Port, 107–8

St Stephen's College, 344

Sainte Claire le Château, 295

Salerno, Battle of, 236

Salisbury, 35, 102

Salisbury Plain, 185

Salisbury, Robert Gascoyne-Cecil, 3rd Marquess of, 50, 115

Salisbury, James ('Jim') Gascoyne-Cecil, 4th Marquess of (earlier Viscount Cranborne): and Baldwin's appointment as Prime Minister, 251; golden wedding anniversary, 327; at Hatfield, 178; house in Arlington Street, 221–2; and Knights of the Garter, 289; and Oxford Group, 324; during Second World War, 335, 339, 350; visits Panshanger, 219, 248, 288, 350, 351, 358; visits Taplow, 57, 161, 176

Salisbury, Robert ('Bobbety') Gascoyne-Cecil, 5th Marquess of (earlier Viscount Cranborne), 126, 192, 294

Salisbury, Alice ('Ally'), Marchioness of (née Gore, then Viscountess Cranborne): character, 266; childhood, 17, 20, 30; debutante, 32, 34, 37; in Egypt, 167; on Ettie, 135; at Ettie's London dinner parties, 117, 178; in Ettie's will, 296; friendship with Ettie, 353–4; godmother to Imogen Grenfell, 113; golden wedding anniversary, 327; at Hatfield, 178; house in Arlington Street, 221–2, 331; Imogen Grenfell's wedding gift, 293; and Ivo Grenfell, 110, 223; and Julian and Billy Grenfell's deaths, 141, 196, 198, 199, 200; marriage, 167; moves to Chelsea, 362; and Nancy Astor, 140; at outbreak of First World War, 180; and Pages from a

Family Journal, 210, 229; during Second World War, 17, 335, 339, 346; visits Ettie in hospital, 352; visits Panshanger, 219, 248, 288, 345, 351, 353–4, 358, 365; visits Taplow, 57, 161, 176, 198; **letters to**, 36, 37, 89, 219, 244, 276

Salisbury, Elizabeth ('Betty'), Marchioness of (*née* Cavendish, *then* Viscountess Cranborne), 126, 294

Salmond, Sir John ('Jack'): career, 256, 257, 285–6, 297, 299, 333; character, 286; engagement, 256–7; marriage, 257–8, 297–8, 299–300; at Panshanger, 270; at Taplow, 277; at Willie's burial, 356

Salmond, Joy, 256, 297, 298, 300

Salmond, Julian: birth, 280; career, 281; death, 374; Ettie's attempt to secure a peerage for, 299; in Ettie's will, 366; at Imogen Grenfell's wedding, 293; and Panshanger, 284, 296; and Princess Elizabeth, 320; sailing, 281; schooling, 108; at Willie's burial, 356–7

Salmond, Monica, Lady *see* Grenfell, Monica

Salmond, Rosemary (*later* Mosley, *then* Lady Ravensdale), 280–81, 357, 361–2, 363–4, 366, 368

Salomé (Wilde), 58

Salonica, 155, 207, 218

Sandhurst, 223

Sandringham, 302, 307, 309, 311–13, 315, 319, 321–2, 342, 369

Sandringham church, 322, 323

Sarajevo, 177

Sargent, John Singer, 133, 167, 236

Sartor Resartus (Carlyle), 67

Sassoon family, 118

Sassoon, Louise (*née* Perugia), 145, 297

Sassoon, Sir Philip: in Ettie's will, 297; gift of a watch, 296; his house in Park Lane, 41, 237, 314; his parrot, 264; Imogen Grenfell's wedding gift, 293; and King George V and Queen Mary, 313, 314–15; on Laming Worthington-Evans, 252; and Louis Mallet, 236, 237; at Oxford, 120; at Port Lympne, 236–8, 245; and Siegfried Sassoon, 267, 268; on Venetia Stanley's engagement, 197

Sassoon, Siegfried, 2, 195, 266–7, 268–9, 300; 'Counter-Attack', 5; *The Heart's Journey*, 269; *Memoirs of a Fox-hunting Man*, 269; 'When I'm Alone', 268–9; **letters to**, 280, 300, 354, 362

Sassoon, Sybil *see* Cholmondeley, Sybil, Marchioness of

Sawley Lodge, 18, 201–2, 253

Scapa Flow, 208

Schloss Eichhorn, 59

Schopenhauer, Arthur, 67

Scotland, 52, 98, 105, 107, 248

Scott, Robert Falcon, 345, 361

Scott-Cockburn, John, 335

seances, 215, 216

Second World War: air raids, 331, 332, 333, 338–9, 350, 364; Battle of Britain, 338; Battle of Salerno, 236; D-Day, 354; Dunkirk, 336; German capitulation, 358; outbreak of, 332–5

Secret Places of the Heart, The (Wells), 159, 282–3

Sefton, Osbert Molyneux, 6th Earl of, 318

Serbia, 177

Shaftesbury, Anthony Ashley-Cooper, 7th Earl of, 20

Shaftesbury, Anthony Ashley-Cooper, 8th Earl of, 20, 100

Shaftesbury, Anthony Ashley-Cooper, 9th Earl of, 156

Shaftesbury, Emily ('Minnie'), Countess of (*née* Cowper), 20

Shakespeare, William, 271, 296, 329; *Henry IV*, 345; *Julius Caesar*, 345

Shaw, George Bernard, 157, 161

Shaw, Robert ('Bobbie'), 141, 180, 181

Shaw-Stewart, Patrick ('Patsy'): character, 212, 225; and the Coterie, 137; death, 224–6, 229; on Julian and Billy Grenfell, 207; at Oxford, 119; relationship with Ettie, 122, 143, 225; visits Panshanger, 170, 218, 219; visits Taplow, 164, 173; **letters to**, 201, 303

She Stoops to Conquer (Goldsmith), 118

Sheringham Hall, 251

shooting, 98, 122, 171, 212, 279, 312, 316, 321

Shredded Wheat factory, 248

Siberia, 66

Sicily, 288

Silsoe, 21, 23, 301

Simla, 57

Simon, Sir John (*later* 1st Viscount), 322

Simpson, Wallis (*later* Duchess of Windsor), 325

Singapore, 297

Sissinghurst, 361

Sitwell, Sir George, 29

Sitwell, Sir Osbert: on Earl of Abingdon, 127; on Ettie, 56; Ettie adores, 261; on Evan Charteris, 76; at Imogen Grenfell's wedding, 295; lunches at the Ritz, 350; memoirs, 359; visits Ettie in hospital, 352; visits Panshanger, 216, 347, 359, 363

Sitwell, Sir Sacheverell, 295

Skelmersdale, Edward Bootle-Wilbraham, Baron (*later* 2nd Earl of Lathom), 33, 34, 104

skittles, 234

Slough, 148

Smith, Frederick Edwin (*later* 1st Earl of Birkenhead), 117, 165, 250, 274–5, 277, 315

Smith, Logan Pearsall, 349; *Trivia*, 213

Snowball, Mrs (Caribbean islet owner), 364
Social Evolution (Kidd), 52
'Soldier's Faith, The' (Holmes), 182–3, 215, 228
Somaliland, 202
Somerset, Lady Katherine ('Kitty'), 233
Somerset, Susan, Duchess of, 199
Somme, Battle of the, 212, 222–3
Sons and Lovers (Lawrence), 268
Sophie, Duchess of Hohenberg, 176–7
Souls, the: apogee of, 85–6; at Ashridge, 43;
    Balfour as 'High Priest', 50, 51;
    characteristics and composition of, 41–8,
    56–8, 62, 104, 253–4; morality of, 62, 65, 84,
    85–6; at Panshanger, 44, 49–50; and politics,
    163–4, 165; at Taplow, 1, 58; their games,
    48–50; Violet Bonham Carter's radio talk on,
    364–5; at Wilton, 43, 44–5; women in, 43, 48,
    49, 53–6, 62; at Wrest, 44
South Africa, 169; Boer War, 42, 100, 110–111,
    125, 161, 214; mines, 68
Soveral, Marquess de, 117
Soviet Union *see* Russia
Spain, 289; Civil War, 329
Special Operations Executive, 344
Spectator (magazine), 301
Spencer, Herbert, 99
Spencer-Churchill, Lord Ivor, 218
Spenser, Edmund, 244
Spion Kop, 110
spiritualism, 216, 242
Spottiswoode (printers), 209
Stack, 105, 106
Stafford, George ('Geordie') Leveson-Gower,
    Marquess of *see* Sutherland, George
    ('Geordie') Leveson-Gower, 5th Duke of
Stair, John Dalrymple, 10th Earl of, 46
Stair, Louisa, Countess of, 46
Stamfordham, Arthur Bigge, 1st Baron, 194,
    251, 273, 298
Stanley, (Sir) Arthur, 199
Stanley, Venetia *see* Montagu, Venetia
Stanley, Victoria, 173
Stanmore, George ('Jack') Hamilton-Gordon,
    2nd Baron: career, 245; character, 245–6; in
    Constantinople, 174, 245; at the D'Abernons,
    332; in Ettie's will, 297; French holiday with
    Ettie (1932), 295; injured during Blitz, 339; in
    Spain, 289; visits Ettie in hospital, 352; visits
    Panshanger, 358; visits Taplow, 244, 245;
    visits Willie after his heart attack, 356
Stanway House, 22, 48, 55, 95, 136, 158, 209,
    226, 258, 328
Steele, George, 194
Stevens Point, Wisconsin, 254
Stevenson, Robert Louis, 107, 274; *Ebb Tide*,
    106
Stoke d'Abernon, 360

Stoker, Bram: *Dracula*, 319
Storrs, (Sir) Ronald, 170, 245
Strachey, Lytton, 212, 266, 270–71; *Eminent
    Victorians*, 42, 226
Straits Settlements, 202
Streatfield, Sir Henry, 223
Stricken Deer, The (Cecil), 263
Stuart, James 'Athenian', 16
Studley Royal, 25
Sudan, 111
Sudetenland, 329
Sudley, Edith, Lady, 17
Suffield, Charles Harbord, 5th Baron, 47
Suffield, Charles Harbord, 6th Baron, 33
Suffolk, 366
Summer Fields (school), 108–9, 141
Sunday Times, 240, 329
Sussex, 160, 281–2
Sutherland, 98, 105, 107
Sutherland, George Leveson-Gower, 3rd Duke
    of, 88
Sutherland, Cromartie Leveson-Gower, 4th
    Duke of, 34–5, 108, 157, 176
Sutherland, George ('Geordie') Leveson-
    Gower, 5th Duke of (*earlier* Marquess of
    Stafford), 112, 241, 248, 265, 279
Sutherland, Eileen, Duchess of, 241, 248
Sutherland, Millicent ('Millie'), Duchess of, 112,
    139, 144, 164, 176, 349
Sutton Courtenay, 207, 325
Swanage, 109, 110, 129
Swaythling, Samuel Montagu, 1st Baron, 197
Sweden, 157
Swift, Jonathan: *Gulliver's Travels*, 106

Taalat Bey, 175
Talbot, Lord Edmund, 85
Talbot, Margaret, 86, 94
Talbot, Lady Mary, 85
Talbot, Neville, Bishop of Pretoria, 125, 294
Tangiers, 202
Taplow: reach, 282–3, 283–4, 289; St Nicholas's
    church, 84, 90, 292, 293, 294; station, 38–9,
    88
Taplow Court: afternoon tea at, 132;
    architecture and grounds, 87–8, 136, 167,
    216, 239; Ascot week at, 93–4, 112, 283–4;
    bought by Willie's great-grandfather, 87;
    breakfast at, 132; burglary at (January 1888),
    89; chauffeurs, 293; Christmas and New Year
    at, 113, 173; and Cliveden, 140; the Coterie
    gather at, 136; Eton parties at, 112, 157, 161,
    176; Ettie as chatelaine, 38–9, 74, 87, 91–4,
    284; Ettie's decoration of, 74, 93; garden
    party for Monica's wedding, 257; graveyard,
    356; housekeeping expenses, 93; Imogen's
    début at, 255; inheritance of, 296, 365, 366; let

to King of Siam (1897), 107; let to Otto Kahn (1922), 248; nursery, 97, 109; as nurses' home during First World War, 198; rental income, 88; Royal Family visits, 154, 198; 'Saturdays-to-Mondays' at, 57, 90, 112, 130, 135–6, 164, 165, 176, 177, 233–4, 244–5, 253–4, 267–8, 277, 341–2; during Second World War, 332, 333, 344; sold by the Gages, 366–7; the Souls gather at, 1, 58; tennis court, 154; visitors' book, 332

Tariff Commission, 163, 328

Tate Gallery, 75

Tatler, 167

Tchekov, Anton, 226

telepathy, 214–15

Temple, Frederick, Bishop of London (*afterwards* Archbishop of Canterbury), 38

10 Downing Street, 178, 190, 329, 341

Tennant family, 118, 215

Tennant, Kathleen (*later* Duchess of Rutland), 295

Tennant, Margaret ('Margot') *see* Asquith, Margaret ('Margot')

tennis, 34, 67, 154, 167, 214, 287

Tennyson, Alfred, Lord, 345

Tewin Water, 169

Thames, River, 34, 84, 87, 88, 92, 93, 149, 161, 264, 282–4

Thames Conservancy Board, 240, 266

Thatcher, Margaret, Baroness, 367

theosophy, 101

Tilbury Ferry, 361

Tilden, Philip, 245–6

Times Literary Supplement, 348

Times, The, 20, 35, 100, 148, 175, 203, 213–14, 240, 344; Ettie's contributions to, 124, 152, 153, 264, 276, 281–2, 328, 338, 359; Julian's letters and poem in, 187

Tintoretto, 113

Titchfield, William ('Sonnie') Cavendish-Bentinck, Marquess of (*later* 7th Duke of Portland), 173

Titian, 113, 270

Tono-Bungay (Wells), 158

Tories, 15, 41, 42, 50–51, 102, 104–5, 251; *see also* Conservative Party

Touraine, 288

Tredegar, Evan Morgan, 2nd Viscount, 332

Trenchard, Hugh (*later* 1st Viscount), 257

Trethewy, Henry, 24

Trevelyan, G. M., 94, 334

Trevor-Roper, Hugh (*later* Baron Dacre of Glanton), 349

Trinity College, Cambridge, 10

Trivia (Logan Pearsall Smith), 213

Turkey, 174–5, 222, 237, 249, 251, 256

Tuscany, 9, 10

Tweedmouth, Edward Marjoribanks, 2nd Baron, 115, 262

Tweedmouth, Dudley Marjoribanks, 3rd Baron, 262

Tweedmouth, Fanny, Lady, 115

Twickenham, 310, 314

Ullswater, James Lowther, 1st Viscount, 366

Unionists, 163

United States of America, 76, 82, 148, 299, 315, 364; *see also* American Civil War; American Declaration of Independence; Americans, Ettie's views on

Uxbridge, 148

Van Dyck, Sir Anthony, 45; 'Panshanger Van Dycks', 113, 170, 270, 362

Vanbrugh, Sir John, 179

Vane, Sir Francis Fletcher, 66

Vane-Tempest, Lord Herbert ('Bertie'), 318

Vansittart, Robert (*later* 1st Baron), 232, 237, 241

Vaynol, 336

Venice, 68, 121, 280

Venizelos, Eleutherios, 237

Vernon, George, 8th Baron, 144, 203–4

Versailles, 21–2

Versailles peace conference (1919), 217, 231–2

Victoria, Queen, 27, 28, 35, 90, 130, 134, 151, 154, 308; Diamond Jubilee (1897), 91, 355

Victoria Eugenie, Queen of Spain, 310

Victoria, Princess, 319, 321

Vie de Jésus (Renan), 106

Vie Parisienne, La (magazine), 306

Vienna, 10, 11, 174, 231

Vincent, Sir Edgar *see* D'Abernon, Edgar Vincent, 1st Viscount

Vincent, Lady Helen *see* D'Abernon, Helen, Viscountess

Vincent, James ('Jim'), 279, 333

Virgil, 82

Waddesdon Manor, 88, 93

Wadham College, Oxford, 263

Wadhurst, 273, 277

Wake, Matilda ('Nannie'), 12, 13, 16, 17, 19, 24, 64, 65, 97, 98, 113

Wales, 332, 341

Walls, Tom, 321

Walpole, (Sir) Hugh, 233, 235, 248–9, 270; 'Absalom', 233

Ward, John, 248

Ward, Margaret ('Peggy'), 270

Warsaw, 332

Washington, DC, 187, 285, 291

Waterford, John Beresford, 5th Marquess of, 277

Waterford, Henry Beresford, 6th Marquess of, 277

Waterford, John ('Tyrone') Beresford, 7th Marquess of, 272, 277–8, 287

Watford, 247

Watling Street, 284

Waugh, Evelyn: *Scoop*, 248; *Sword of Honour*, 349

Weather in the Streets, The (Lehmann), 271–2

Webb, Beatrice, 48, 115–16, 131, 134, 157–8

Webb, Sidney (*later* 1st Baron Passfield), 115, 157

Weigall, Lady Rose: on Apethorpe, 12–13; death of her brother, 14; guardian of Ettie, 14, 17, 24, 27–8, 28–9, 37, 221; their mutual dislike, 29, 31

Welbeck Abbey, 22, 163, 165, 176, 288, 302, 335, 339

Welby, Emmeline ('Nina'), 68, 84

Wellesley, Lord Gerald (*later* 7th Duke of Wellington), 332

Wellington, Arthur Wellesley, 1st Duke of, 10, 11

Wells, H. G., 2, 131, 158–9; *Ann Veronica*, 158; *Love and Mr Lewisham*, 158; *New Machiavelli*, 158; *The Passionate Friends*, 158; *The Secret Places of the Heart*, 159, 282–3; *Tono-Bungay*, 158

Welwyn, 169, 247, 284

Welwyn Garden City, 247–8

Wemyss, Francis Charteris, 10th Earl of, 54, 55

Wemyss, Hugo Charteris, 11th Earl of (*earlier* Lord Elcho): character, 71; at Ettie's London dinner parties, 117; golfing holiday with the Grenfells (1904), 112; and H. G. Wells, 158; at Lord and Lady Ancaster's, 231; marriage, 54, 55; parliamentary career, 71; pursuit of Ettie, 71–2, 75; at Sheringham, 251; and the Souls, 43, 48; visits Taplow, 57, 141, 161

Wemyss, Anne, Countess of, 77–8

Wemyss, Mary, Countess of (*earlier* Lady Elcho): appearance and character, 55, 328; and Balfour, 54–5, 146; at Cassiobury, 133; death, 328; deaths of her sons, 203, 208–9, 229; and Edward Marjoribanks' death, 262–3; on Ettie, 124; at Ettie's London dinner parties, 117; and Ettie's relationship with Archie Gordon, 146; in Ettie's will, 296; friendship with Ettie, 72, 258, 324, 328; golfing holiday with the Grenfells (1904), 112; and H. G. Wells, 158; at Hunstanton, 190; and Ivo Grenfell, 224; and Julian Grenfell's death, 196–7; marriage, 54, 55; and Nancy Astor, 140; at outbreak of First World War, 180; and *Pages from a Family Journal*, 209; paternity of her children, 62; at Sheringham, 251; and the Souls, 43, 44, 46,

49, 50, 53, 56, 62; at Stanway, 258, 328; visits Panshanger, 217; visits Taplow, 57, 141, 157, 161, 197, 244, 267; **letters to**, 142, 156, 165, 229, 232, 240, 255, 258, 277, 310–311, 323, 324, 328

Wendover, Robert ('Bob'), Viscount, 192

Wenlock, Beilby ('Bingy') Lawley, 3rd Baron, 62–3, 66, 73

Wenlock, Constance, Lady: appearance and character, 63; *crise de coeur*, 63, 64; on Ettie, 29, 55–6; Ettie visits with Gladys de Grey, 56; and Evan Charteris, 75, 77; on George Wyndham, 83; in India, 73, 74, 75, 155; influence on Ettie, 62, 63, 74; marriage, 62–3; moral outlook, 63–4; and the Souls, 43, 63, 86; **letters to**, 79, 102–3

Wessel, Denise (*earlier* Lady Churston, *afterwards* Duchess of Leinster; 'Denise Orme'), 355

West, Sir Algernon, 25

Westminster, Hugh Grosvenor, 1st Duke of, 37, 41, 88–9

Westminster, Hugh ('Bendor') Grosvenor, 2nd Duke of, 124, 179, 254, 261, 275, 276, 285, 287–8, 295, 318

Westminster, Katherine, Duchess of, 149

Westminster, Loelia, Duchess of, 295

Westminster Abbey, 239, 310, 319

Westminster Review, 203

Westmorland, John Fane, 11th Earl of, 9–10

Westmorland, Francis Fane, 12th Earl of, 12

Westmorland, Vere Fane, 14th Earl of, 250, 295

Westmorland, Adelaide ('Adza'), Countess of, 15

Westmorland, Diana, Countess of, 295

Westmorland, Priscilla, Countess of, 9, 10–11, 11–12, 13–14, 15, 16–17, 18

Weygand, Maxime, 237

Weymouth, Henry Thynne, Viscount (*later* 6th Marquess of Bath), 254

Wharton, Edith, 1, 133, 247, 285, 295–6, 299; *The Age of Innocence*, 295; *The Glimpses of the Moon*, 296

Wheathampstead, 345

'When I'm Alone' (Sassoon), 268–9

Where There is Nothing (Yeats), 135

Whigs, 15, 20–21, 24, 33, 41, 101–2, 103, 126

Whipsnade Zoo, 325

Whistler, Rex, 332, 354

White, Henry ('Harry'), 43, 49, 57–8

White, Margaret ('Daisy'), 43, 49, 70

White, Percy: *The New Christians*, 115

White Lodge, Richmond Park, 152

Whiteslea Lodge, 278–80, 281, 297, 330, 332–3, 337, 365

Whittinghame House, 22, 54, 256

Widener, Paul, 171

Wigram, Clive, 1st Baron, 298, 321, 322
Wilde, Constance, 44, 58, 59
Wilde, Oscar: barred from Taplow, 362; dedicates 'The Birthday of the Infanta' to Ettie, 58; socialises with Ettie, 2, 58, 59, 60; and the Souls, 44, 57–8; sues the Marquess of Queensberry, 362; *A House of Pomegranates*, 58; *Lord Arthur Savile's Crime*, 58; *The Picture of Dorian Gray*, 58; *Salomé*, 58
Wilhelm II, Kaiser, 179–80
Will to Believe (James), 108
Wilson, Sir Charles (*later* 1st Baron Moran), 357, 369
Wilson, Sir Henry, 233, 237
Wilton House, 22, 43, 44–5
Wiltshire, 281, 307
Wiltshire, Augustus Paulet, Earl of (*later* 15th Marquess of Winchester; 'Wilty'), 33, 34, 38, 42, 104, 110
Wimbledon, 13–14, 15, 17, 148, 313
Wimbledon (tennis) Championships, 287
Wimborne, Ivor Guest, 1st Viscount, 82, 86, 146, 222, 231
Wimereux, 187–9, 190, 197
Winant, John, 358
Winchester, 150
Winchester, Augustus Paulet, 15th Marquess of (*earlier* Earl of Wiltshire; 'Wilty'), 33, 34, 38, 42, 104, 110
Winchester, Henry Paulet, 16th Marquess of, 223, 250–51, 318
Windmill Hill camp, 185
Windsor, 88, 102, 148, 172; Frogmore Cottage, 310
Windsor Castle, 115, 131, 148, 155, 168, 173, 303, 304, 307, 311, 313, 321, 326; St George's Chapel, 357
Windsor, Robert Windsor-Clive, 16th Baron *see* Plymouth, Robert Windsor-Clive, 1st Earl of
Windsor, Alberta ('Gay'), Lady *see* Plymouth, Alberta ('Gay'), Countess of
Winterton, Edward Turnour, 6th Earl, 5, 144, 231
Witness of God and Faith - Two Lay Sermons (Green), 65–6, 67
Woking, 290
Wolverton, Edith, Lady, 219, 220
women: attitudes to pregnancy, 95–6; Constance Wenlock's categorisation of, 63–4; debutantes, 32–3, 166, 254; imaginary Cabinet of, 222; at Sandringham, 312; in the Souls, 43, 48, 49, 53–6, 62
Women's Tariff Reform Association, 163
World Disarmament Conference (1932), 297
World Economic Conference (1933), 299

Worst Journey in the World, The (Cherry-Garrard), 345
Worthing, 281
Worthington-Evans, Sir Laming, 251–2
Wrest Park: as American country embassy, 114, 213; art collections, 114; Balfour visits, 111; Bron Herbert inherits, 114; damaged by fire (1916), 213; despoiled by Essex Timber Company, 301; Ettie's children at, 212; Ettie's 'Great Good Place', 18, 21, 22–3, 27, 213; Ettie's orphaned childhood at, 17–18, 20, 23–4, 29, 30, 62; Ettie's parents at, 11, 13, 14; gardens, 21–2, 44, 62, 81; Kitchener visits, 112; 'Le Petit Trianon', 22, 25; rebuilding by Lord de Grey, 23; sold to John Murray, 249; the Souls gather at, 44; as wartime hospital, 213
Wuthering Heights (Brontë), 106
Wyndham family, 83, 215
Wyndham, Diana (*née* Lister), 184, 202
Wyndham, George: appearance and character, 82–3; career, 82–3, 85, 291; and Chesterton, 157; death, 85; death of his son, 184; at Ettie's London dinner parties, 117; and Gay Plymouth, 85; marriage, 83, 85; on the middle-classes, 44; relationship with Ettie, 83–4, 85; and the Souls, 43, 62, 84–5, 165; visits Taplow, 57, 84, 161
Wyndham, Madeline (mother of George Wyndham), 215
Wyndham, Pamela ('the Babe'), 84
Wyndham, Percy (father of George Wyndham), 215
Wyndham, Percy (son of George Wyndham), 184
Wynyard Park, 130, 138, 152, 288, 361

Xenia, Grand Duchess of Russia, 310

Yalta, 310
Yeats, W. B., 2, 131, 159–60, 161; *Where There is Nothing*, 135
Yonge, Charlotte, 248; *The Little Duke*, 106
Yorkshire, 21, 25, 85, 114, 366; *see also* Sawley Lodge
Young Melbourne, The (Cecil), 263
Young Visiters, The (Ashford), 233
Young Women's Christian Association, 315
Younghusband, (Sir) George: *The Relief of Chitral*, 107
Ypres Salient, 191, 206

Zeppelins, 221, 302
Zeus, 124
Ziegler, Philip, 80